Tales of Endearment

Tales of Endearment

MODERN VINTAGE LOVERS AND THEIR EXTRAORDINARY WARDROBES

NATALIE JOOS

pH powerHouse Books   Brooklyn, NY

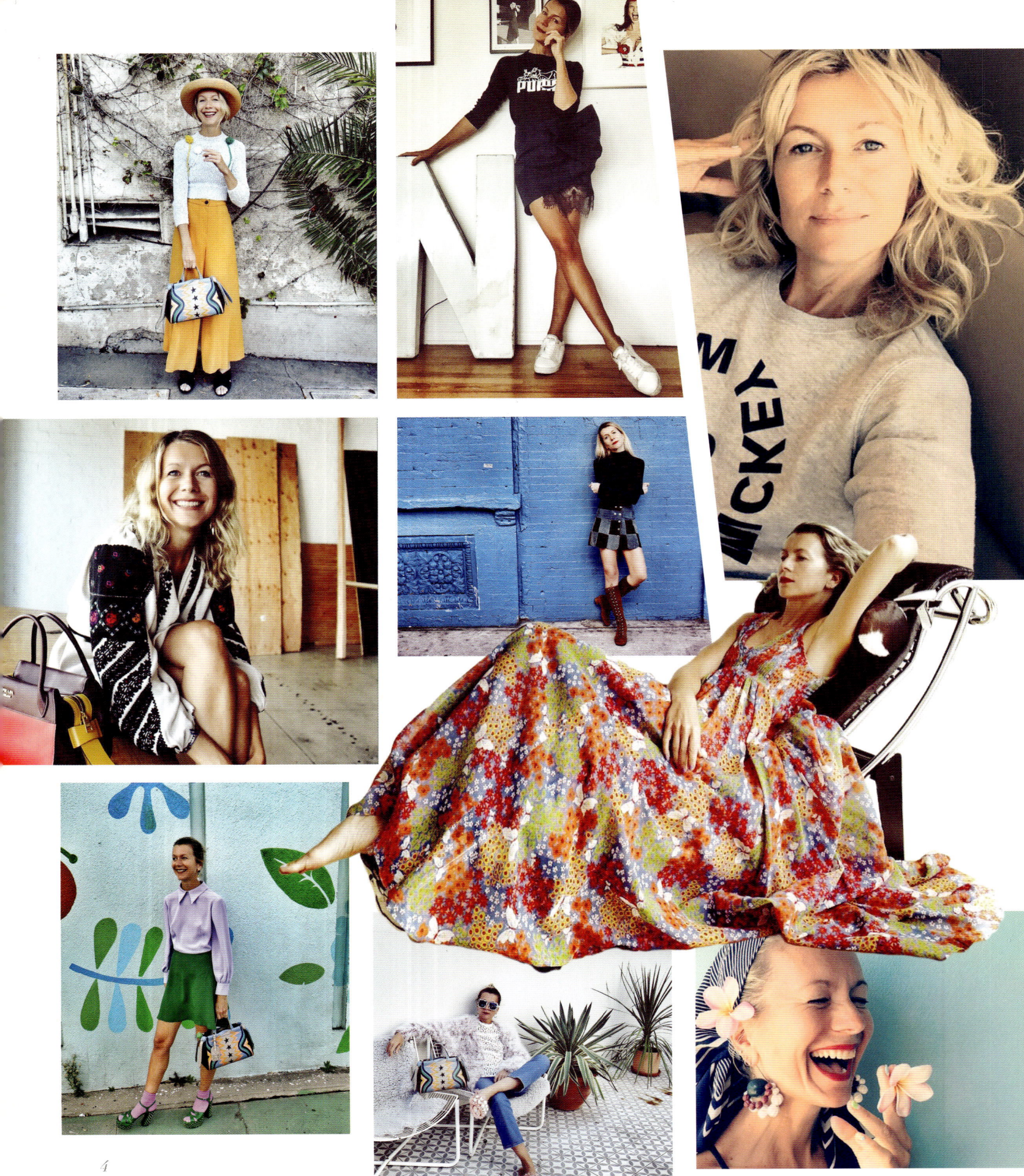

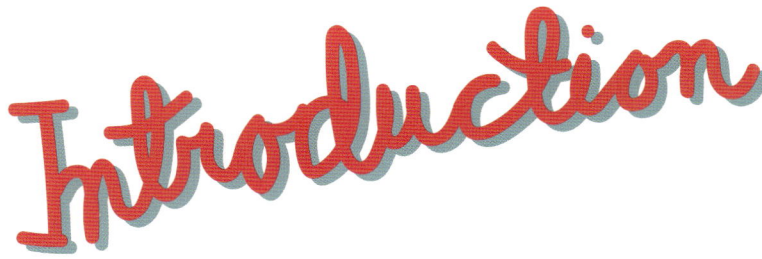

Introduction

There weren't many style blogs out there in 2010. In fact, the fashion landscape was quite grim. The economic crisis had put an alarming halt on frivolous spending and the industry's notables tread with cushioned caution. I was jobless—no one was splurging on casting agents anymore and the phone had stopped ringing. It worried me, but I also appreciated the mental space my newfound "professional freedom" had created. When work is no longer a burden, the mind goes to fortuitous places. I had millions of ideas and so much time.

Tales of Endearment was one of the first fashion blogs to make vintage a central focal point. I began generating content primarily to show designers and fashion consultants all the amazing vintage pieces I came across—inside my closet and in my friends' wardrobes, during my travels to stores around the world, and at online shops like eBay. My Muses quickly became as inspiring as the vintage pieces that lead me to tell their stories. Soon I was diving into the world of a new vintage devotee every week. I traveled, photographed, interviewed, and wrote persistently for the next six years. The overwhelming response I got finally encouraged me to compile an exclusive printed edition.

The *Tales of Endearment* book you now hold is a collection of photos and stories featuring 58 die-hard vintage fans. It celebrates the men and women that buy, collect, wear, and love vintage clothing. They come from all walks of life but share one uniting passion: a love for the discarded, the recycled, and the nostalgic. Each one of their "Tales" reveals a common drive to explore the past and revive its many abandoned designs. From 70s rock 'n' roll T-shirts, to Edwardian mourning jackets, to mod suede skirts, each garment in these extraordinary wardrobes was handpicked with love, gratitude, and a green conscience, and when worn well, has the power to inspire future generations.

In essence, *Tales of Endearment* identifies with the notion that "everything old becomes new again" and the remarkable people who hold it dear. They are the real-deal vintage connoisseurs, historians, collectors, sellers, enthusiasts, and aficionados. Sourced by word of mouth and recruited by me to share their priceless knowledge and styling talent. The final picture is an amalgam of yesterday's colors, shapes, prints, and patterns that have been passed on and reinterpreted as tomorrow's cutting edge. But what's more: vintage is the most sustainable form of fashion, and it is my hope that this message prevails and mobilizes you to dig for your own treasures.

Tales of Endearment

CATHERINE KRONE

HANNAH BHUIYA

DEE HILFIGER

MAXINE ASHLEY

PAZ LENCHANTIN

CATHERINE BABA

AMY VAN DORAN

J.J. MARTIN

JESSE JO STARK

GREG BANKS

PATRIZIA MARRAS

STELLA MAXWELL

ABIGAIL SPENCER

ALESSANDRA CANARIO

ERIN WASSON

ALIX BROWN

ISABEL MUSIDORA

ANDREA VILLARROEL LUA

ANGELA PHAM

CULLEN MEYER

CONSTANCE ZIMMER

DEBBIE CHU

SHELLY LYN SUGAWARA

DENNIS BALMACEDA

DJUNA BEL

ECE SÜKAN

ELEANOR WELLS

LAURA HELMS

OLIVIER CHÂTENET

GEORGIANA BOBOC

HAYETT MCCARTHY

STEFANIA & MICOL SABBADINI

DAMIAN YEE

ELIZA DOOLITTLE

KYLEIGH KÜHN

LANGLEY FOX

MIRIT KONOWIECKI

LENKA TSITSISHVILI

LINDA RAMONE

JENNY BACQUING

MARGOT

WENDY HENRY

TENNESSEE THOMAS

EMMANUEL DEMUYNCK

PAIGE ELKINGTON

PAULA GOLDSTEIN

STAZ LINDES

SHIVA ROSE

ALDENE JOHNSON

STEVEN ONOJA

VALY BAX

DESANKA FASISKA

ZOË BLEU SIDEL

SASHA SPIELBERG

WARIS AHLUWALIA

MARYAM MALAKPOUR

HEIDI MIDDLETON

SABRINA MARSHALL

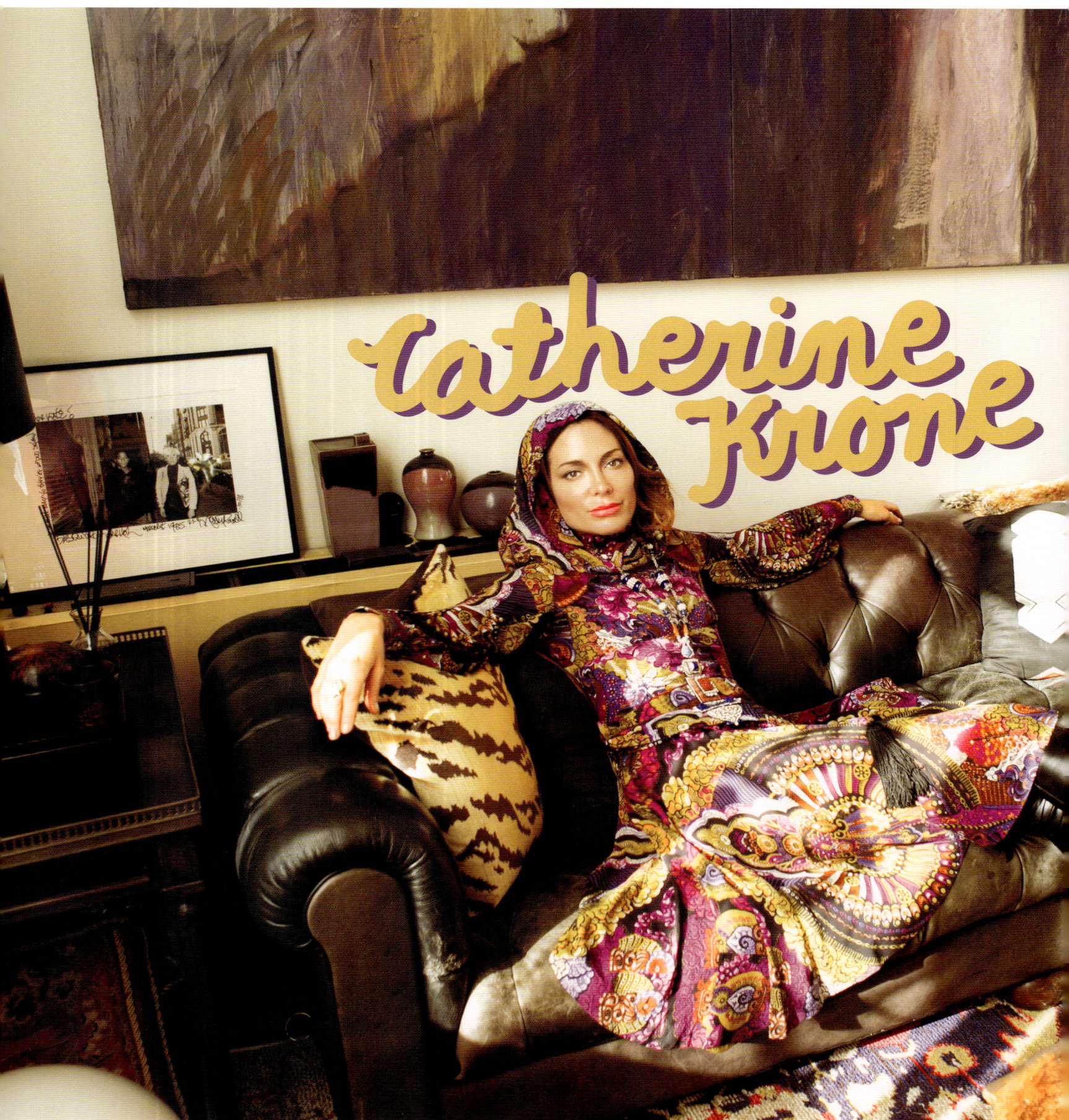

CATHERINE KRONE
DON'T MAKE GOD LAUGH

"There's that old Woody Allen quote: 'If you want to make God laugh, tell him about your plans.'" Catherine says it jokingly because I just asked her what the future holds, and she's "not a good planner." The man she met on the plane to Art Basel may very well be fiancé number five, but "who knows?" She's had to plan four weddings so far and each time it got harder to come up with a new theme, dress, and location "as any repetition would have felt wrong." Growing up, she always wanted to be a professional chef, and studied for years at the best schools to become one, then hated it once it turned into a job. Now she only cooks "serious feasts for friends." And tomorrow she might come across that highly coveted, yet dreaded Paul Poiret piece that's missing from her collection and be faced with an existential crisis. She owns garments by every major designer in history, except Poiret. Obtaining anything with his name would be her brass ring and the end of her archiving ride. So no, she doesn't want to make god laugh right now.

Catherine Krone never planned on being an orphan. Her father, the famous advertising guru whose "Think Small" image for Volkswagen was named, "the #1 campaign of all time," passed away after battling cancer in 1996. Her mom later died unexpectedly in a car accident while on vacation. She not only left Catherine all the family's properties—how to become a landlady and real estate developer overnight—but also a massive, priceless wardrobe. "I was 23 years old, and as her only child I quickly became overwhelmed with, well, all her *stuff*, and she had a lot of stuff, in part due to the fact that she was not expecting to die. A significant part of that was a storage room full of really incredible clothing, from Fortuny dresses to Geoffrey Beene gowns. So I have just been adding to her collection, essentially. I specialize in Civil War to Victorian-era clothing and textiles." She now calls the collection the "Krone Archive," and lends the pieces to designers, stylists, and friends who have fancy parties to attend. "I hope to make it more of a full-time thing," she adds.

But it's no real surprise she sustained, and grew, her mother's legacy. Vintage was always in her blood. "My mother and I did a lot of treasure hunting in thrift shops. I was buying vintage from Antique Boutique with my allowance or chore money from age 12. At 15 I was working at nightclubs in New York and back then, the more unusual and unique your look, the cooler and more accepted you were. Now scrolling through Instagram I feel like everyone wants to look like a Kardashian. Sad!" Catherine loves vintage because she finds that no one buys it "because it was seen in a current magazine, or on a celebrity. It's a direct reflection of the wearer's own taste. It takes thought and effort." And of course there's nothing like the disappointed look on people's faces when you're wearing a one-of-a-kind piece. "I live for a good opening, event, or gala dinner," she smirks, "so I can wear a fabulous vintage gown that no one else in the room will be wearing. Ahahahahaha!"

Catherine is one of the most profound, beautiful, and unique women I have met; a little absent-minded and dreamy on the surface, but never not endearing. Her friends unanimously describe her as being "trustworthy, reliable, caring, warm, generous, and kind," and I can only agree. She cares less about taking these photos than showing me all the dresses she thinks I would like, and wants to gift me. She's at her best when she can share her passion, and pays little attention to the trials of materialism. "Losing my family and some of my closest friends—my oldest and closest friend died right after my mother, and my steady high school boyfriend was violently killed right after my father died—has made me value *things* less and less. Stuff is just stuff; friends and lovers are what I treasure beyond all else."

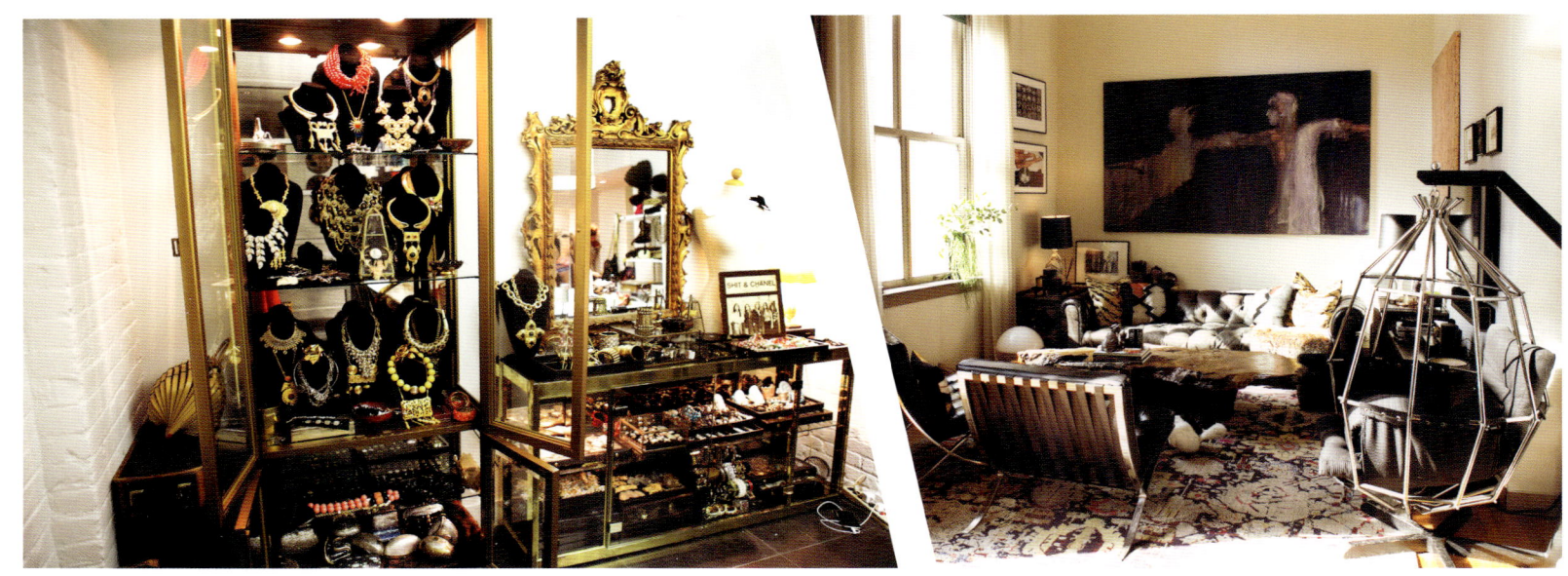
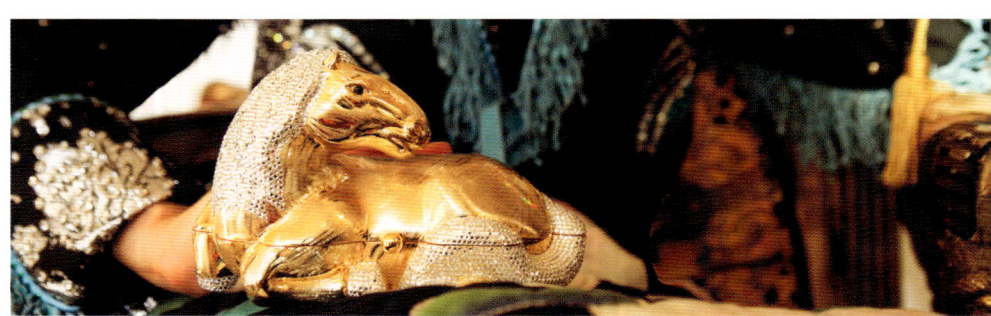
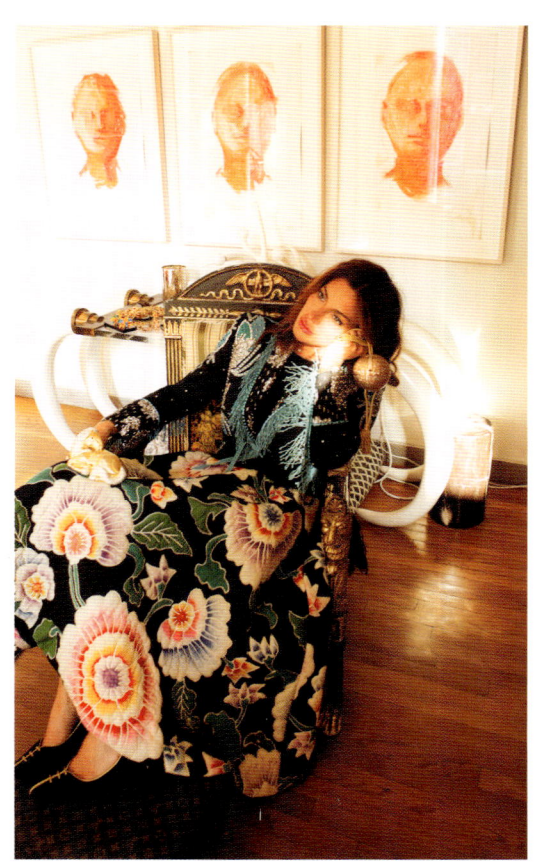
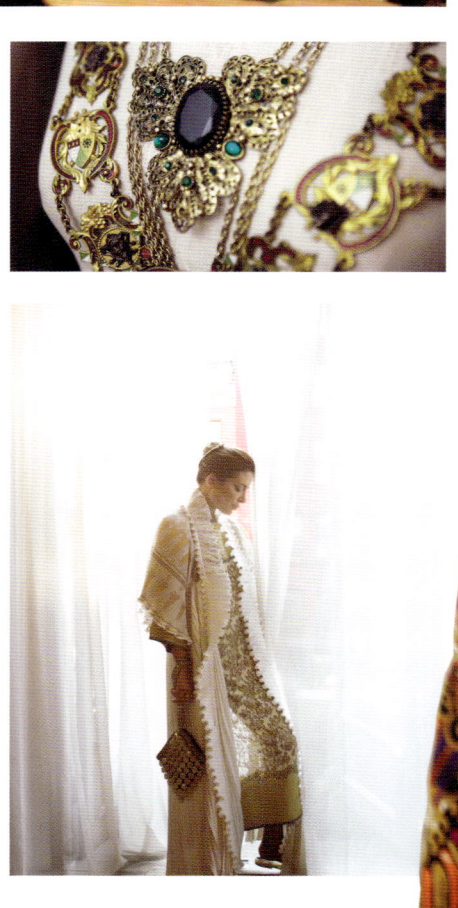
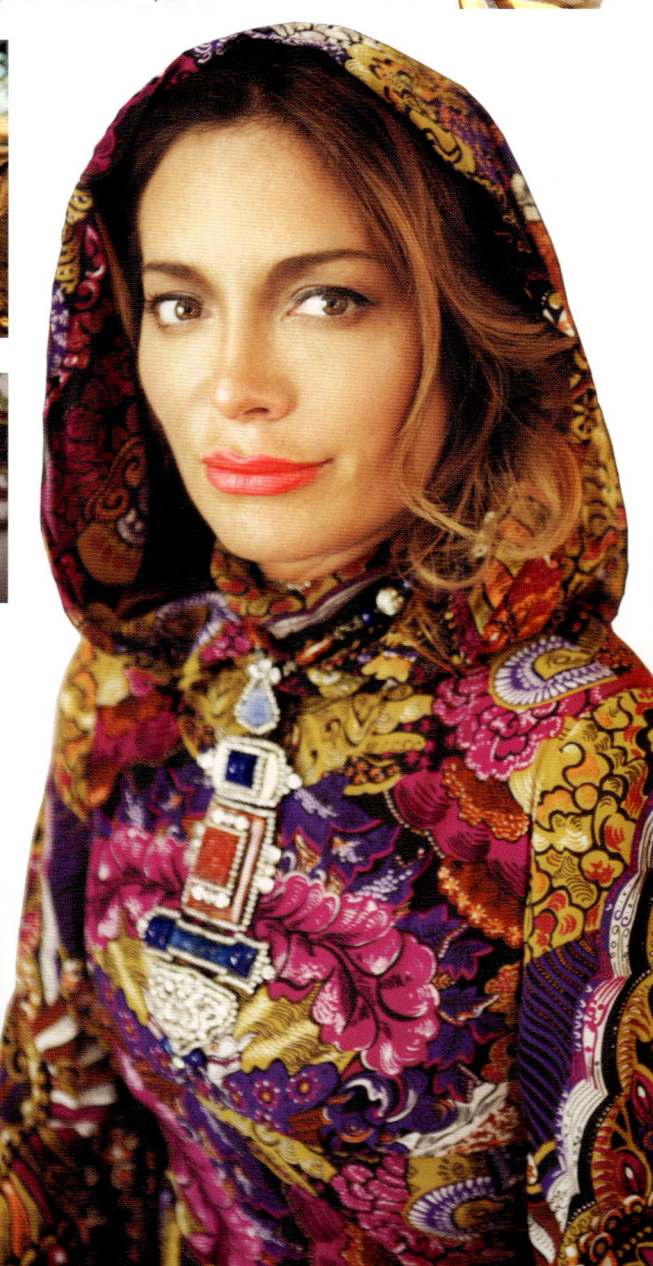

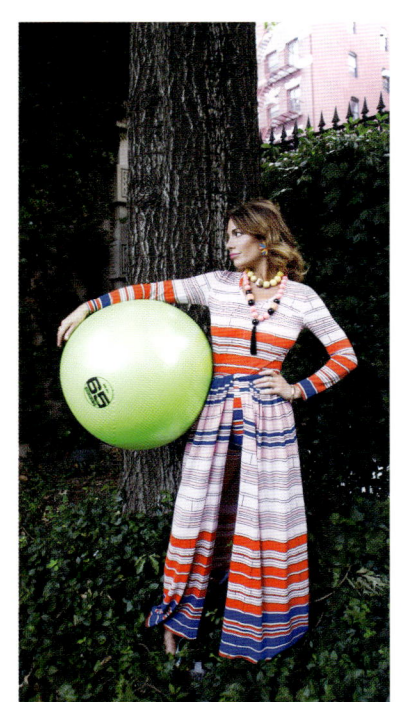
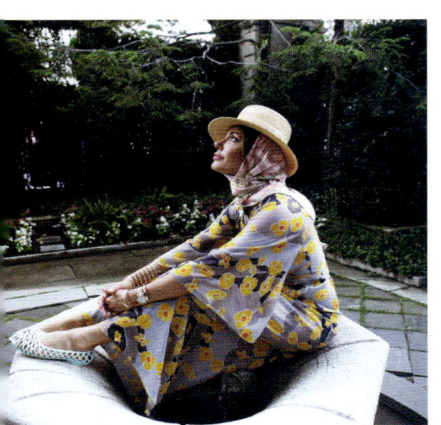
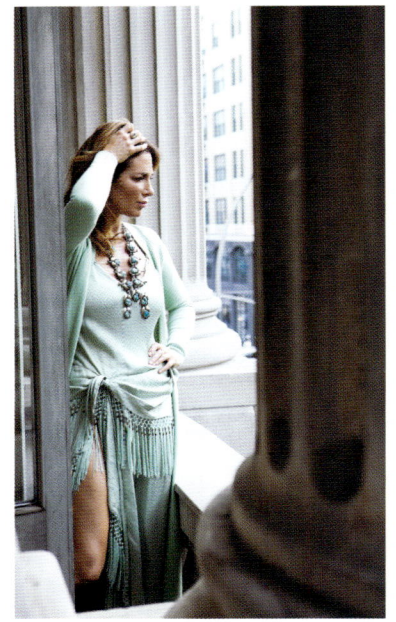
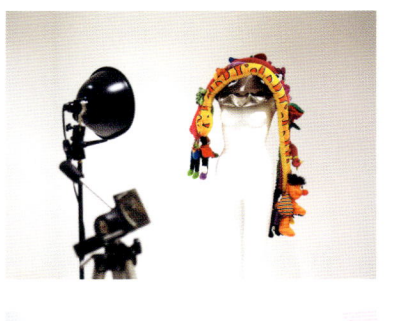
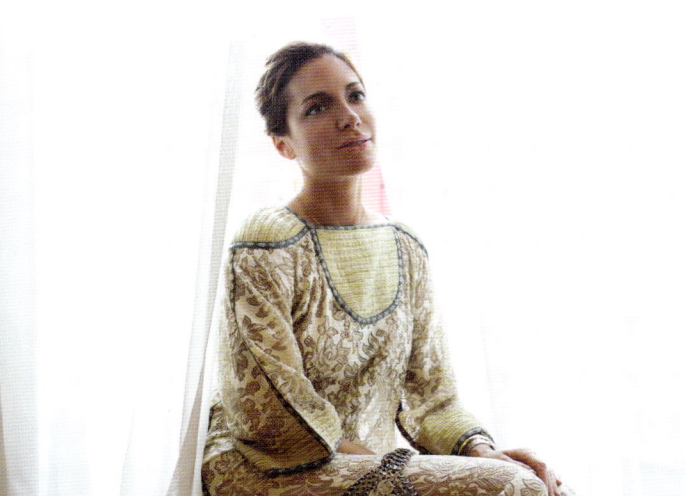
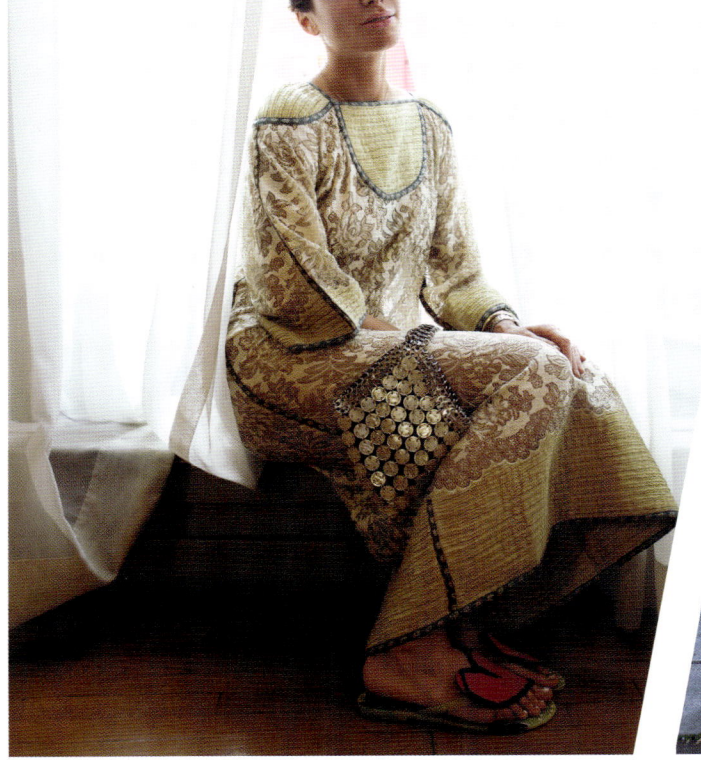
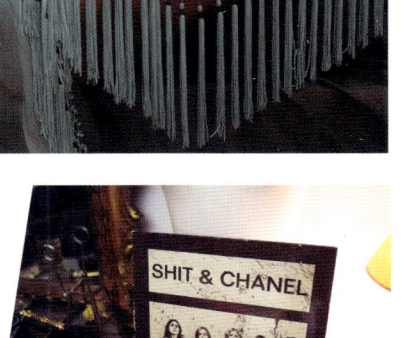
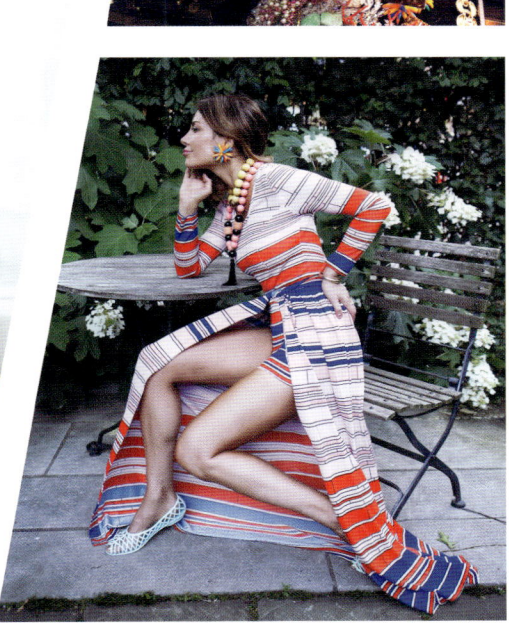
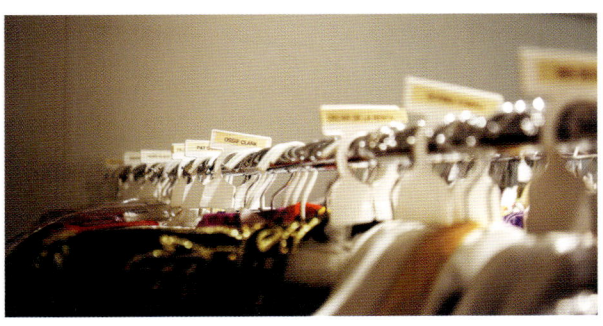
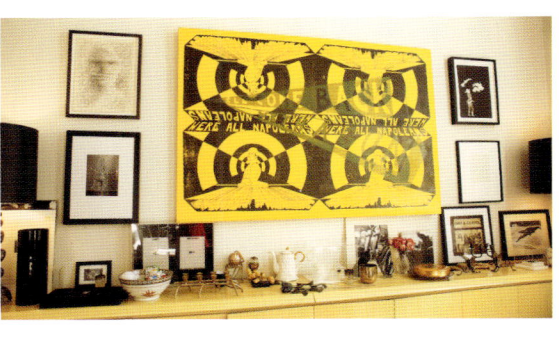
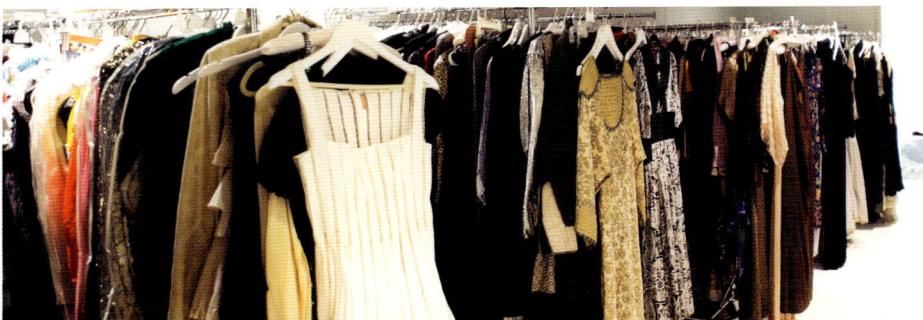

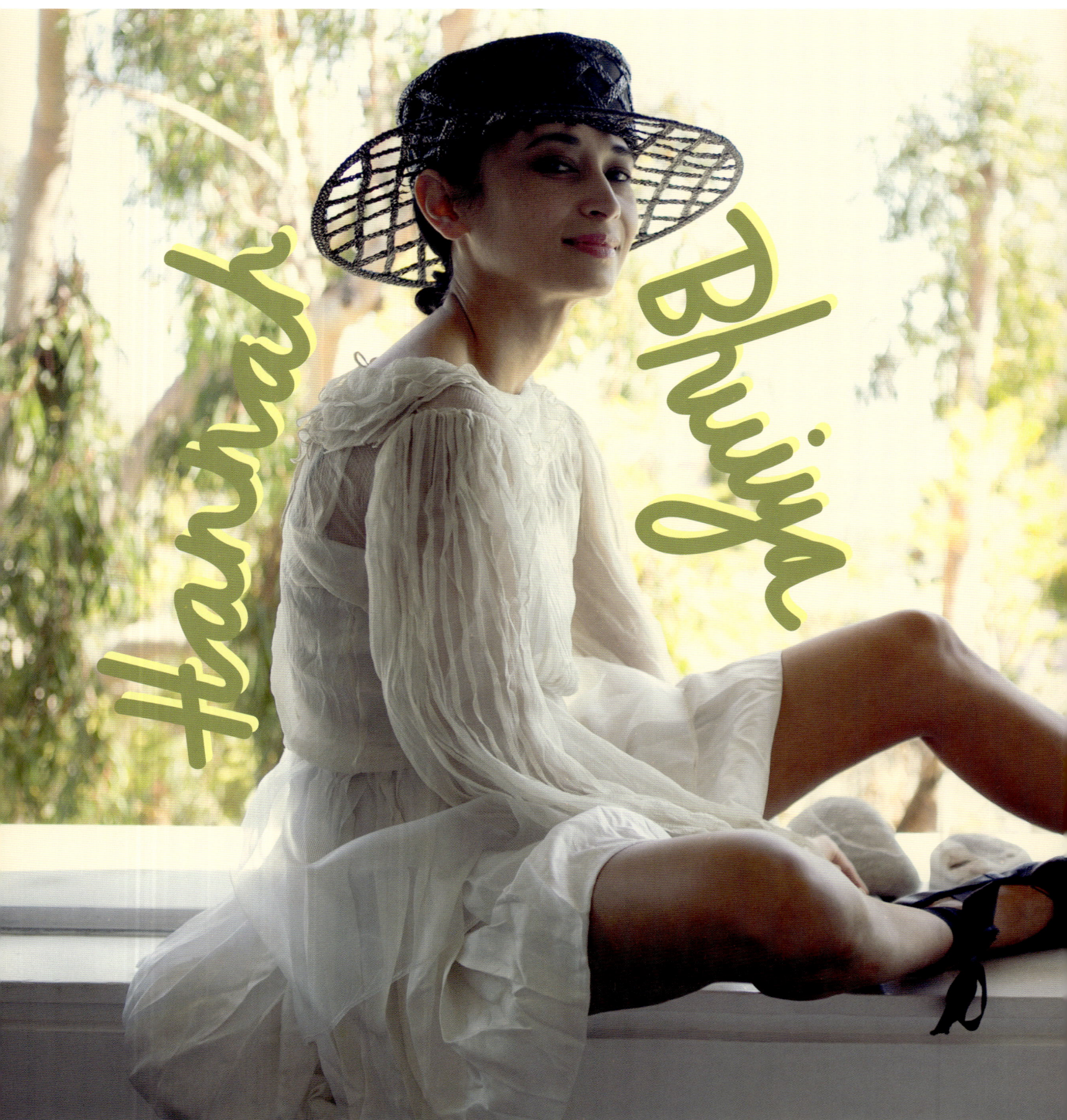

HANNAH BHUIYA
FAUX-BOURGEOIS CHILD IN PETER PAN COLLAR

It's hard to write about another writer. I've been sitting here for a few minutes, thinking of the ways to do her justice, but I cannot find words more eloquent and colorful to describe my friend Hannah than she uses. If you read her answers to my many questions, you would understand the depths and nuances of her self-perception. She's a rare bird with a tenacious drive to paint pictures, a storyteller, a reader, a dreamer, a rapturous architect of feelings and sentences. She's a visual creature, on both ends of the attraction. She's not content with mere pleasure or success. The complete image has to have cache, speak with the correct intonation, and drive a certain car. In Hannah's world, presentation and intellect are more revealing than facts.

Hannah Bhuiya didn't want to be a ballerina, or a doctor, or a musician. She wanted to live inside the Yves Saint Laurent ads of the 80s, perfectly chic but with a dark side, a classic Parisienne. "At the time, I didn't know who Helmut Newton was," she thinks back, "but I know that this was the imagery I saw and wanted to grow up into. And of course I had not seen [Luis] Buñuel's *Belle du Jour* either, but now that I have, that's the feeling. Looking rich, but also being wild."

And every day of her current life, whether she's cloaked in a cape in Venice immersed in the library of Coco Chanel, or in her Minnie Mouse bathing suit tending to her tan by the pool of the Chateau Marmont, she plans to succeed. She does not leave the house without the right lipstick, or an evident attempt to look properly interesting. The clasp on her penny loafer that matches the lapel of her blazer, a stack of books worn as an accomplished handbag, a silk foulard adorning the Peter Pan collar of her vintage Ungaro dress, it's all in the details and it's never not a little bit wry. And when you ask, she will describe with great delight why you stared in the first place. "Curating a look is always about drawing out the textures and contrasts in the main garments, and then throwing in something surprising underneath."

Hannah was born in London but grew up in New Zealand. Her father is Indian and her mother, Irish and Italian. She doesn't talk much about them. It is my feeling that she shelved her years of fashion deprivation to make space for more vibrant, lyrical memories. "I didn't have a messy or rebellious teenage stage," she complains, "I was in a Catholic school uniform and stuck in suburban New Zealand, with nothing to rebel against and no one to rebel against it with." She color-coded her marbles, decorated her room, dug for stones and rocks, experimented with nail polish and eye shadow, but mostly read, to escape. "Each novel or book was a tablet of experience," she muses, "an everlasting gobstopper chewed in solitude, which had flavors that could then be brought back in the memory at any time."

When she moved back to London for college she felt she could finally breathe, and delved deep into the underbelly of the vintage world. "London really taught me and gave me everything," she says thankfully. "Finally I was free to hunt, and construct myself from what I found." She couldn't always afford everything, but she was obsessed with the classics. "I could (and can) tell the stitching of a Valentino jacket at 20 paces. I also bought things for future lives—such as my huge pink Pucci-esque caftan, straight out of a Slim Aarons photo—which was unwearable in London, but is perfect for poolside LA."

I finally managed to write about my friend Hannah. And as I sit here a few hours later, wondering whether I should watch *The Voice* or not, I can see the beauty, but also the pressures, of an existence as demonstrative as hers. She gave up her life as a successful stylist in Paris for that of a struggling—but uber-relaxed—screenwriter in Los Angeles. The film script she cowrote is finally going into production, but who knows where the next figment of inspiration will come from? Hollywood was the perfect blank slate, and she still feels the novelty of all its differences from other cities. But when the act of survival becomes a form of art, noble and poised, there is even greater honor in the performance.

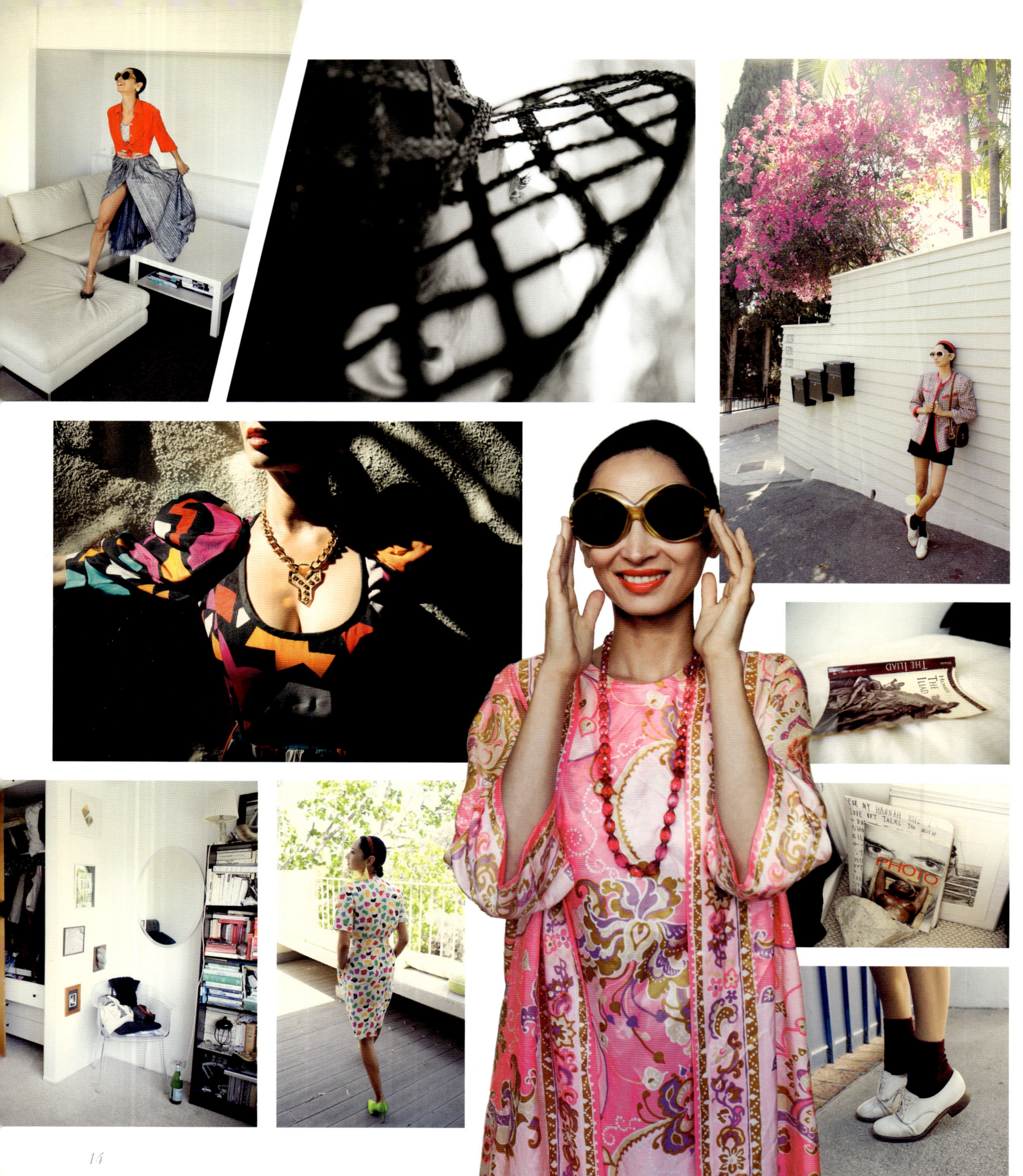

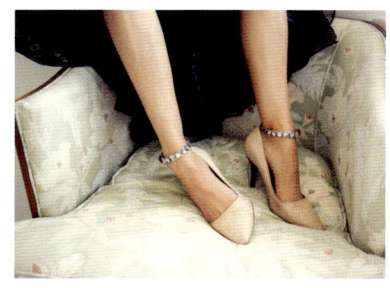
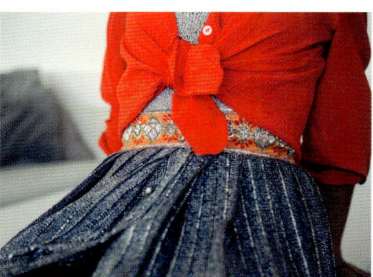
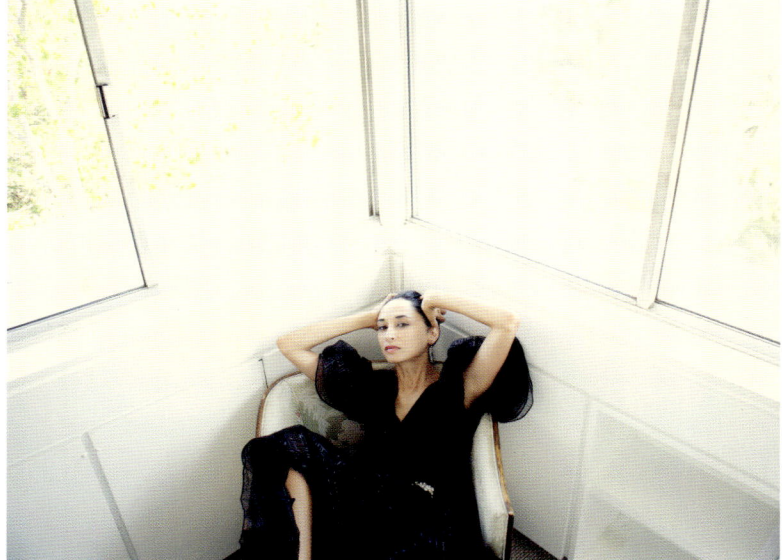
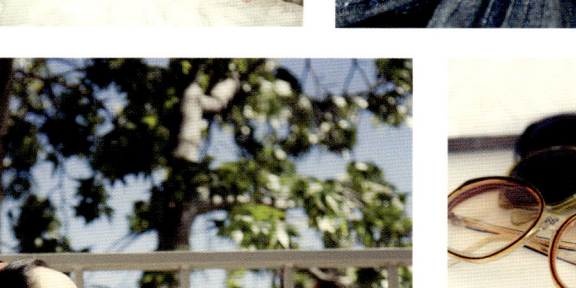
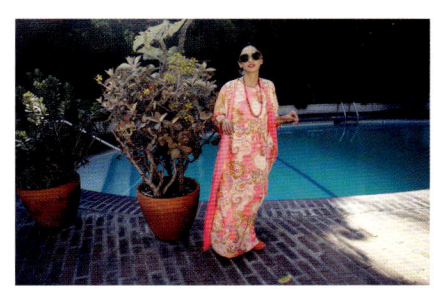
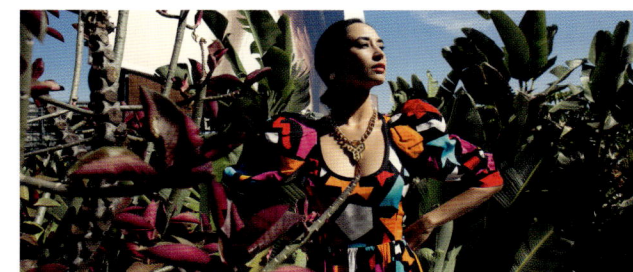
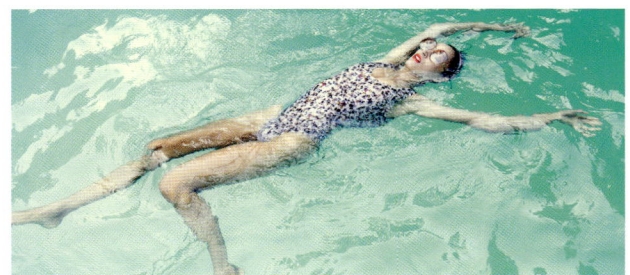
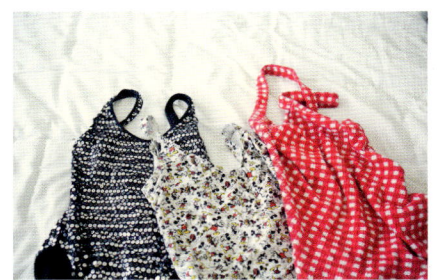
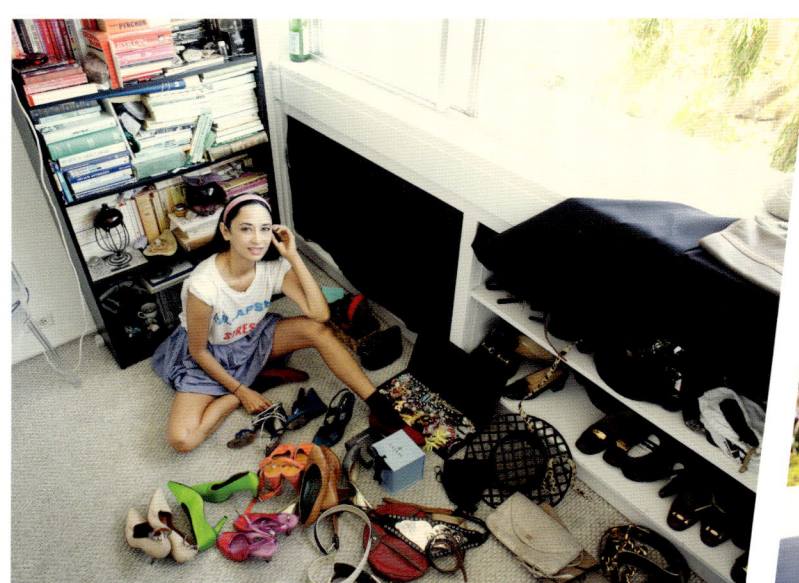
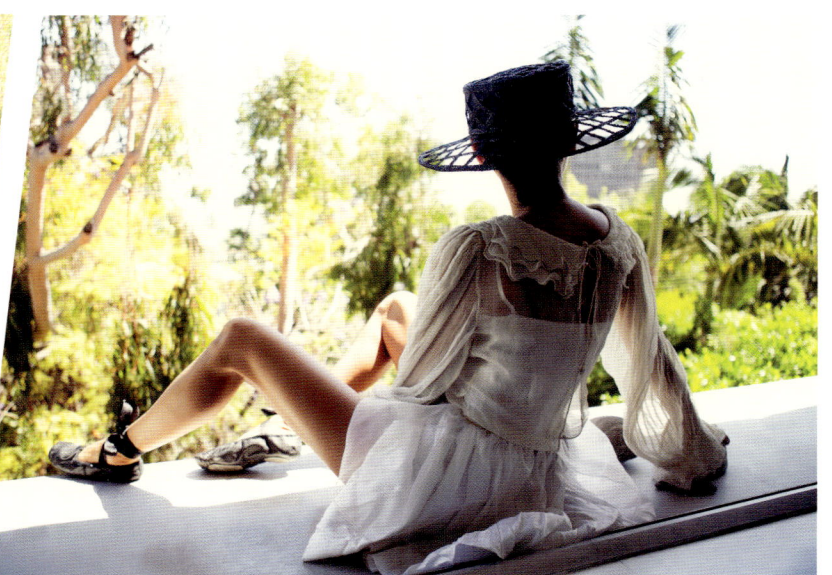

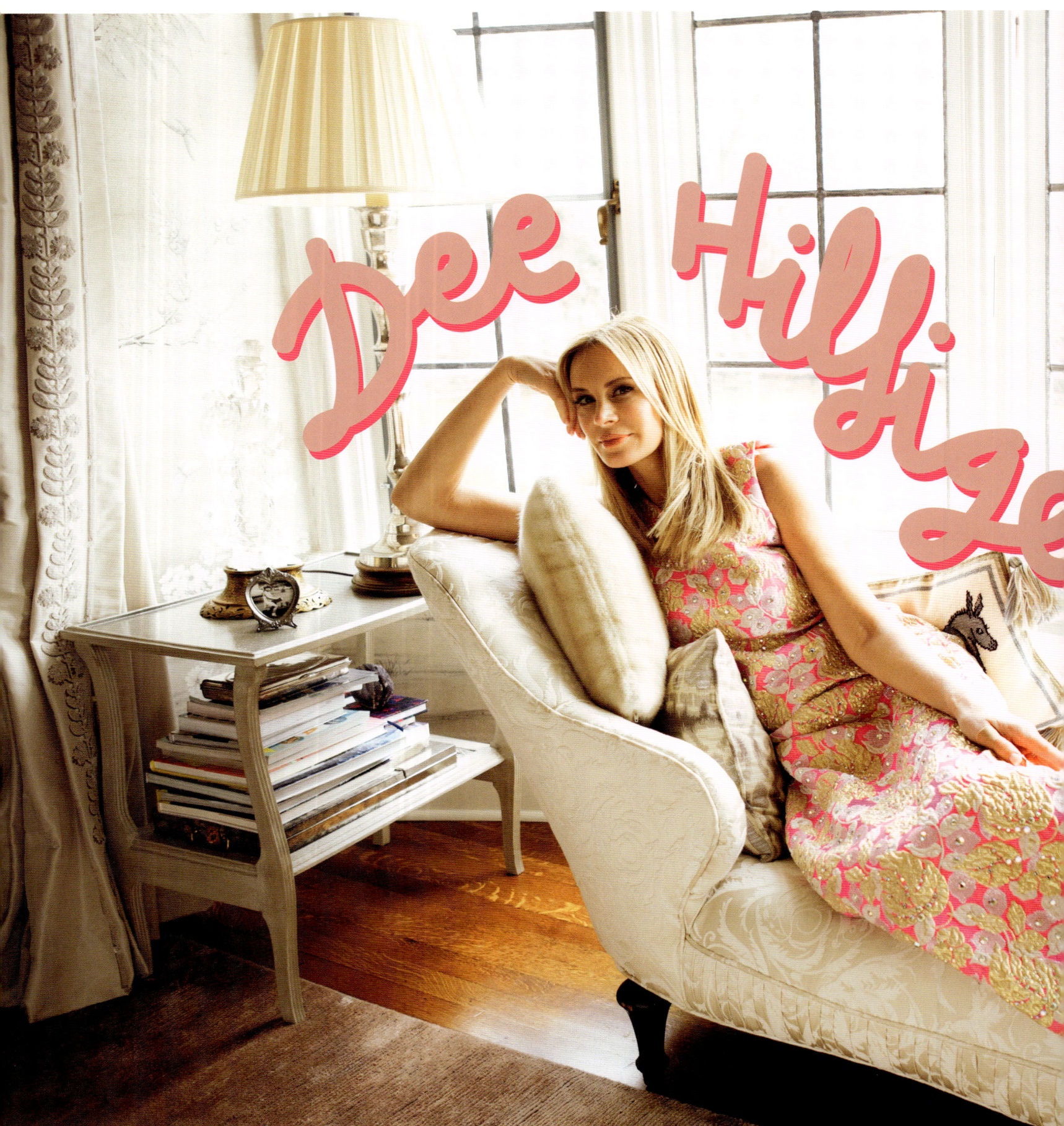

DEE HILFIGER
TOO YOUNG FOR A UNIFORM

It's early December in Greenwich. As the year draws to a close, the Hilfiger's pre-war Normandy home is in a state of near-hibernation, like a Norwegian goose gearing up for the long trek southwards. The verdant, decorative bushes in the front lawn are covered in oatmeal-colored linen sacks. The gardeners are scaling the peripherals of the roof to clear away autumn's leaves from drainpipes and gutters. Inside the house, time seems to have stopped, or at least be half asleep. Where one would expect to see a giant, ornate Christmas tree stands a vase with flowers, and an artificial, imperfect little tree with adhesive white lights is gently revived, but confined to the kitchen. Trunks are cleaned, gifts are packed up. The family is off to their home in Mustique for the holidays.

Dee is still having her makeup done when the housekeeper ushers me upstairs to the dressing room. It was Mr. Hilfiger himself who had told me about his wife's vintage collection. And as I step into the room, I understand in one instant why. Lined up against the walls of this beautiful, soft-white space, shimmering and sparkling in the morning sunlight, are mannequins wearing the most exquisite 1960s designer dresses: Paco Rabanne, Oscar de la Renta, Valentino, pieces I recognize and have admired for years. "These days I source my vintage pieces primarily online," she says, "and I'm always on the lookout for clothes with a timeless quality to them, things that still translate well today."

Deniz Caroline Ocleppo Hilfiger, 50, grew up in Rhode Island. Her father was a radiologist born in Turkey, and her mother a microbiologist, born in the U.S. She studied Communications at university in Texas, but moved to Paris and London to model. She met Tommy on a beach in Saint-Tropez two years after her divorce from Italian tennis player Gianni Ocleppo. She was living with her two sons in Monte Carlo at the time and Tommy had four kids from his own previous marriage—now they're a family of nine! The latest addition: their son Sebastian, who's eight.

Aside from the house staff and her makeup artist, Dee is alone in the house. I'm amazed but also puzzled by the equestrian theme of the interior. While it definitely feels warm and welcoming, it has an unquestionable masculine quality. I lose count after about two rooms, but I wonder how many antlers have actually been rescued. "We don't hunt," says Dee categorically. "And I don't ride horses anymore. Our home just has such a clear aesthetic at its core—all that beautiful, carved oak; to me it feels like a European country home. When we decorated it we really just tried to develop that innate DNA."

Christmas is the toughest time of the year for Dee. There was much time spent penning holiday wishes to every family member, friend, acquaintance, employee, doorman, bartender, and then waiting in agony to find out who she had forgotten. Most of their kids have families of their own now, and she has seven godchildren. It gets really hectic, especially getting all those people off to the island and finding suitable presents. "The tree is decorated when we get there," appreciates Dee. "I don't know where they get it, but it's a big old pine and it's super charming and cute in a Caribbean way, not the fancy thing you'd expect in Connecticut." She looks forward to spending time in the sun, and unpacking her yellow Mexican wedding dress for the New Year's party, but mostly she can't wait to see the last gift unwrapped, and a smile on everyone's faces...because that's when *her* vacation really begins.

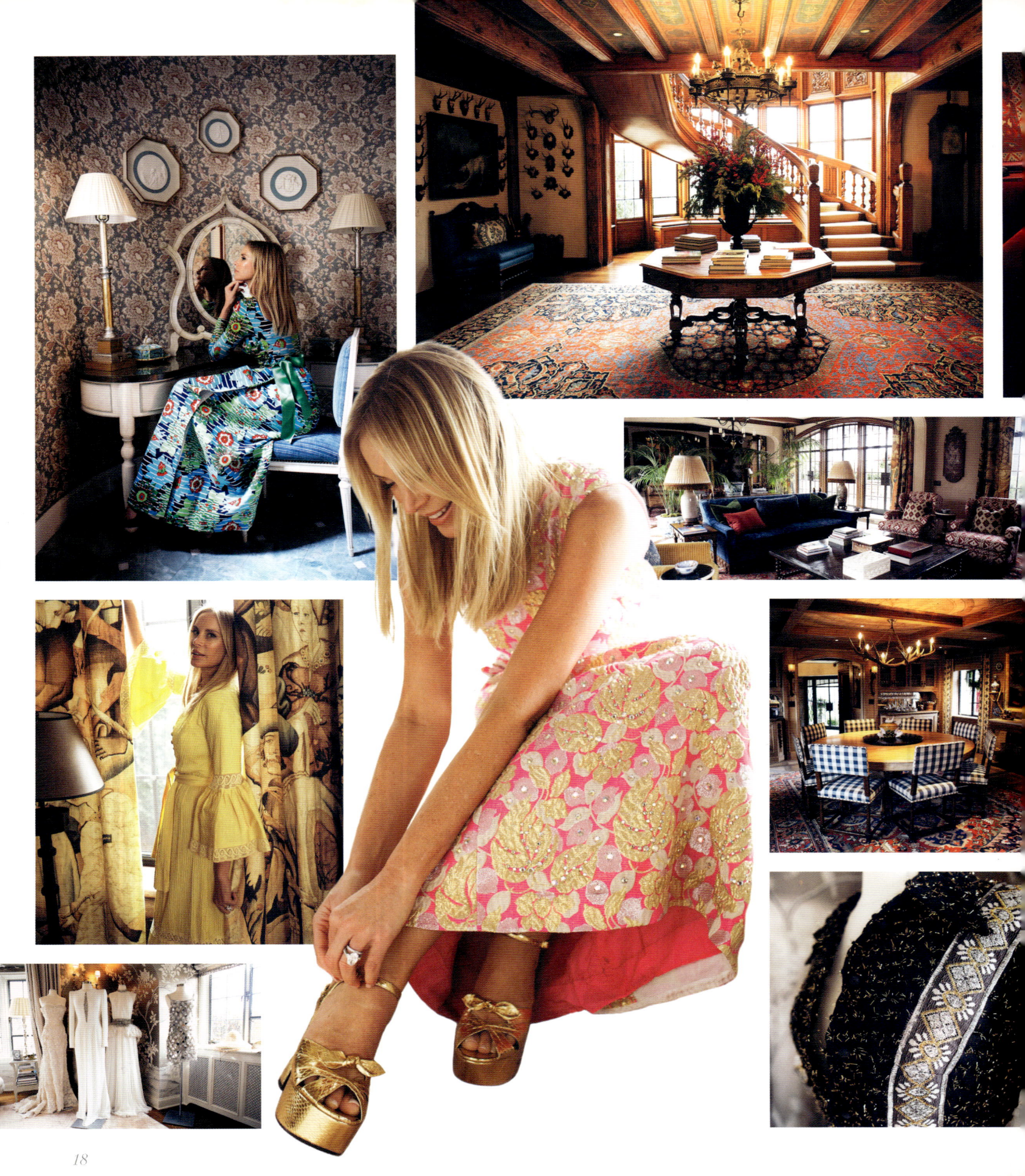

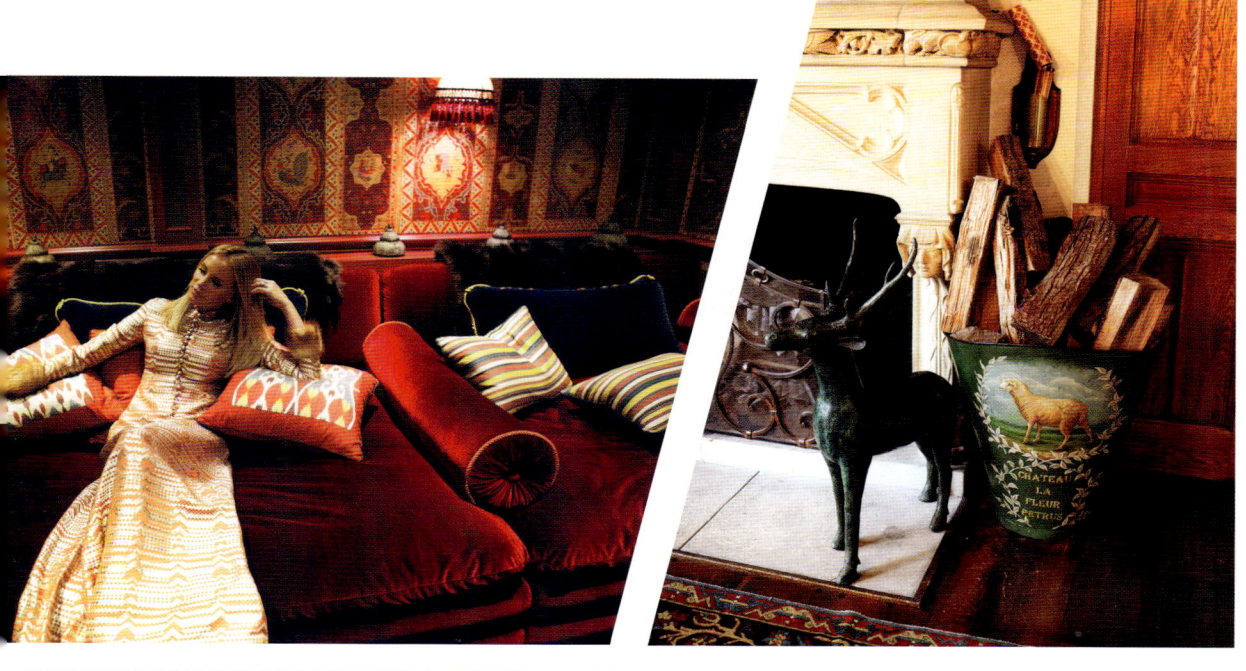
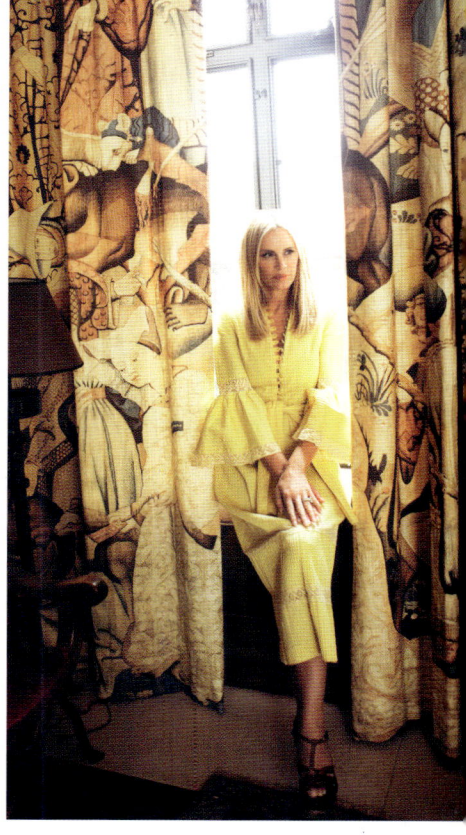
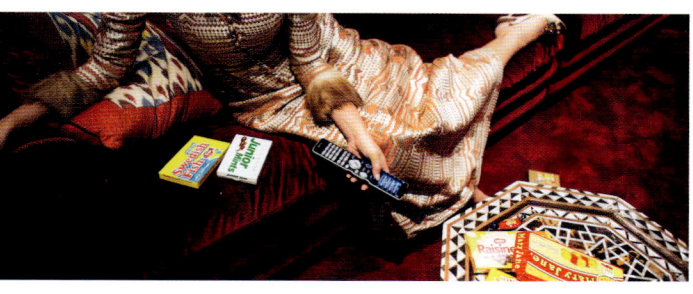
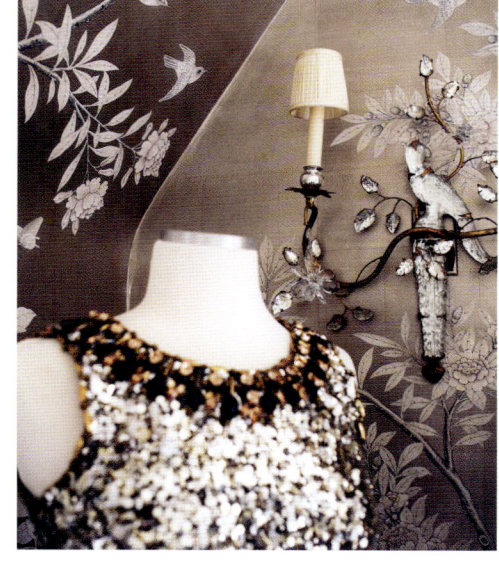
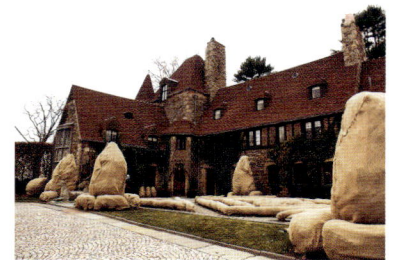
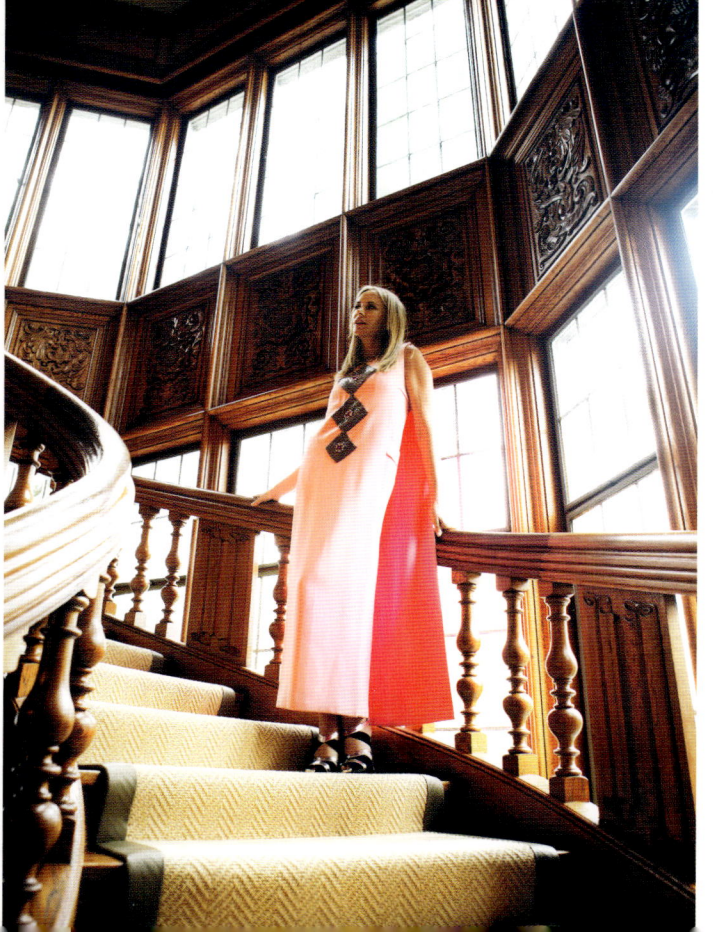
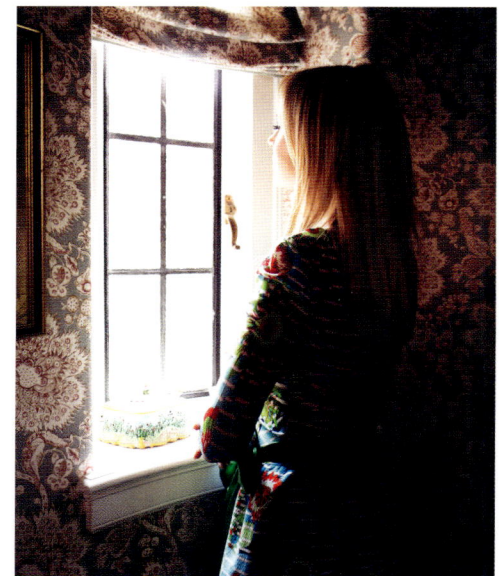
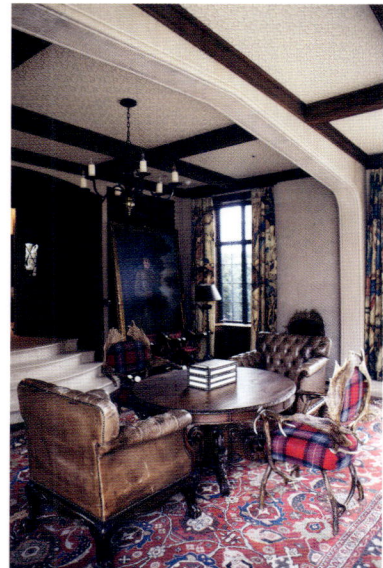

MAXINE ASHLEY
WE DON'T NEED ANY NEW CLOTHES

I could turn around right now. I don't even have to knock on the door. I can tell them later that their music was too loud, or that the dog was barking, and that they didn't hear my calls. I'm just not confident that there is anyone behind this door who loves vintage. I just took a 50-minute train ride up to the Bronx, walked the cold streets to Sherman Avenue, entered an apartment building that has seen so many layers of paint, smoke, and intrigue it looks like something out of *Scarface*, rode the elevator up five floors, and am now standing here in front of mystery door number nine with my tail between my legs. It takes a minute before she answers too, and that's when I *really* think we've got our wires crossed. The living room is empty, apart from a black futon couch and a television. Maxine is still in pajamas and seems in no rush to put clothes on. And she's asking me the kind of questions that make me wonder if she even knows who I am, as in: *What are you doing in my house?*

There's a guy here too, the roommate. His name is Raylon. He's stirring around in the kitchen, cooking something that smells like fried cheese. I also meet a woman whose voice sounds just like Maxine's. It takes me a while to figure out that Tiffany is not just Maxine's manager but also her mother, and literally looks not more than five years older. "My mother had me at a very young age," Maxine explains when she sees the astonishment on my face, "15 specifically. She wasn't supposed to live past the age of 20 or have children because she had a bad heart. But she beat all the odds, had me, and I'm blessed to still have her til this day. My mother is also one of seven kids. Let's just say I have a huge family and we're all young. No one in my family is really over 40 yet besides my grandma and she is in her early 60s." Most of them live in this very building, on different floors.

"You sure you don't want coffee or tea or anything? No? You're good?" asks Raylon. I wouldn't mind some coffee. "With almond milk?" Sure! "I'm not lactose-intolerant," interjects Tiffany. "I just don't like milk." Maxine agrees: "Milk is nasty." This little household of "Nuyoricans" as Maxine calls them, is starting to grow on me, despite the fact that we still haven't talked vintage. We're sitting around the kitchen counter chatting about the party in Williamsburg Raylon used to manage, Maxine's disastrous hangover yesterday—she woke up at 5 p.m!— and the superintendent who painted their door shut from the outside and accidentally held them hostage for a few hours. Before long I have a plate of Yucca, purple and white Cassava, sautéed onions, fried cheese, and salami in front of me, and it tastes incredible. I went from wanting to run, to wanting to move in, in a matter of minutes. "Yeah, that's the point," laughs Maxine. "We got another bed! A queen-size, double, you know."

Maxine Ashley had been on my radar for a while. She's a promising new artist, and one of Pharrell's new protégés. She sounds like Beyoncé, no joke; her new EP will blow your mind. I was also intrigued by her look. It's urban, sexy, suave, and kind of hardcore-raver too: different, refreshing, and unlike anyone else's in this book. When we finally slide open the doors of her closet, I am relieved and impressed: there *is* a lot of love here. Personally she describes her wardrobe as "cozy, high fashion, bummy, street wear." In other words: "I'm an oxymoron." And she loves thrifting. "I usually go for whatever catches my eye and looks like something I can't find anywhere else," she explains. Vintage shopping is an addiction: "Looking through clothes and finding gems, I just looove the thought of wearing something so old and rare," she gushes, "wearing an article of clothing that has more history than myself. Plus I love buying recycled clothes as opposed to buying new, new, new. We don't need any new clothes."

After lunch we visit grandma downstairs. One of Maxine's cousins is there too—she's pregnant. We take pictures by the Christmas tree and proceed onto the rooftop. She loves the view here, but will soon have to say goodbye because she's moving to Los Angeles. Coincidentally, so am I. And as I'm walking back to the subway, I realize something important: the passion, dedication, and appreciation we feel for vintage is what binds us, no matter the size of our wallet, the shape of our body, or the color of our skin. The love is just as deep, even if it looks totally different on the outside. Yesterday I photographed a society girl in designer gowns at a mansion, today an R&B artist in 80s baseball shirts in the Bronx. But if you sat them in a room together and asked them to describe how they *felt* about their wardrobes, you wouldn't be able to tell them apart. It's not about taste or money or age; it's a lifestyle.

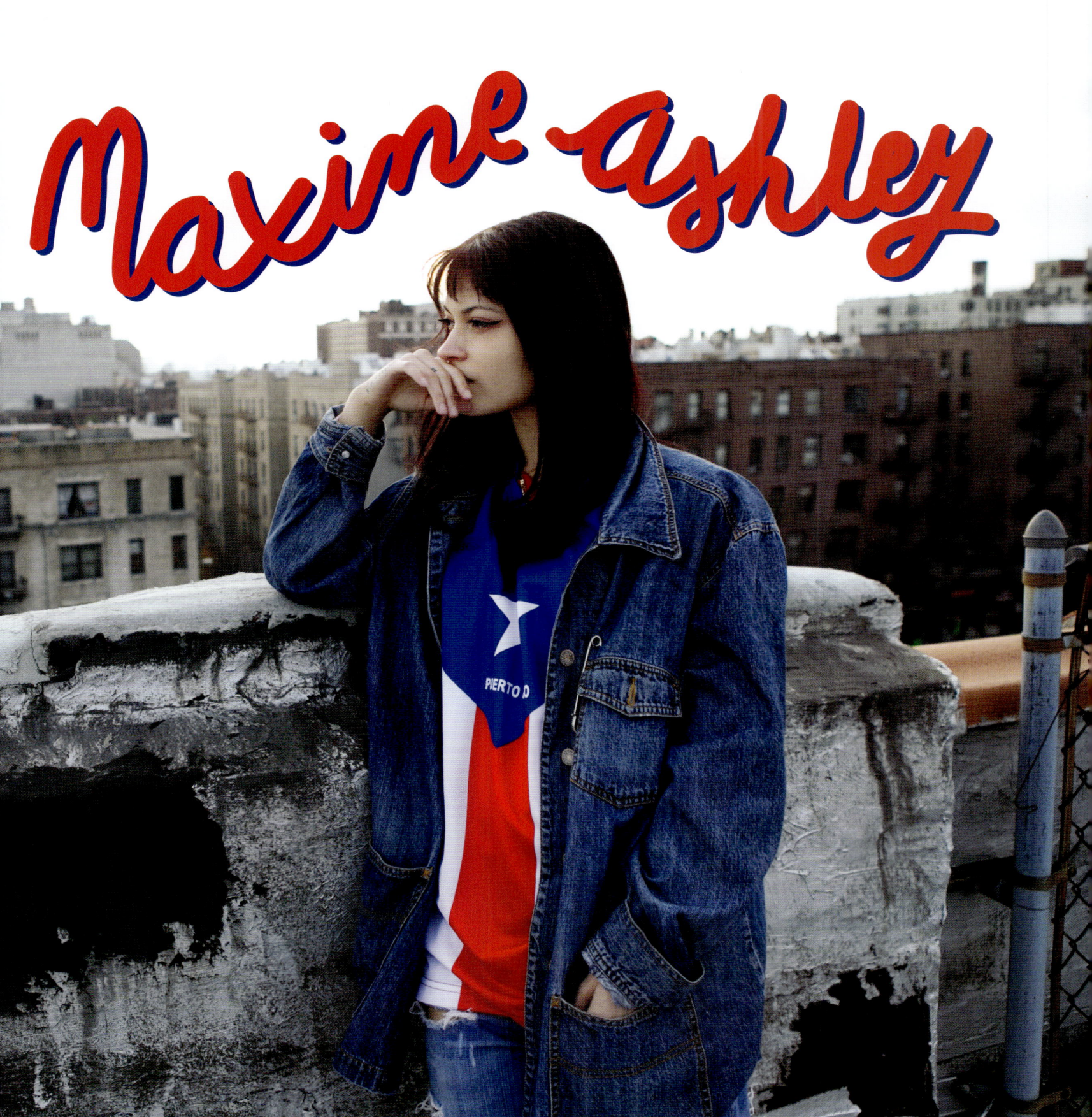

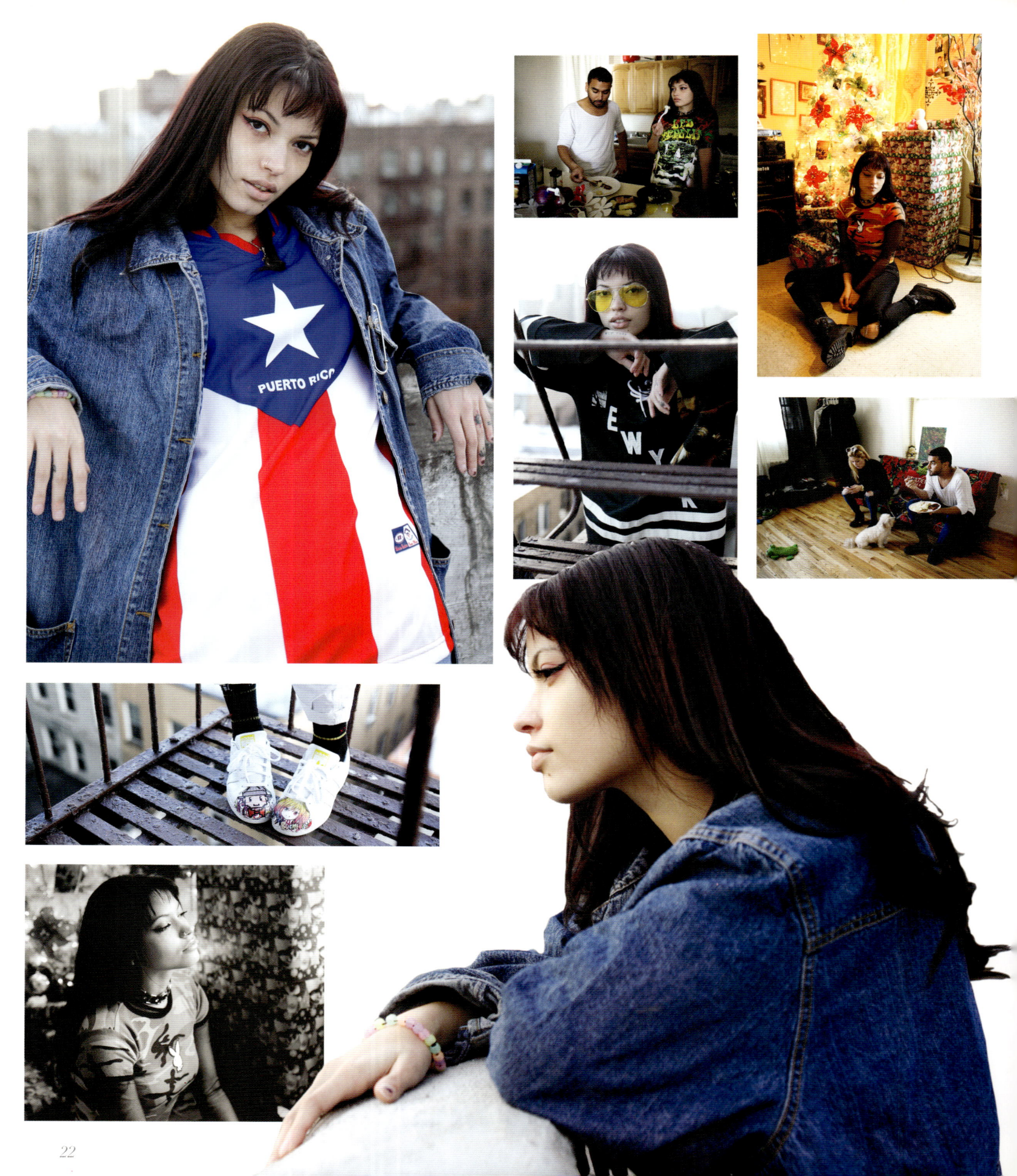

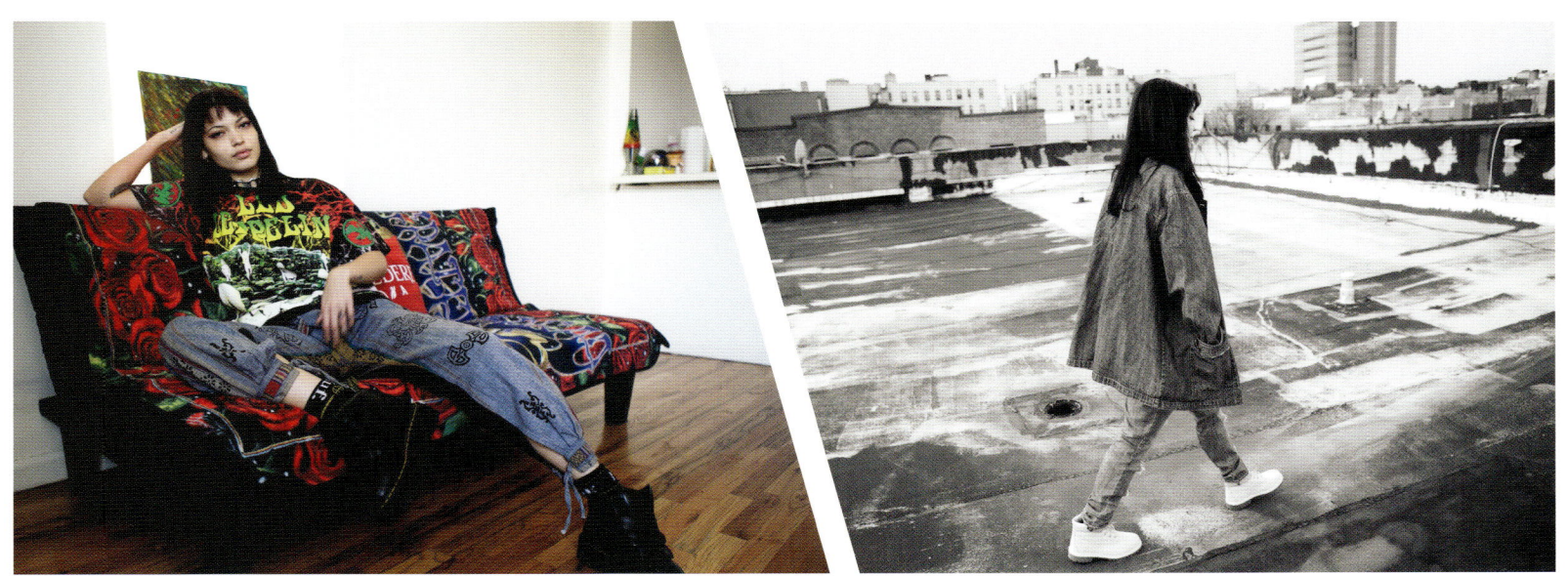
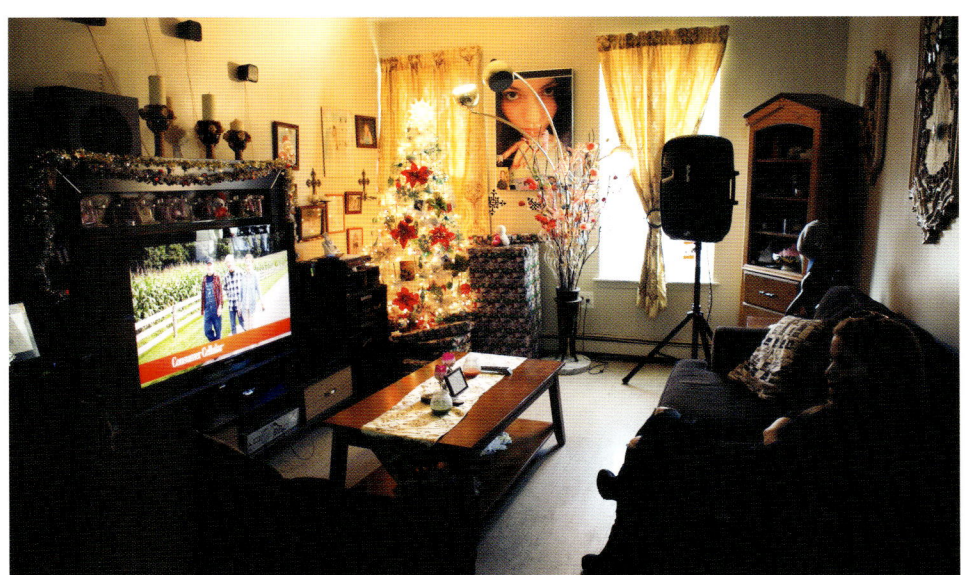
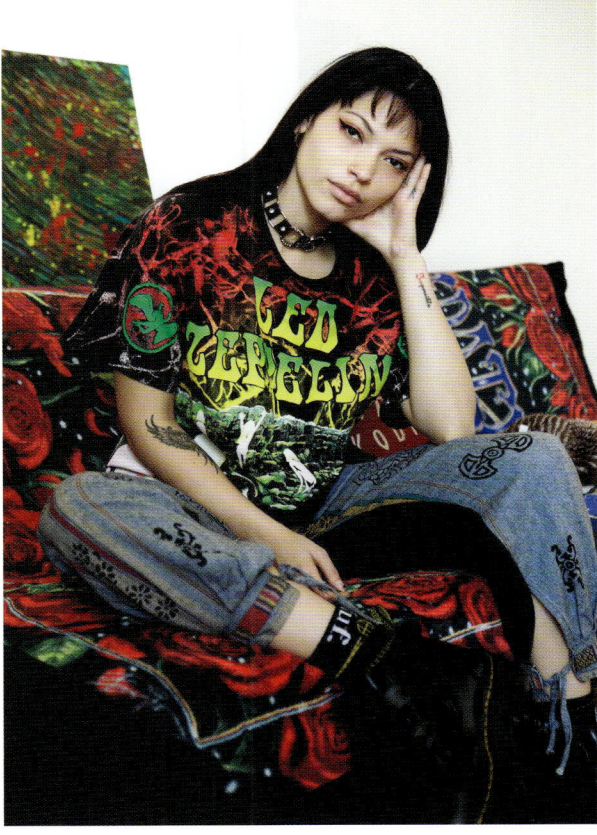
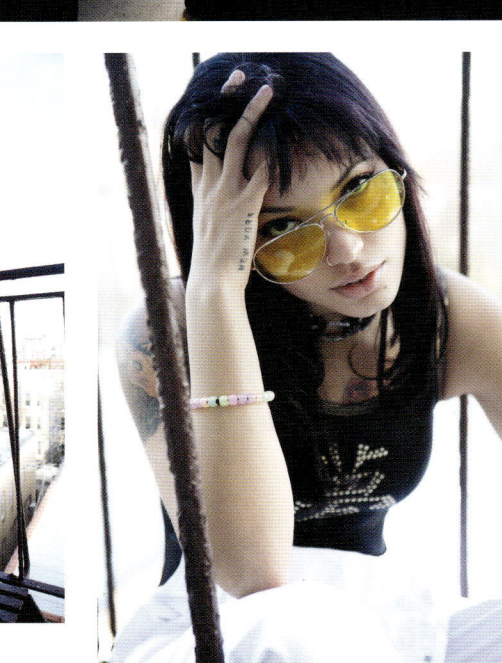
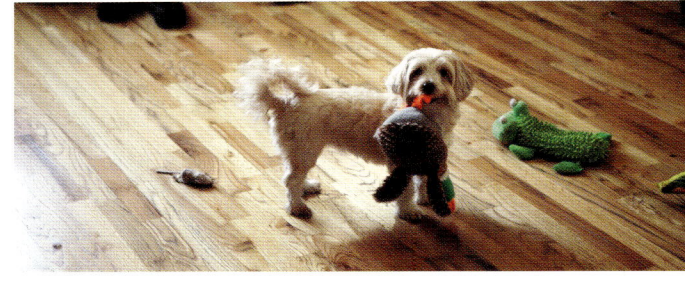

23

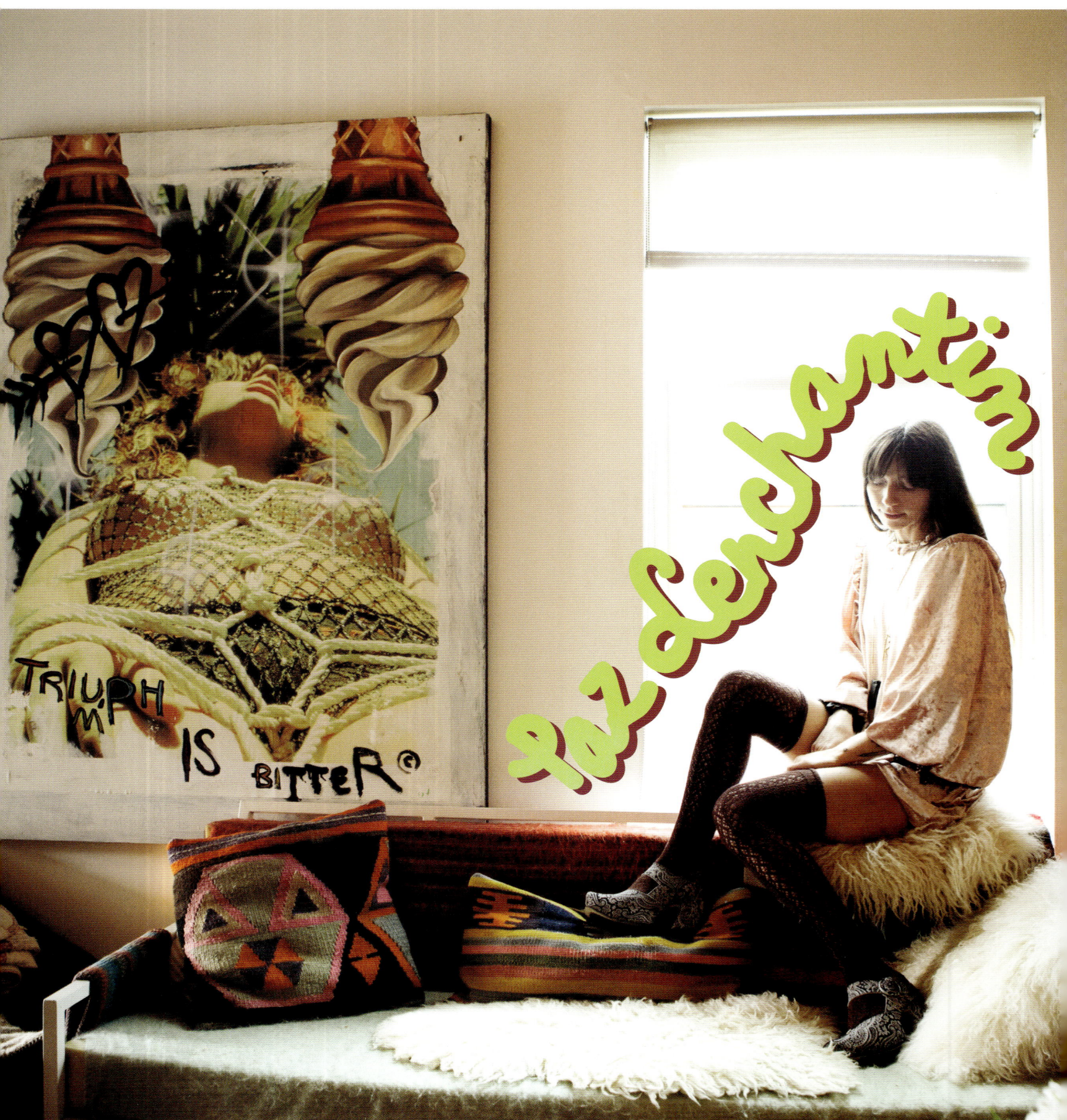

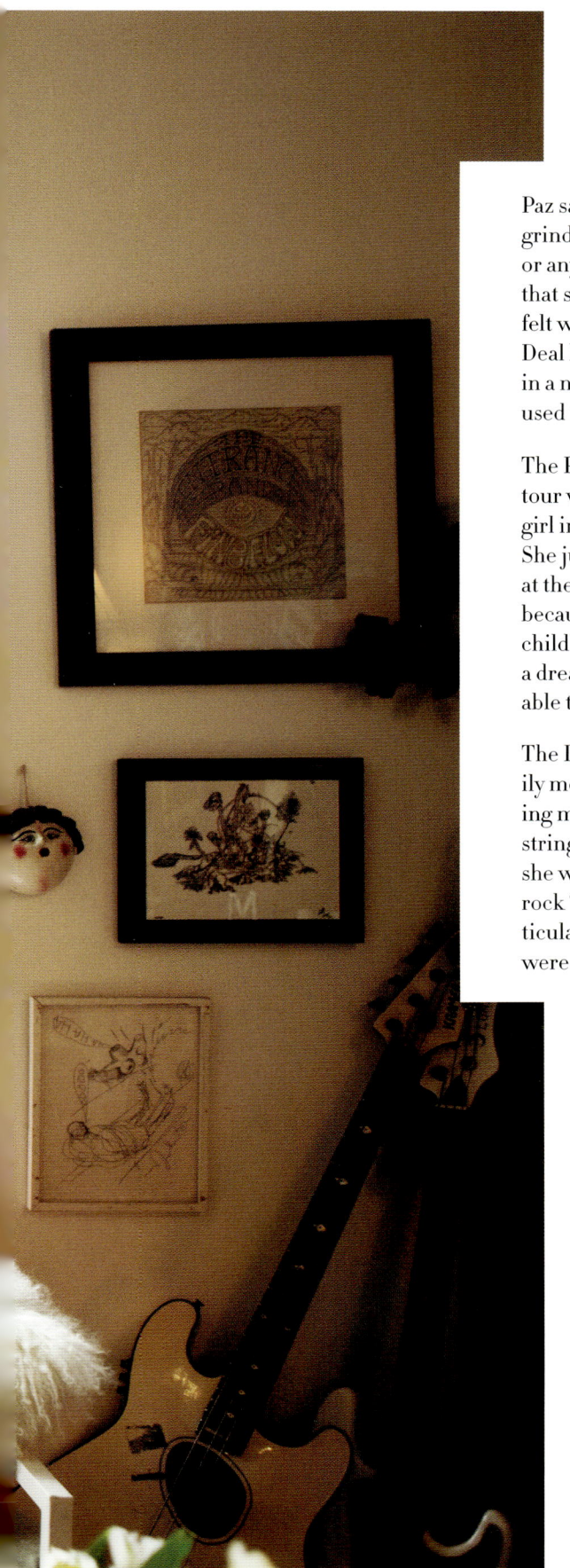

PAZ LENCHANTIN
LIKE A PLUMBER

Paz says she feels like a plumber. She's at the kitchen counter, grinding some espresso beans and fixing us a cup of coffee. There's nothing wrong with her pipes or anything. The water seems to be running fine in this little duplex on the Venice Canals. It's just that she's had some pretty big shoes to fill as of late, and it took a while for her to rebuild what she felt was broken. I'm talking about her stepping-in as the new bass player of the Pixies after Kim Deal left in 2014. The fans had a hard time with the sudden transition, but she finally "feels like it's in a new place," and she's "finally accepted into the band, without the nostalgia about how things used to be."

The Pixies just got back from South Africa and Australia. For the next year they will be on a world tour with their latest album, *Head Carrier*. Paz doesn't mind the long hours, or the fact that she's a girl in a boy's world. As long as she can keep making her stop-motion films on Super 8, she's happy. She just finished their latest music video for "Classic Masher," and won the "Avant-Garde Award" at the 2017 Audience Awards so, suffice it to say, she's good at it. "I knew I was gonna be a musician because everyone called me a musician before I had a chance to be anything else," she says of her childhood ambitions. "One of my favorite parts about being a musician is that it requires me to be a dreamer and to keep on dreaming. Sometimes I dream about making films. I hope one day to be able to score a beautiful film."

The Lenchantins were classical pianists in Argentina—Paz means *peace* in Spanish—and the family moved to California when Paz was still a child. "I was raised in a classical environment, studying music at a very young age, starting with piano and violin," she says. "My siblings also played stringed instruments. Part of our upbringing was to play music together as a family." And perhaps she would have continued the virtuous path of a concert-violinist had she not been seduced by rock 'n' roll. At about 12 years old, she was at a grocery store in the Valley when she heard a particularly enticing song on the radio. "I was with my friend at the time, so I asked her dad who we were listening to; he laughed and said, 'Why, this is the Beatles!' I had no idea who they were, but I became instantly obsessed. I bought a bass and figured out all of Paul's basslines on my own. He's still my hero."

But it wasn't a complete departure. When it comes to her stage presence, Paz still holds to certain standards, like a Wimbledon champion to his white uniform. "It is a prerequisite for the orchestra to perform in your 'concert black,'" she claims, "I still abide by this rule. I still perform in my concert black; it gives me a sense of separating life on and off stage." When she's not playing, she wears colors, and her words become almost poetic. "I like the colors you see when you're dizzy, or through a window in the rain," she muses. "I like the way painter Gustav Klimt uses gold combined with deep reds and oranges. I like textures made of velvet and lace. I like Moroccan colors; their colors of spices are both earthy and dreamy." The Victorian era is her favorite. It's all vintage, all the time: "I remember the first time I *wasn't* wearing vintage," she thinks back and then laughs, "I went to school with the price tag still attached."

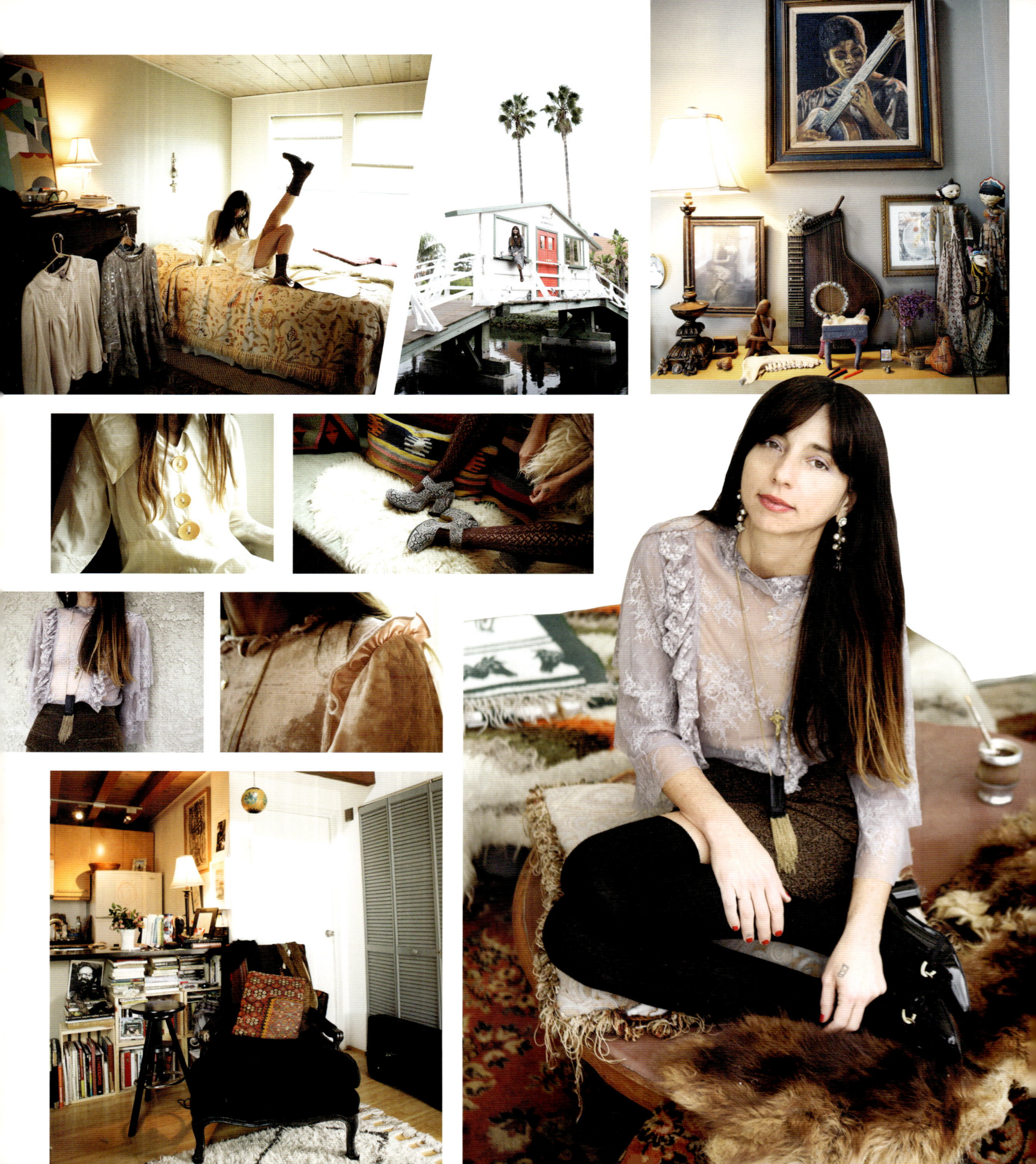

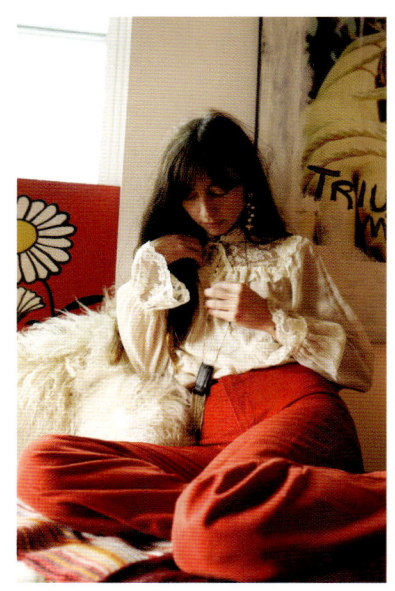
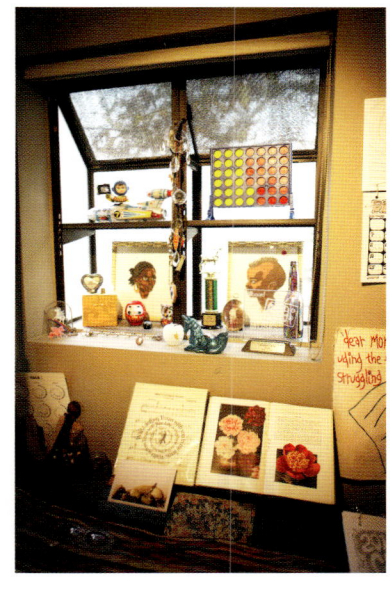
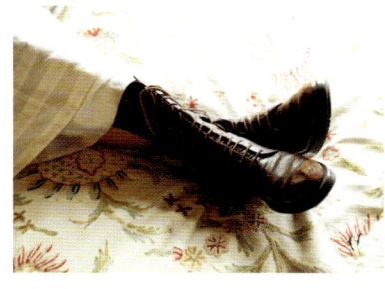
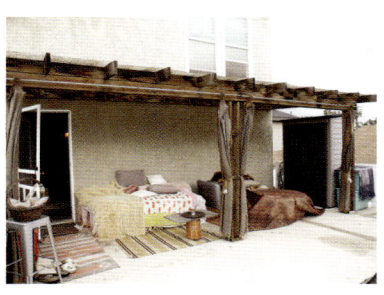
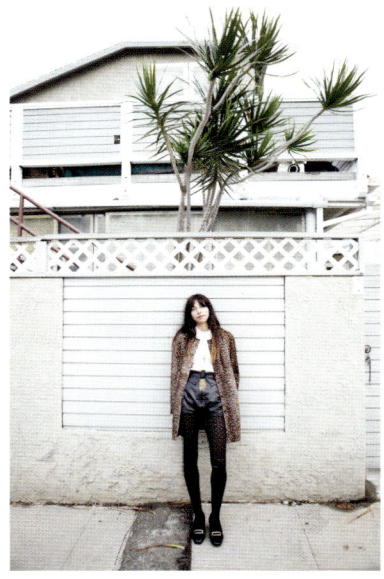
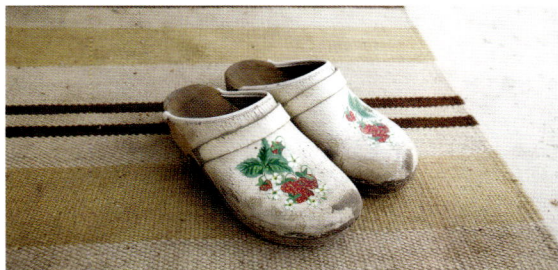
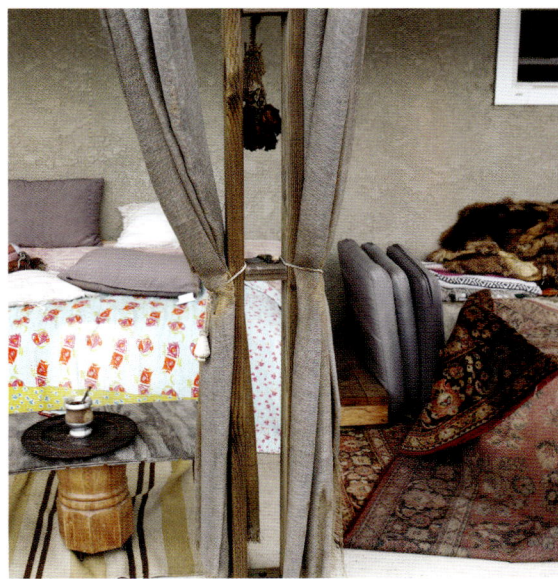
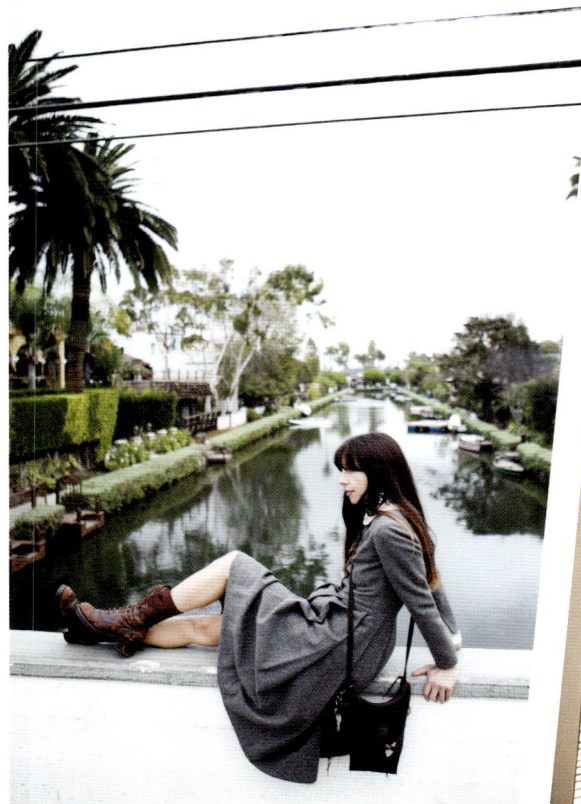
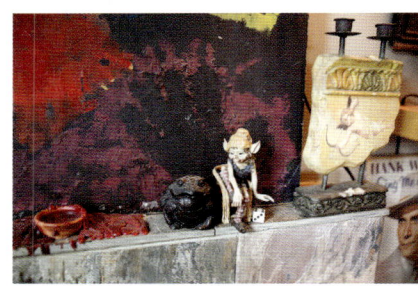
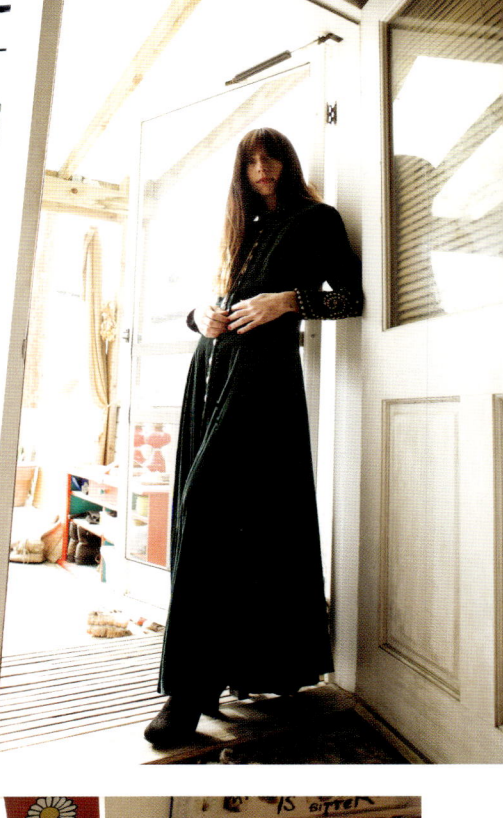
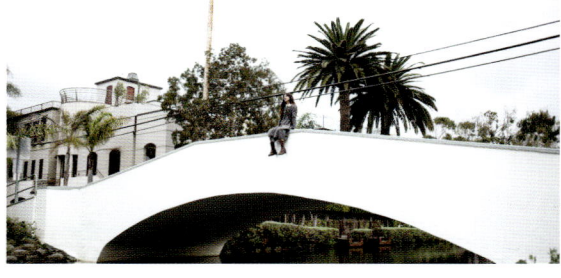
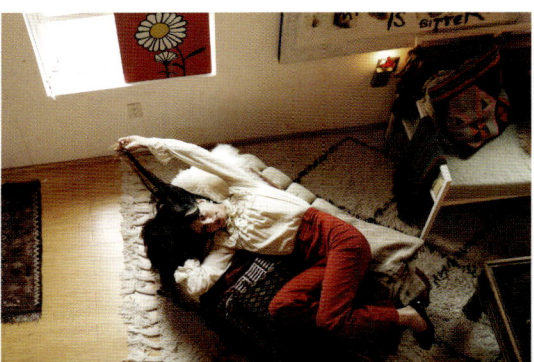

CATHERINE BABA
DIVINE INTERVENTION

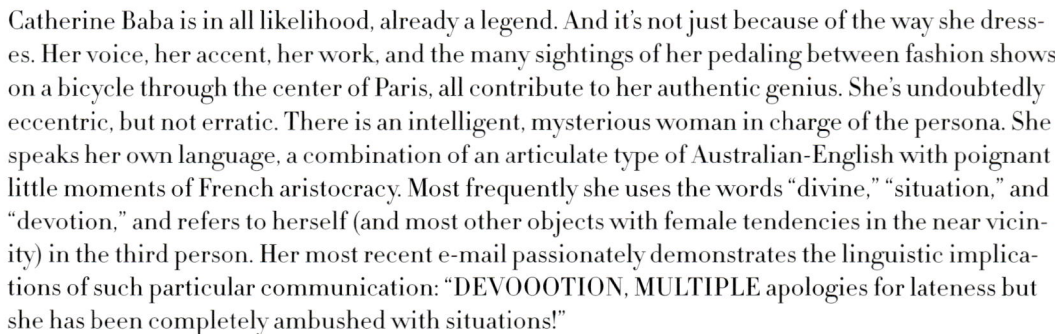

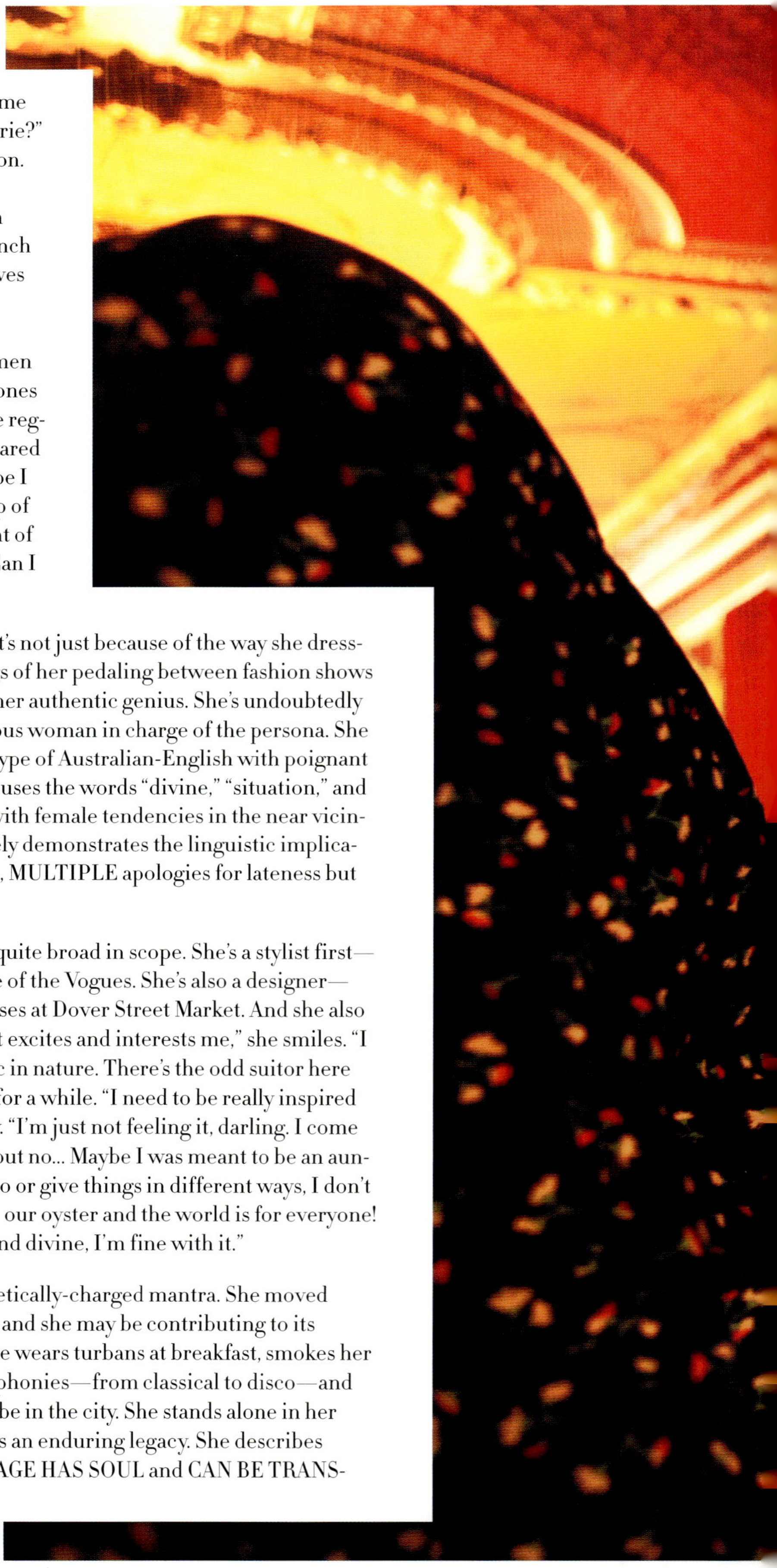

"Do you really want me to get on a table, chérie?" She looks around the dining room with a pained expression. I can tell the suggestion intrigues her, but perhaps not in those heels? And not in her favorite restaurant? We are on the top floor of Lapérouse, an infamous, 18th-century French bistro on the riverbank of the Seine in Paris. Catherine loves it because it's "haunted by poets." The story goes that rich French men would take their mistresses to dine here, and when offered diamond jewelry (as adulterers do), the women would scratch the mirrors above the banquets with the stones to make sure they were real. Catherine and her friends are regulars here. "I'm afraid I will ruin the table for them. I'm scared I'll slip and all the glasses will fall," she hesitates. "Or maybe I can sit on her?" She points at the mantel and climbs on top of it. She refers to it as the "chi-chimney," and asks with a hint of excitement: "Are we feeling her? Should I stand on her? Can I see?" I show her the screen of my camera. "J'adore!"

Catherine Baba is in all likelihood, already a legend. And it's not just because of the way she dresses. Her voice, her accent, her work, and the many sightings of her pedaling between fashion shows on a bicycle through the center of Paris, all contribute to her authentic genius. She's undoubtedly eccentric, but not erratic. There is an intelligent, mysterious woman in charge of the persona. She speaks her own language, a combination of an articulate type of Australian-English with poignant little moments of French aristocracy. Most frequently she uses the words "divine," "situation," and "devotion," and refers to herself (and most other objects with female tendencies in the near vicinity) in the third person. Her most recent e-mail passionately demonstrates the linguistic implications of such particular communication: "DEVOOOTION, MULTIPLE apologies for lateness but she has been completely ambushed with situations!"

Hyphenated and unfettered as she is, these situations are quite broad in scope. She's a stylist first—she works for magazines like Dazed & Confused and some of the Vogues. She's also a designer—she has her own line of superior, vintage-inspired sunglasses at Dover Street Market. And she also designs costumes for cinema. "I do all and any project that excites and interests me," she smiles. "I am living my dreams." The situations can also be romantic in nature. There's the odd suitor here and there, but for the most part she's decided to be single for a while. "I need to be really inspired by a man," she explains. And kid situations? Not right now. "I'm just not feeling it, darling. I come from a family of eight, and I have 15 nieces and nephews, but no... Maybe I was meant to be an auntie. Pourquoi pas? I don't think I'm being selfish. If I can do or give things in different ways, I don't think I need to help populate the population. The world is our oyster and the world is for everyone! I don't believe in borders. Just as long as everyone's chic and divine, I'm fine with it."

She's most certainly in the right place to uphold her aesthetically-charged mantra. She moved from Sydney to Paris because it is "the capital of couture," and she may be contributing to its Bohemian, laissez-faire mentality in significant spurts. She wears turbans at breakfast, smokes her cigarettes with tip filters, collects kimonos, listens to symphonies—from classical to disco—and undoubtedly owns the most sophisticated vintage wardrobe in the city. She stands alone in her niche, which makes her all the more powerful and ensures an enduring legacy. She describes vintage just as I would describe her superior taste: "VINTAGE HAS SOUL and CAN BE TRANSFORMED ETERNALLY!"

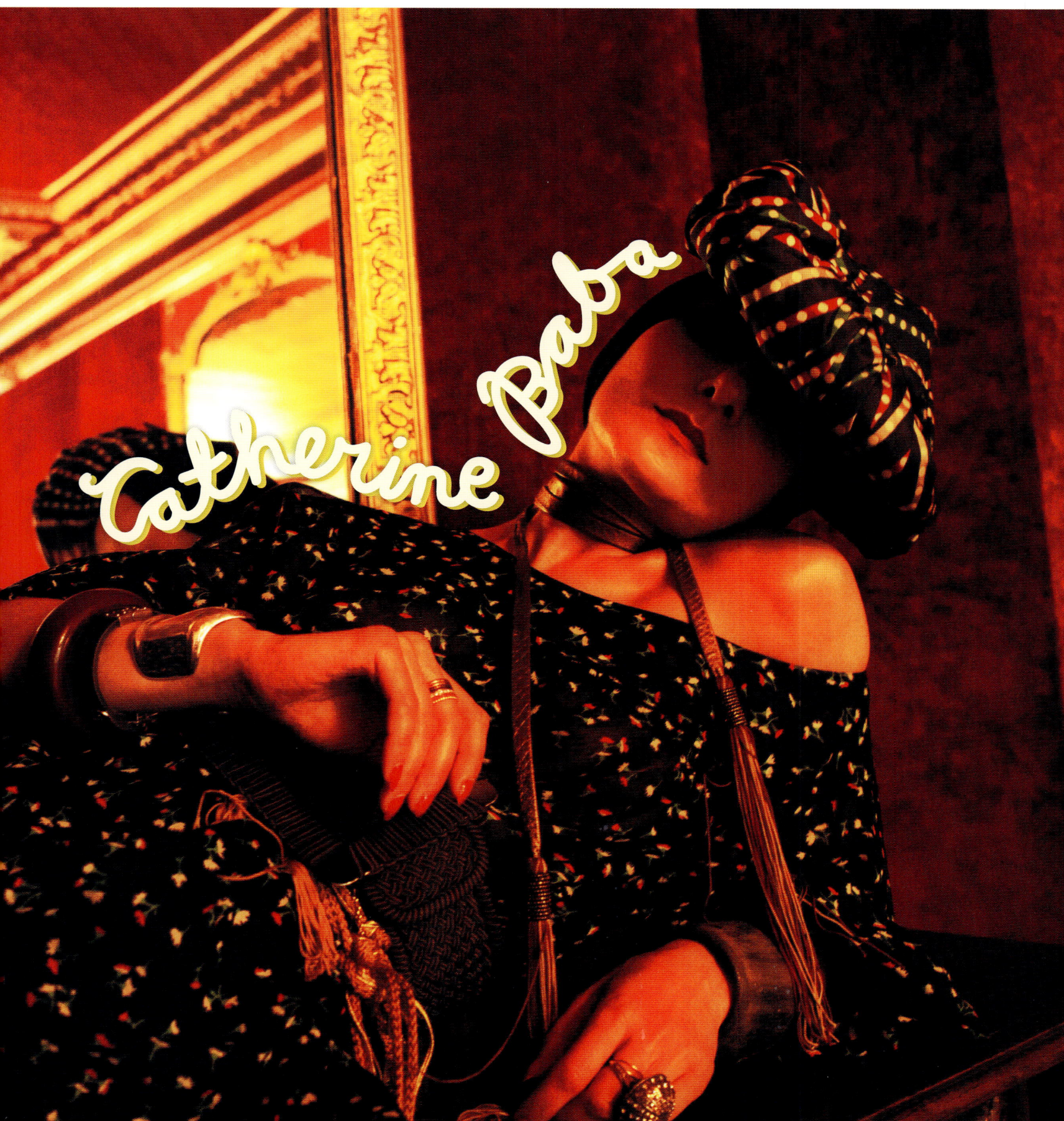

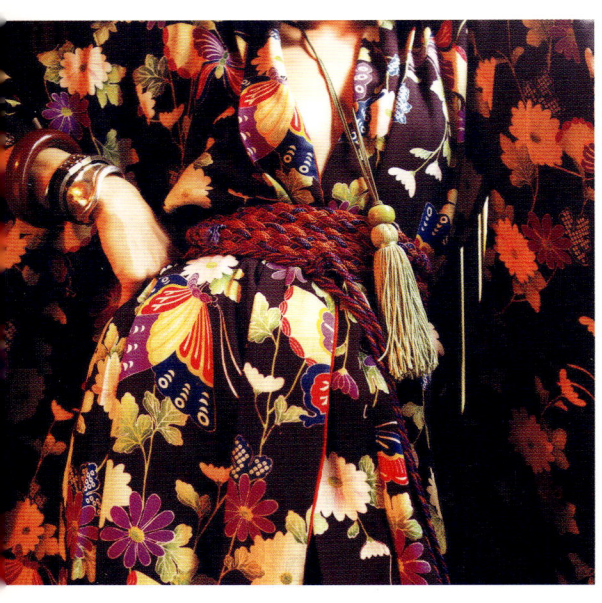
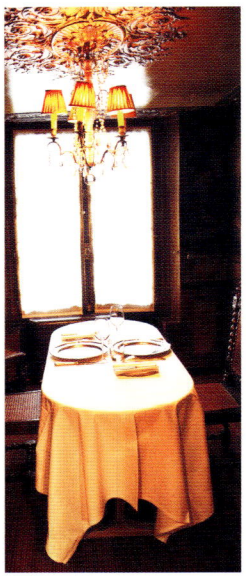
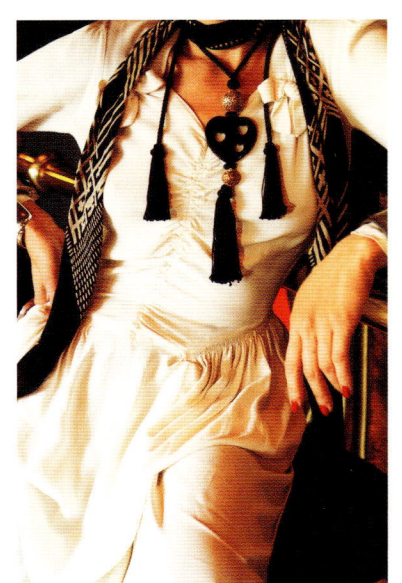
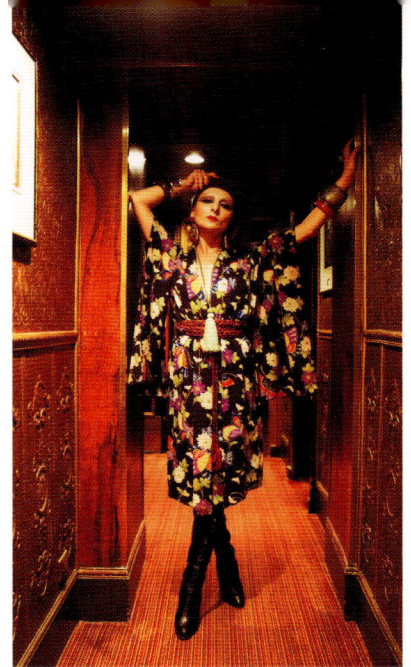
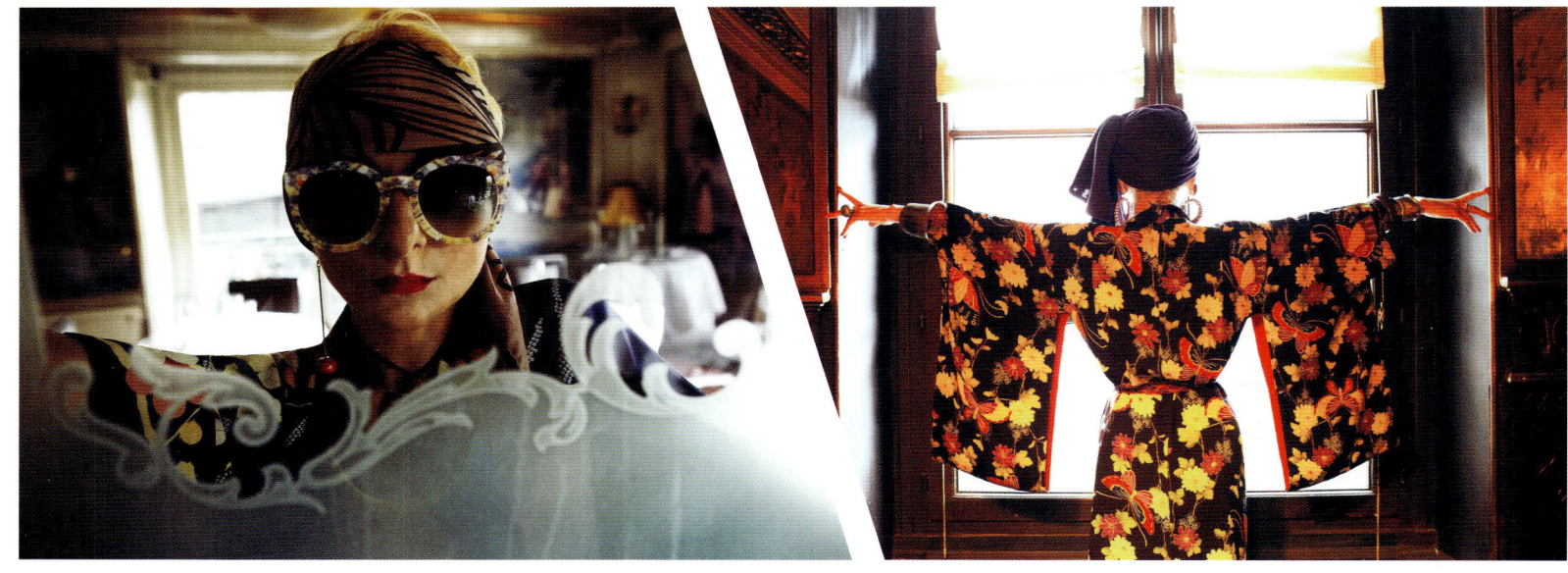
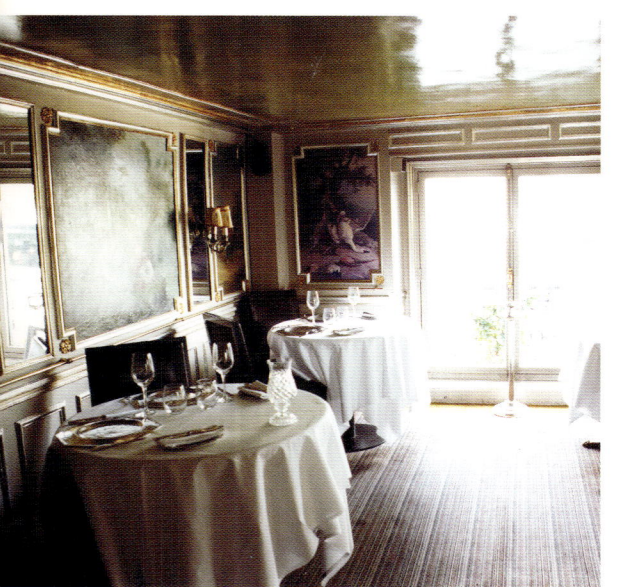
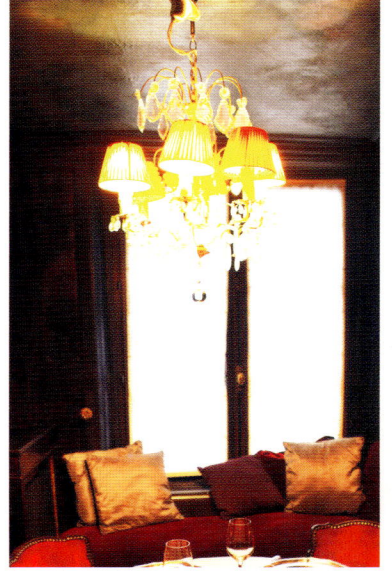
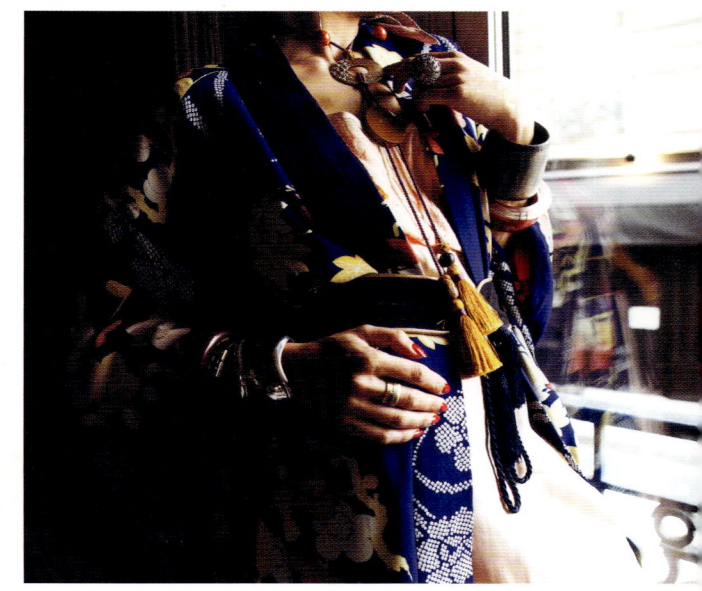

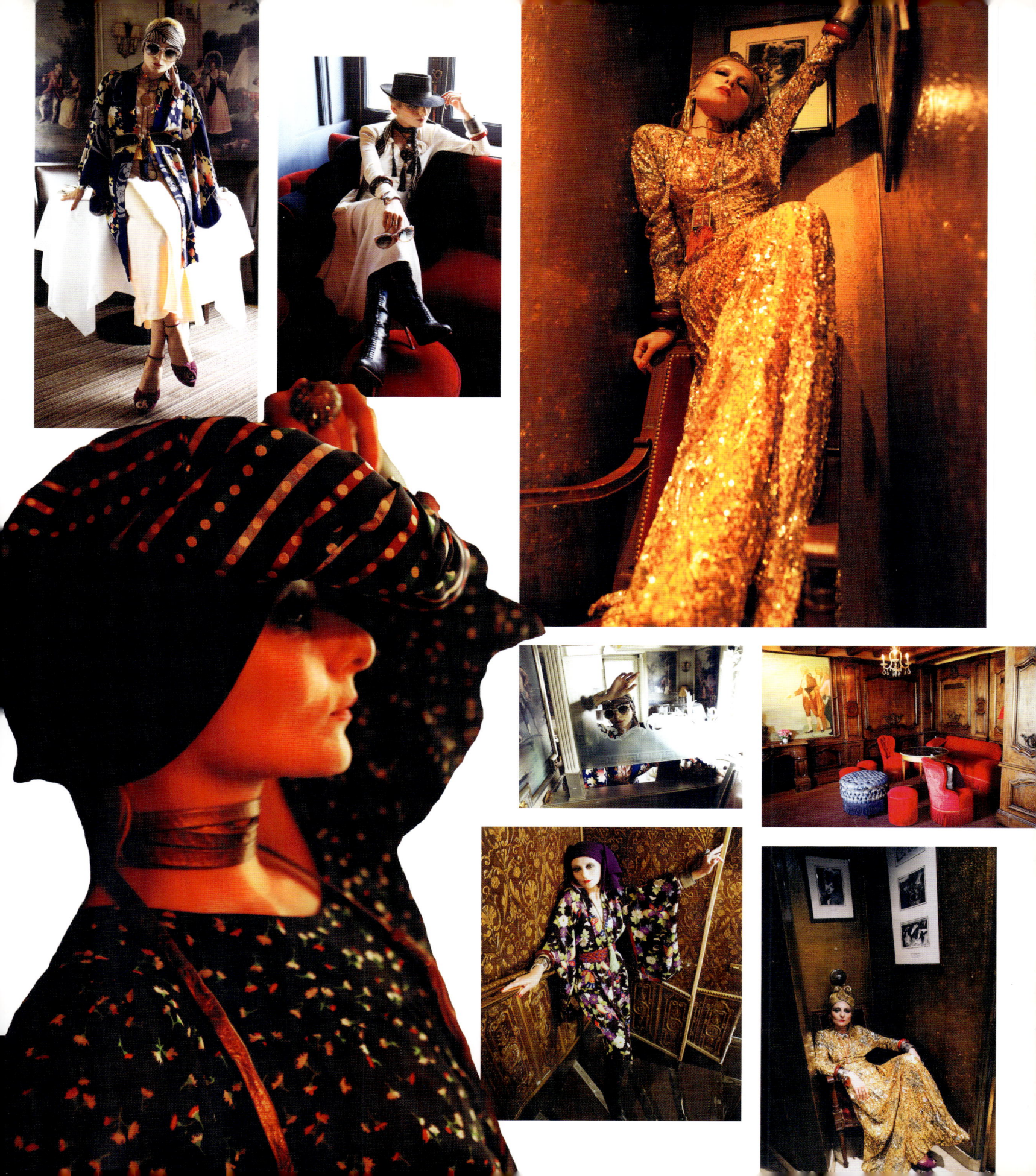

AMY VAN DORAN
THE MATCHMAKER

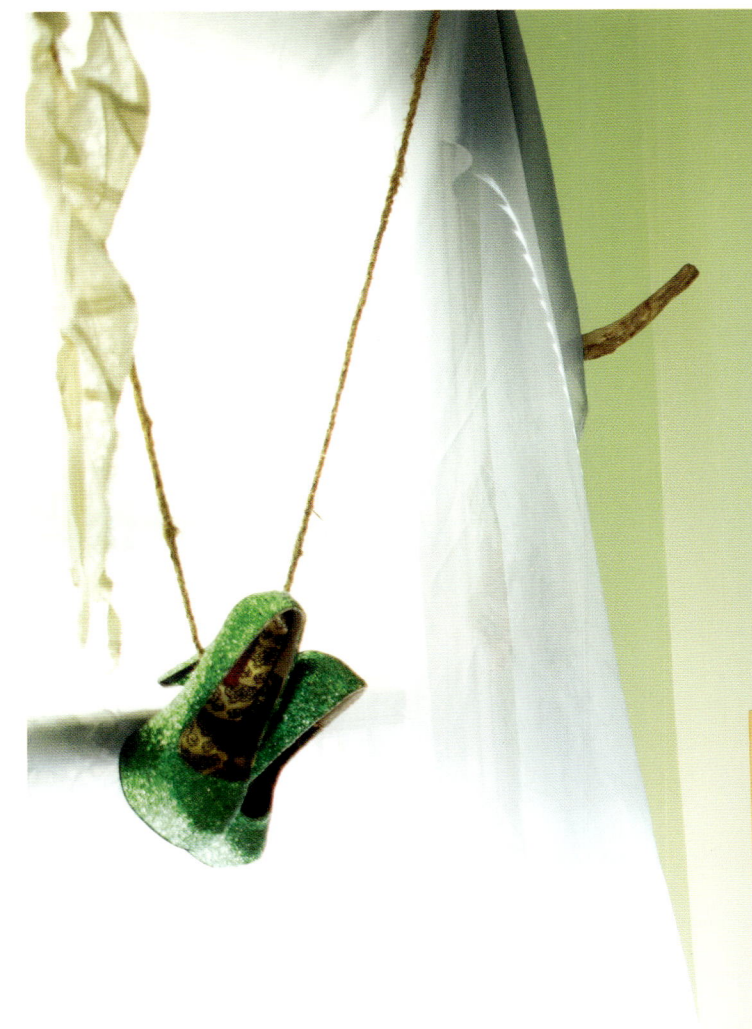

I wonder what it takes to become one of Amy's clients, what arduous, heart-wrenching process one has to go through to become part of her exclusive Modern Love Club Rolodex. She's quite mysterious about it. She only takes on 16 clients at a time and sees them for six months, "or until they fall in love, whatever comes first." Maybe my being single and dropping subtle hints isn't so subtle after all, and she sees right off the bat that I am a lost cause. I get it. Why jeopardize a perfect marriage-and-baby track record by taking on a faulty client? This professional matchmaker is not taking any chances, even if she thinks that "love is the most important thing in the world," and she wants "everyone to get a chance to experience it." So I move on. To the color of her hair to be exact.

It's orange now, and I can't help but ask if it's real or a wig. She assures me it's real. Her natural color is brown but it only made an appearance when she had a regular job. In high school it was purple, pink, and green. It's just another expression of her personality, her way of saying: "Hello stranger, I would like to know you, please say hi!" She learned how to own her weirdness from a very young age. "The harmony between my interior self and my presentation was a long journey," she says, "and I feel so grateful to have come home to myself." Her general rules for fashion are "A: There should always be a joke built into the outfit. B: False eyelashes solve all existential problems, and C: More is more is more."

Amy Van Doran grew up on a junkyard in Cape Canaveral, Florida, raised by a junkman grandfather and former circus performer grandmother. They adopted her. She led a free, surreal, and strange childhood. She tells me about the day she wore a garbage bag taped on like a dress to school and it started to rip in the middle of the day, and shows me a family portrait in head-to-toe Victorian dress. And she remembers going thrift shopping, digging for costumes, and imagining living different lives so no one would make fun of her. She wanted to be a basketball player, an artist, and a performer. "I'm happy to say that two of these things are still a part of my life!" she laughs. She studied film and acting, but eventually ended up at Matchmaking Institute—yes that's a real thing! "It's very popular now," she winks.

Amy is actually much more normal than she willingly demonstrates. She's a small girl with a sweet voice and a mild sense of humor. We have pleasant conversations about her white baby poodle Juniper Prancer, who's blind and incontinent, the stuffed "elephant" who's always "in the room," and the funny characters she performs today: a mermaid, a homemaker in apron, Pippi Longstocking goes to Boca Raton, and "Barbarella mixed with the jewelry of an anthropologist wife from the 50s." So, what about her own love life then? Apparently dating comes easy to her. She refers to her guys as "gentleman callers," and always seems to have a few floating around. I casually mention that my ex lives around the corner from her, and she pauses: "What's his name?" And with a slight tone of danger she adds: "Just to make sure I haven't matched or slept with him…"

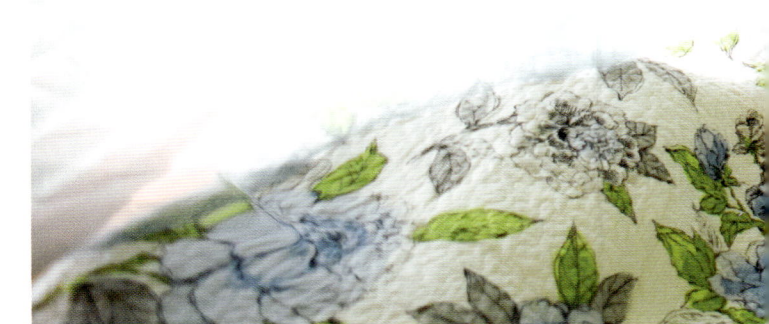

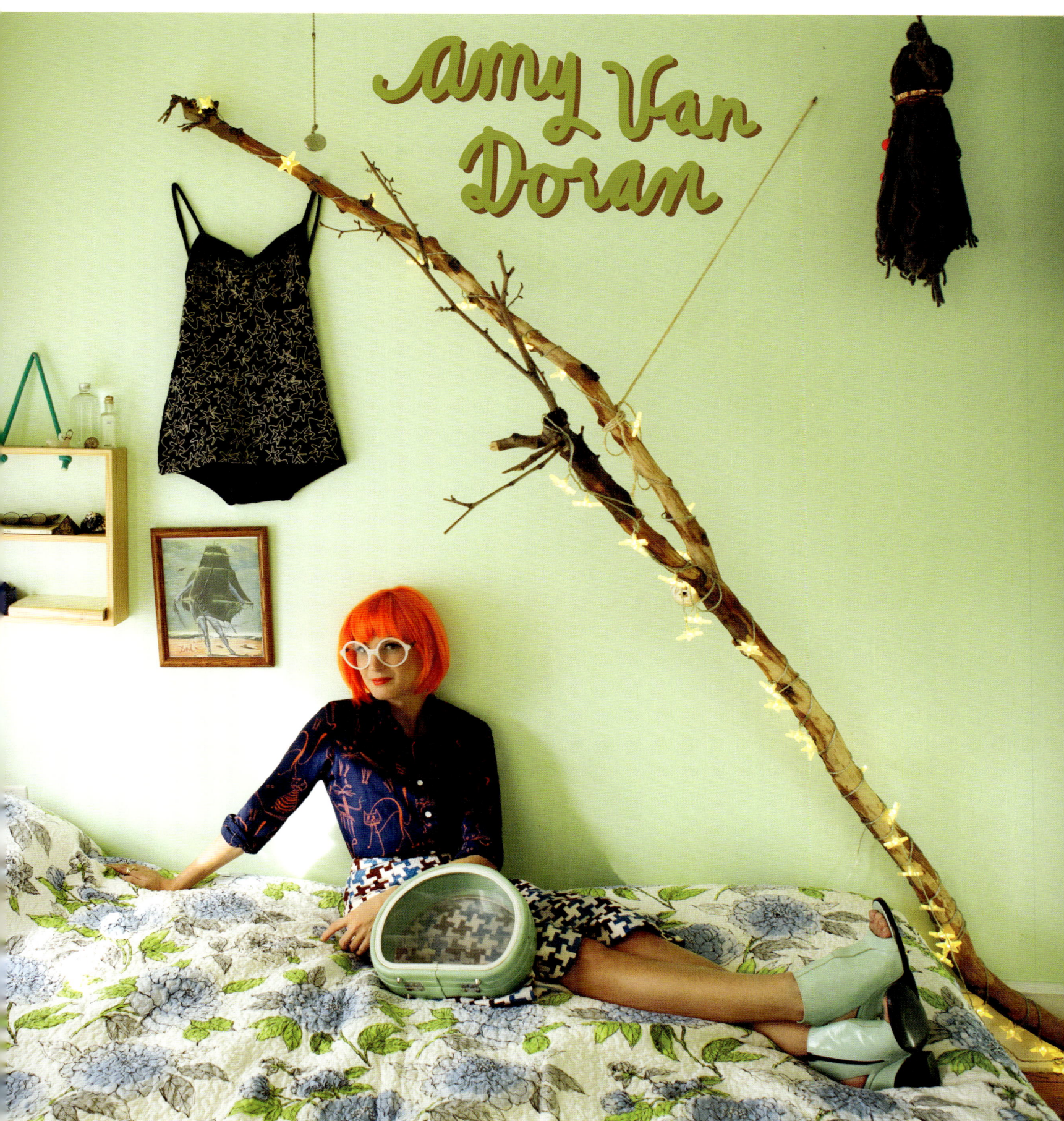

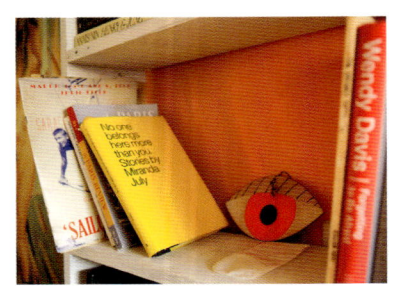
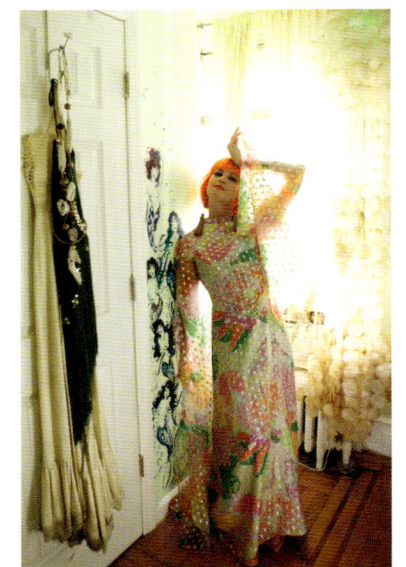
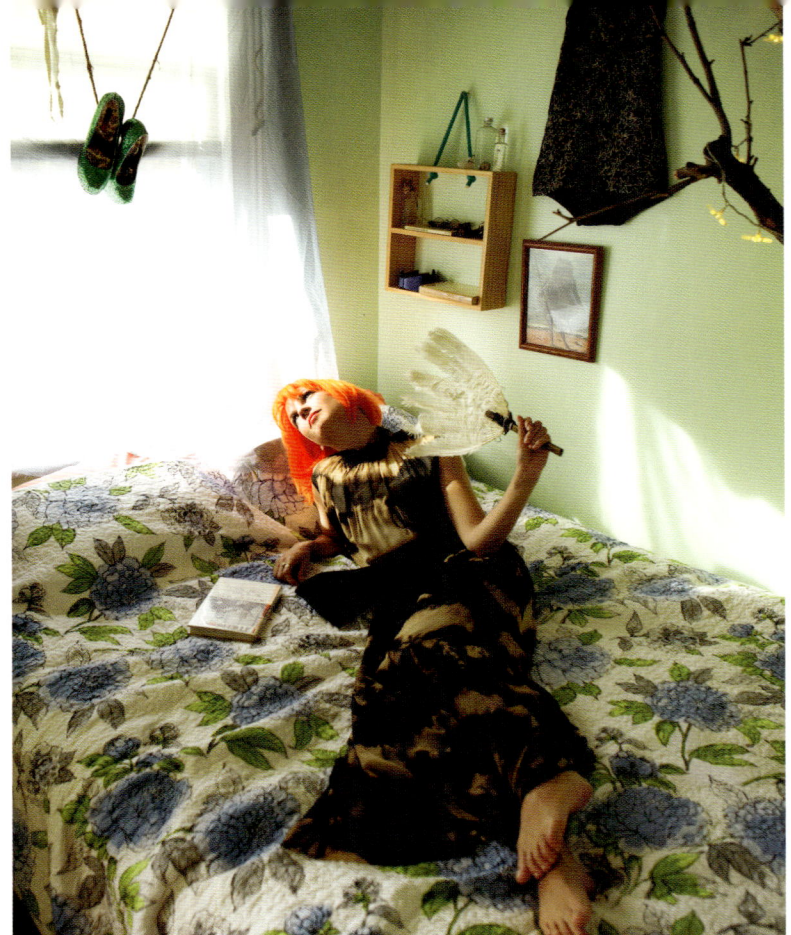
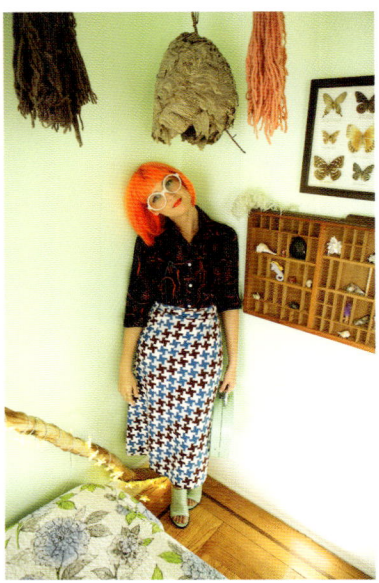
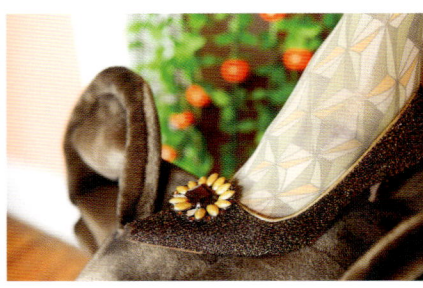
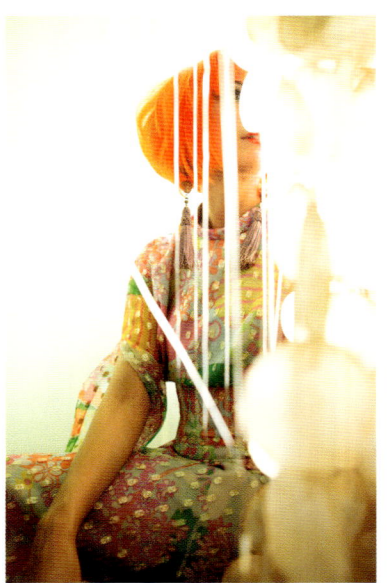
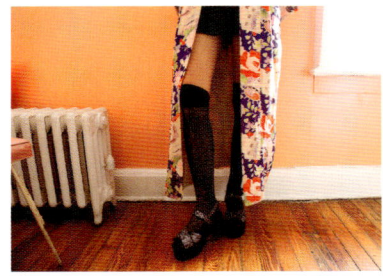
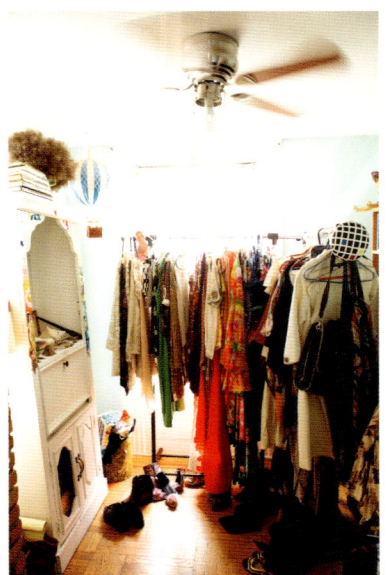
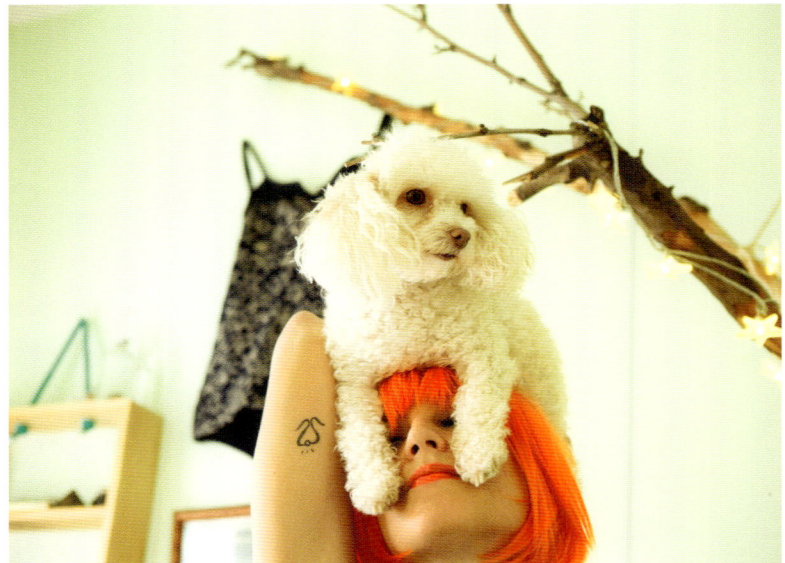
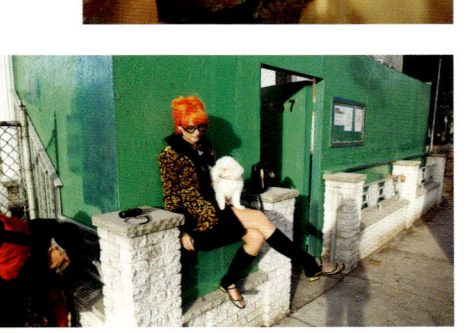
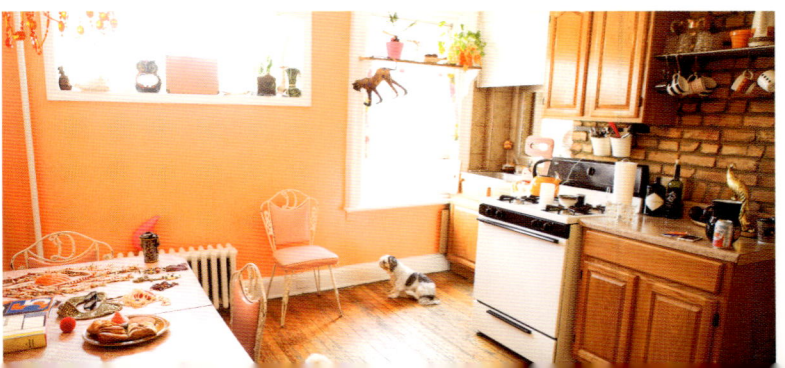

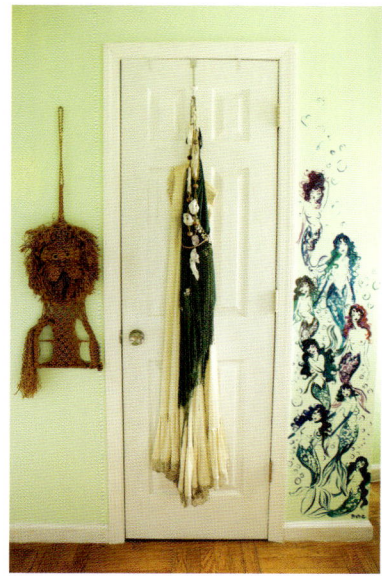
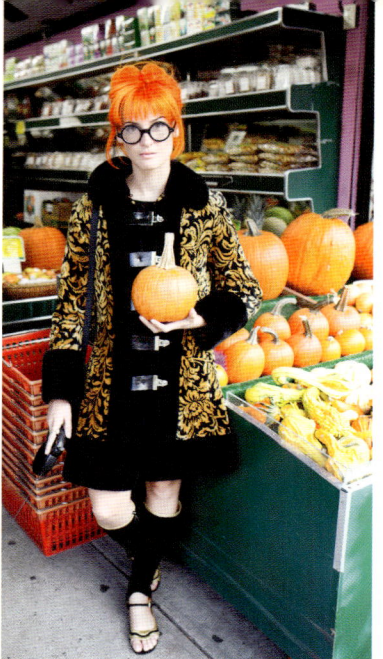
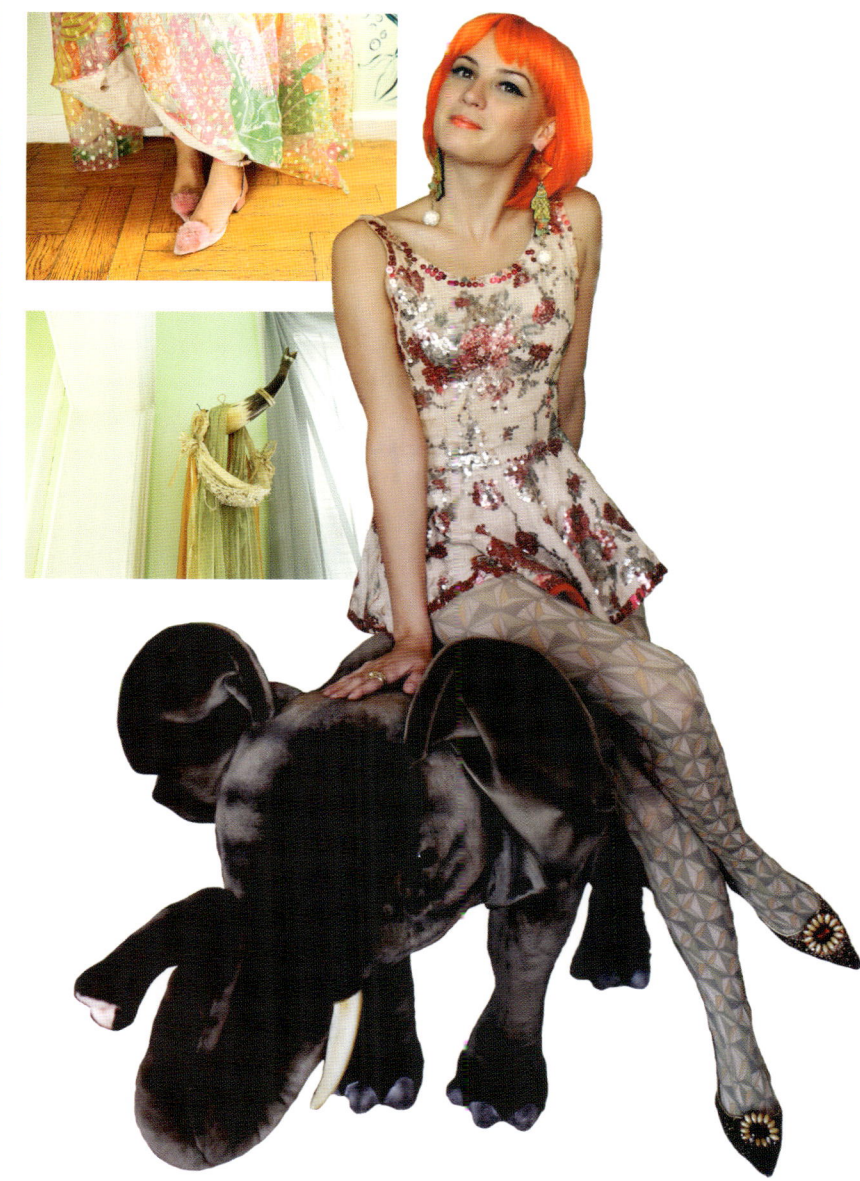
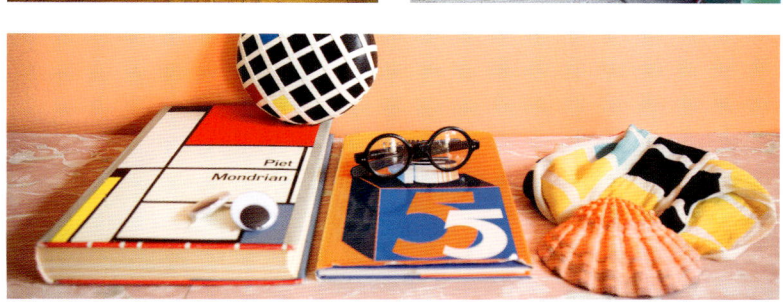
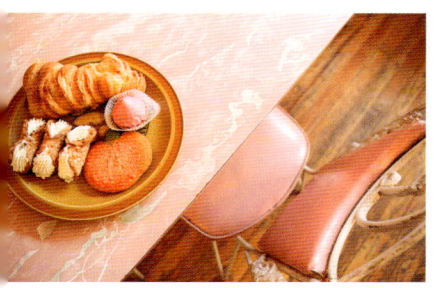
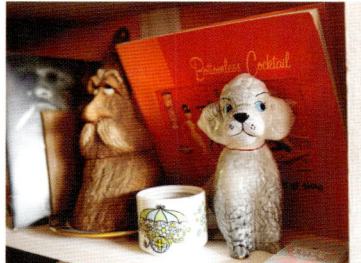
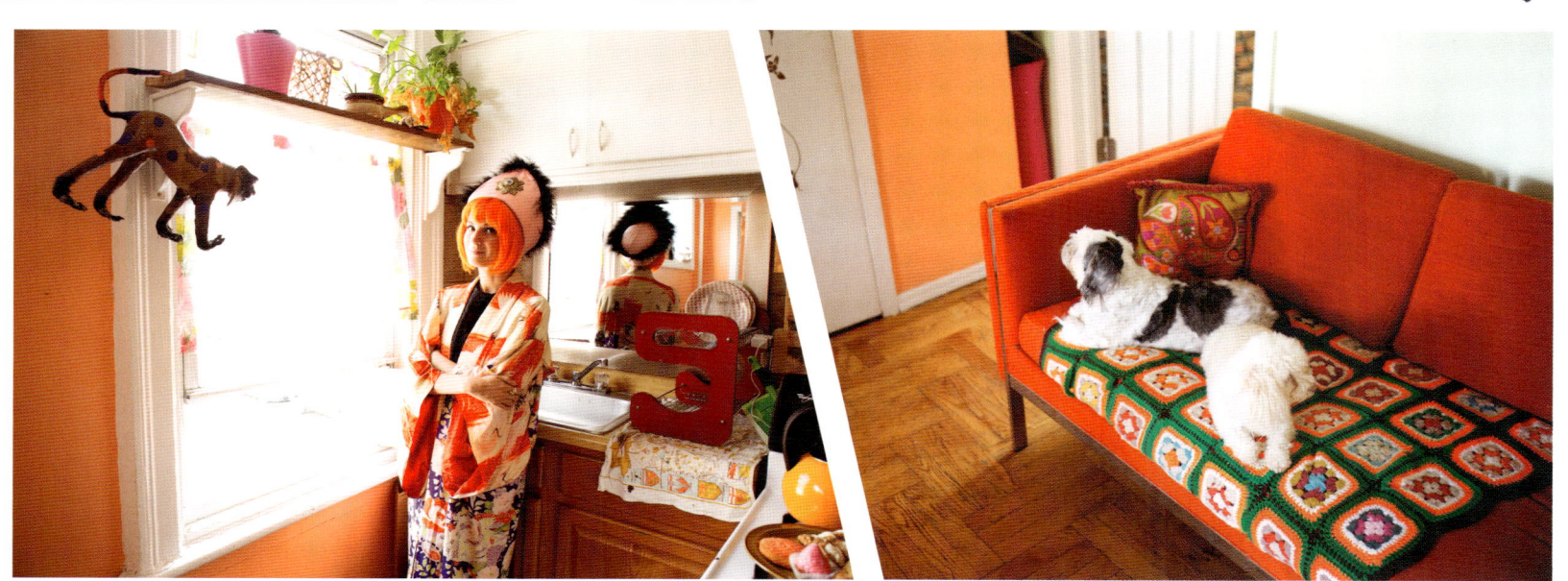

J.J. MARTIN
THE MAXIMALIST

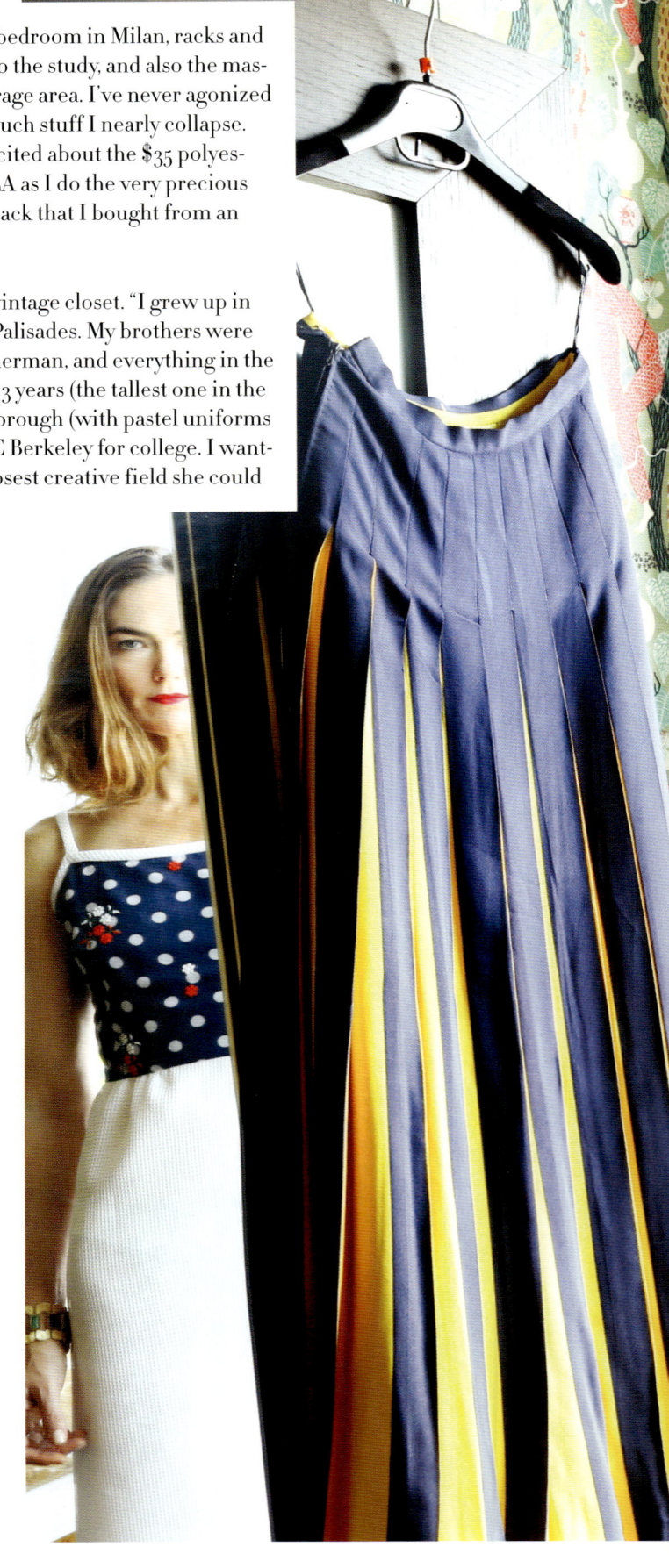

J.J.'s wardrobe takes over the entire wall of her bedroom in Milan, racks and closets in the guest room, the corridor leading to the study, and also the massive basement in their apartment building that she transformed into a storage area. I've never agonized more about anyone's collection. I end up stacking my poor arms with so much stuff I nearly collapse. "To be honest I am not really a snob about vintage," she shrugs. "I get as excited about the $35 polyester coat with the psychedelic neon print that I found at the garage sale in LA as I do the very precious Valentino couture dress from the 80s with the illusionistic embroidered back that I bought from an important dealer."

Jennifer Jane Martin's story starts about 6,000 miles from her illustrious vintage closet. "I grew up in Los Angeles," she begins, "in a small town on the West Side called Pacific Palisades. My brothers were surfers and beach volleyball players, my dad was a very big hunter and fisherman, and everything in the family revolved around sports and outdoor activities. I was a gymnast for 13 years (the tallest one in the history of the universe!) and I went to a stuffy all-girls school called Marlborough (with pastel uniforms and saddle shoes, which by the way, I really appreciate now), then up to UC Berkeley for college. I wanted to be in fashion but had no clue how anyone did it." So she got in the closest creative field she could find: advertising. She worked at a few boutique ad agencies in San Francisco and New York before she landed at Calvin Klein, a prestigious feat but not a fulfilling one. "I never saw the designer, and everyone was wearing black all the time," she frowns. "I would show up to work in wacky outfits I'd found at the Chelsea Flea Market and my boss would just shake his head.

And then she met her husband, a sophisticated Italian man who lived in Milan. "When Andrea asked me to move in, I spent three months in six hours of one-on-one Italian classes per day—I am *horrible* at languages—and found a job at CoSTUME NATIONAL. But her journalism career started at *FWD*, the first online fashion news reporting service. "It was a grueling, very low-brow, gopher job—but it was full immersion and hugely educating. I used to sit in the back of taxicabs between fashion shows banging out my reviews on my Sony Vaio, and then run into a hotel to hook up to an internet cable to send them off. It all paid off though. Suzy Menkes was a big fan of what we were doing, and six months later she asked me to write for her at the *Tribune*. I wrote regularly for her for almost ten years."

The stream of information doesn't end there. While we play dress-up, the tips keep rolling in:
1. To all the single fashionistas out there: marry an Italian man. When I ask J.J. what Andrea thinks of her maximalist outfits, and if he ever begs her to "just wear a little black dress," she laughs. "Italian men are hysterical! They are the only heterosexual men on the planet you can actually take fashion advice from. He likes my outfits, but not my pear shaped ones. He wants something a little less maternity and more sexy. (I think he's referring to my Marni moment five years ago.)"
2. Do your own decorating. Don't leave it up to the architect unless you want your house to look like a Knoll catalog. J.J. bought most of her furniture at the few vintage dealers she found in Milan. She befriended each one and would stop in on them once every two weeks. She has some important pieces, but mainly she would just scoop up any furniture pieces that struck her eye. "I am obsessed with chairs and have

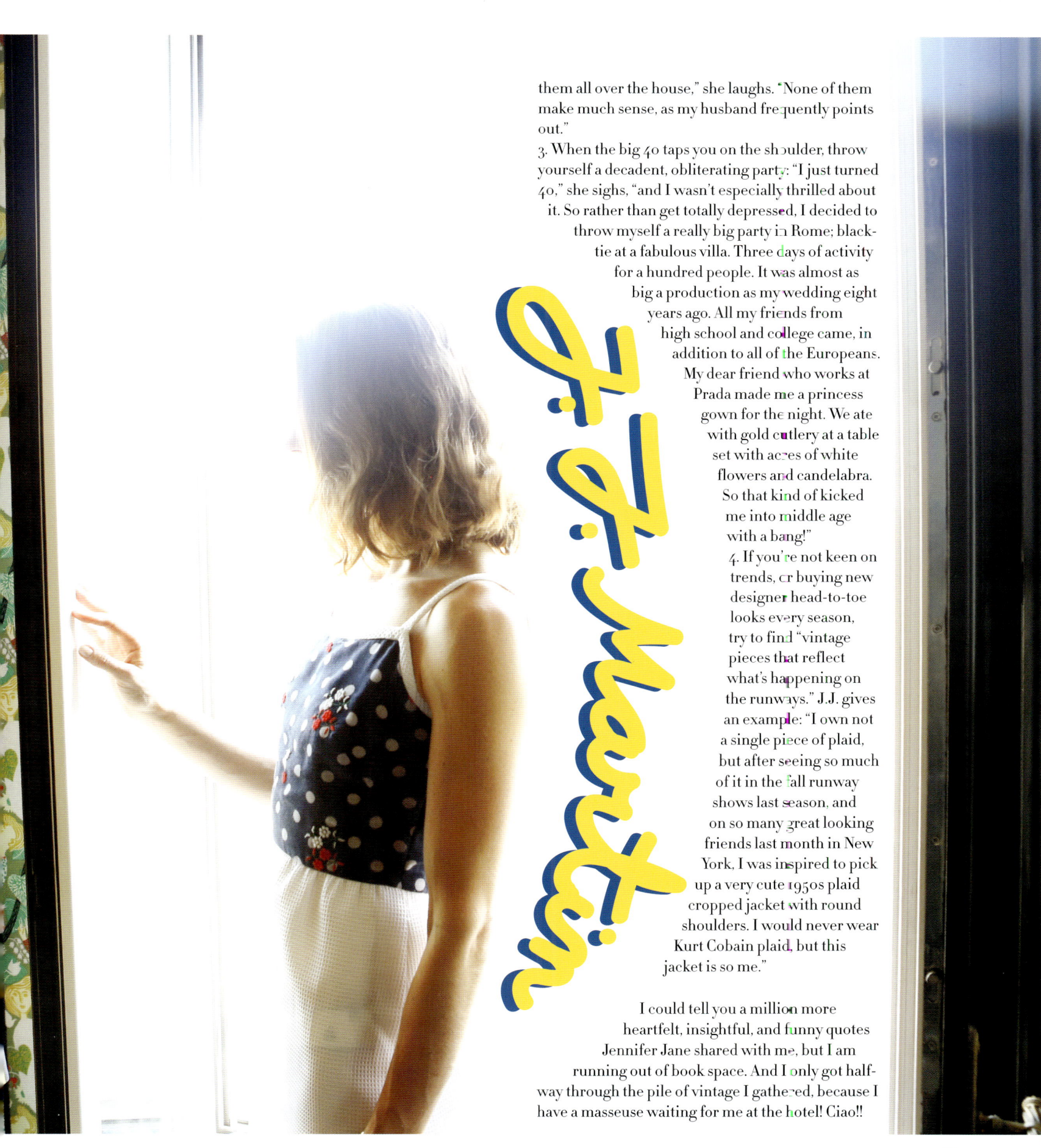

them all over the house," she laughs. "None of them make much sense, as my husband frequently points out."

3. When the big 40 taps you on the shoulder, throw yourself a decadent, obliterating party: "I just turned 40," she sighs, "and I wasn't especially thrilled about it. So rather than get totally depressed, I decided to throw myself a really big party in Rome; black-tie at a fabulous villa. Three days of activity for a hundred people. It was almost as big a production as my wedding eight years ago. All my friends from high school and college came, in addition to all of the Europeans. My dear friend who works at Prada made me a princess gown for the night. We ate with gold cutlery at a table set with acres of white flowers and candelabra. So that kind of kicked me into middle age with a bang!"

4. If you're not keen on trends, or buying new designer head-to-toe looks every season, try to find "vintage pieces that reflect what's happening on the runways." J.J. gives an example: "I own not a single piece of plaid, but after seeing so much of it in the fall runway shows last season, and on so many great looking friends last month in New York, I was inspired to pick up a very cute 1950s plaid cropped jacket with round shoulders. I would never wear Kurt Cobain plaid, but this jacket is so me."

I could tell you a million more heartfelt, insightful, and funny quotes Jennifer Jane shared with me, but I am running out of book space. And I only got halfway through the pile of vintage I gathered, because I have a masseuse waiting for me at the hotel! Ciao!!

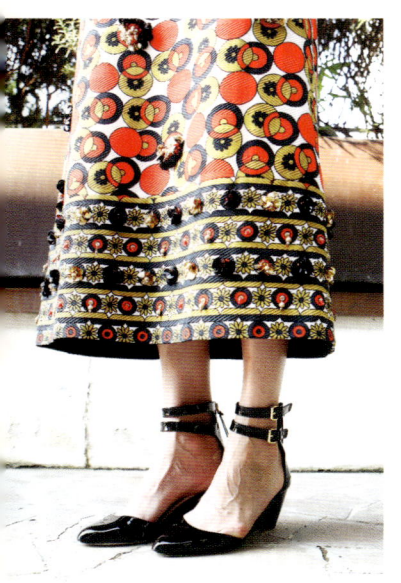
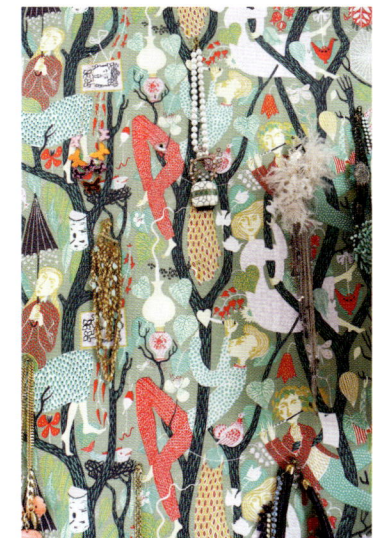
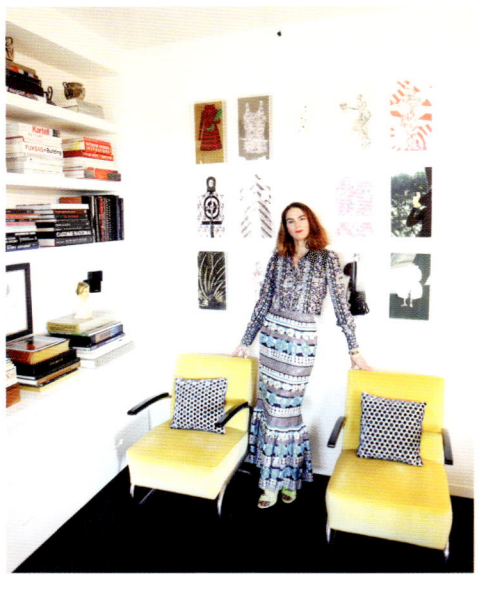
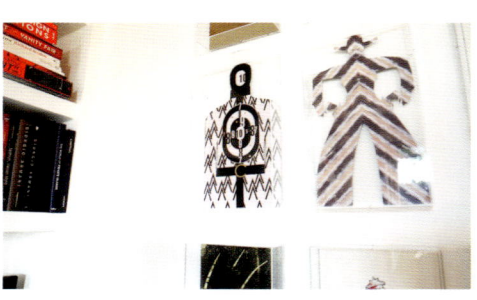
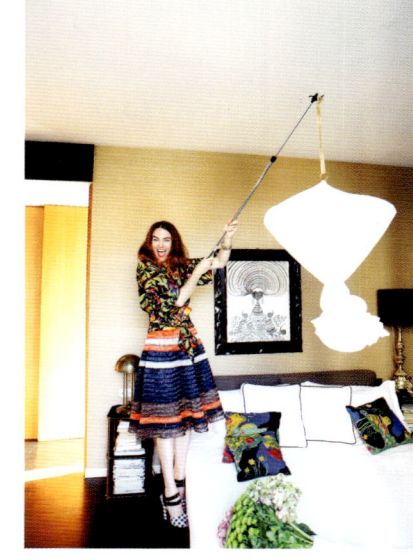
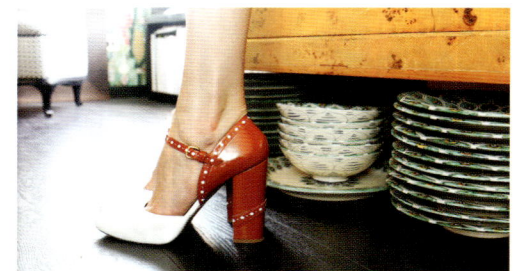
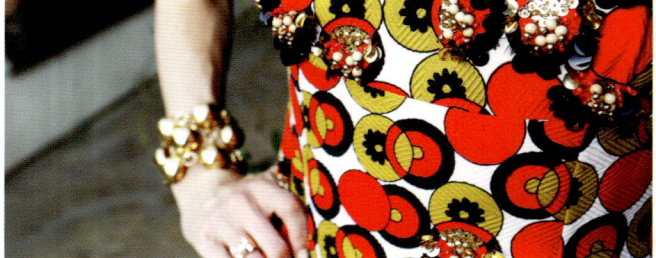
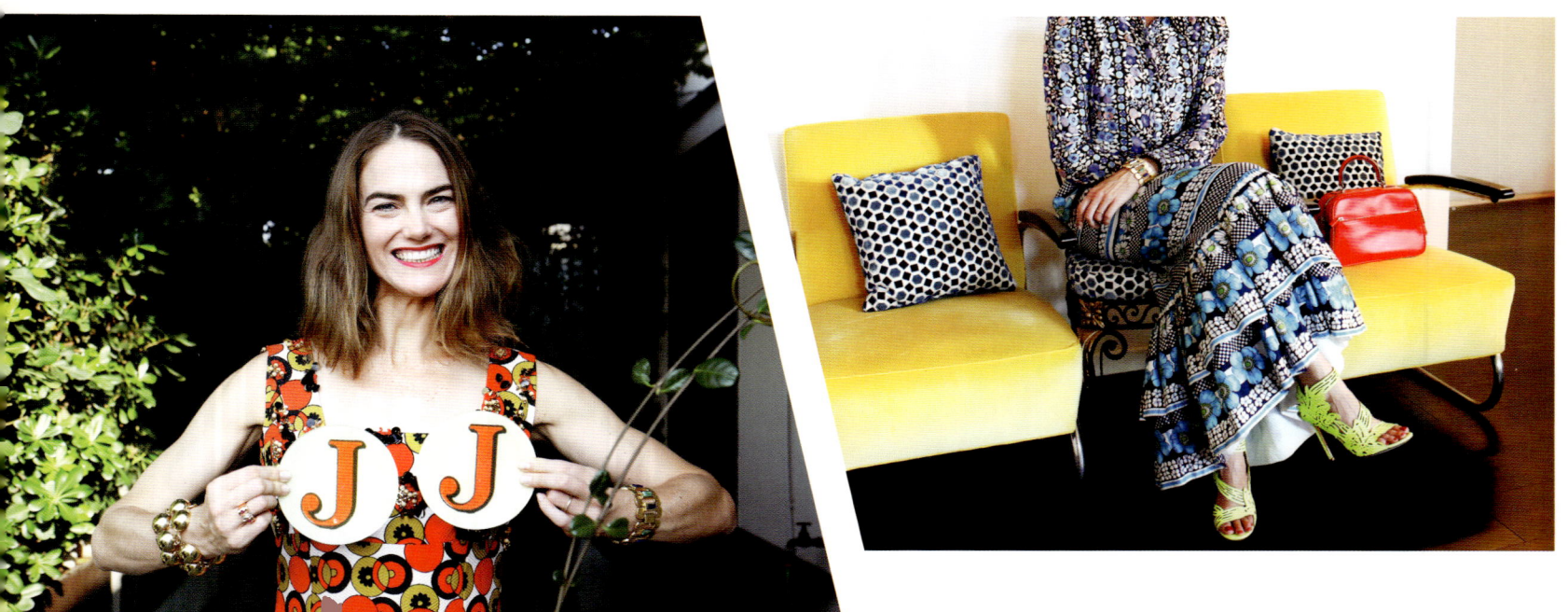

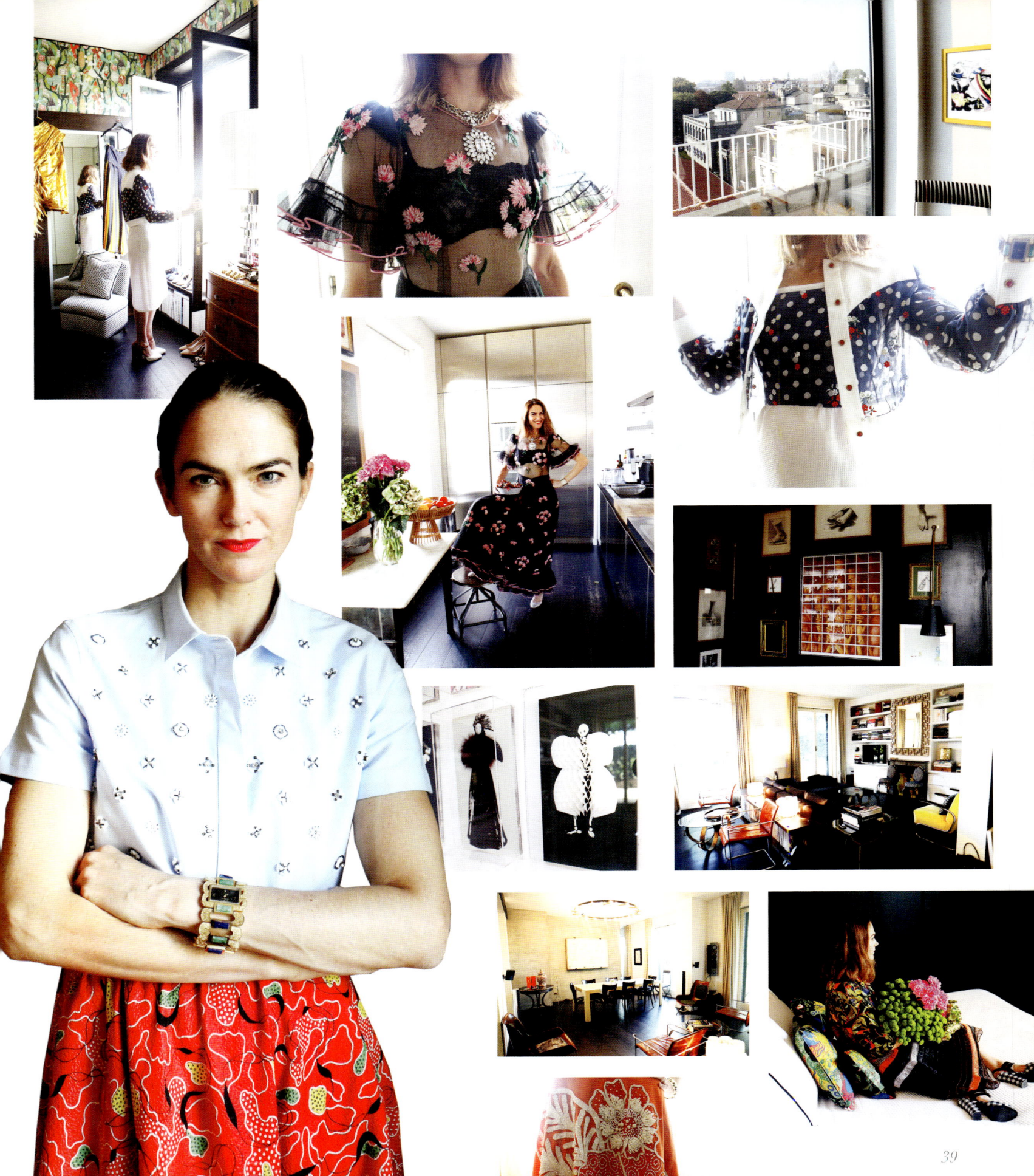

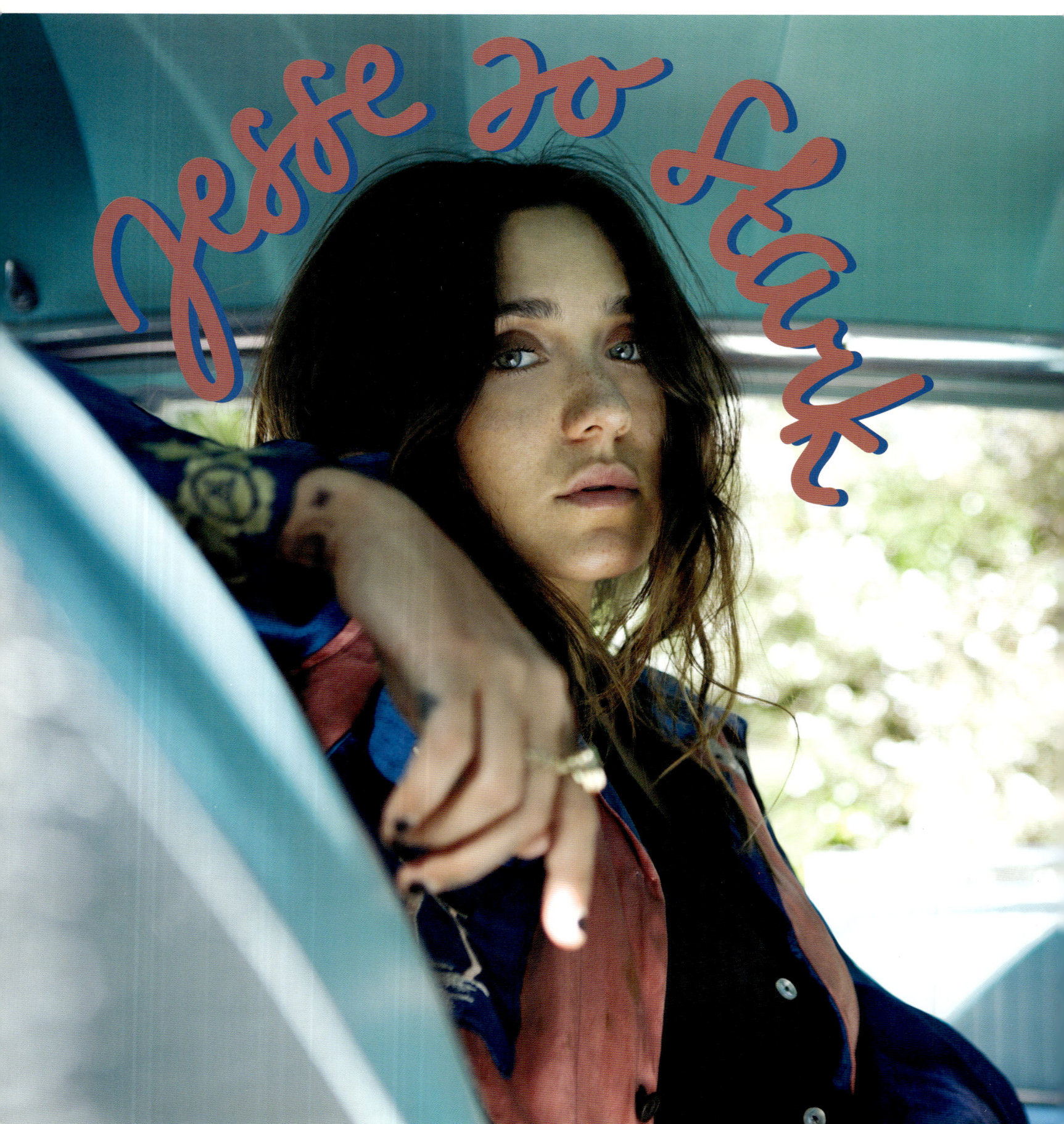

JESSE JO STARK
CHROME HEART

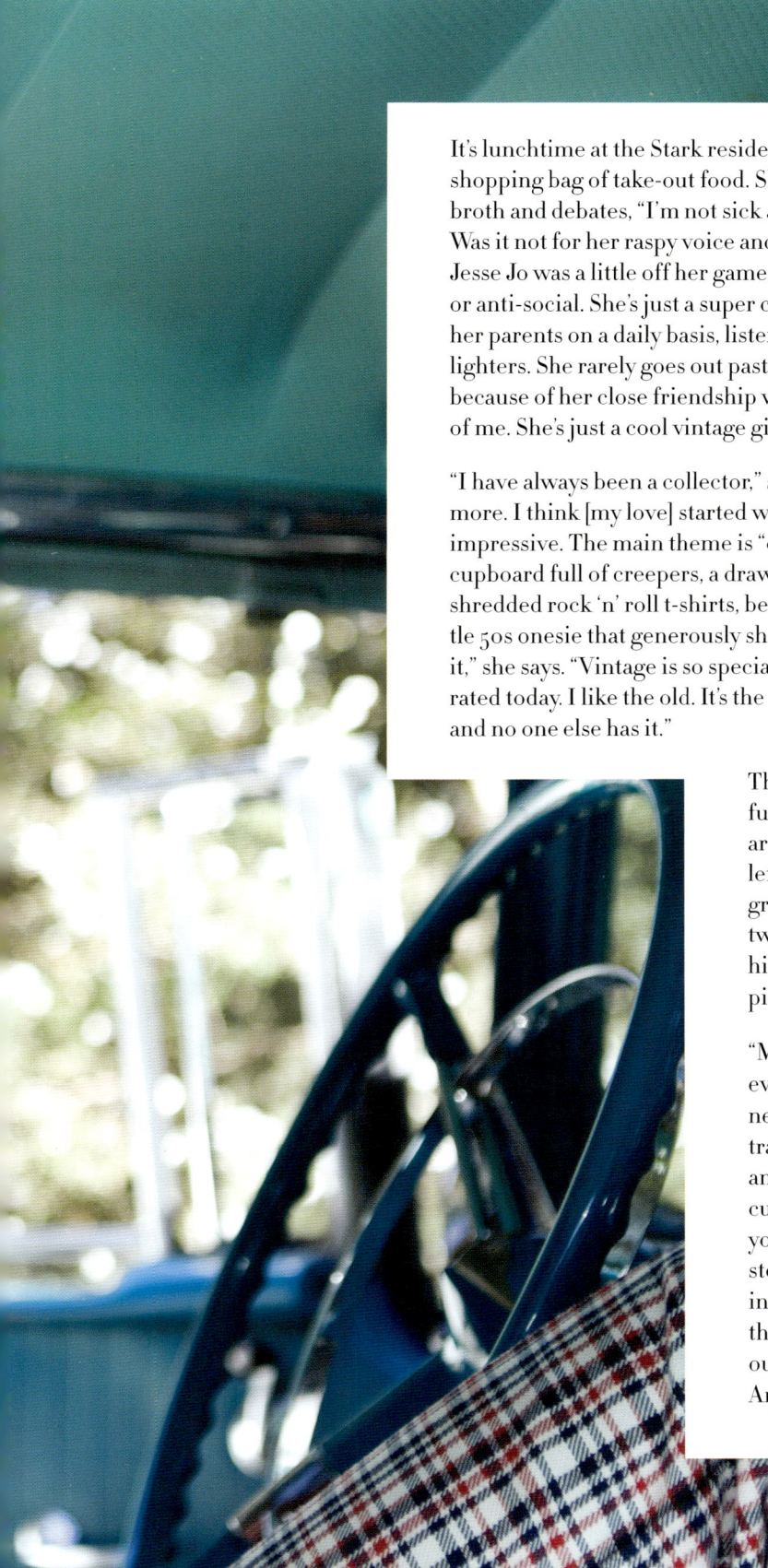

It's lunchtime at the Stark residence and the restaurant just dropped off a large shopping bag of take-out food. She hovers her face over a giant bowl of steaming broth and debates, "I'm not sick anymore, but I'm not quite there yet, you know?" Was it not for her raspy voice and the sporadic cough, I would not have noticed Jesse Jo was a little off her game. She's a quiet girl, but not because she's sick or shy or anti-social. She's just a super chill homebody. She lives in sweats, hangs out with her parents on a daily basis, listens to country music, plays the guitar, and collects simple things like lighters. She rarely goes out past 11 p.m. And even though you might think she's a "girl on the scene" because of her close friendship with Bella Hadid, that's the furthest from the girl who's sitting in front of me. She's just a cool vintage girl, through and through.

"I have always been a collector," she says. "It started with vintage T-shirts and has moved towards way more. I think [my love] started when I had my own money to buy my own things." Her closets are impressive. The main theme is "comfort," but it swings across many decades and hemlines. There's a cupboard full of creepers, a drawer full of Kappa track suits, racks brimming with western shirts and shredded rock 'n' roll t-shirts, beautiful 30s chiffon dresses, varsity jackets, 90s Gaultier pants, and a little 50s onesie that generously showcases her amazing legs. "It's all about the feel—and if I know I need it," she says. "Vintage is so special because it is rare, and rare is cool. Everything is so fucking oversaturated today. I like the old. It's the best feeling when you find that perfect jacket that fits you like a glove, and no one else has it."

The roommates may have all moved out, but it's still and always will be a full house here in Santa Monica. There's at least two assistants running around, a housekeeper, her mom, two dogs, and the only live-in person left, her boyfriend Matt. "I love a full house," laughs Jesse. "That's how I grew up: tons of people around. But I am really digging that it's just the two of us now. I like that now I can be naked and no one's looking but him!" Matt DiGiacomo aka Mattboy is an artist who does one-of-a-kind pieces for Chrome Hearts, Jesse's family's business. It's one big love affair.

"My dad started Chrome Hearts almost 30 years ago now—we make everything in the USA. My parents oversee every aspect of the business, and have always done it their own way. I guess it's never been very traditional but it has something special that is impossible to describe and that everyone loves. It's not just jewelry—we do everything from cut-and-sew, leather furniture, and eyewear, to every other weird thing you can think of." An ebony and silver toilet plunger with diamonds, or sterling-silver corn on the cob holders? They have it. "Chrome Hearts is in my blood," she continues. "I grew up at the factory. I started working there daily when I was 18. I design alongside my parents, creative direct our magazine, shoot alongside my mom—and I'm still learning it all." And we're all watching.

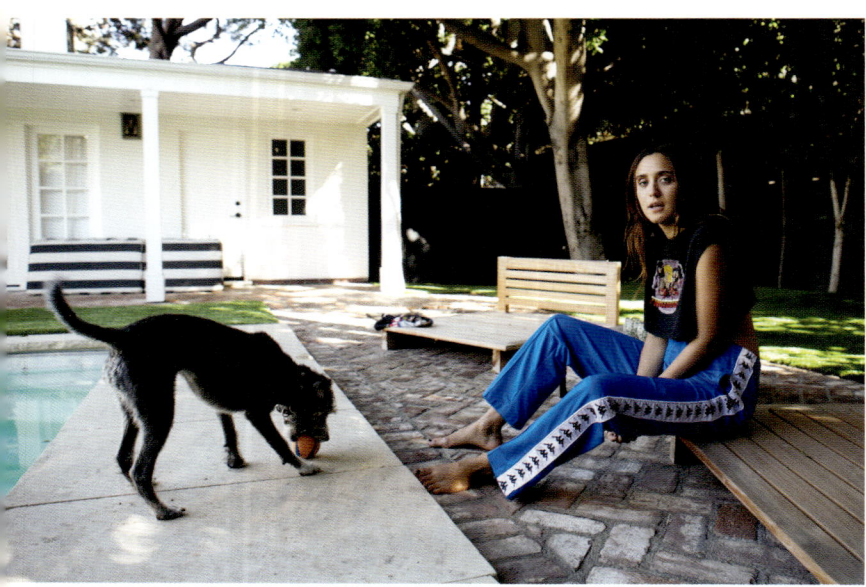
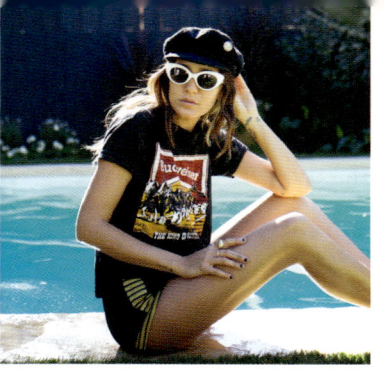
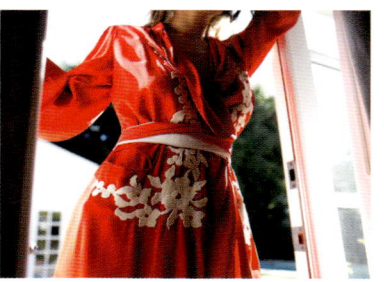
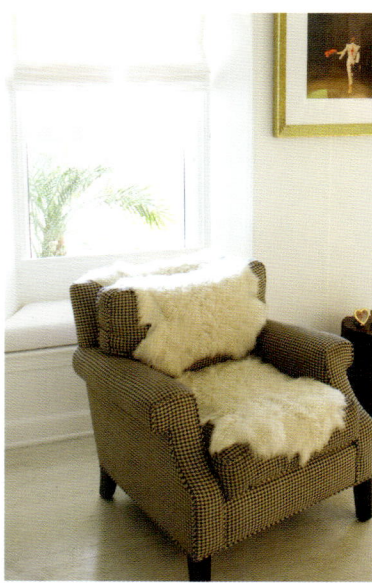
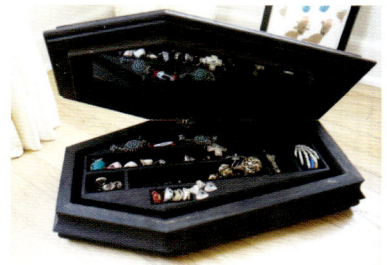
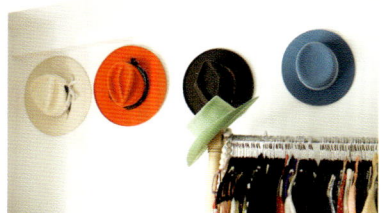
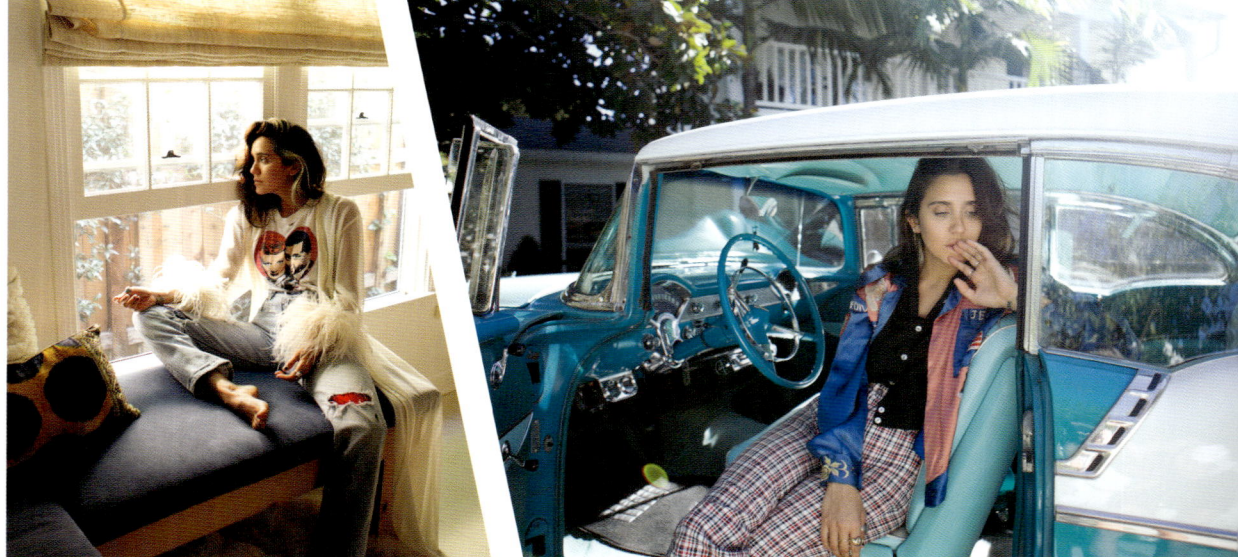
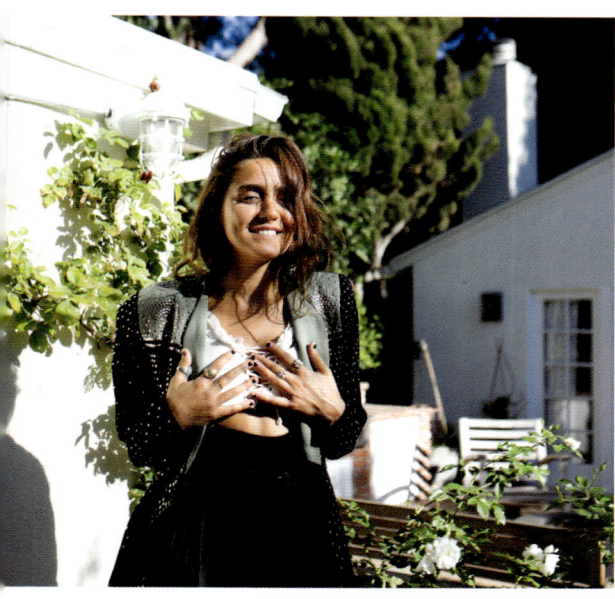
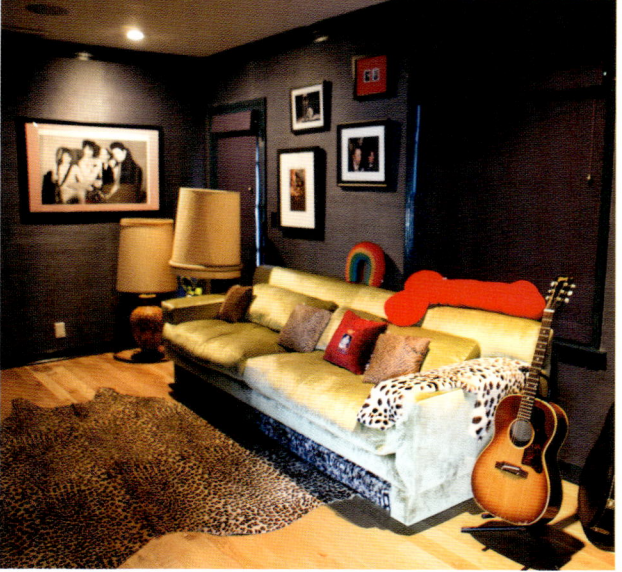
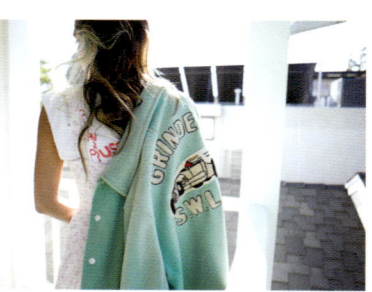
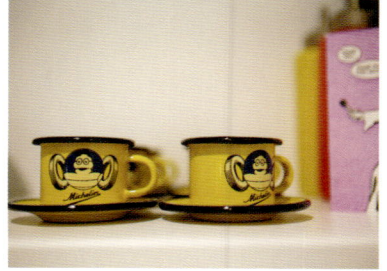

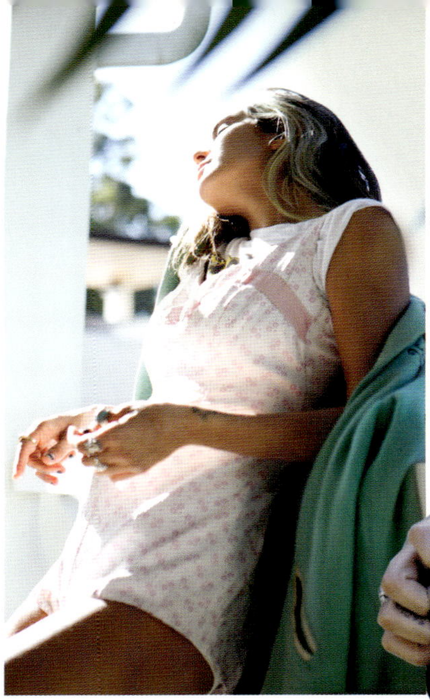

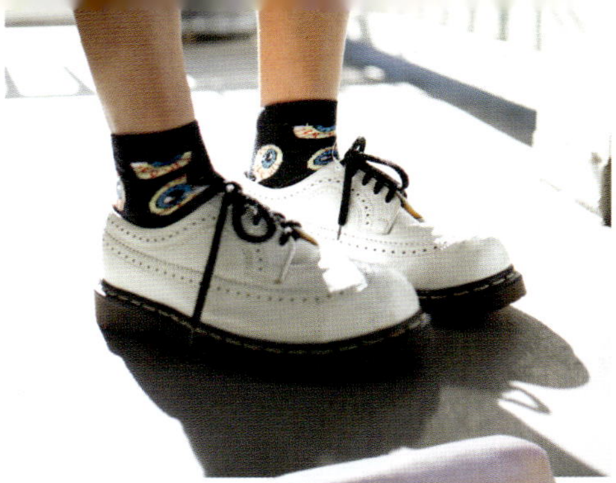

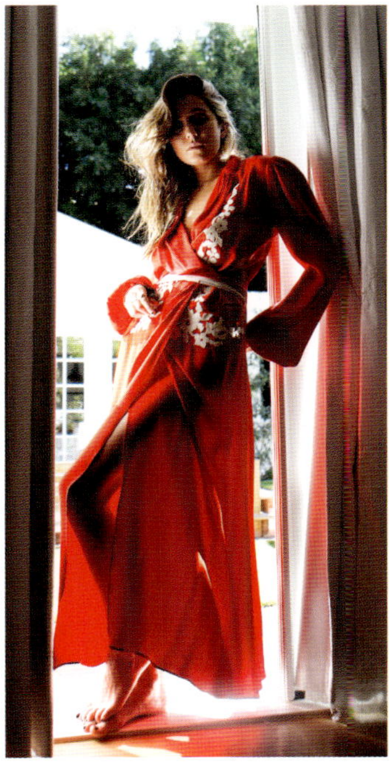

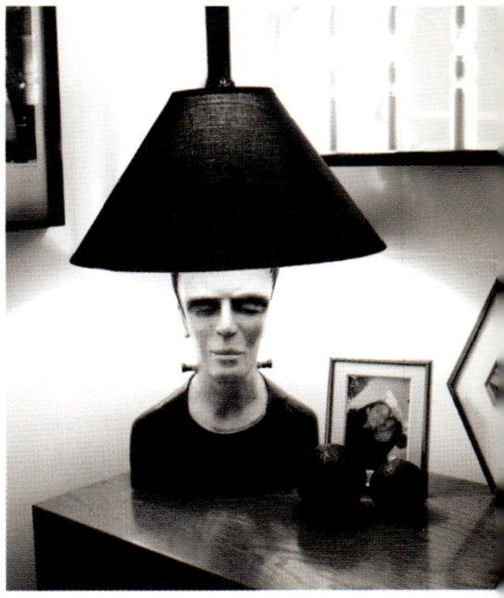

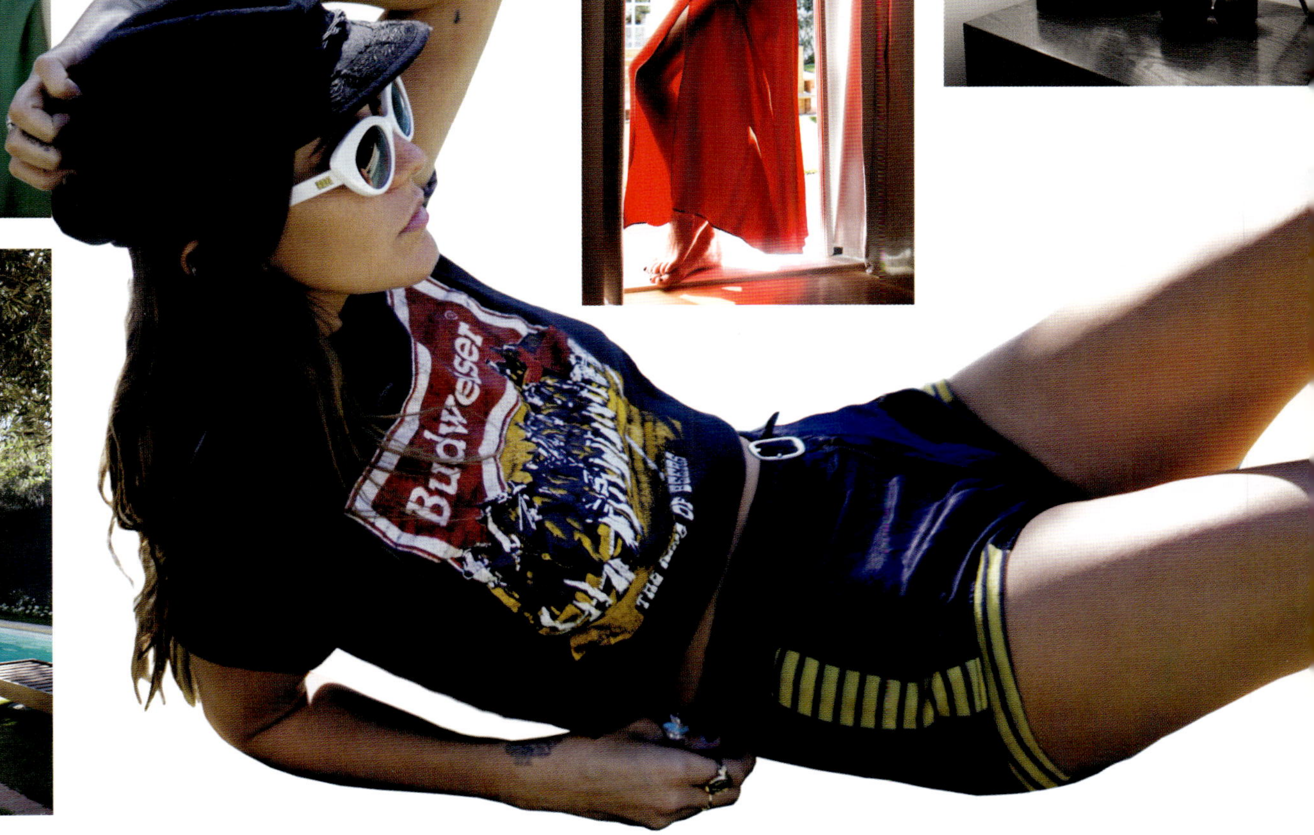

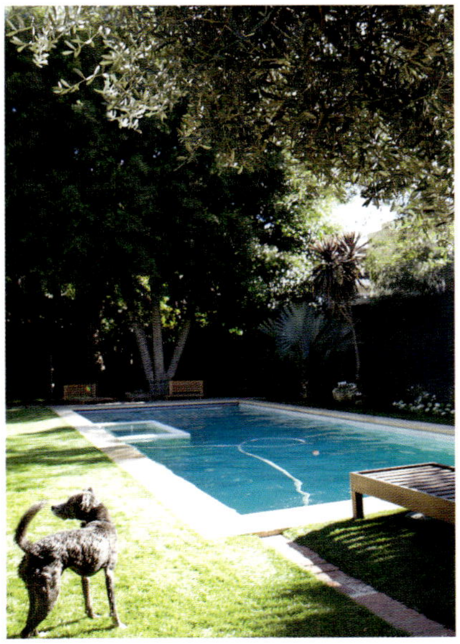

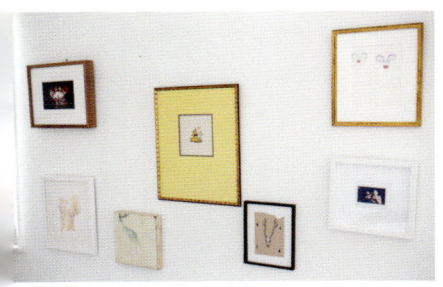
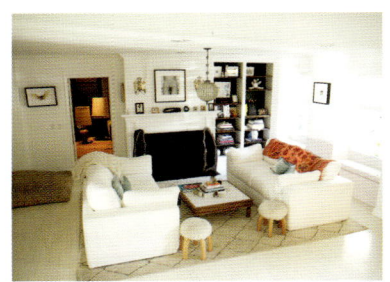
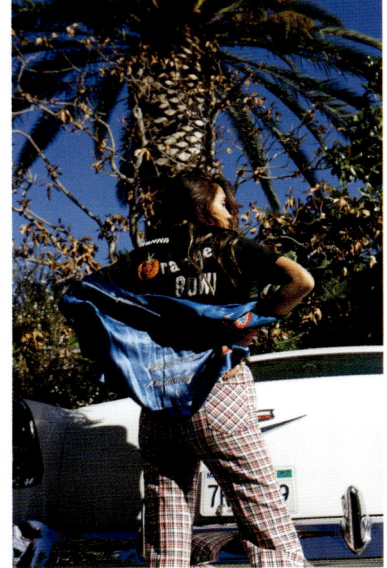
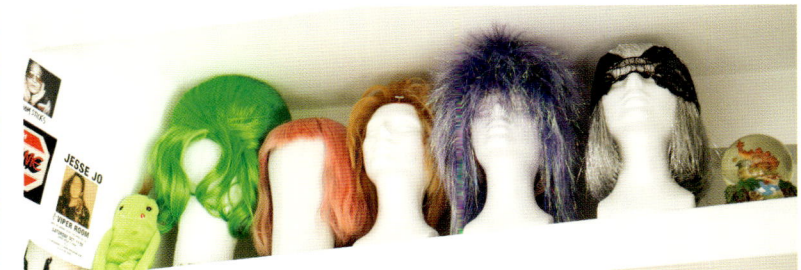
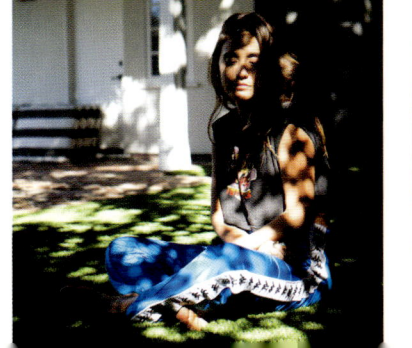
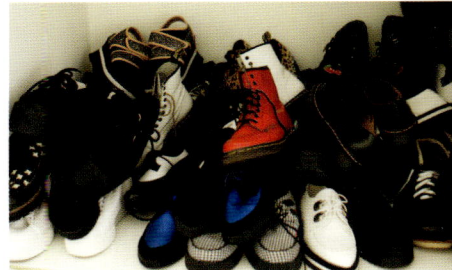

GREG BANKS
ONE GIANT ARCHIVE OF SWAG

The tale of Gregory Banks, Jr. is too large for this book, at least not for 500 words. If at any point in his music career, Greg becomes famous—and he will—and all the photographs that have been taken of him on the streets of New York City are compiled into one giant archive of swag, someone ought to write a movie script. It might start the day he was born at the St. Thomas Development housing projects in New Orleans, the fifth son (of nine children) to a single mother, with his father in prison. It might include a scene of his fondest childhood memory, the day his mom bought a house for the family. To Greg, it felt larger than life even though, at 11 years old, he had to share one room with his five brothers. And what about his first instrument, the trumpet that cemented his musical calling? Or his uncle Michael, who always wore amazing shirts and reptile skin boots, and introduced him early on to vintage style?

There are countless cinema-worthy stories—past, present, and undoubtedly future—but perhaps the most pivotal event in his life, however brutal and devastating, was also the most meaningful. "Hurricane Katrina left me with nothing but my talent and the voice of God," he recalls. "I had no clothes, no friends, all the photographs of my childhood were gone. We had to move into a one-bedroom apartment with 25 people, piled on top of couches and air mattresses. I had nothing superficial to guide me anymore. That's truly where my authenticity was born." He knew then that life had to be about *his* truth. He couldn't hide behind anything because, at any moment, it could be taken away. "From that moment on, I said, 'I have to push for it, I can't be a victim of my circumstances. I have to be greater than that.' And I started to write music. To express myself."

He moved to New York shortly after, met his wife Marlene, who is also his manager, and settled in a duplex loft in Brooklyn. He looks like Jimmy Hendrix, Lenny Kravitz, James Brown, and Prince rolled into one feverishly-stylish package, enhanced with his own personal staples: rings, stones, neck scarves, and "eloquent ruffles!" He thanks New Orleans for shaping his sartorial identity, and New York for giving him the balls to own it. "Growing up seeing the Mardi Gras Indians, and the different styles of West African, French, and Spanish culture, the colors, and the architecture, showed me that I could mix colors and patterns. There's no name for it; that's just who I am," he smiles. "And New York gave me that edge. New Orleans is really calm and chill and laid-back, but New York has that grittiness. New York took what I thought I knew and transformed it into something revolutionary. It gave definitiveness for what I was doing. New York showed me consistency."

I don't know who will write the script of Greg's life and I don't know who would play his part, but hopefully the recordings I made during our shoot will be useful, because to hear Greg speak is a revelation itself. He's like a poetic preacher. When I ask him about having kids, he muses: "If you give up on your dream how can you teach a child to begin to dream? They may not understand the hardships that come with the journey, but they will definitely understand the rewards, because they were the witness to it all." When I ask him to describe his own style, he states: "My style is sewn into the tapestry of my life." And his ethnicity: "I am a host of cells derived from the heavens." And just when you think you're dealing with some celestial being, he comes down to Earth with: "When I want to relax, I have sex, lift weights, and write." Oh! A script, maybe?

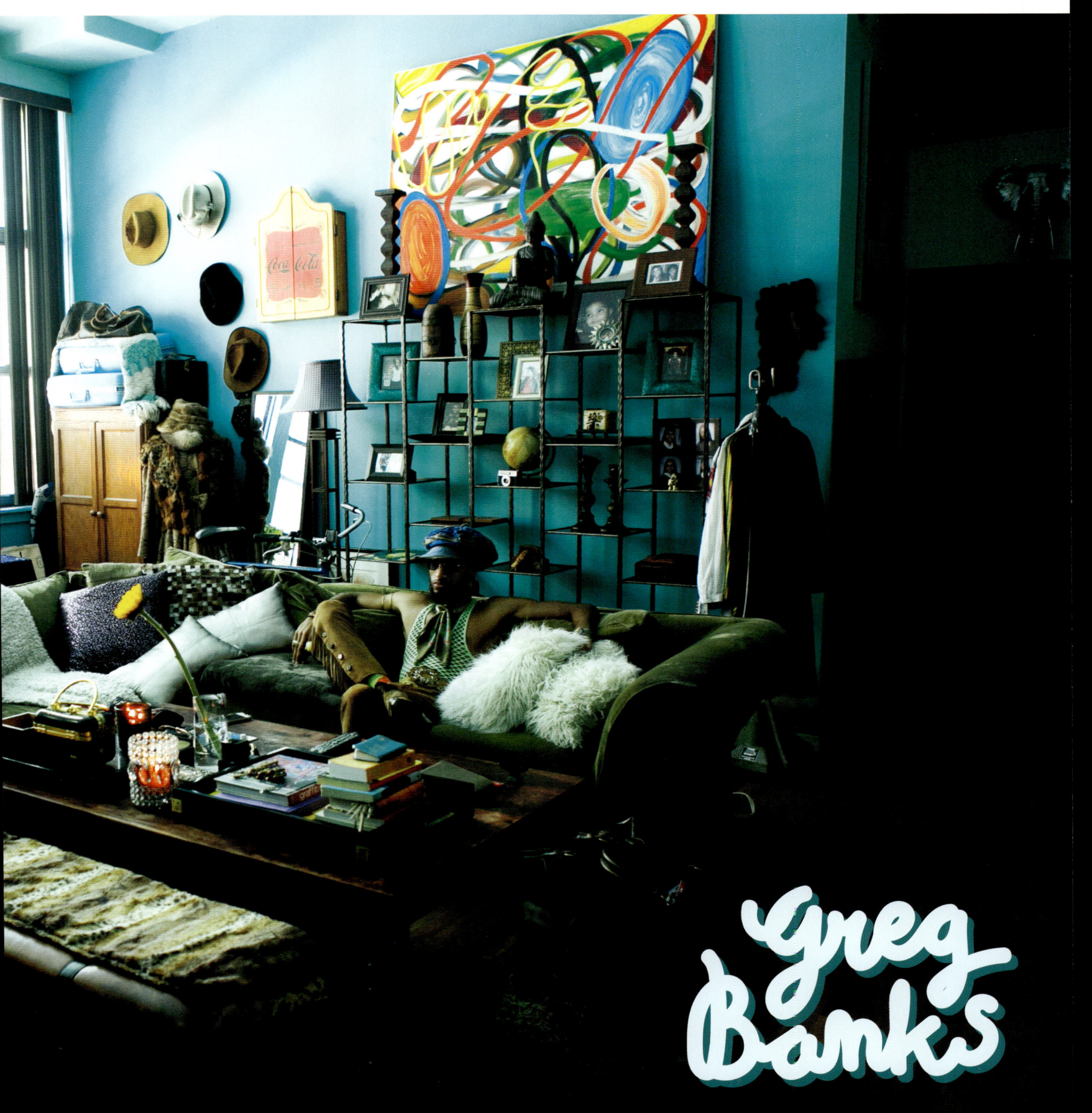

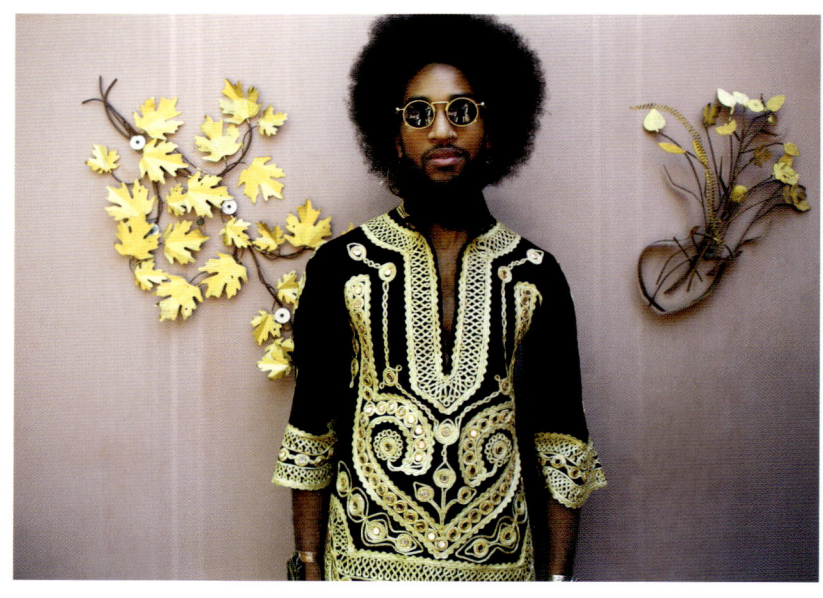
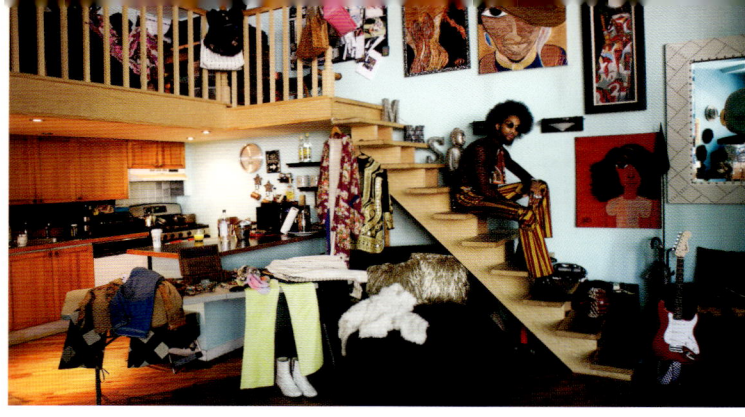
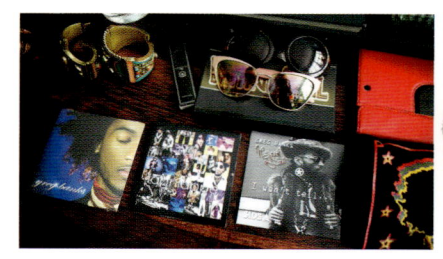
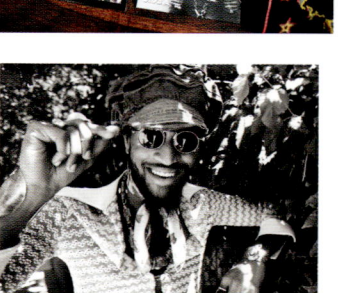
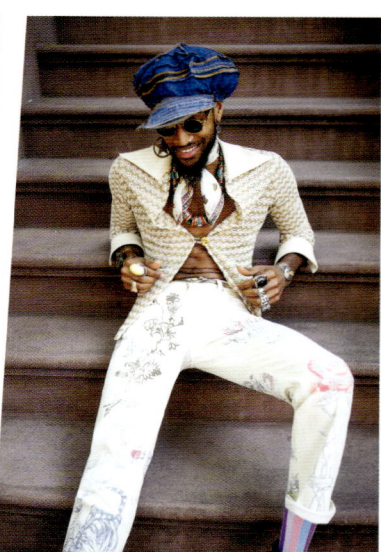
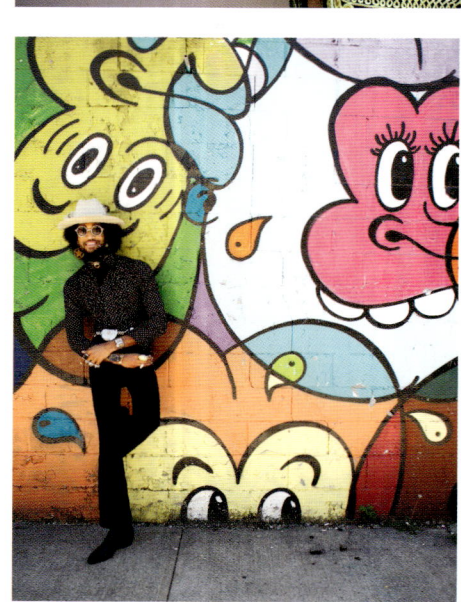
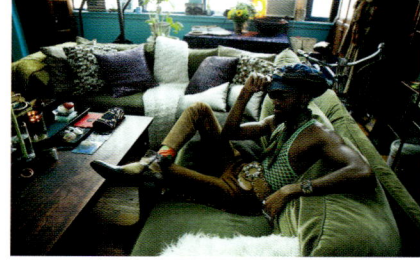
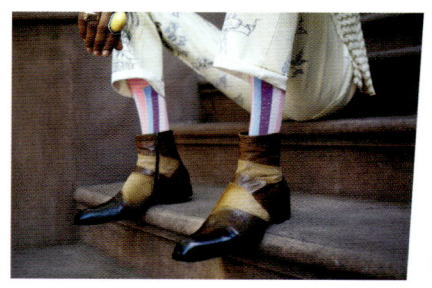
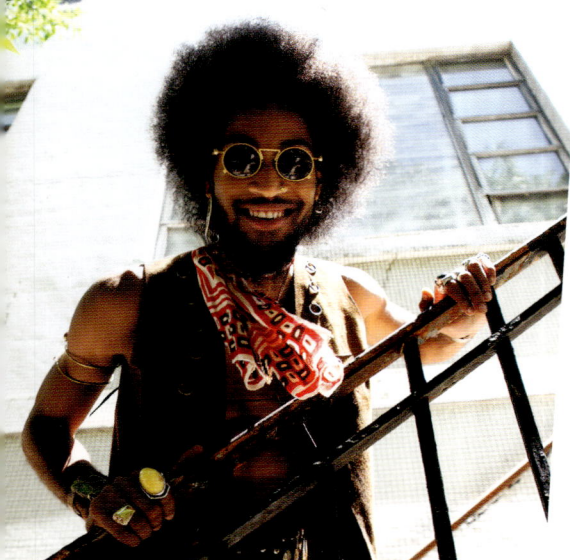
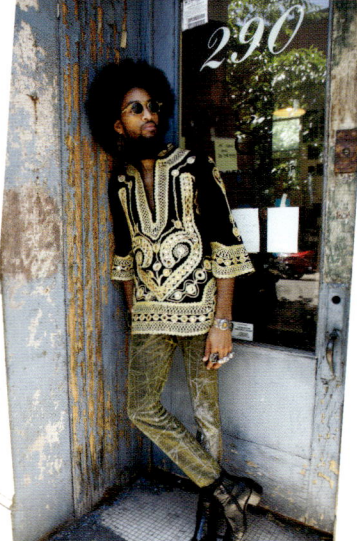
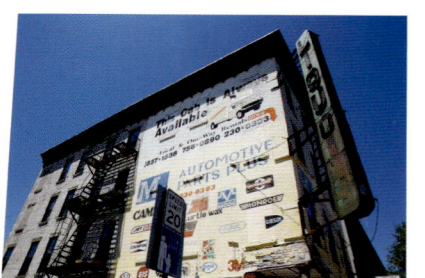
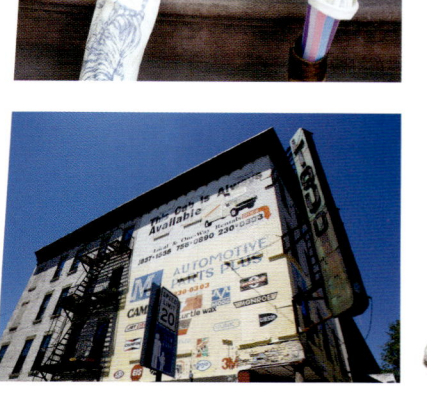

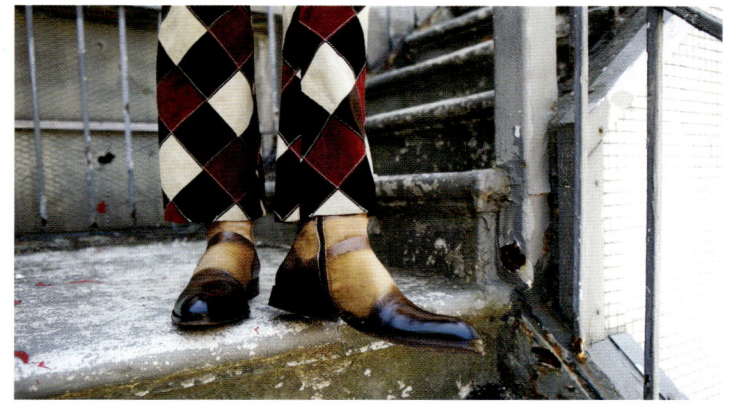
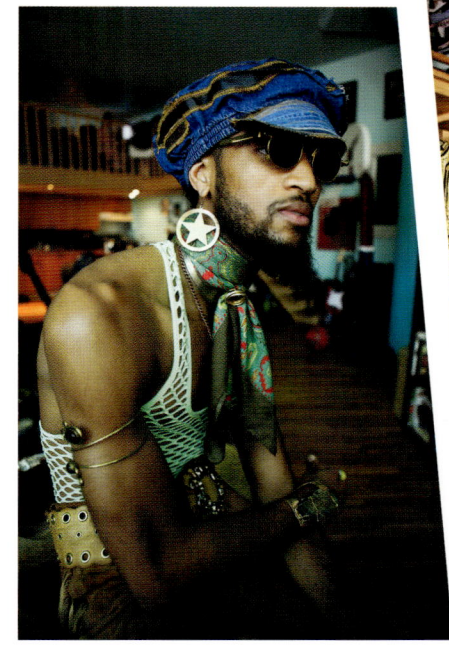
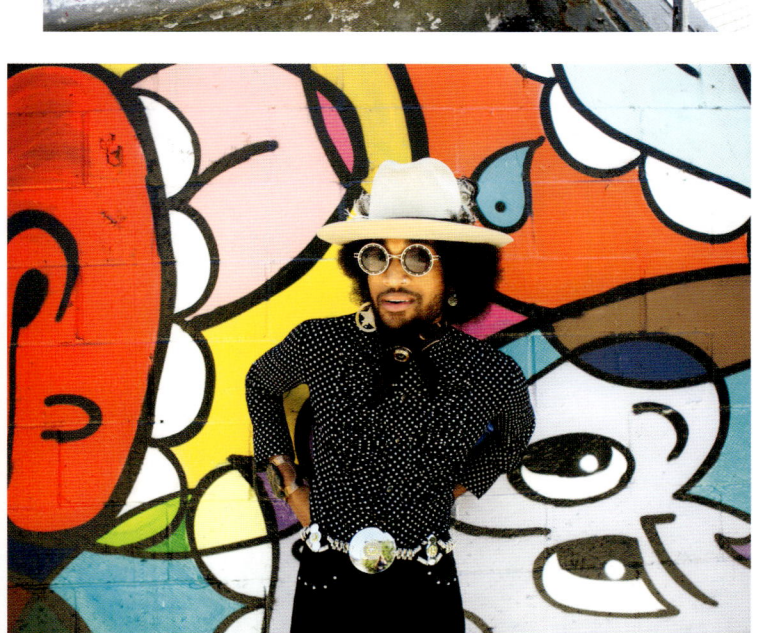
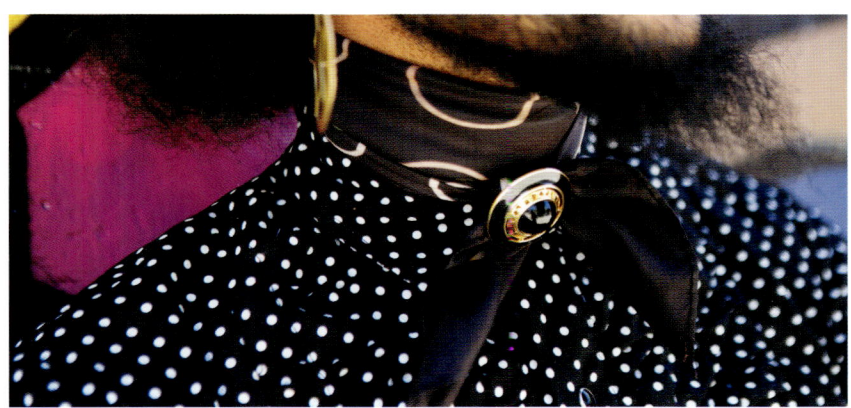
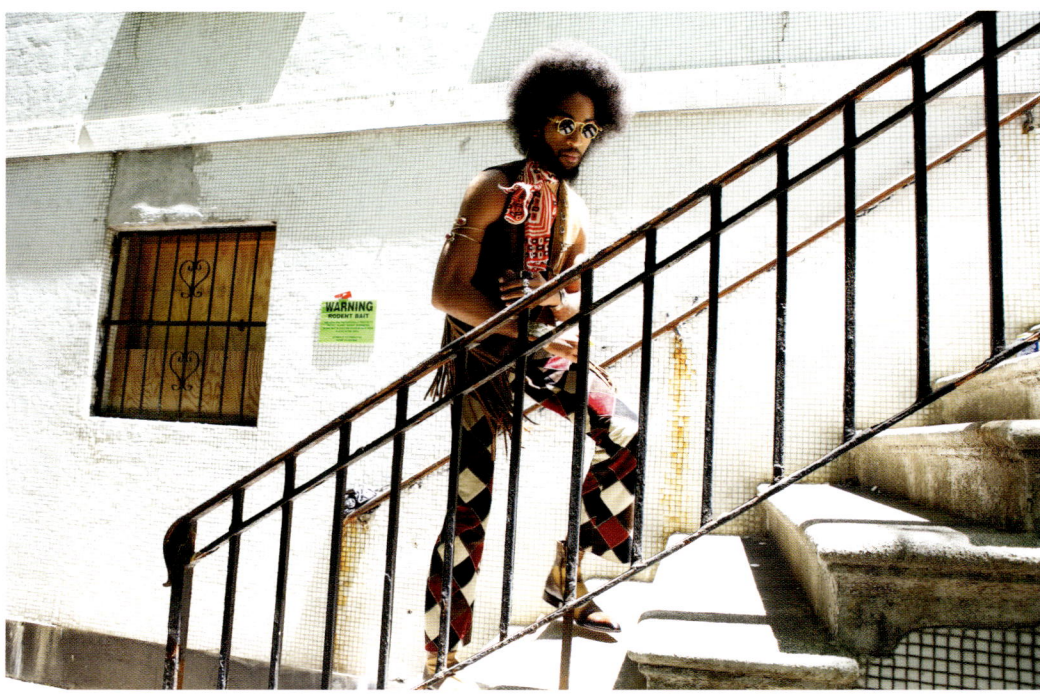
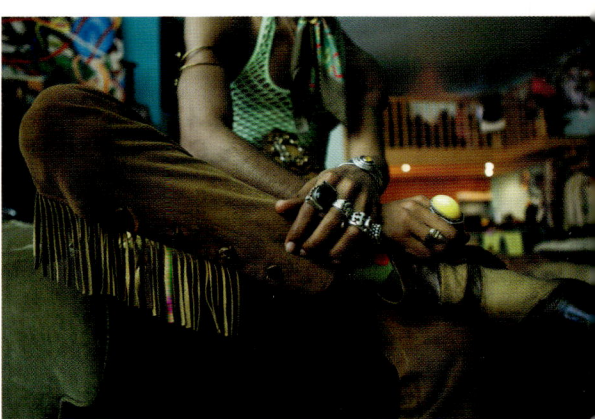
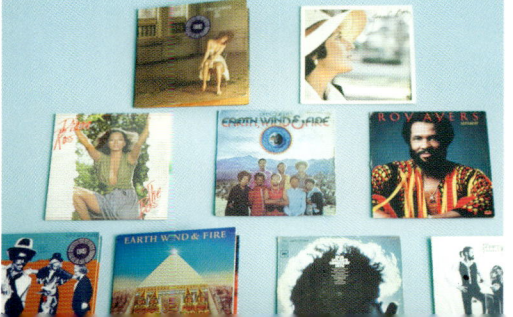

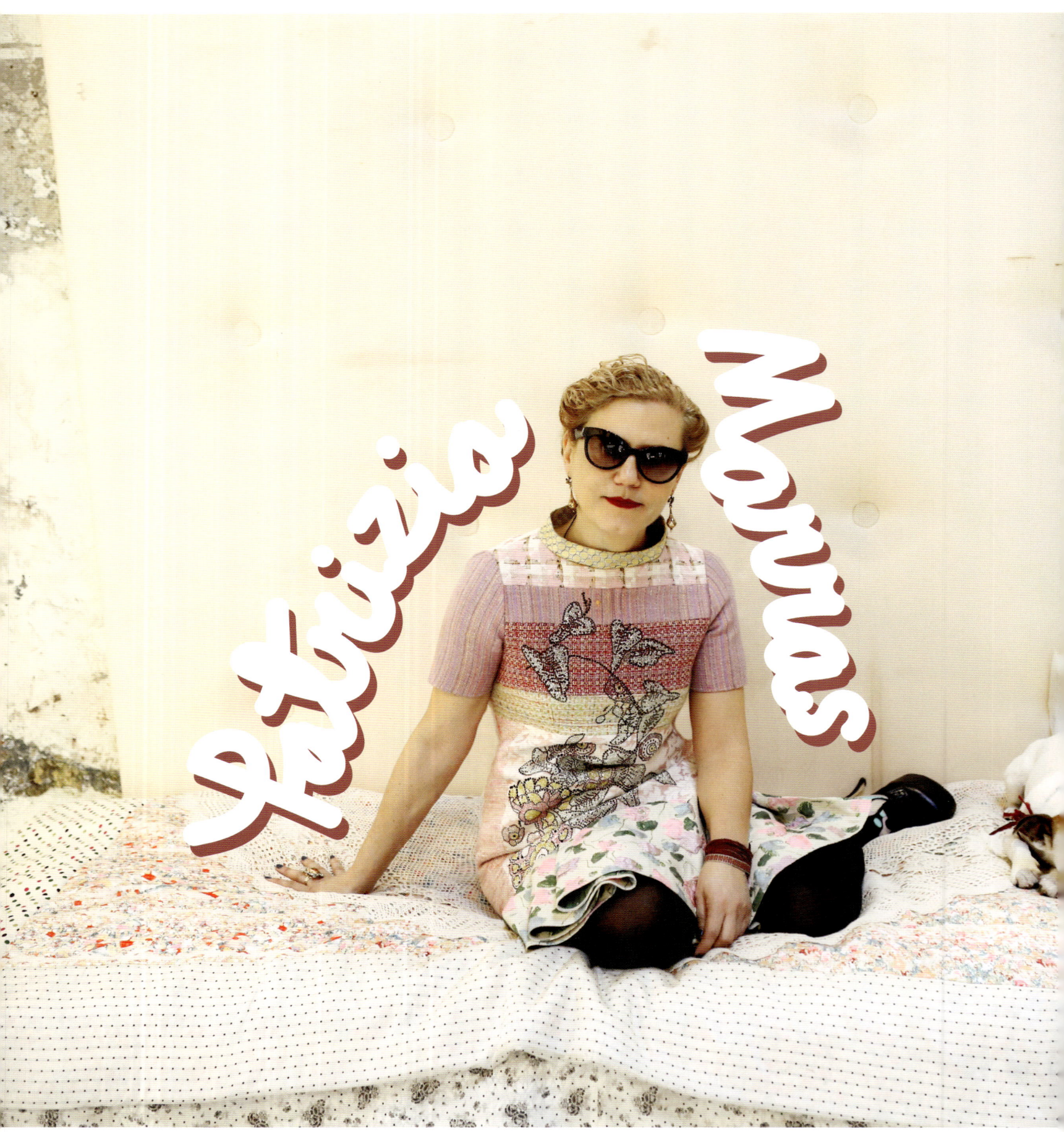

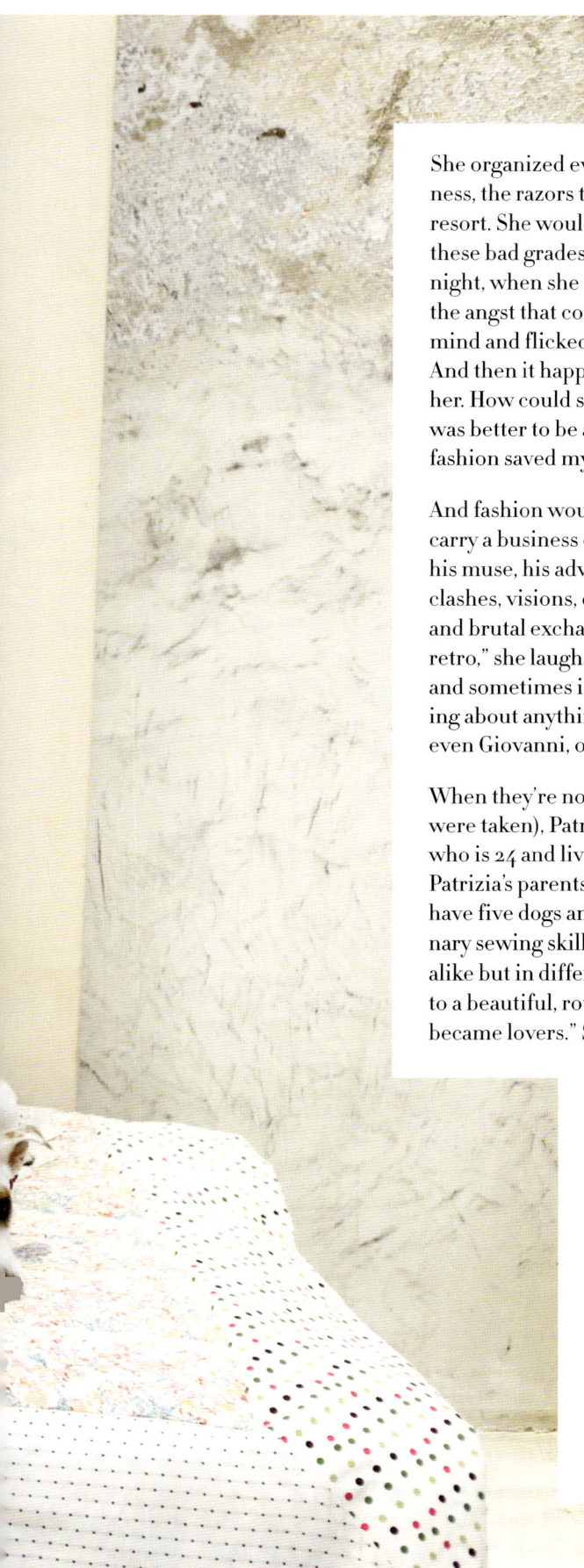

PATRIZIA MARRAS
THERE IS NO FUTURE WITHOUT PAST

She organized everything: the bathtub, the darkness, the razors to cut her veins. Suicide was her last resort. She would never graduate high school with these bad grades, and the thought of failing was too shameful and heavy a burden to bear. Tonight, when she came back from school, she would end her wretched teenage life and resolve the angst that consumed her so deeply: Resigned to her seat on the bus home, she quieted her mind and flicked through a magazine: pages and pages of the usual pretty girls in pretty frocks. And then it happened. She came across a picture of the new Byblos collection, and it halted her. How could she buy this amazing outfit if she wasn't around tomorrow? "I decided that it was better to be alive to wear it!" She looks back with a sense of gratitude, "I can really say that fashion saved my life."

And fashion would eventually *become* her life. As the wife of Antonio Marras, Patrizia doesn't carry a business card or a specific title. She does everything, from design to planning. She's his muse, his advisor, his lover, and his greatest adversary. "Fashion is a work of meetings and clashes, visions, dreams, and harsh reality," she says. When they start a new collection, a vivid and brutal exchange of opinions takes place. "I fight with Antonio because I am nostalgic and retro," she laughs, "and he—like a real case of Dr. Jekyll and Mr. Hyde—sometimes is extreme and sometimes is conservative. Sometimes he does what comes into his head without worrying about anything or anyone, and sometimes he wants to listen to anything anyone has to say... even Giovanni, our gardener. What a hell!"

When they're not traveling abroad or working at their atelier in Milan (where these pictures were taken), Patrizia and Antonio live in Alghero, Sardinia. The couple has two sons, Efisio who is 24 and lives in Paris, and Leonardo who is 19 and attends art school in their hometown. Patrizia's parents both live in the house and are in charge of the grounds and the animals. They have five dogs and 20 cats! Growing up, she was impressed by her mother and aunt's extraordinary sewing skills, and the princess dresses she and her sister wore. "We were always dressed alike but in different colors," she smiles. She was 14 when she met Antonio. "He was engaged to a beautiful, round, and buttery woman (very typical Italian mamma)" she recalls, "and we became lovers." She professed his love for him six years later and hasn't left his side since.

Patrizia's look is distinctive and consistently garnished. She never leaves the house without earrings, dark sunglasses, a big handbag, and lipstick, even just to run to the supermarket. Her silhouette is undeniably 50s, preferably juxtaposed with men's shoes. And she has a very large collection of vintage. "Any dress is more beautiful in its original creation," she says. "If I think of the fashion of the 20s with Zelda Fitzgerald, the Golden Years in Hollywood, and Charles James, up to the 50s with the new look of Dior, how can you appreciate what we see around us today? Copies of copies of copies without thickness, research, and quality!!!" Vintage plays a big role in her design work too. "It is decisive," she declares. "Because there is no future without past, because we need to know and respect what has been done before us, because now we have a great advantage: we can tap into all there was and review, we can mix styles from different eras and styles of different countries. That's fashion, baby!"

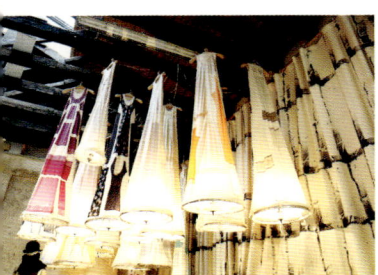
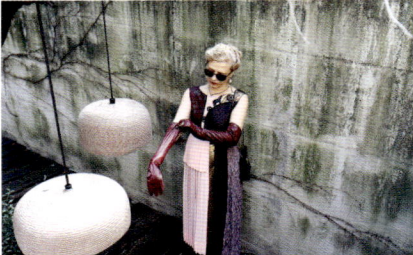
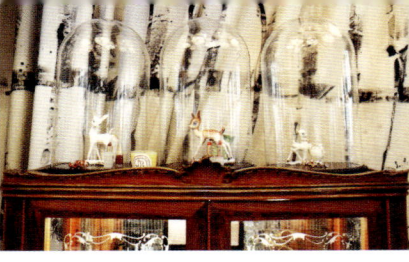
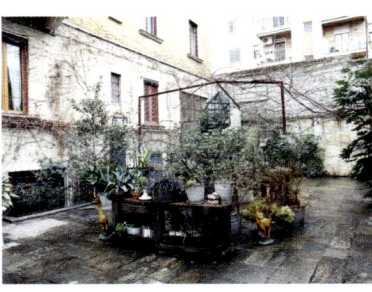
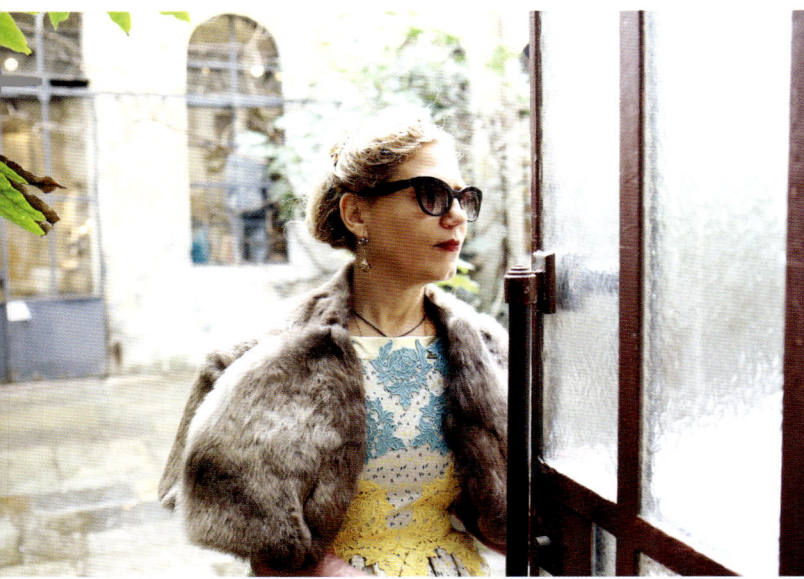
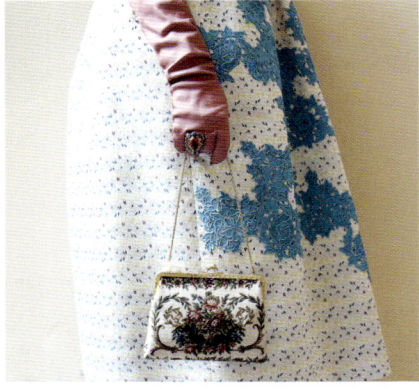
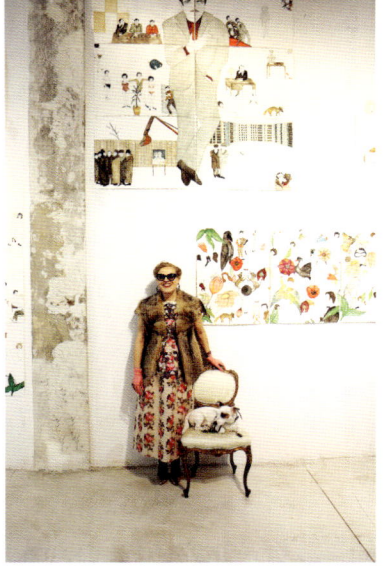
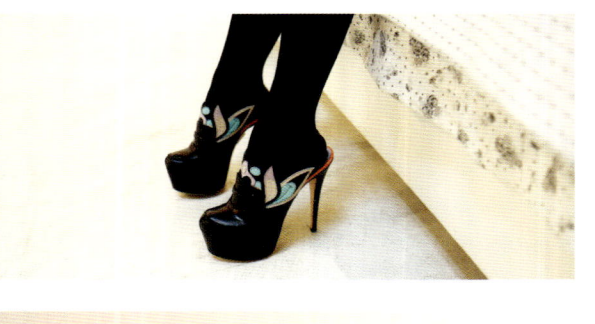
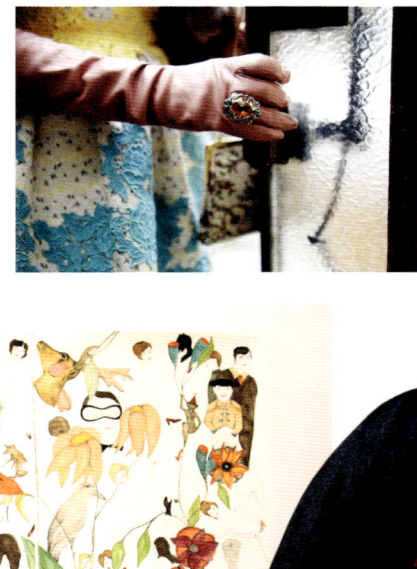
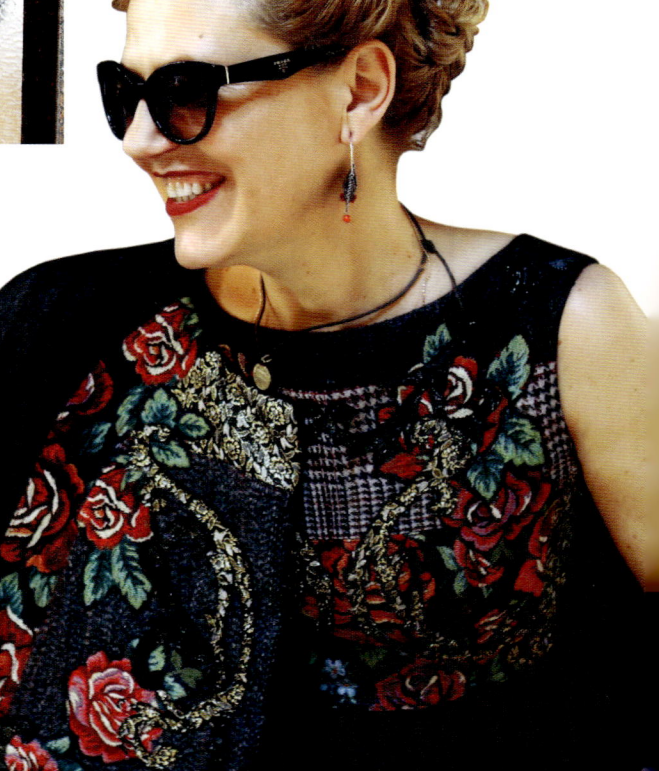

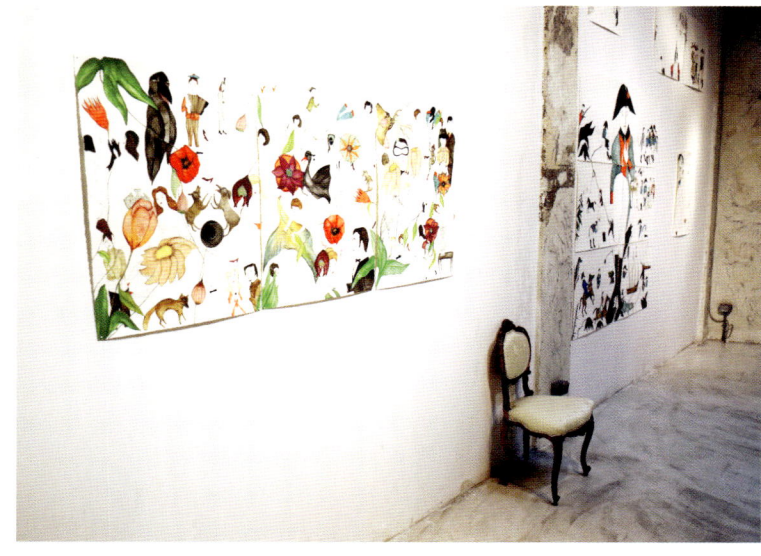
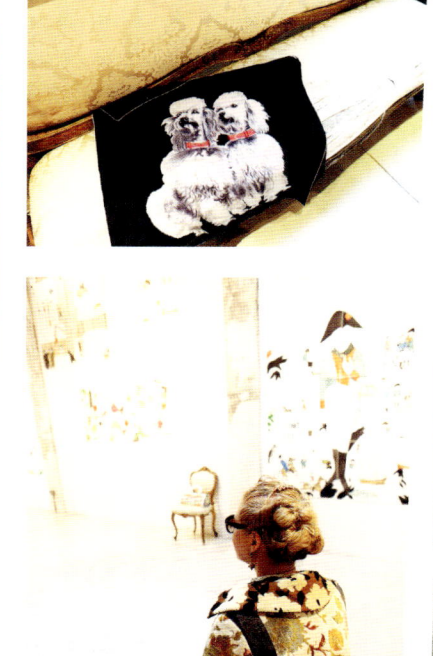
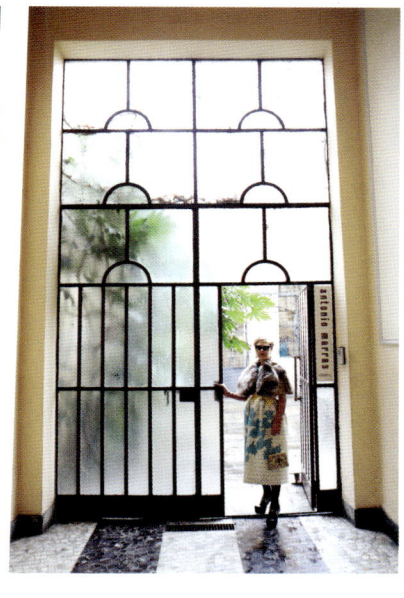
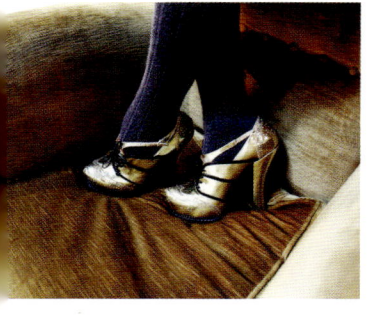
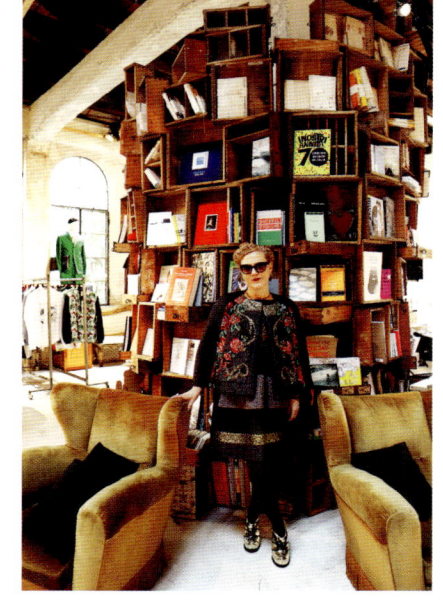
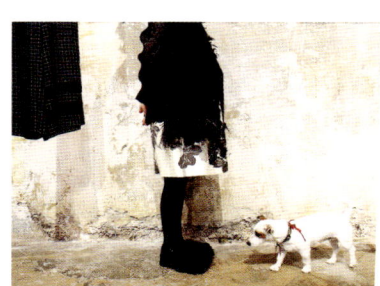
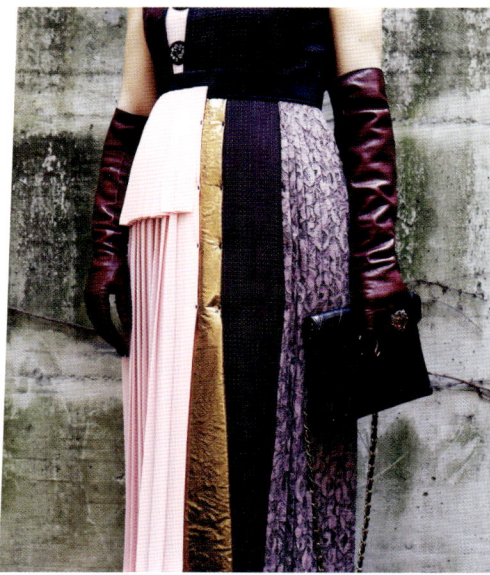
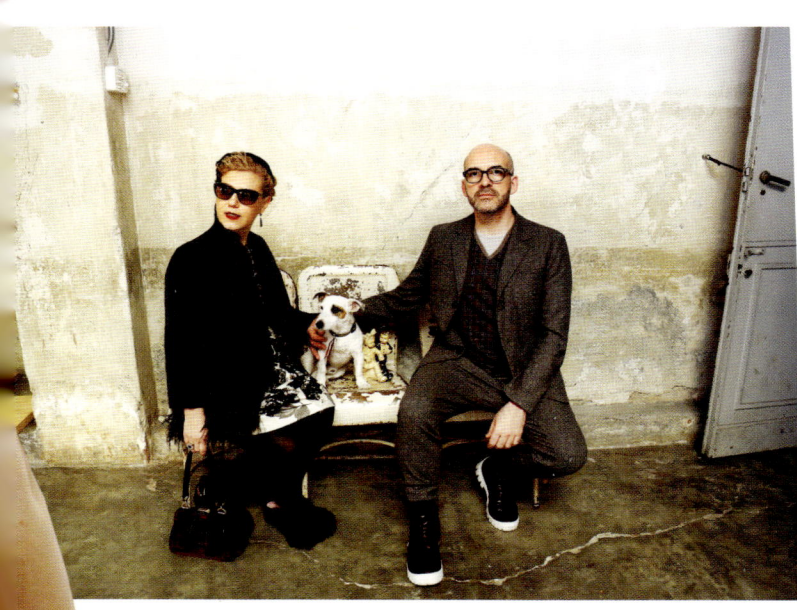
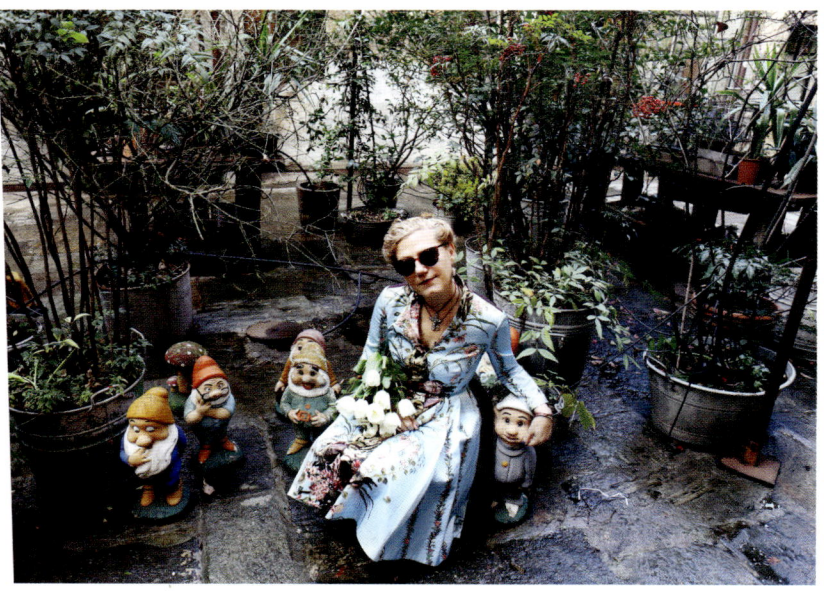

STELLA MAXWELL
IT'S A HANG

Something's wrong with the camera. Even when I turn on the autofocus, the image is blurry and I can't change the aperture. I try every button, lever, and switch, but nothing's working, except, ironically, the battery. This is extremely unfortunate timing for a technically-impaired amateur. It's 2014, I am at the Rose Bowl Flea Market for the very first time—I've been dreaming about this moment for years—and Stella Maxwell is locked in a loving embrace with Jeremy Scott a few feet away. How am I to capture these sweet, historic junctures with failing equipment? I moan, desperately pivoting to locate people with big cameras, in hopes there's a real photographer among our midst. "David is here!" exclaims Stella, with noticeable concern for my anguish. "Do you want me to call him?" I thank the heavens, and the ever-so-gratifying concept of having a photographer for a best friend. "It's fantastic!" laughs Stella with reference to her own fortuitous situation. "It's like having someone to document all the beautiful moments of my life!" A few minutes later, like a *deus ex machina*, David Mushegain appears and clicks the lens in place. That's all it was.

Twenty-one-year-old Stella Maxwell lives between Los Angeles and New York, so the odds of her catching the monthly Rose Bowl in Pasadena are more favorable than mine. She goes every chance she gets, even if she describes her relationship with vintage as, "just friends." She loves it, but it's not a must. "Is the Rose Bowl the cheapest market? For sure, no. Is it fun? For sure, yes," she claims. "There are so many vendors that you can always find at least one thing. Even if it's salt and pepper shakers you never knew you wanted. But honestly I think a lot of people go to just walk around and socialize. You will always run into friends. Or enemies!!! Just kidding. No enemies. But really you can run into anyone and everyone there. It's a hang." And she's right. Over the course of our two-hour shopping/shoot we bump into Annabelle Dexter-Jones and Andre Saraiva, Jeremy Scott, a few stylists, and Stella's cute model friend Staz. What's missing though is food and toilets. And quality. Besides a few expertly-run stands like Shanana Mil & Co., Fuzzy Bellas, and Vintage Rosemond, I am having a hard time finding the great pieces. Everything seems to be recycled bulk and it gets exhausting after a while.

Stella was born in Belgium to Irish parents—her dad was a diplomat for the European Union—who relocated to New Zealand when she was 13. In 2009 she was scouted by a modeling agency and began to travel the world. The Fashion Spot has a job-per-job, almost-to-the-minute rapport of her career so far. It mentions Testino, British Vogue, Alexander McQueen, Luella, and more. She's not the tallest, and with her short, blonde hair definitely not the most marketable, but she's certainly one of the most beautiful and coolest girls I've ever seen. Her dewy, fresh skin, full lips, and big, blue eyes remind me of a baby Claudia Schiffer, and it's absolutely impossible to take a bad photo of her. I love how David describes his first meeting with her in Paris. It sums up exactly—minus the love story—how I experienced shooting her: "You don't have to pry the photograph out of her like some hidden treasure. It's just there for the taking, and that is such a gift."

It's also clear that Stella is destined for great things. Whether it's making music, or buying a puppy, or making her favorite fruit salad with chili and lime, I am confident she will find a way to pour her heart into it. When I ask her if she collects anything, she thinks for a second and responds, "Well, maybe I collect love. I try and surround myself with the most amazing friends. I love my friends a lot. I don't collect them, but I love them." She just got back from a surfing trip to Indonesia and can't stop talking about it. "Indonesia is incredible!" she cries. They rode around on motorbikes, crossed suspension bridges, visited little fishing villages and beautiful temples, and braved jungles. But then she gets serious: "Can we please take a little moment to send love and thoughts to the families affected by the recent volcanic outburst in Indonesia? Natural disasters, or any disasters that cost lives, are such a tragedy. Sometimes we see things in the news and they are there for a moment in our lives. But for people affected, the effects of these disasters go on for years and years. It's important to keep things in perspective. We are discussing my style and where I shop. And that's beautiful. There is a time and place for that, and fashion has done wonderful things for people. But let's not lose sight of who we are as people; at least, who we strive to be. And for me, compassion and love and caring are such important qualities. Our actions really define who we are as people. Our actions outshine what we are wearing. True style is in how you carry yourself."

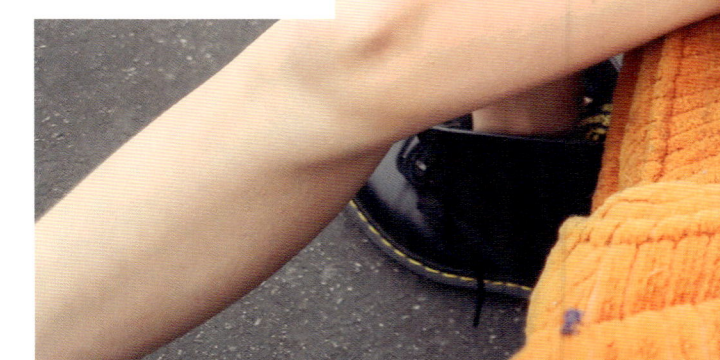

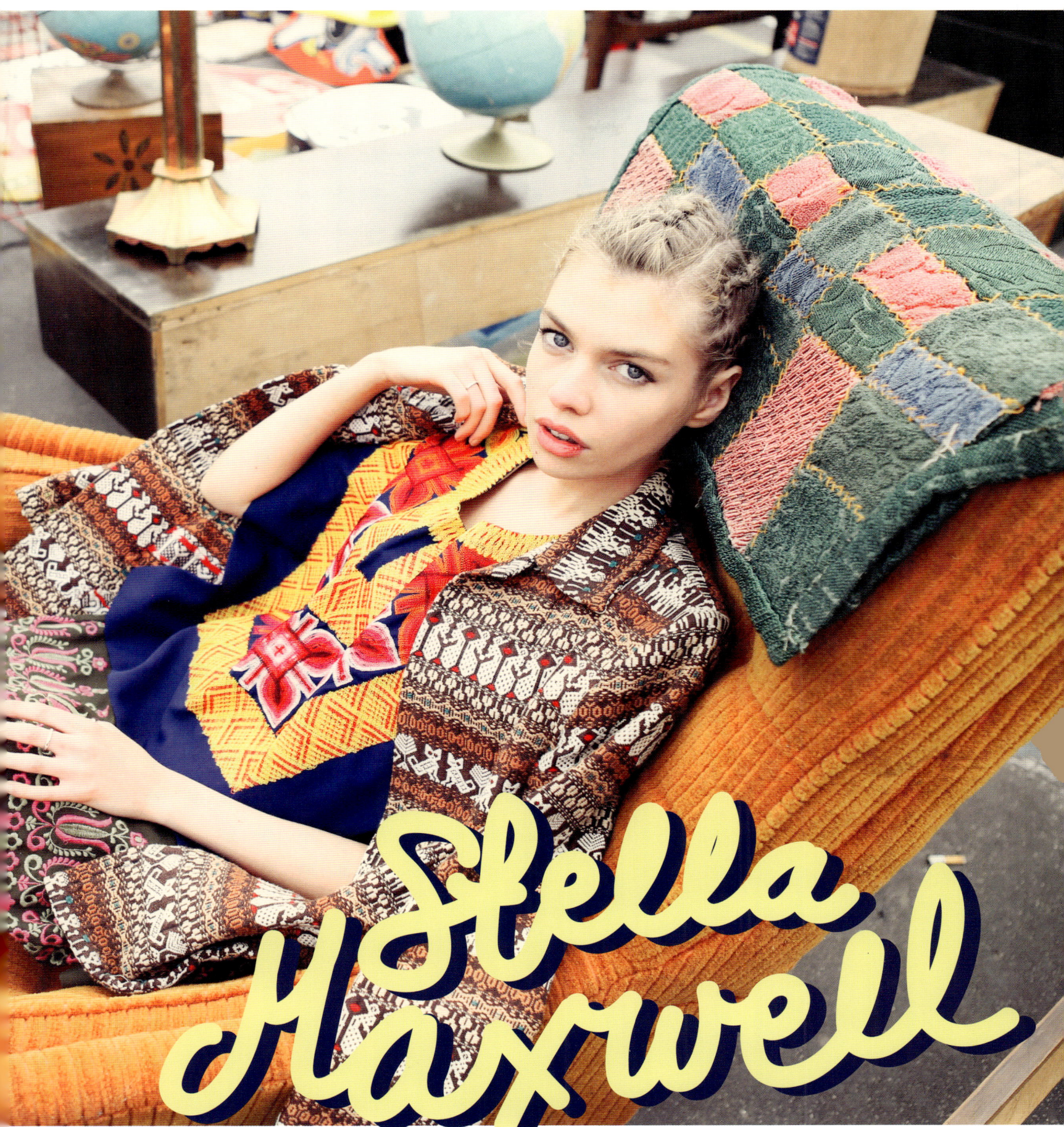

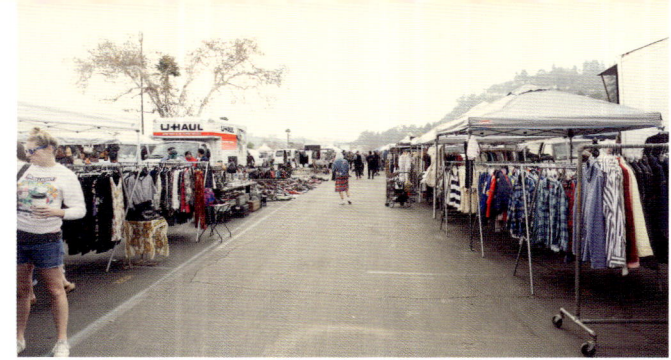
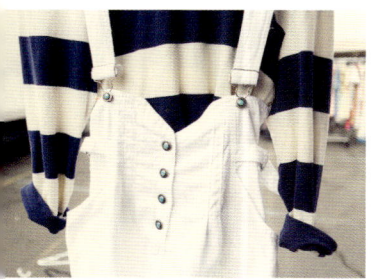
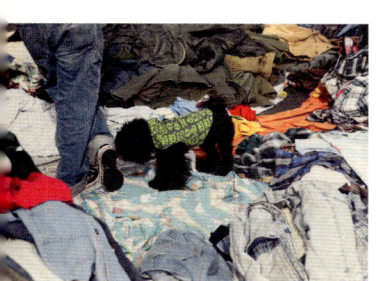
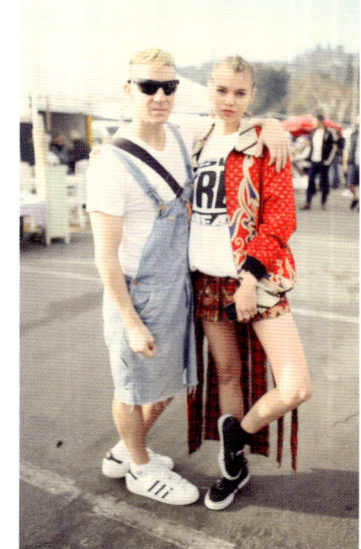
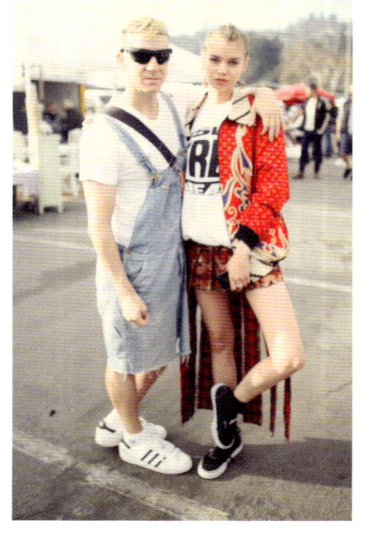
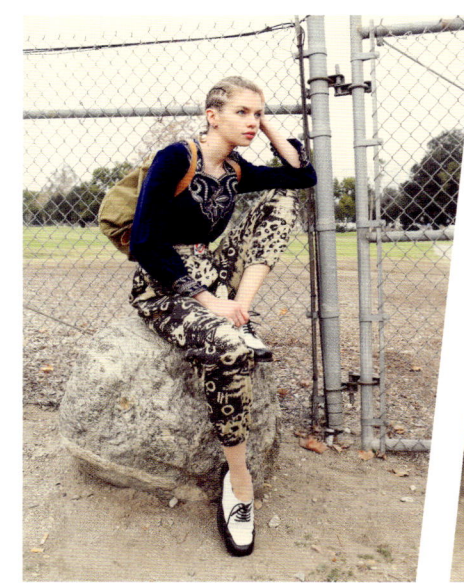
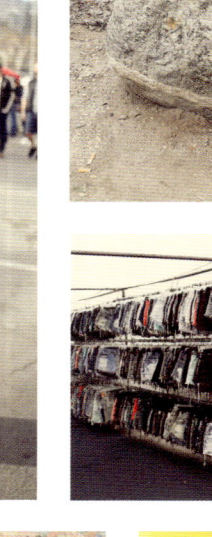
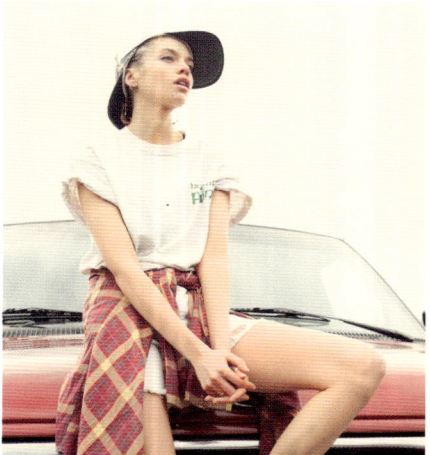
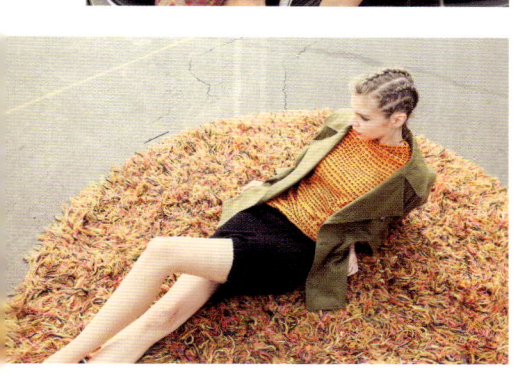
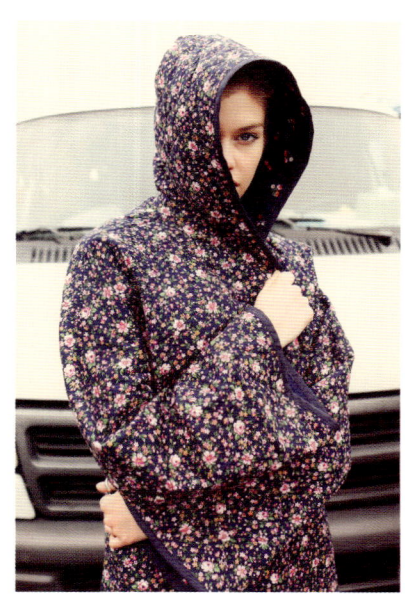
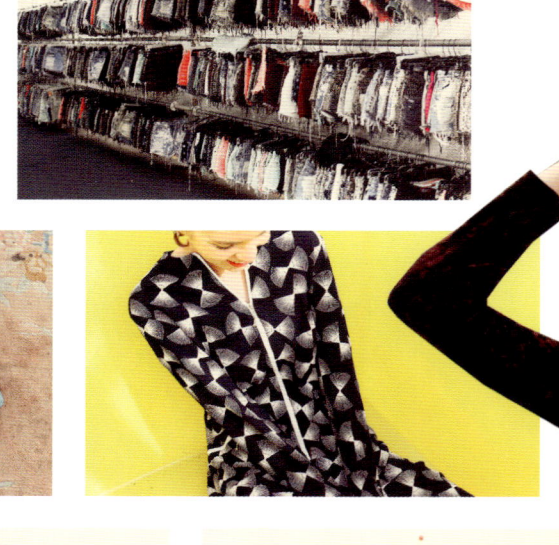
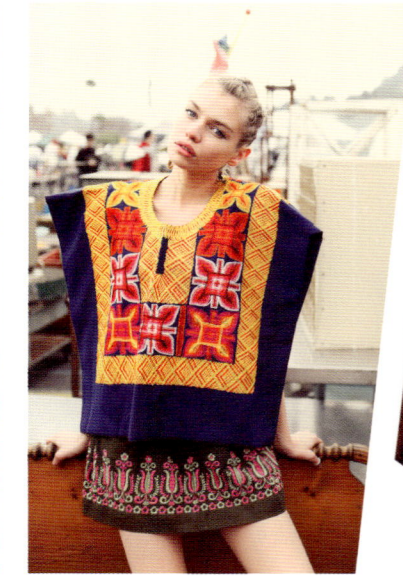
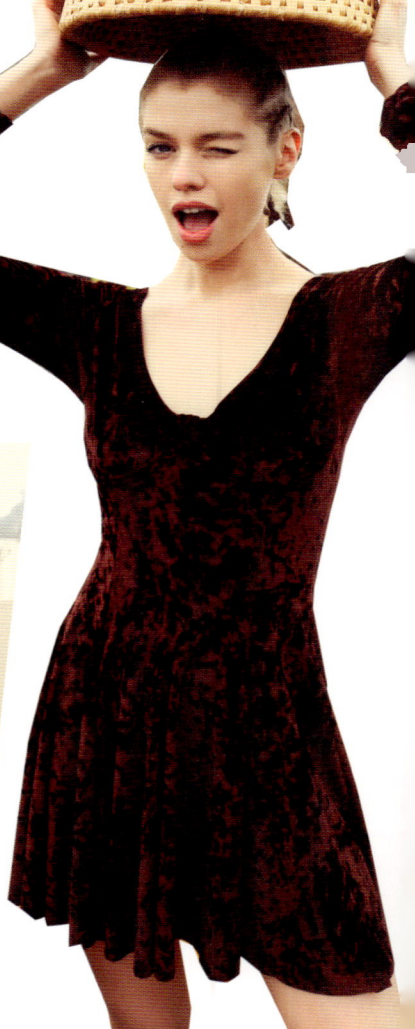

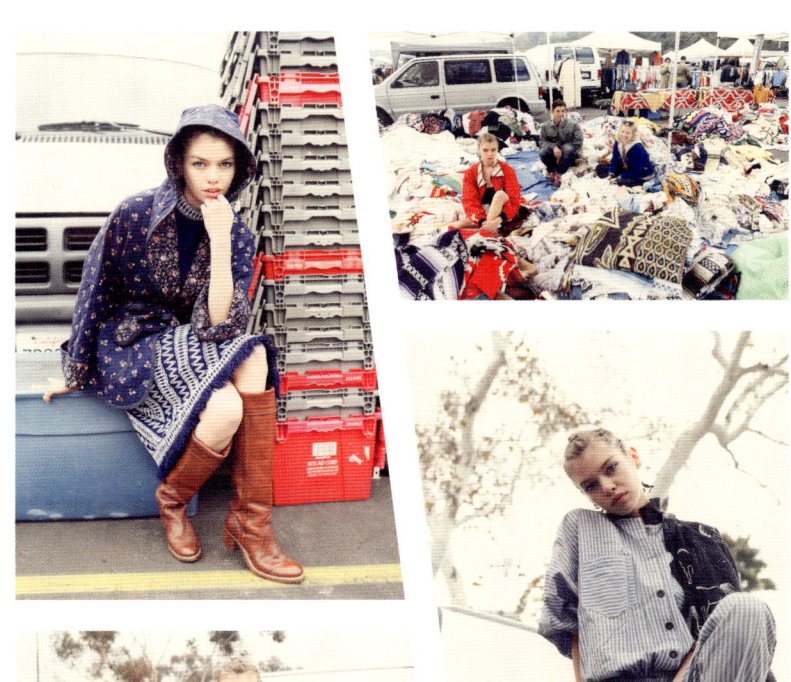
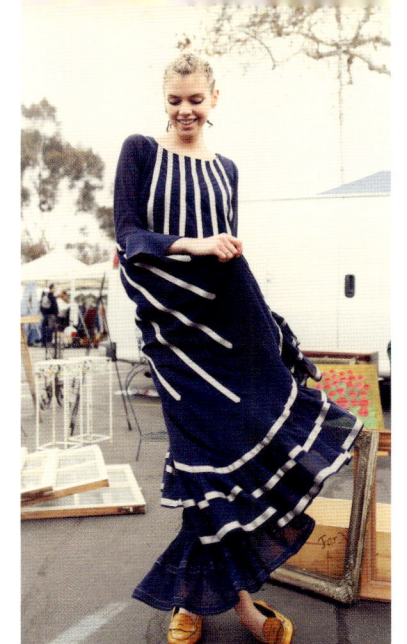
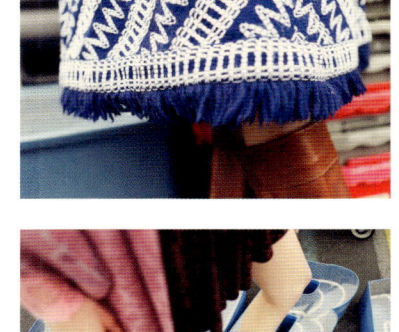
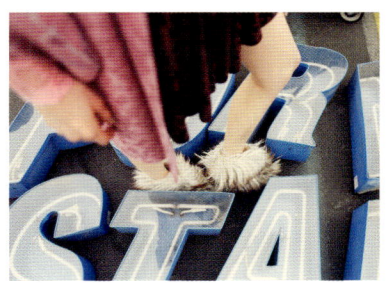
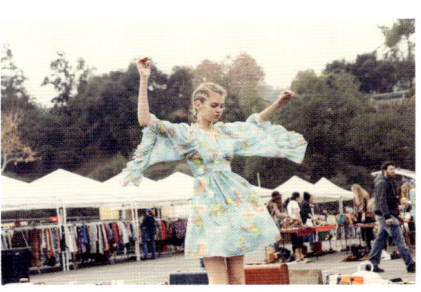
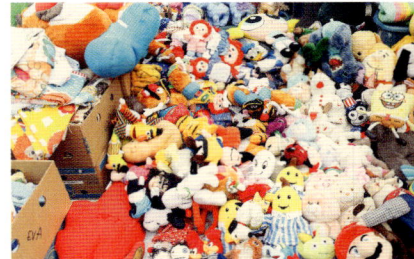
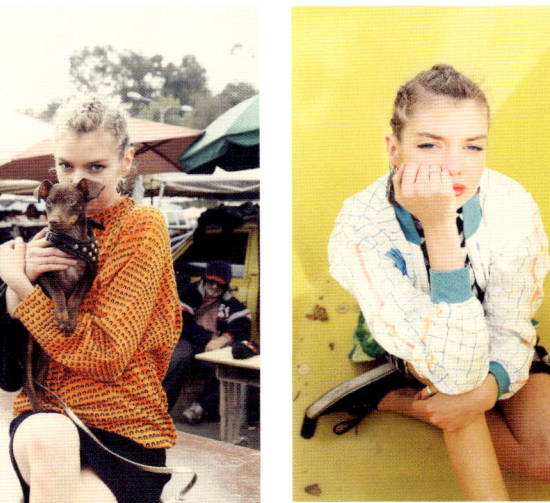
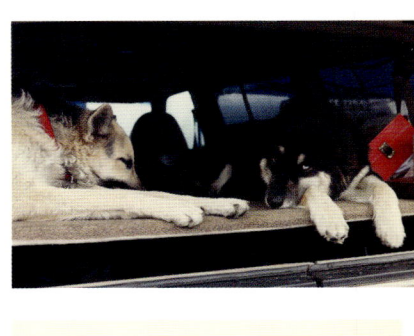
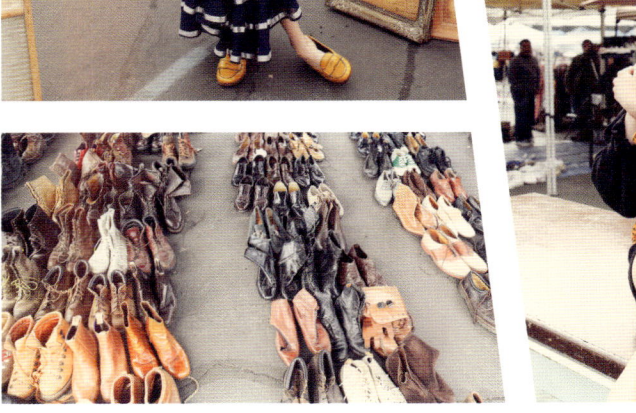
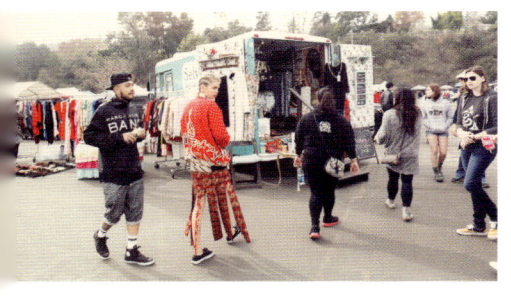
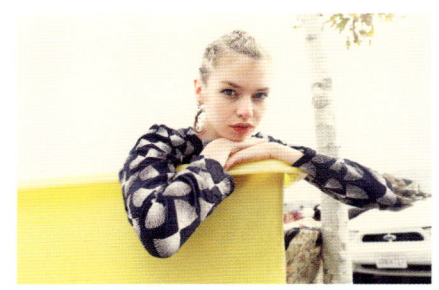
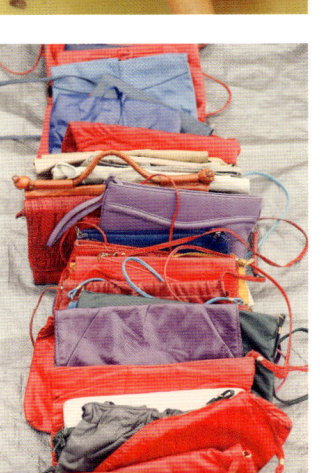
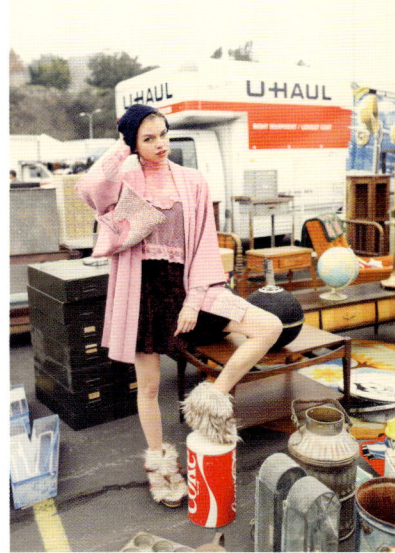

ABIGAIL SPENCER
TIMELESS

The film crew is still here. They've fabricated a provisional interview booth in the guesthouse at the back of the driveway. I poke my head in to find Abigail, but her chair is empty. The camera guy is in the middle of a sound test and the producer is flipping through the pages of her questionnaire. "She's in the kitchen," I'm told. They haven't finished her makeup and hair yet, which sincerely worries me. If we're supposed to start my Tales shoot in half an hour, she'll literally have to race through the SundanceTV interview—and that's just a preposterous notion for the 35-year-old actress. "My nickname was The Boss," she told me earlier." And not like Bruce Springsteen. I was always hoarse from talking too much." Shit.

Abigail Spencer's acting career started on *All My Children* in 1999. She was 17 years old, fresh off the boat from Gulf Breeze, Florida, when "opportunity knocked" and she ditched college to say yes to her role as Becca Tyree, a young video producer with a massive head of dark curls, clear braces, and multiple boy crushes. It would be silly to list the rest of her TV roles, because it's endless. Most recently she played Ray Velcoro's ex-wife on *True Detective*, a rival attorney on *Suits*, and Amantha Holden on *Rectify*. She just got back from Vancouver, where she's been filming the first season of *Timeless* for the past few months. Which reminds me: *How much more time is this interview going to take?* I press my flushed face against the window and give the crew a wretched, anxious look. "Two more questions!" they motion.

We're about 45 minutes behind schedule, but Abigail's not the least bit fazed. While the camera's still rolling, she dashes to her closet, shimmies right into a black-and-white polka-dot 60s minidress, and stages a sexy secretary on the Spanish steps of her back door. "I choreographed all my high school musicals," she winks. "I was creative and constantly coming up with some harebrained scheme and roping everyone into it." Next she climbs on the toolshed in a bright-red vintage chiffon gown and gives me Snow-White-Goes-to-Hollywood. And then she suggests that I shoot her from outside, on the front lawn, while she stands in the window in a white cotton pique dress. She's literally unstoppable.

It was her mother who built vintage into the seams of Abigail's childhood. "She and I would study *Vogue* pattern books," she remembers, "so I was always studying the origin. She made most of my clothes growing up, and has a heightened sense of style for sure." Abigail's always looking for Ali MacGraw when she shops vintage, or a "great designer in good condition at a great price." She attributes the words "classic, modest, timeless" to her style, but admits others have described her as having the style of a "hip old Grandpa." Or in her own words: "I indeed have a *Prairie Home Companion*—meets—Hasidic-Jew side."

It's a near miracle, but we finish the shoot in under an hour. Abigail's energy is otherworldly. I can only blame genetics—she's the daughter of five-time U.S. champion surfer and East Coast legend, Yancy Spencer—because the past year has been tough, juggling two shows in different locations, and running a household with an aging dog, 8-year-old son, and live-in boyfriend. "I've been tremendously and continually sick this past year. It was too much. Living on planes and going non-stop, so I'm homebound now and looking to strengthen my mind, body, and immunity. It's all for nothing if I don't feel well." Amen.

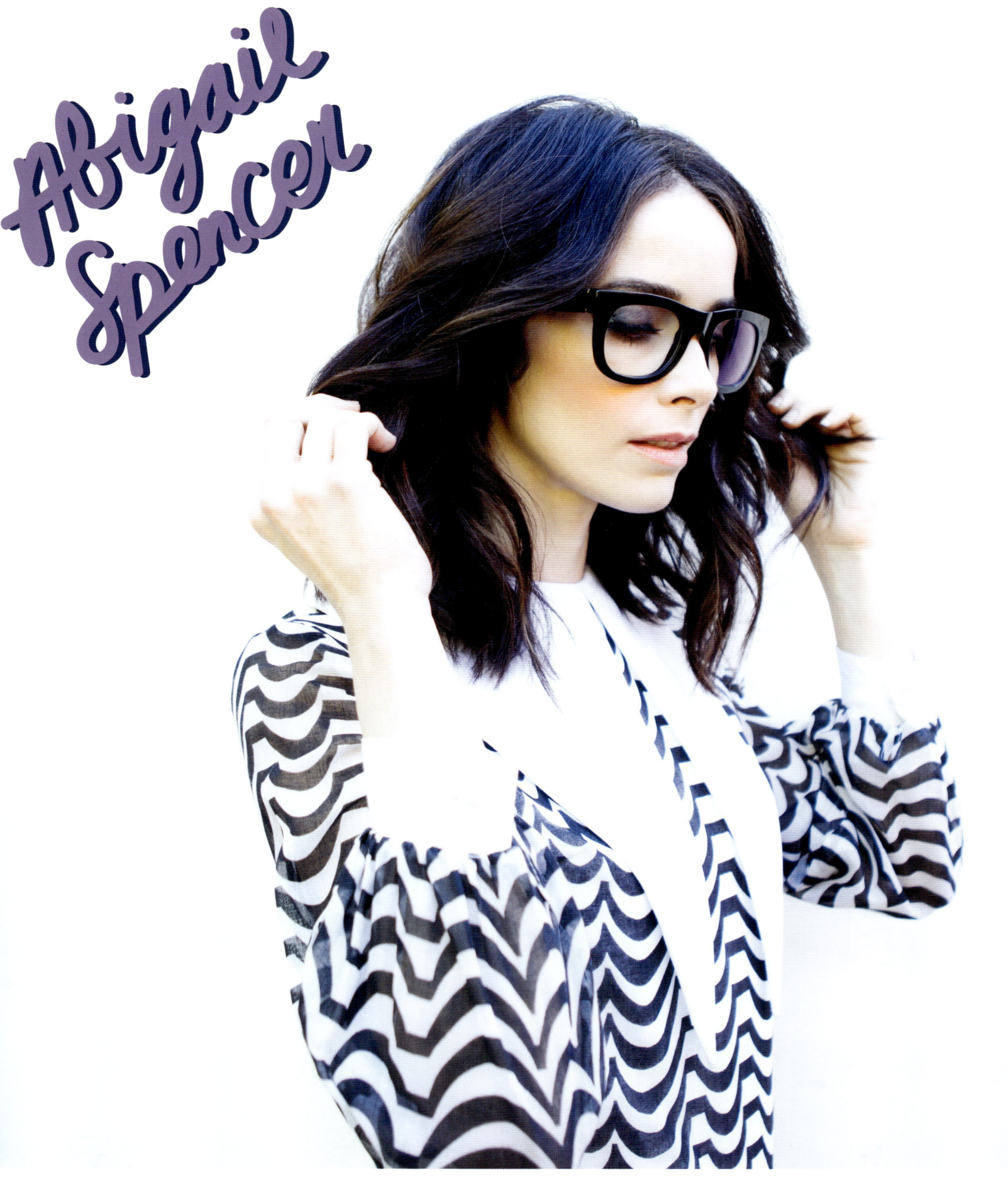

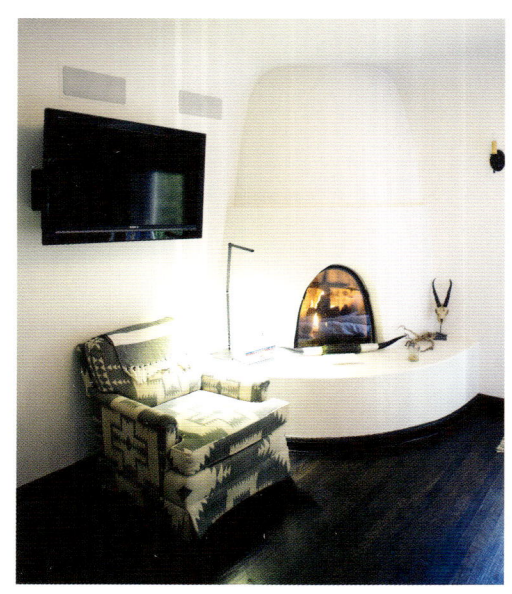
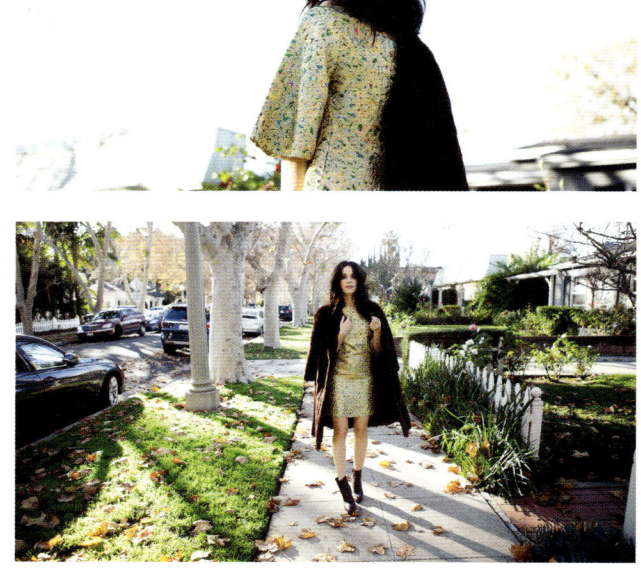
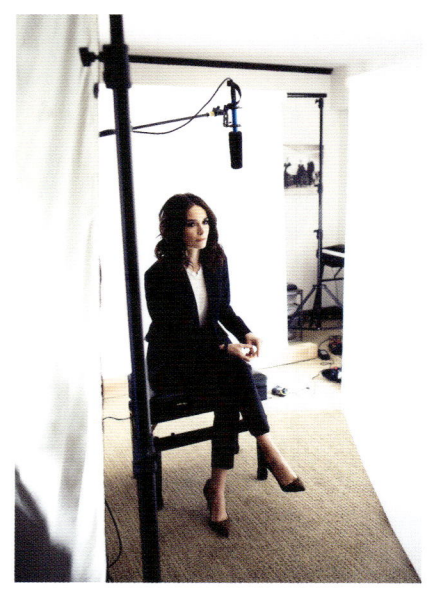
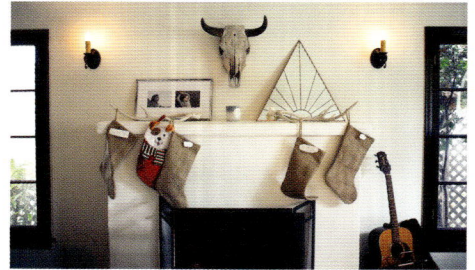
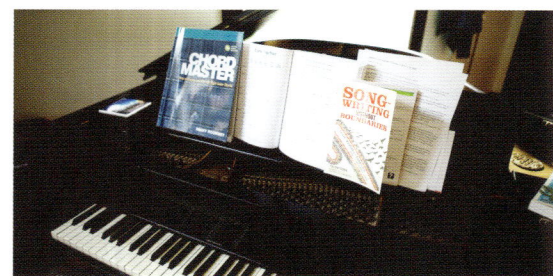
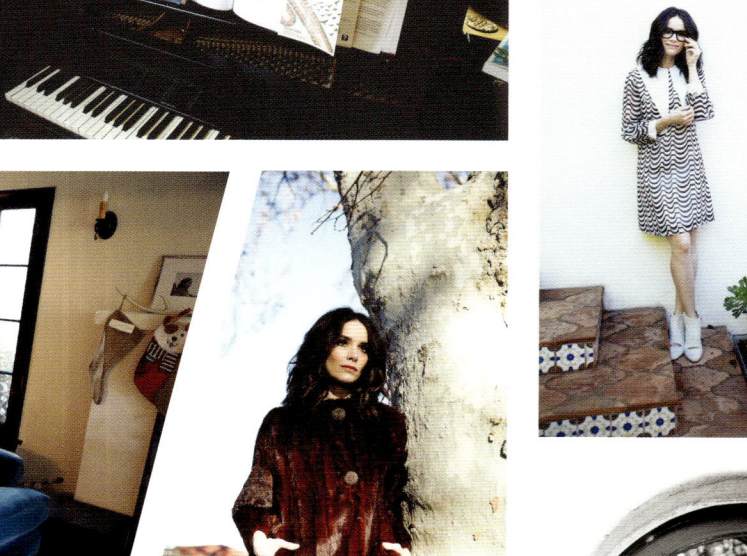
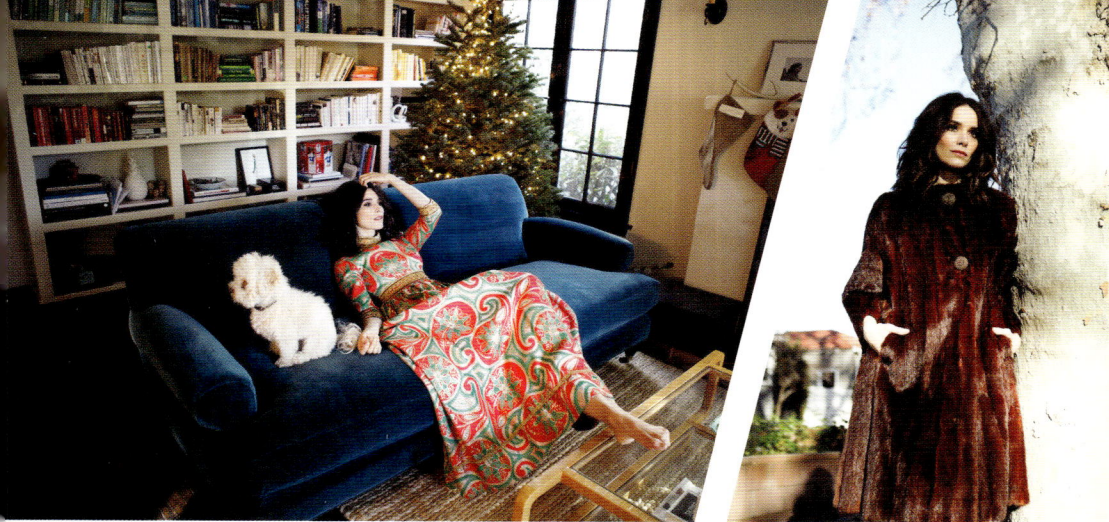
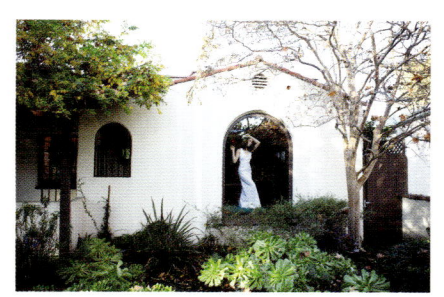
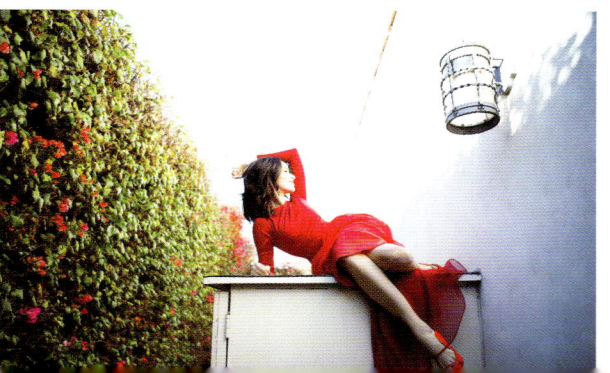
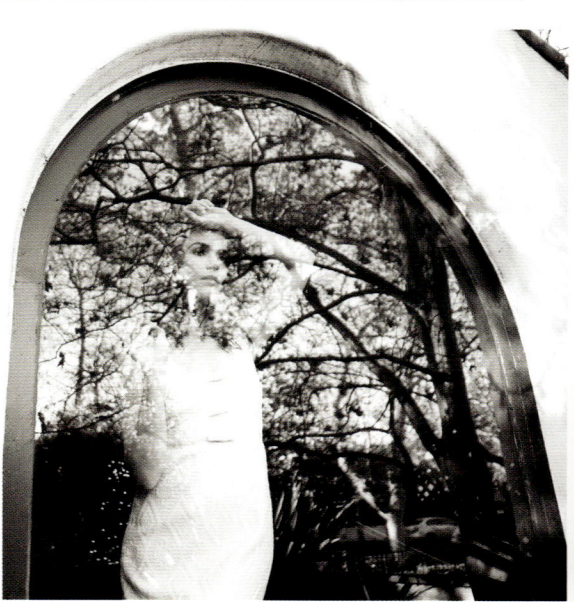

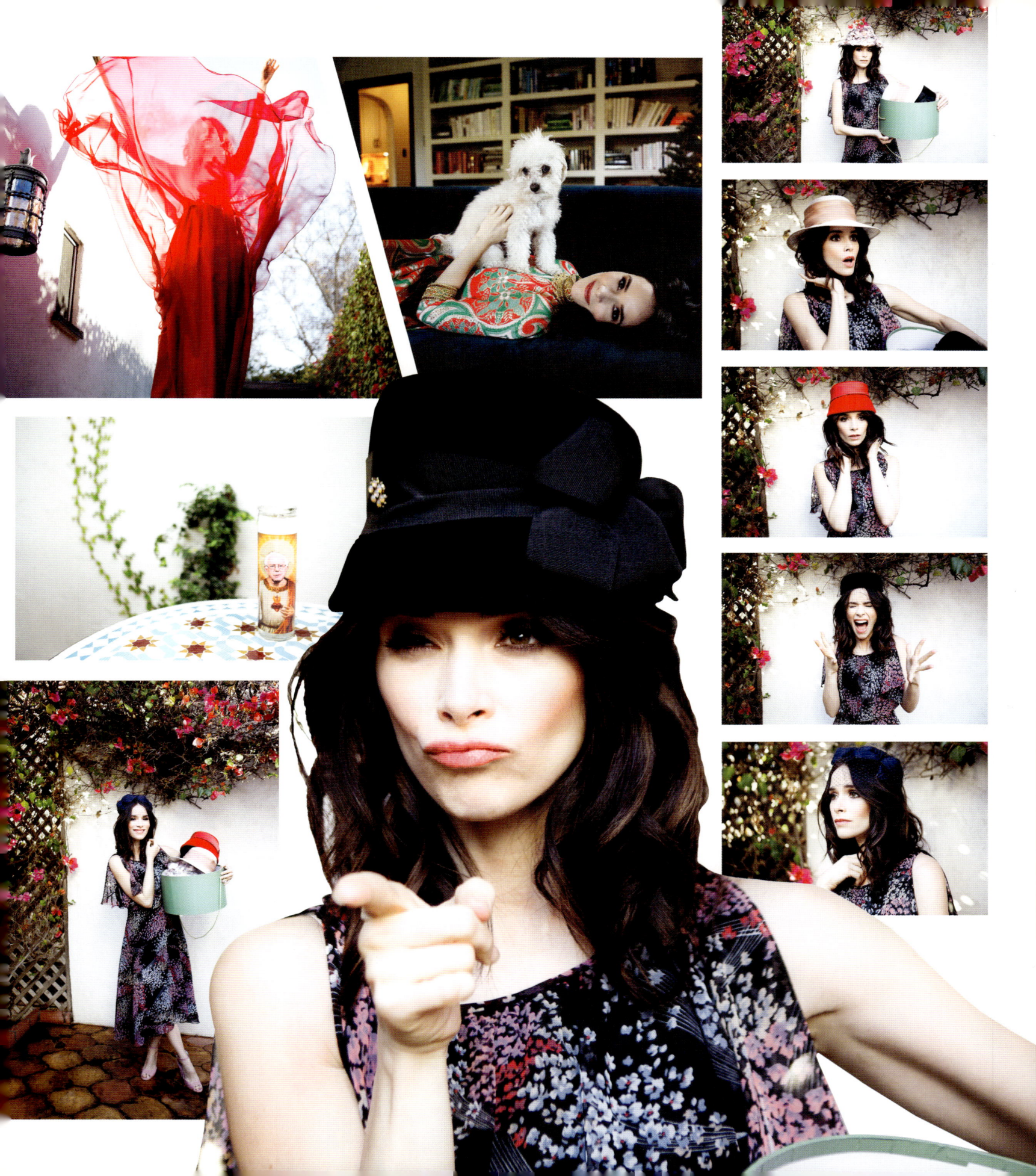

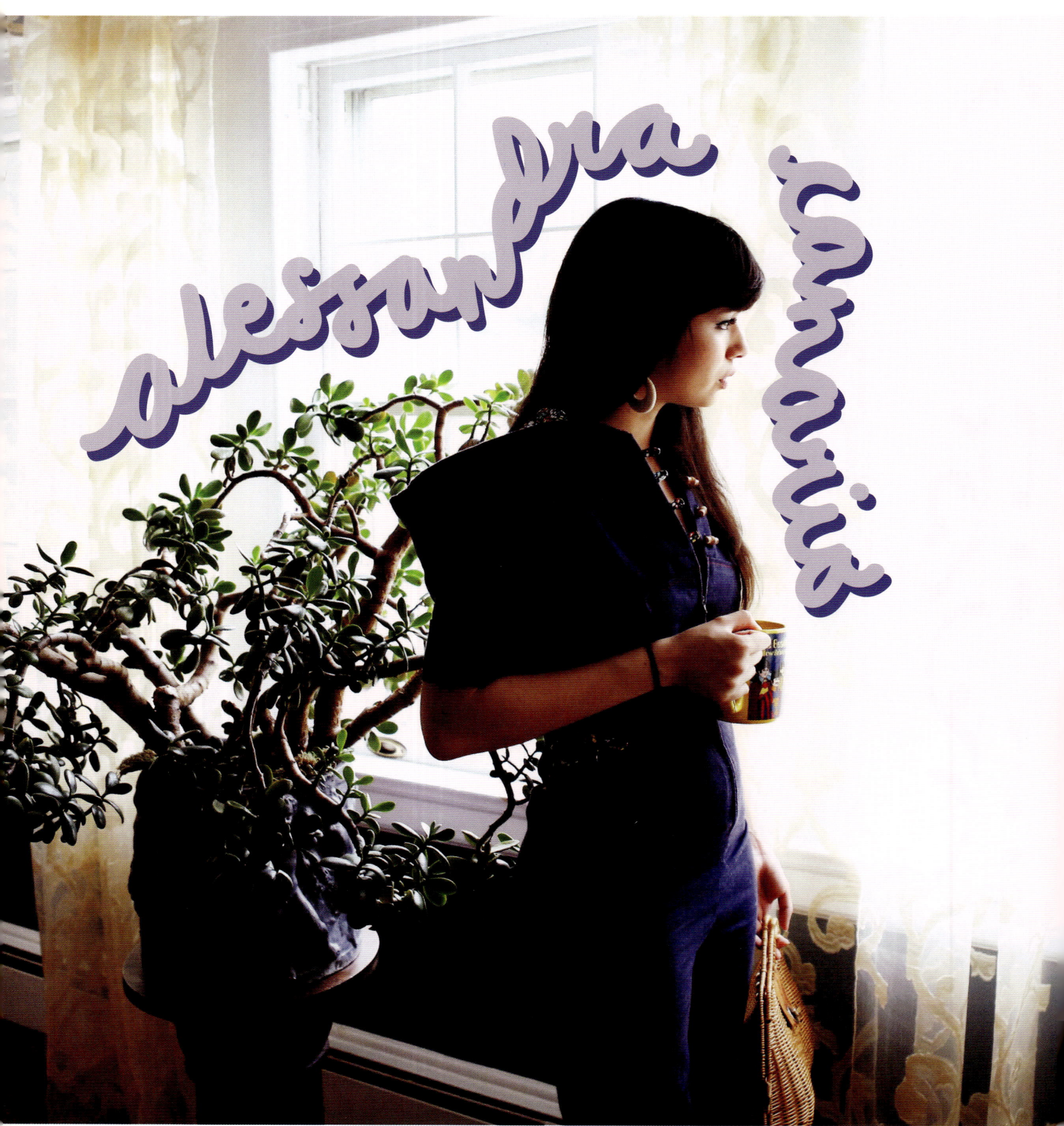

ALESSANDRA CANARIO
PURPLE HAZE

On a drizzly afternoon in Montclair, Alessandra Canario is waiting at the end of the platform of the New Jersey Transit train track. It's hard to miss her in her dark denim 70s jumpsuit. She's a stunning girl, with curves and lips and hair that have surely shattered many a boy's heart into a thousand bewildered pieces. She's that dangerous combination of adorable and exotic. She warns me about the car—"it's purple"—but the small 2012 Honda parked in the lot is less sci-fi than cute. It suits her. And she has no problem pushing the pedals in her high, rose-printed platforms. "Oh my god!" she screams when we pull out into a line of traffic. "That guy has the same steering wheel cover as me!" I catch a glimpse of an implausibly similar, shaggy, purple thing in the front seat of the other car and start laughing. "That's never happened…" she gasps.

Ally takes a detour to show me some obscenely huge mansions, pretty tree-lined streets, and the schools she attended since her parents moved to Montclair from the city. She tells me she loves her neighborhood when it rains. "It's nice but I could never raise my children here," she says determined. "The 'keeping up with the Joneses' mentality is not productive for individuals like me. I prefer to be in a more remote, less crowded area like upstate New York. I feel like the area outside of my country house was my ideal living environment." Poems, books, and postcards have been written about that house—it's called Moonhaw and located in West Shokan—and it seems to have strong emotional and magnetic power over Ally. She still feels very connected to the land and has visited every other year (since her dad sold it in 2004) to check if new people have moved in. Her childhood memories are often overwhelming and vivid, and have become the object of her recent obsession: to study history at Skidmore College, which is just two hours away.

Ally is a contemplative, serious teenager. Though she may be pretty, she doesn't want to belong to any group, least not the popular girls. She has (or needs) very few friends, and feels she is often irrelevant, an outsider, especially because of the way she dresses. "It's funny, you would think it's hard to forget the girl in a disco jumpsuit. But I now have two best friends, Maddie Carr and Lauren Peressinni. And I guess I am not completely forgotten about since I won 'Best Dressed' in the yearbook! I got used to weird looks in school for my vintage clothing, but towards the end of high school people started asking curiously about it and complimenting my confidence to wear what I do." The highlight of her social life is an active Instagram account with 3,000 followers, where she posts her impeccable looks, and tries to get connected with the vintage world.

Girls like Ally are rare. She has a remarkably clear understanding of her passions and dreams. She fell in love with history in middle school and got intrigued with all things old: first antiques, and eventually clothing. "I can't remember my first piece because, once I discovered I could bridge my two loves and physically live in history, my obsession with buying many pieces at a time graduated to rarer pieces when I was able to work to pay for them." Up until a few months ago she was a sales assistant at Speakeasy Vintage in Montclair, where she learned the ropes of the trade, got first dibs, and modeled new pieces that came in. Her closet has become a perfectly-curated collection of colorful dresses and funny pants from the 60s and 70s era. "because it embodies a time when the search for individuality and self-expression was paramount. The clothes were as bold as the movement." Through college she will intern at Another Man's Treasure in Jersey City and ultimately—the dream—work as a researcher at a costume rental shop.

At the house, mom Susana is rushing off to her next makeup appointment, and sister Sabrina is just getting back from school. She comes upstairs in between episodes of *Gossip Girl* to watch her big sister in action. When I ask her to join us for a picture, Ally warns me: "My sister hates vintage. She thinks it's creepy to wear clothing that someone else previously wore, especially if that person is deceased." (Sabrina is one of the popular girls.) There's also a very curious dog, Teddy (Roosevelt), and beautiful cat, Taquito. Dad, Thomas, a wine distributor and avid cook, is working in the city. They're a friendly bunch, a mix of Mexican and Brooklyn-Italian warmth and hospitality. We eat pork and rice for lunch, drive out to Ally's favorite green spot and talk about her other passions: hiking, and bowling! "I was the varsity girl's captain of the high school bowling team," she surprises me. "I have a vintage bowling bag for my ball, named Purple Haze after the Jimi Hendrix song!" I could write on an on about Alessandra. It's baffling how someone so young already has such an intrinsic story. But I will just end with her favorite quote by Robert A. Heinlein: "A generation which ignores history has no past—and no future."

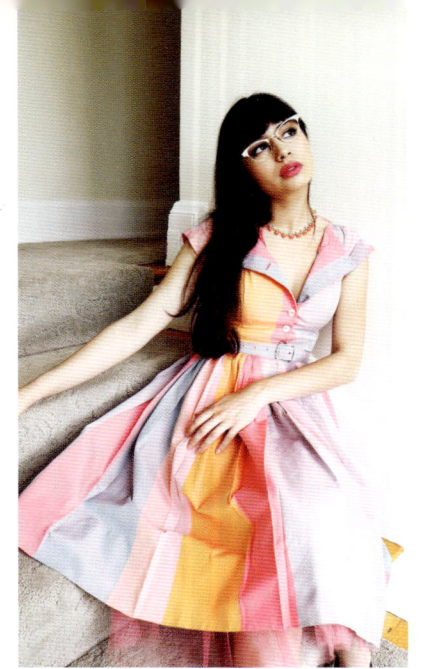
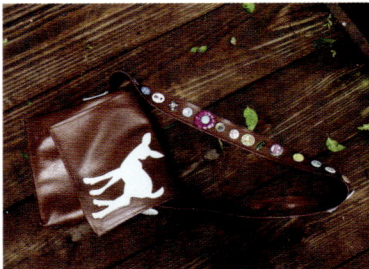
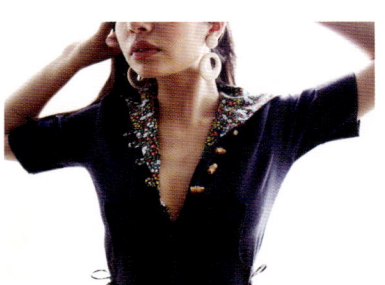
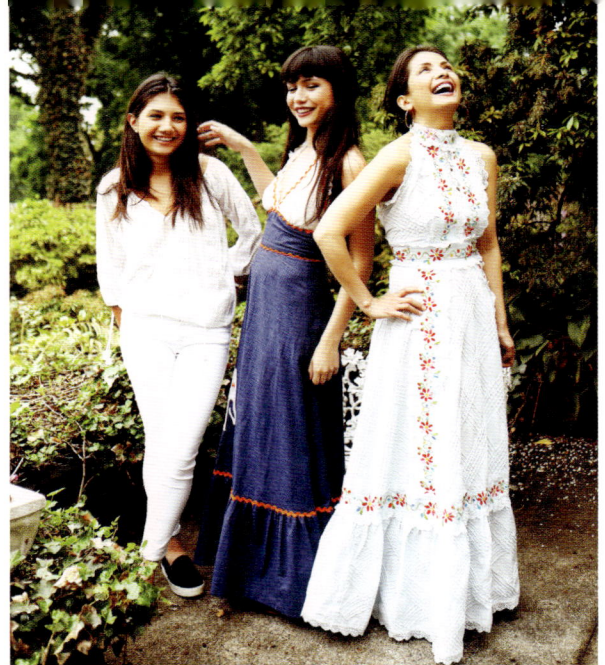
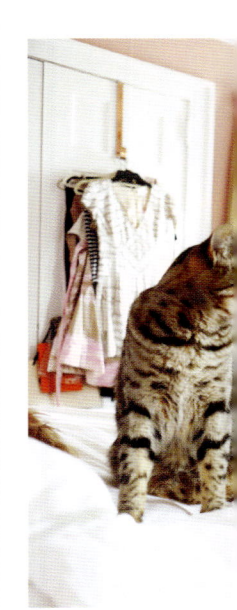
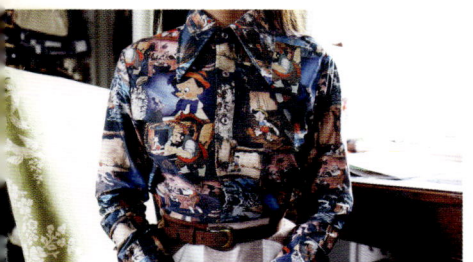
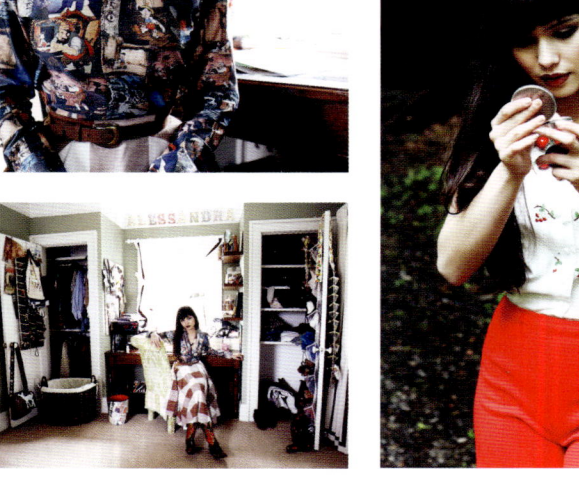
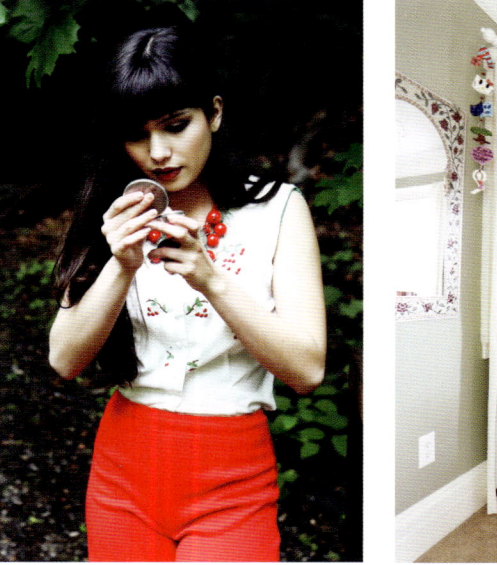
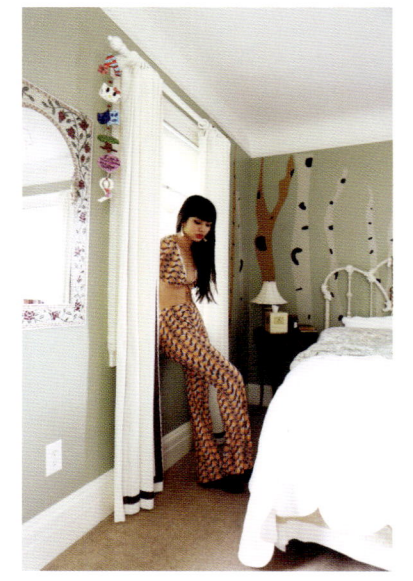
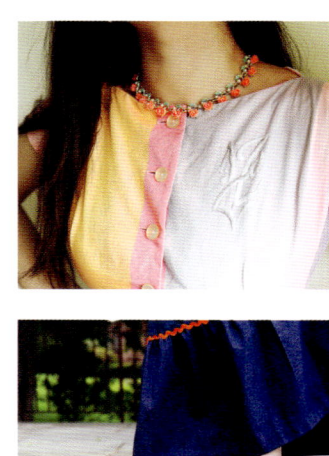
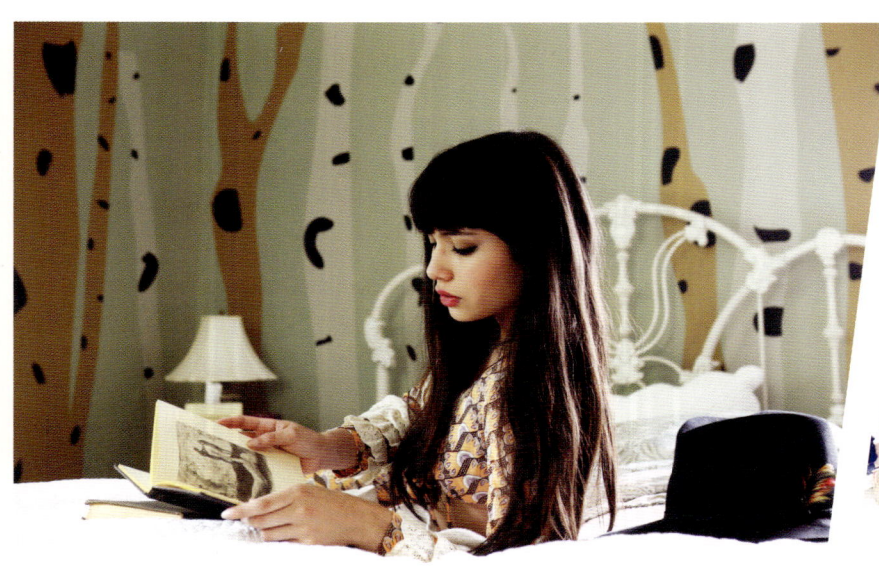
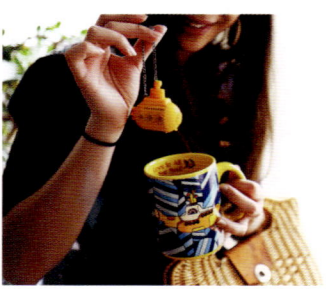
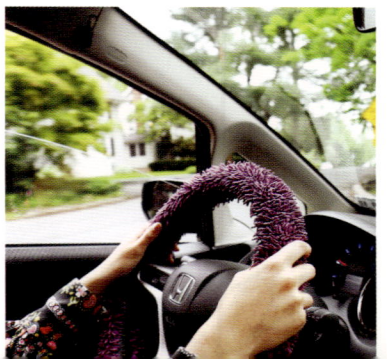

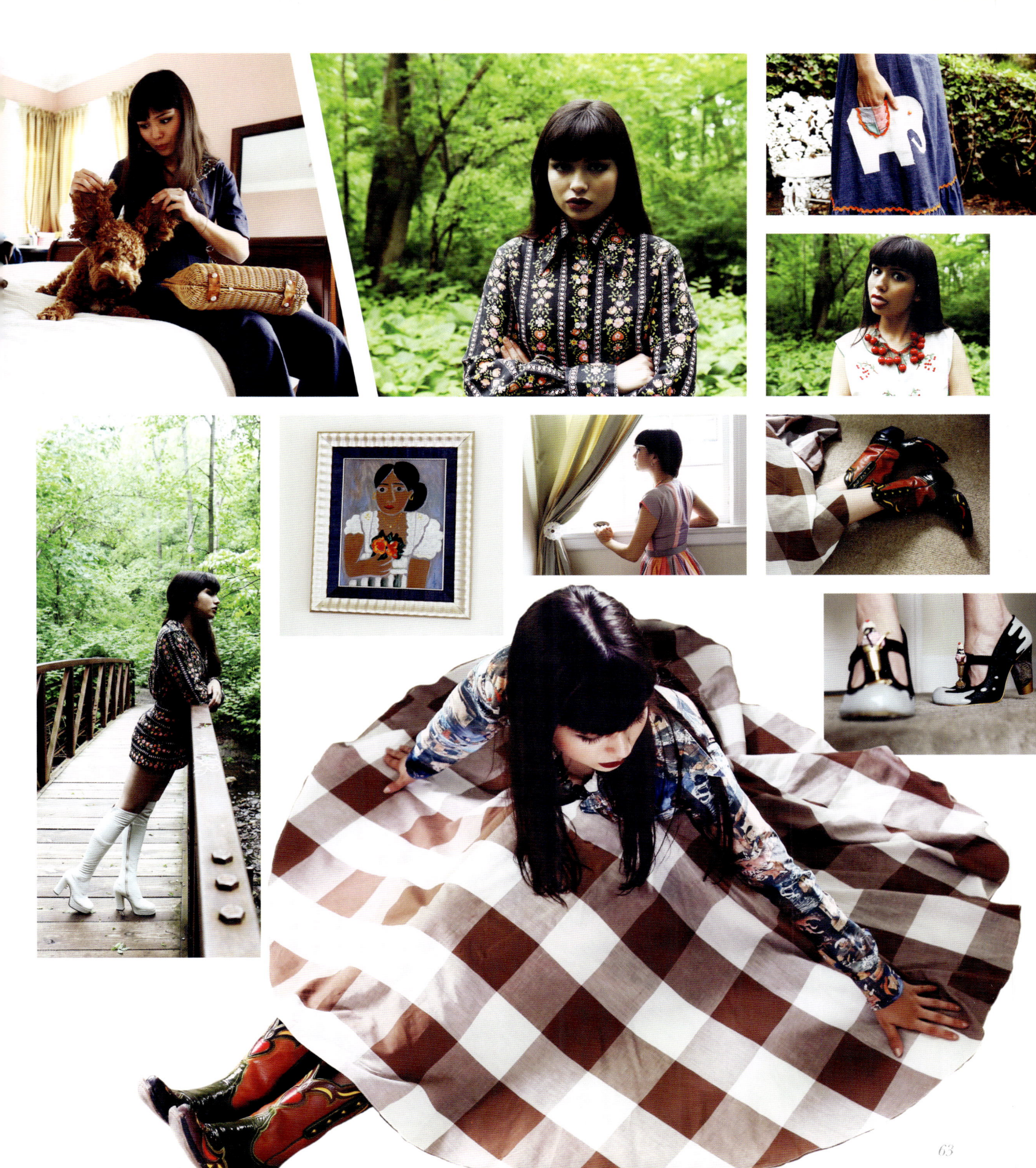

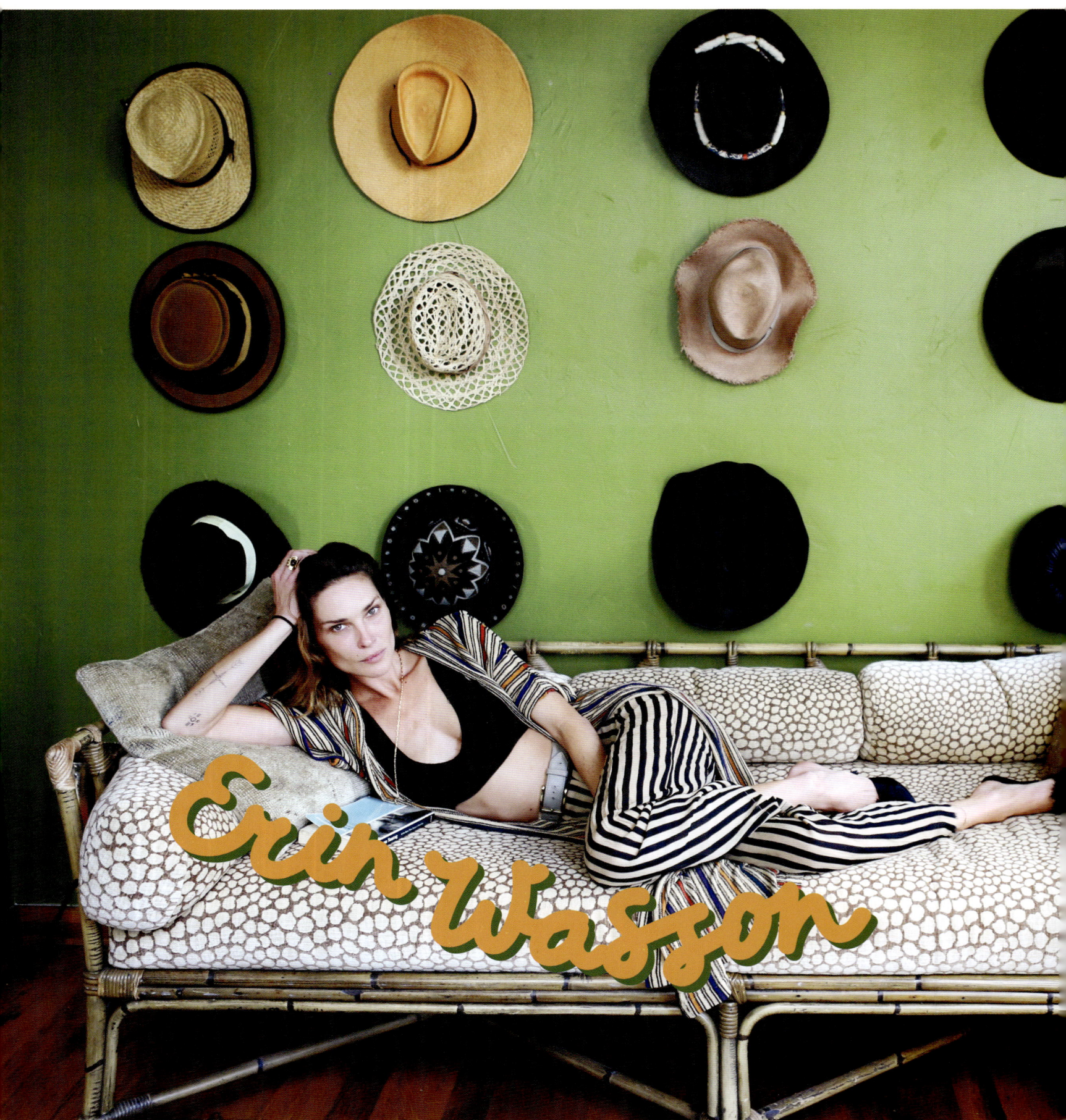

ERIN WASSON
LITTLE MOMENTS OF FUCK YOU

Seven girls, five bottles of wine, three sheepskin rugs, a sleeping dog, and a crackling fire. It's the stuff chick flicks are made of. But this gathering has all the trappings of a sorcerer's circle, with philosophical, spiritual, and herbal banter bouncing around the room like a dirty tennis ball. I don't know who steered the conversation to monkey witchcraft and animal abuse in Victorian England—I am half asleep at this point, next to a kindred pit bull, and my participation is dwindling—but suddenly we are discussing the incredulous story of an elephant named Mary who was hanged in early 20th-century Tennessee because she had killed her trainer. Yes, *hanged*. I'm watching Erin as Emily continues to propagate the incident with photo evidence on her iPhone. She rolls her eyes, shakes her head slowly, takes another sip of her red wine, and shrugs: "Well, that's the dumbest thing I ever heard."

One is never *not* sure with Erin Wasson. She wears her heart on her sleeve, especially when she feels cornered. Even in her most diplomatic of voices and wordings, you'll know exactly what she thinks. Like when, the following morning, red-wine stains still on the glasses in the sink, she not-so-secretly hopes to get out of our photo shoot, "because I really don't want to be thinking about fashion right now..." and I remind her, as a dear old friend and house guest, of the earlier promise she made. She says she doesn't dress up anymore, but I know vintage plays a huge part in her life and her work, so I am relieved when she finally twirls up the stairs to get dressed. "I think when I was younger I simply just experimented more," she admits when she shows me an old Dries Van Noten robe. "I would throw crazy shit on together that didn't match but somehow worked. I'm just more lazy. Or maybe I'm just closer to my real self and don't want to waver too much." Nowadays it's jeans, T-shirts, cowboy boots, and accessories: "The bag, the jewelry. The extra shit. Nothing too girly or frilly, like a tutu??" she laughs. "My style is simple with little moments of 'fuck you' I suppose. The older I get, the more boring. But I do get a kick out of being the least dressed-up person at a party."

Trust me, even in her most modest of sartorial choices it's hard to miss this 34-year-old Texan. For starters: that hair. She wears it big and curly and natural, like a lioness. And then those startling eyes and cheekbones, both undeniable and unparalleled in the business. Even after 20 years of modeling—she won the *Dallas Morning News* model search at 15 after her father sent in one of her catalog pictures—she's still a powerful vision, and a name to be reckoned with. And she's not just a pretty face; she never was. She has a few collaborative design projects under her belt (Alexander Wang, RVCA, Pacsun), launched her own T-shirt and jewelry line, had a role in a vampire movie, and appeared as a mentor on Rihanna's *Styled to Rock* TV show with Pharrell and Mel Ottenberg. People just want a slice of the Wasson pie. "I think I'm hired because I live it," she ponders. "The 'thing' I'm selling is a piece of the lifestyle. I don't fake the funk. Maybe a rarity in this day and age."

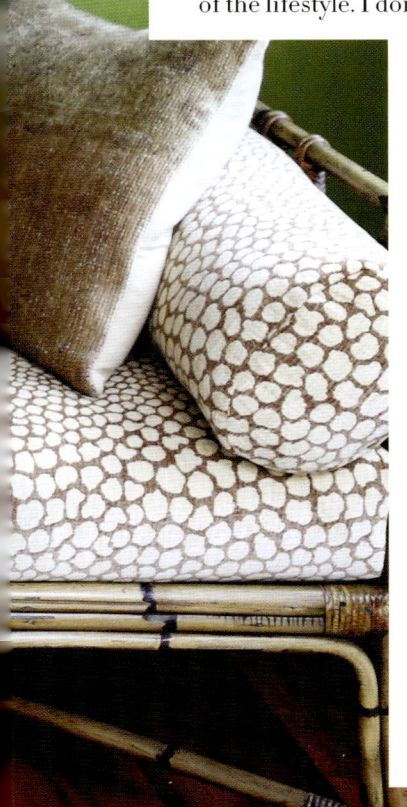

She's getting into it now. The laughs have become bigger and the outfits more elaborate; vintage will do that to a person. "Vintage is authentic and unique," she declares, "two things that are very important to me. My first piece was a beautiful long black dress with cool cut-outs from a shop in Deep Ellum. I would wear it with chunky amber jewelry and a belt made of a seat-belt clip and beer-bottle tabs. My prized possession is a tin-soldier style vest from Alexander McQueen, maybe seven years ago? Maybe six. It's just divine." She shops at Narnia in New York, Scout and Catwalk in LA, Dolly Python in Dallas, Style Station in West, and Feathers in Austin, but her most recent digs happened in Santa Fe, where she went on a post-Christmas unwinding mission with Cream, "the greatest animal I know, my superglue." She scoured the pawnshops off the reservations and all the antique jewelry shops, in search of Native-American inspiration for Low Luv. She bought a pocketknife made of mammoth bone and new Stallion boots at Nathalie's.

These days she calls Venice Beach home. She moved into her two-story house off Abbott Kinney a few years ago. "I took it over from Sophie B. Hawkins and her wife. Remember her?" she smirks. "They left so much shit behind. Like all these light fixtures!" Her nomadic days are over. She still has the loft in the East Village though. "I will never get rid of that place," she swears. "I rent it out to friends now." Work is steady but much more sporadic, which has freed up time for things, like buying a horse—"her name is Malin"—and dating? "Dating is difficult no matter where you are in the world," she finds. "The older you get the more stuck in your ways. And we all have issues with commitment because I think the world is moving so fast to begin with. Who knows. I'm no love doctor." Maybe one day she'll finish college. She quit after one semester of English Literature to take the plunge and model full-time. Back on the couch in front of the fire that night, she breathes deeply and says with a sigh of relief: "Thank god it all worked out, man..."

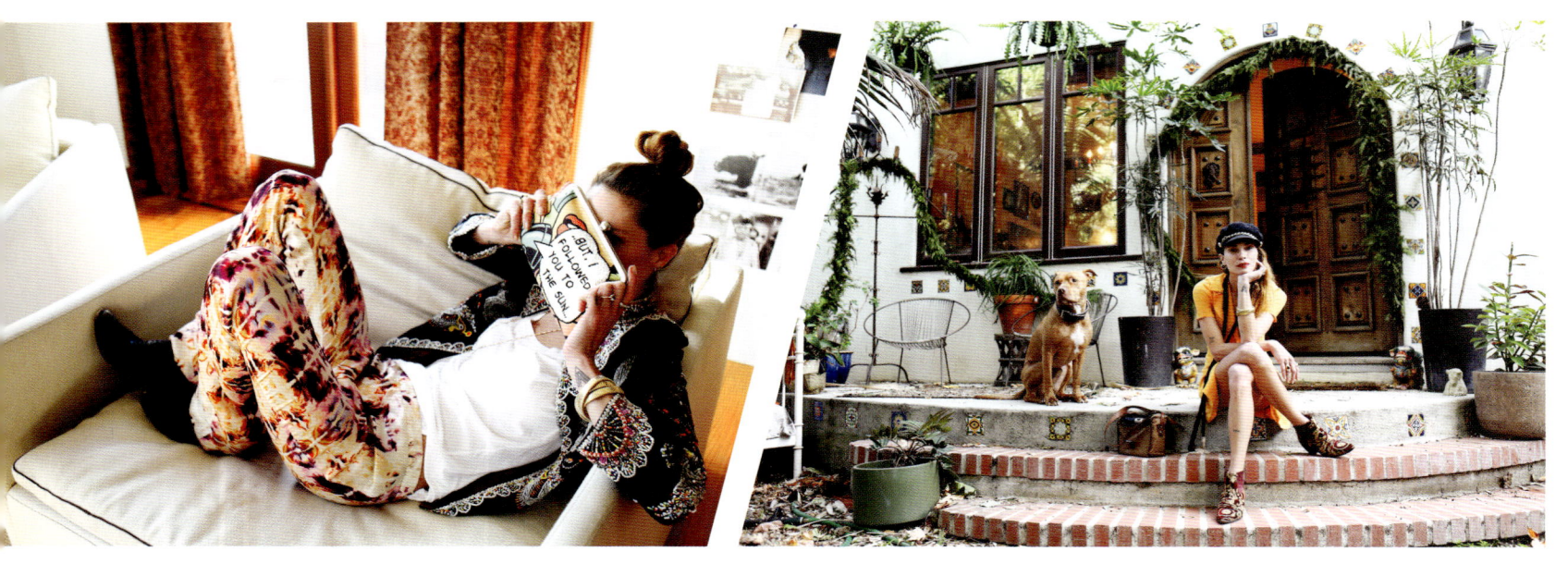
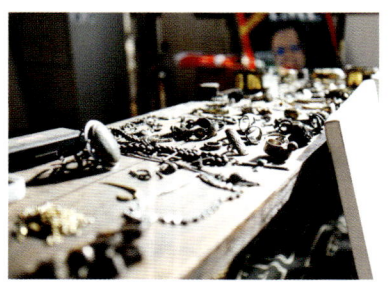
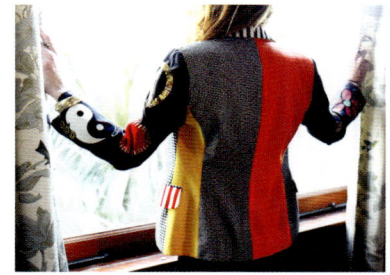
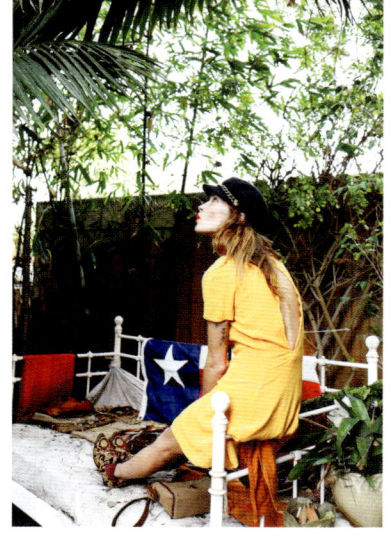
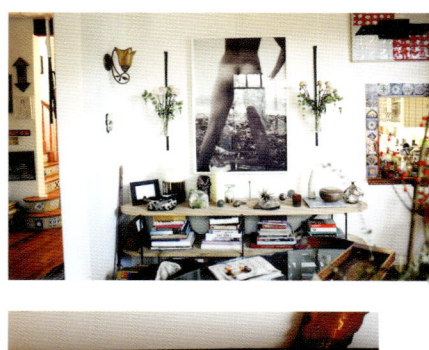
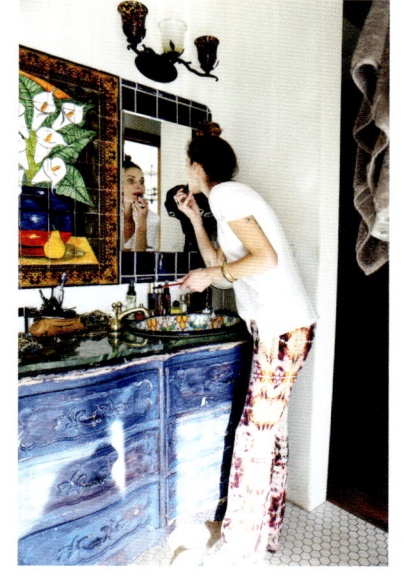
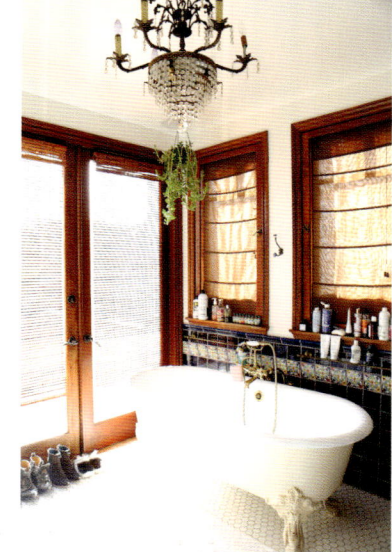
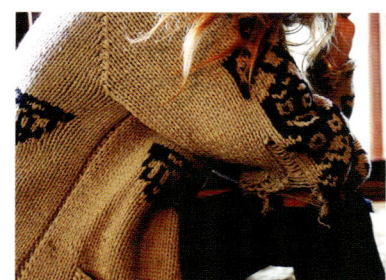
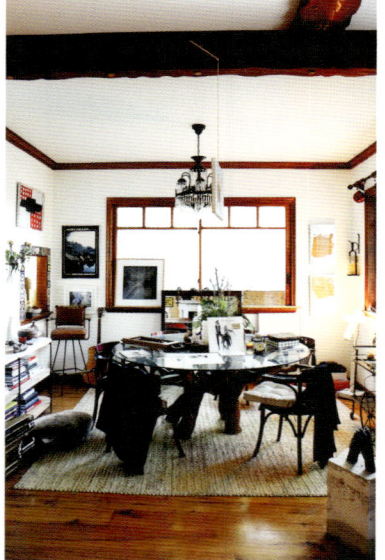
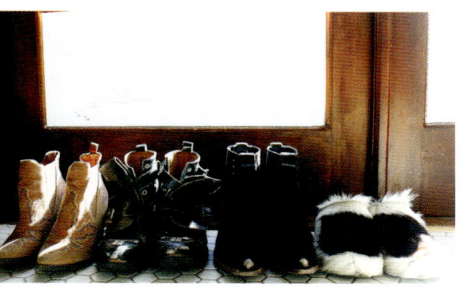
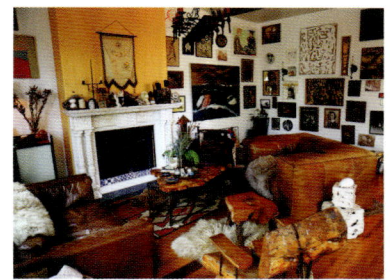
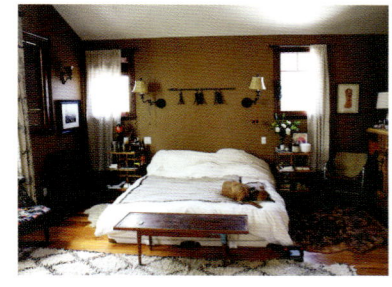
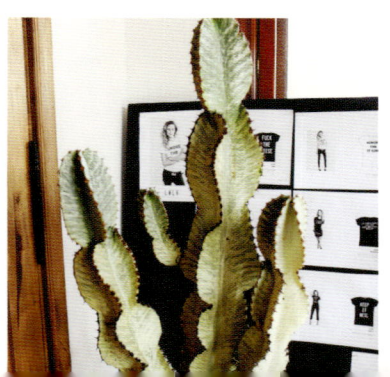

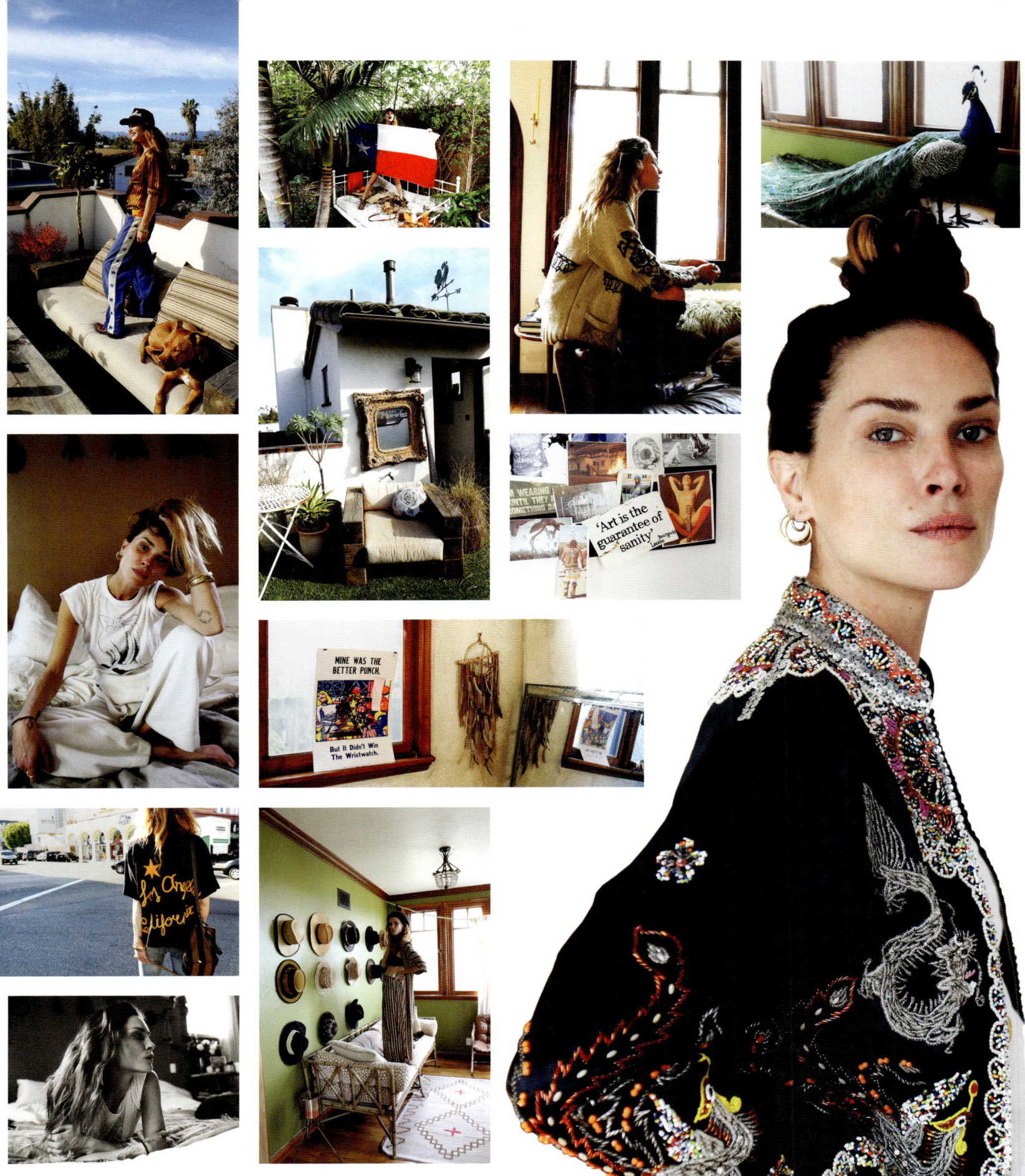

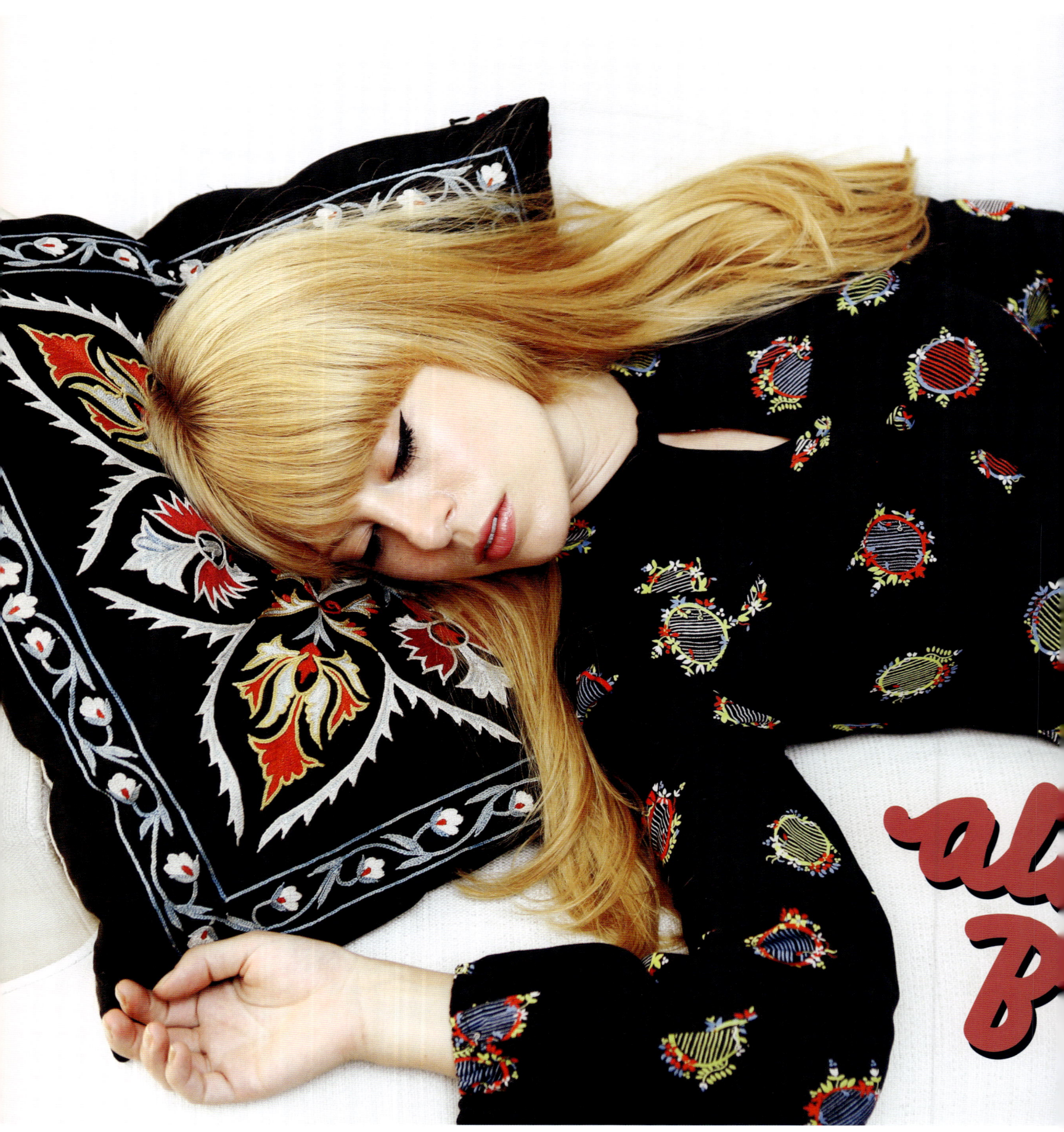

**ALIX BROWN
EVERYTHING ALEX CHILTON EVER TOUCHED**

I immediately spot the birdcage—I get really excited when I find animals in a house. It's one of those cute white cages, on a stand, with a tiny seed feeder, a cuttlefish beak, a mirror, and a swing. I press my nose against the metal for inspection. Then I realize the bottom is missing. And there is no bird. Is the cage a piece of art, perhaps? Before anyone has a chance to relieve my befuddlement, I contemplate the bird's tragic ending and its owner's grieving reluctance to let go—hence the birdcage, still intact, posthumous, like a widow who keeps all her husband's suits hanging after he passes. "She's a Blue-Capped Cordon Blue Finch from Africa," interrupts Alix. "My roommate thinks it's funny to let her fly around the apartment." Even so, this might just be a fantastical extension of the denial, because when I look around the SoHo loft there is still no bird.

Twenty-nine-year-old Alix Brown was definitely born in the wrong decade. Had she been conceived 50 years ago, we may have thought her thick blonde bangs were a sign of the times, not the skillful work of the hairdresser around the corner (the only one who can tame her curls). And we may have considered her choice of sassy, suede miniskirts a matter of mod survival rather than her latest obsession. Alix effortlessly channels all the qualities she admires in her style icons: "The classiness of Catherine Deneuve, the sexiness of Anita Pallenberg, and the badass-ness of bass player Carol Kaye." Throw in a little Brigitte Bardot, and a smidgen of Amanda de Cadenet (do you see it??) and you have the quintessential, modern go-go girl. "I like 60s mod mixed with 70s glam," she declares. "With platforms."

And the look has inspired the lifestyle—or vice versa—from a very early age. She dropped out of school when she was 16 to travel and play music. "Not saying kids, that's the thing to do, but it worked for me!" she quickly adds. After growing up in Atlanta and Memphis, she settled in New York, because she often visited with her dad as a kid and fell in love with "its dirtiness." Her fondest childhood memory is discovering her parents' old records and in turn, she now owns a huge collection that moves with her around the world. She mostly likes 60s and 70s rock 'n' roll, soul, psych, punk, power pop; "Roy Wood from ELO, Lou Reed, Iggy Pop, Bowie, Ramones, Arthur Lee, and everything Alex Chilton ever touched." She plays bass guitar, and DJs with Tennessee Bunny and for the Grandlife Hotels. For the past two years she has been working full-time as a researcher/buyer for What Goes Around Comes Around, one of New York's finest vintage stores. She got into vintage as soon as she was big enough to fit in her mom's clothes.

"Do you want to smoke some weed?" she asks after a couple of outfit changes. I happily decline while she takes a few puffs from a roach. It suddenly dawns on me why the mood is so mellow. Her slow and sexy tone of voice, the way she saunters around the room, how easily she poses... It's all second nature and indispensable to the beatnik life that was laid out for her. She takes a cigarette break, changes records, takes me up on the roof, and tells me she would love to shoot for *Playboy* one day. "The *Playboys* from the 70s are sooooo cool!" she sighs. Downstairs her ex-boyfriend just arrived, wearing "the nice shirt." I had almost forgotten about the bird, when something blue and fluttery sheers over our heads, and lands on one of the pipes in the ceiling. She is indeed blue, and tiny. And very much alive.

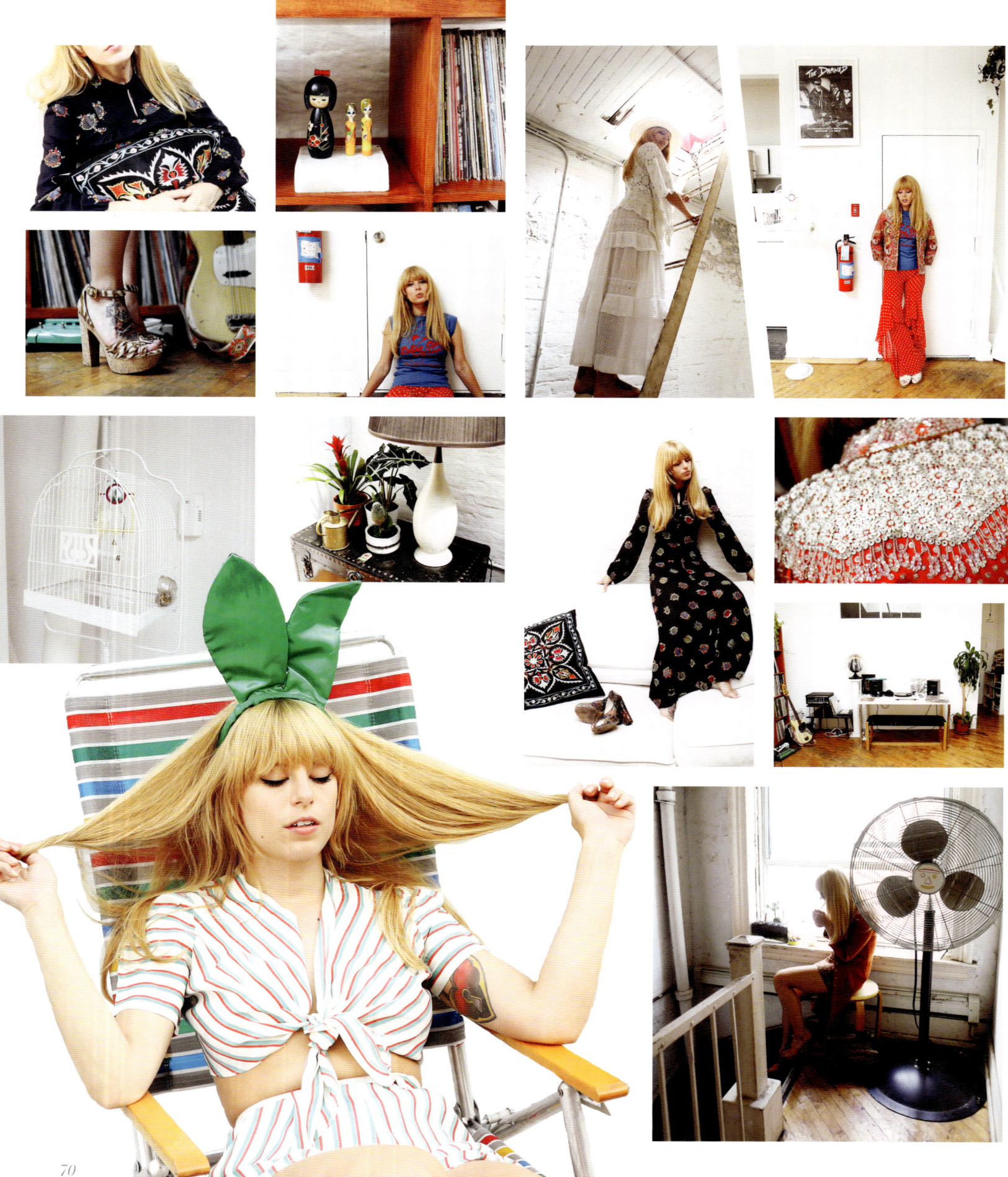

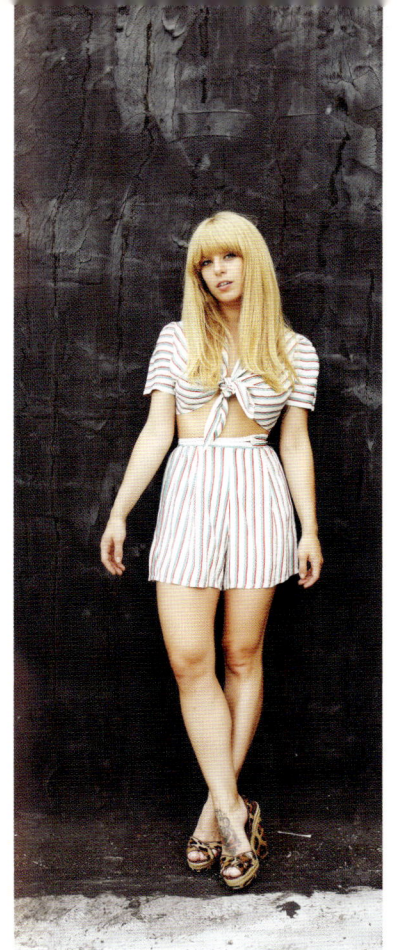
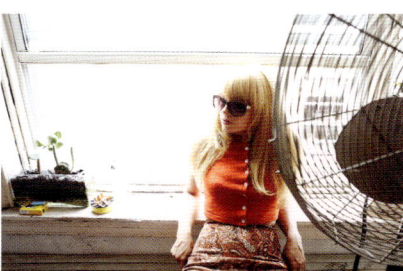
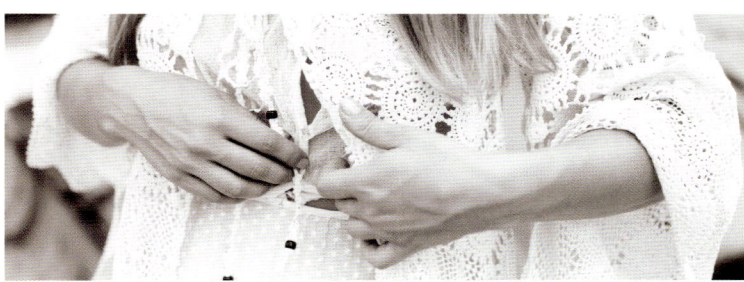
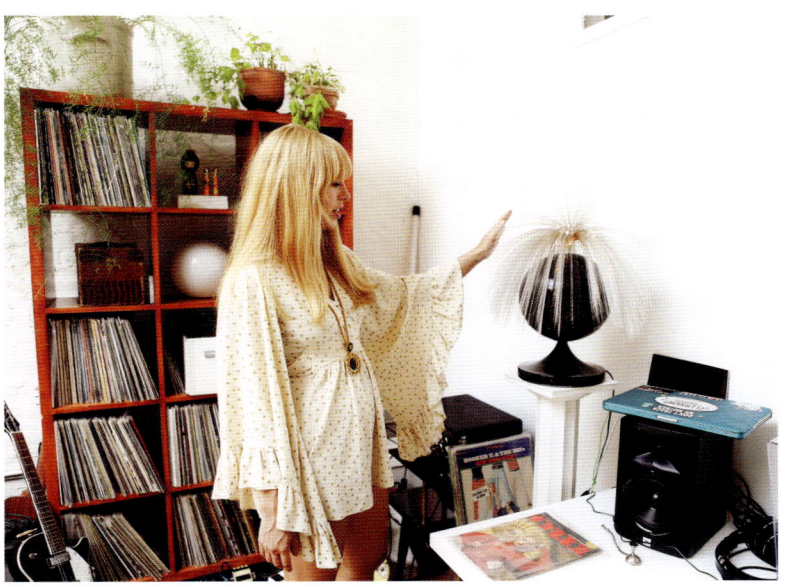
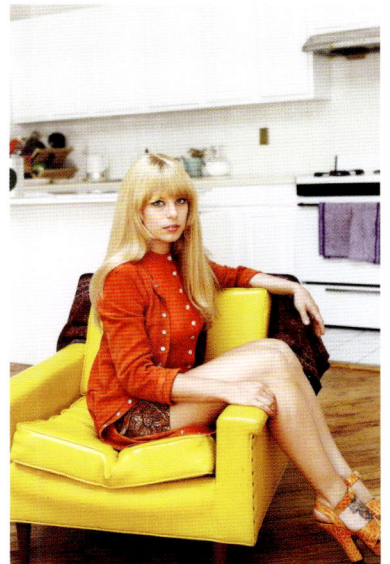
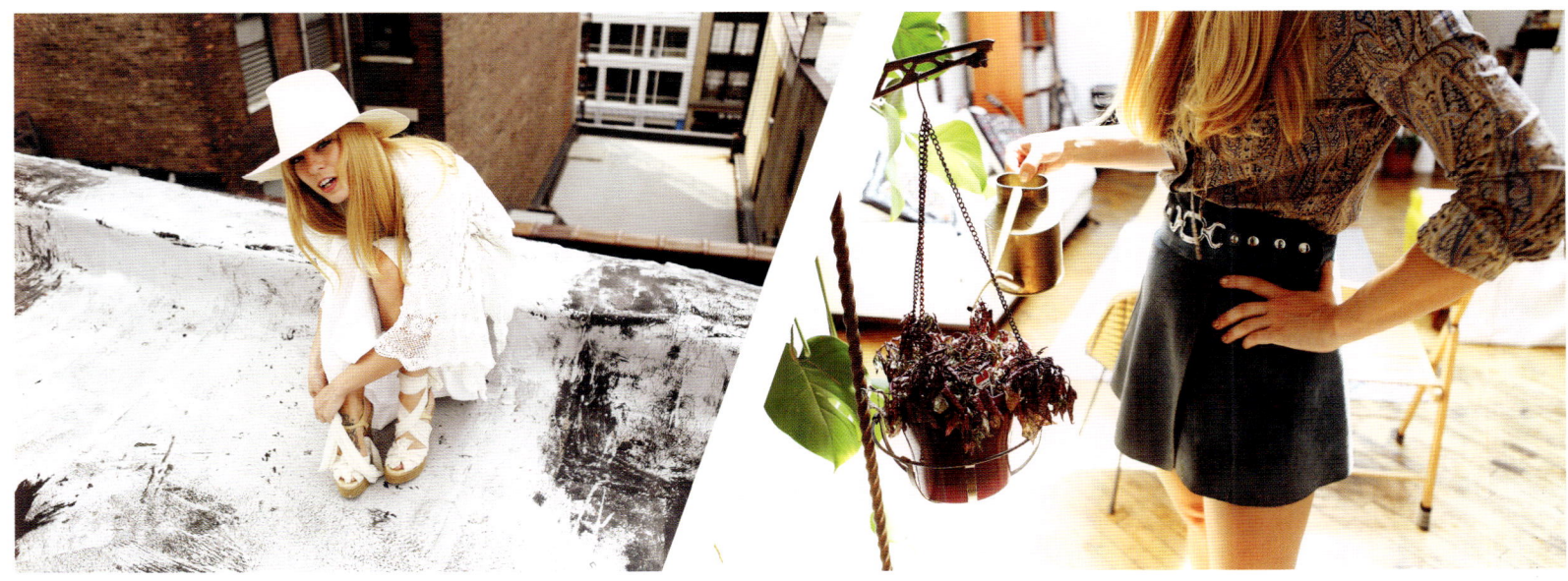
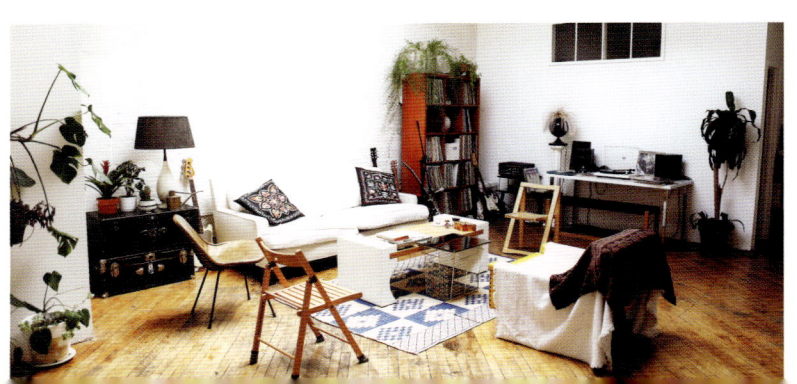
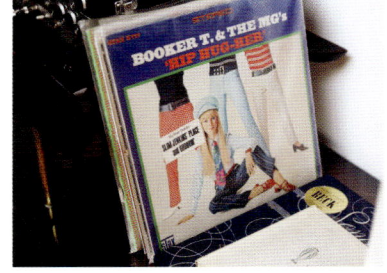
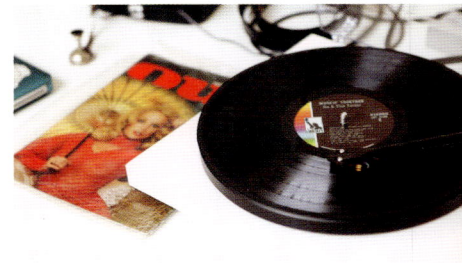

ISABEL MUSIDORA
DARKNESS WITH A CHANCE OF PASTEL

Isabel Musidora does not seem to belong in this sunny surfer's paradise. She has alabaster skin, perfectly coiffed, dark-auburn hair, painted-on eyebrows, an undeniable penchant for the theatrical, and a wardrobe that consists exclusively of dark clothing, with the exception of a few pastel moments for summer. She only wears authentic 1920s garments, and tries to emulate every little detail of the era. She scours the Internet for images of early Hollywood starlets, like Theda Bara and Pola Negri, and even listens to the music. She lives it. She breathes it. "The 20s were quite a culturally-revolutionary and artistic time," she says, "and that is clearly reflected in the fashion of the era. There's an air of androgyny, drama, bohemia, decadent hedonism, and romance injected into everything. It's truly irresistible to me." Her look is so pure and magnetic she turns heads everywhere she goes. "I feel really distinctive when I'm walking down the street, dressed how I dress, and looking like something people have only seen in pictures," she says with an air of poise and pride. "Being able to capture the essence of what you admire from the past through clothing is the ultimate gratification."

Despite her complete and utter surrender to the era, she wouldn't actually want to *live* in the 20s. "Nothing sounds worse to me!" she squirms. "A lot of people who are into vintage stuff will say they wished they were born in a different time. I can't imagine how awful it must have been. Look at the technological advances we made, the medical treatments, our evolved values and ideals. The internet has done me so much good in my life, and when people say it's ruining our minds it just really annoys me." Instagram has been an invaluable tool for Isabel. She's racked up more than 30,000 followers through sheer ambition and dedication. She gives personal makeup and hair tutorials on her YouTube channel, makes artistic films with interesting collaborators, and connects with like-minded people from all over the world. She met her best friend online, a photographer in Australia; they FaceTime every night. "The first time I went to Australia to visit, we walked into this antique store together and they had two of the same 20s ring! So now we share twin rings with each other across the world, and I can't ask for anything more special than that."

Mom is driving us around Santa Barbara in her car. It's not my first time here but I forgot how beautiful and old this town is. When I ask Isabel if she ever felt cast-out because of her eccentric choices, she's quite secure: "I think growing up here, where I was a bit of an ostrich, and isolated in my fierce quest for unique self-expression, has only fostered my sense of individualism. Being the only one in my immediate peer group to explore this kind of expression was ultimately good for me, because I never really had a chance to compare myself to them. I was just happy to do my own thing." And it was all set in motion when she was about 10. Her first piece of vintage was a bubblegum-pink chiffon prom dress she found in a local antique store. Around that time, she also became obsessed with her favorite accessory, a giant Styrofoam chicken with rainbow feathers that she affixed to a headband. "It made me feel like the pictures I'd seen of Carmen Miranda," she remembers. "I would even wear it to school, paired with yellow-lens sunglasses." She also wore cat ears from fifth to eighth grade. "Every day for three years!" echoes mom from the driver's seat. And she enrolled in a local school for aerial dance when she was 13. "Dance is my other creative pursuit in life," she smiles. "I feel like dance and fashion go perfectly hand-in-hand in that they both involve conveying a feeling using your body as a medium."

We stop to eat lunch by the Old Mission. And as I am sitting here watching and listening to Isabel, I am astounded by her grace and maturity. It's hard to believe she's only 17 years old, my youngest muse to date. We talk about her plans for college, the only subject that's a little foggy. "I'm actually taking some time off from school at the moment," she confesses. "I didn't want to jump into my future too hastily, especially since I'm at a point where I have no idea what I want to do with my life. I'm sure I'll stumble into some career-path that I'm wildly passionate about, when the time comes." I am also reminded of Alessandra Canario, the young girl I photographed in New Jersey. She was about Isabel's age, and I see such incredible similarities. Both are strong, determined, and nonconformist girls with a clear, unwavering, and enunciated sense of self. They have sculpted their singular image in accordance with the aesthetics they most identified with. They never let society, peers, or the media dictate their choices or feelings. They created their own beautiful world, and dwell in it with such self-awareness that nothing or nobody can ever topple it. Perhaps Isabel says it best: "The only opinion that matters about your appearance and expression is your own."

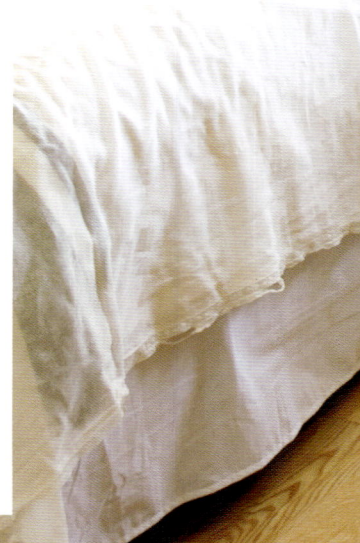

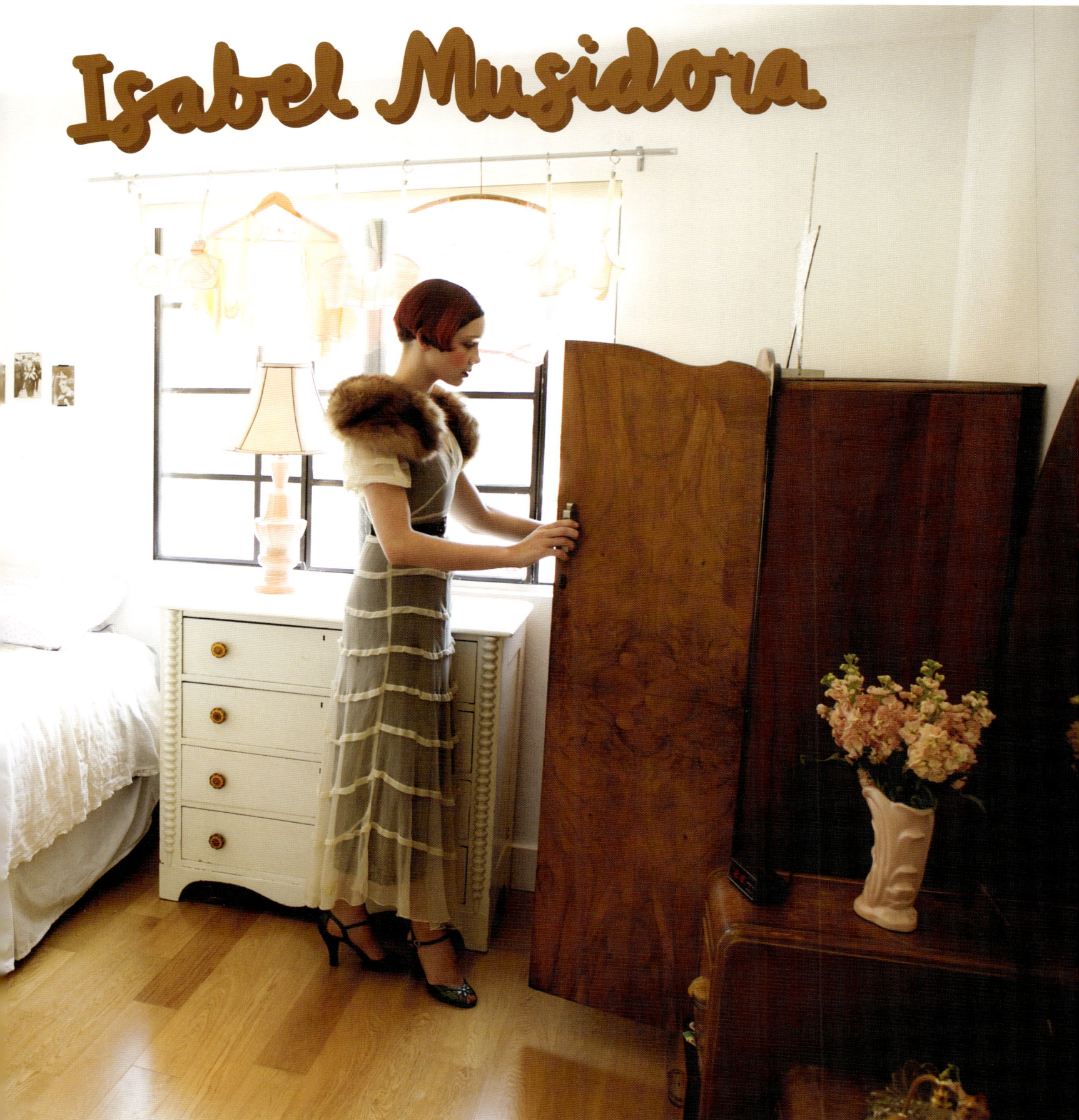

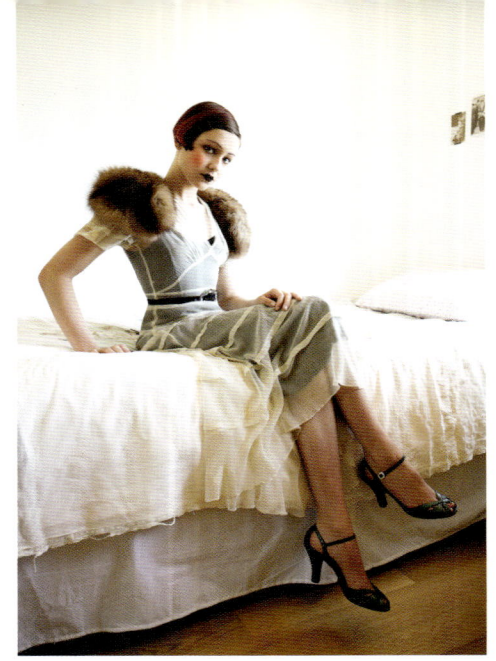
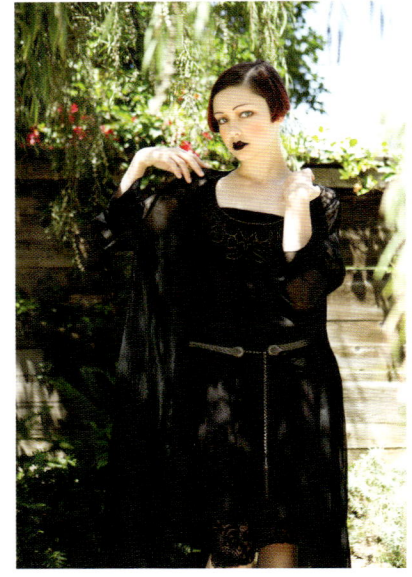
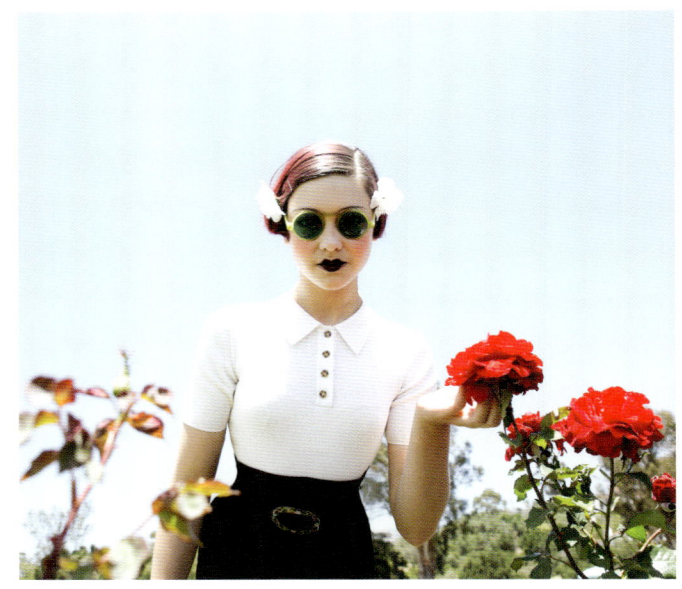
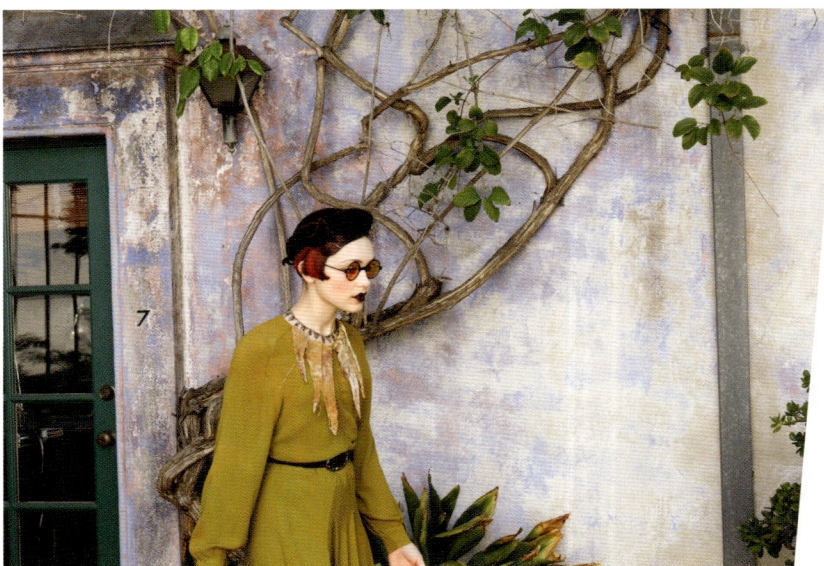
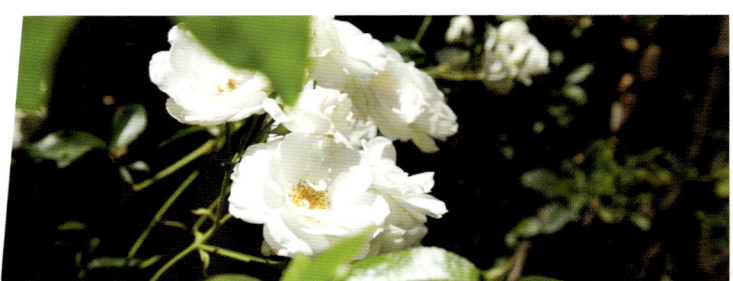
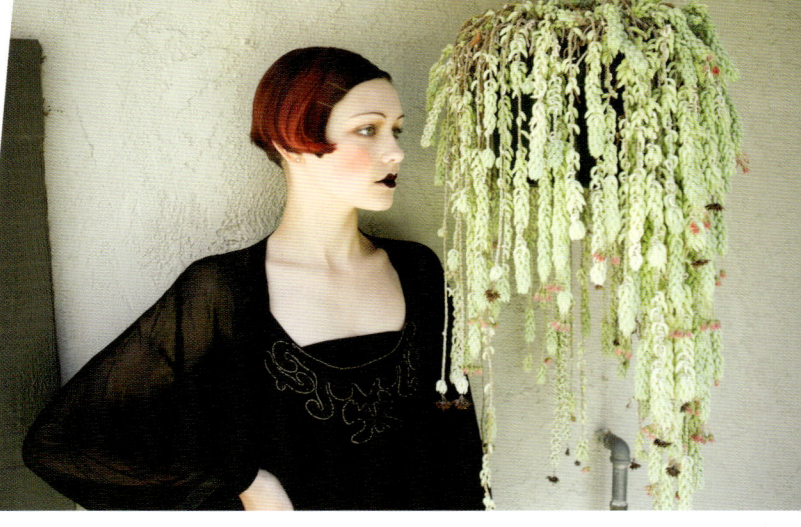
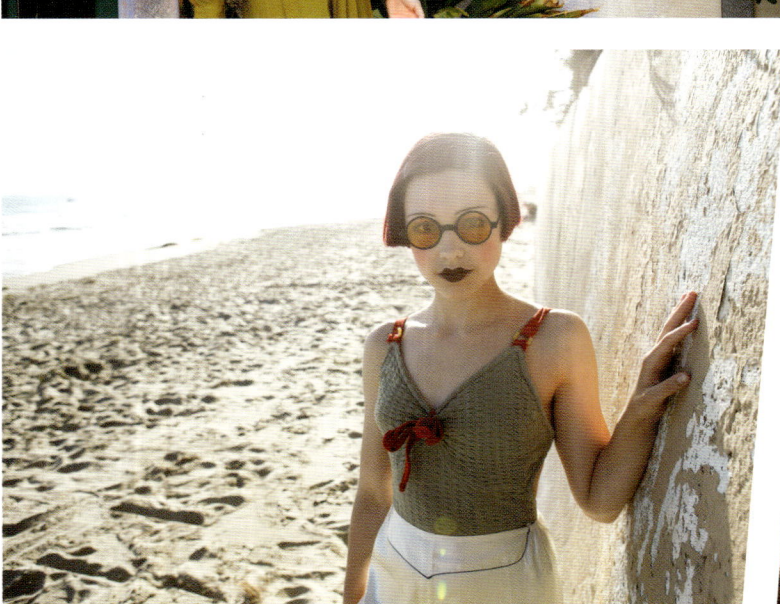
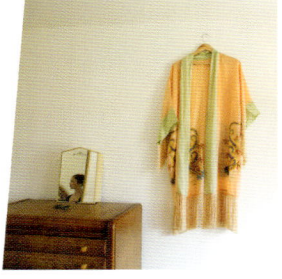
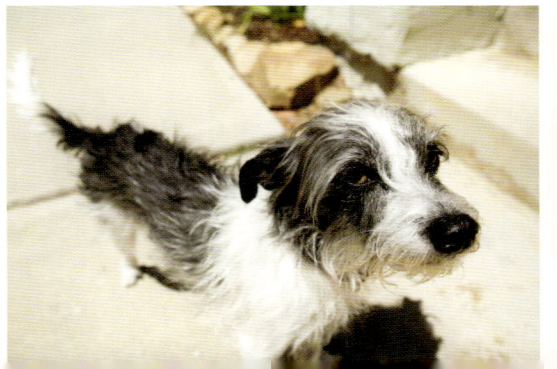

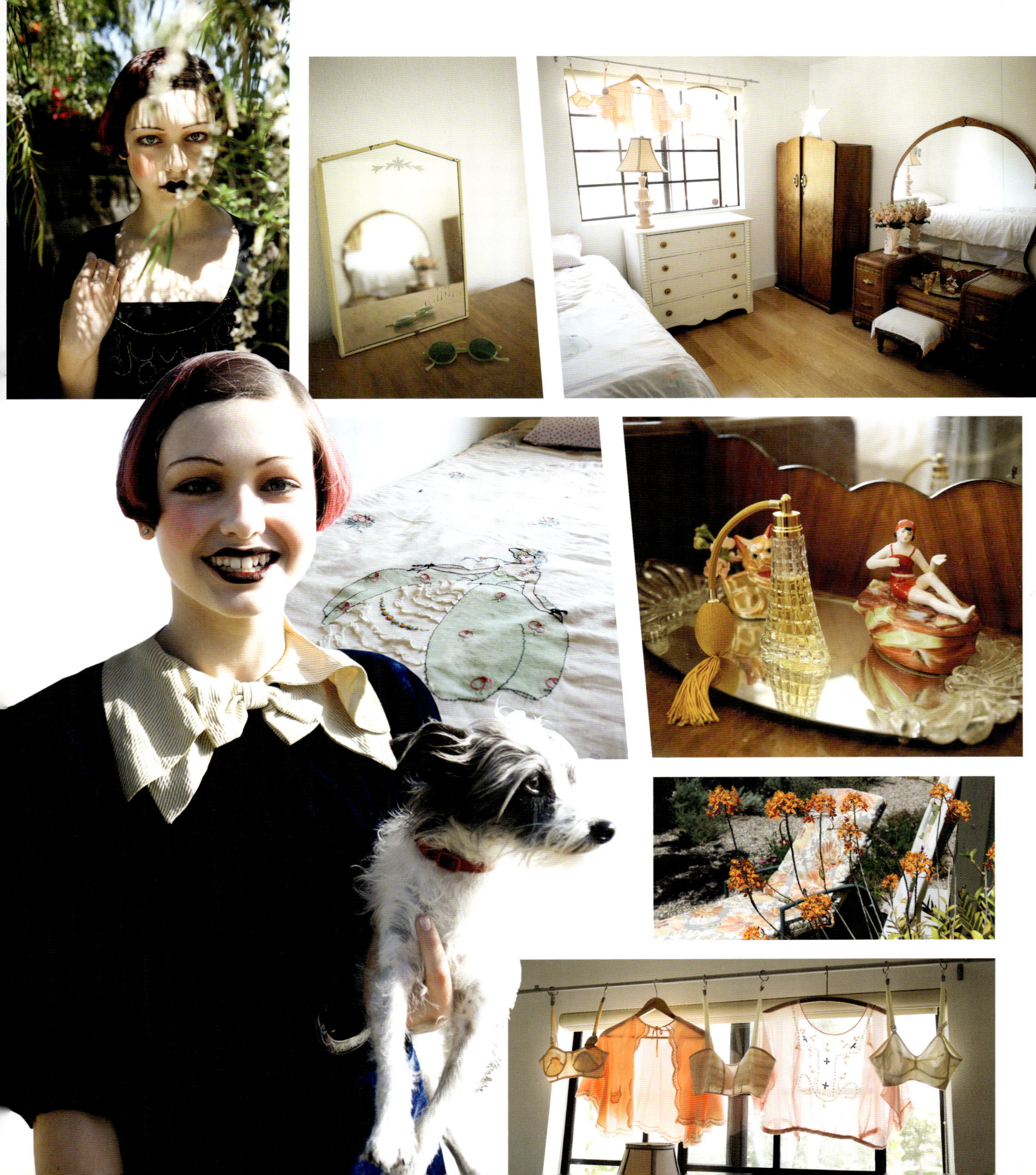

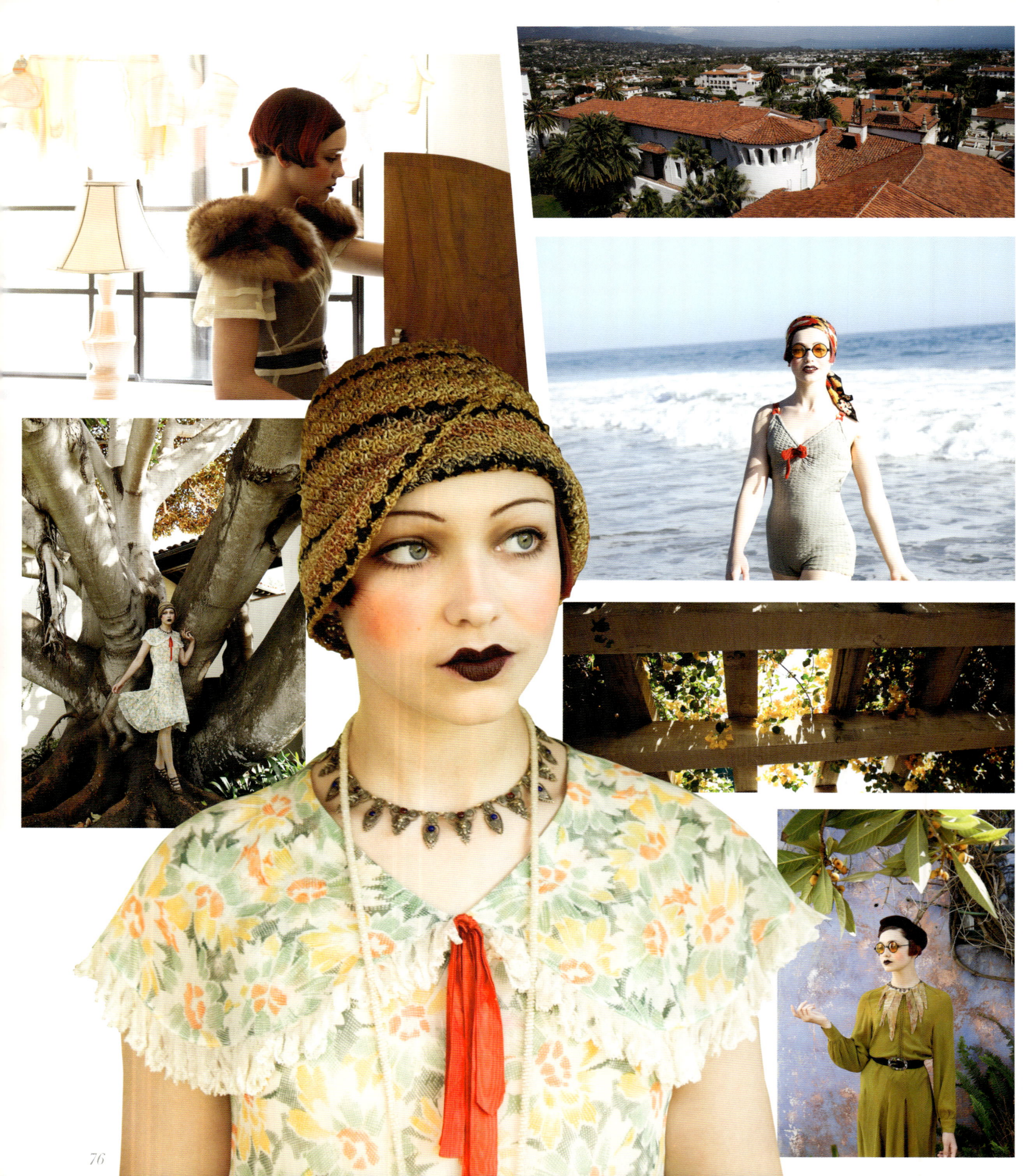

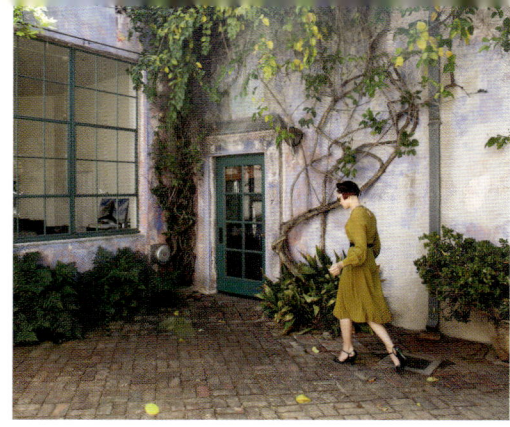
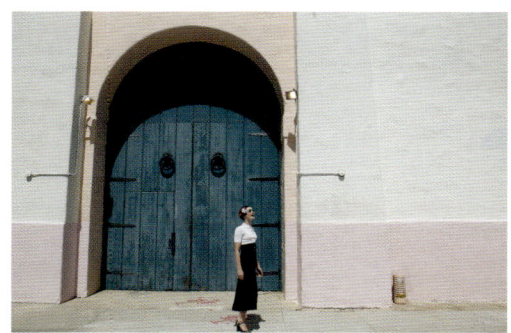
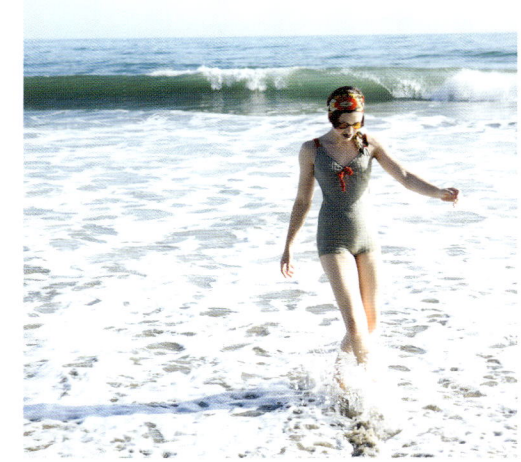
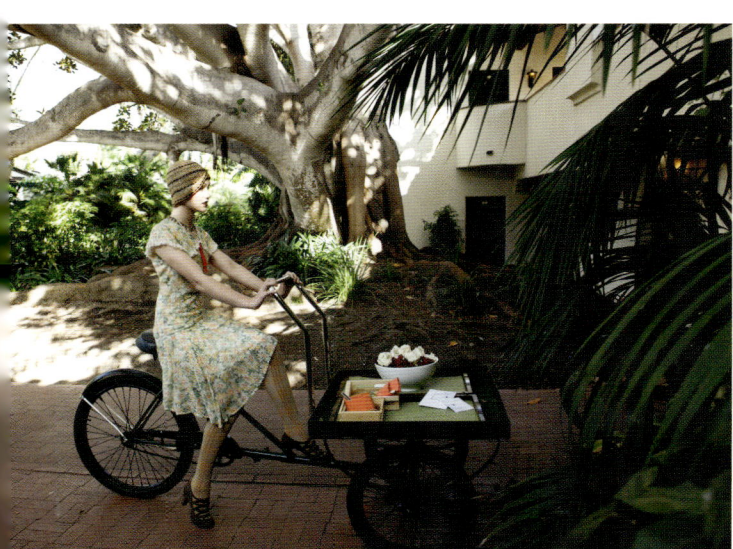
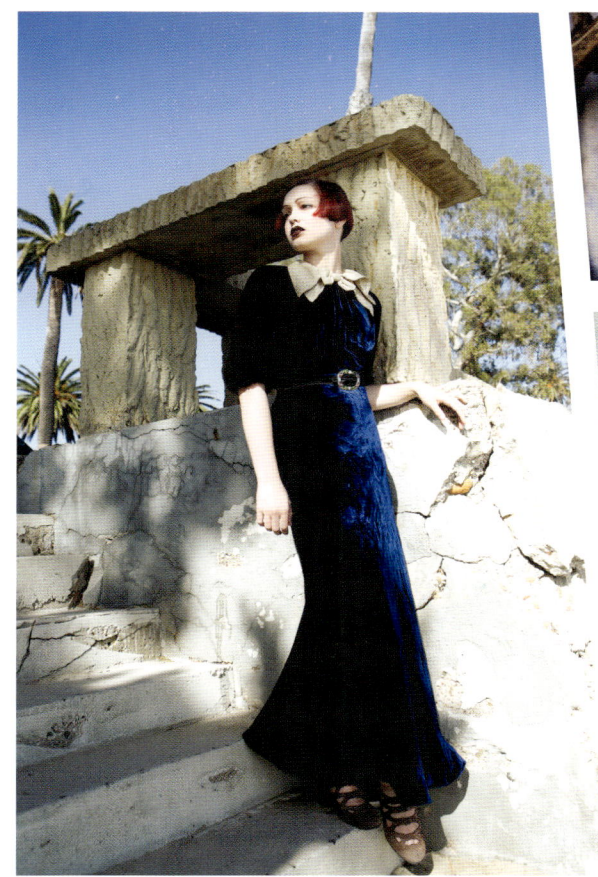
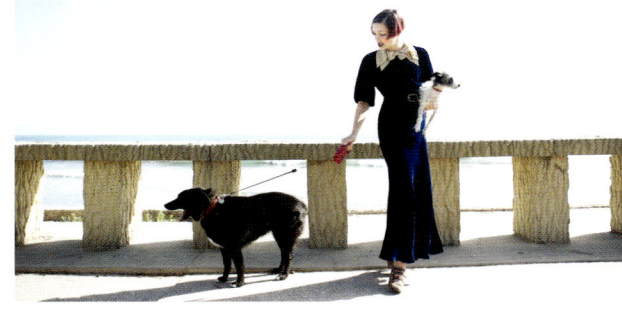
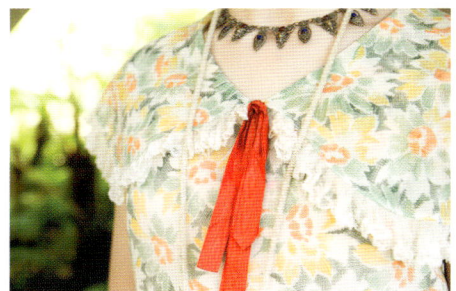
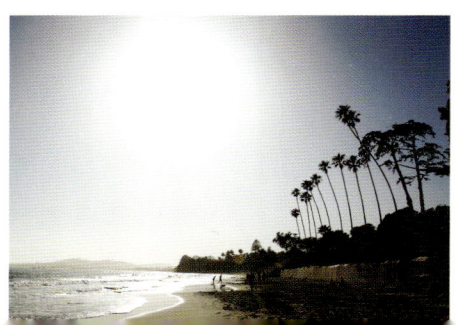
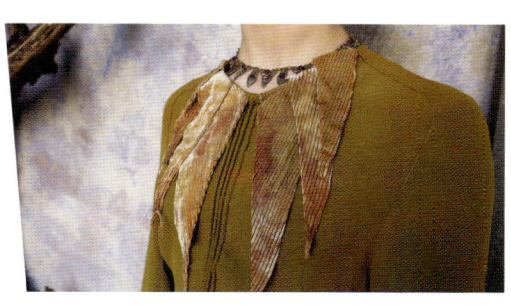
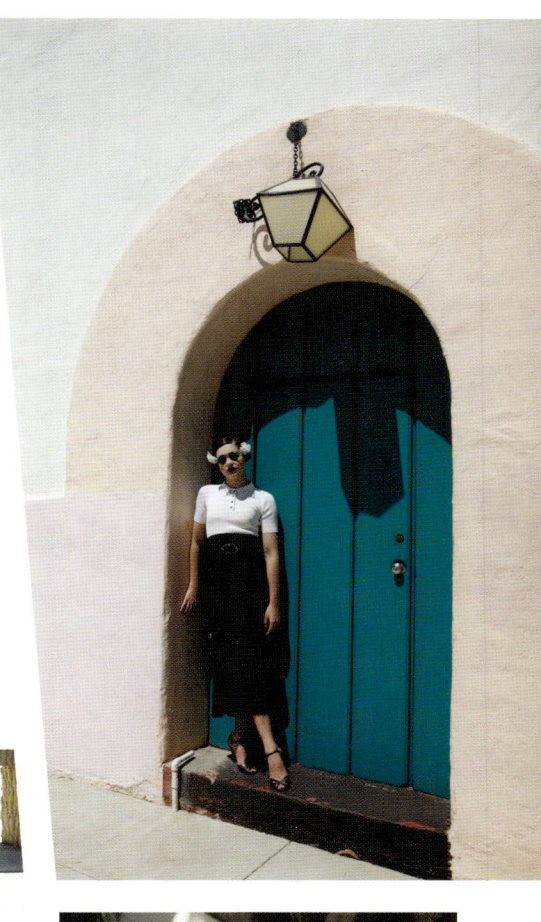
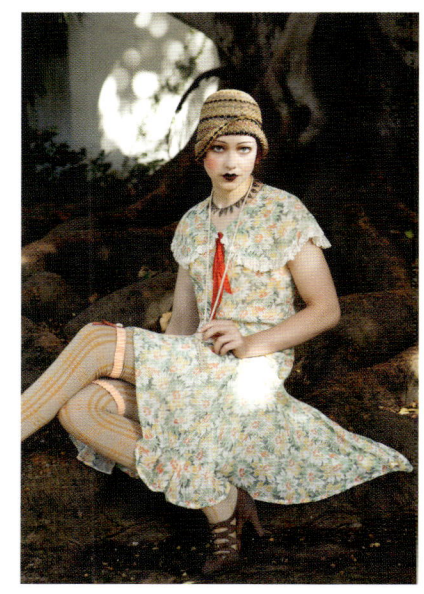

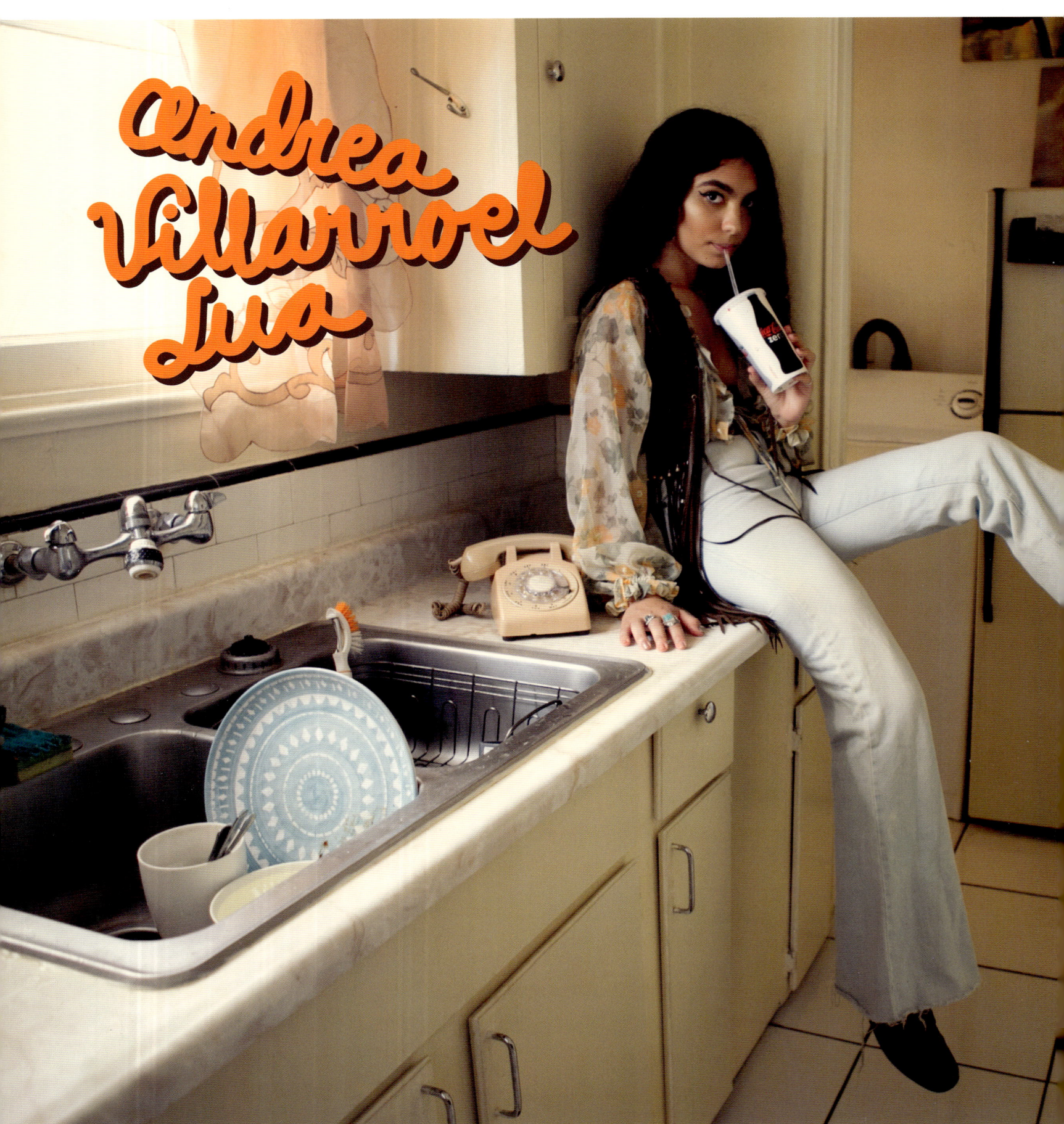

ANDREA VILLARROEL LUA
THE COACHELLA EFFECT

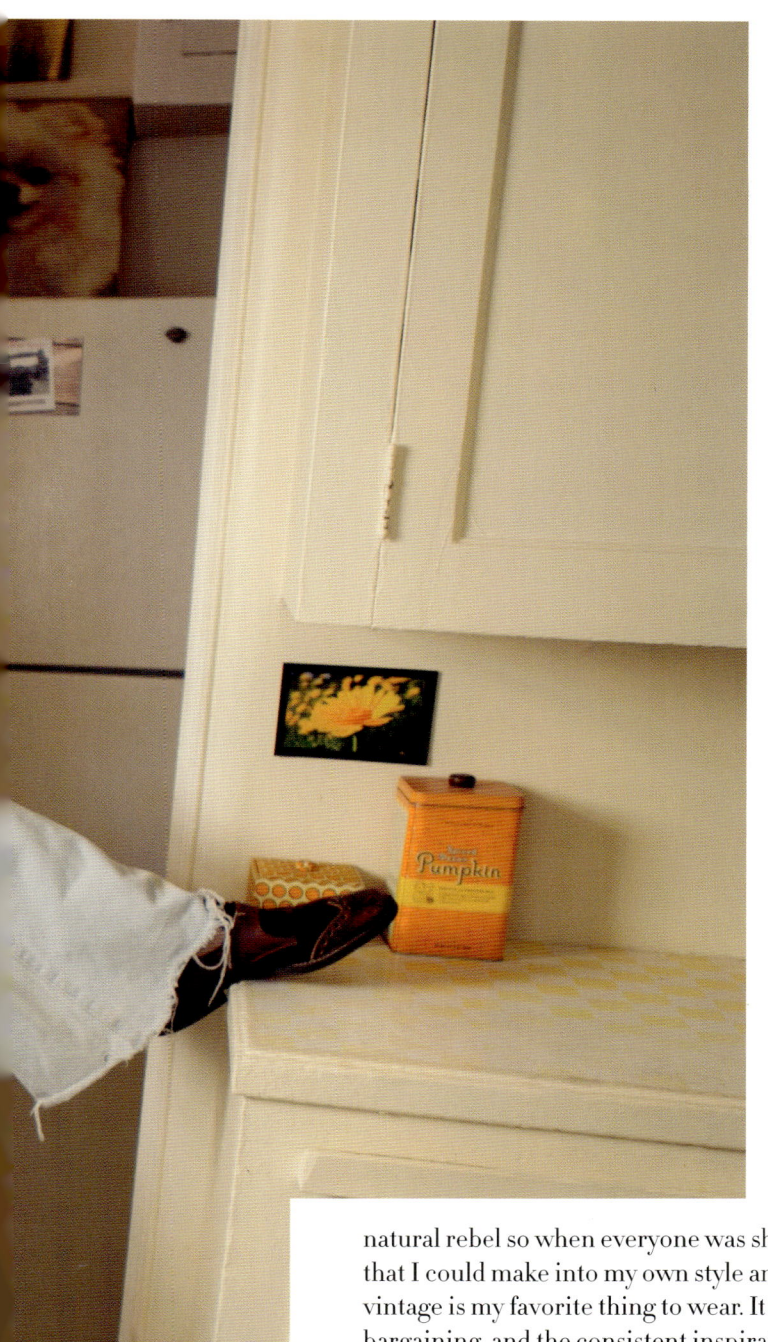

On a sunny afternoon in South Central, LA, three 21-year-old girls sit cordially in a cluttered, cottage-style bedroom. It's a snug little scene of hushed voices and the mono sound of Tame Impala coming from a laptop in the living room. Shaiya is putting the finishing touches on Andrea's thick, black cat-eye makeup, while Adrienne, phone in hand, watches from the bed. It's a familiar setting if you watch television and high school dramas, but for most adult women this is reminiscent of a beloved, fading memory. There will never be a time again when all you had to think about was boys and grades. Yet for me, today, it's about something else entirely: a three-hour discovery of a girl I met at a vintage fair.

Andrea Villarroel Lua just turned 21. She's the daughter of a Venezuelan papa and a Mexican mom, born and raised in Palm Desert, California. "It's definitely a big one!" she winks when I ask if she got drunk on her birthday. "I was in Morelia, Mexico with a family friend and I hung out with them. It was a chill day. I wore a flower-print dress and flower crown and went to a little park. I did go out to a bar that weekend and have a few drinks." She's not new to the party circuit anyways. She practically grew up at the Coachella festival because her dad bartends all over the Valley. "He introduced me [to the festival] at the tender age of 14," she smiles. "Every year since then, I have attended and seen it expand and have seen some of the greatest rock 'n' rollers too. We can thank them for my looks and my music taste!"

It was her crazy, beautiful hair that struck me first. It's big and loud and unbearably healthy-looking. Funnily, she says, it was straight until she was 10 years old. "I have been growing it out for about five, six years and it is a lot of work!!" she groans. "My goal is to one day donate it to a child with cancer; I think it would make them very, very happy." Her girlfriends concur: Andrea is a sweet girl with a big heart who believes in doing good for people, animals, and the environment. It's one of the reasons she loves vintage so much. It's recycling! "I am a natural rebel so when everyone was shopping at Forever 21, I raced to my local thrift shops in search of clothing that I could make into my own style and that visually represented me as an individual. Ever since then, I feel that vintage is my favorite thing to wear. It is nameless and yet fashionable." She loves the hunt, playing a character, bargaining, and the consistent inspiration. "I look for genuine pieces, doesn't matter what decade," she explains "I currently lean towards 1960s and 1970s because of my natural hippie ways. I have connected with that era of clothing because it was so vivid, broad, and yet original."

This is not your ordinary, run-of-the-mill, little shoot for these girls. It's work. They ran FIDM's bi-annual fashion magazine Moda and know the drill. I'm not only impressed with the looks, but also with their professionalism and efficiency. They planned, fitted, and executed each outfit to the smallest detail—from the hat down to the toenail color. Notes were taken on Post-its and stuck on each garment like flash cards. It's fun to watch Shaiya give posing instructions while I shoot Andrea. They're like a team of editors in waiting. "In five years I see myself deeper into my career, traveling, and passionately working for what I am striving to do in the fashion industry, and I'll also be done with university. I am avidly working on creative endeavors as well as studying. In 20, who knows? Maybe your next style icon."

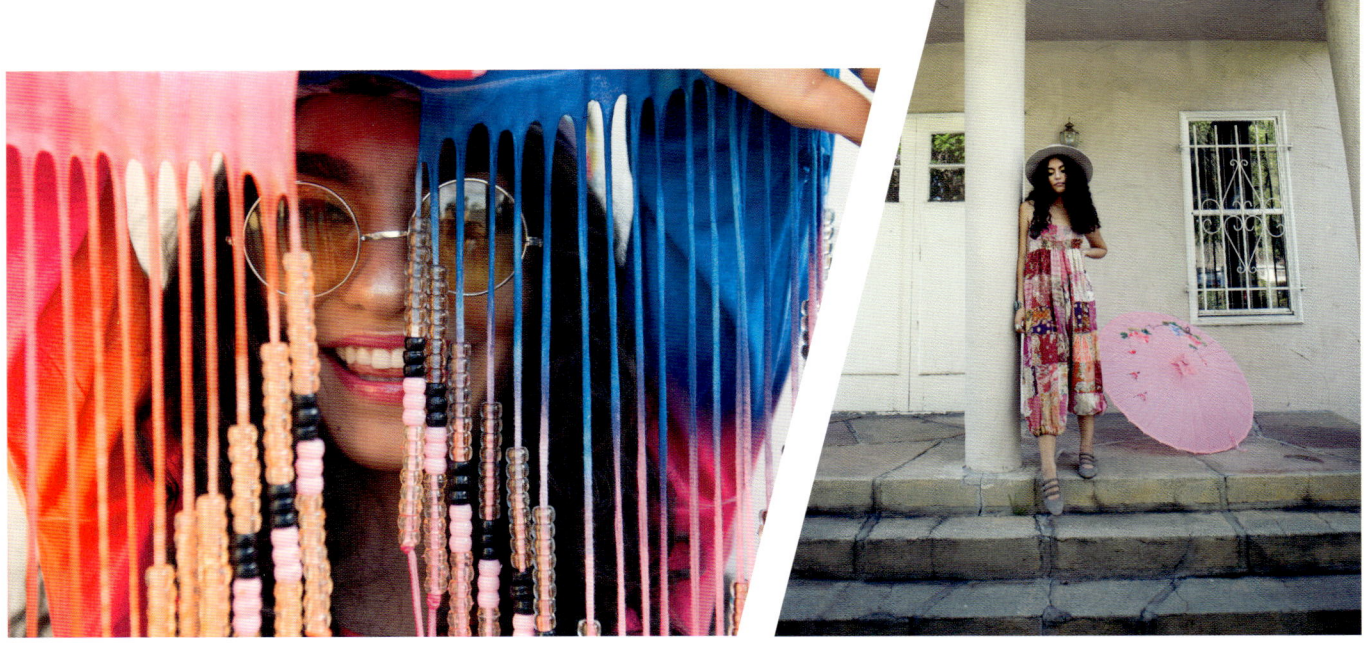
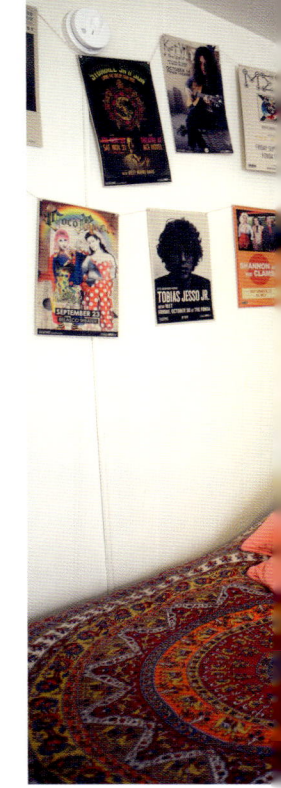
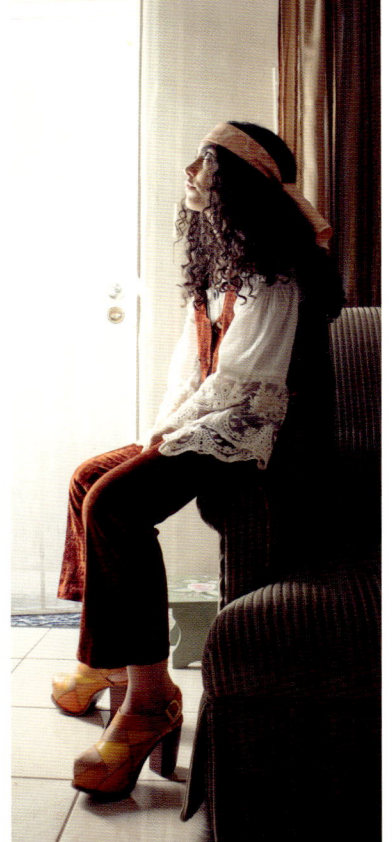
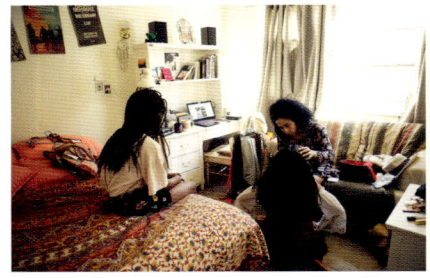
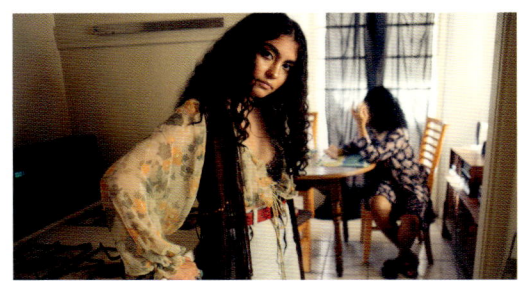
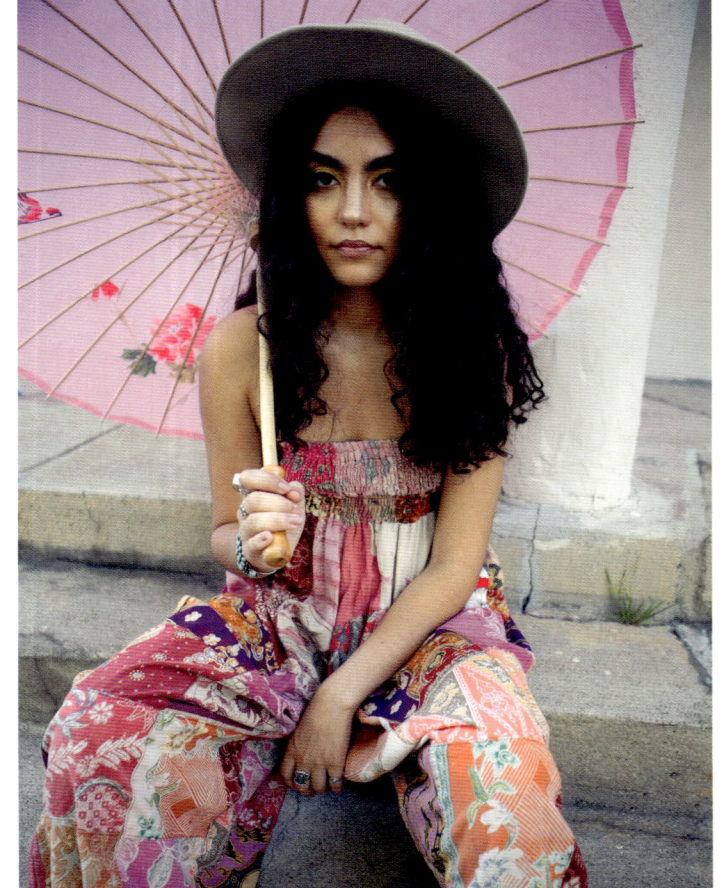
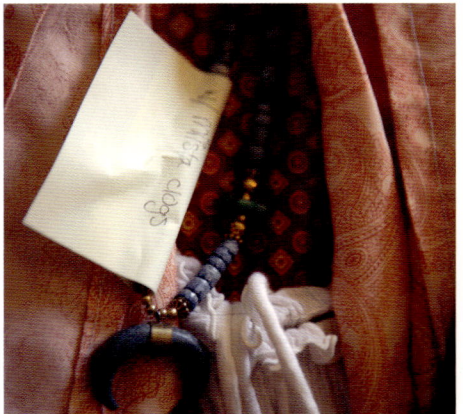
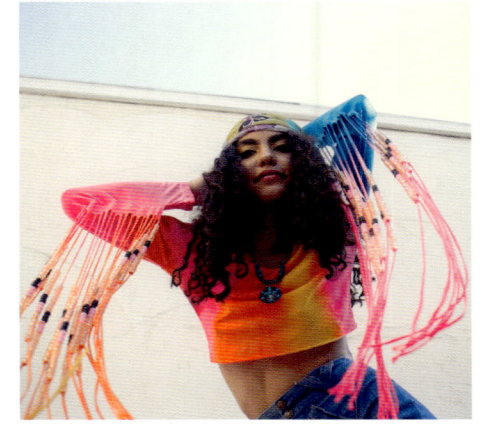
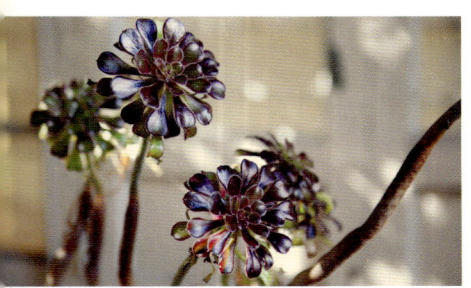

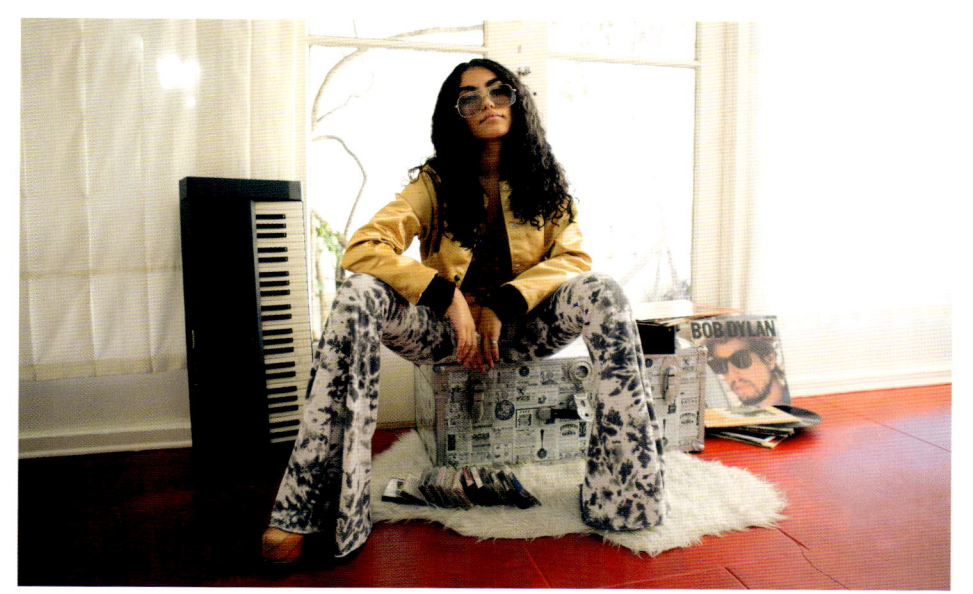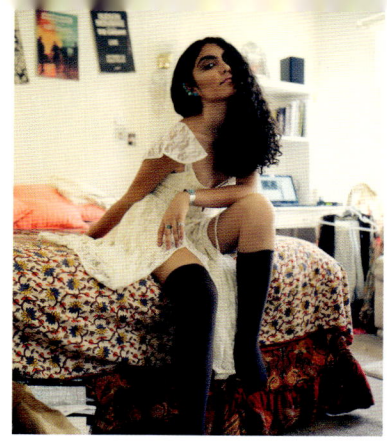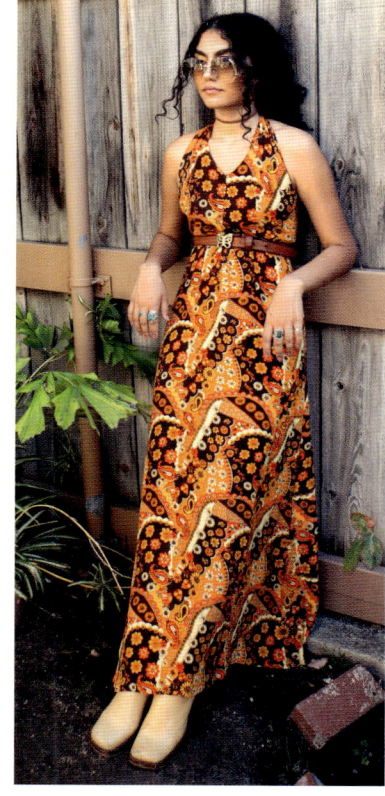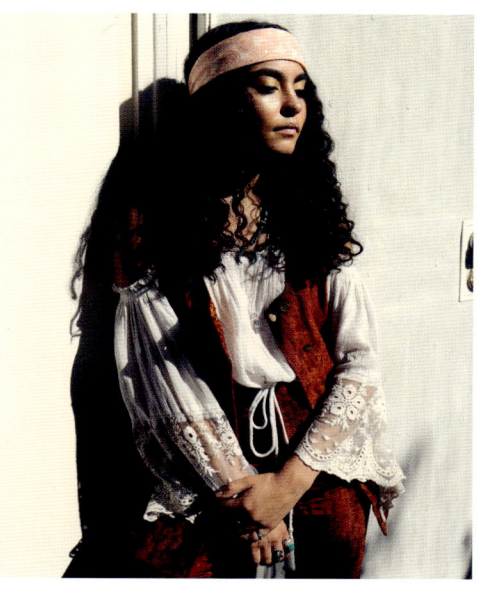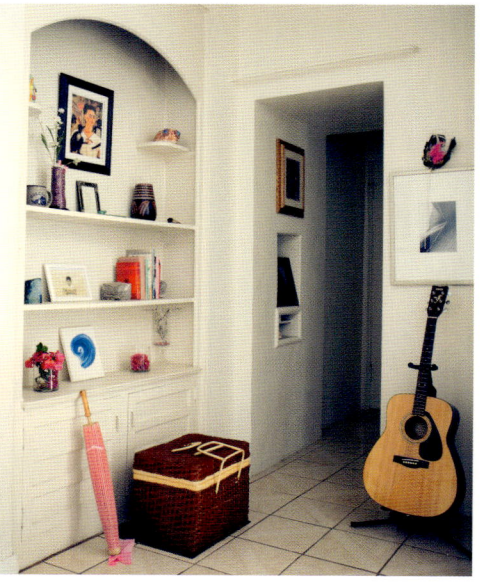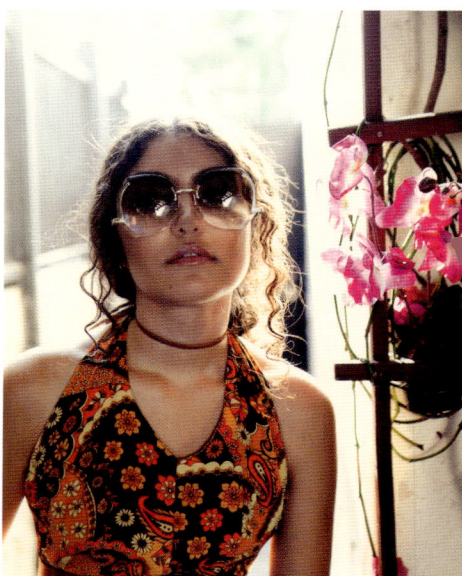

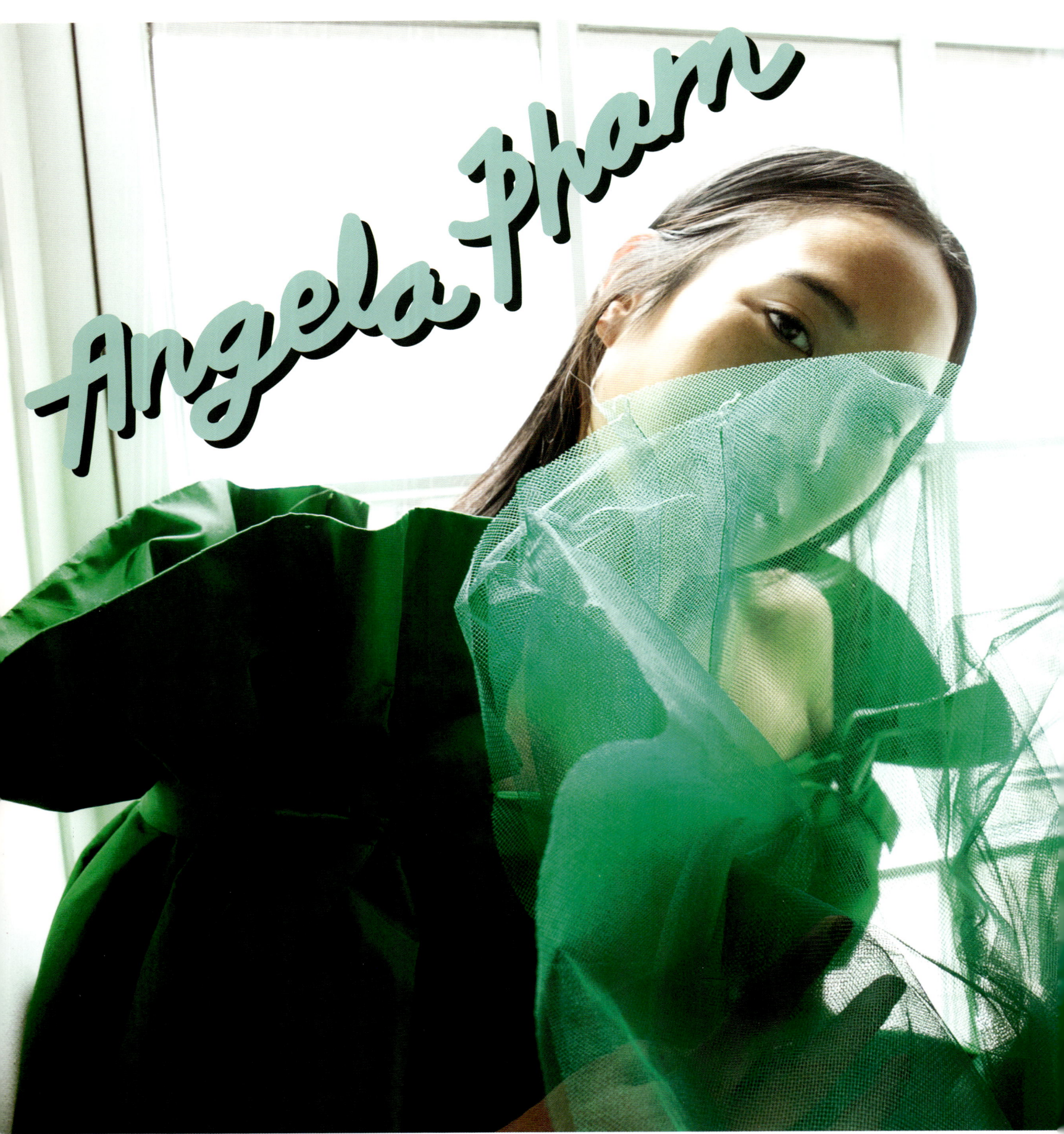

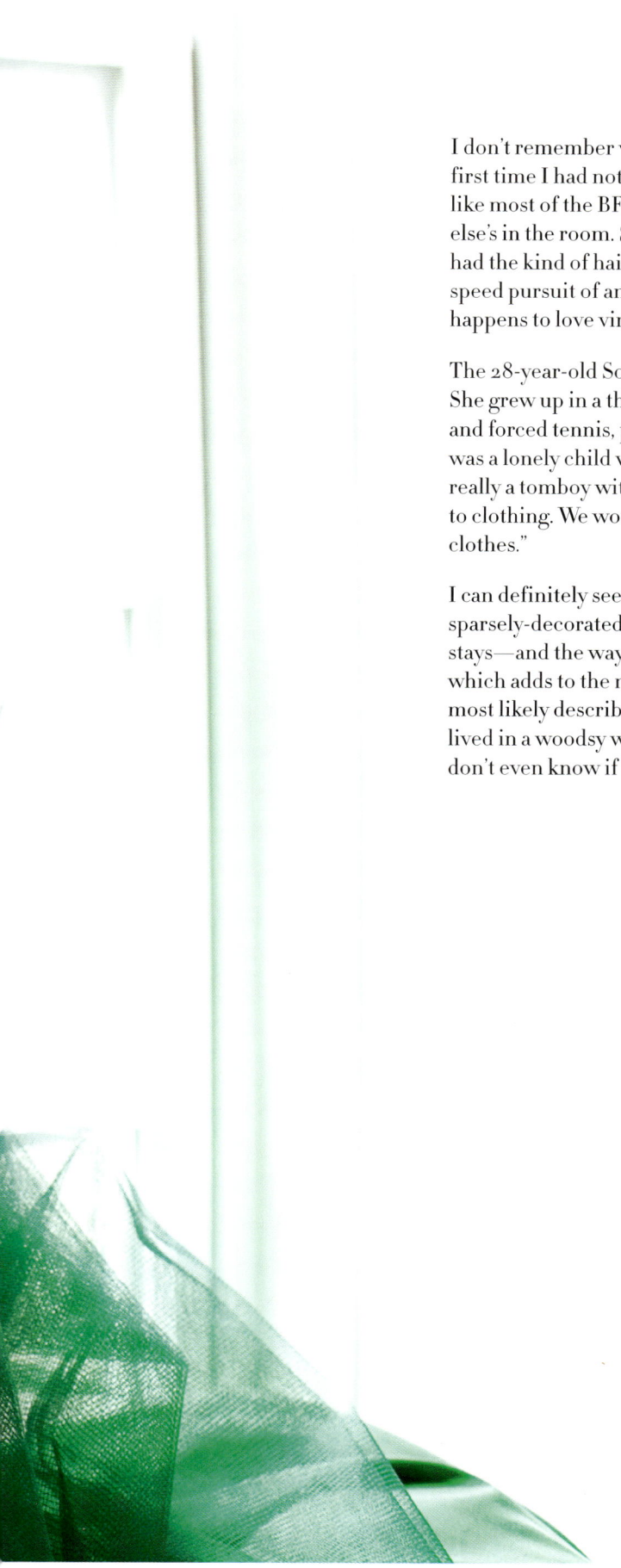

ANGELA PHAM
CLOTHES WERE JUST CLOTHES

I don't remember what she was wearing that night, but I knew it wasn't the first time I had noticed this party photographer. She was discreet and patient like most of the BFA guys, but her outfit screamed style louder than anyone else's in the room. She was probably the best-dressed person there, and she had the kind of hair that wins awards. I found out later, after I dashed in high-speed pursuit of an interview, that Angela Pham not only dresses well, she happens to love vintage shopping more than she does food.

The 28-year-old SoCal native wasn't groomed to become a fashion maven. She grew up in a thrifty Vietnamese immigrant household with a rigid routine of discipline and forced tennis, piano, and language lessons. Nobody cared about clothes or makeup. "I was a lonely child who just wanted to emulate my older brother," she thinks back. "So I was really a tomboy with not an ounce of femininity. My mom had a very pragmatic approach to clothing. We would just shop at discount stores like T.J. Maxx or Ross. Clothes were just clothes."

I can definitely see remnants of a strict, modest upbringing in her minimal décor—the sparsely-decorated modern space is her own; the other, her boyfriend's, where she often stays—and the way she politely answers questions. She's cautious and doses her words, which adds to the mystery. She tells me how she feels like an introvert but her friends would most likely describe her as happy and extroverted. It sort of makes sense if you know that she lived in a woodsy world of imaginary pet wolves as a kid. She wanted to be a wolf-biologist: "I don't even know if that's a thing."

It wasn't until high school that Angela discovered vintage and adopted an appetite for her own individual style. "I suddenly loved going thrift shopping, to fill my wardrobe with pieces that would reflect my uniqueness," she remembers. "It was my favorite activity, and I would spend hours at a Goodwill or Savers. I would buy my prom dresses at thrift stores."

And she still has a masterful knack for finding the gems. Her closet in Williamsburg is filled with dramatic finds from eBay, Etsy, and any of the thrift stores she might pass while driving. "I can't explain that feeling of intense elation and giddiness when you stumble upon a hidden treasure: either a great vintage shop or a perfect vintage piece, the right designer, the suspiciously low price, the ideal fit... Vintage clothes and vintage shopping is simply just FUN for me!"

It is my guess that Angela will soon be forced to come out from behind the camera. Her flair for urban luxury is too conspicuous and unique to remain secondary. One look at her Instagram page and it is clear that she found her calling, and a way to quietly turn her passion into a game of fashion. It's not even a matter of time. Just geography.

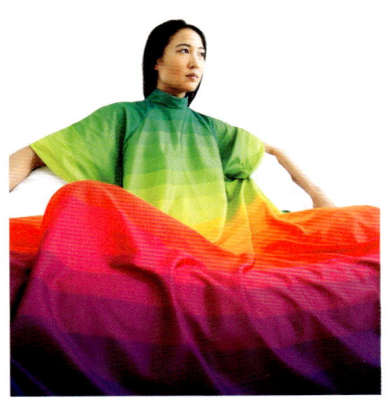
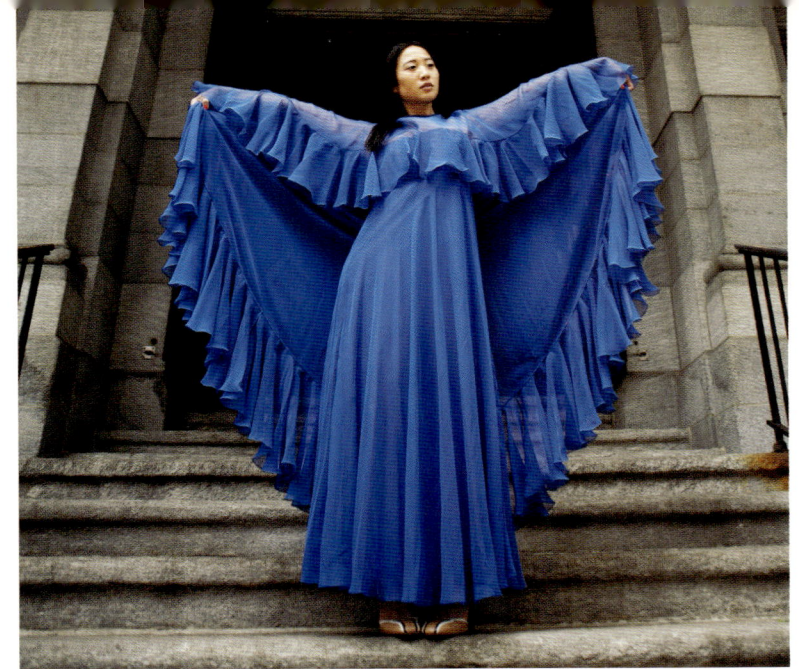
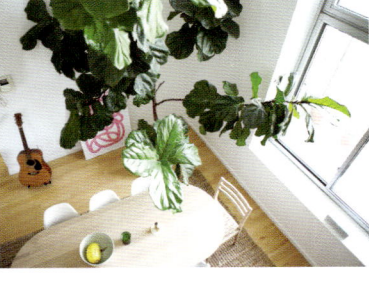
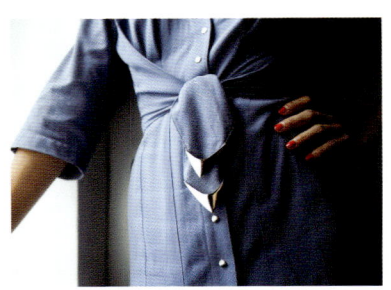
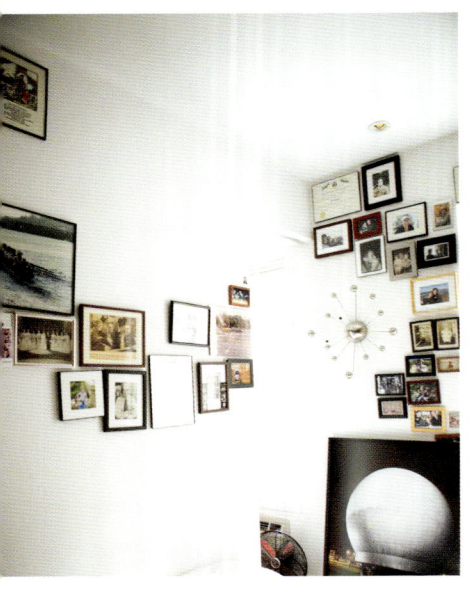
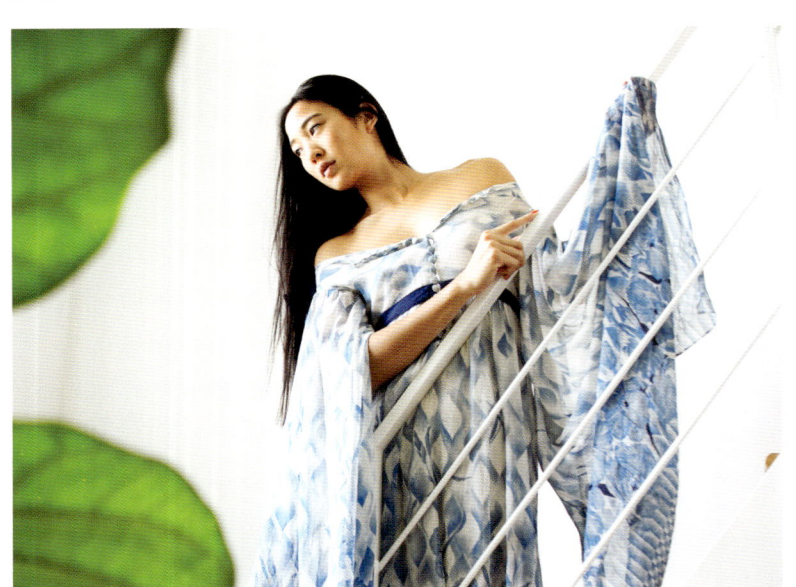
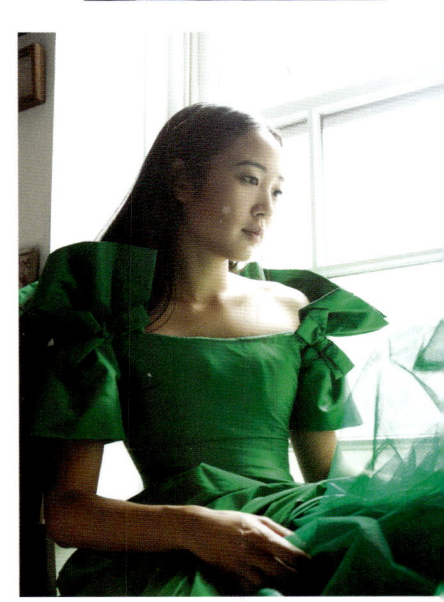
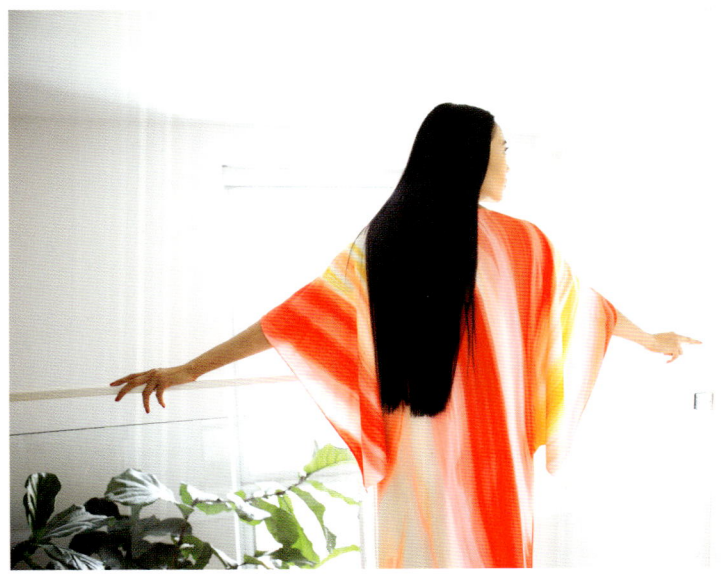
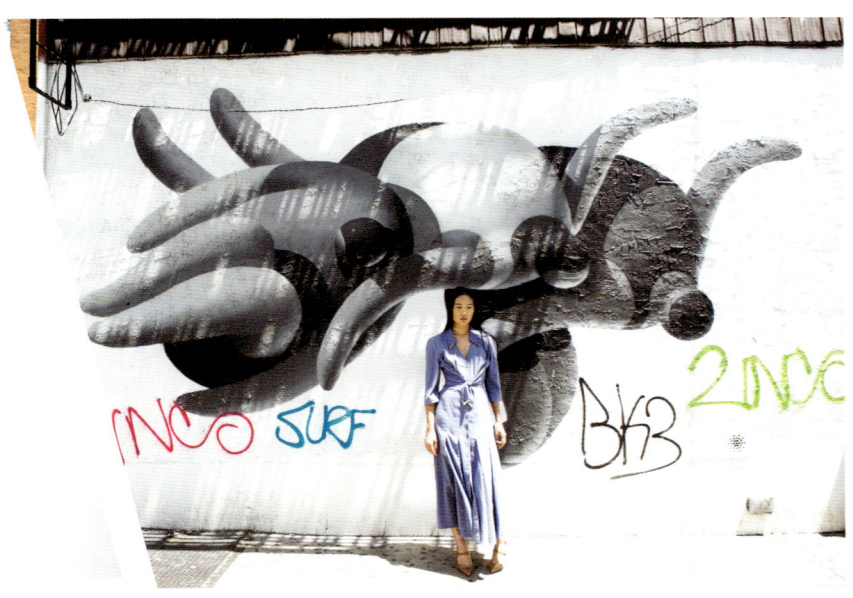

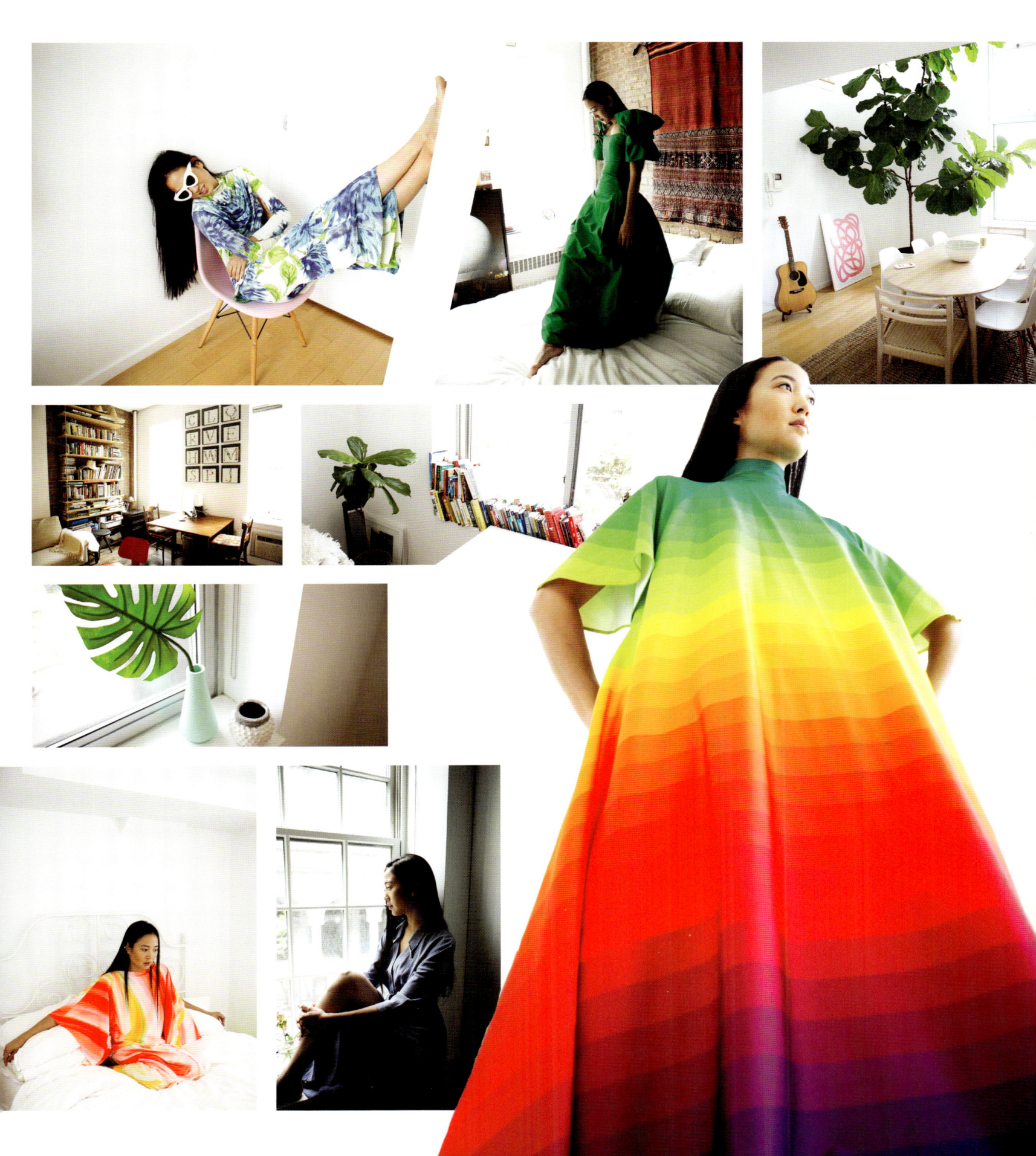

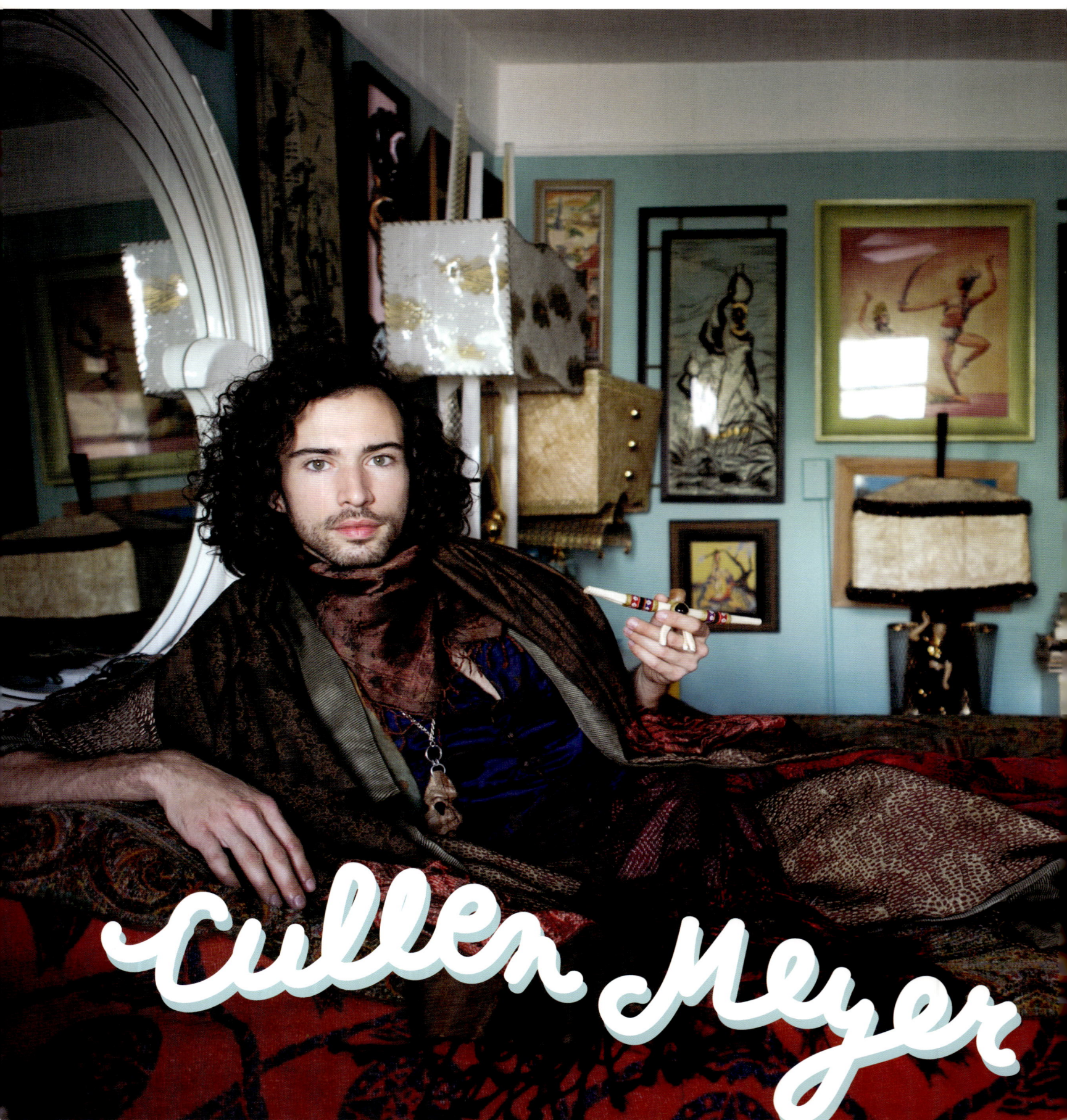

CULLEN MEYER
A ONE-INCH PIECE OF RIBBON

Cullen Christian Meyer was never going to be an ordinary child. He was destined for a far more sophisticated path of personal manifestation. It's as if he created his first fashion memory in the birth canal, when he changed out of his tattered womb pajamas to appear decently in front of his parents. Robert and Effie received him with open arms and began to foster creative genius. After a few years of covert practice, Cullen was ready to make his debut as an avowed master of transformation. At three he convinced his nursery school teacher to grant him exclusive permission to wear costumes during class. At home he constructed elaborate forts utilizing appliance boxes and Christmas lights and dwelled inside his illuminated creations with great satisfaction. While maintaining his dream of becoming a veterinarian he started to explore the arts. He sang, acted, painted, performed, designed clothing, and integrated all the forms into new arrangements. But above all, his appearance commanded immediate attention.

There was one thing standing between him and his next achievement: his private school uniform. By the time he was seven, his "innate sense of style was demanding emergence like a sprout through concrete." The only pieces of the militant look that allowed for choice were his footwear and neckties, but that wasn't enough. Cullen needed vestiary freedom. He successfully persuaded his parents to release him to the public school system, and that meant: a new wardrobe. Effie, who was an excellent shopper and always game for a makeover, felt her flourishing son's predicament and offered to drive the 90 miles from Milwaukee to Chicago. They walked into Urban Outfitters, a rare bird of retail at the time, and returned with a set of garments that would titivate his look, 70% of which were vintage.

And there was another thing to overcome: his weight. By freshman year in high school he was a seasoned performer, but often typecast. He tore into a rigid diet that cut out white flour, sugar, and any processed food, and resized his portions. He did not even eat cake on his birthday. He shed a hundred pounds in a year and promptly received a modeling contract. He also wrote and published a weight-loss and eating book for teens, "the only one by a teenager for teenagers." By senior year he was designing and creating 90% of his own clothing, including his prom outfit, and was also performing in a band. Barely 18, he moved to New York City to continue his journey. He studied at NYU but transferred to Parsons School of Design after sophomore year. His senior thesis show got him nominated for a Designer of the Year Award, featured in the windows of Saks Fifth Avenue, and offered a full page in Women's Wear Daily.

His discovery of vintage clothing unleashed a completely new wave of strategic enterprises. He became a regular fixture at the 5 a.m. line of antique dealers at every local estate sale. "I would even enlist my parents to come with me, give them a trash bag, and teach them what I was looking for, or make trade deals with other shoppers." He distributed homemade flyers in the fancy buildings Uptown and made friends with the doormen in hopes of getting dibs on clearances. He worked with a number of renowned vintage clothing dealers, set up at countless shows across the country, and pioneered "the formal integration of the inspirational aspect of vintage clothing into the global, trend-forecasting industry." And he had just one rule: "A label is a one-inch piece of ribbon."

Ultimately, for Cullen, it all boiled down to one thing: *How do I reach people and heal them with my artistic knowledge?* Cullen looks at vintage clothing as a medicinal object, similar to what a shaman would use for transformation, as a piece of history that comes with a spirit of other people who have worn it. He calls his art of dressing, "Shamanic surrealism aka mind-fuck magic aka Visual Alchemist." He's a creator. He art-directs his world with very tight palletes and coordinating patterns to evoke an otherworldly level of cohesive, visual storytelling. "When I look down at my outfit every day, it reminds me that life is one big lucid dream, and my experience with the world reflects that magic. There is a wonderful sense of freedom to look like one has just walked out of a painting." When he enters a room and people look at him, he's creating a state change. He's making people think, because their brains cannot connect all the visual references into one image; it transmutes judgment into curiosity.

But it doesn't end with his body. Cullen's Greenpoint apartment is the vessel that propagates the spells. "My home is my art, my altar, and my shrine; everyone and everything inside is sacred." He looks at his interior objects as a choir. Each individual piece is a treasure, a note he rediscovered in a moment of ecstasy—but the real magic happens when they all find each other. His home is a world from which he draws to better articulate and manifest his imagination.

So where does the journey lead to next? Cullen's existential intention is to never go to sleep the same person he was when he woke up, which makes the expanse of time implied in that question a wild musing. "However," he interjects, "if we create our own destiny with the spells of our words, then I would have to say that I see myself as a fully realized being who completely embodies the divine proportions, structures, and magic of nature; a captain of love through the lens of inspired beauty that I may share the joy of my heart and experience in whatever I create. And when I fully embody that vision, I will lead a massive empire of creation." So you see, Cullen was never going to be an ordinary adult.

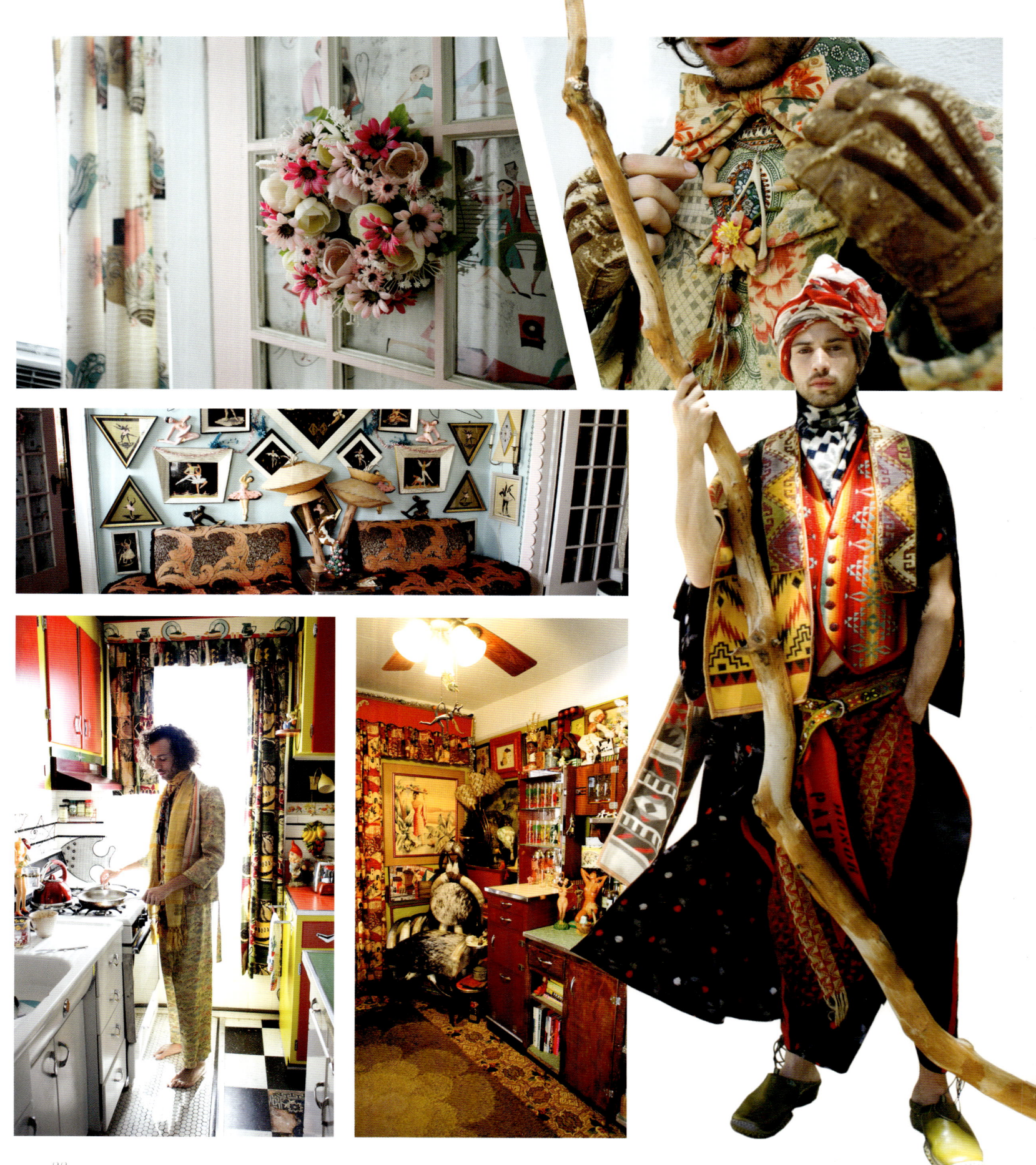

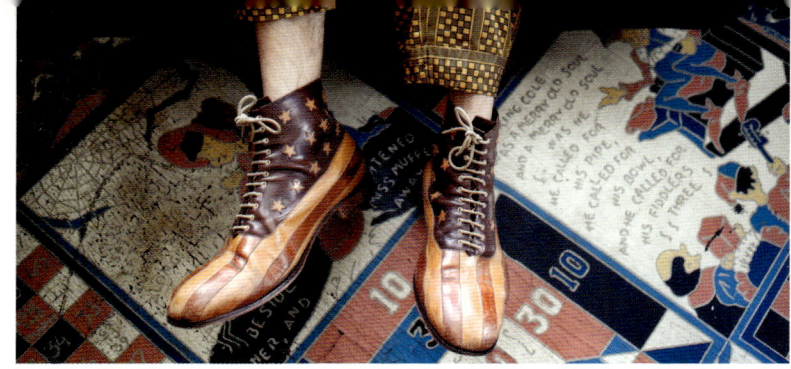
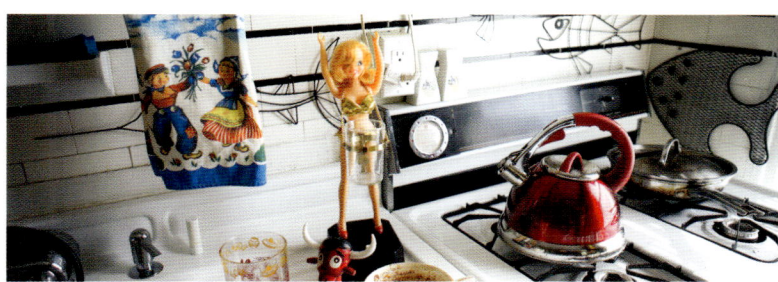
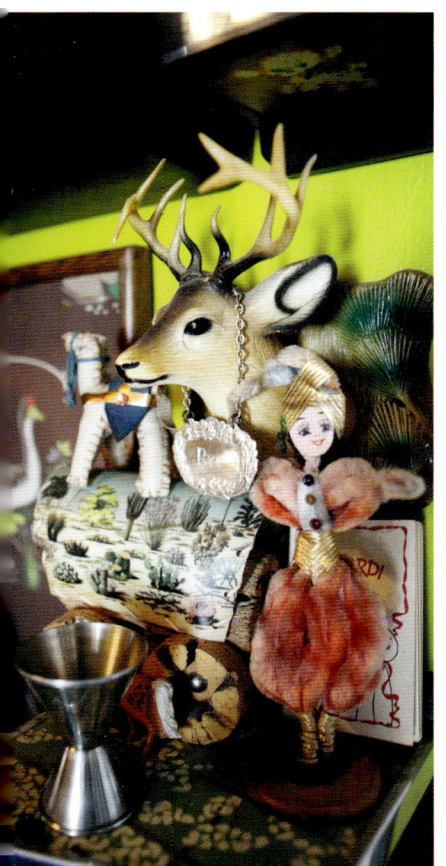
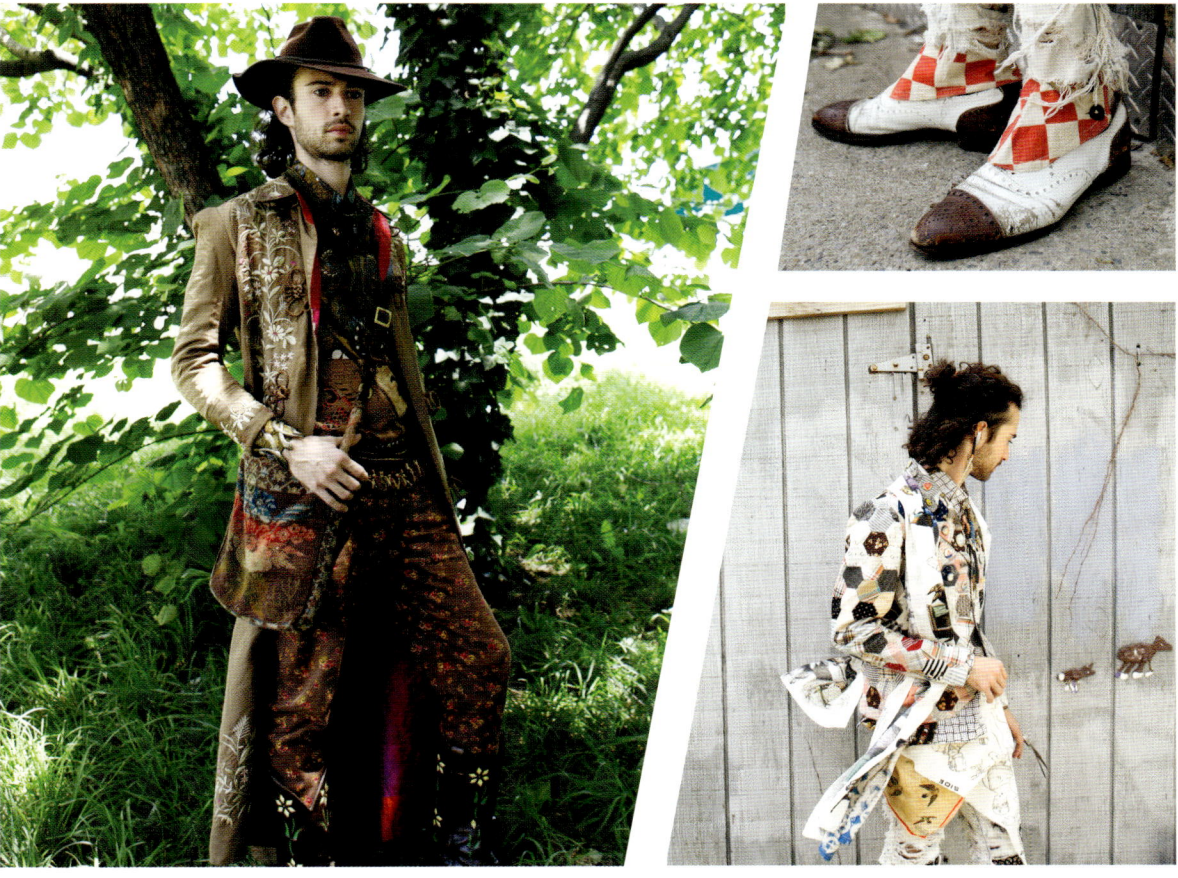
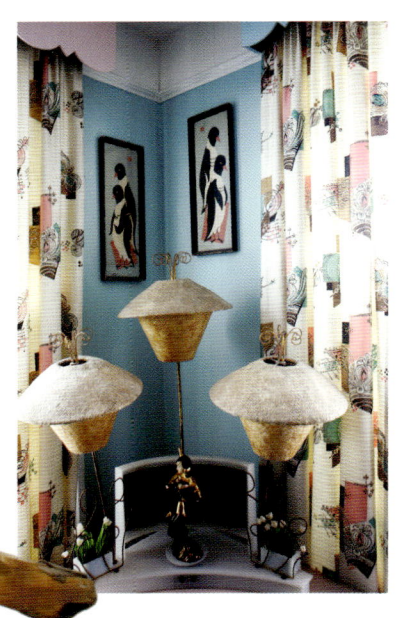
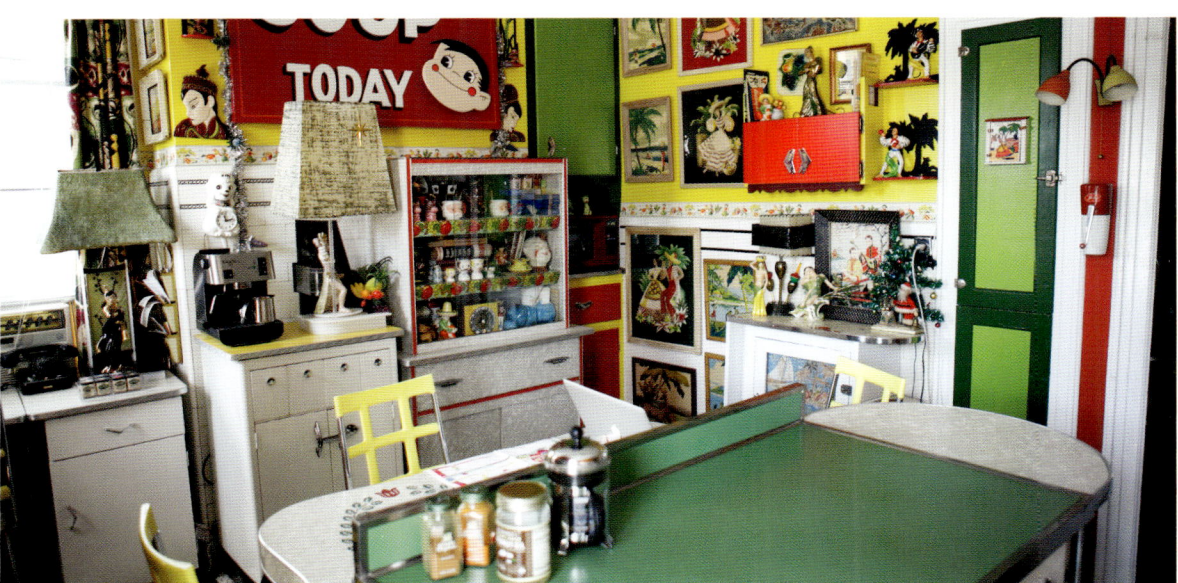

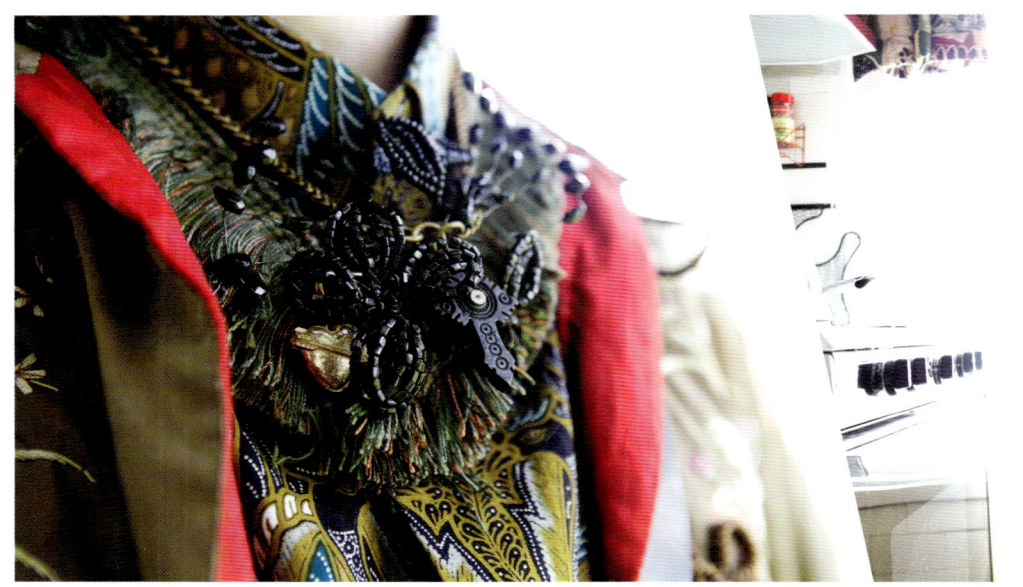
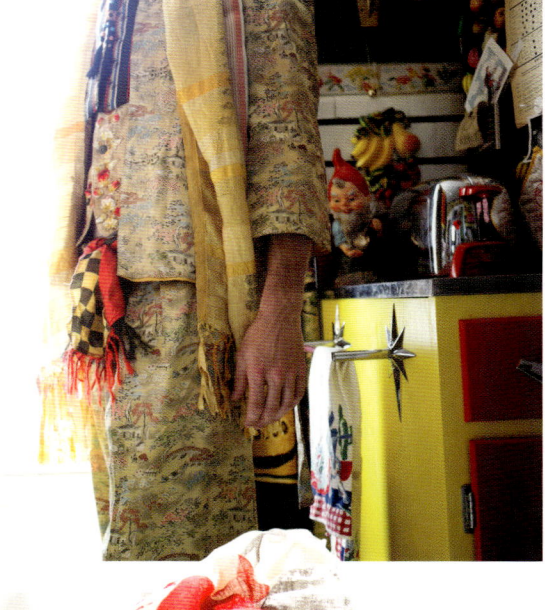
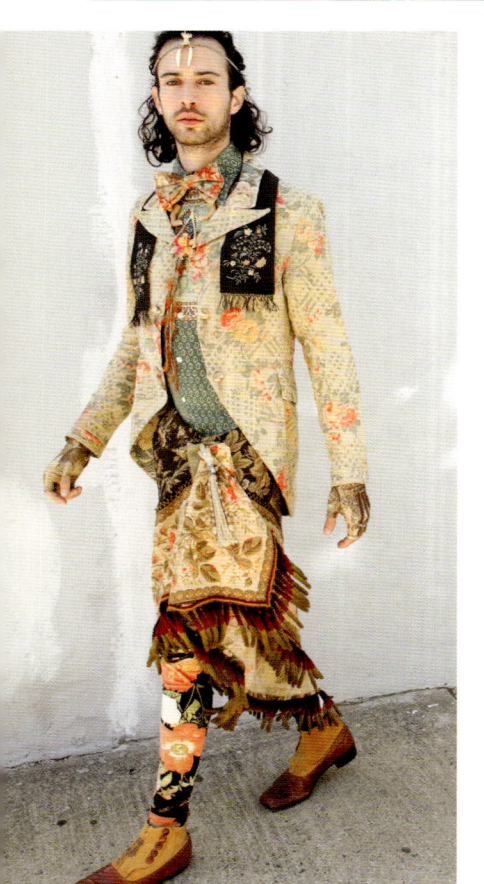
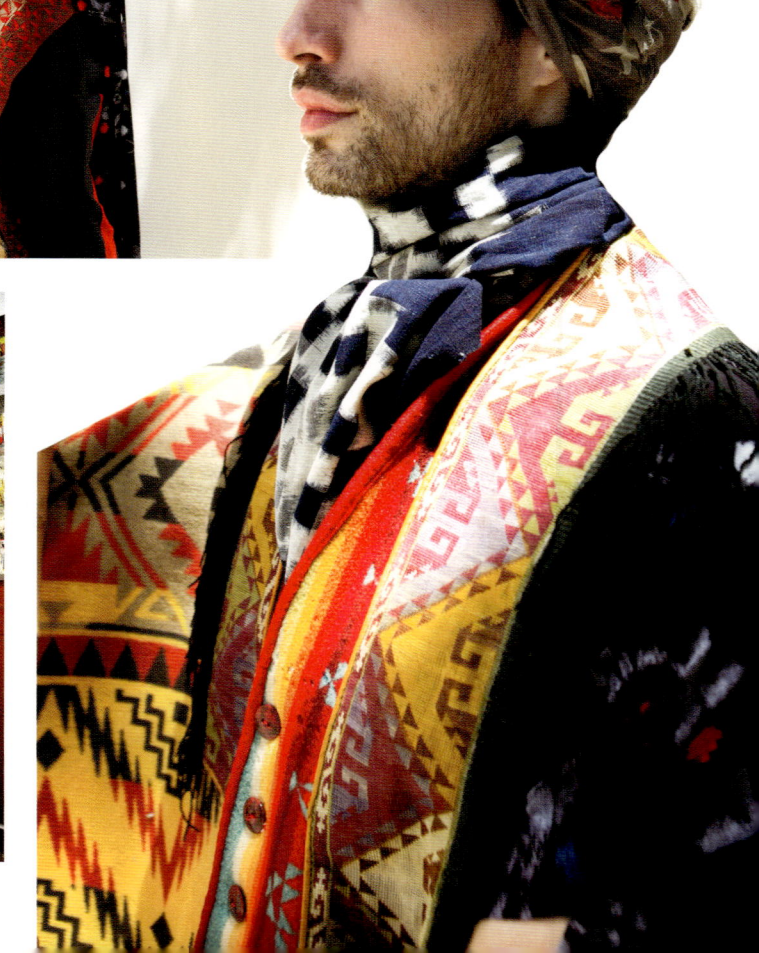
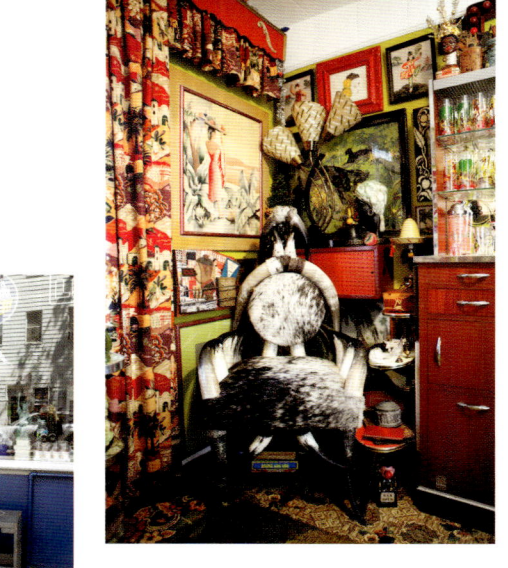
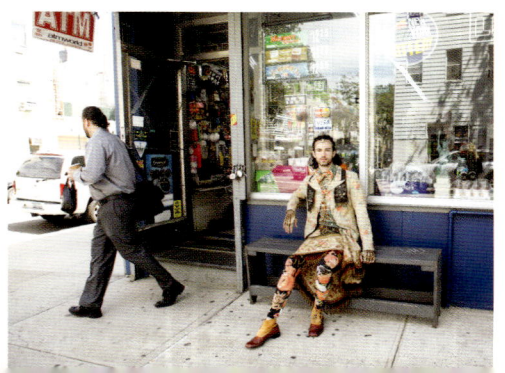

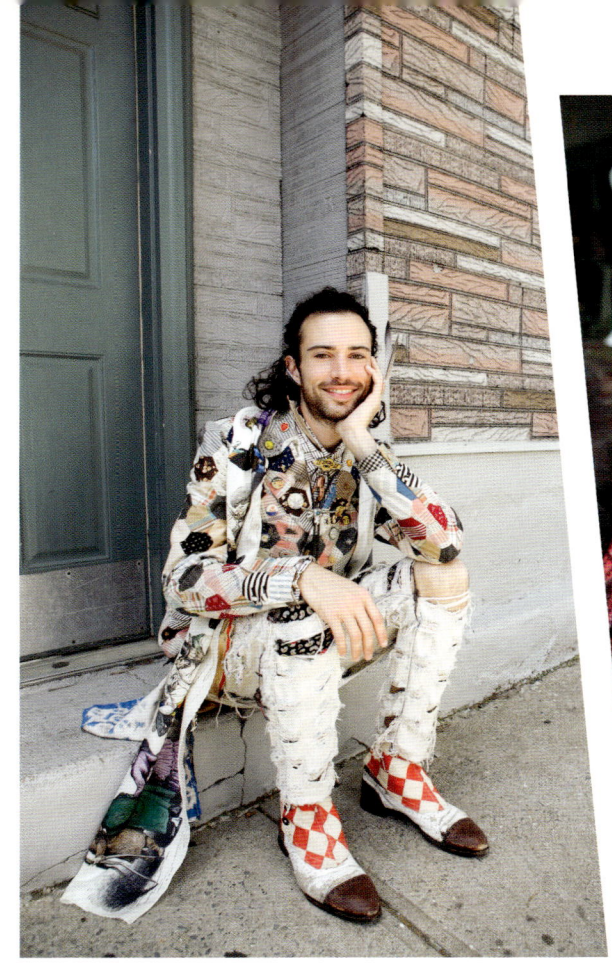
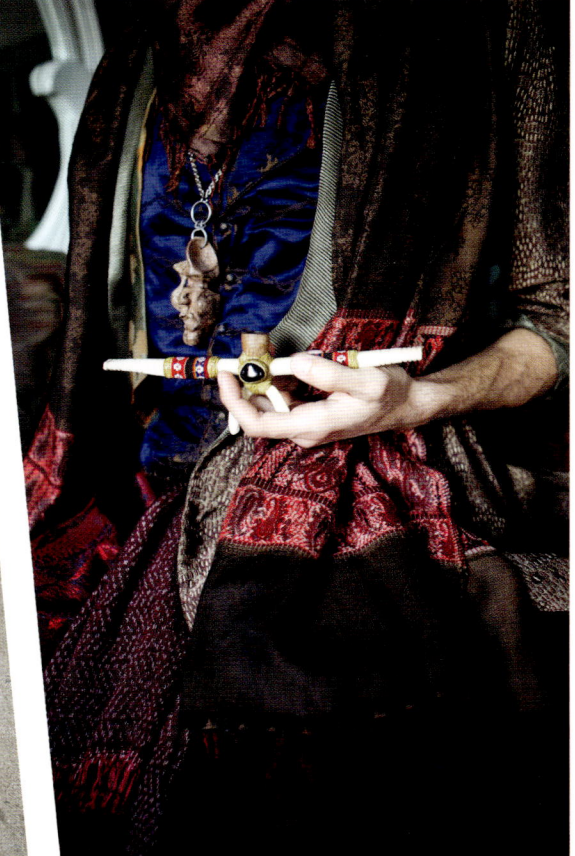
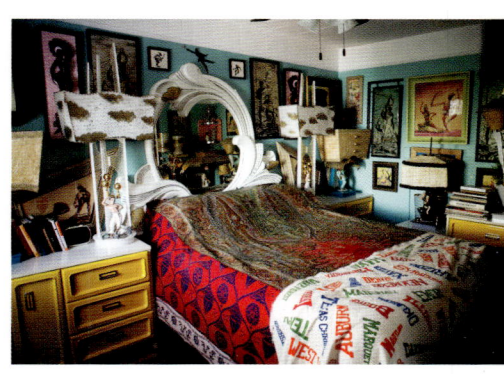
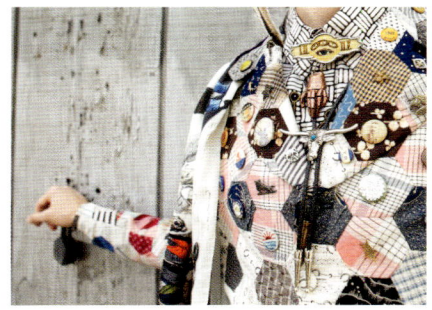
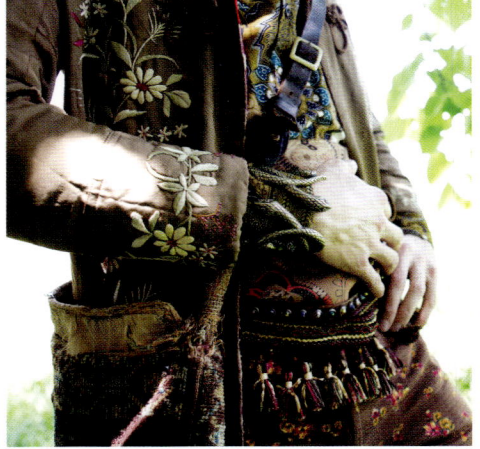
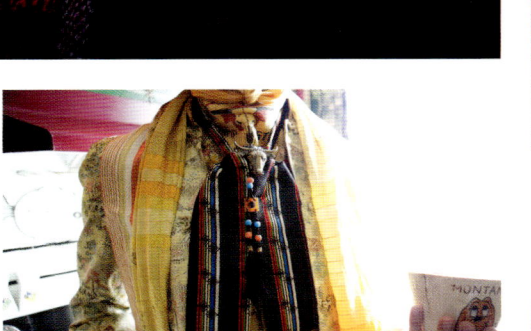
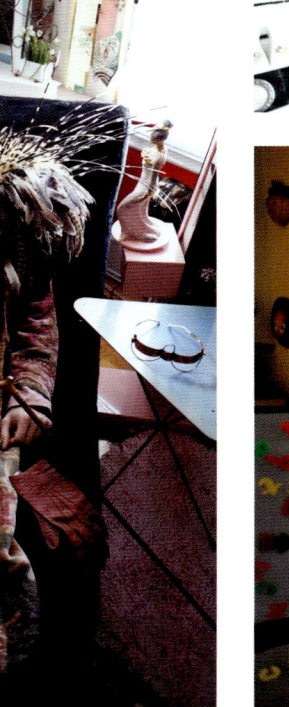
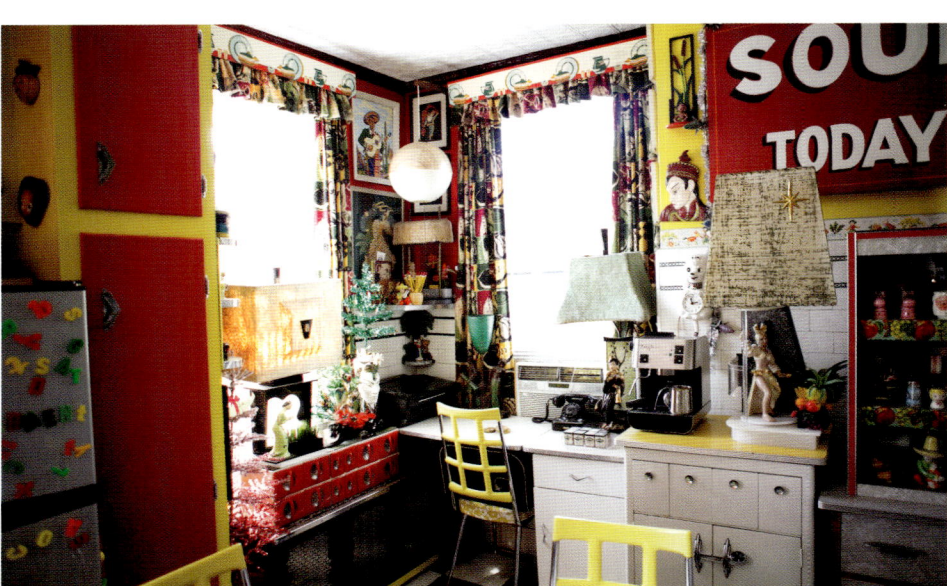

CONSTANCE ZIMMER
SHE HATED WORKING OUT

By the end of season two, Janine Skorsky had long fled Washington and her job at Slugline. She knew too much, and had to disappear before somebody made her. Zoe Barnes was dead, Lucas Goodwin was in jail, and then killed—she could be next. But when your character is dormant, milling about in hiding somewhere near Ithaca, and she's the only person who can really bring down that *House of Cards,* how do you resuscitate her? Constance Zimmer must have rewritten her character's comeback a hundred times in her head, because, wasn't she great as the abrasive journalist? If only she knew what the script guys had in mind, or how to whisper in their ears. "As far as I'm concerned," she shrugs, "as long as my character's still alive, I'm holding out hope to head back to that show."

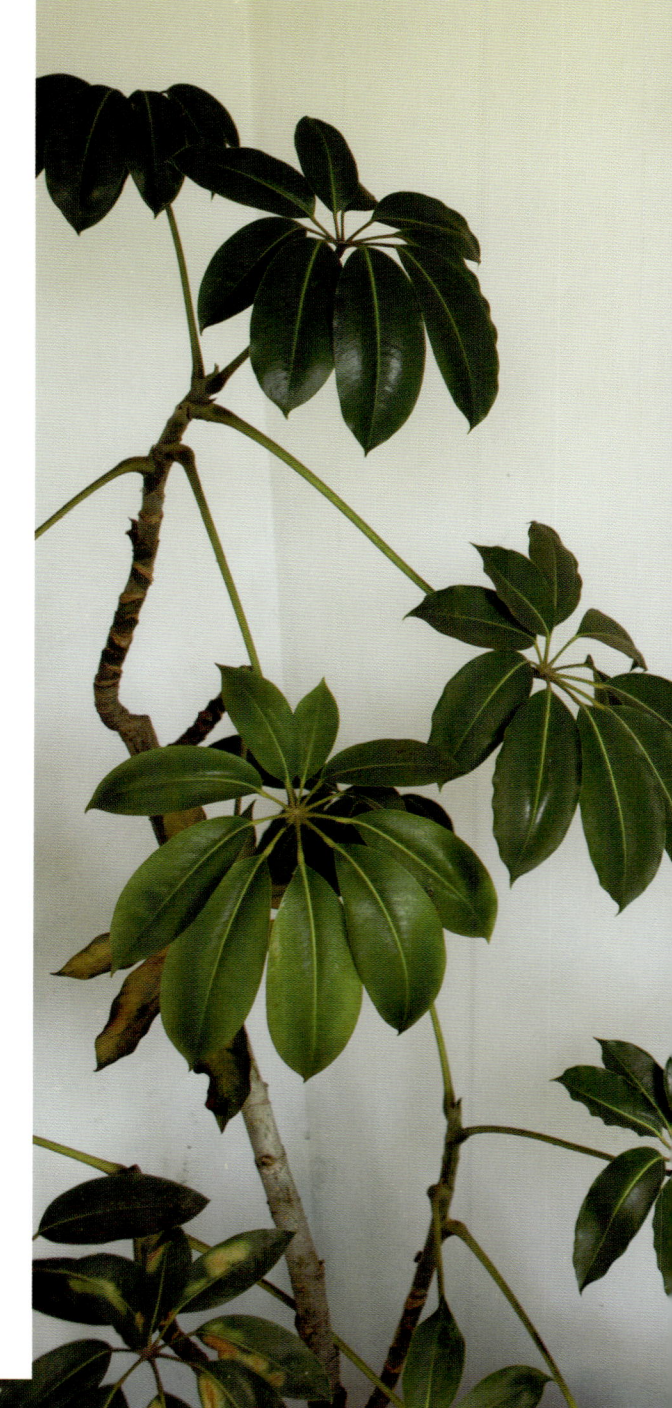

In the meantime though, she's playing a mean boss on Lifetime's series *UnREAL* and also directing her first episode. When I arrive at her house in Studio City, Constance and her assistant are in the middle of phrasing a Quinn King Instagram giveaway, but it doesn't seem to have the desired result. "Dammit, no one's doing it right!!" she grumbles in frustration. In order to win the show's merchandise, her fans have to comment with an #Quinsult quote and their T-shirt size, but most of them do either/or. I'm also a little shocked at the answers. "Get the fuck out of my fairy fort!" is a popular one. "Now that's a good bitch," another. I also read, "Welcome back meat puppet," a few times. All I can think is, *Why haven't I watched this show??*

Constance Zimmer is one of the fortunate women that have been making a living as an actress for more than 20 years. She was headed for a life as a professional gymnast, but that took a drastic turn when she auditioned for a school play. It was the catalyst that propelled her onto the small screen. (All the better, because she hated working out!) Her family moved closer to Los Angeles so that she could pursue acting. She attended the American Academy of Dramatic Arts in Pasadena, and later Stella Adler before she started to pound the pavement. Before long, she had an agent and began starring in commercials and sitcoms. Did anyone see her in Seinfeld in 1998? Or in Beverly Hills 90201?

It's a few days until Christmas and dad—his name is Russ and he's a director—warns his wife to hide the skateboard. Colette, their nine-year-old daughter, will be back from school any minute and it's not gift-wrapped yet. The house looks like an old Spanish Colonial but it was actually built in 2007. "It's a wannabe," laughs Constance. "We have fun details, like arched doorways and crown moldings reminiscent of the 1920s, but with all the modern upgrades, like big closets and bigger rooms in general." Her wardrobe is modest with a few hidden gems, specifically the dresses she inherited from her husband's grandmother. She would live in baggy jeans every day if she could, but that's only because vintage shopping requires time, and she doesn't have any. "I get excited when I can wear a vintage dress on the red carpet; I just haven't had the time to scour thrift stores lately. I think my style is definitely eclectic or feminine tomboy, if that's even a thing. I try to emulate a vintage vibe, even if I'm wearing all new clothes, by throwing on a vintage scarf or shoes."

Constance is a funny woman. She's down-to-earth and curious, and doesn't take herself too seriously. She was "always a ham," and remembers the days when she and her sister would dress up like elephants and put on full productions, in German, when visiting their grandparents. And as much as I would have loved to witness those early days, I think I would much rather have Janine back. What are you waiting for, guys?

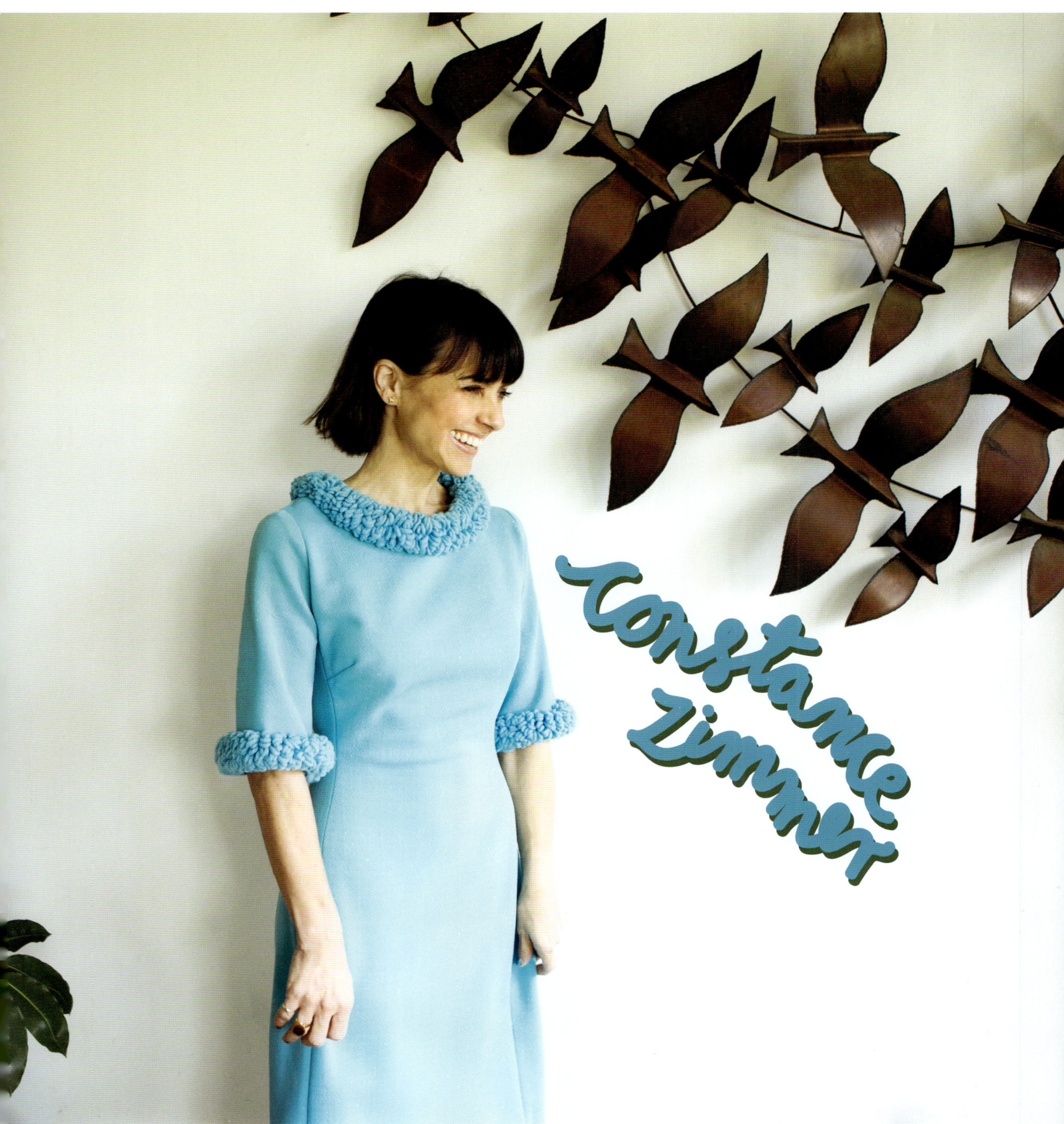

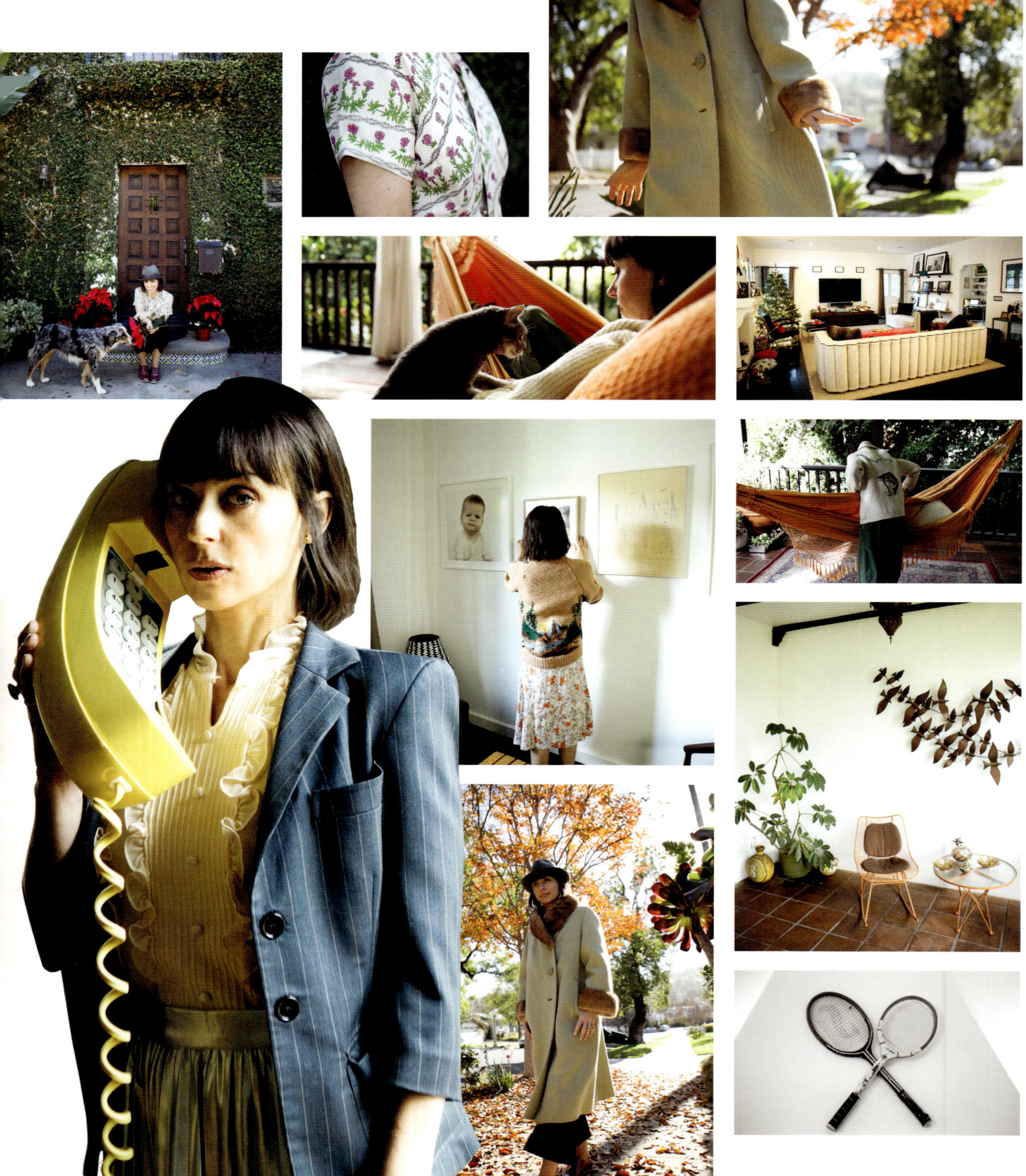

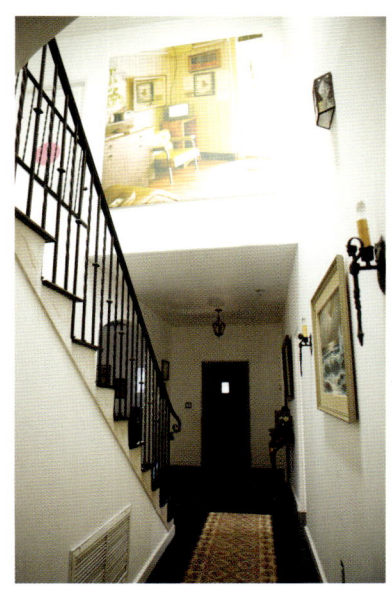
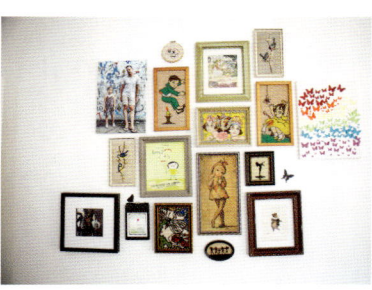
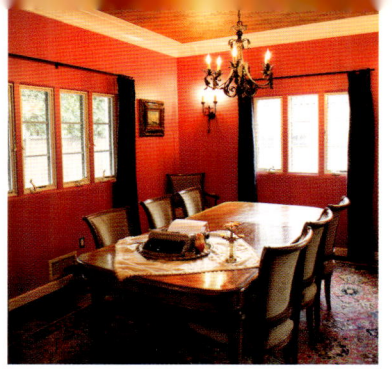
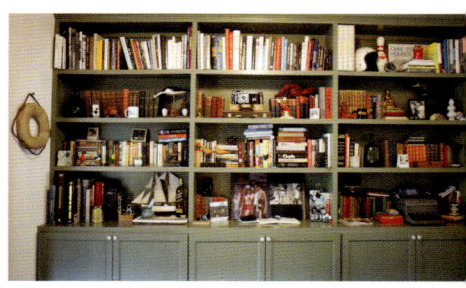
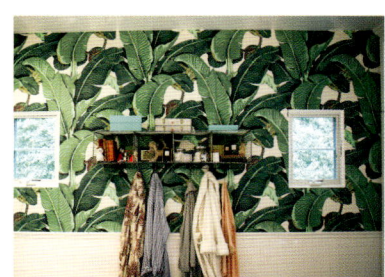
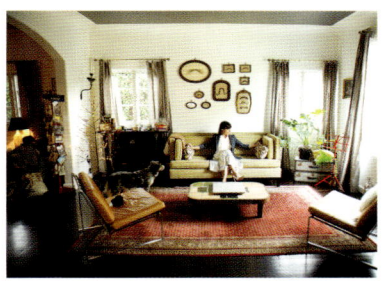
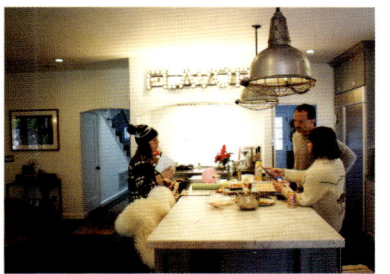
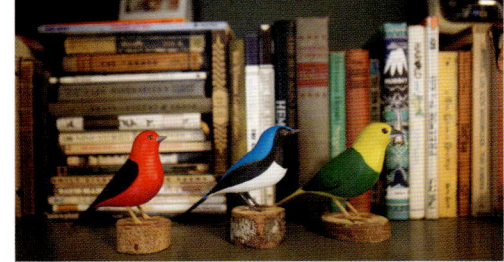
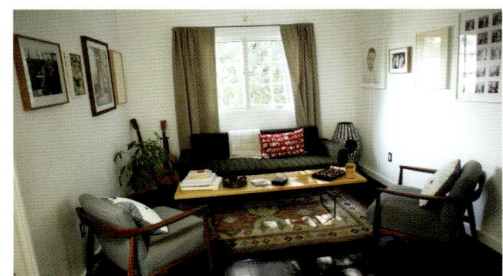
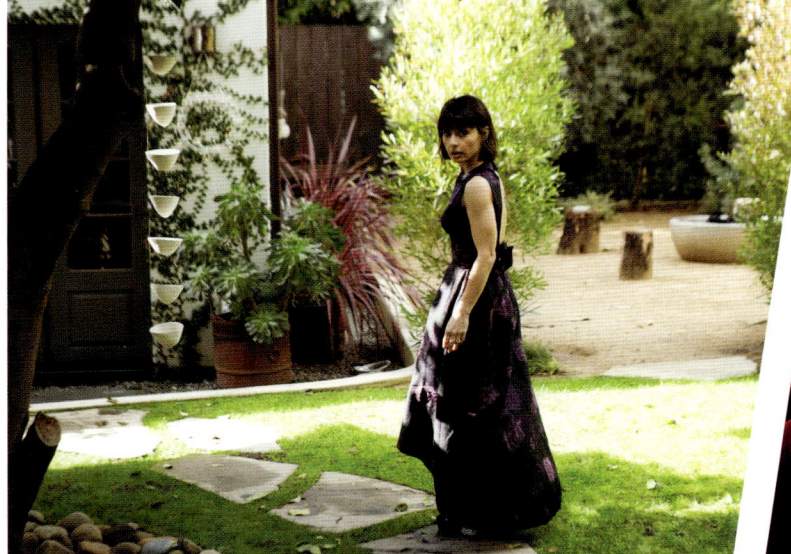
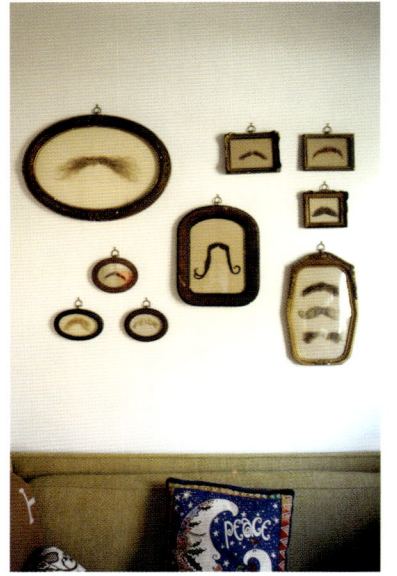
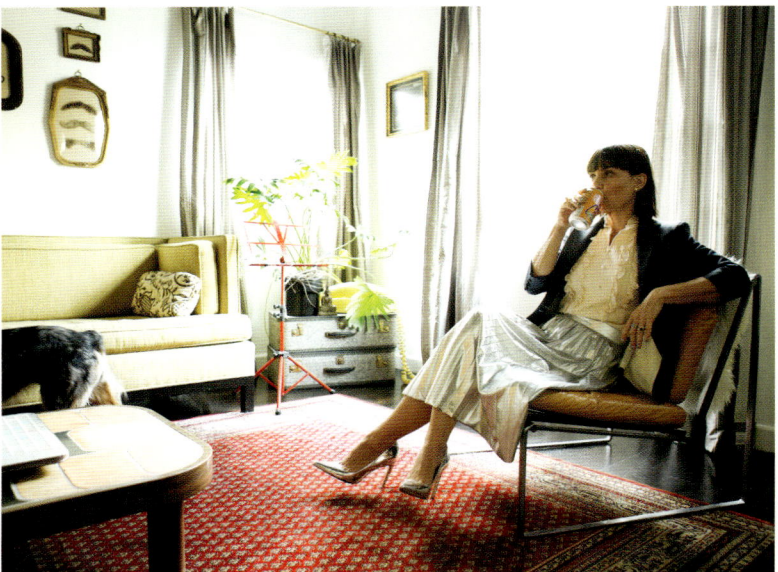
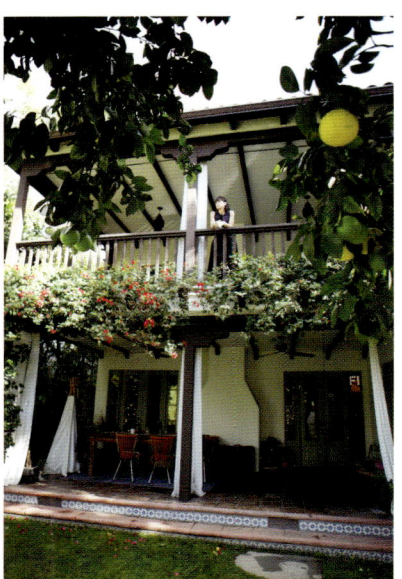

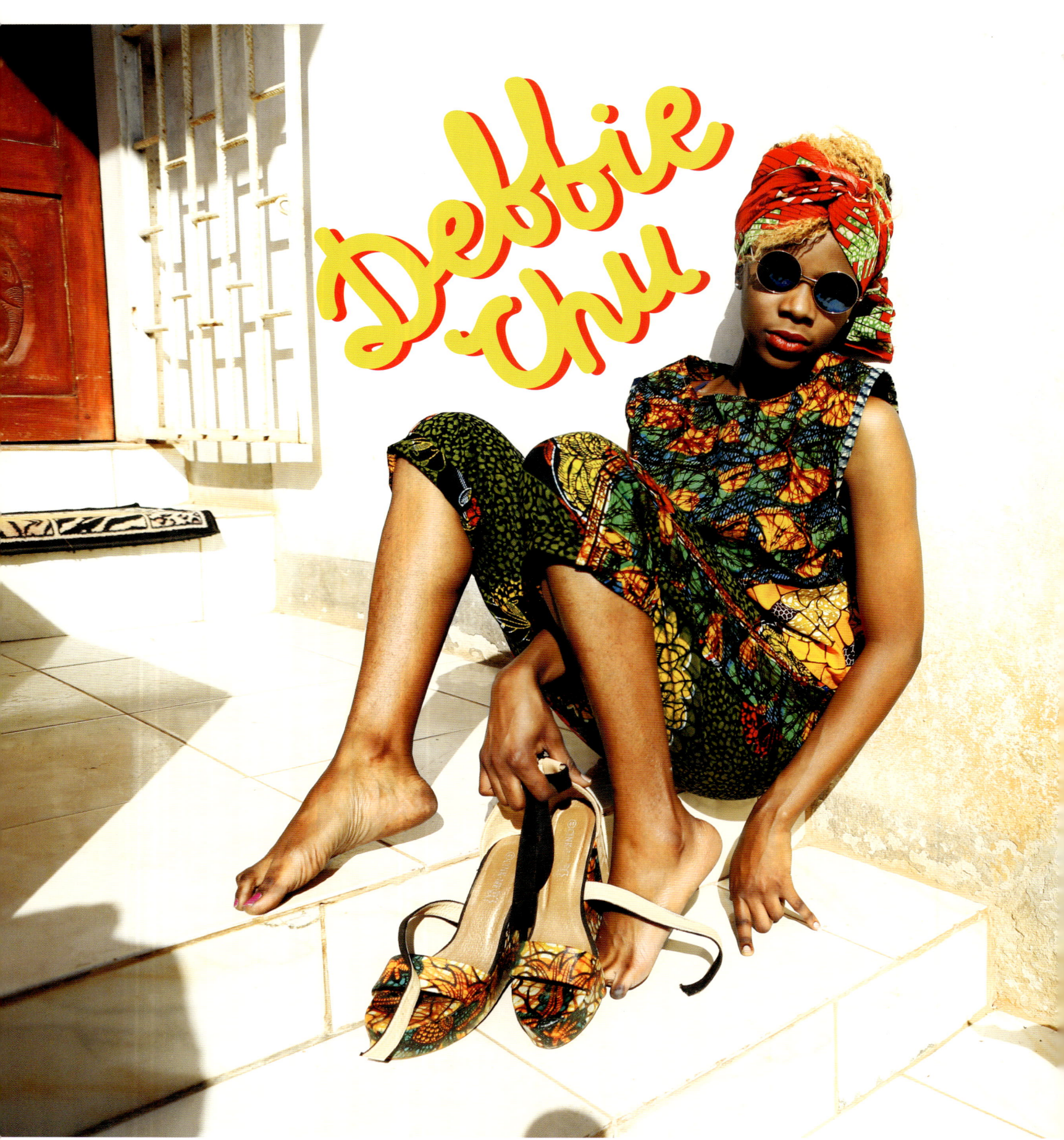

DEBBIE CHU
THE VINTAGE QUEEN OF ZAMBIA

In just five hours I will be on a plane back to New York, but I insist on squeezing in a shoot with Deborah Chuma this morning. She was hard to miss at my workshop days earlier: khaki shorts, brown booties, a boxy, embroidered sweatshirt, those wild, blonde 90s tresses gushing generously from a fedora, and her equally colorful girlfriend Nandi in fashionable tow. They both sat behind me, literally starstruck, because they had seen my 15-second cameo on *House of DVF*, and couldn't believe I was in their hometown. "The first few minutes of the workshop I couldn't even pay attention!" she told me afterwards, pressing her flushed cheeks lavishly against mine for an assailment of selfies. I didn't even know they *had* E! here. "We have DSTV," she explains. "You have to buy and pay for it with a monthly subscription. It's expensive for a low-income family. It comes with so many channels. Us fashion lovers can watch *House of DVF* on E!, Fashion TV, *Fashion Bloggers* and *Project Runway* on Lifetime." Today she's supposed to be at Nandi's graduation, but the prospect of being featured on my website annihilated every promise. "Nooo, our friendship of 10 years is strong!" she assures me, when I send her a concerned message on WhatsApp. "I've bribed her. I will make up for it with lunch. Plus, she ditches me all the time too! LOL!"

Debbie is a talented, young designer. At 23, she is part of a new, fashion-forward generation that has the opportunity and ambition to look outside the borders of its sheltered country. Her work is interesting and shows great promise. Her aesthetic and style are also unusual for Zambia. She mixes vintage fabrics with chitenge, and her patterns are anything but traditional. The week leading up to my visit, for example, she made me a dress from her grandmother's curtains, a vintage skirt she found at the market, and a blouse she had lying around. "I didn't go to college to study fashion and design," she tells me, "because you see, in Zambia we don't have fashion schools. Me and mum planned for me to study abroad, but then the year I completed high school, she got sick and passed away. I've always been a positive child. Mum might have died, but these dreams of fashion designing won't."

In Zambia, the closest thing to a being a fashion designer is learning how to tailor. And that's what she eventually studied. "I work from home. My first workplace was my bedroom. But now I've moved to the dining room." She was raised by her grandparents—she was their first grandchild—and lives in the main house with her grandmother, an aunt, her son Emmanuel, and her grandmother's father. "Yes!" she cheers. "My great grandpa is 102 years old. We are so blessed to have him. He's such a joy, with lots of stories." Next door lives her uncle Chibuta and his family of five, which explains all the gutted cars in the driveway: "He's a mechanic/engineer, so he's now made our once-upon-a-time neat, clean yard into his workshop..." There's also a boarding house on the compound with seven bedrooms that are being rented to university students.

Vintage is big in Zambia, and Debbie loves it. But it's not the kind we consider. "We don't have thrift stores," she explains. "We have second-hand clothes heaped together on the ground, sold alongside the road in a marketplace. It's called *salaula* and such business has boomed in Zambia. Odd clothes are sold as cheaply as one or two cents. You can find brands like Chanel for two dollars or less. But you have to have patience." Her earliest fashion memory involves a vintage Valentino shirt her late "Grandpa Mr. Chuma" gave her when she was 11 years old. "I didn't know who Valentino was, but coincidentally, that very night I am watching TV and this new show comes on that was profiling international designers and clips of their work and I noticed the same brand on my grandpa's shirt. I watched my first runway show on TV and it was Valentino, and I had a Valentino shirt!"

This visit is everything I hoped for, and more. Debbie has allowed me a rare glimpse into the real life of a Lusaka family. There are so many more questions I want to ask, like why she never mentions her father, or why all the houses in the city are fenced off and walled in, or how her mother died, but I don't need to. I am so utterly grateful for the past two hours. I have come to know a girl with humble hopes and dreams, who loves Gospel music and poetry, whose childhood is "bittersweet," but tangled with memories of friendship and neighborhood games, who's in love with a boy named Nathaniel, "my best friend, my gift," and whose five-year plan is to "provide employment and help, put food on the table for my family and other Zambians." As far as my driver goes, he never shows up. At least not when I asked him to. "You should always tell people to come half hour before you want them there," Debbie laughs. "But don't worry, my uncle will drive us." And just in that second I realize, this is not just a young woman's reality; this is how the world turns.

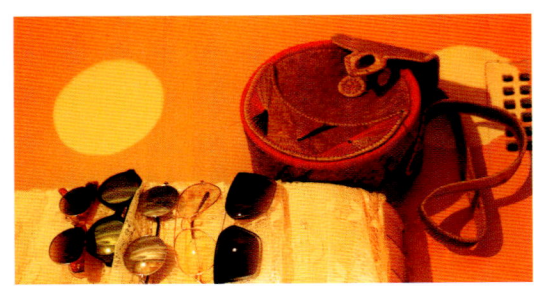
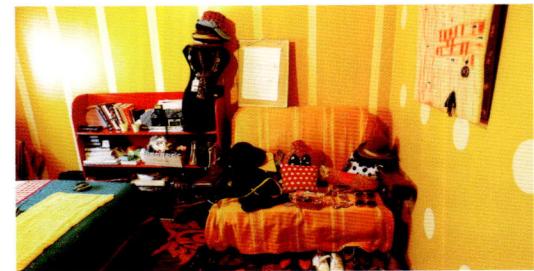
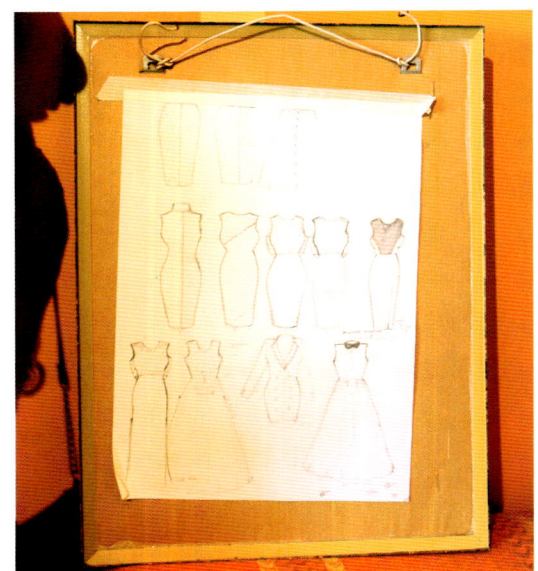
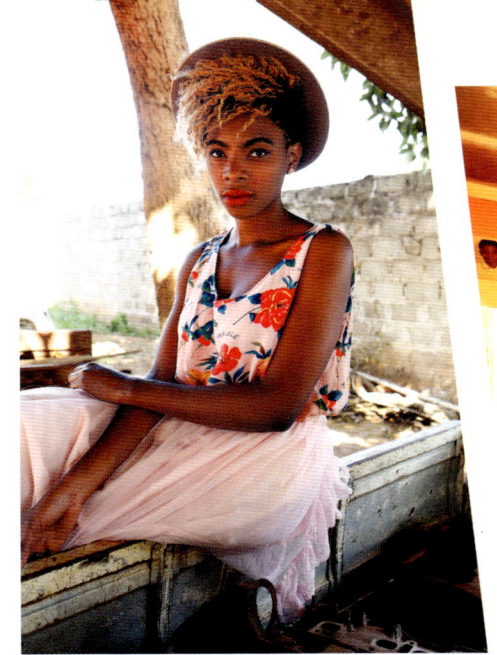
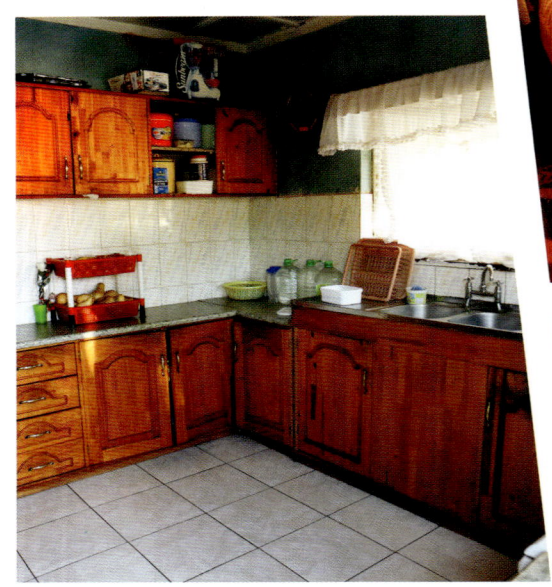
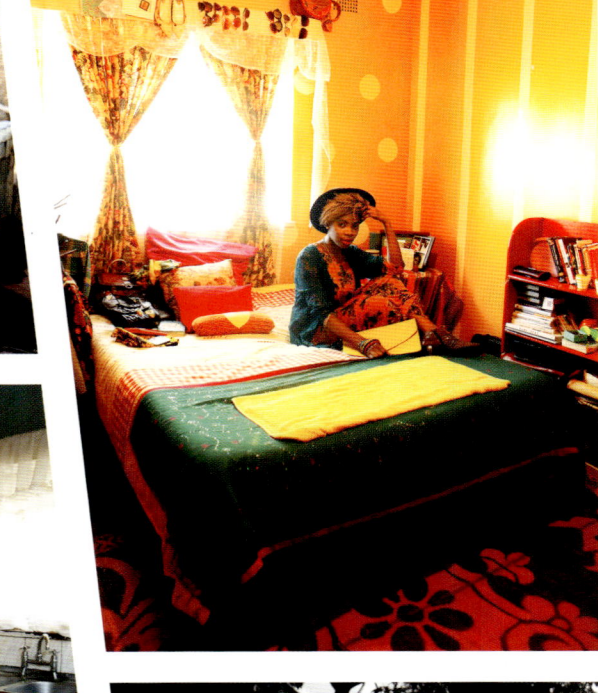
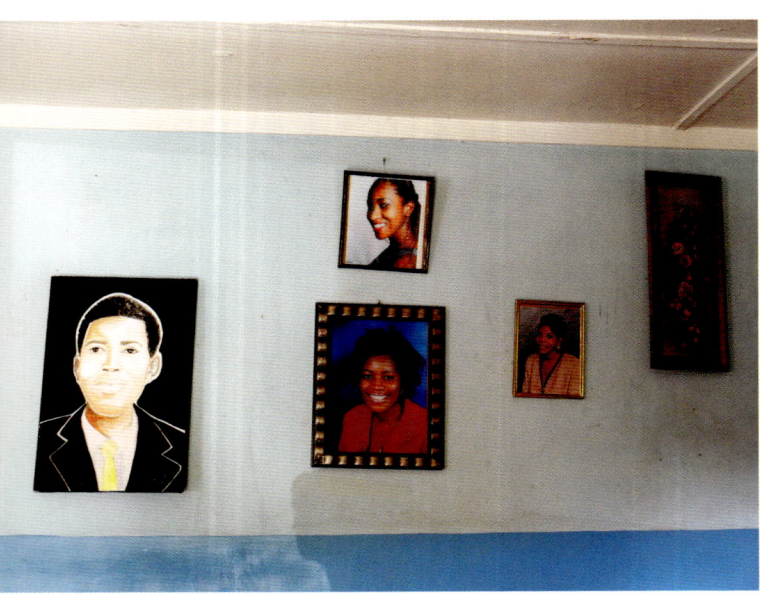
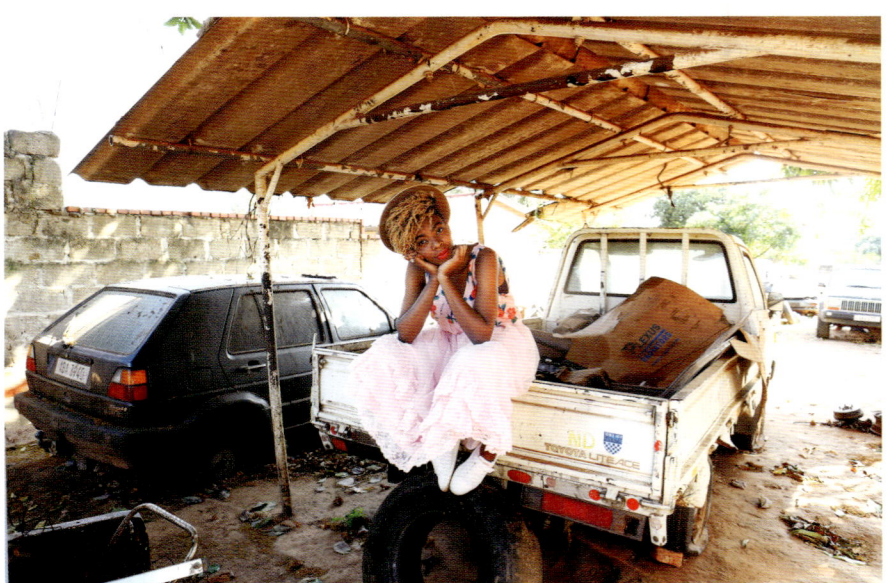

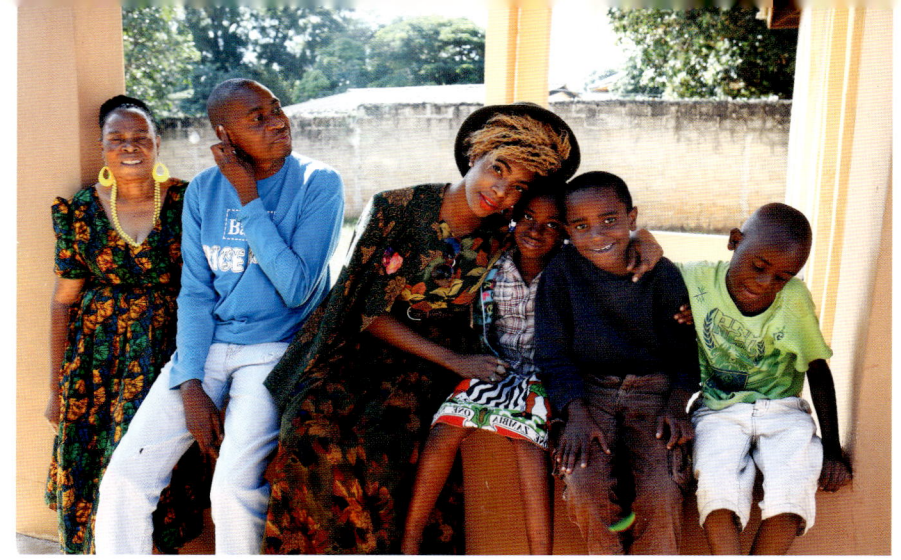
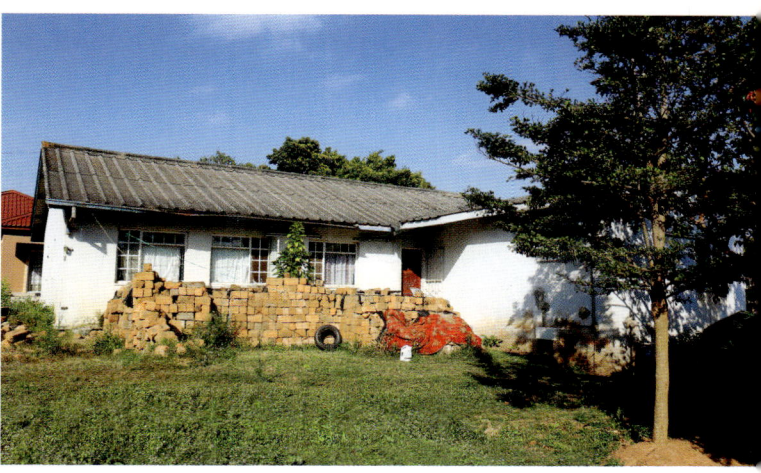
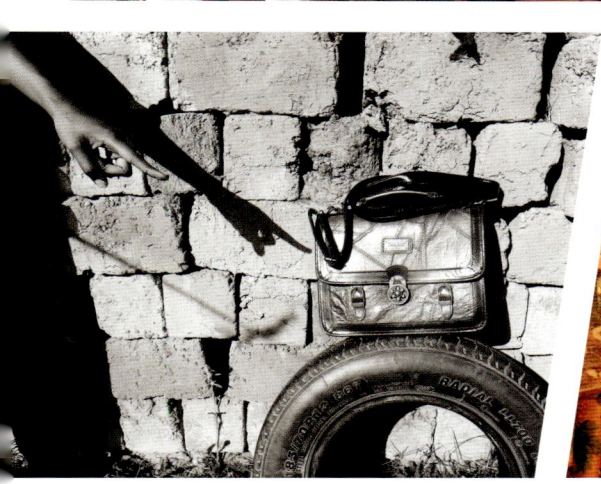
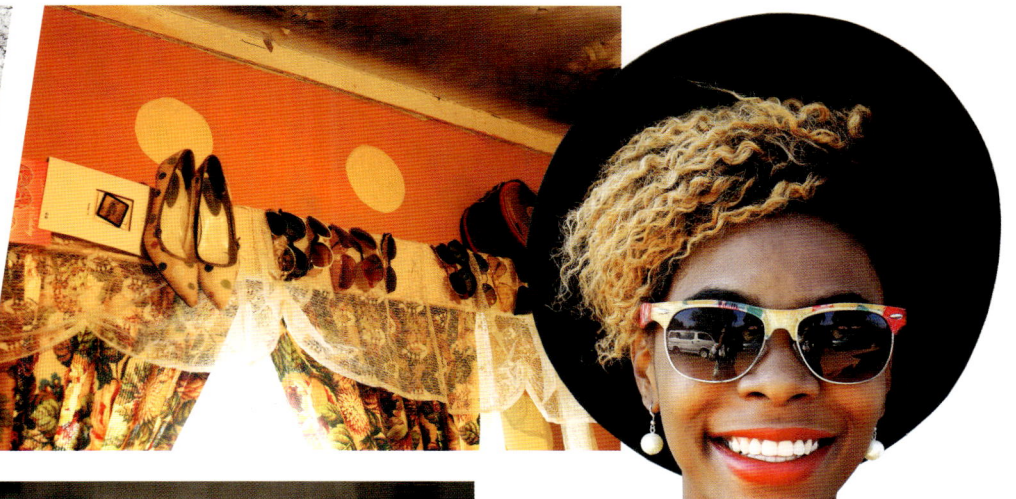
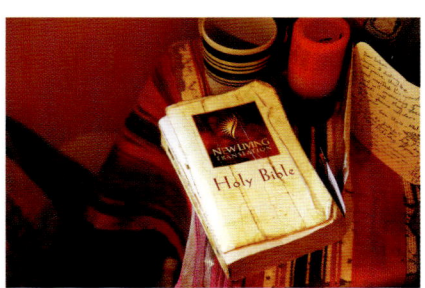
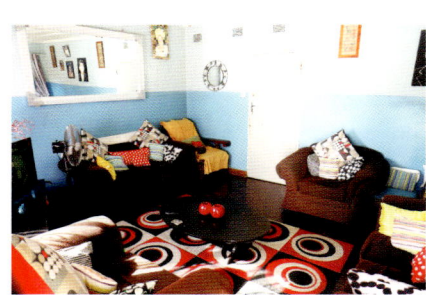
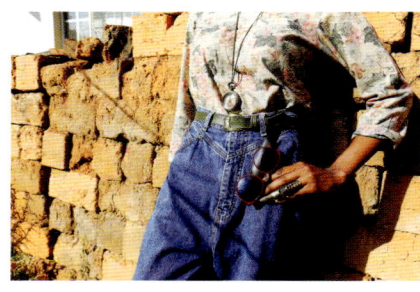
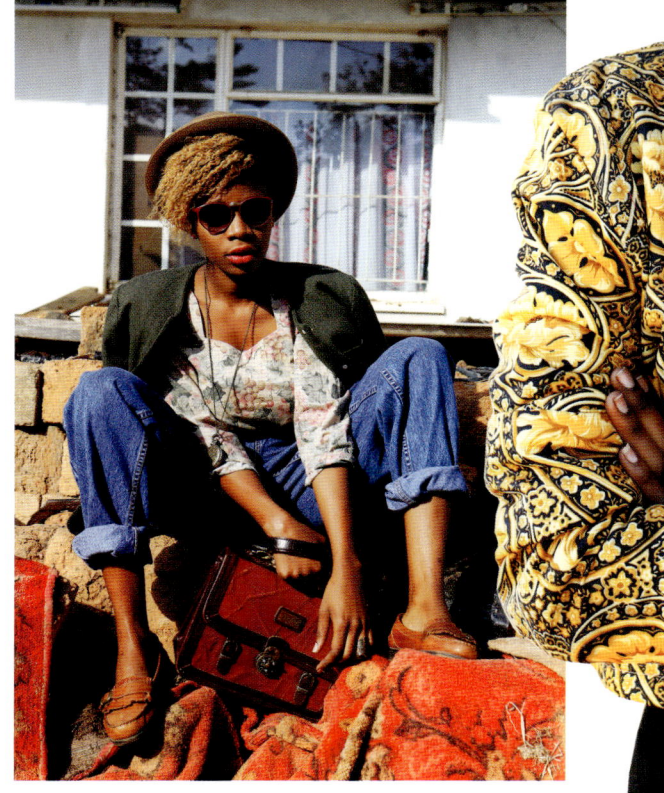

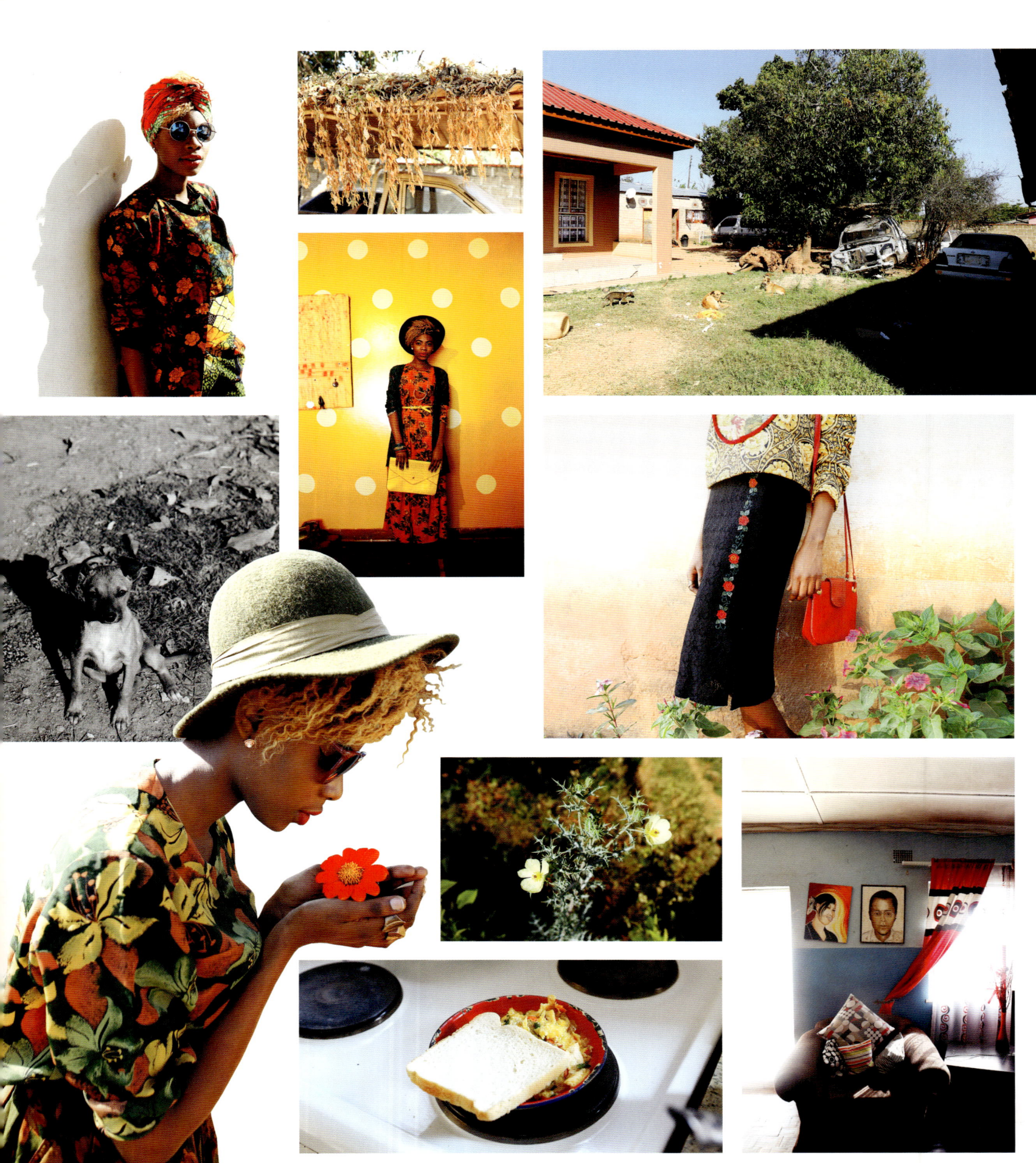

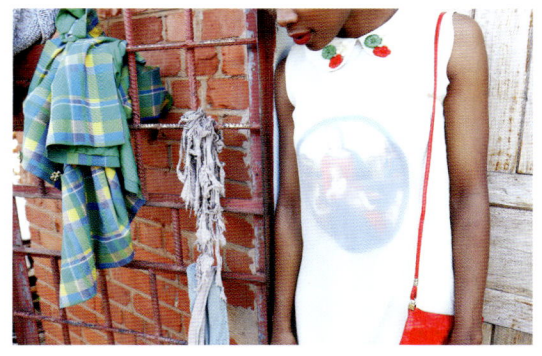
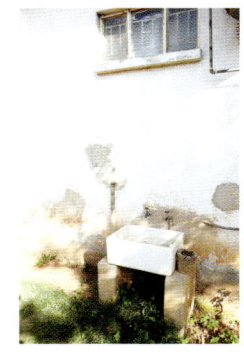
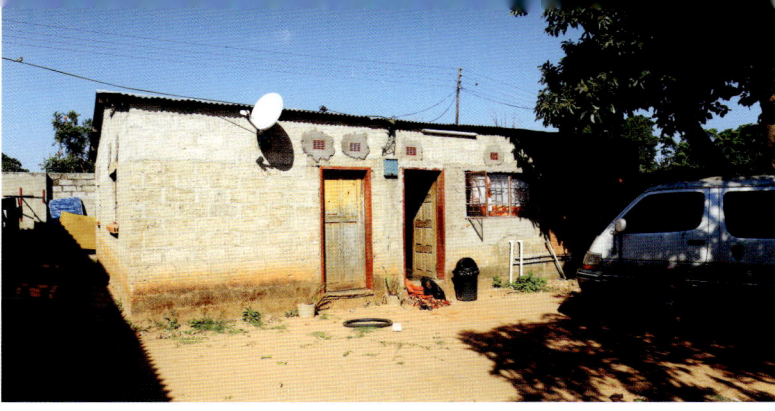
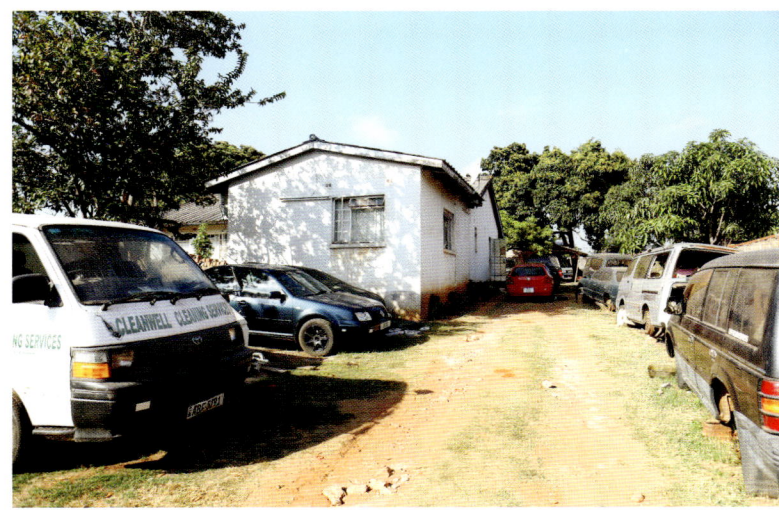
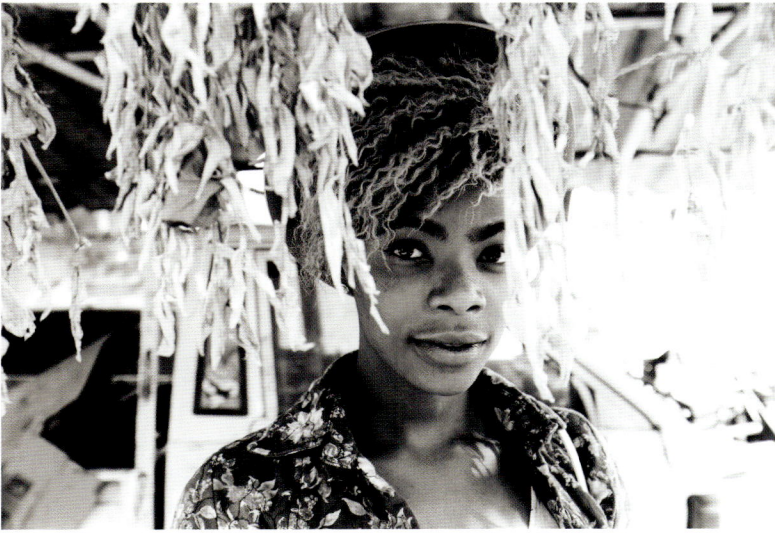
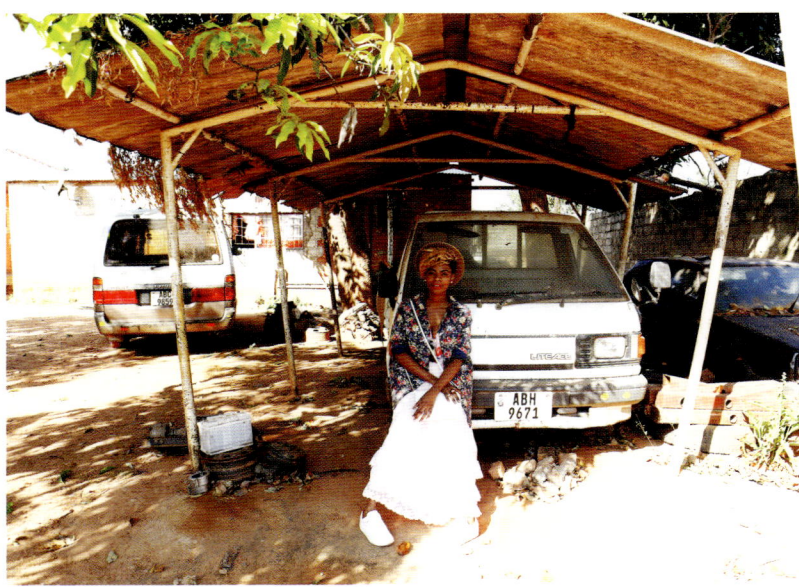
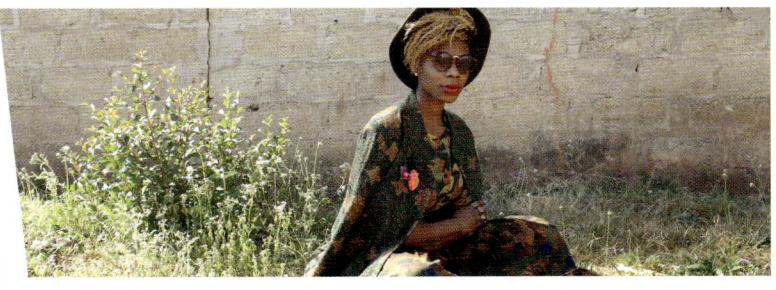
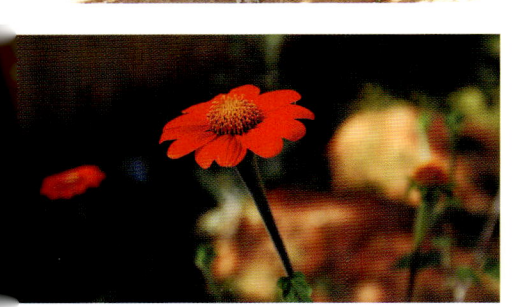
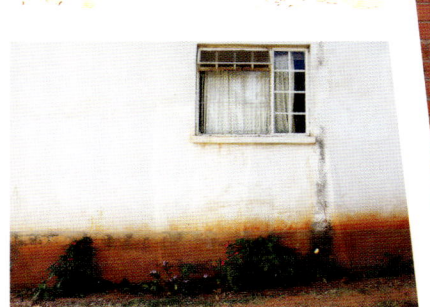
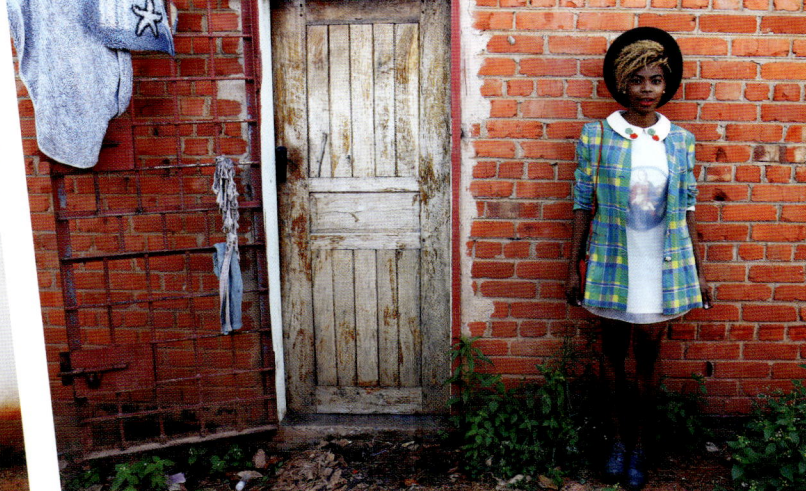

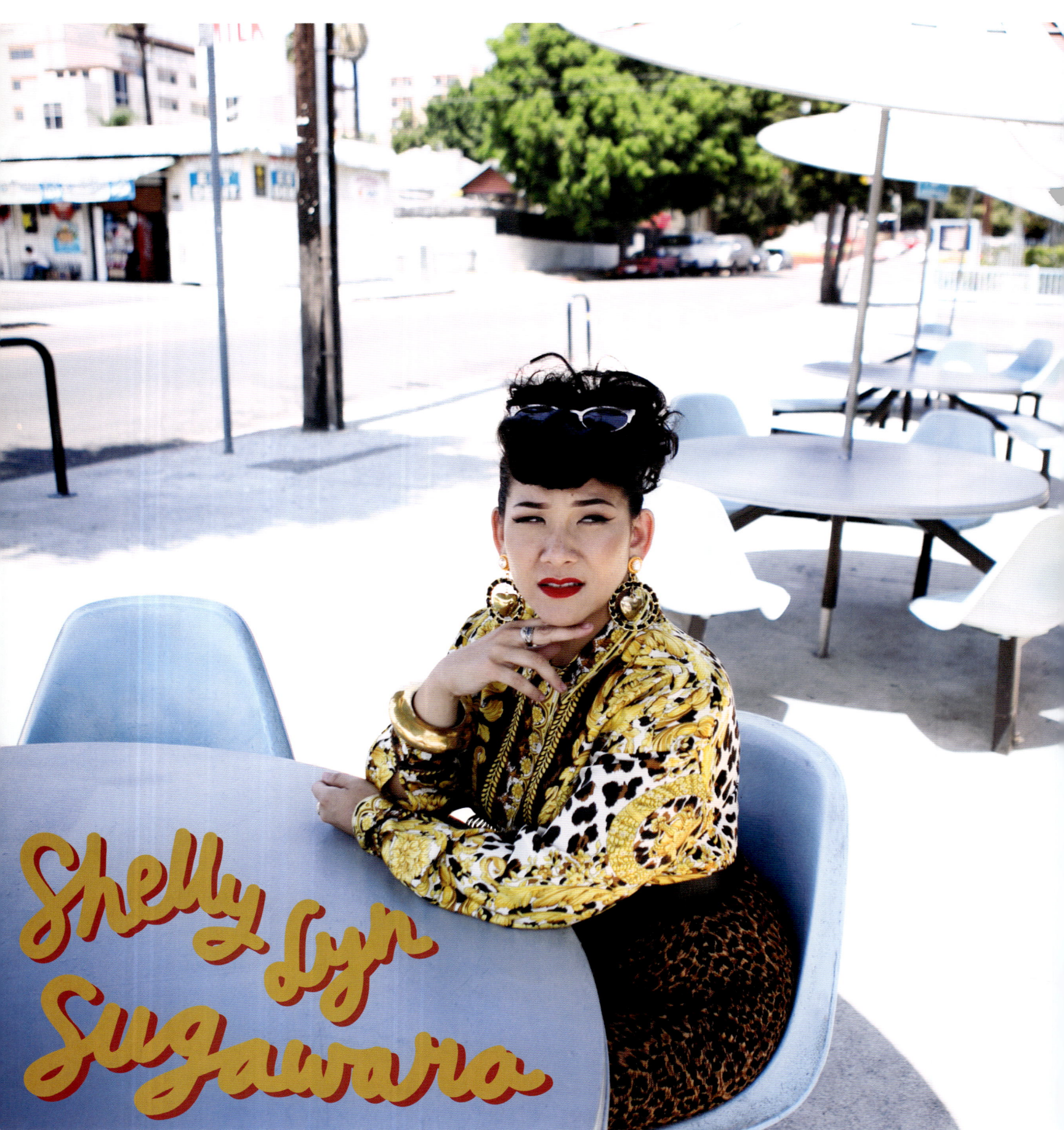

SHELLY LYN SUGAWARA
SERVING STYLE WITH A SMILE

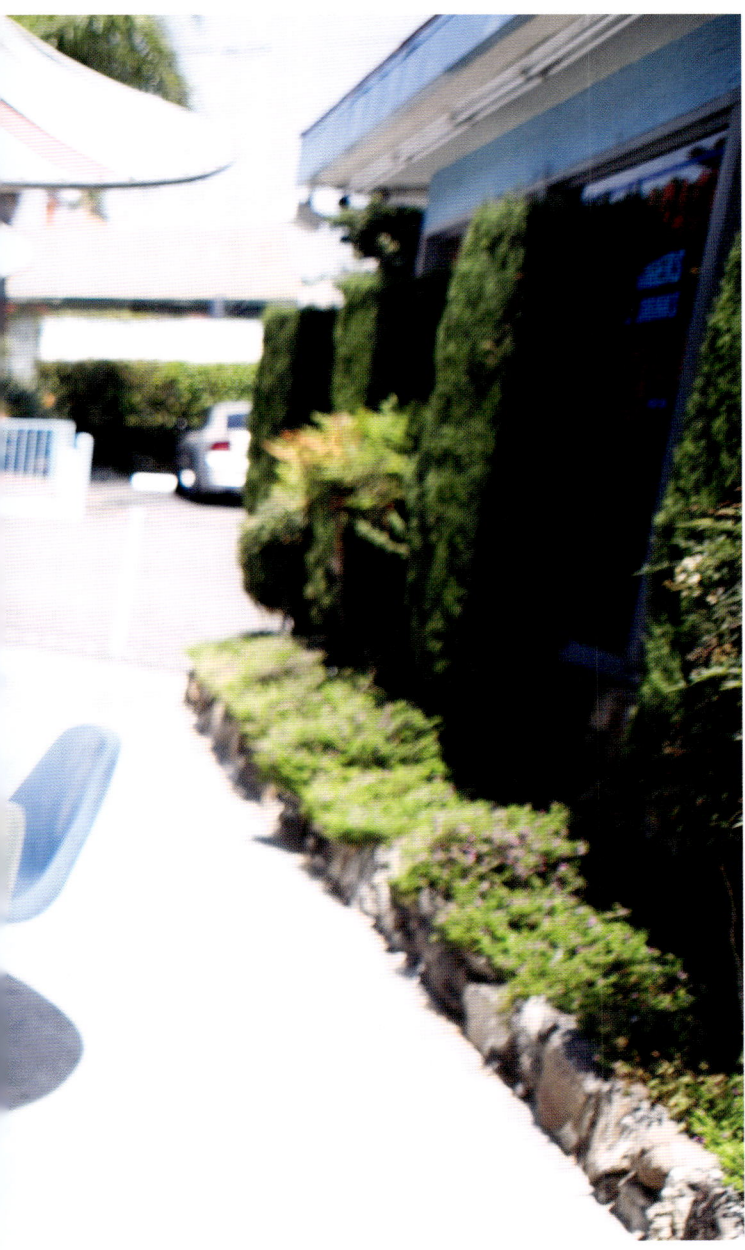

"My mom and her 1970s maroon-and-white polka-dot polyester pantsuit," she decides, when I ask what her earliest fashion memory is. "I remember the anxiety and torment I experienced on my way to school, thinking about the ridicule both she and I would face as she showed up in the conspicuous garment. Mind you, this was well into the 90s. I felt my heart racing as we pulled up in the parking lot; I couldn't escape my feelings of impending doom. I remember my mom opening the car door and stepping out of our wood-paneled station wagon—which was an embarrassment in itself—head held high, with her glorious French twist and her signature fringe swoop. She smiled at me and totally disarmed my anxiety and embarrassment. At that exact moment I realized the true power of presentation and how confidence was the key to making anything look good—even an outdated, itchy, polka-dot pantsuit! I was in total awe of my mother's beauty, and how delivering the diva all came down to serving style with a smile."

This is just one of the countless, sweeping memories Shelly Lyn Sugawara relives today. Her reveries of Kauai, Hawaii, sound like verses from the Bible, or excerpts from a long and winding poetry medley. She'll look at you with her sparkling eyes and big old smile, and say things like: "The beautiful colors of the island have forever painted my memories, and have gifted me a lifetime of inspiration." She's half-German and half-Japanese. Her mom's side of the family has been in Hawaii for more than a hundred years, "even before Hawaii became a state." She'll talk about her family with such fervor and celebratory nostalgia that you wish you could take them all out for dinner.

Her grandmother Yasuko, for example, sounds like the chicest, feistiest little lady, "incredibly glamorous, her eyebrows always painted on with perfect precision, and her pout always the prettiest shade of pink." It was in grandma's wardrobe that Shelly Lyn discovered vintage. "By the time I went through everything," she remembers, "I ended up with a closet full of beautiful clothing, and a heart full of treasured memories—both of which I still have most of today." Grandma also encouraged seven-year-old Shelly to show her skill as a future artist, by equipping her with a stack of wax paper and "a handful of gloriously beautiful gold-colored wands of lipstick, each tube a different hue of pink." Shelly felt "like a mini-Picasso going through a pink period."

Shelly lives in Boyle Heights now. She has two cats; one named Sir Duke Dukerson Kitty Extraordinaire, after her uncle Duke who died the day she found the sick kitten, and the other, Kimchi. When I ask if the neighborhood's safe, she points at some of the illegible graffiti on the concrete walls. "Those are gang signs," she whispers. She feels sufficiently snug, even with the squatters who occupy the grimy house next door. She works at The Way We Wore, one of LA's best vintage stores, during the day, and designs her own jewelry line at home. "I decided I wanted to create consciously and use primarily vintage findings," she explains. "Vintage pieces have a richness and beauty to them that contemporary pieces lack."

So, you see: Shelly is the real deal, and if you ever meet her, she will no doubt dazzle you with her grandiose smile. Her outfits are serving "90% sass and 10% sparkle," so it's no wonder her friends say she lights up a room. And doesn't this page look a little brighter too?

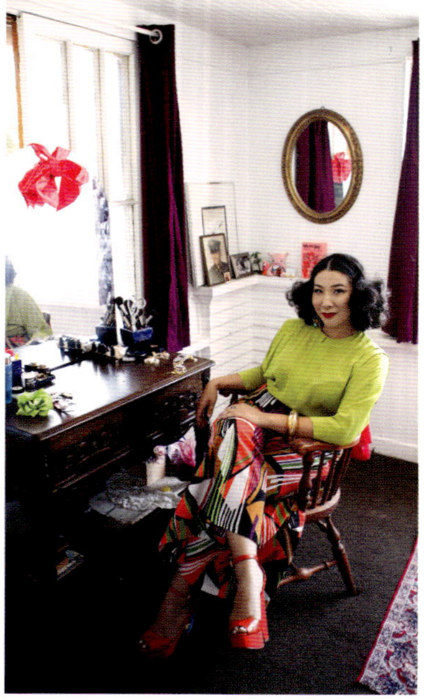

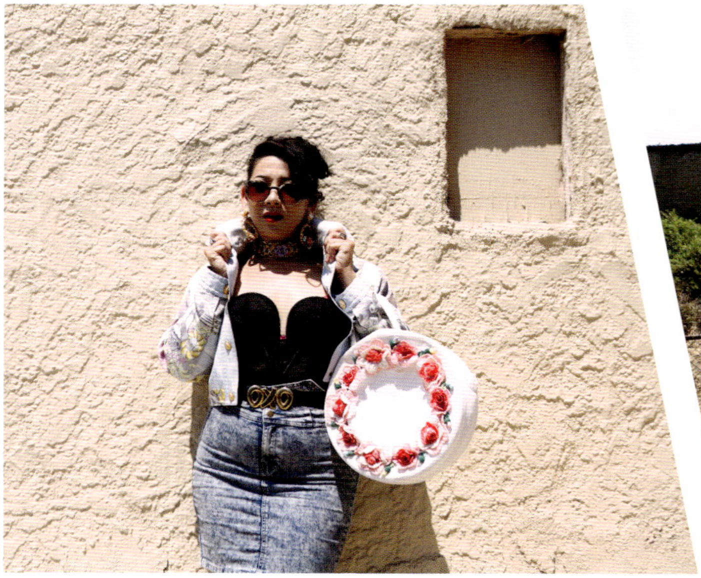

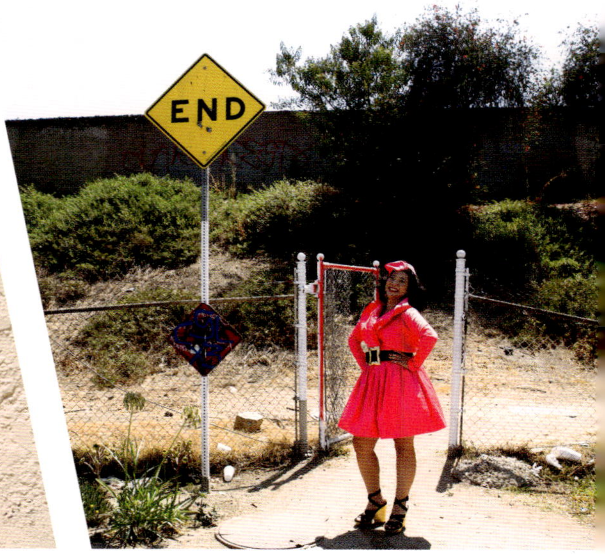

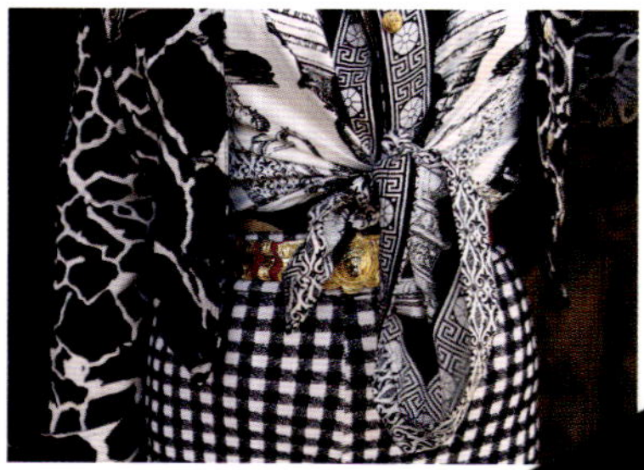

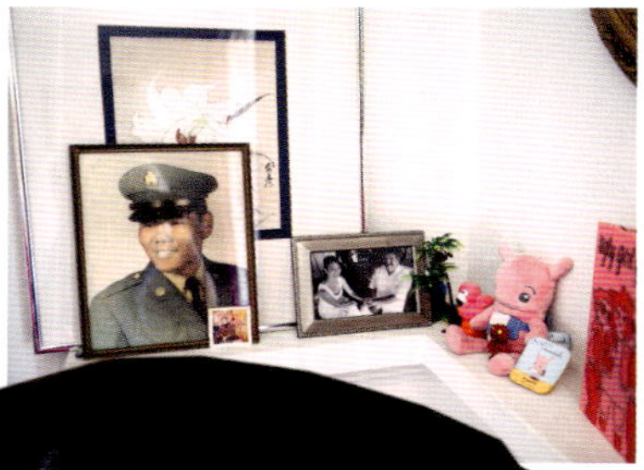

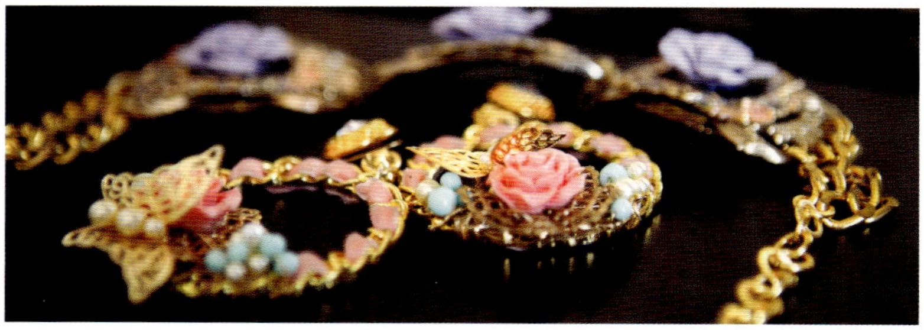

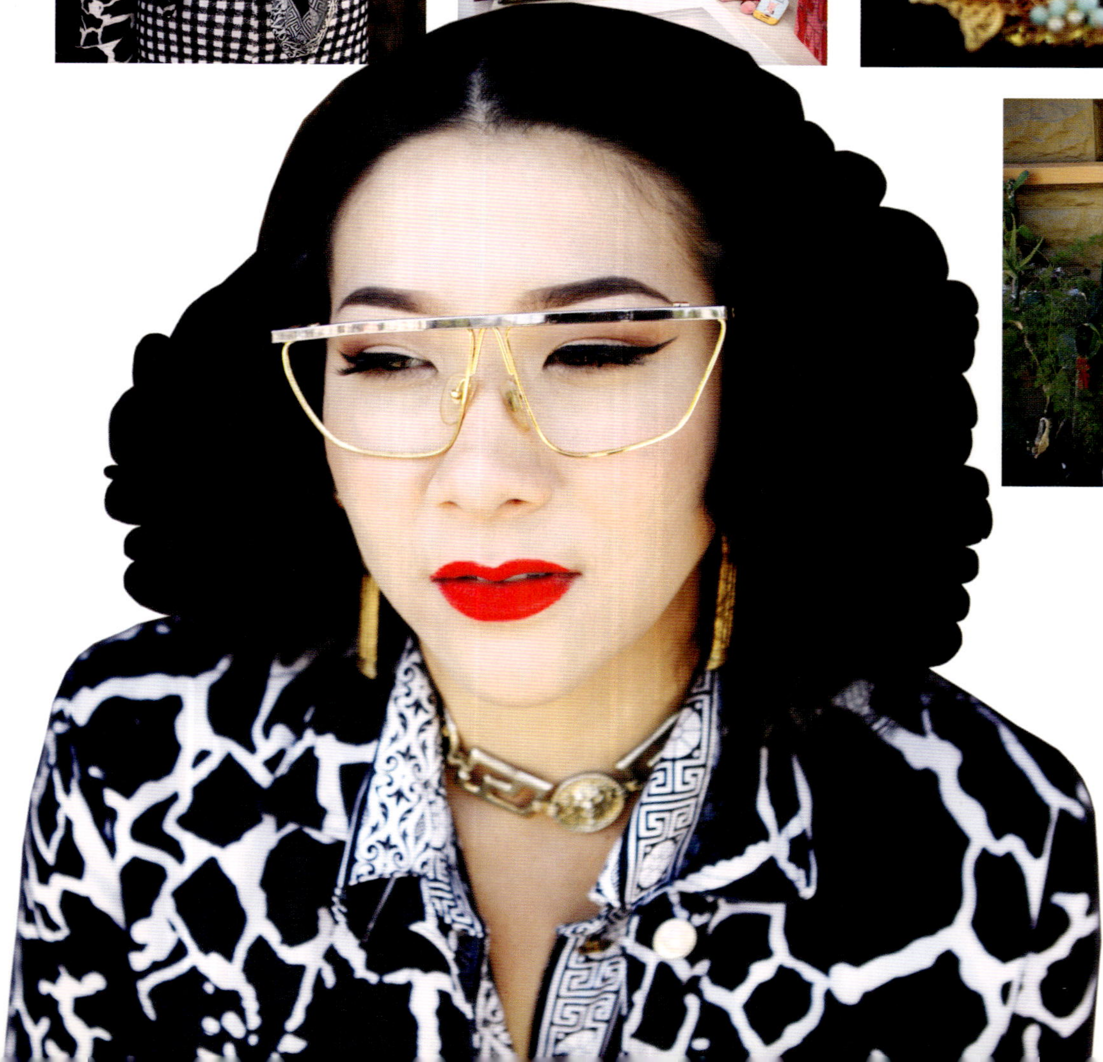

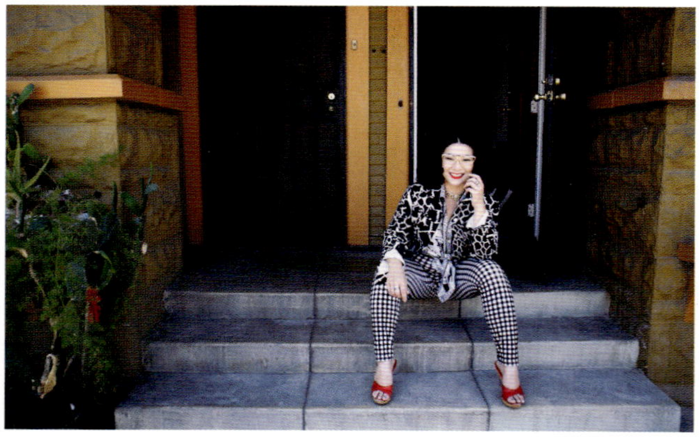

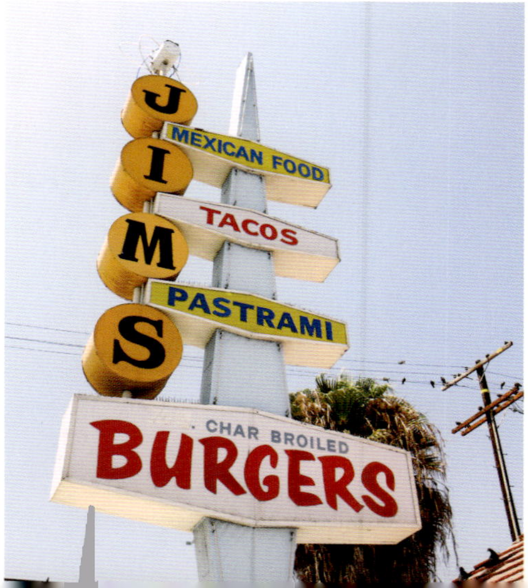

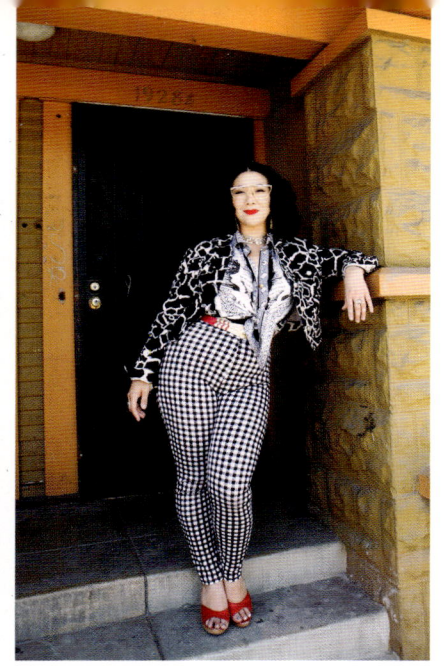
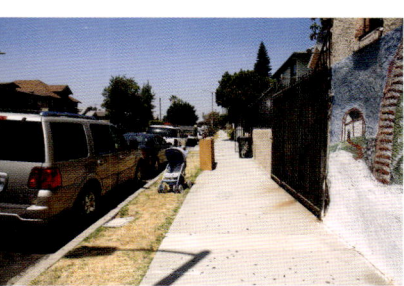
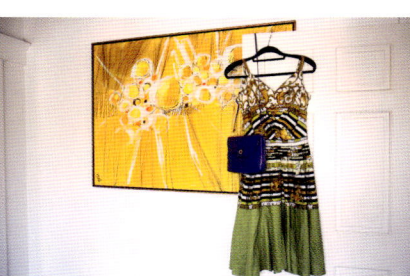
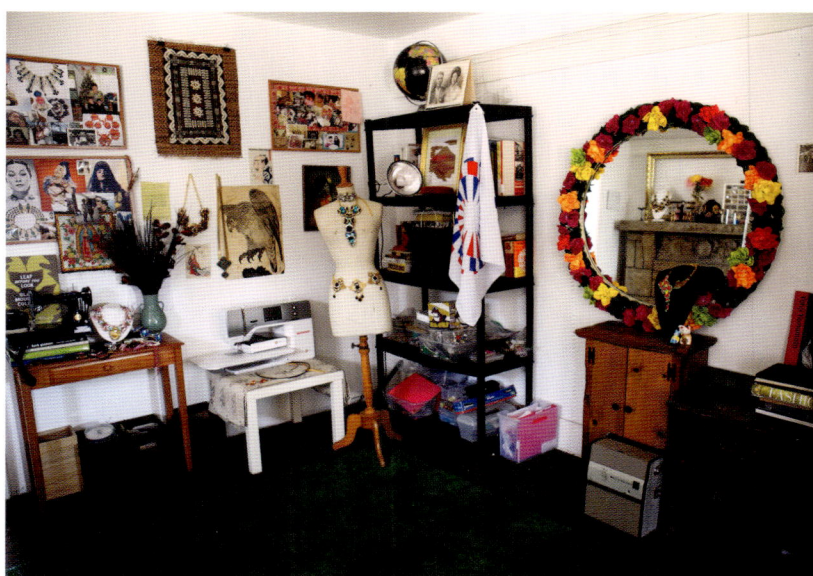
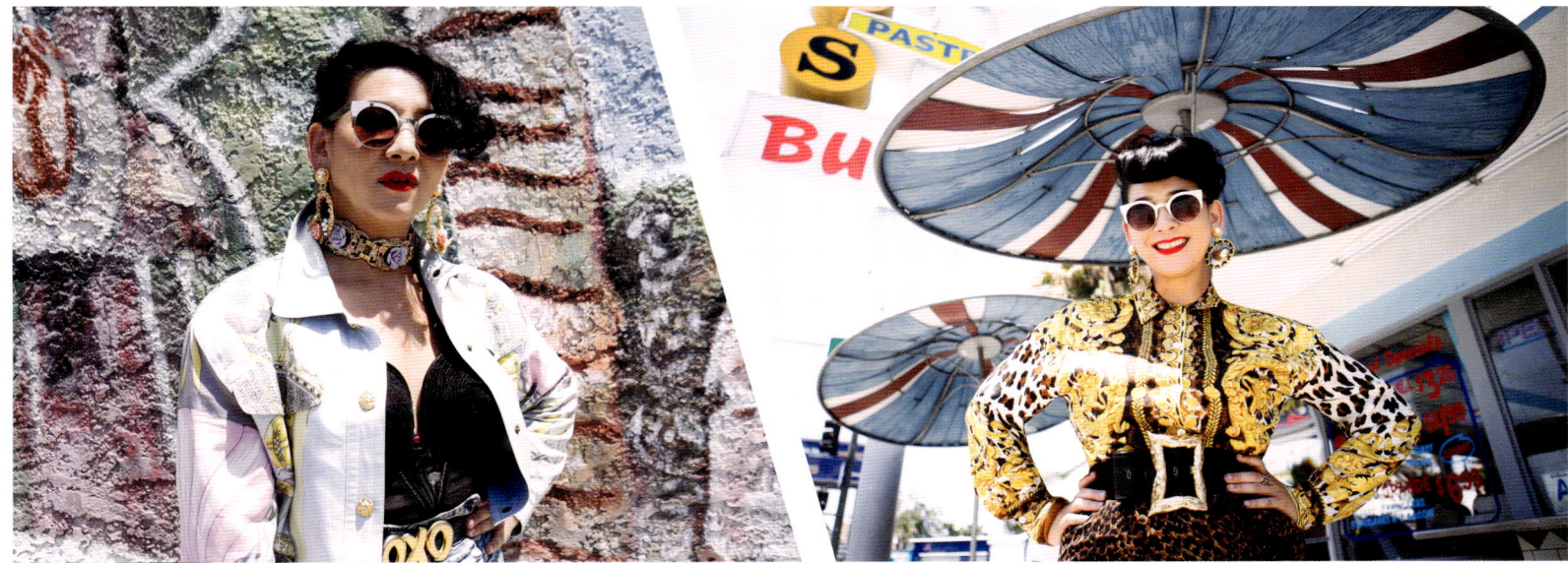
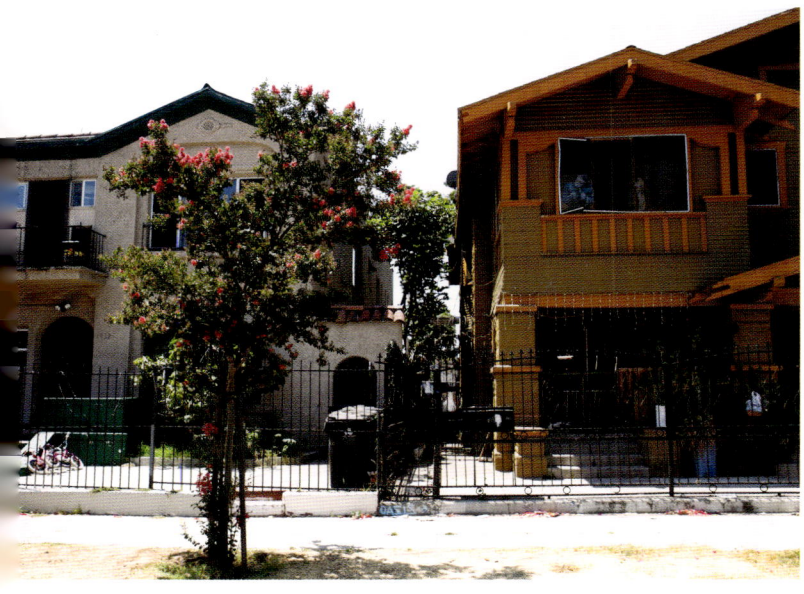
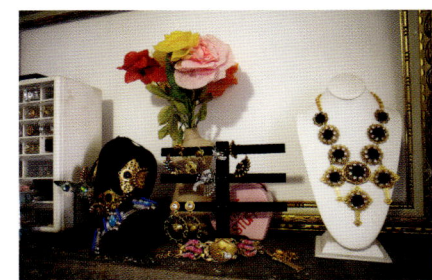
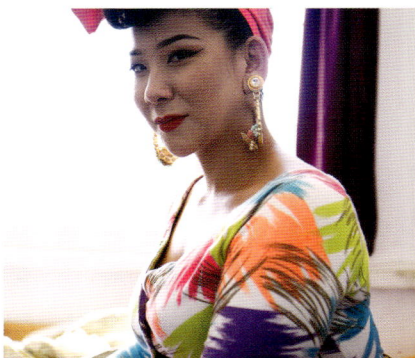
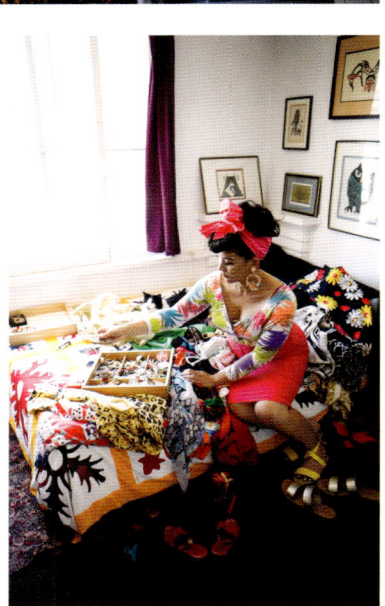

DENNIS BALMACEDA
EVERY LAST BUTTON

The Balmaceda residence does not have your typical husband and wife arrangement. Dennis is undoubtedly the man of the house—this is *his* furniture in the room, those are *his* hats on the wall, and that is *his* music playing on the radio—but it's far more sophisticated than that. Dennis is like the Frappuccino of alpha males. He's a dude with a penchant for flare. He loves his cats—he calls himself a proud "father of three" and "that weird guy with cats." He grew up with two older sisters whose magazines were his prime sources of fashion in the 90s. And he, not his wife, takes up all the closet space. "Gia is about to kill me because of my clothes," he laughs. "Recently, we moved from a one-bedroom apartment into a two-bedroom with two walk-in closets to accommodate all of my vintage. My poor wife has a small capsule wardrobe of like 20 pieces, and the rest is all mine. Oops!"

It's a healthy and perhaps natural obsession, because as a full-time menswear blogger, Dennis lives and works for his clothes, and he treasures them to the point of hoarding. He recently purged 25% of his closet and donated it to charity, so he believes that disqualifies him as a clinical case, "It was really, really hard for me to part with my things," he admits, "but I did it. When you don't grow up with much, every last button seems to matter." Dennis has no memory of his real mom, and his dad passed away in the Philippines when he was four. His aunt and uncle adopted him when he was just nine months old and emigrated with their family to the States. "I was treated like one of their own," he says with a sense of relief, "but in some ways I felt one step removed. I grew up with many cousins, mostly on my dad's side, and I was very close with them. But it was hard to see them with biological parents and siblings. I think growing up the way I did made me appreciate the little things and always feel grateful."

Anyone who follows the sartorial dealings of Dennis Balmaceda online will attest to his tenacity and insatiable desire for good content. He's a perfectionist without trying to look perfect. There's always that nice balance between street and classic, much like his style icons Johnny Depp, James Dean, Andre 3000, and his own father. "My dad always wore great, tailored, American legacy brands," he remembers. "I like to emulate the way he dressed and learn about the brands he was so faithful to. I also loved professional wrestling, and I'm not embarrassed to admit that it's still something I follow to this day. My flare for the dramatic is probably influenced by the bombastic, colorful wrestlers I idolized as a kid."

Dennis started blogging in 2008, two years after graduating high school and while working a less-than-fruitful job as a travel agent. He saved up money for a digital camera and started posting his daily outfits on Facebook. "I remember getting very low likes and negative comments," he complains, "because people thought I was just being weird and vain. Then a friend of mine told me about Lookbook and I discovered Tumblr and suddenly, I had a real platform and community to foster what I was doing." He created a blog called *Look Rich, Shop Cheap* in 2010. "My reputation of being the thrifty, vintage blogger really began here. I think my appeal is that I look like a regular guy who is confident in dressing how he wants. I've never been your typical drop-dead-gorgeous, boy-next-door, model-looking Blogger. I was just a racially-ambiguous brown kid who a had small bedroom and dreamed of collaborating with brands." Case in point.

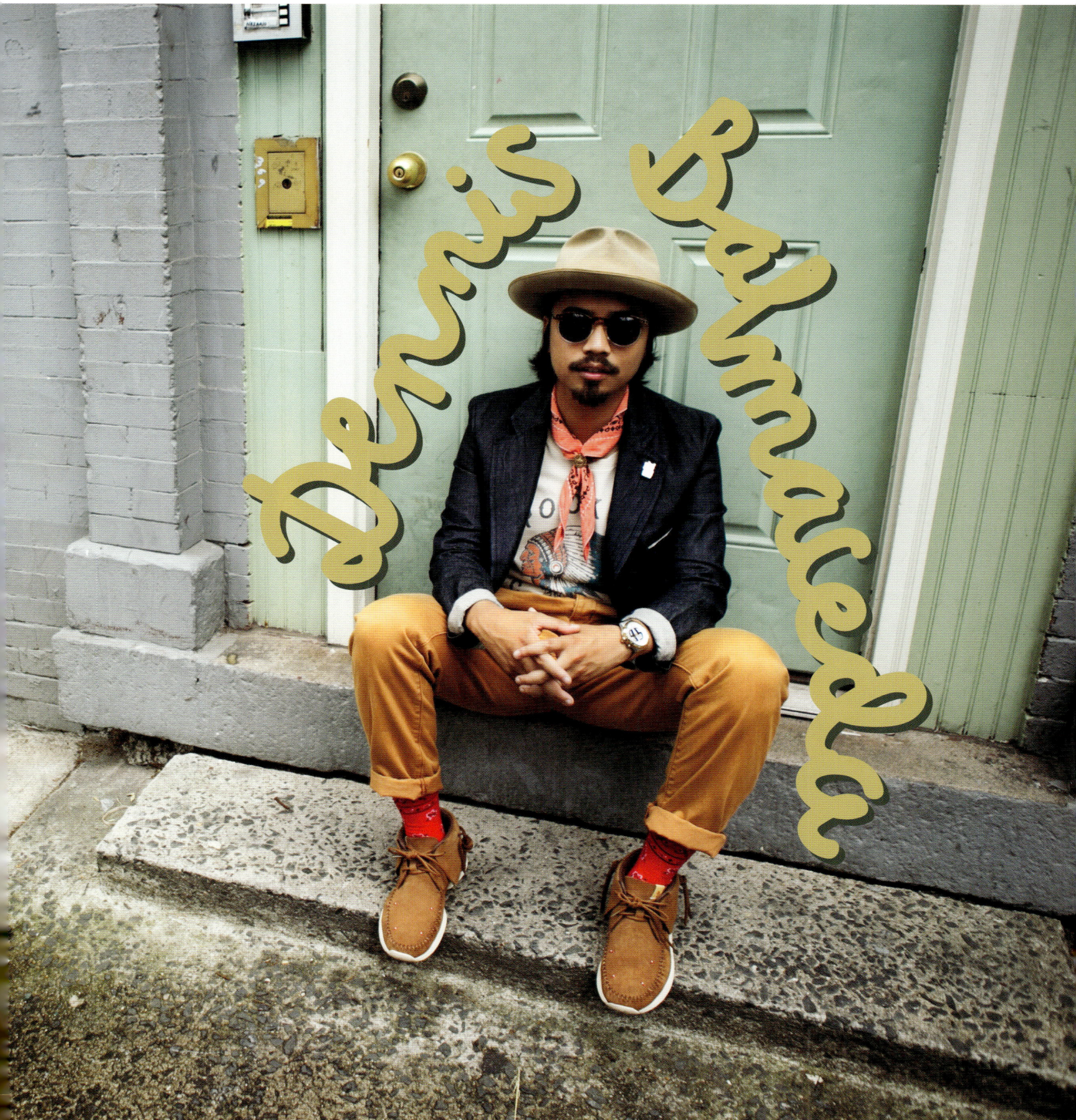

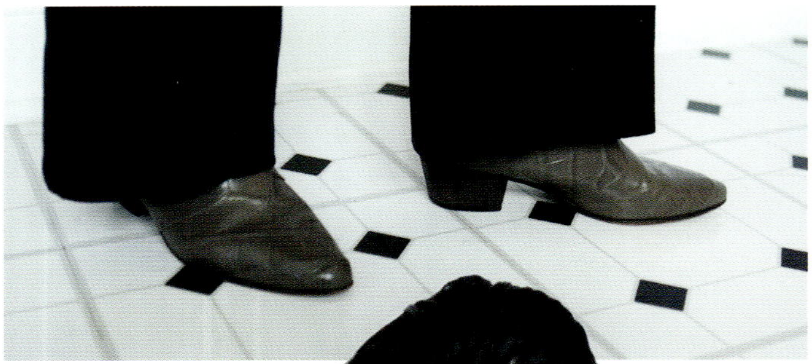

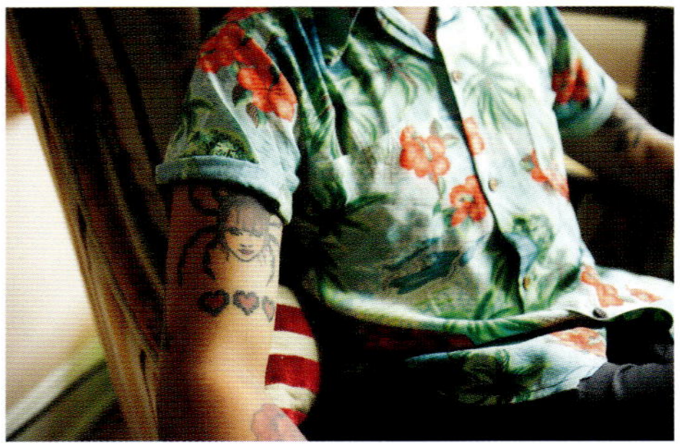

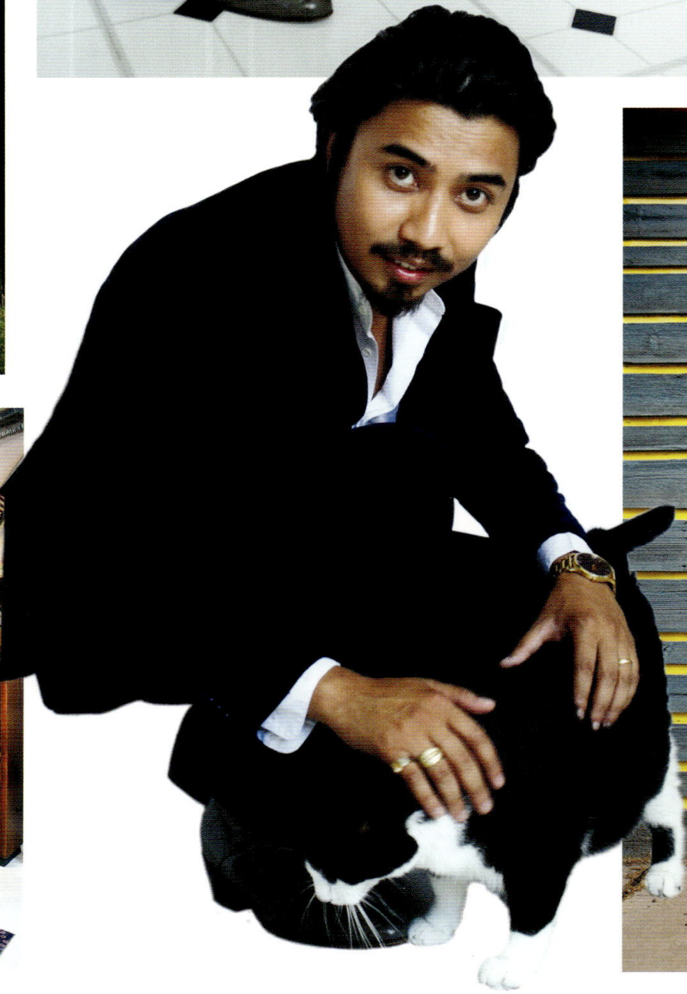

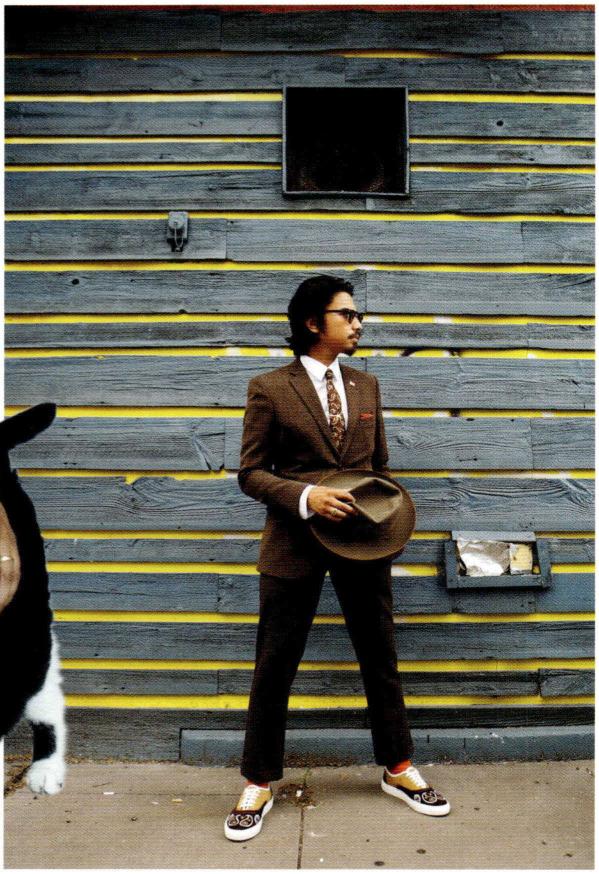

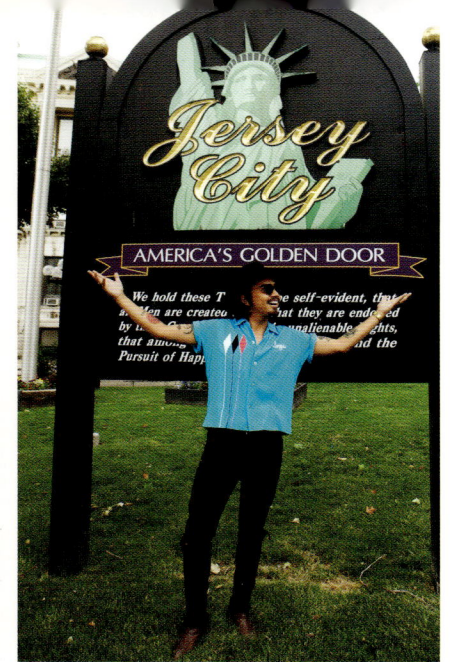
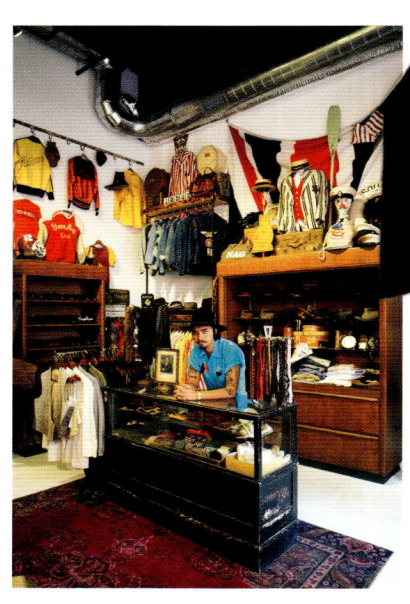
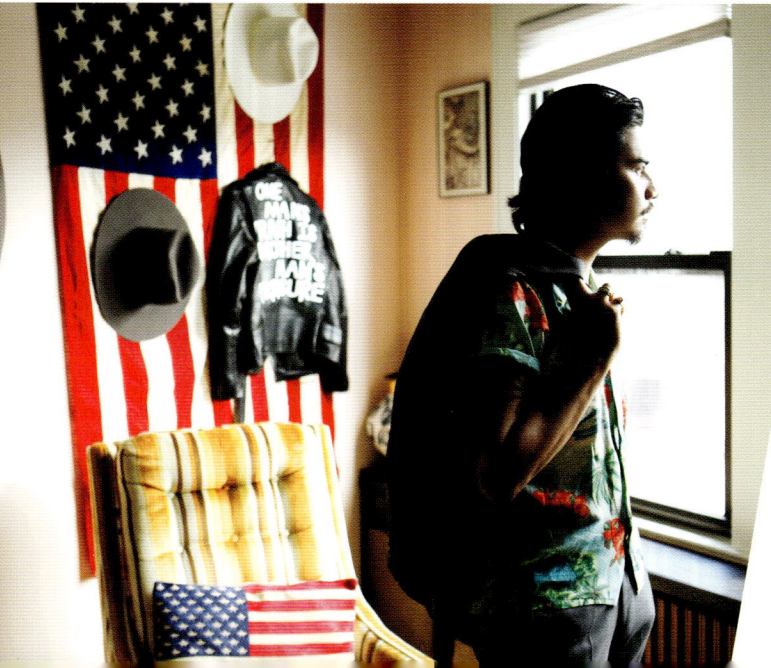
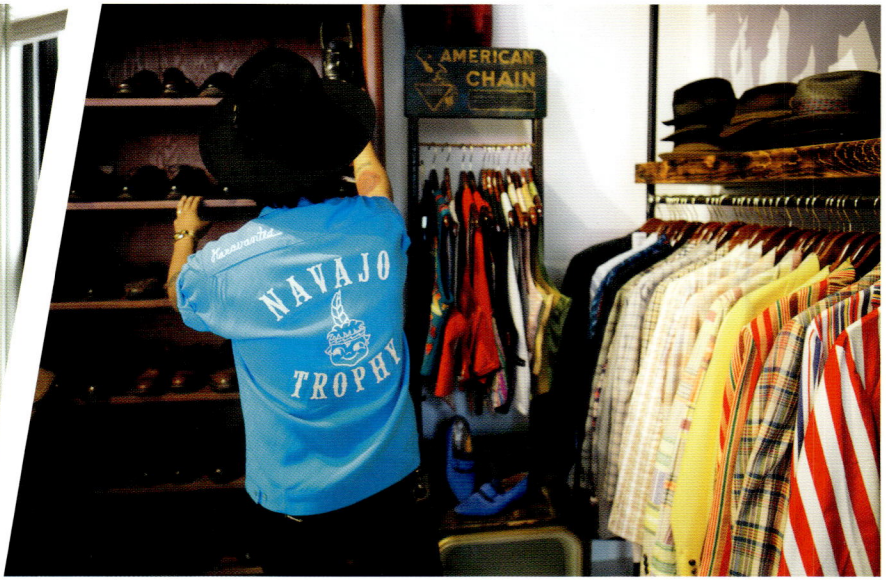

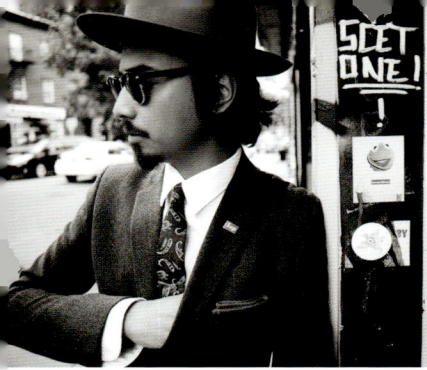
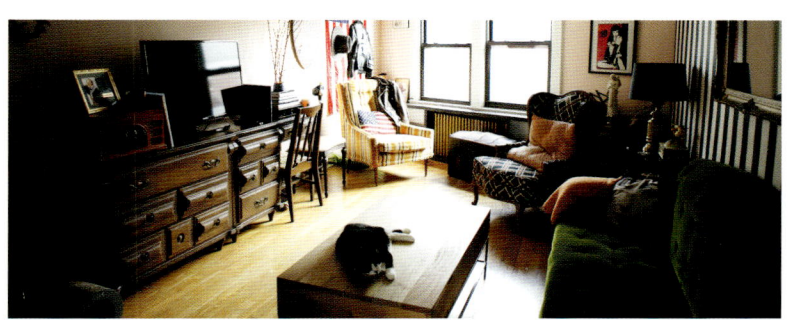
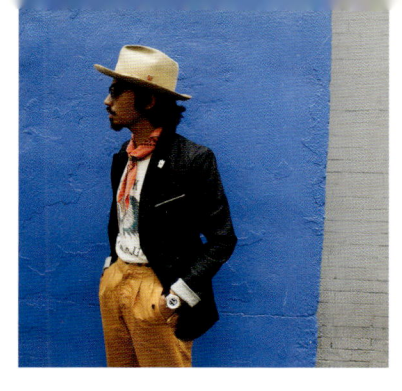
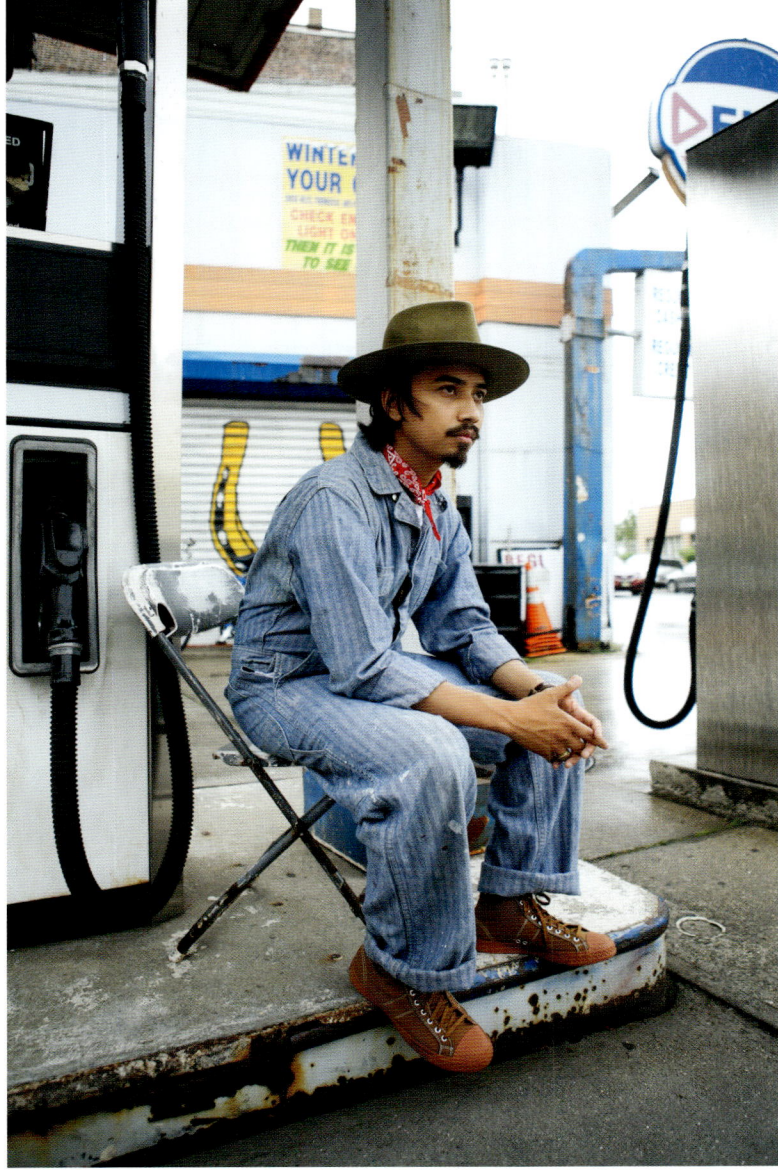
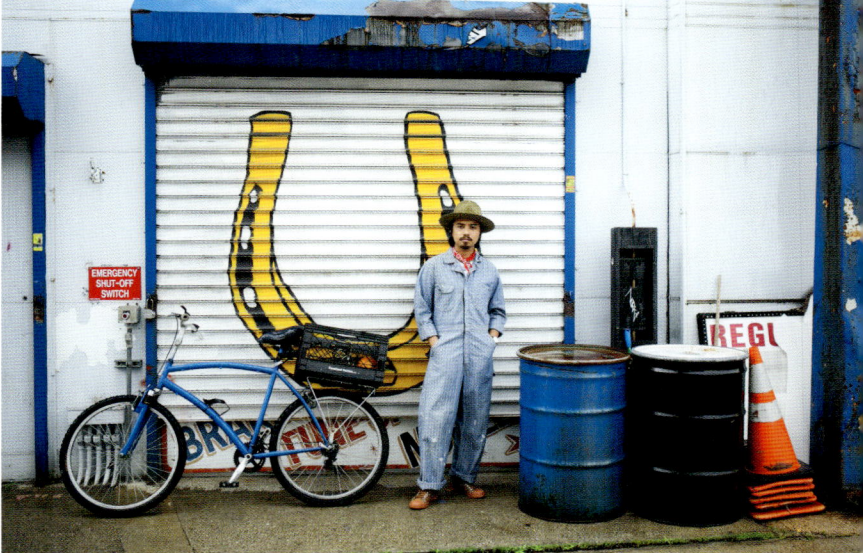
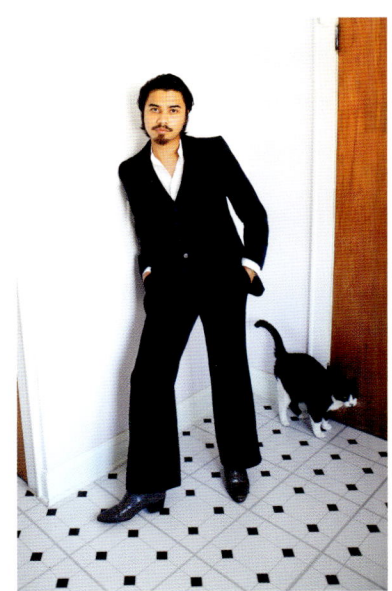
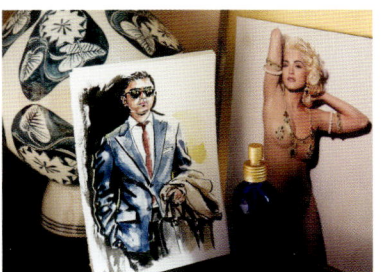
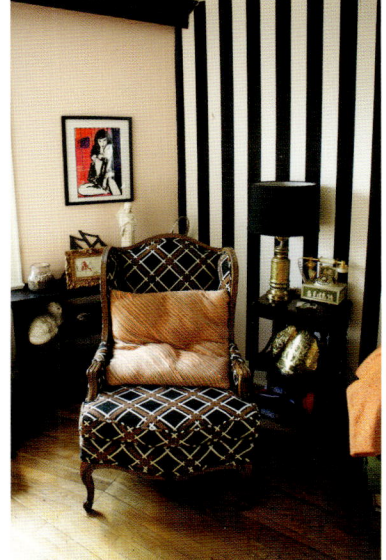
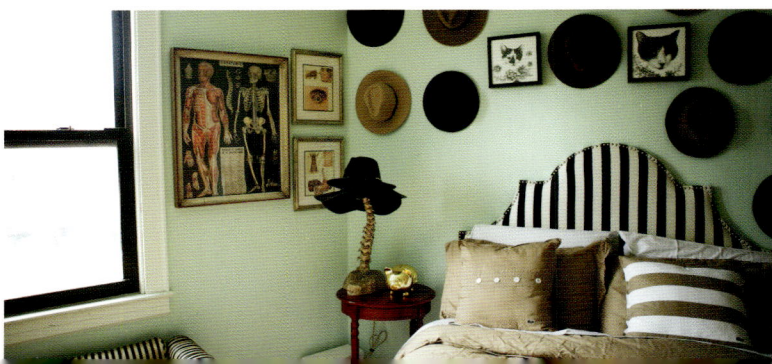
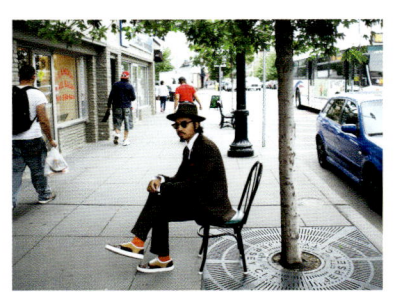

DJUNA BEL
GLAMOUROUS TOMBOY

She calls it "Cameltoe City," that awkward moment when you're trying on a vintage jumpsuit in the dressing room and realize it's too short for your torso. Djuna is that enviable combination of tall and small. If she ever had a nickname in high school—she's not aware of one, but is certain she was made fun of—it could have been anything from Bean Pole to Supermodel. "Honestly, my WHOLE teenage life was a fashion disaster," she cringes. "I went from basketball shorts and skate shirts, to desperately trying to fit in and not being able to find pants long enough or slim enough for my string-bean body." It's one of those physical, grass-is-greener-on-the-other-side inconveniences she soon learned to use to her advantage: "I never mind when things are very, very, inappropriately short."

Djuna Annajna Bel, 33, grew up between Groningen, Holland, and Santa Cruz, California. Her family traveled a lot when she was young. "We spent some time in Bali, Indonesia, and all over Europe," she remembers. "It seemed a bit harsh to try to adjust to Western life since my early, early childhood was very free." Her first fashion memory occurred at the airport in Jordan. "I was obsessed with all the amazing jewelry the women wore," she recalls. "I tied toilet paper around my wrists, neck, and ankles and called them my jewels for the whole flight. I was a weird kid..." She moved to New York at the age of 17, worked briefly as a model, opened a vintage store called Fox & Fawn, took on a few wardrobe assisting jobs to pay the bills, and moved to LA in 2010. That's when she took the plunge and dove into styling full-force. She's one of the cool girls in LA, and surprisingly less hyphenated than most. She lives in Highland Park with her artist/designer/sculptor fiancé, Nicolai Haas.

"We didn't grow up with much money so I was always a thrift shopper," she says. "But when I finally realized that vintage was cool—maybe my freshman year of high school—it really changed my fashion life." Djuna has amassed an impressive vintage collection that spans a few closets in her Highland Park house, the basement, and two shipping containers in West Adams that together take up about 700 square feet. "Honestly, I think I am a hoarder," she fears. "I like dressing myself up, but I love finding things that I know would look amazing on other people. Working in the industry has really helped. Now I buy those pieces for "work" and less because I am just an obsessed collector. I am always looking, but less for a specific piece and more for something that inspires me: color, shape, something that is truly unique. I want something that no one else has."

Djuna's home is the LA modernist's take on a tree house. It has sunken and elevated levels, wooden floors and decks, multiple exposures, luscious, tropical surroundings, and a few happy cats nestled in the window. The couple has just finished remodeling the interior. It was a formidable operation but it paid off. "I'm so excited to spend time here!" gushes Djuna. "Lately I'm really into watching TV at home. We have a really nice set-up and I realized I have been deprived of cable my entire life—I have been missing OUT!" She plays records for fun, makes blood orange mimosas like a champ, and organizes dinner parties. "We might be adding a pool next!" she hopes. "I may never leave my house again!"

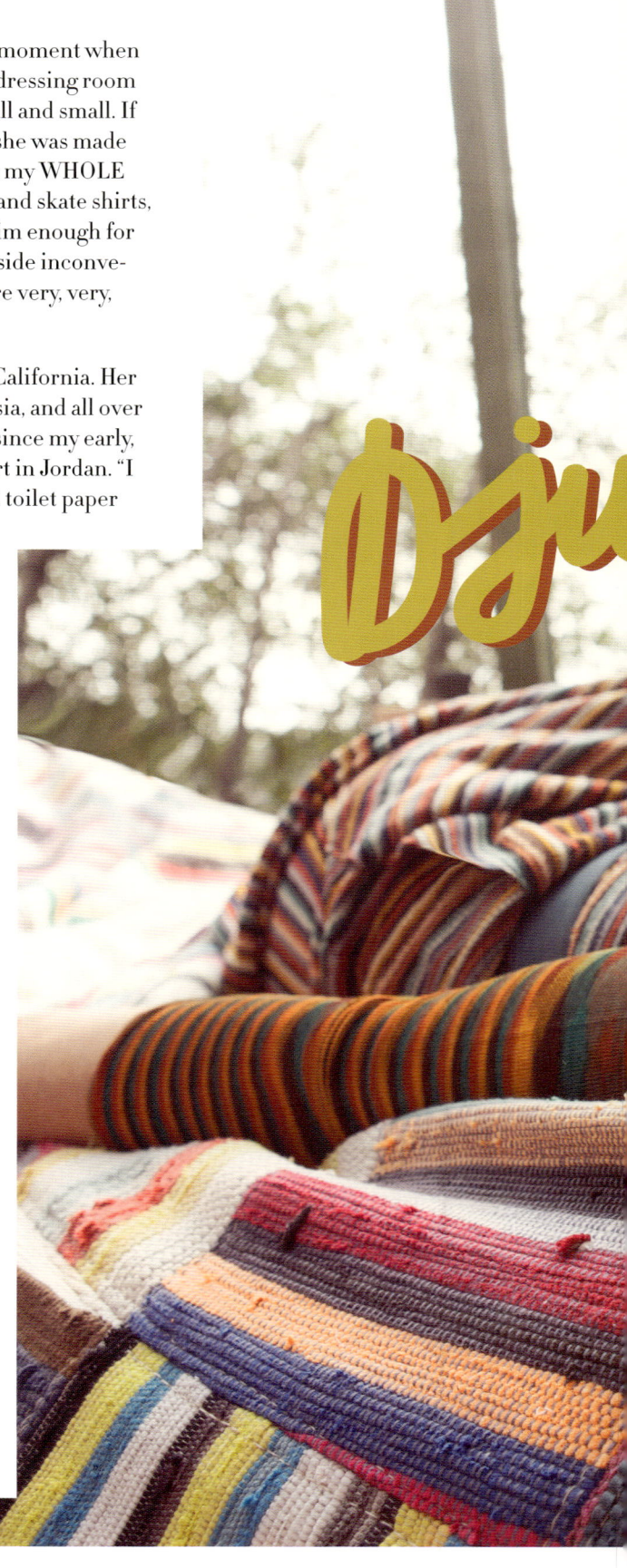

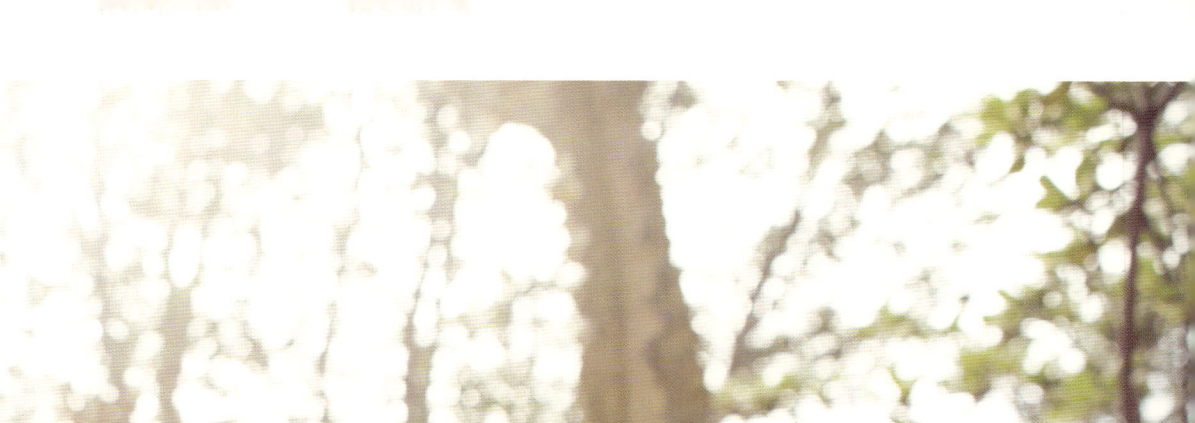

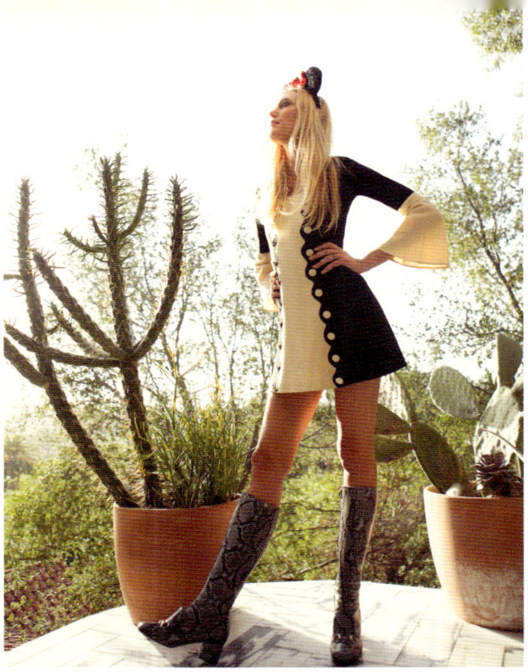

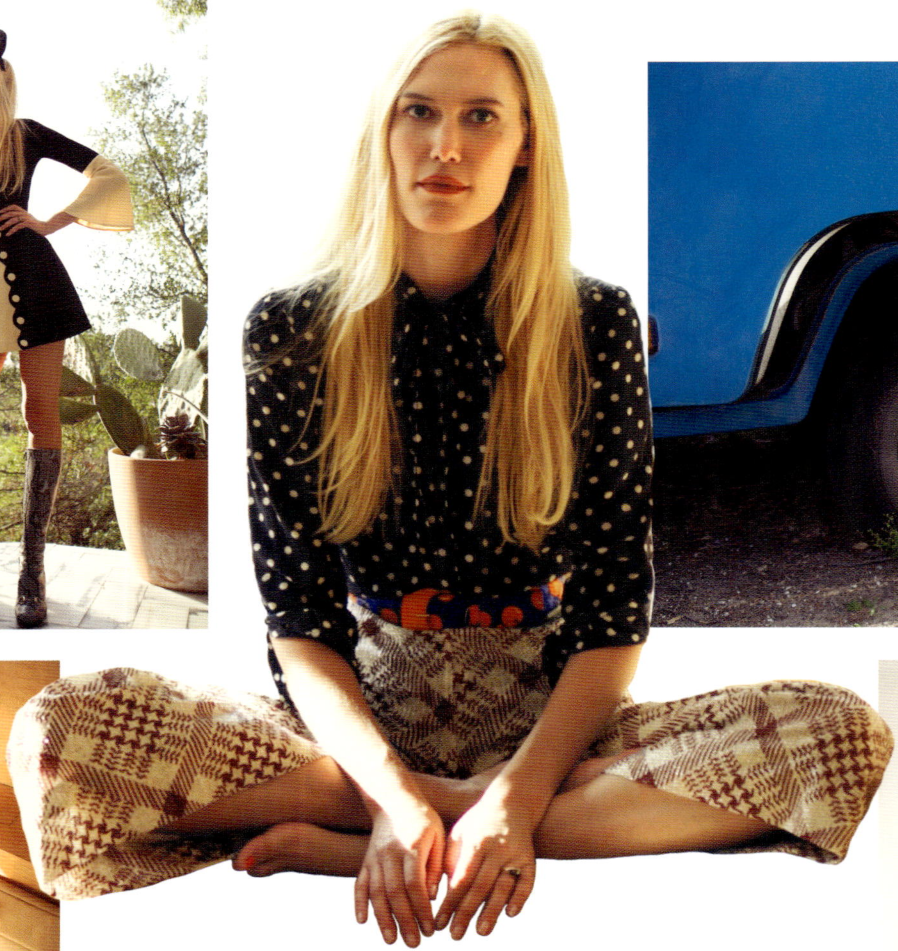

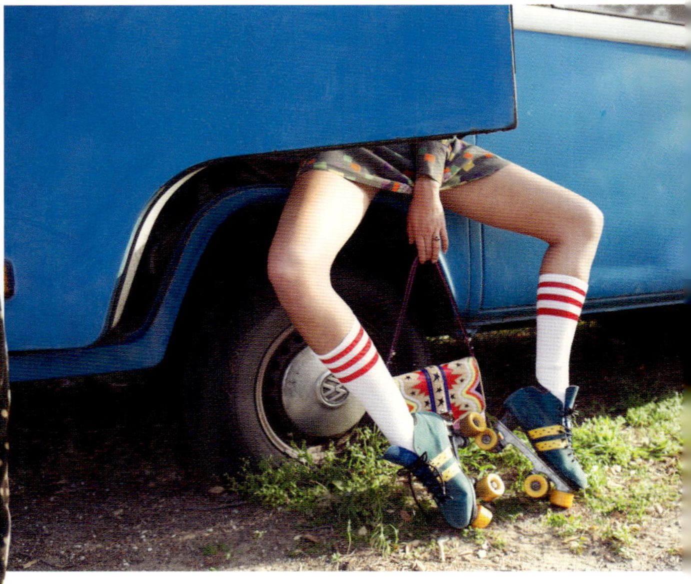

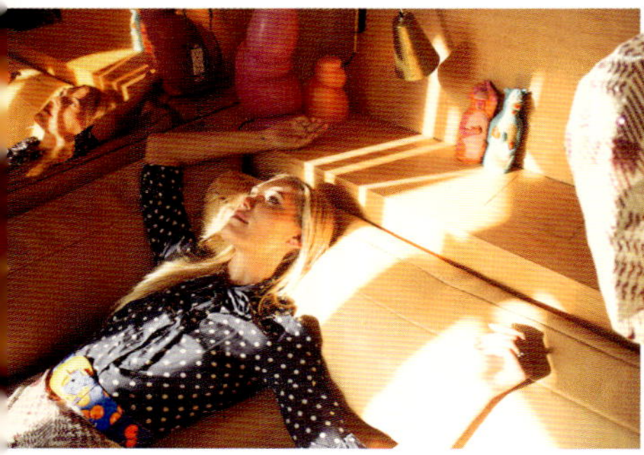

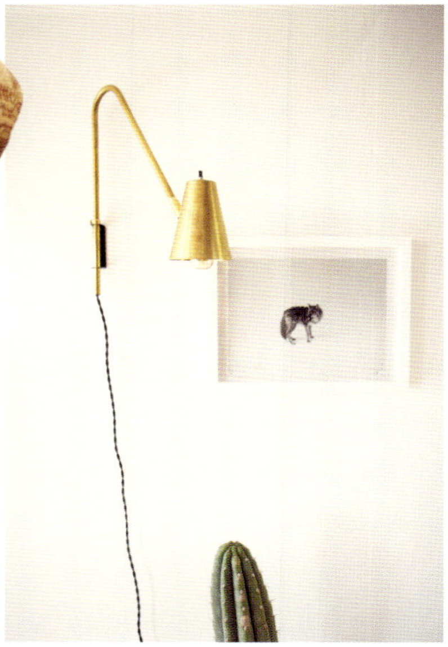

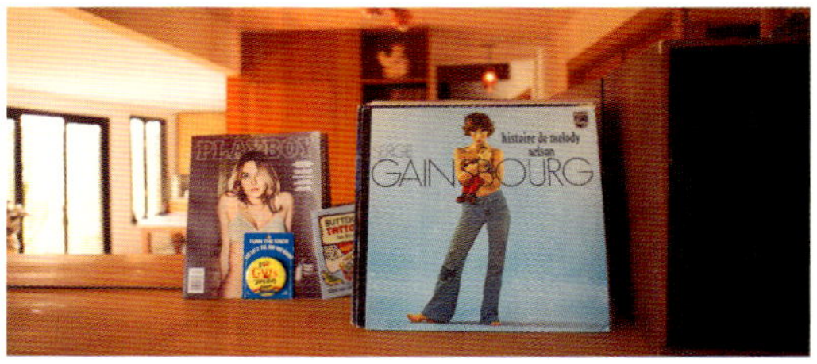

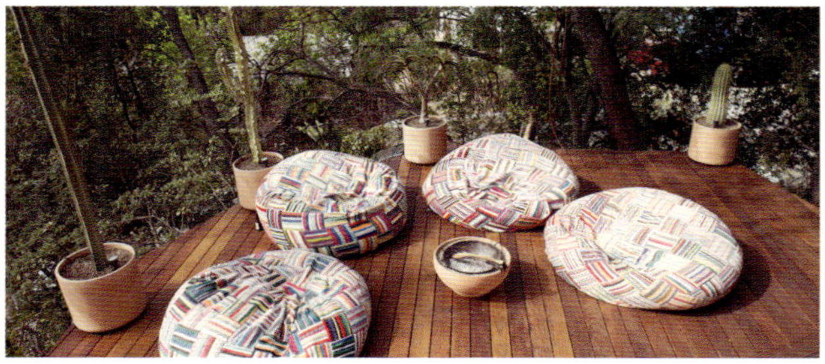

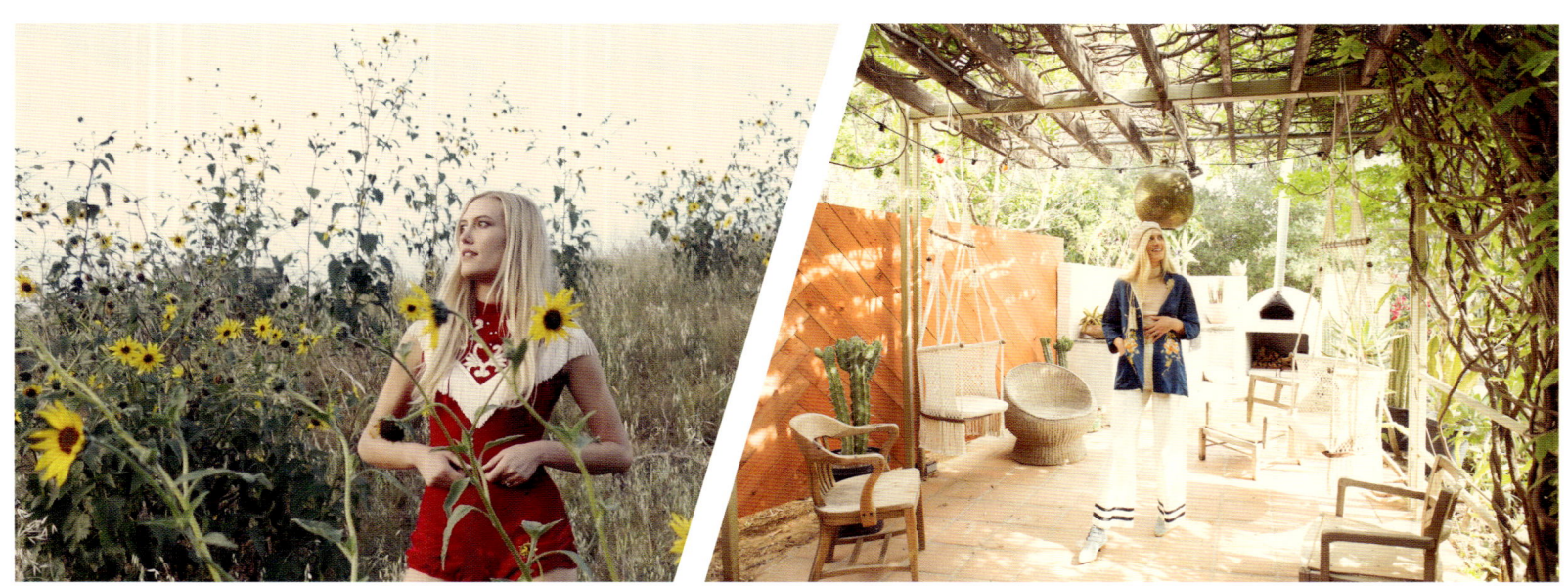

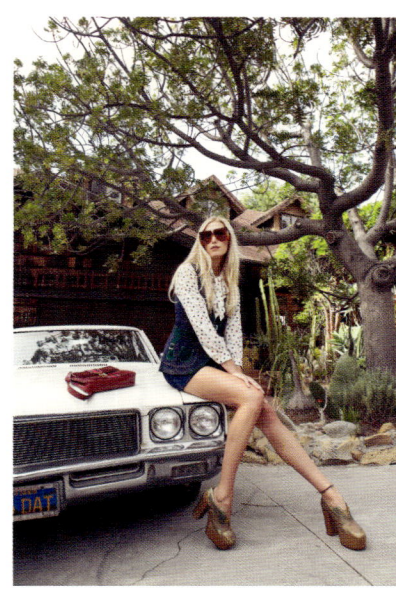
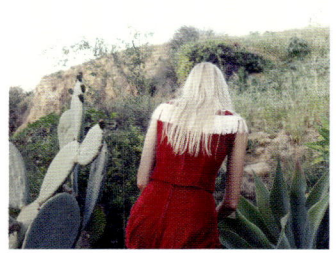
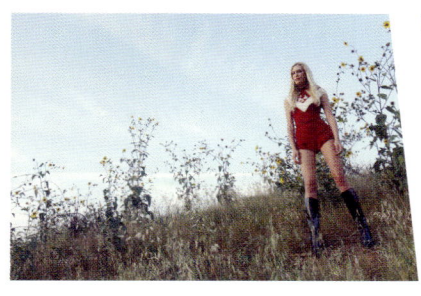
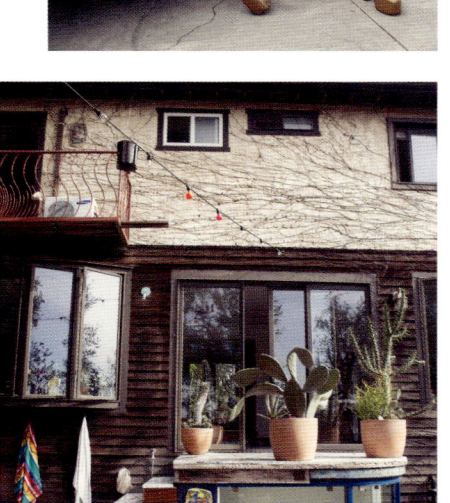
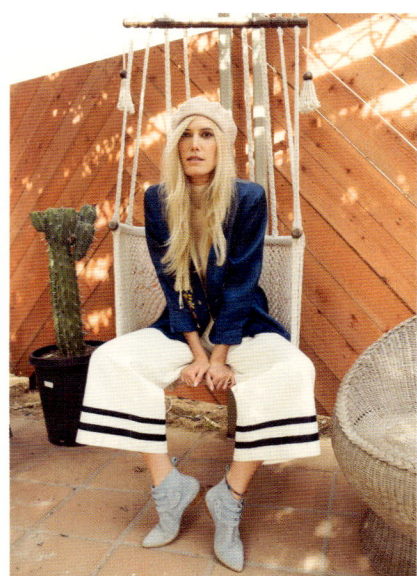
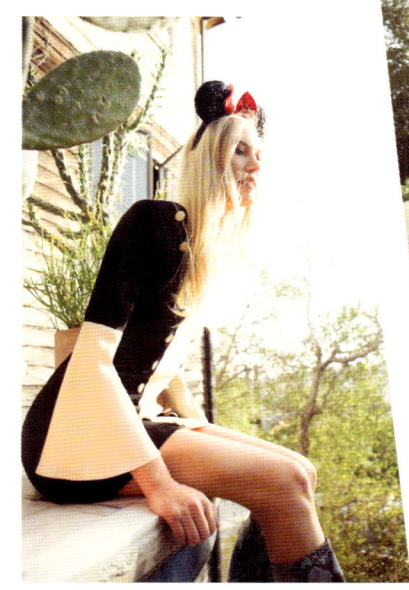
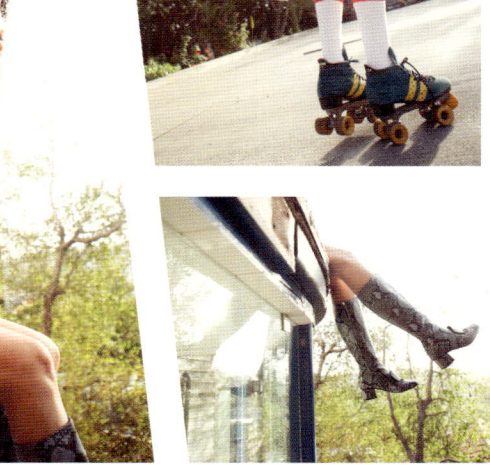
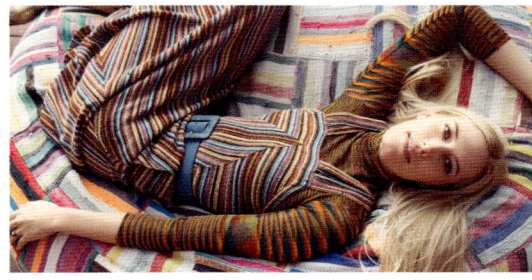
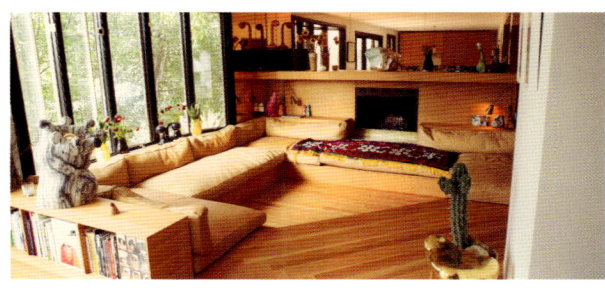
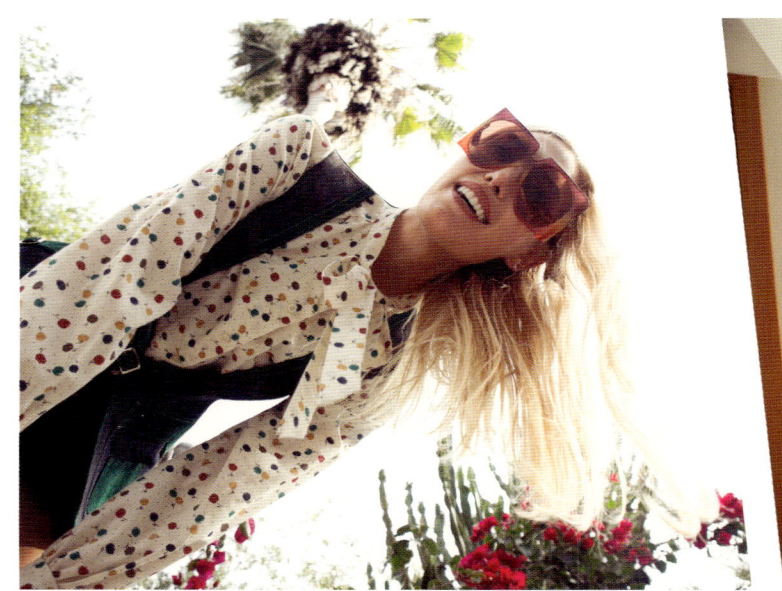
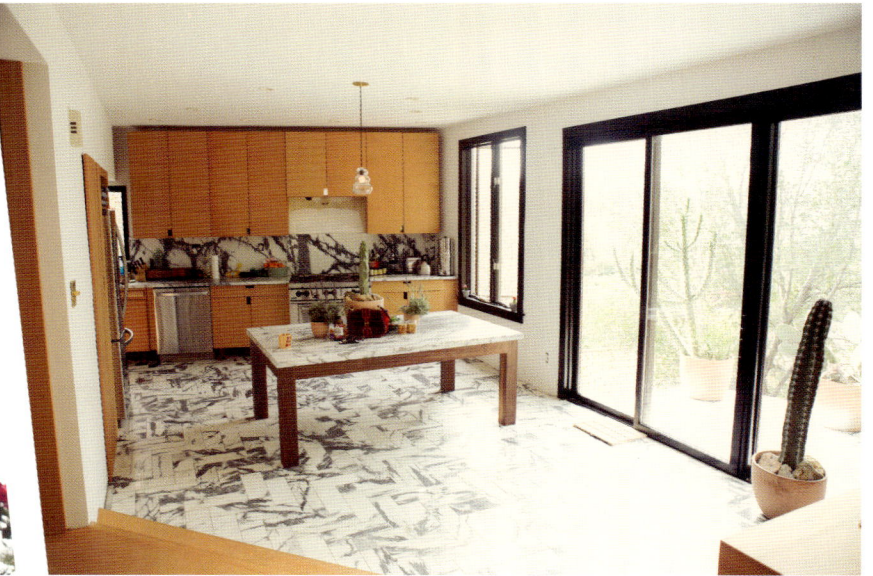

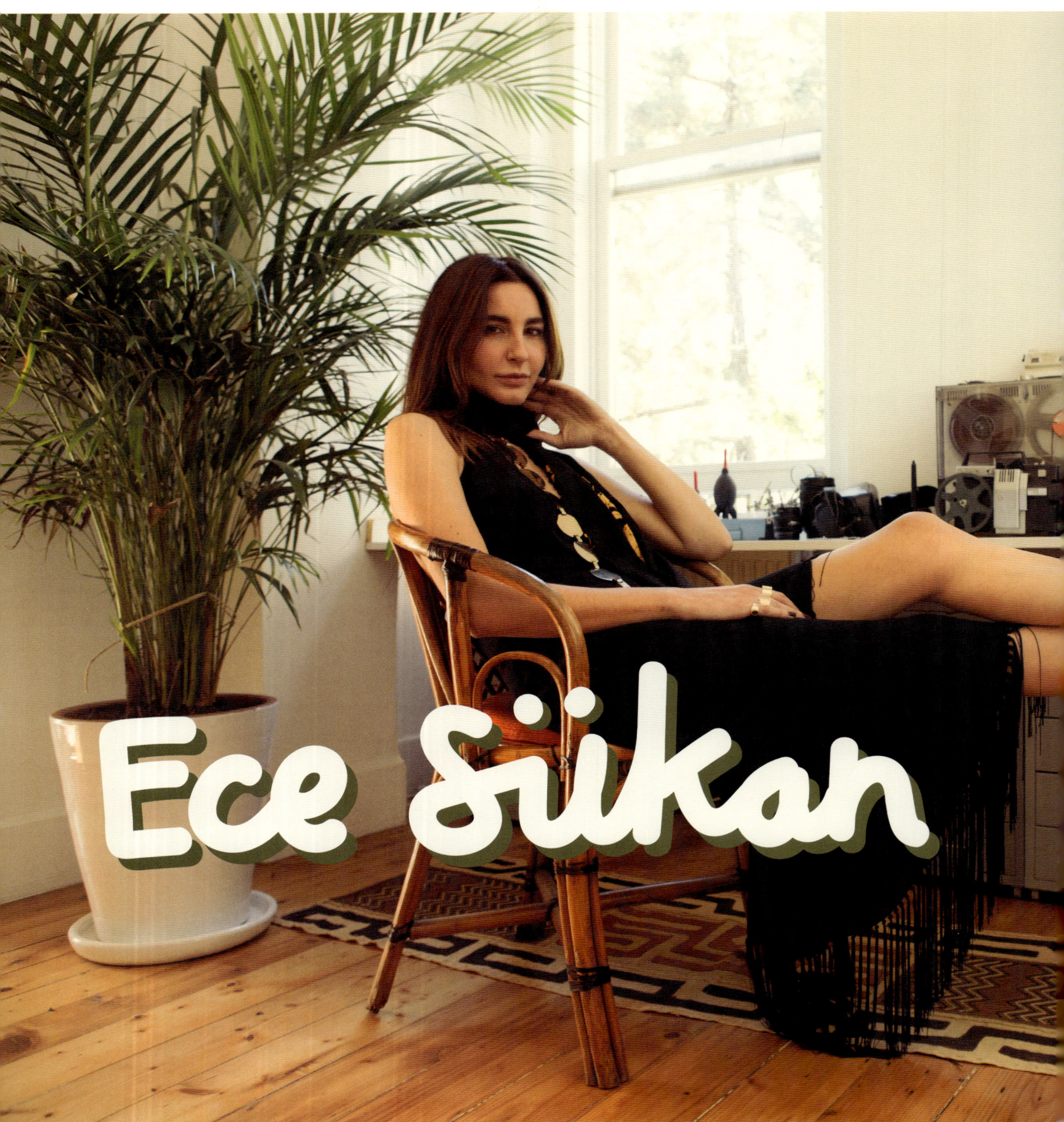

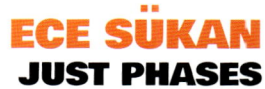

ECE SÜKAN
JUST PHASES

It's only by chance that I catch Ece Sükan in Instanbul. I'm on a 48-hour layover to Georgia and she's between Milan and New York mostly, with a few stints in Turkey to visit family, clean up her archive, redecorate her studio, and work on her new project, Pera64. And it's also only by chance that I found out she's a massive vintage collector. Growing up behind the theater curtains, she watched her mom perform plays in impressive costumes and adopted a kindred eye for style and nostalgia. Ece started collecting seriously when she studied Fashion Styling at FIT in New York and opened Istanbul's first high-end vintage store two years later.

Ece's mom was an icon back then, and instilled not only a love for fashion, but also a love for the stage. "I was 'the kid' doing the ballet, doing the children's movies, dubbing TV series, including Pippi Longstocking! I had a TV show as well, with the most famous pop singer on national TV! It was sci-fi, the year was 2026." And even though an acting or fashion career seemed like the obvious path for her—she was obsessed with fashion magazines and decided early on she would be a stylist—Ece went on to study Psychology. "Back then, there were no options [for fashion] in Ankara," she explains, "and psychology was my other interest. I was a pretty good student. I graduated university with honors. And the university we're talking about is one of the most difficult-to-enter and hard-to-finish in Europe."

We meet in the Galatasaray/Cukurcuma area at her brother Arslan's apartment. It's mid-November but we don't need jackets yet. The afternoon sun is blaring through the third-floor windows, casting a soft, yellow sheen on the walls and wooden floors. Her studio is still under construction so she brought some of her collection here. Ece has incredible taste and the kind of style that makes her look, and feel, like a confident, modern woman—and sexy if I may add. (Sorry boys, she's taken!) She blends the past with the future to make it "now," and she doesn't have a uniform, just phases. "Typical doesn't exist with me," she states. "Or, let me say, a typical outfit of mine also changes with different periods. For some time I might be obsessed with wearing dresses, then jeans and shirts, then pants and coats." She shops instinctively, and designer names are just a bonus, not a must, even if her vintage clients demand it.

It feels peaceful and safe in this apartment, but outside these walls, the city is brimming with dissonance and unrest. President Erdogan was reelected a few days ago, despite the fact that he is extremely unpopular with the creative class. Ece worked as the Editor-at-Large of Turkish *Vogue* when it launched, and still writes for *Hurriyet* newspaper. "It's actually hard times, both psychologically and business-wise," reflects Ece in a deep and serious voice. "But at the same time, there is an amazing young generation, and potential, and spirit. Creative industries are obviously affected by the increasing authority of the government. So many journalists and writers are in prison right now! Freedom of speech doesn't exist anymore. How can a creative sector be creative with these fears and threats?"

It's a pertinent question that not only affects Turkey. The issues we face today impact us on a scale larger and more global than at any time in history. Even the very planet itself is at risk. "It is so depressing what's going on in Turkey and also in the world!" remarks Ece. "The only upside of everything that's happening so horrible around us could be reminding ourselves that we are all going through an awakening of collective consciousness. And something bright shall come out of this darkness, I believe. We need peace in the world... and we have to earn it, I guess."

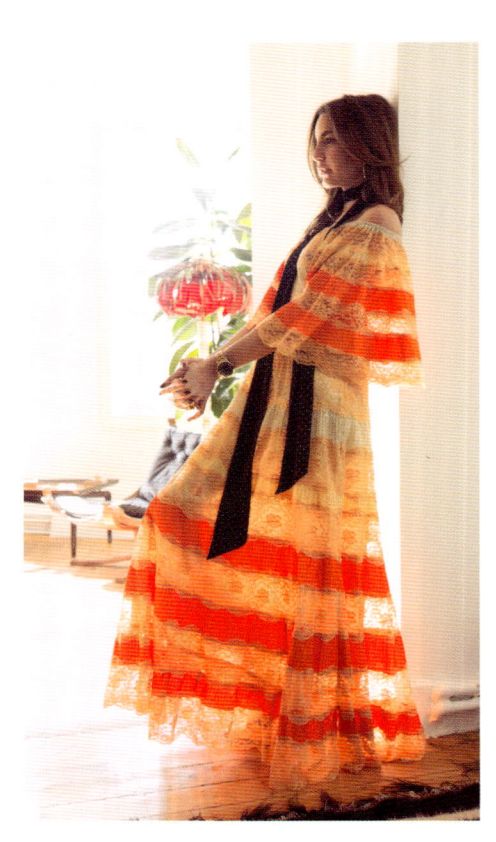
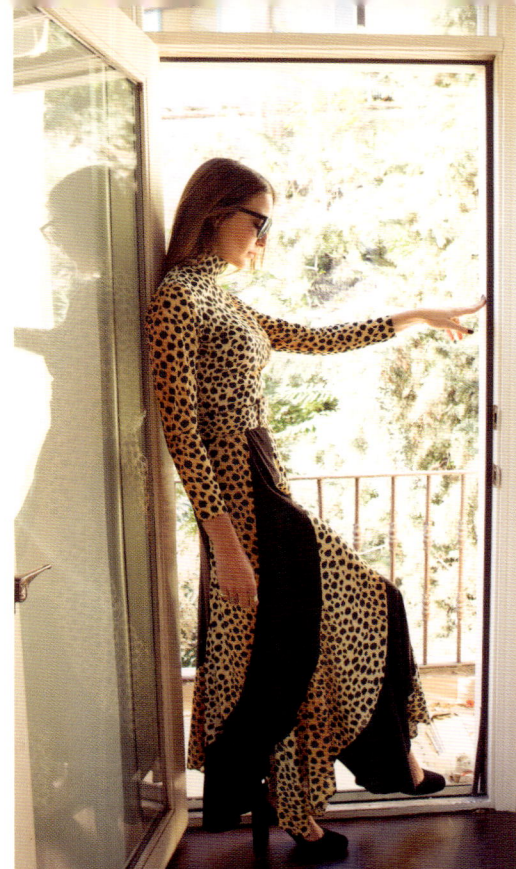
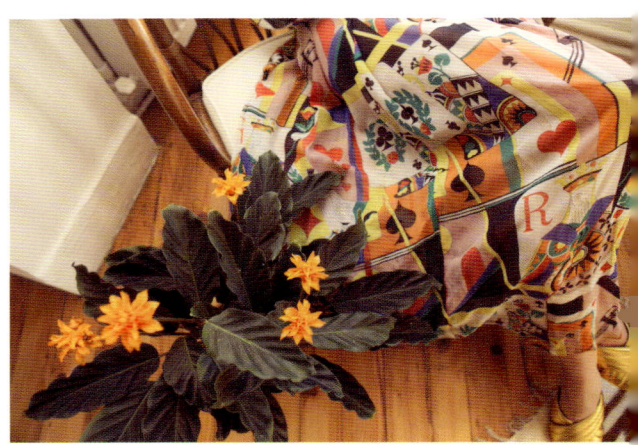
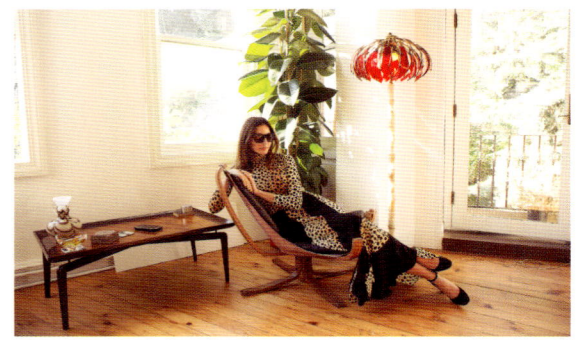
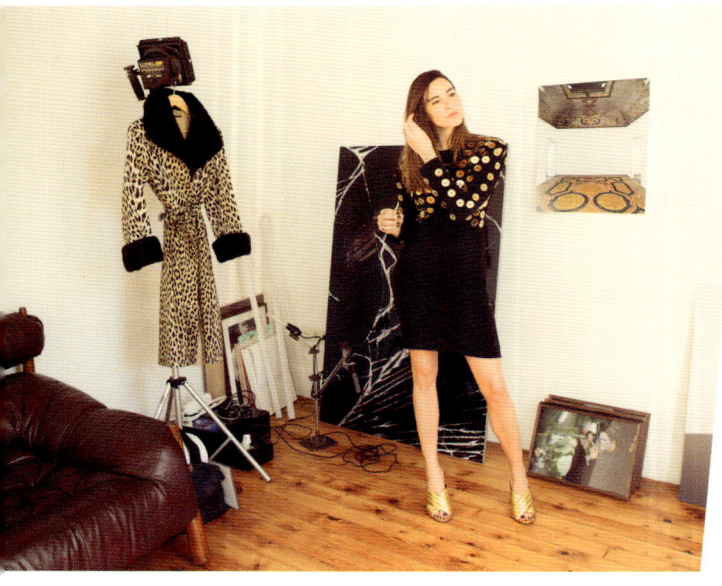
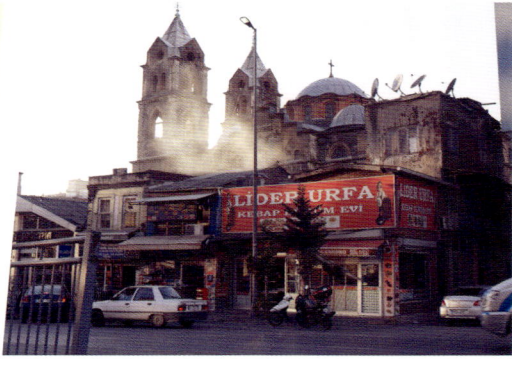
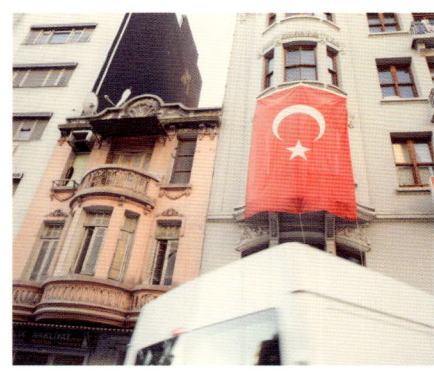
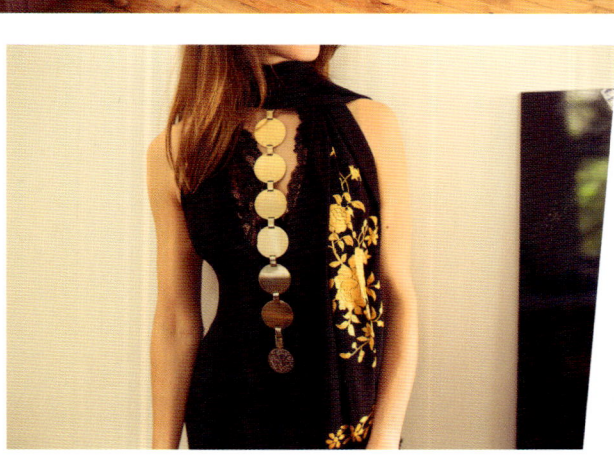
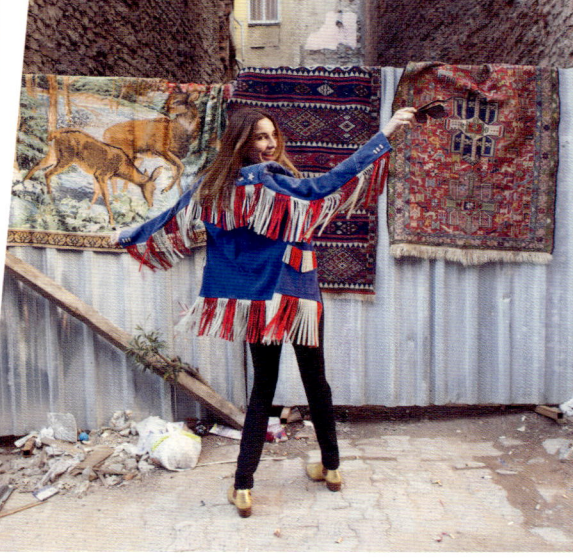
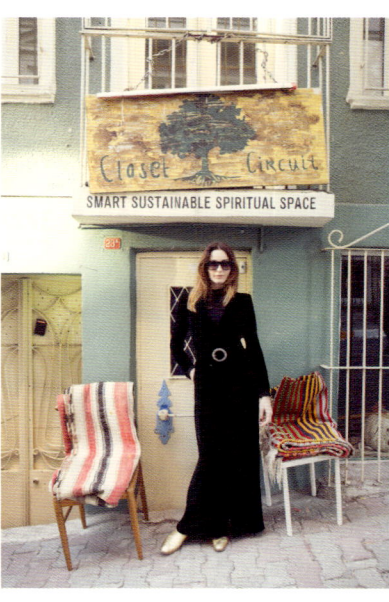

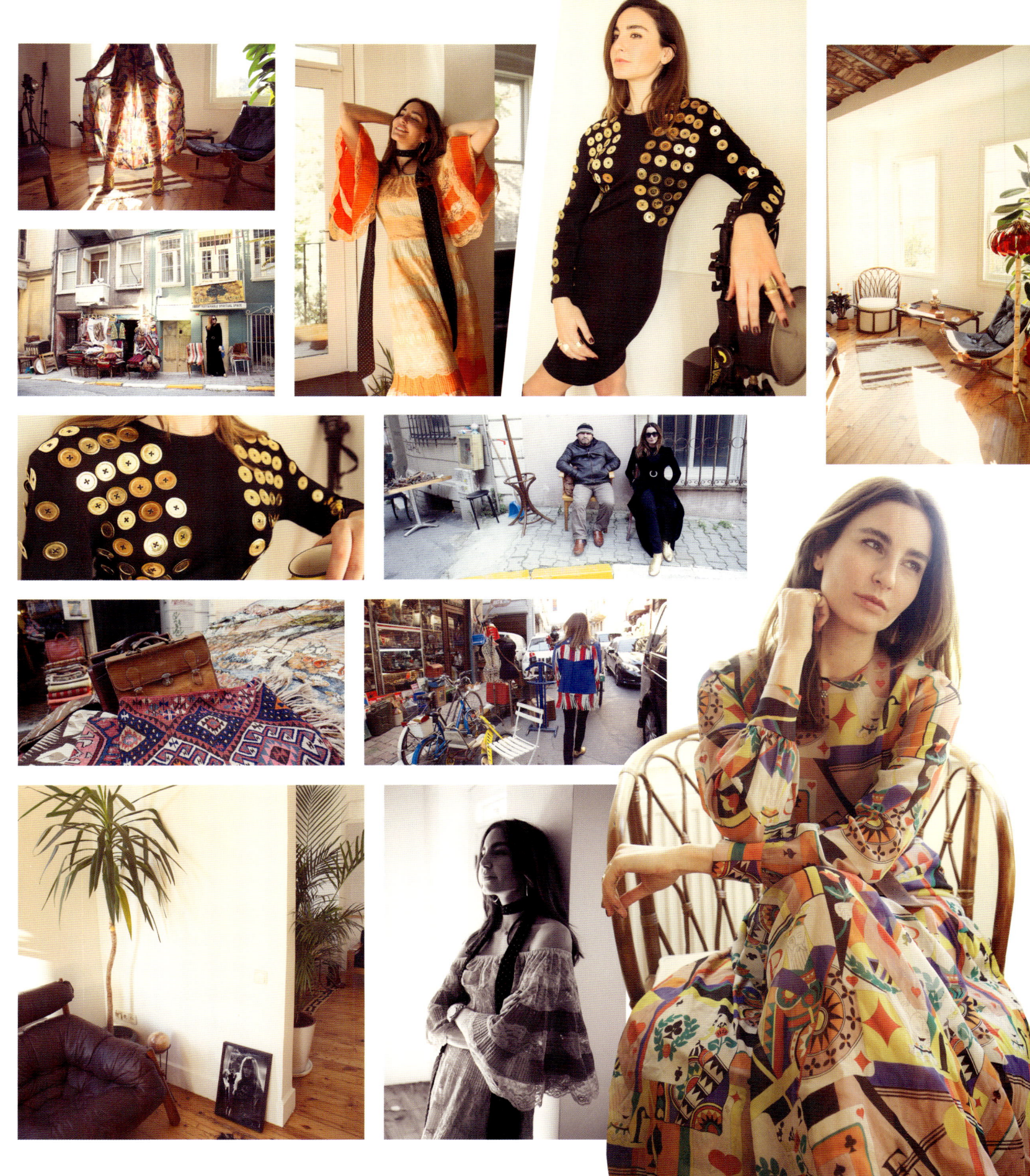

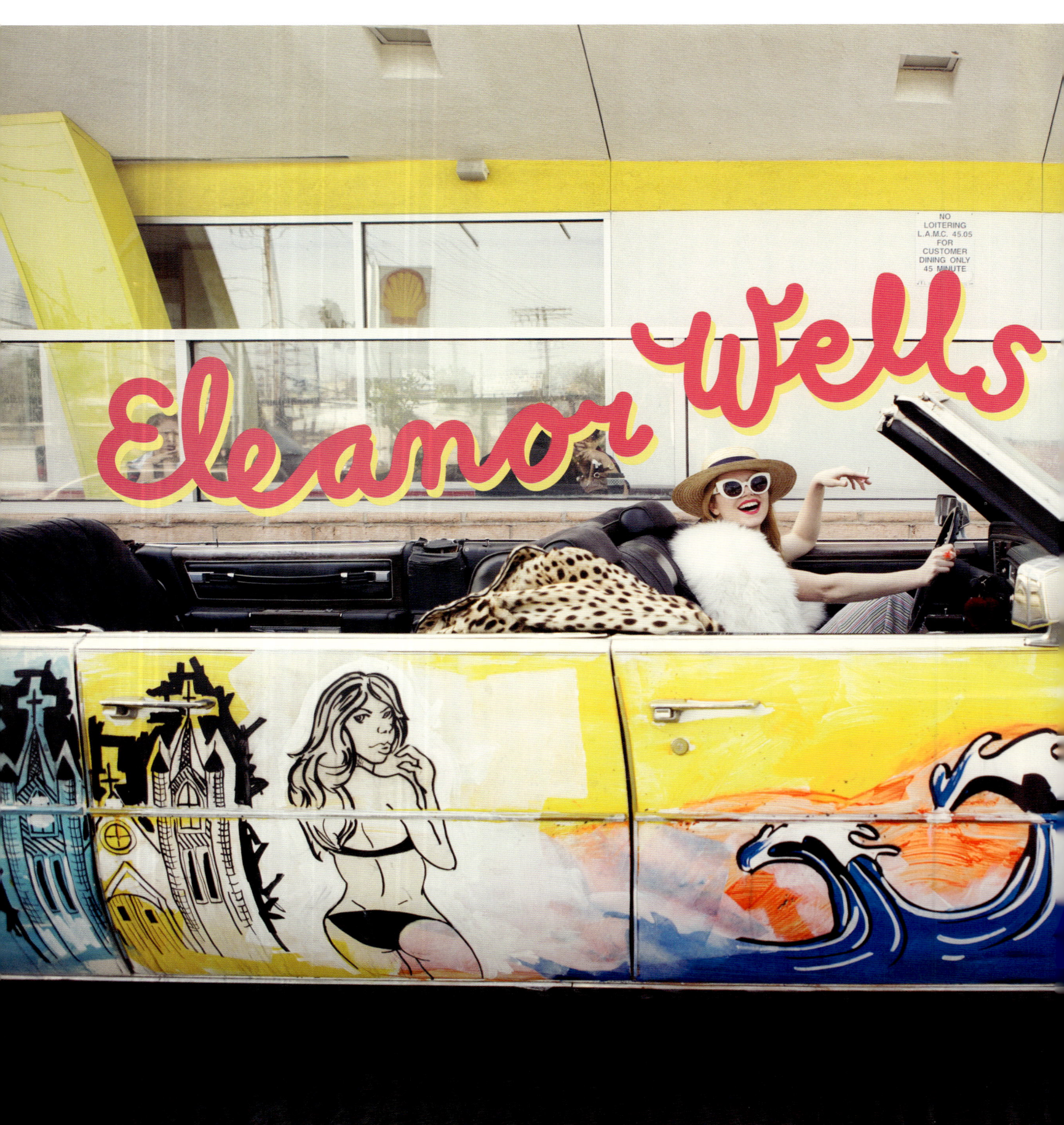

ELEANOR WELLS
ONE TOO MANY MINT JULEPS

She had told me about the car when I first met her: a convertible, stretch limousine she bought at auction at the police impound for $500. She described its splendor in great detail. It had all kinds of amazing hand-painted, quasi-religious art on the body, rear-facing back seats, and a spectacularly loud engine. And it ran well too. She would drive her "disco steed" around the neighborhood and get cheered on by little boys and grown men in wife beaters. It was a conversation piece for sure, and her ride to Burning Man, and it defined her essence in one motorized instant: Eleanor Wells likes to have *fun*.

Growing up on an old farm in Louisville, Kentucky, "the friendliest place on earth," Eleanor spent most Sundays after church at the racetrack. She learned how to place bets without losing money, and dodge the onset of an ironic allergy to horses. The yearly Derby was—and is—a highlight in her sartorial existence. "Louisville is somewhat old-school in that people still dress up there," she smiles. "It's also a rather progressive Southern town so there's an element of flamboyance to fashion." Last year, after one too many mint juleps, she climbed on the horse statue in the paddock and nearly got arrested. "Honey, you best believe I hopped up on it, arranged my dress, and got *the* most epic photo I will ever, *eeeeever* have!" she cheers.

She knew she wanted to be an actress when she was six. "Being the youngest of four, it was tough getting heard," she recalls, "so naturally I gravitated towards an extracurricular where I had the microphone, so to speak. I started attending a young people's conservatory at eight and asked Santa Claus for an agent at nine. I was always in a play, sometimes two at once." In high school she assumed she would attend the conservatory, but her parents wouldn't have it. So she chose to go to a school in LA where she thought she could still pursue acting on the side. "Little did I realize," she rolls her eyes, "the 'biz' has little to do with what I loved about theater." She became obsessed with the costumes instead, and got to study "the real deal vintage too, not reproductions. Because of theater, I learned the silhouettes from the 1400s to the present."

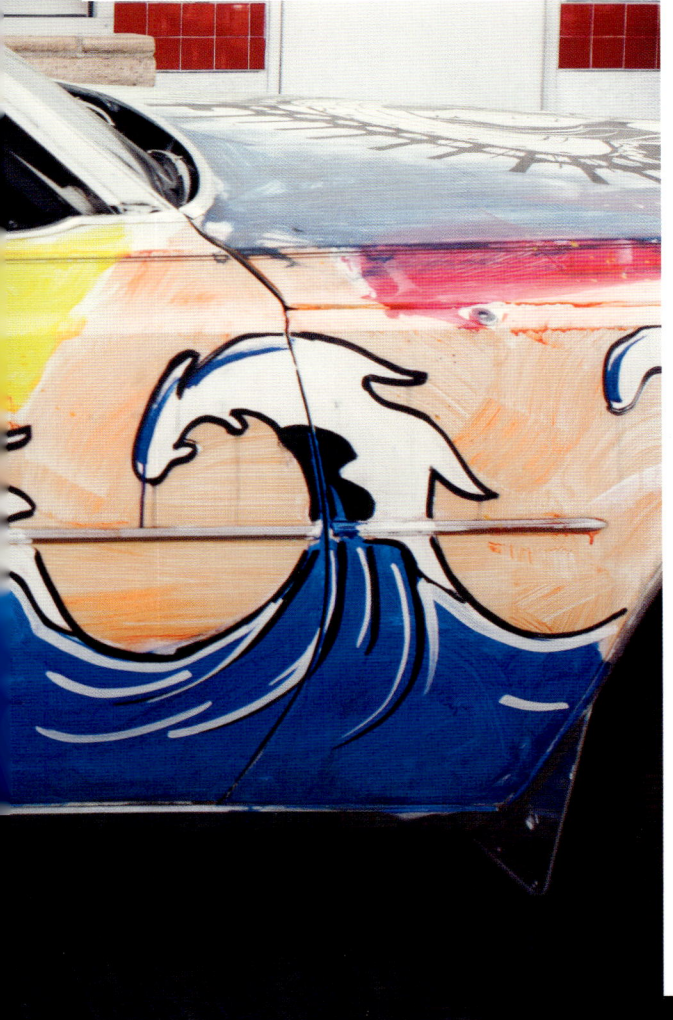

Lately she's been gravitating toward "clown chic" to describe her look. "I like taking an outfit just over the top enough to let people know I don't take myself too seriously," she laughs, amused. "My best and worst fashion moments are blurred because they both occur when I really don't give a damn. For instance: I shaved my head in sixth grade so I looked like a little dude. In an effort to feminize me a bit, my older sister took me shopping for makeup. Hellllo turquoise eyeliner! Around the same time, I had a black-and-white tracksuit with tear-away pants. I wore it to a middle school mixer, and in the middle of a dance circle, I ripped off the suit to reveal my cute tee and one-inch-rise jeans. I think I may have rocked a whale tail around then too; that's when your thong strings are above the top of your jeans."

I'm not surprised Eleanor has become one of LA's most devoted nightlife personalities. She calls herself "The Duchess of Disco," and organizes underground parties. She also dances for DJ Harvey and gets to make all the stage costumes. "I fell into styling because of my own personal style," she continues. "I still can't believe I get paid to play dress up. I also rent out pieces from my vintage archive. If a girl needs a gown for an event, she can come over and I'll style her head to toe! Finally found a way to fund my shopping addiction!"

I love being around Eleanor. There's always that slight hint of danger and excitement when she shows up, because you know she's open to any and all ideas of fun. She's well-spoken, open-minded, and wholeheartedly cracks up about something every couple of minutes or so. She tells her stories with elevated enunciation and never talks shit about people. She's the most spontaneous girl I know. We've eloped to the most random events together. We saw Saint Pablo in Inglewood, hobnobbed at the Veuve Clicquot polo match, celebrated Halloween at a seedy, underground loft downtown, and hung out in the basement of a recent murder scene. But most of all, she's the one of very, very few girlfriends that will drive to the West Side to see me, and that's a pretty impressive feat.

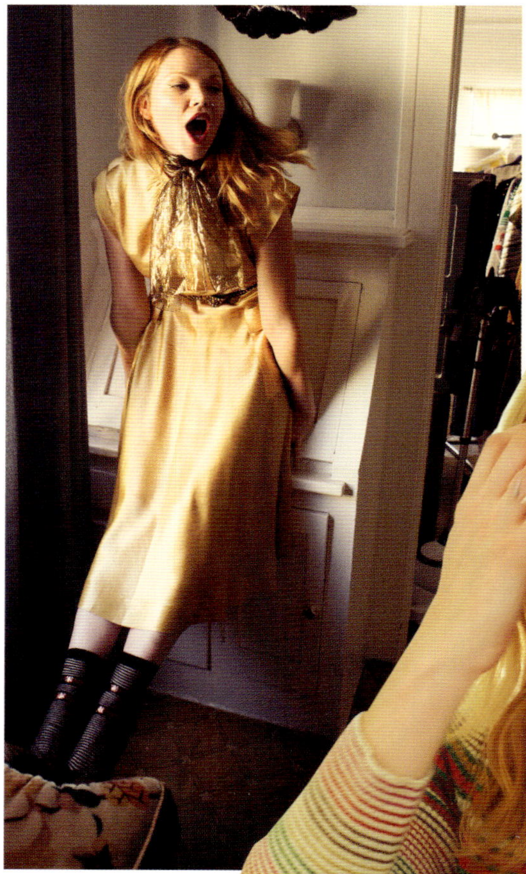

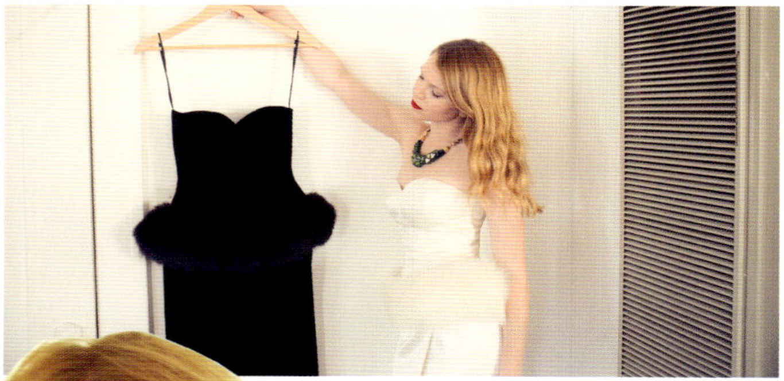

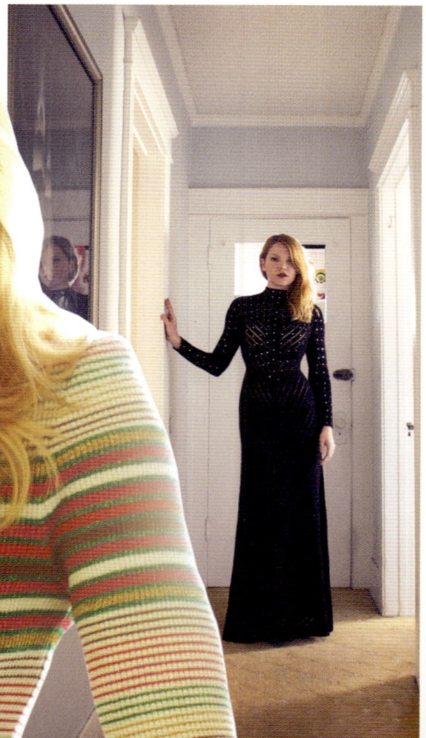

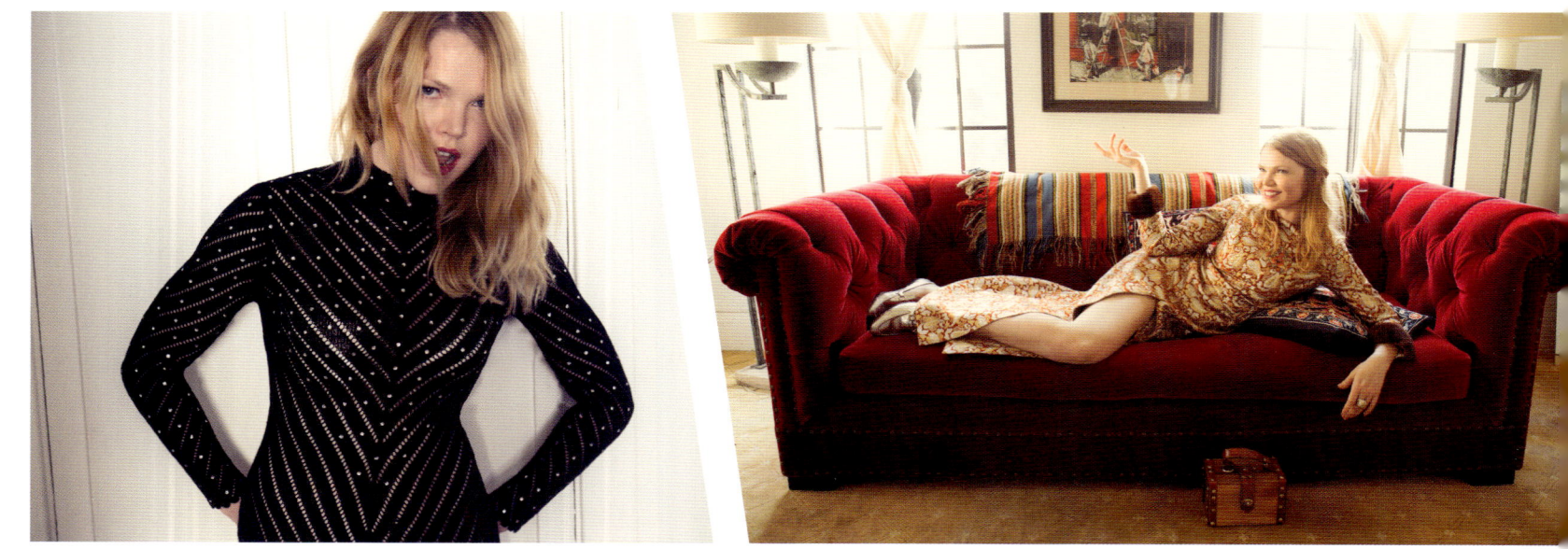
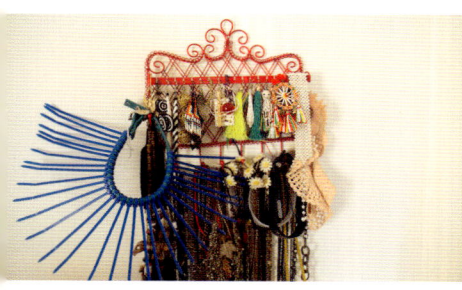
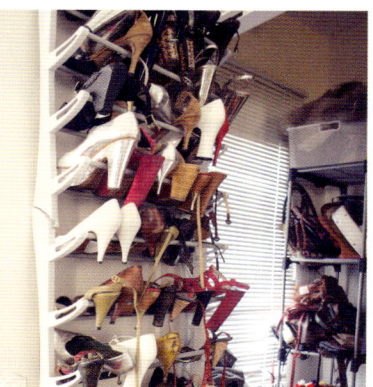
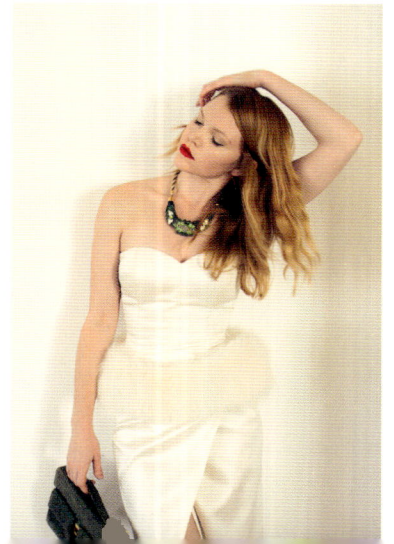

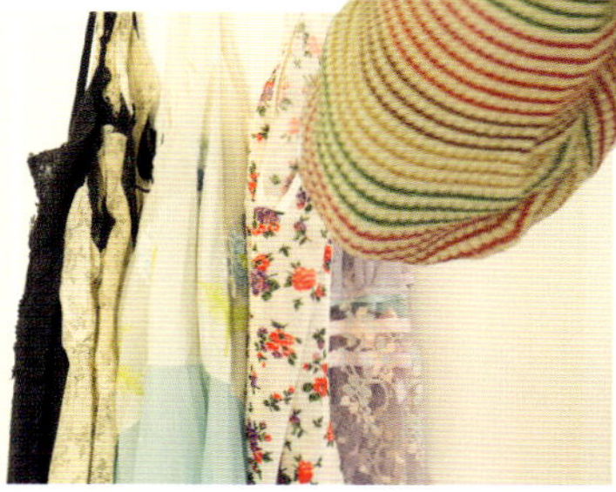

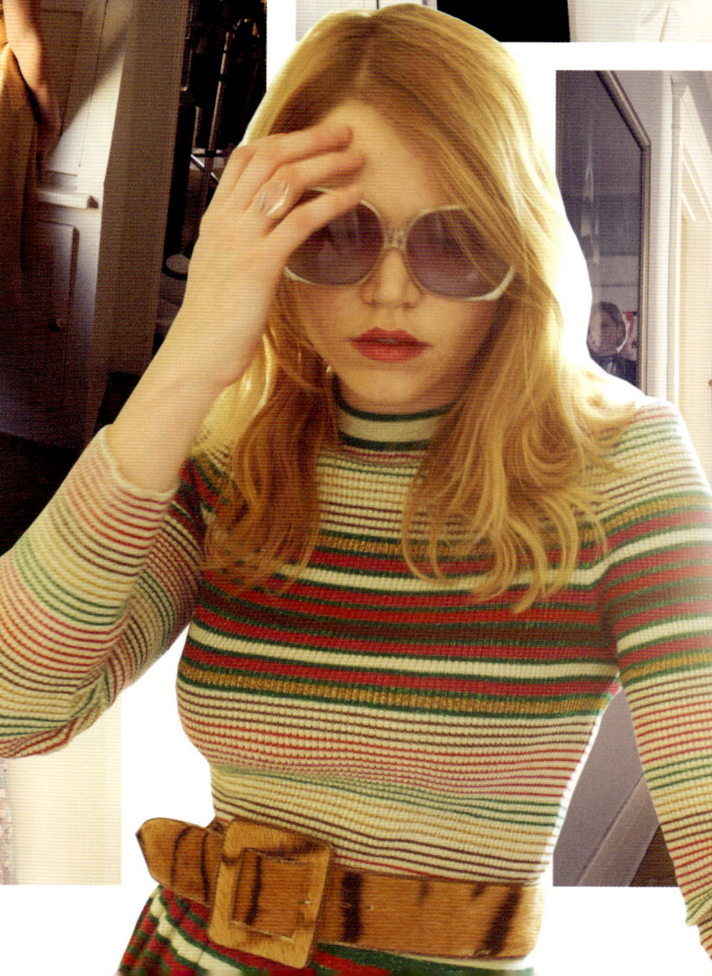

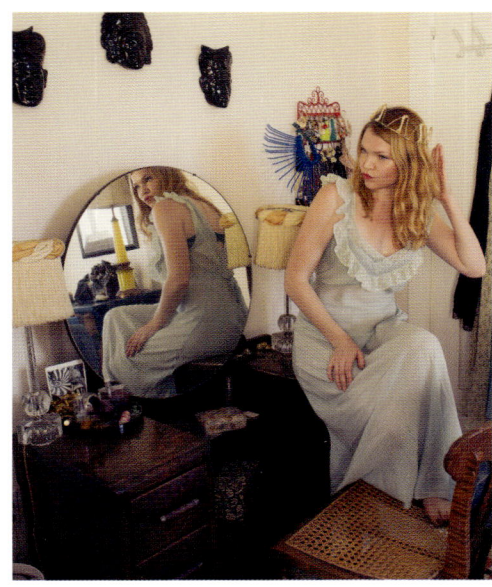
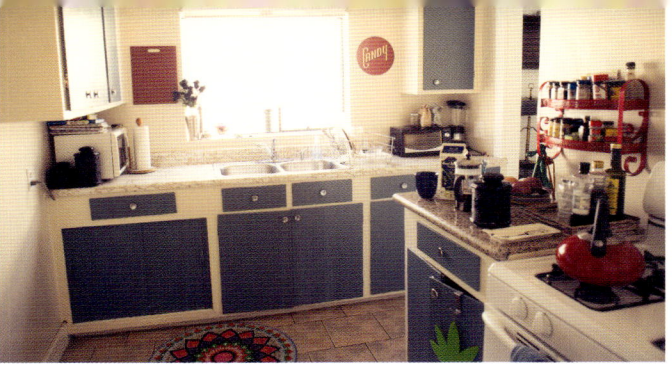
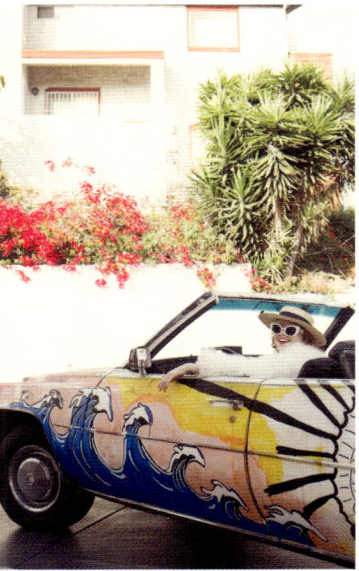
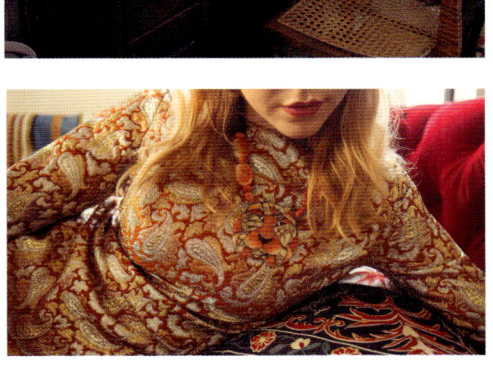
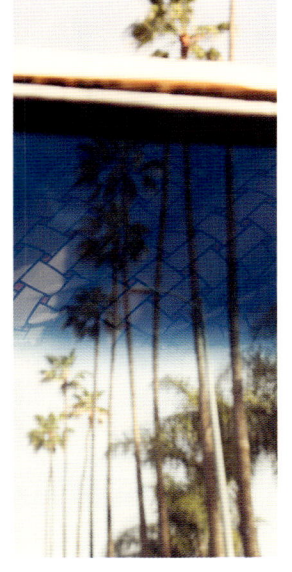
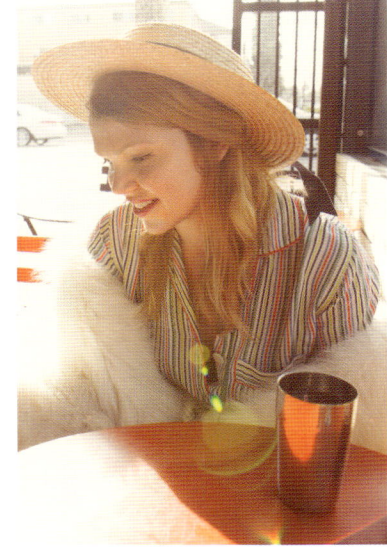
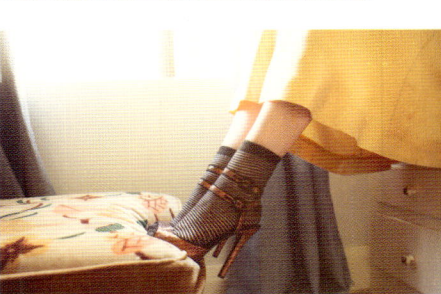
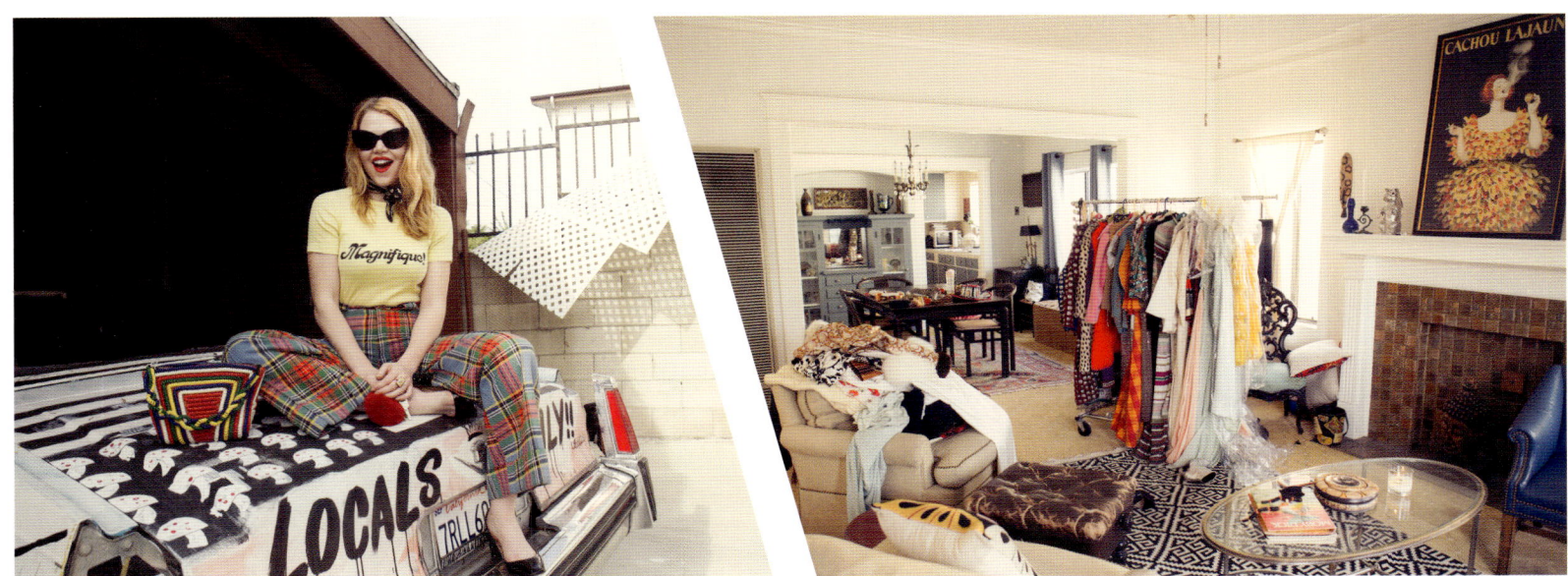
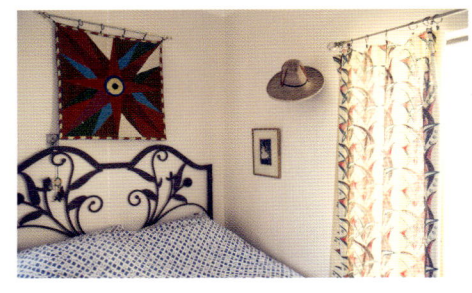
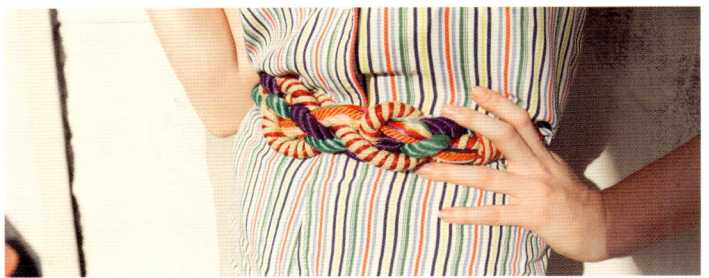
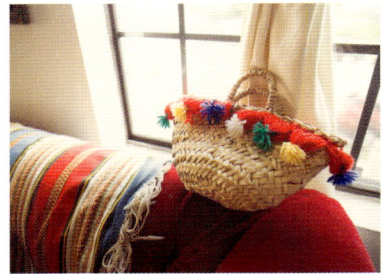

LAURA HELMS
ROUND TWO

Five years pass before I photograph Laura a second time. She has since moved out of her teeny two-door place in Greenpoint and upgraded to reign as queen in a sprawling duplex apartment inside a converted seminary in Prospect Heights. In 2012 I described her as a "medieval nobleman's daughter," a girl with golden locks, theatrical frocks, and two adorable cats. She was 28 years old then, armed with several arts and history degrees and working on a dissertation for her final year at the London College of Fashion. Her wardrobe was a study in itself, albeit confined to the peripherals of a small bedroom, a complete and riveting exploration of every era and a celebration of her grandmother's legacy.

Fast-forward through several books, a few museum exhibitions, a film about Thea Porter, and the passing of her grandmother, and Laura McLaws Helms now calls herself a "Fashion and Cultural Historian, Author, Creative Director." Laser and Misha (the cats) are still around, her hair is still the same, and her shape is just as godly as I remember. She even gives the same answers to my questions. The queen hasn't changed—she just found a new castle. "It is definitely my dream apartment," she smiles blissfully. "I looked for two years before finding this magical place. I knew from the moment I walked in that I couldn't live anywhere else and I've now been here for almost two years."

The basement is her sanctuary now, a giant walk-in, multi-room closet, gloriously and luxuriously expended and organized. Pants and jeans remain absent; it's only dresses and skirts here. And there's no difference between night and day. "I never feel out of place in an evening gown in the day time. I'm always wearing fur, sequins, capes, and lace even just to go to the deli. I exist in my own weird fantasy world, so this is sort of what the inside of my brain is like, this room." She buys most of her clothes on eBay and doesn't care about labels or brands. "My favorite thing is to go on eBay and see what I can get for $20, including shipping, and see what's ending in the next hour. If something is fun, flattering, and affordable, then I will wear it regardless of brand."

When you ask her about vintage ethics, she has a concise response: "In general, I find it easier to source pieces that appeal to my own sense of fantasy and glamour through vintage, rather than new. Not only are new designs lacking in the magic and drama I seek, but they are usually poorer quality for the price, and the garments and textiles are often produced in environmentally-damaging ways with poor conditions for the workers. As someone who is very passionate about the environment, I could never reconcile purchasing something new that is so destructive to our earth, when there is so much available on the secondary market (which I luckily much prefer)."

Laura had a five-year plan in 2012: "Living part-time on my farm in the mountains of North Carolina, writing books on fashion and cultural history, and finding new and innovative ways to bring history and art alive." Maybe my visit is a reminder that she has not completely succeeded. Today she still dreams about that "little escape from the city" where she'll be able to write and grow her own food in a lush landscape. Alas, life throws odd curve balls now and again: "In the last five years many things happened that I could never have imagined: a serious accident that left me in a wheelchair for eight weeks, many close family and friends' illnesses and deaths, new work opportunities, and now after everything, I might finally be in the right place to make the part-time rural life a possibility." I think that calls for a new visit, and new answers.

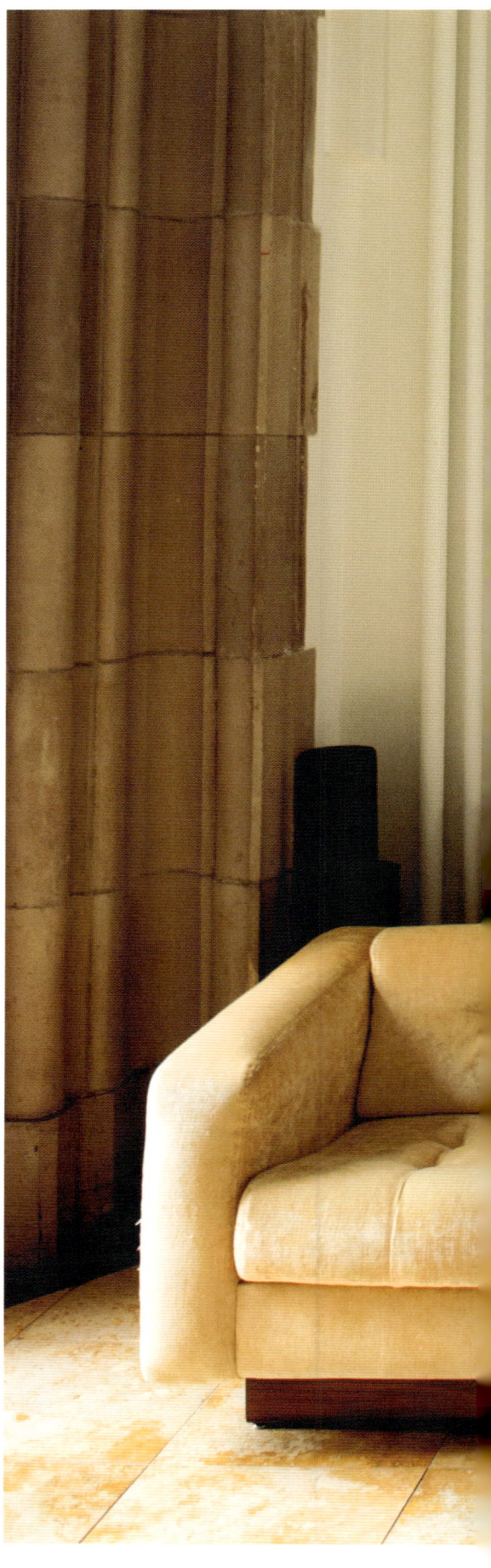

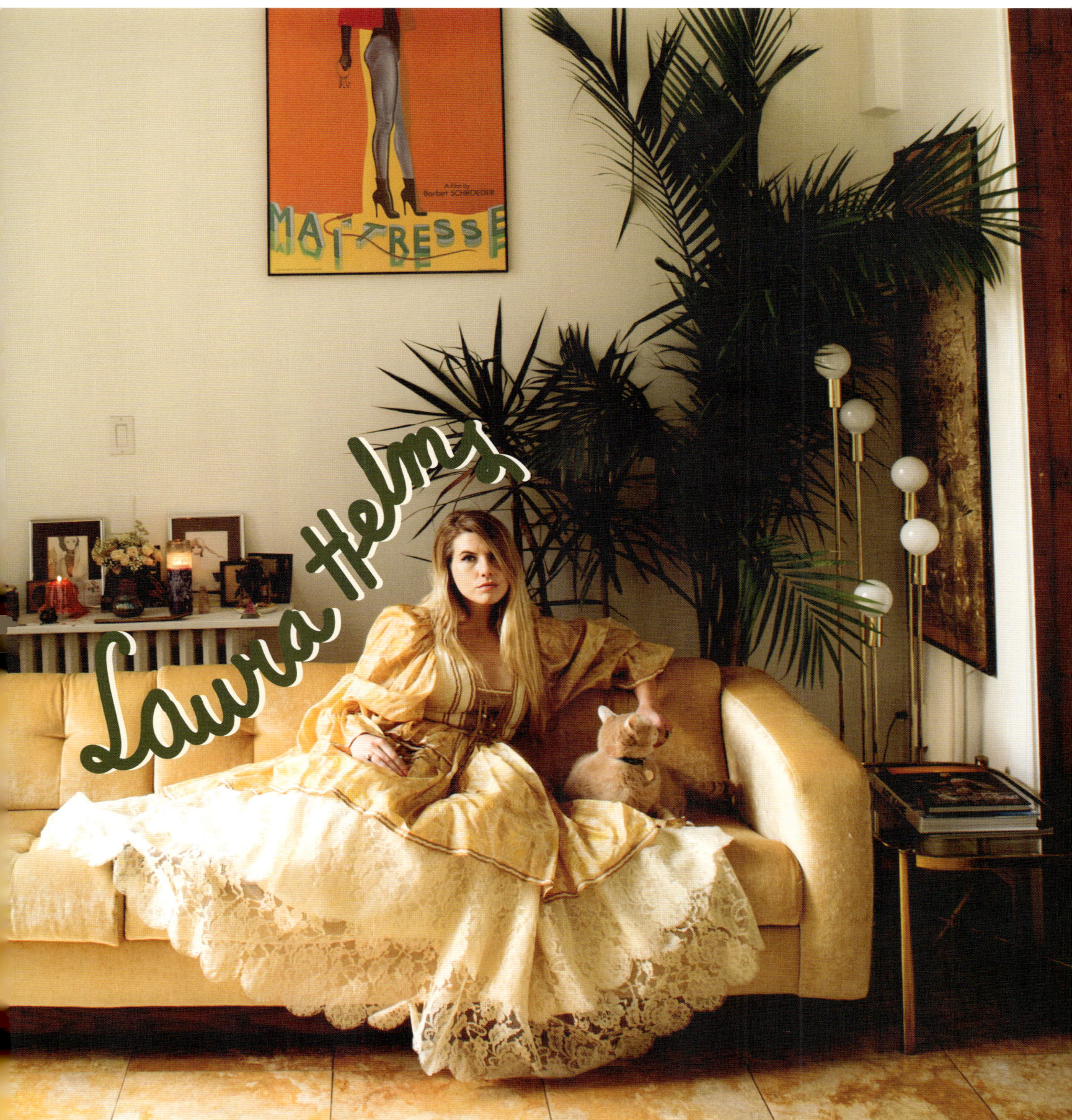

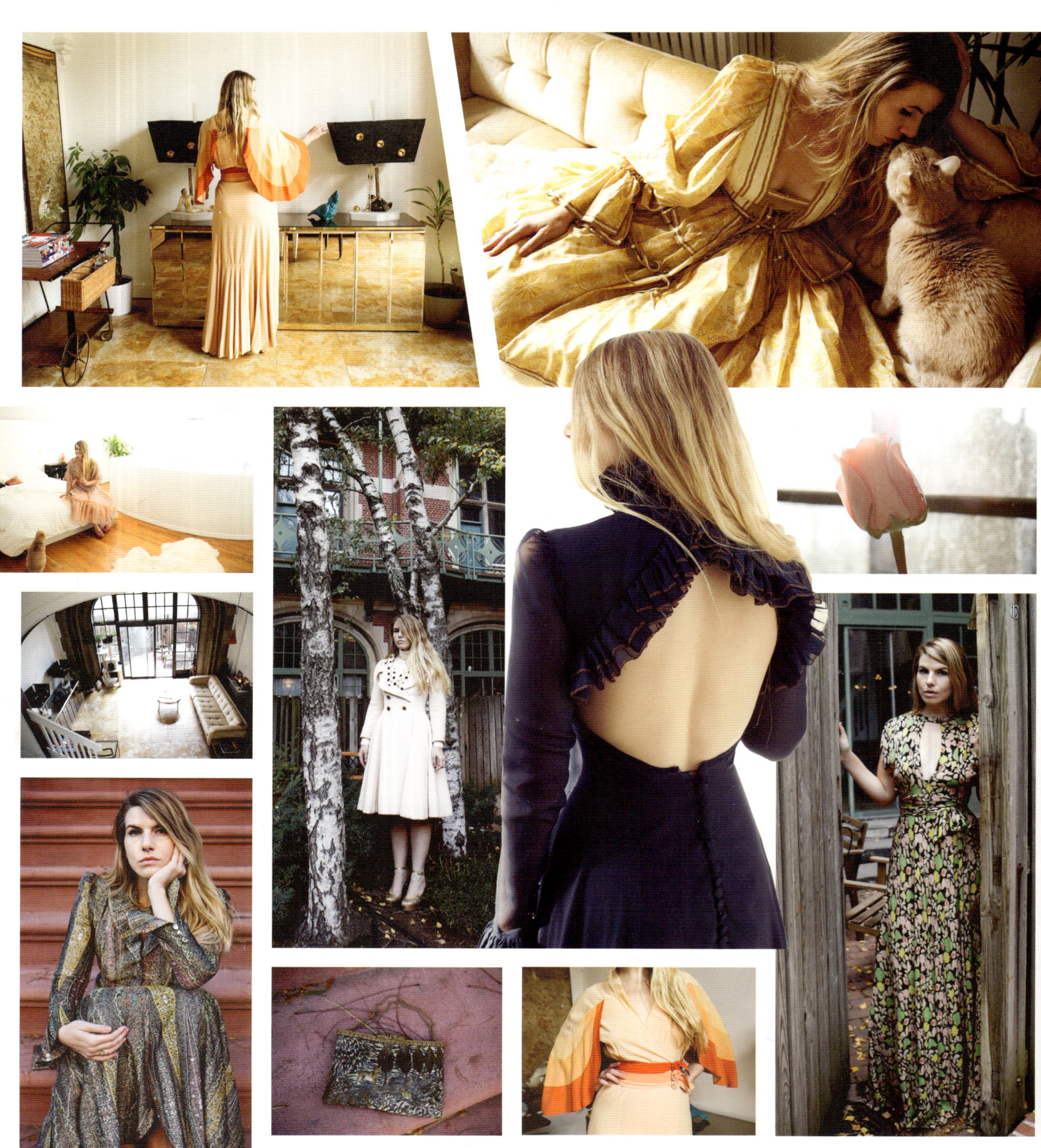

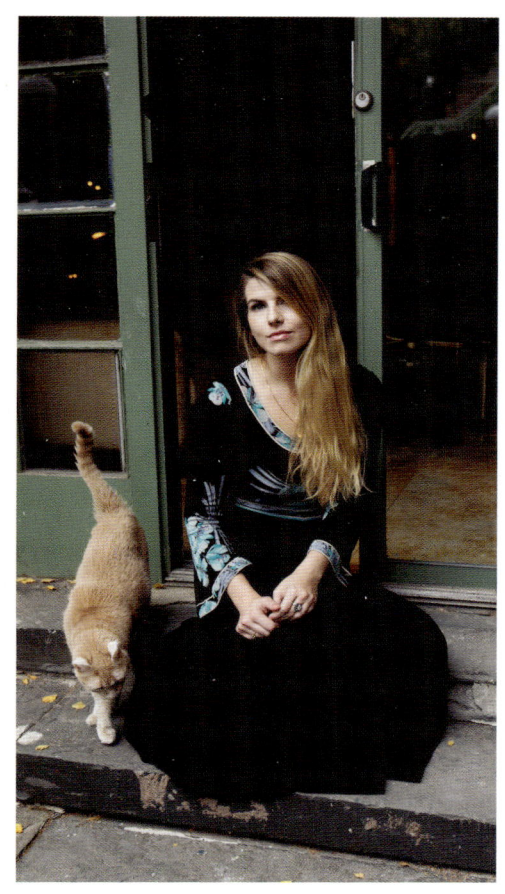
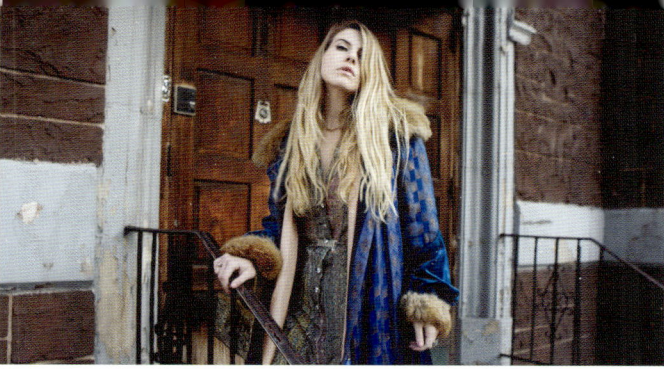
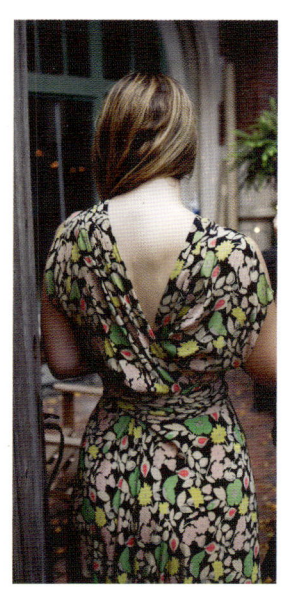
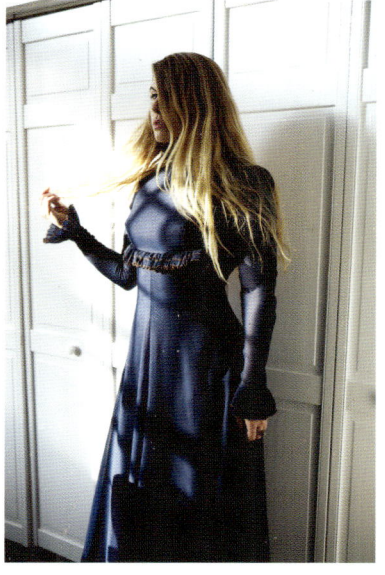
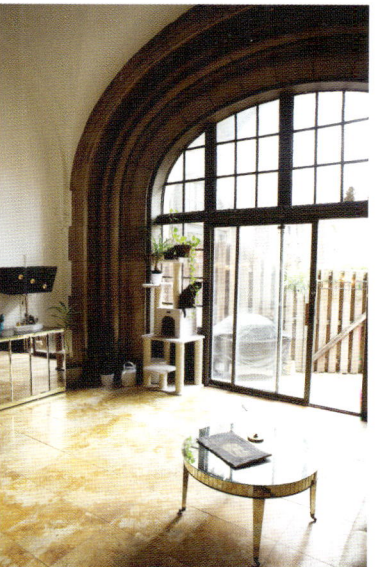
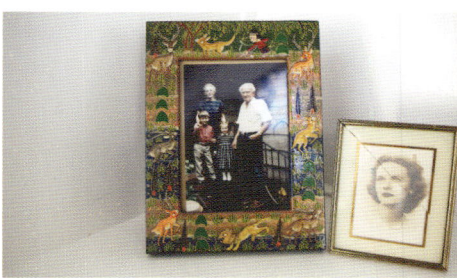
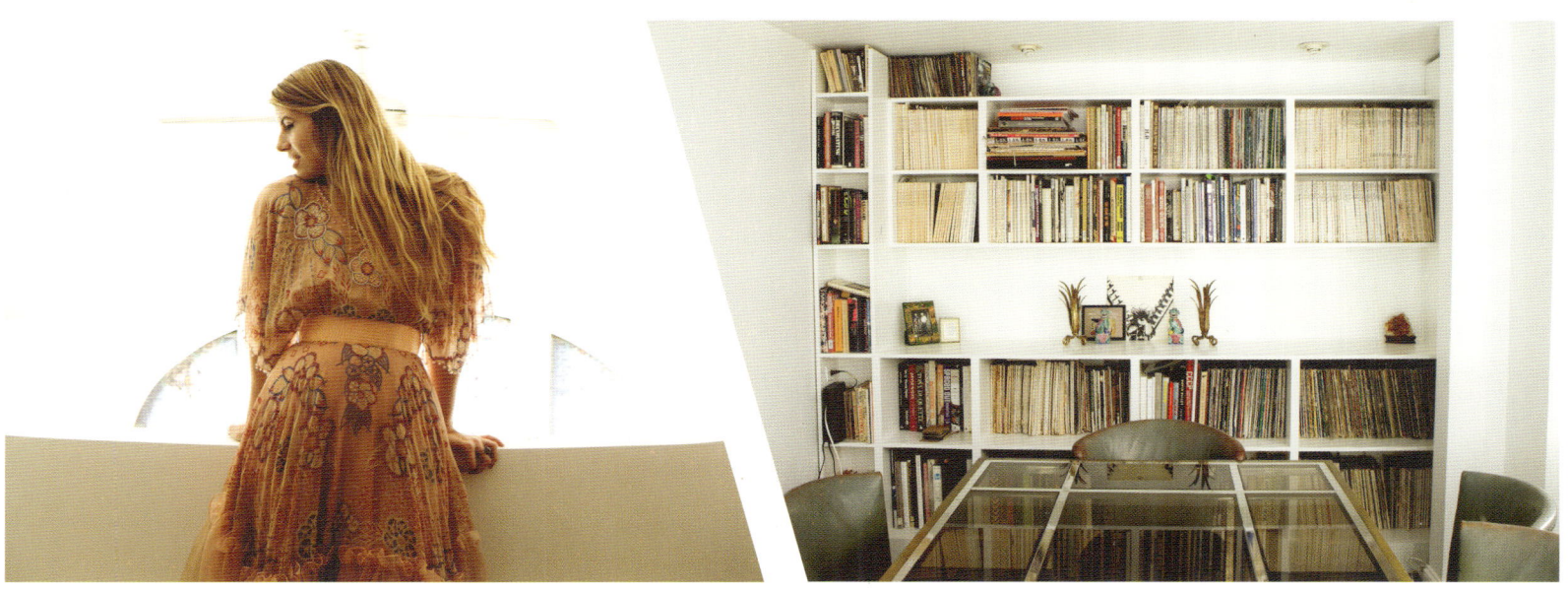
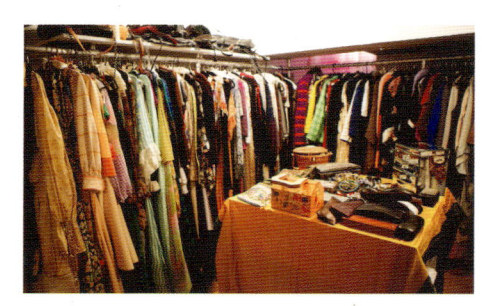
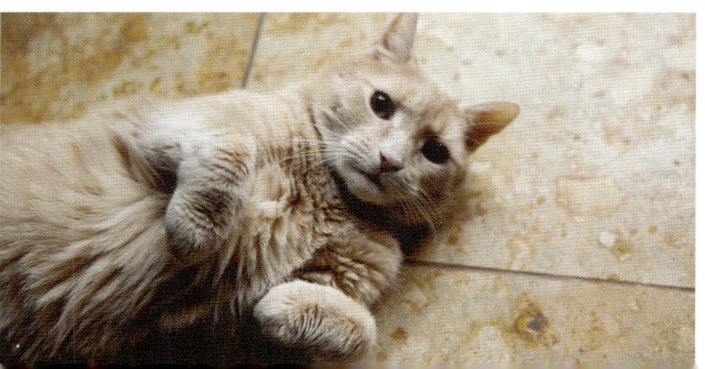
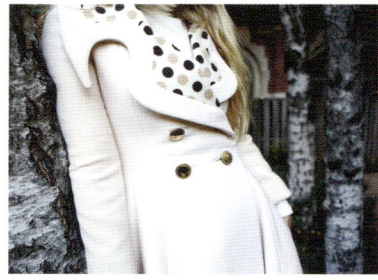

OLIVIER CHÂTENET
ADVICE FOR THE DAPPER MAN

It's not easy to find men who wear vintage well. Often the look becomes too dandy or plastic, and crosses the awkward line into Halloween territory. The jeans might be too tight, the lapels too wide, or the prints too loud. Even for the straight man that dwells in the peripherals of the fashion industry, it is too close a call. Instead he finds solace in the soft confines of a threadbare concert T-shirt, a leather biker jacket, or a simple button down. And that's all fine, because he'll feel better about choosing the green, inexpensive shopping route, but is it worth the effort of sifting and trying if you end up looking like everyone else?

The rare man that wears vintage *well* has an innate sense of style and a thirst for quality that transcends the limitations of time—like Olivier Châtenet possesses. The 58-year-old collector has always had a sophisticated affinity for old clothes. He spent his childhood drawing historic scenes, particularly from 18th century Versailles, and styling himself and his friends up in his grandpa's discarded clothes from the trunk in the basement. At 14, he was already shopping the flea markets around Paris and dressing like an adult. His look is versatile but comfortable, "a real mix of sports garments, Charvet made-to-measure, modern designers, and rare vintage menswear."

Oliver has a covetable, priceless magazine archive that spans many decades and multiple shelves at his Strasbourg Saint-Denis apartment. He has lost count, "Thousands for sure!" he laughs. He started with French *Vogue*, then dove head-first into the postwar, new-generation publications like *Elle* and *Jardin des Modes*, and added foreign editions later. "That is how these documents gave birth to my passion for photography leaders like Avedon, Penn, Helmut Newton, Guy Bourdin, and many, many more," Olivier explains. "Also this is the way I made a bridge with my vintage archives, as I found many pictures of garments I have. All this iconography helped me a lot to date and document my collection."

Perhaps the biggest feat of his career was the Yves Saint Laurent movie he consulted for in 2014. It brought all his fashion knowledge into play. After reading the script, Olivier advised the director, Bertrand Bonello, on how things were done in the professional atelier environment of that time. The film depicts the life of Yves from 1967 to 1976, at the height of his career. "I worked in this fashion world for so many years," says Olivier, "that I know very well how everything is codified: the way you talk to a master designer, especially from the YSL generation, the way you do a fitting, the way you prepare a runway show, and so on." He also worked closely with the costume designer Anaïs Romand. The main character, played by Gaspard Ulliel, wore several of Olivier's personal archive suits.

So what styling advice does a man who has so much experience, interest, insight, and taste give to his fellow man struggling to find the right balance with vintage? "Well, style is always difficult to advise on," begins Oliver, "especially for men. I would avoid vintage head-to-toe, and would prefer sportswear instead of urban-style pieces. Think timeless 60s Steve McQueen: a sheepskin jacket, a cashmere sweater, and a pair of white corduroy is the best way to dress when you want to forget what you wear. Effortless style is a secret that works!"

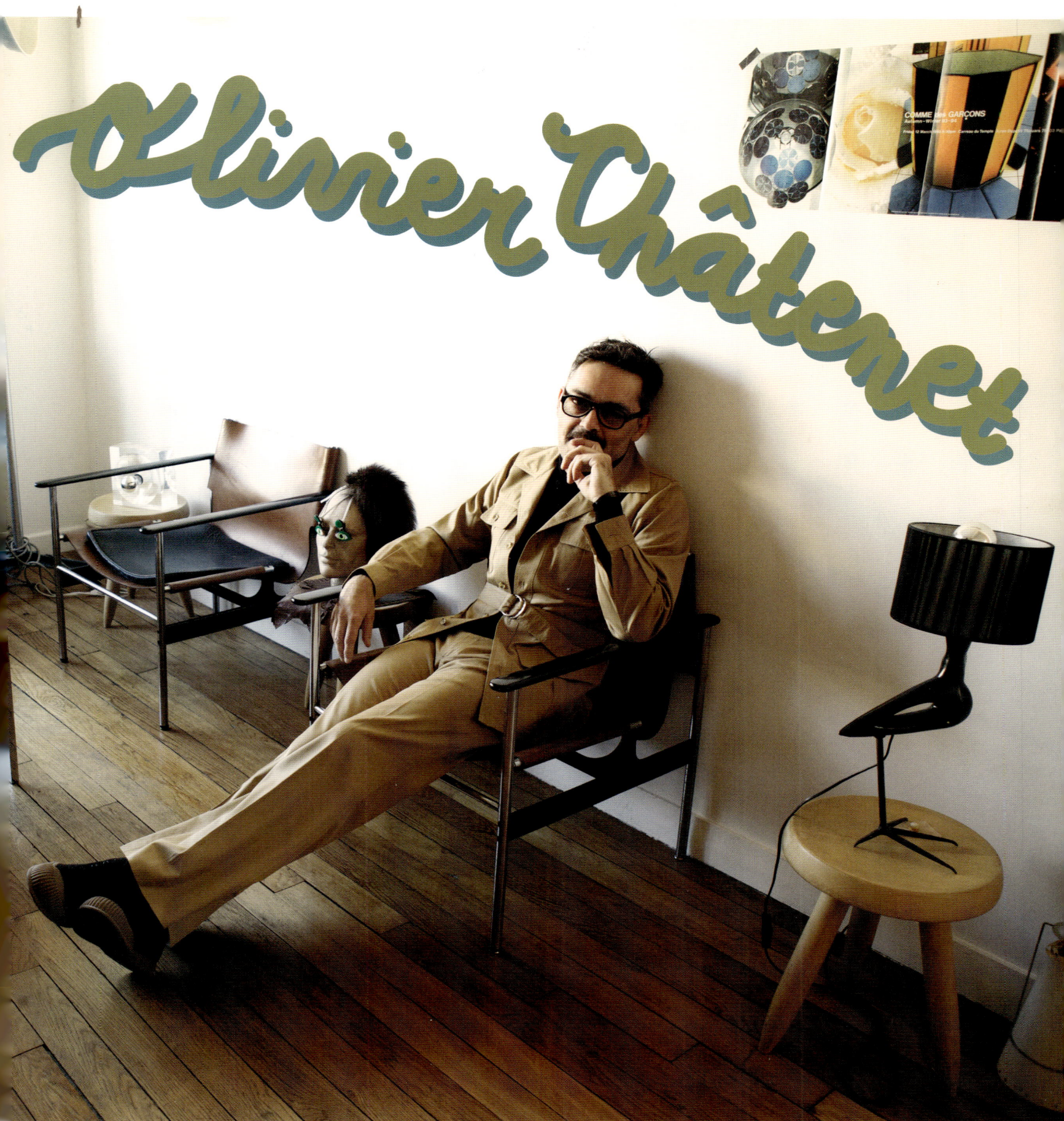

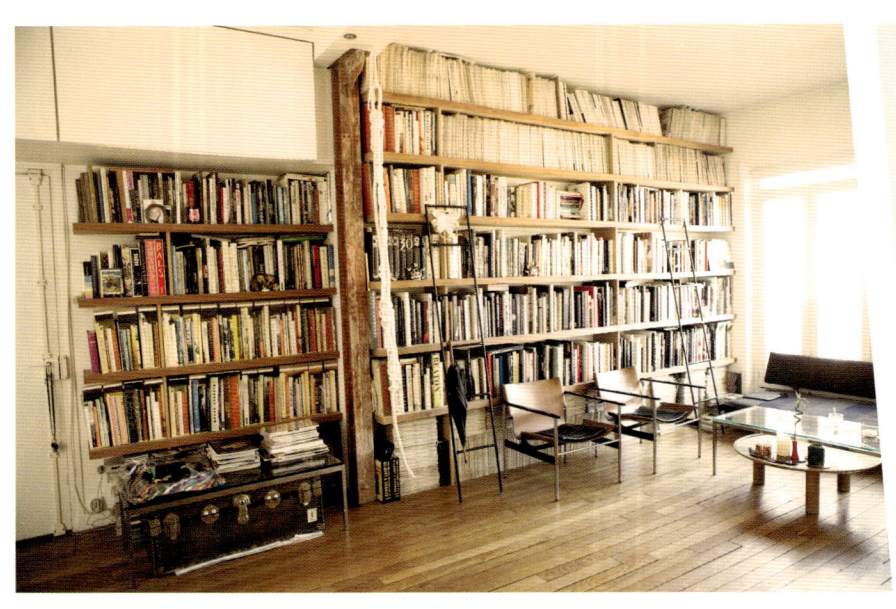
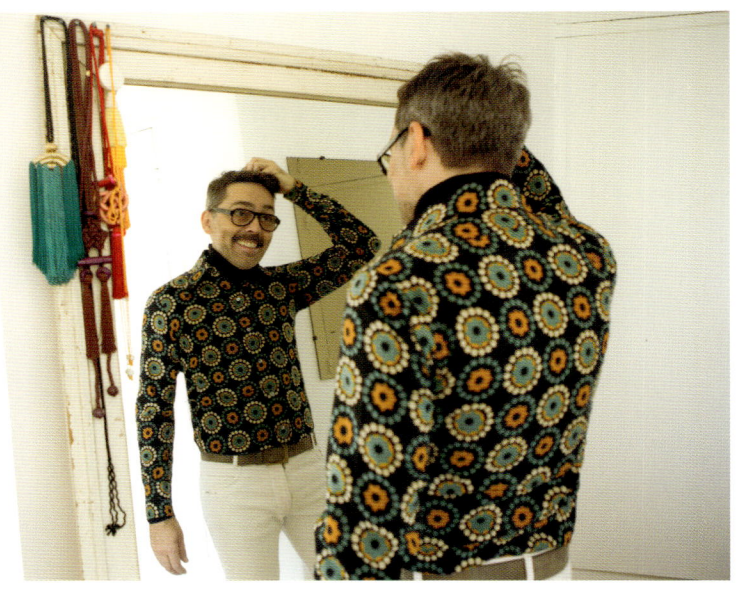
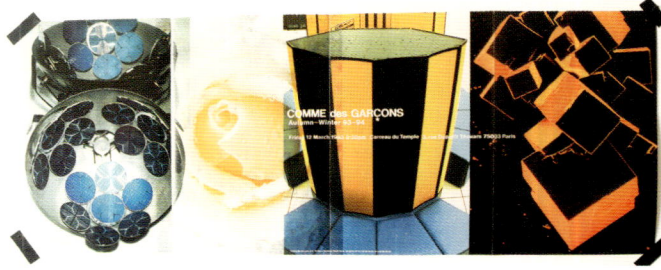
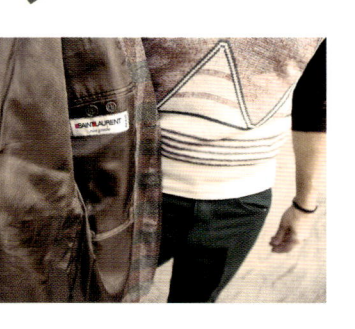
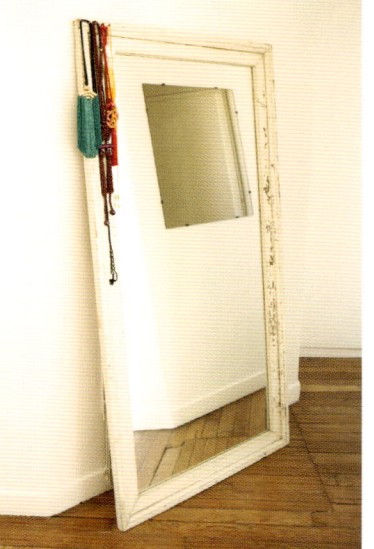
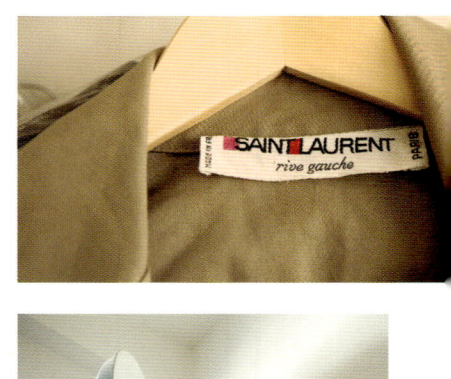
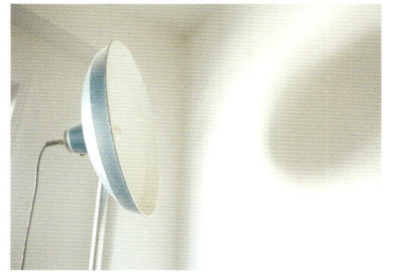
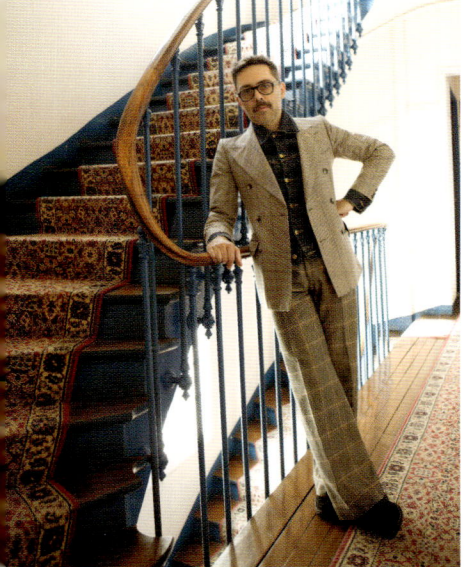
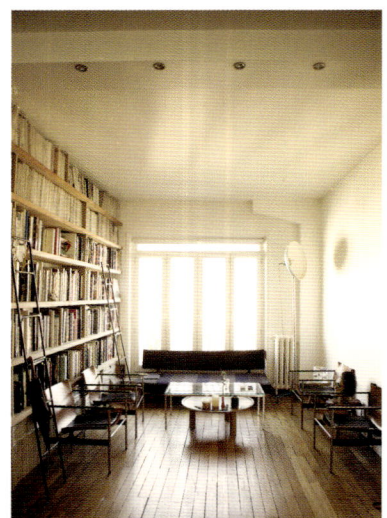
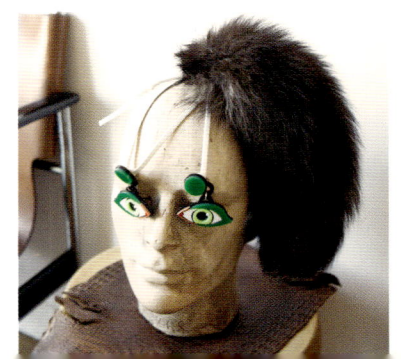
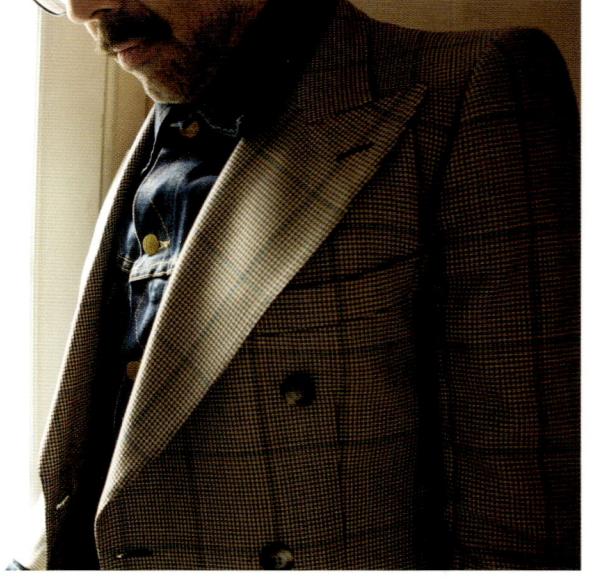

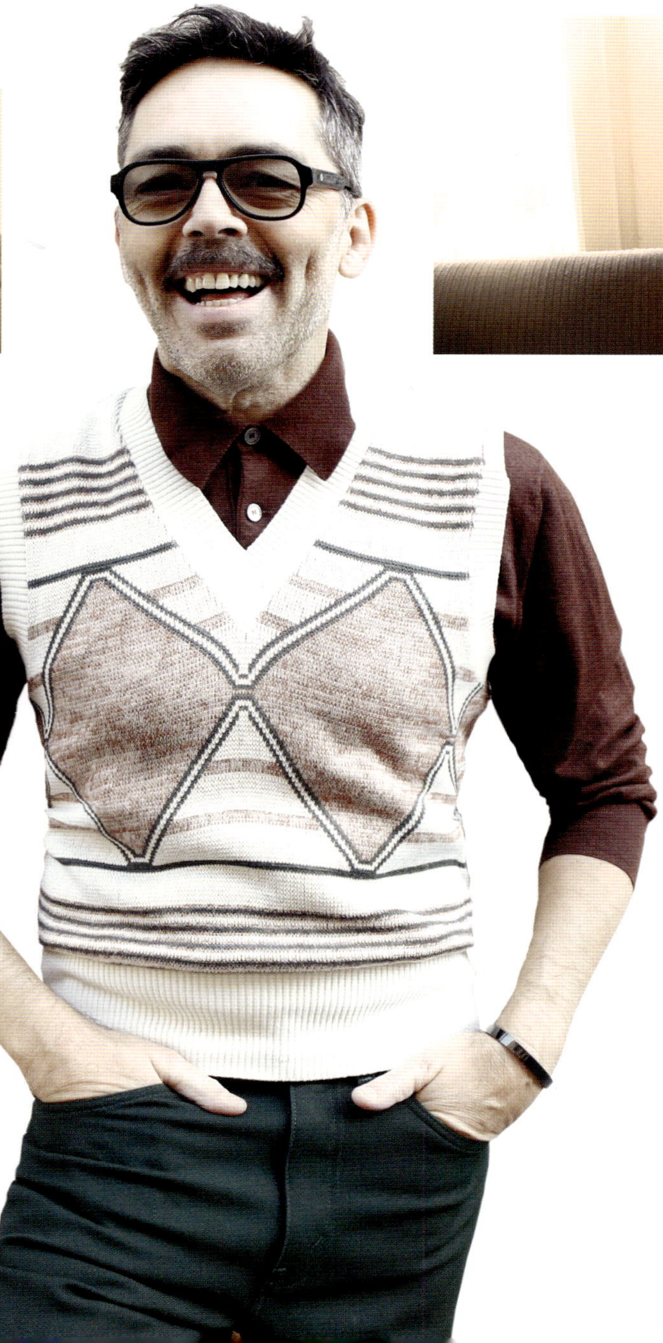

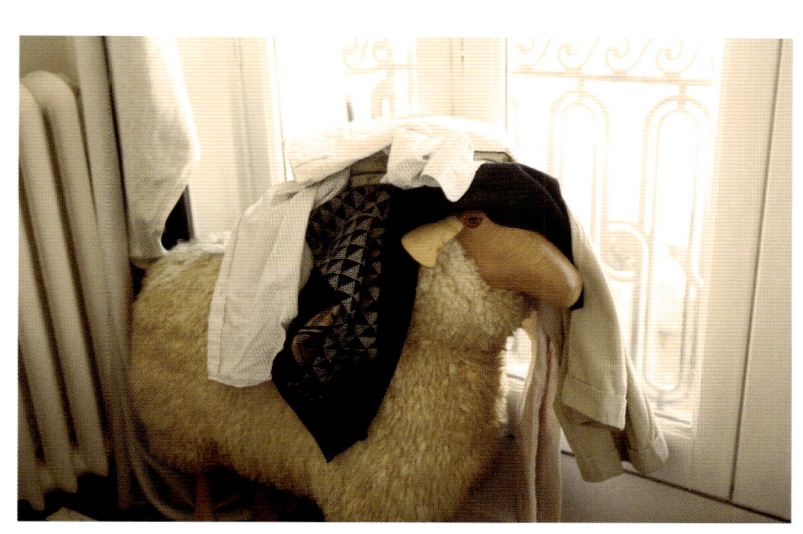
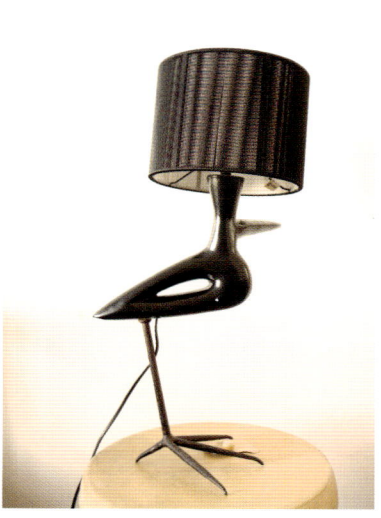
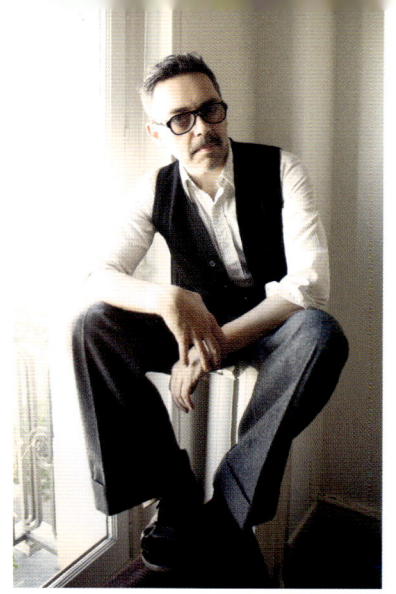
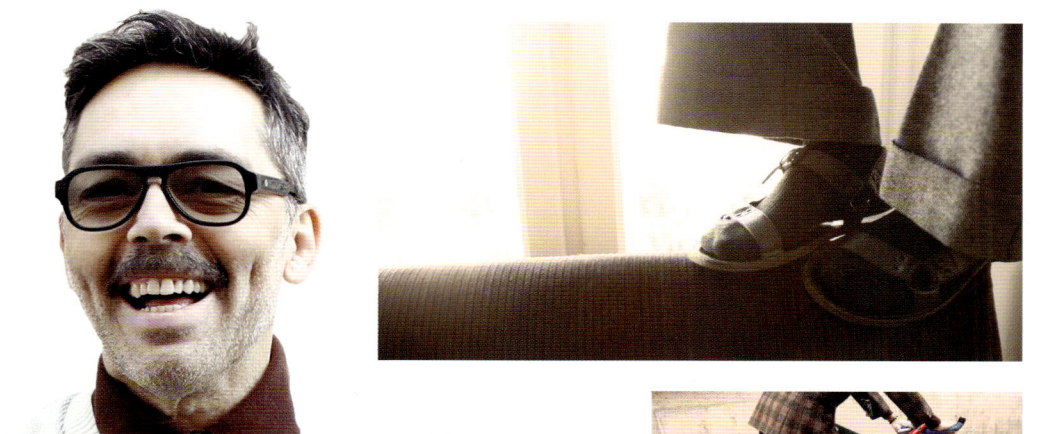
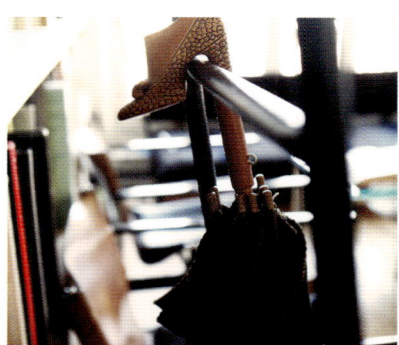
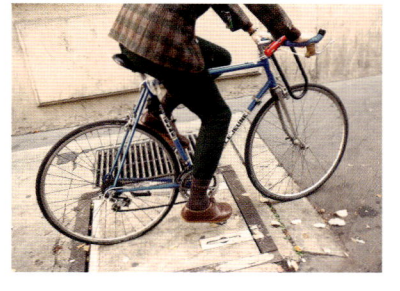
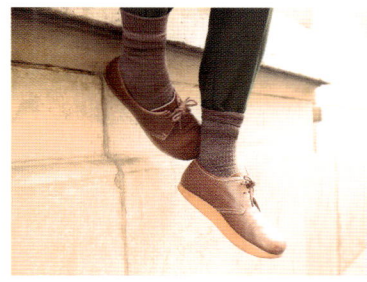

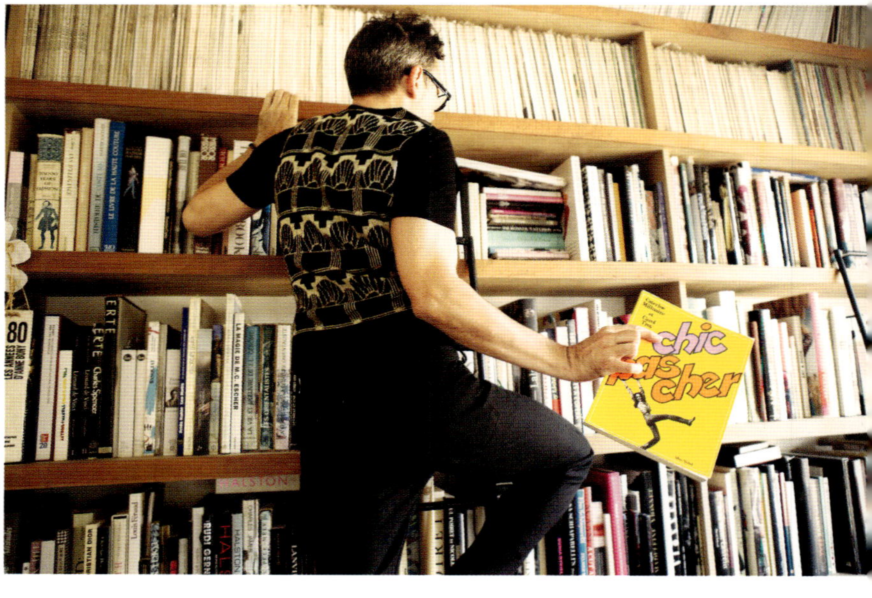

GEORGIANA BOBOC
A "WE" TYPE OF GAL

The apartment is miniscule, no more than 375 square feet, if that: adorable, cozy, and unmistakably girly. There's a large baroque chair on one side of the room, a bright blue lady's bicycle in front of the kitchen island, pastel floral wallpaper in the living room, a cute, white vanity by the sliding door, and a queen-size bed tucked away in the deepest depths of a tiny, dark bedroom. The place feels like Rapunzel's refuge, crammed with things frilly and shiny and colorful. And if one tried to imagine who lived here, she would probably have the allure of a Disney character, with big curly hair, red lips, diamond necklaces, and giant skirts. Her name might even be Georgiana.

It's hard to imagine a boy living here too, but he does: Sébastien, Georgiana's 30-year-old boyfriend of over a decade. And I have to ask—*where does he keep all* his *stuff?* There isn't a trace of testosterone in this ornate little bubble. When she pulls away curtains, we find boxes with shoes ("Boy, I love shoes. Quirkier the better!"). When she opens drawers we find trays with costume jewelry ("Everything with rhinestones is fascinating to me, especially cabaret jewelry, necklaces, and tiaras"). When she opens cabinets we find sunglasses, hats, and funny handbags. The couple is desperately looking for a bigger house, and they want to get married, because he is the love of her life, and her best friend. "I am also lucky enough to work with him for various projects," she smiles. "He takes most of my photos and now edits some of the video content that we started to create last spring."

Georgiana Boboc is a fashion blogger. She launched *vintage-traffic* as a school project and an outlet for her fashion writing, but it quickly became more. Georgiana's sartorial outbursts are hard to miss, and her fans are incredibly supportive. Now she devotes the blog and all her social media full-time to her love of vintage, her eccentric outfits, and frequent travels. Vintage first inspired her when she tried on her mom's and aunt's granny dresses. "Vintage is all about being unique and irreplaceable," she says. "Why would I want to wear the same things as anyone else?! Every time I go thrift shopping, it's like treasure hunting. And how fun to carry a bag full of goodies that come from so many different eras and tell so many exciting stories?"

Georgiana is 29 years old and originally from Romania. She was always a happy kid, despite the fact that her parents suffered a tough existence. "They didn't have much," she says. "They were obliged by circumstance to limit their lives to modest things. I didn't experience the communist era, but my family educated me in such a way that I would later appreciate my freedom in all its shapes." She wanted to be a secret agent growing up. "My father printed me an FBI badge that I kept for years and years," she laughs. "I showed it every time I was in trouble. That was pretty unrealistic, unlike my current position which is all about not keeping secrets, and digitally spreading all sorts of daily news from my life."

Blogging has become a very lucrative business, but vintage isn't and never will be, so I ask her if she feels like she needs to compromise her image to make ends meet. A lot of very successful girls started out selling vintage—Nicole Warne of Gary Pepper Vintage, Jessica Stein of Tuula Vintage, Sophia Amoruso of Nasty Gal—but they all abandoned their core identity for a commercial strategy. "In order to succeed in this harsh industry these sorts of marketing compromises are legit," says Georgiana. "To be digitally successful nowadays means you have to determine your market—either high-end or fast retailing—and influence your public by promoting your choices. Vintage is not really positioned in any of those camps, and it is certainly not the best way to make money. As far as I'm concerned, I will never quit wearing vintage and posting about it on my blog. It is part of my style identity, and when I am creating content I always do it because I am truly passionate about it. The main purpose is to remain as transparent as possible and create high-quality content, whether it is sponsored or not."

Who knows, maybe her financial future lies in the hands of the beauty business. She most certainly has the face and the hair for it. And don't you think the apartment needs just a little bit more of a woman's touch, with say, makeup? Sebastien, better start clearing out your underwear drawer!

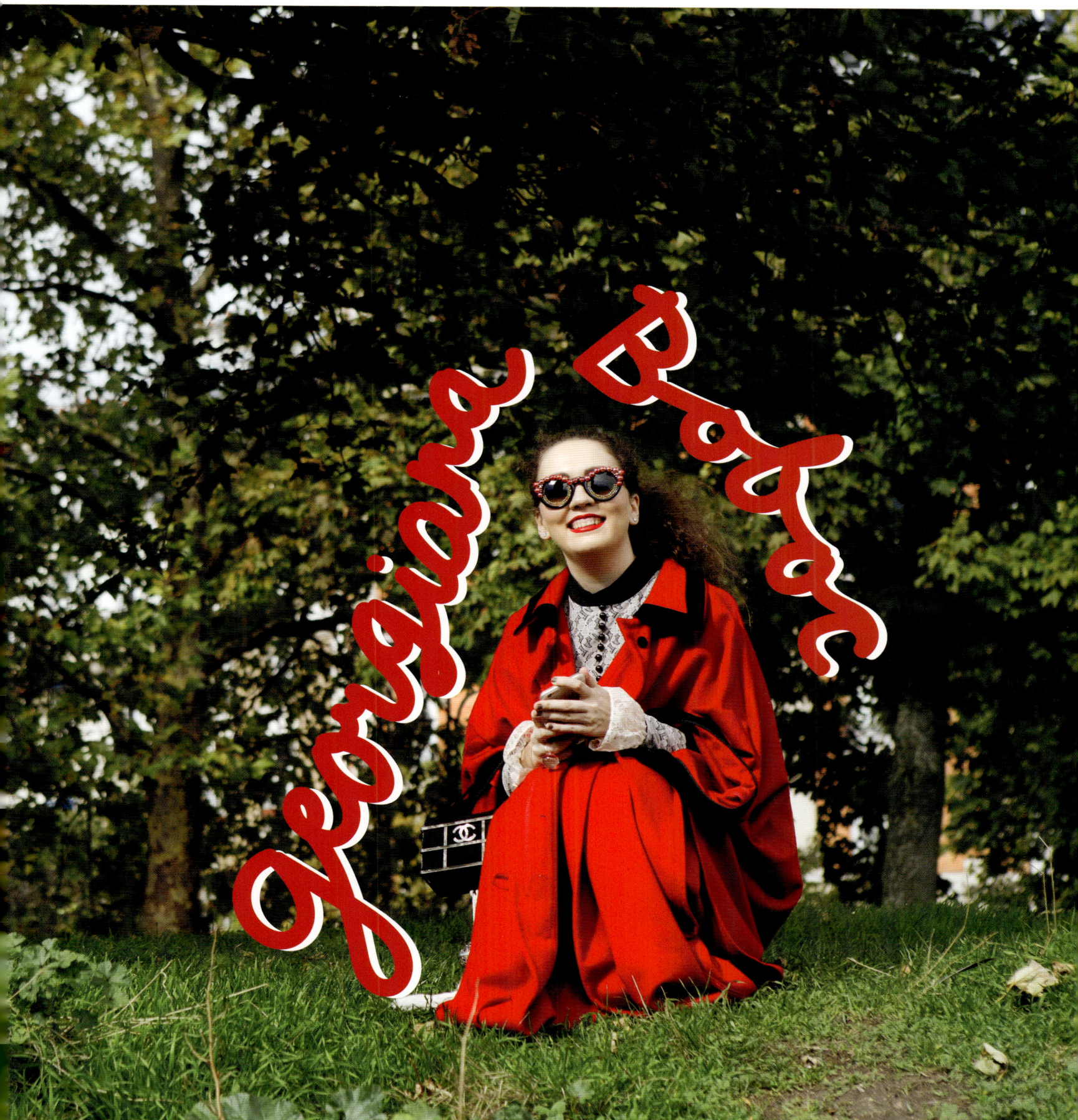

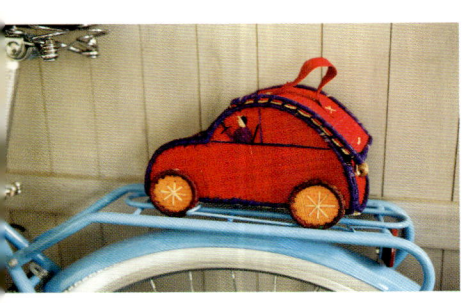
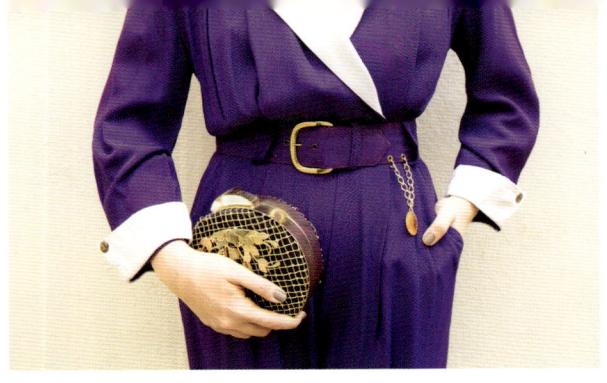
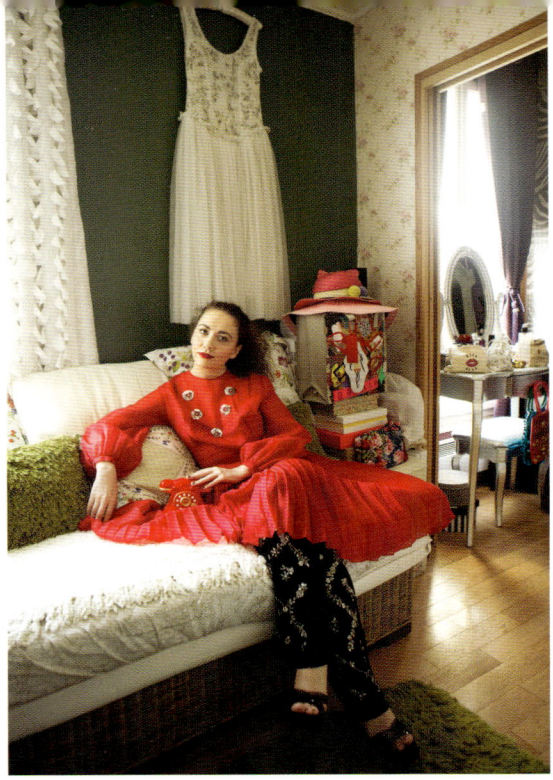
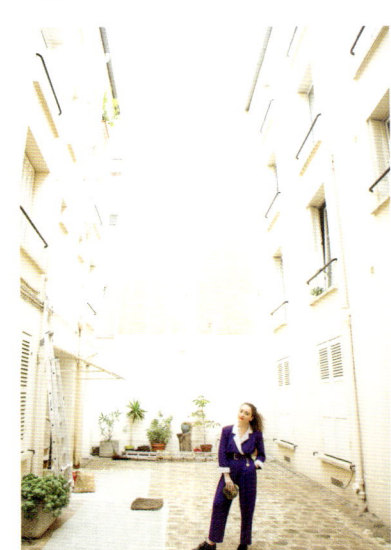
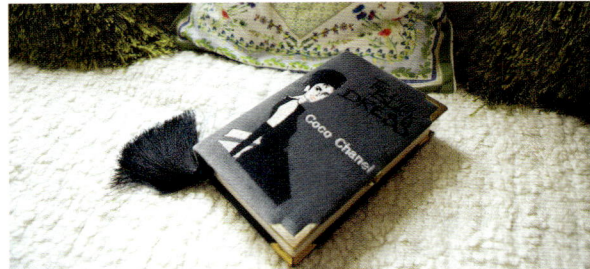
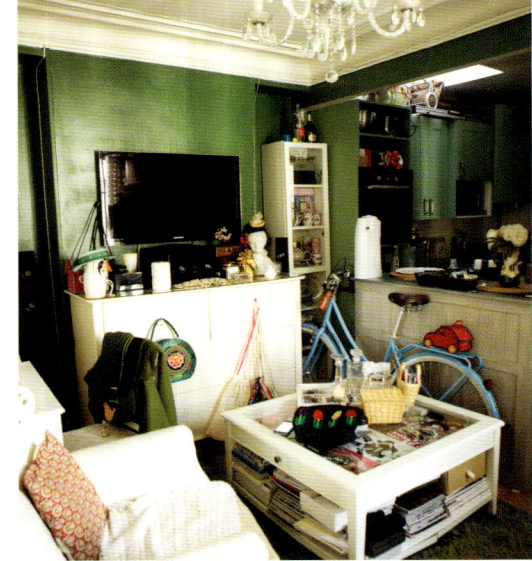
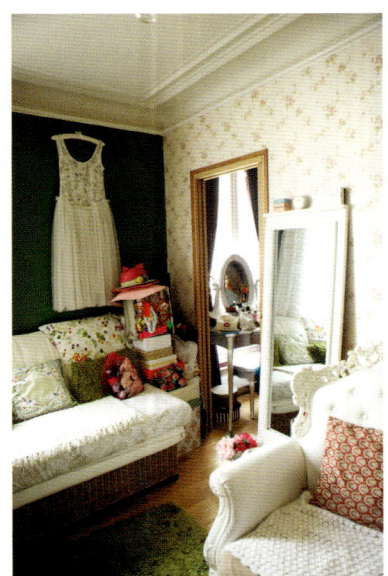
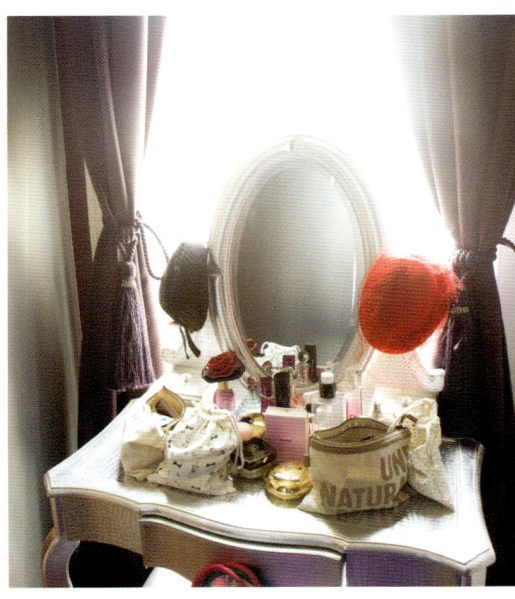
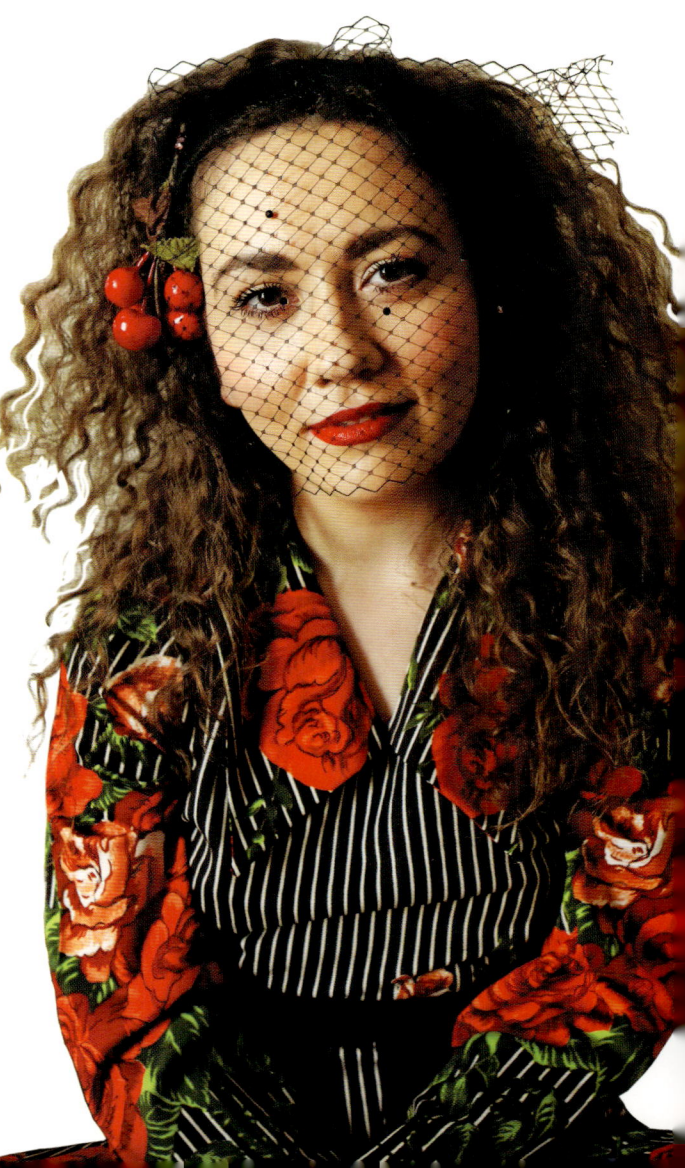
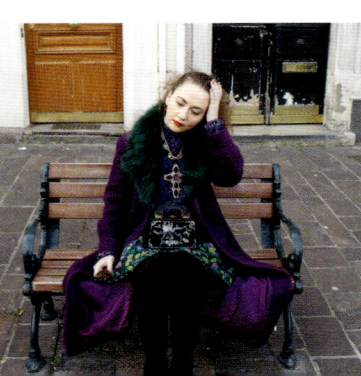

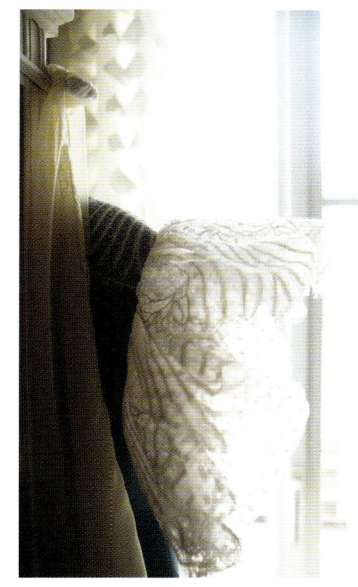
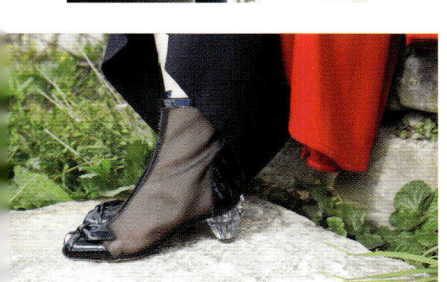
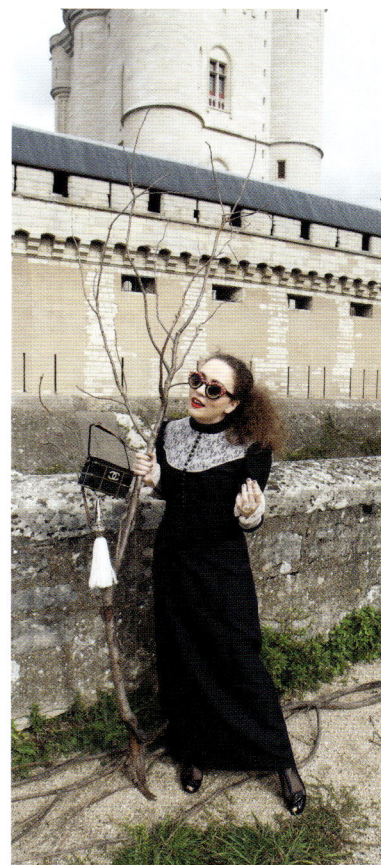
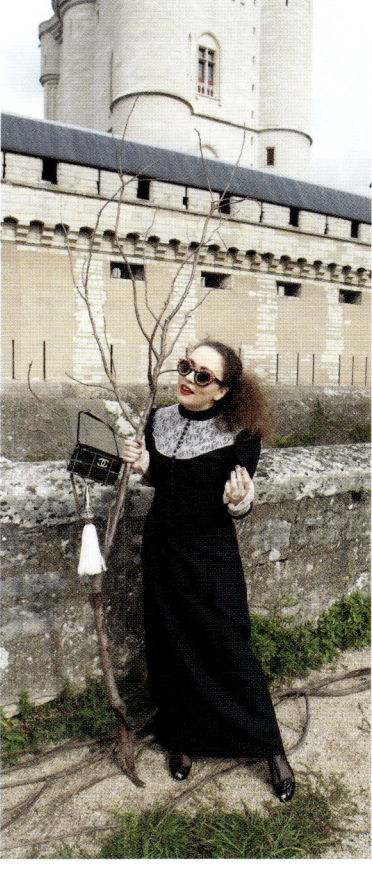
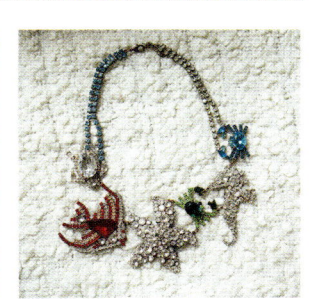
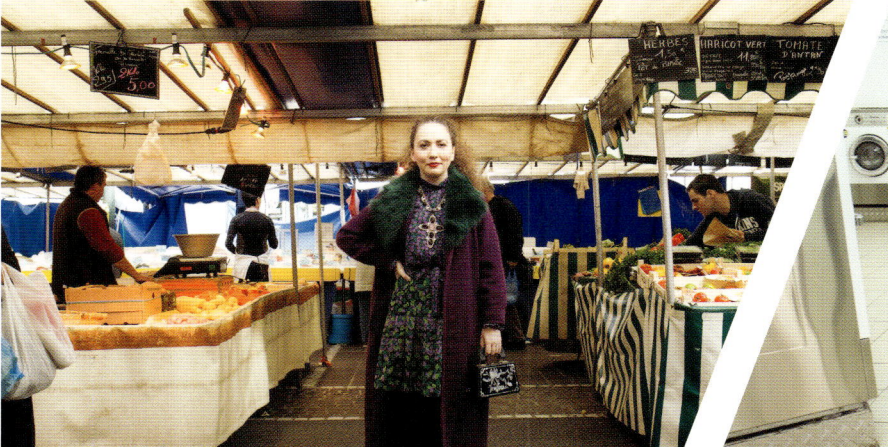
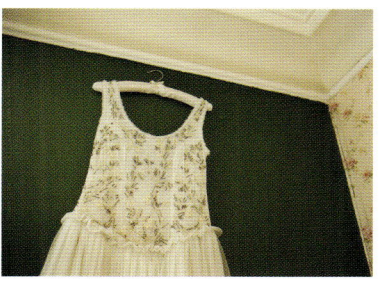
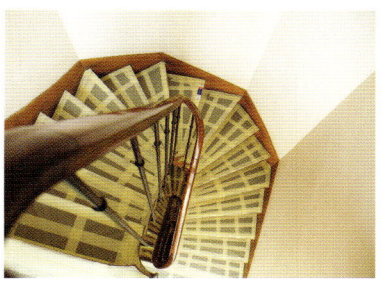
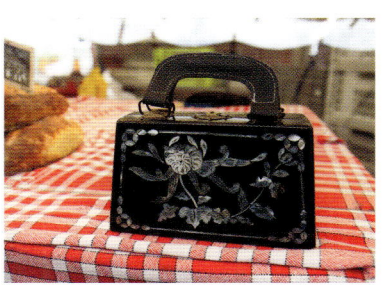
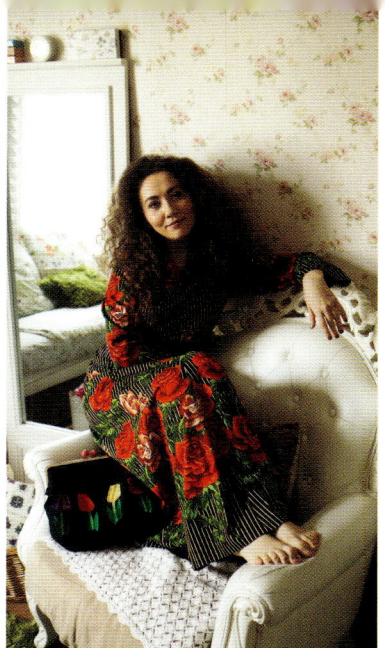
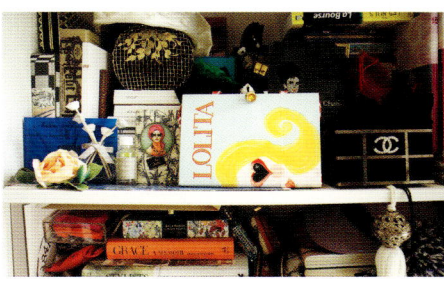
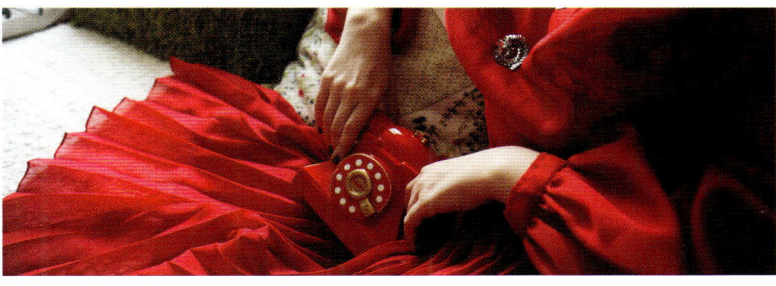

HAYETT MCCARTHY
MODEL CITIZEN

Hayett is on hold for the Céline show in Paris. It's a big deal, because booking and walking a show of this caliber could jumpstart her budding modeling career in ways she never imagined. And for a girl who's barely five-foot-eight, any push like that is priceless. There's not much else she can do but wait though, so here we are, in her small bedroom in North London, sitting on the bed, discussing her French accent and long hair. She's from Lyon originally, the only child of an Algerian mom and a British dad whom she says are both single parents and very close to her, "in a brotherly kind of way." It's raining outside—no surprise there—but we're keeping cozy. Hayett decides to make me her favorite drink. It's not a cocktail—although we both agree that would be splendid just about now—it's matcha tea. She loves the act of preparing it. She has all the wooden utensils and cups needed to be an excellent matcha-preparer. "It's very strong though," she warns, "makes me feel queasy sometimes." She also loves the smell of it and tells me her childhood memories retain a lot of olfactory information, like "a single cigarette my mum would light or the smell of stale tobacco or the smell of dried lavender," which all remind her of home. At one point she even had her mind set on becoming a "nose" in Grasse in the South of France, testing perfumes, but "sadly it requires not smoking or drinking and I wasn't about that at all at 18," she laughs.

Hayett's mom was also a model, "in the 80s, before the times when models were treated as people," claims Hayett, and thanks god those times have changed. As a kid she would look at her mom's test shoots and tiny pictures in Marie Claire and think she was a supermodel. Her own career path has been "full of rejection and acceptance," she says, but she's in good hands at IMG. (In the two years after this interview Hayett went on to become the face of Burberry and booked hundreds more shows and editorials!)

It's ironic though, how someone who loves vintage shopping so much doesn't have the patience for it. Hayett started thrifting out of necessity first, because she didn't have the funds to buy new clothes, but "now the times have changed—old habits die hard—and you will still find me at Goodwill and vintage stores," she smiles. The only thing is, she will never spend more than 30 minutes looking. She claims to have no discernable style either, no uniform. "Every day is new," she says. "I'm insatiably curious and influenced by music and what genre is stuck in my head as I'm getting ready." And if you believe her, those playlists could be anything from Detroit/Hacienda acid house to 70s punk.

Hayett is a cool girl. She most definitely has a style. I'd say it's mod with a touch of Amy Winehouse. I love how lanky and awkward she is, and how she started the hashtag #randomrubberglovesseries, posting pictures of rubber gloves she finds in the street all over the world. In the next few months she'll have to get rid of Othello, the big black cat she got from a friend, "because he wouldn't stop meowing, did everybody's head in." She never did book that Céline show, but you know what? She swears by her motto "forever changes," and that's a fail-proof formula.

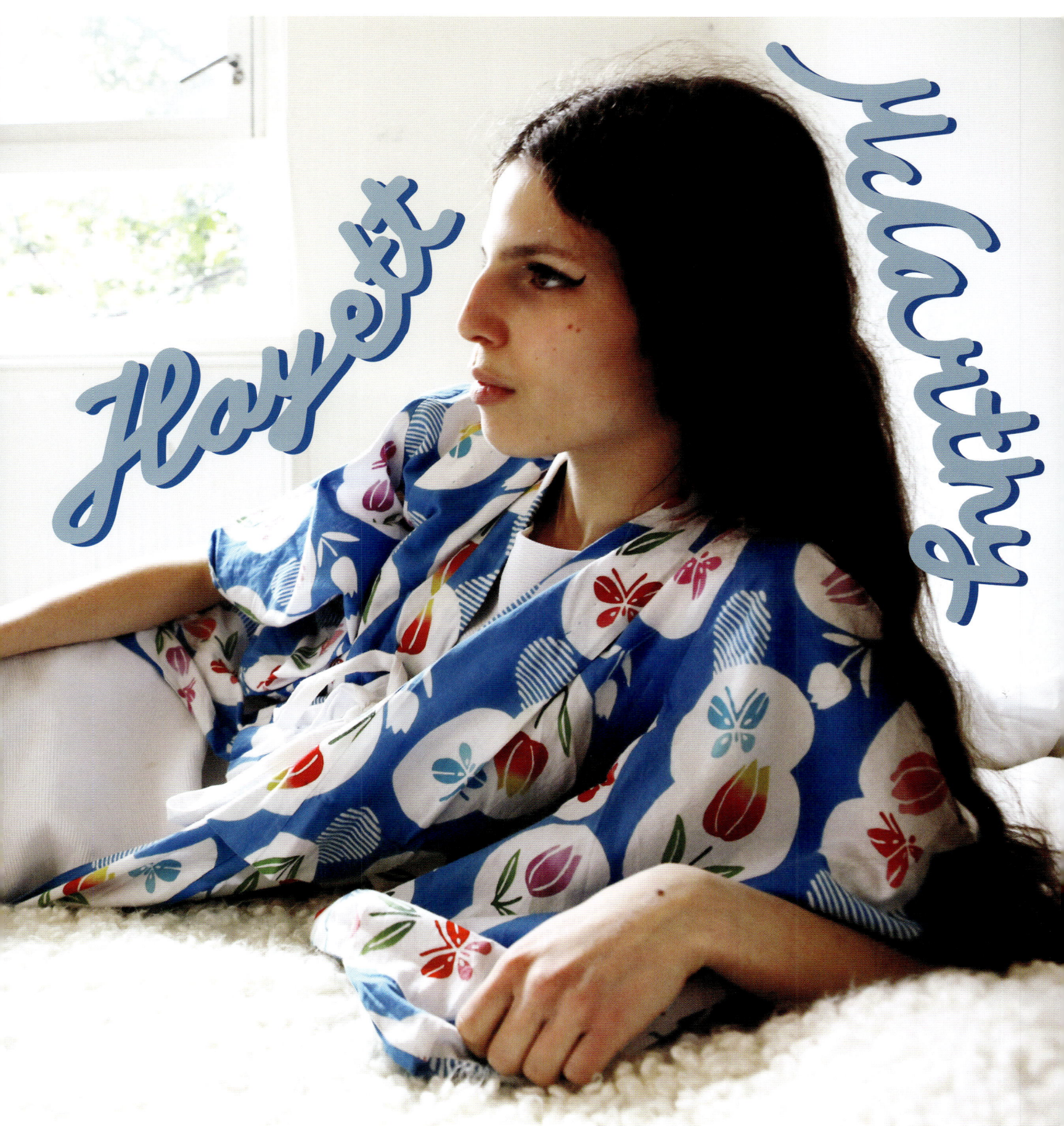

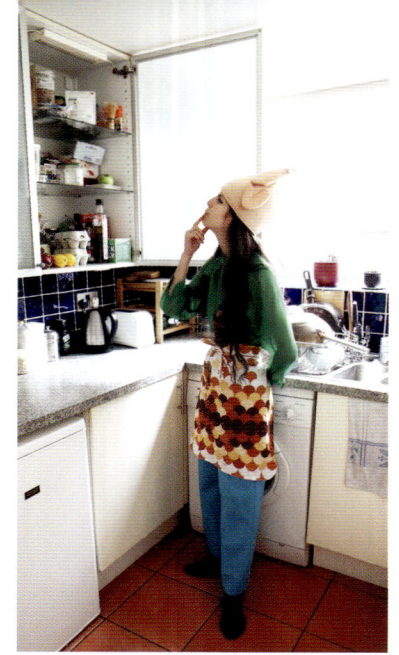
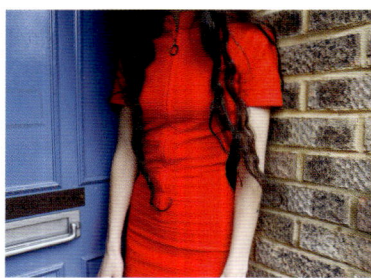
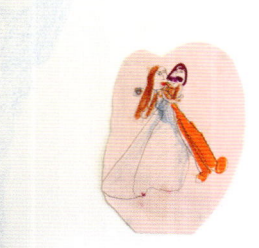
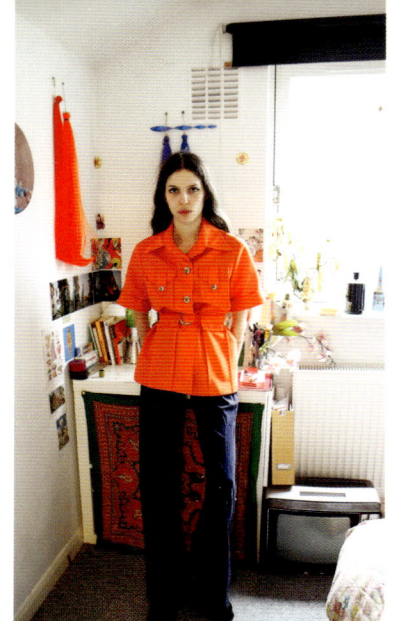
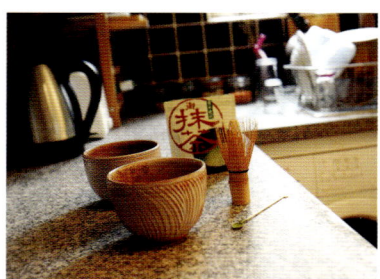
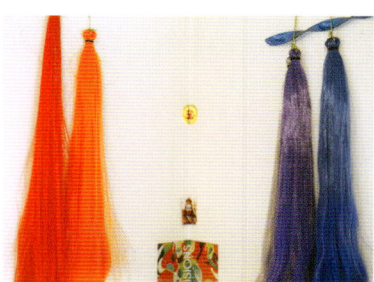
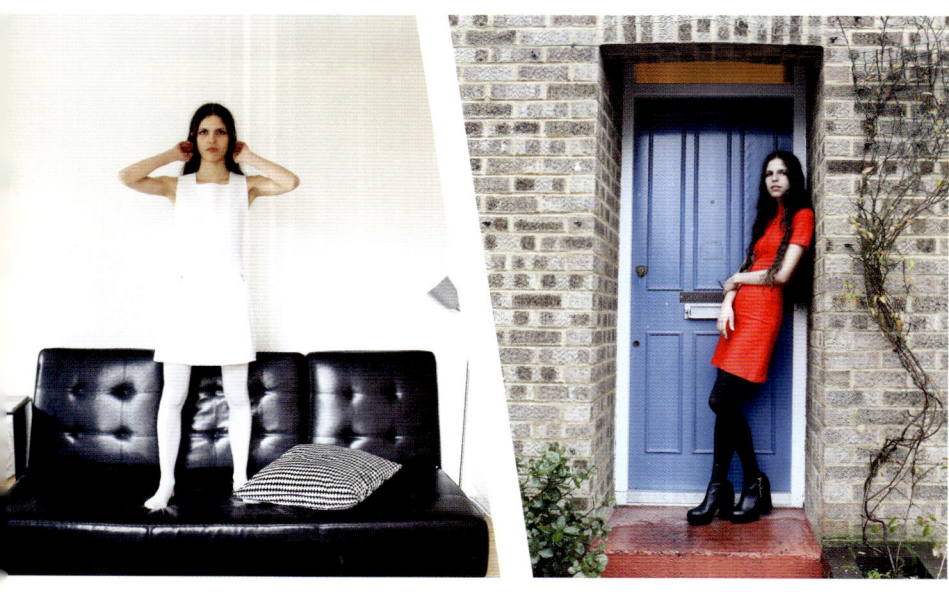
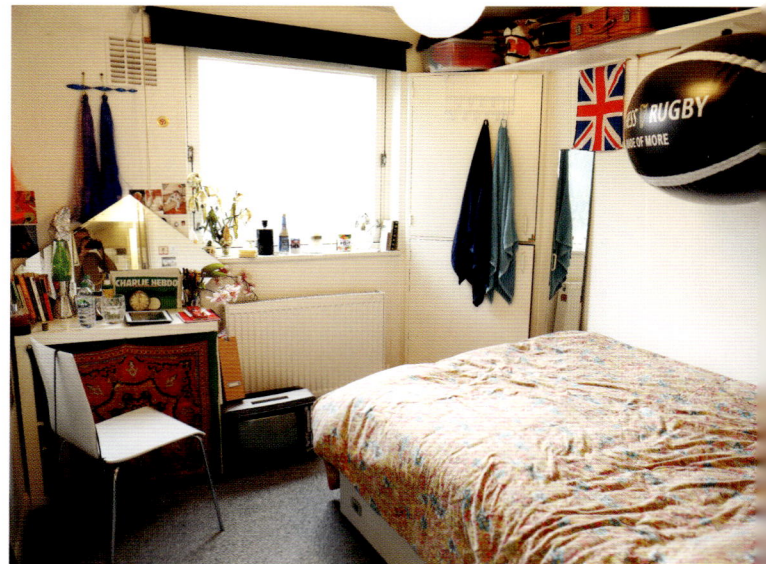
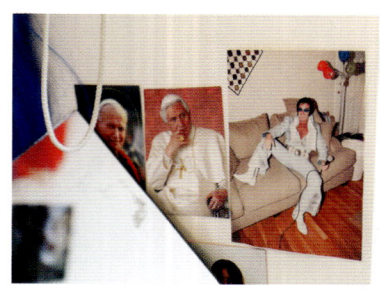
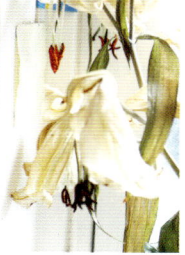
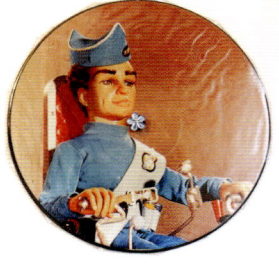
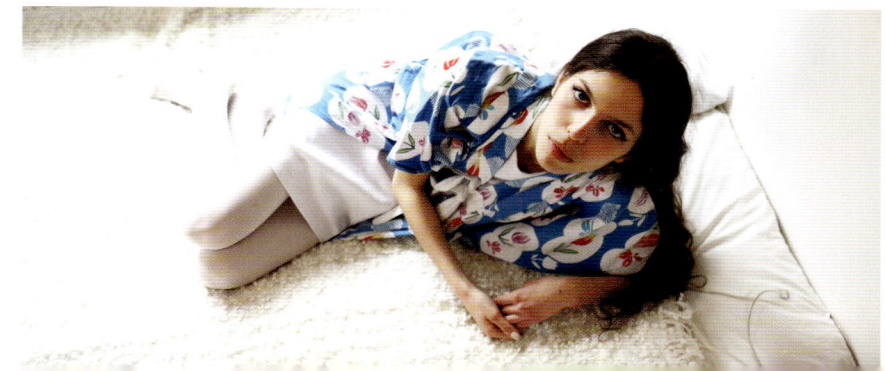
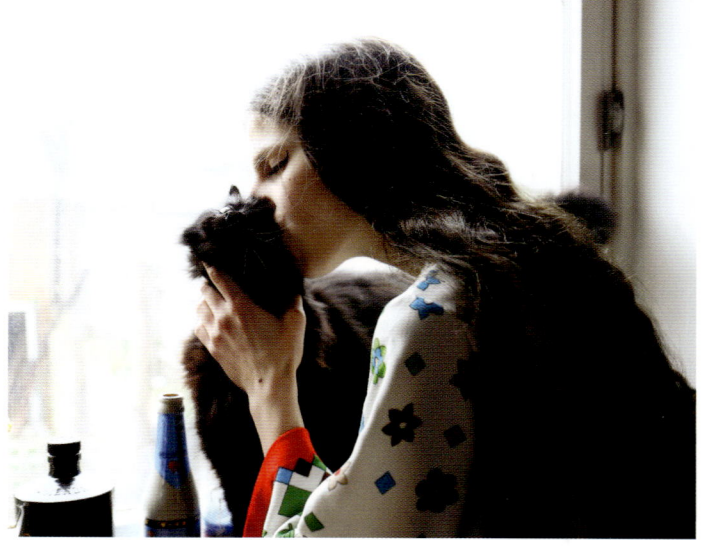

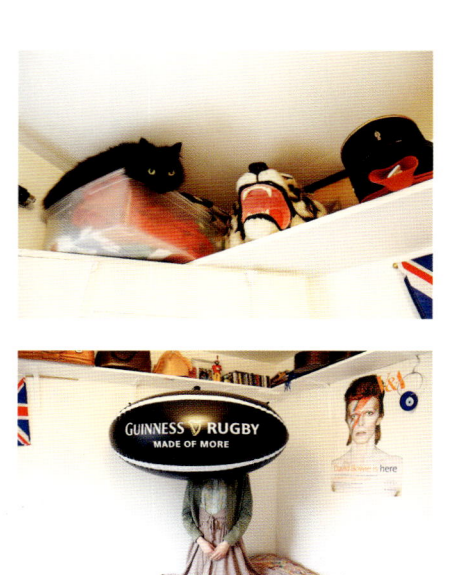
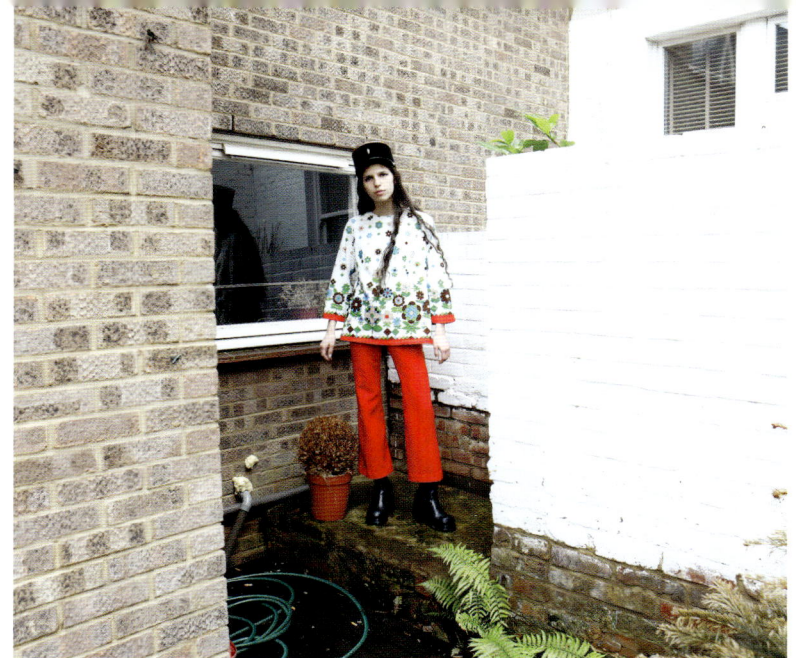
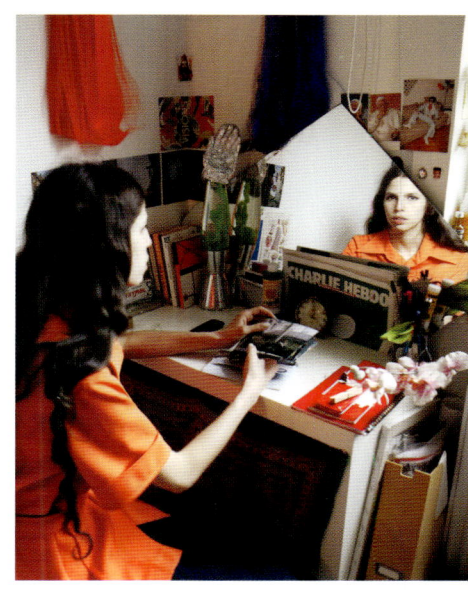
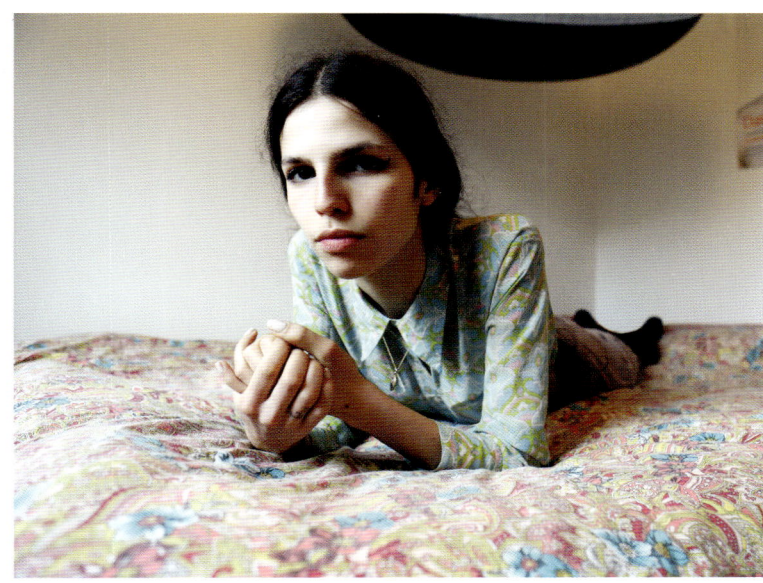
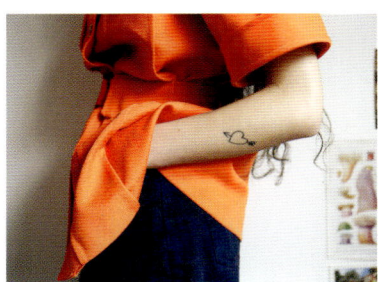
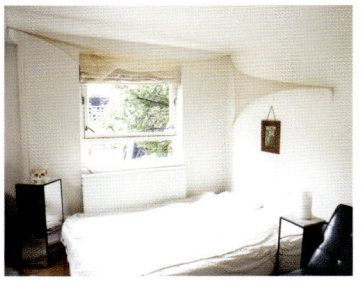
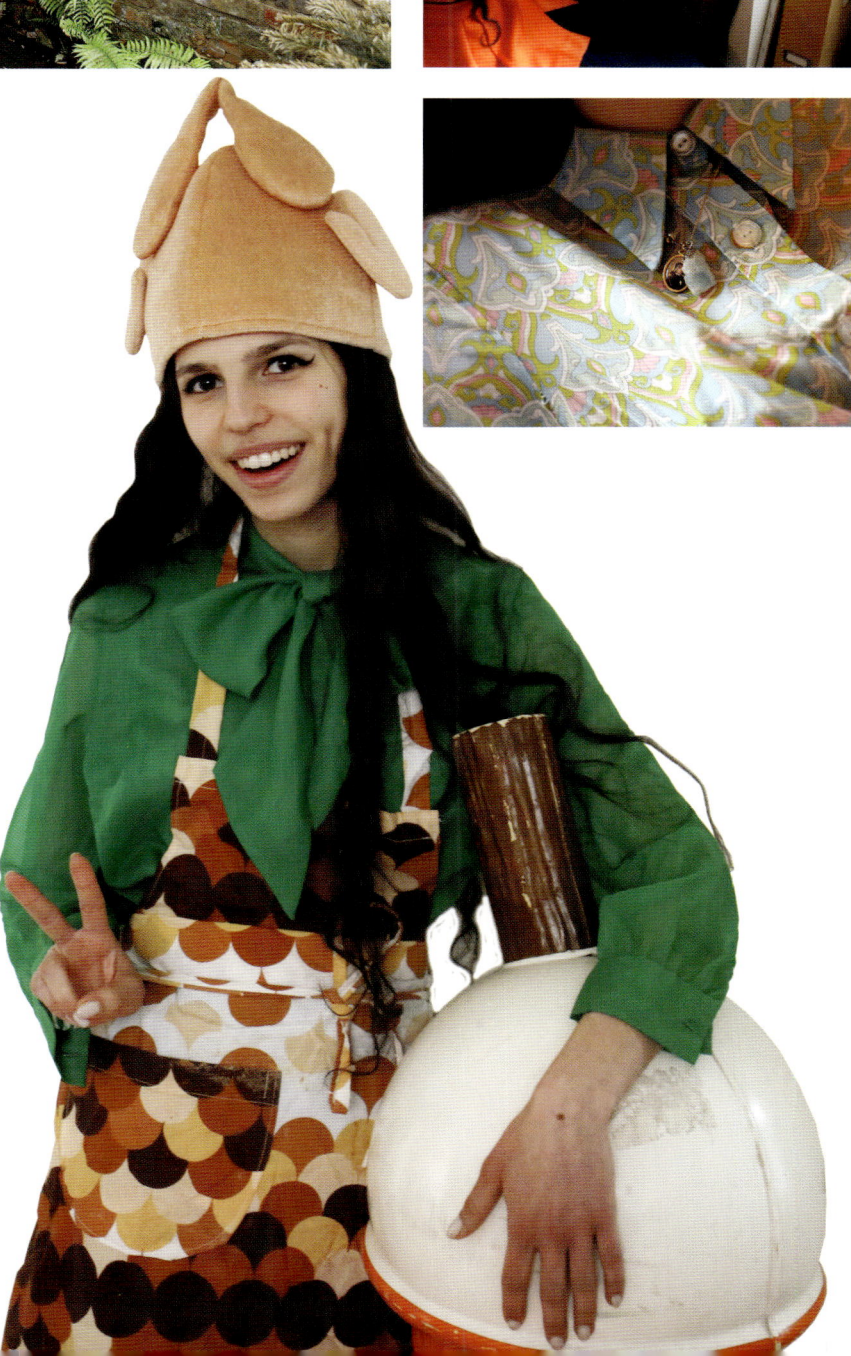
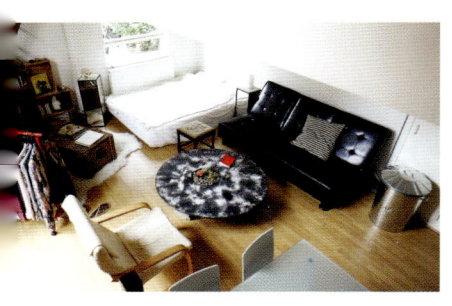
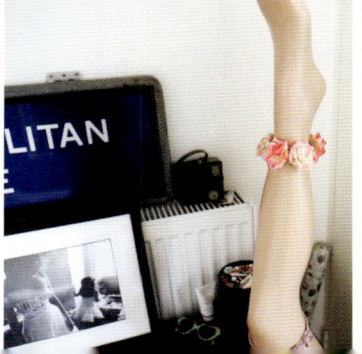

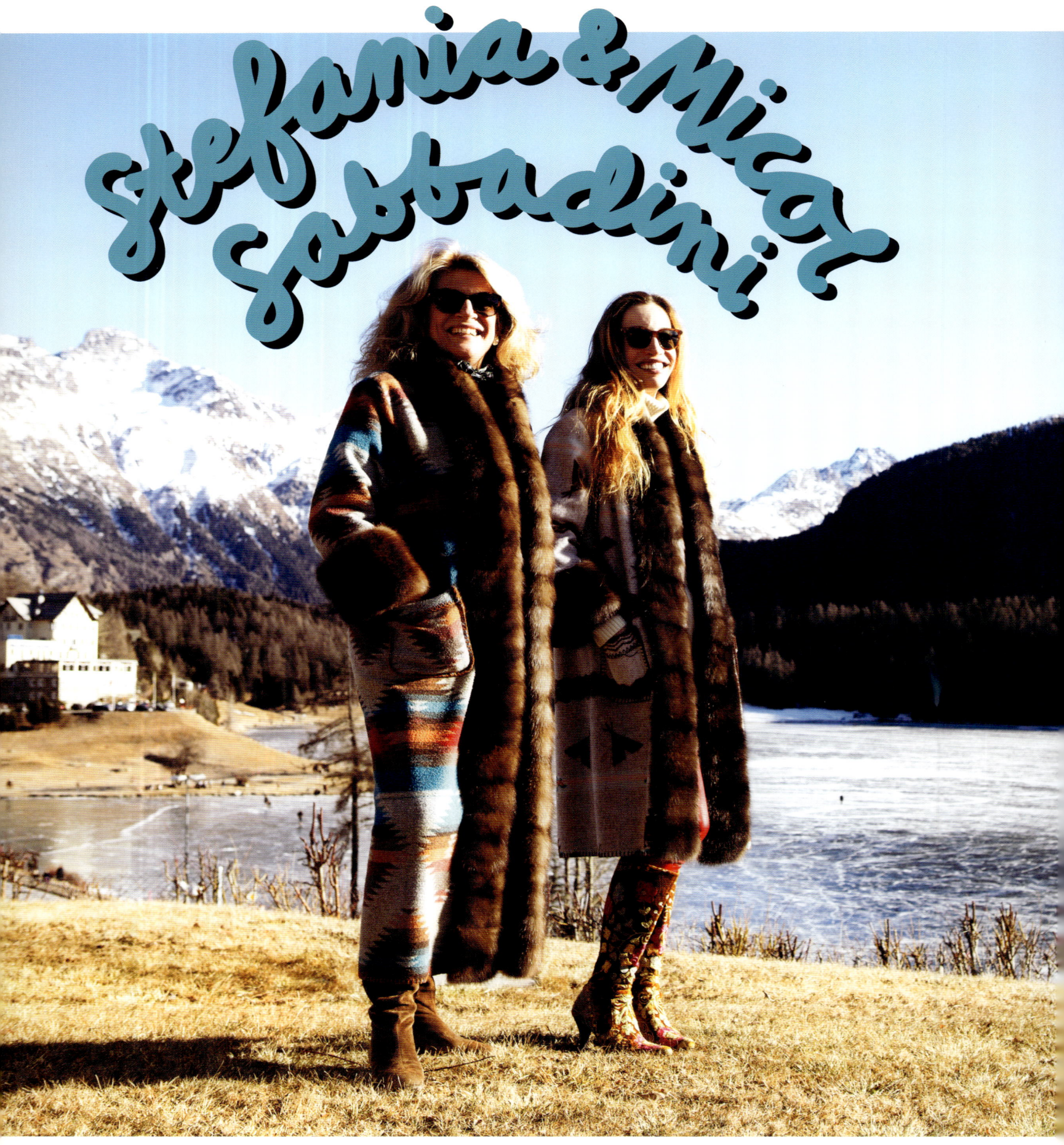

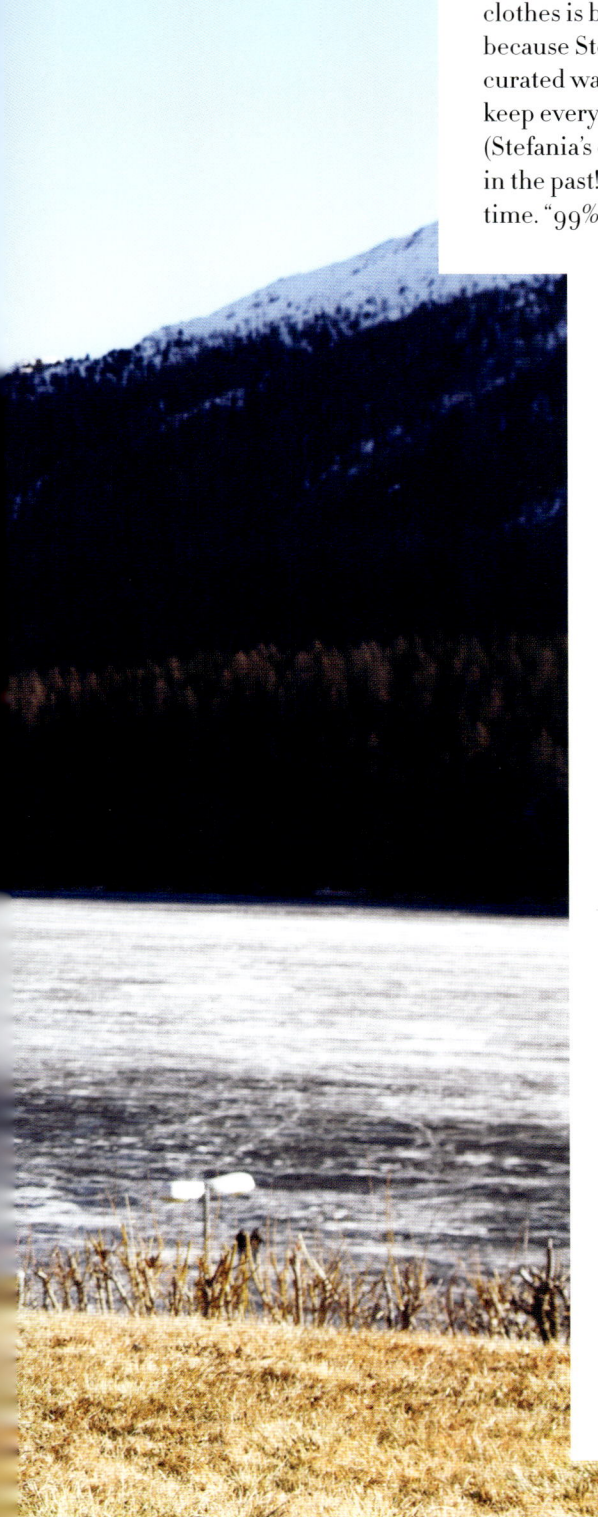

STEFANIA & MICOL SABBADINI
WHEN YOUR MOM IS YOUR GREATEST STYLE ICON

When your mom is your greatest style icon and her closet is just a stone's throw away in the next room, the very thought of having dibs on such an organically amalgamated collection of vintage clothes is both a burden and a blessing: a burden, because Stefania (mom) is neither ready nor willing to part with every piece of her carefully curated warbrobe; a blessing, because eventually, Micol (daughter) knows that she will. "I keep everything," smiles Stefania, "because I know Micol loves to go 'shopping' in my closet." (Stefania's collection of vintage Ralph Lauren is so big that Ralph himself has requested access in the past!) The mother/daughter legacy dynamic is strong, but it's contained by the order of time. "99% of my vintage things are from my mom's closet," admits Micol. "I patiently wait for her not to fit into them anymore or to say, 'This is no longer appropriate for me.'"

Micol and I are meant to be in Hawaii right now—kite surfing and taking photos of waterfalls and black sand beaches—but the weather reports looked less-than-promising. So, rather than risk getting stuck in avalanches of tropical, torrential rain, we decided to spend our Christmas holidays in St. Moritz, where her parents have their second home, a showroom for Sabbadini Gioielli at the Palace Hotel, and a furniture/gift store across the street. And I think we made the right decision. There's plenty of snow, sunshine for days, and a magnificent slew of friends and family from all over the world to visit and party with.

The Sabbadini family is tight-knit. When they're not vacationing in St. Moritz, they all live in Milan. Alberto is the unarguable patriarch of the house. He's a jeweler, part-time art collector, and the designer of the incredibly crafted bed I am sleeping in. "He's slightly controlling, and will never admit he is wrong, but he is by far the most loving father anyone could ever have!" laughs Micol. Stefania and Alberto have been together 42 years, and married for 35. She was studying law, but when they met she quit and now calls herself a "full-time wife working with the husband." A few years ago she launched her own line of coats made of Native American blankets that sell at the shop. Pierandrea, Micol's older half-brother, is visiting with his wife and two daughters. "We are complete opposites on most character traits and interests," claims Micol, "except for sports. We both 100% adore sports and each other." These are Stefania's most treasured moments, "when we are all together, working or on vacation, but only us. We have sooo many things to speak about, and we laugh a lot when we are together."

When your mom is your greatest style icon, she's also bound to instill a few important grooming and life lessons. Micol learned "to always wear matching bra and underwear, to use moisturizer every day, and to start taking care of my skin at an early age. To not care about what people say or expect me to do or be, and just be happy." Stefania agrees. She wants Micol to "smile always, in the face of bad days, because life is beautiful, even when you have clouds around you." And sometimes you have to learn the hard way, like she experienced firsthand on her second date with Alberto: "I arrived to dinner at a friend's house in a dramatic evening dress and everybody was wearing pants and a blouse. I felt soooo bad that it never happened again. Better to be more casual than too dressed up!"

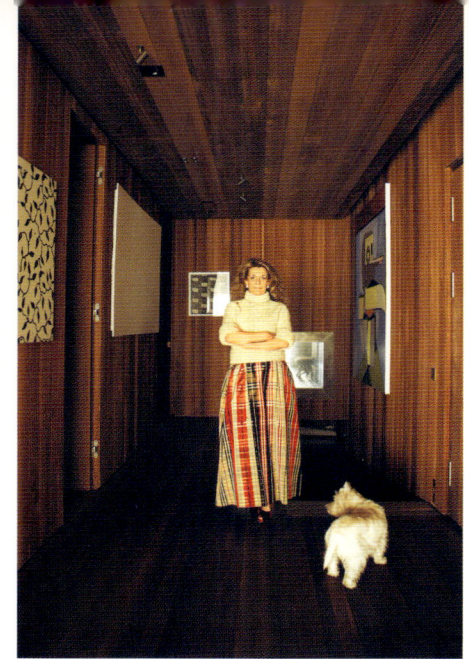
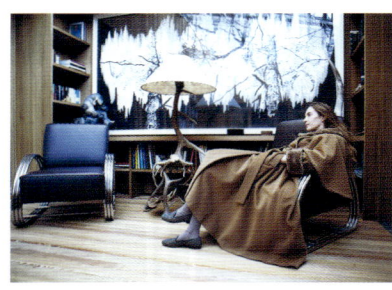
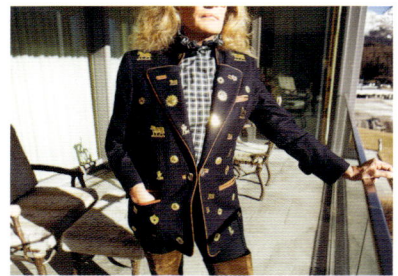
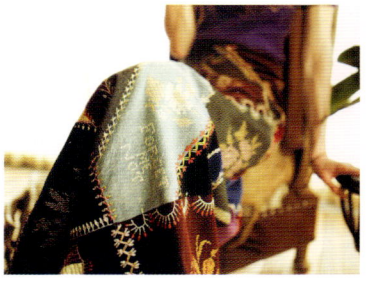
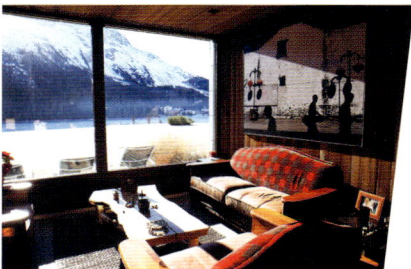
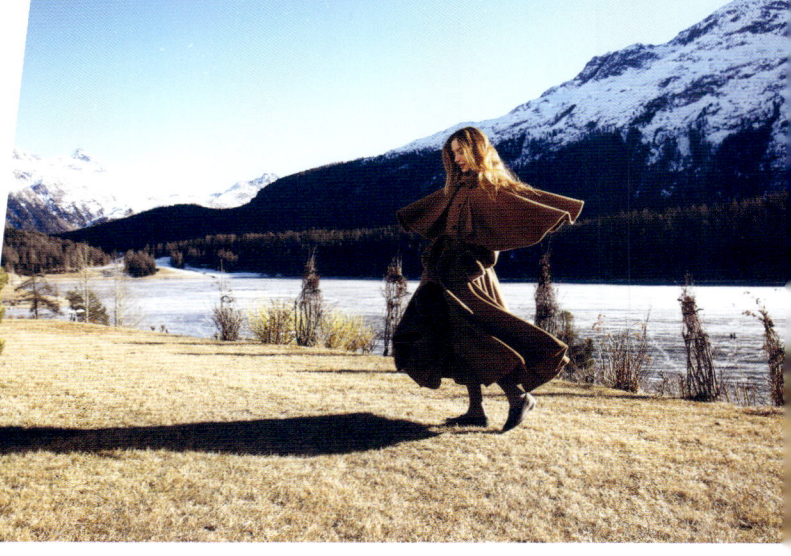
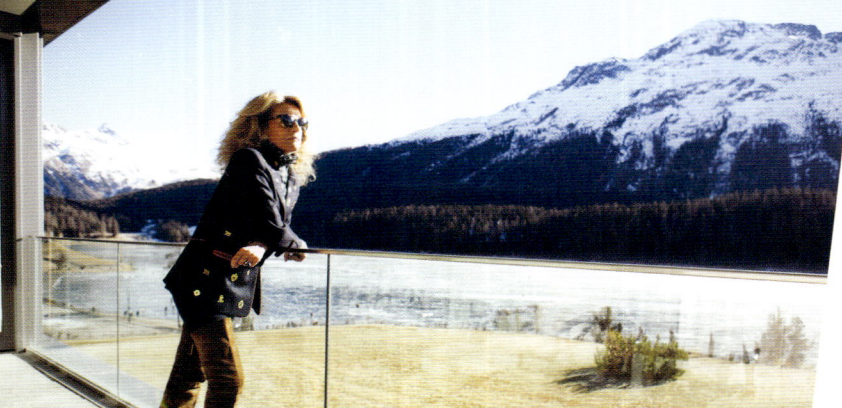
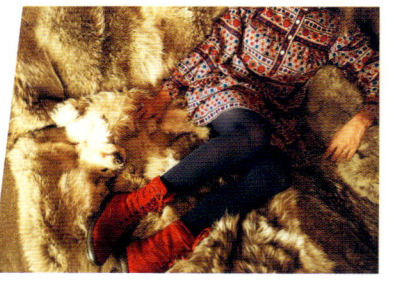
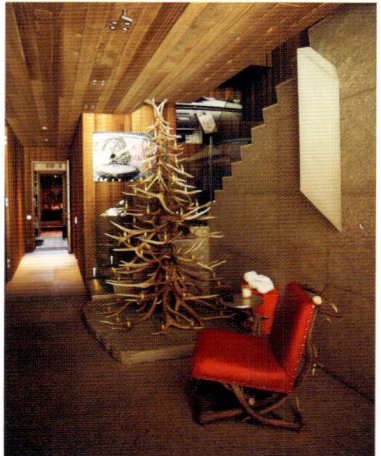
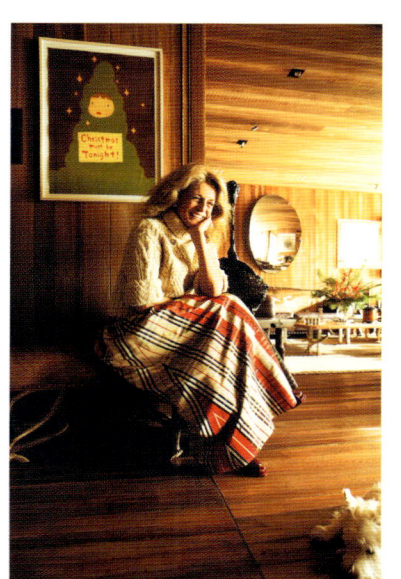
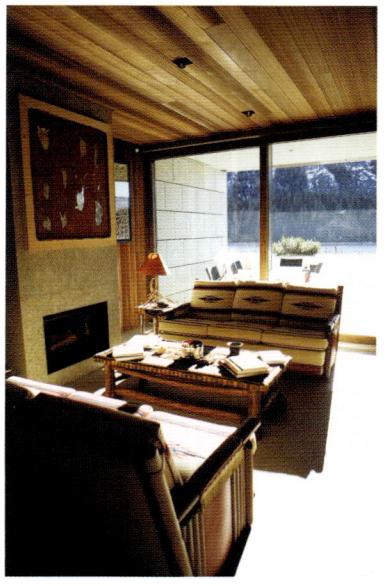
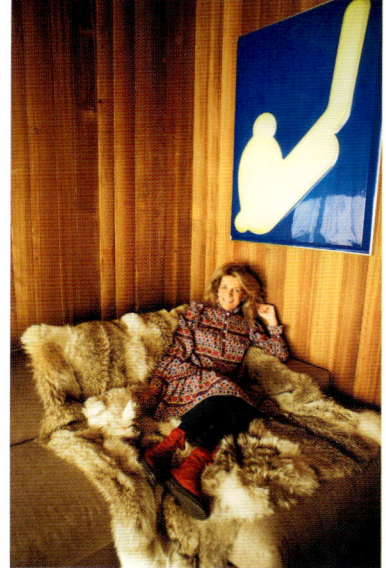
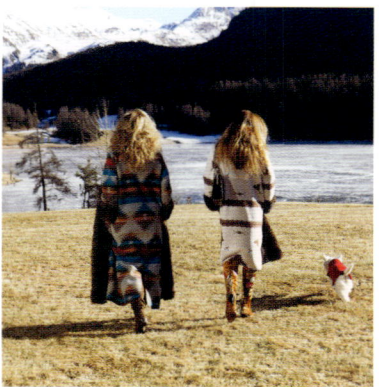

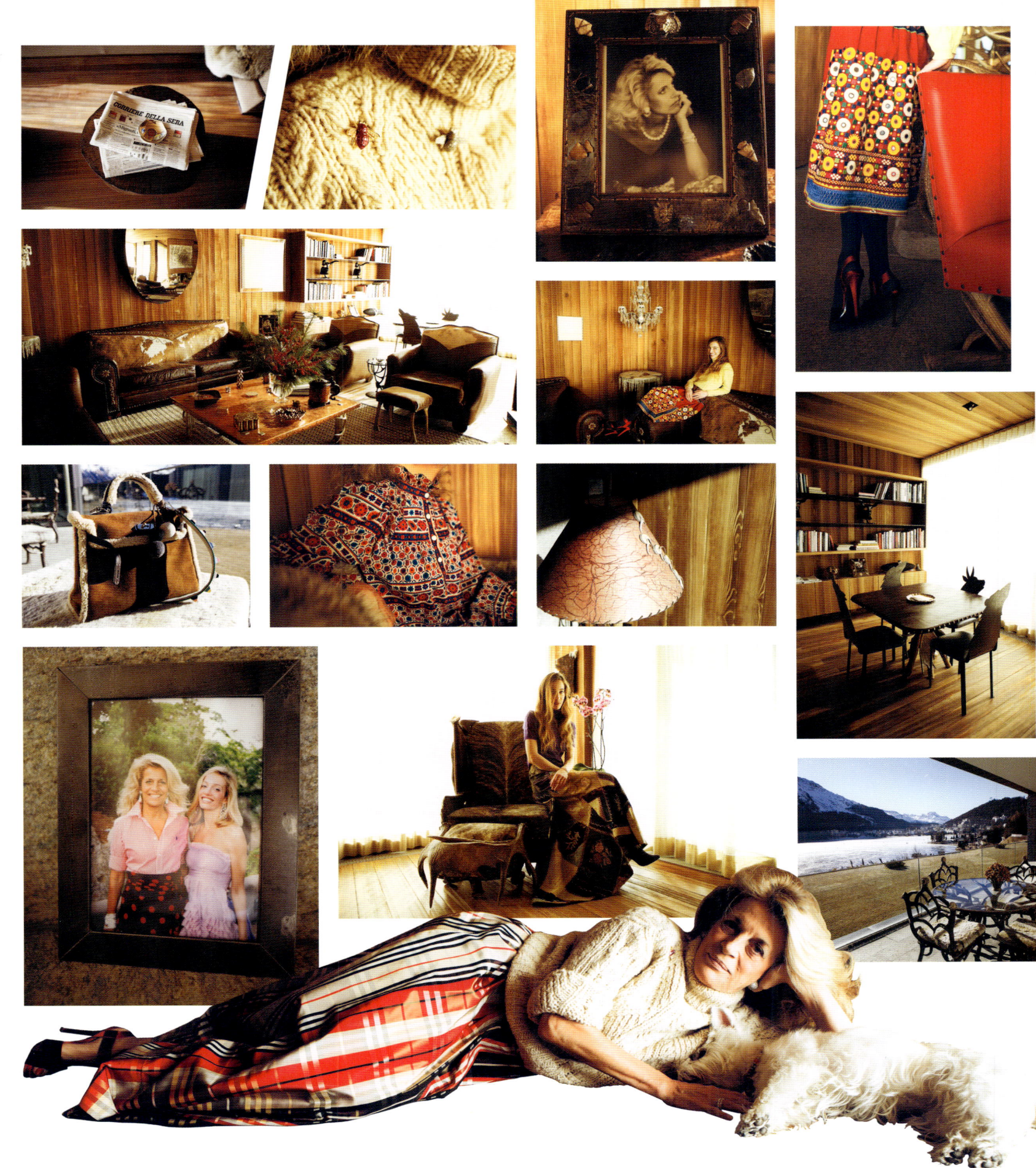

DAMIAN YEE
A JAMAICAN IN PARIS

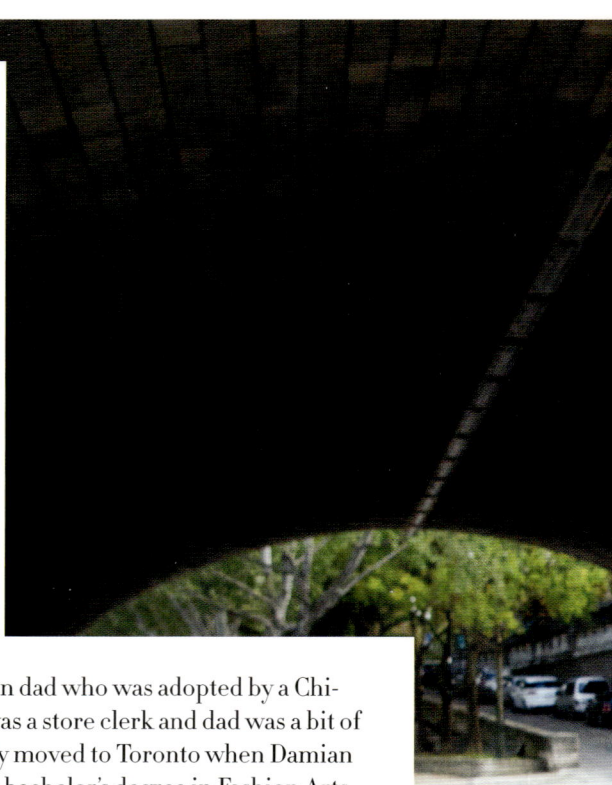

As he pulls out suit after suit from the closet, he discovers more and more moth holes. "Merde," he whimpers when his favorite 80s Gaultier jacket appears, ravaged. Perhaps it's the price to pay for living in a luxurious, dark, antiques store on Boulevard Saint-Germain. It's a beautiful place, but the resident couple has more or less become part of the decor, and been forced to comply with its commercial environment. "We always have to be dressed up when the shop is open," grins Damian wagging his finger. "So no lounging during the day in track pants! Even though I don't own a pair..."

For a young boy in Jamaica who spent his days climbing the hill behind his house, playing well into the night, and imagining being an explorer of unchartered forests, living in Paris may not have been a realistic goal, but when Damian Paul Yee laid eyes on Yves Saint Laurent's iconic oversized pink bow, it sealed his fate. One day he would dance with Christian Louboutin at Le Palace, design 50 outfit changes for a movie that went to Cannes, and dwell on the banks of the Seine in a vintage kilt. It was just a matter of time, talent, and the right trajectory.

Damian is the second-youngest son of a Chinese-born mom raised in Jamaica, and a Jamaican dad who was adopted by a Chinese family. The couple had five kids before they got married, and had six more later. Mom was a store clerk and dad was a bit of a gambler; he built a few casinos in the north of the island but alas, lost everything. The family moved to Toronto when Damian was 12. He spent some time in New York during his teenage years and came back to finish his bachelor's degree in Fashion Arts.

That's when he won the "Jeunes Createurs de la Mode" competition as Canada's representative. "That trip confirmed Paris," he remembers. "I came and fell in love with the city, and actually showed up late at the competition show because I was out exploring. I went out every night to Les Bains Douches at the time when Prince, Grace Jones, Sting, Mickey Rourke, and all the stars were partying there like regulars." The young Jamaican boy had arrived.

Style was everything in those days, and vintage the easy-access, affordable go-to. Damian was first drawn to vintage by watching Cyndi Lauper's "Girls Just Wanna Have Fun" video, and music was a big influence in general. He names Paul Weller, Sade, and Madonna as his style icons. "As I got older I would mix designer clothes from Matsuda, Yohji Yamamoto, Comme des Garçons, and Gaultier with vintage pieces." He wears a lot of suits, old and new, and tapers all his pant legs to fit him just the way he wants.

Despite the fact that he skipped classes frequently himself, Damian eventually became a fashion teacher at three schools: La Chambre Syndicale de la Couture Parisienne, Parsons Paris, and Paris College of Art. "I teach third and fourth final years," he explains, "so the students are basically preparing their own collections. I give creative consulting and technical help, as well as honing their vision to become a coherent concept and line-up." As the former Creative Director at Guy Laroche, Damian is more than expertly equipped to educate these kids.

So what about that movie? "I had worked with the director Olivier Dahan before, on one of his comedy musicals called *Mozart Opera Rock*," he begins, "and when he finalized *Grace of Monaco*, he wanted someone with a fashion couture background to oversee Nicole Kidman's costumes. We had a real couture atelier working for eight months on her changes." The film was not so well received, mostly because the press did not think Nicole was a convincing Grace Kelly. "Plus," Damian adds, "I guess there was also a lot of talk since the family did not like the portrayal of Grace as the savior of Monaco." But the fashion was sublime. Check!

At the shop, Damian sits down with a cup of tea. As we discuss today's pictures, and a satisfactory course of action to attack the moths, his boyfriend joins us—a sophisticated, sarcastic Frenchman named Francis Dorléans. You may know him as the author of *Snob Society*. They've been together almost 25 years. The bell interrupts us a few times and I begin to understand what it's like. "The decor changes every couple of years so it feels like new," Damian comments. "And of course you learn not to be attached to things because everything basically is for sale." Except those darned moths.

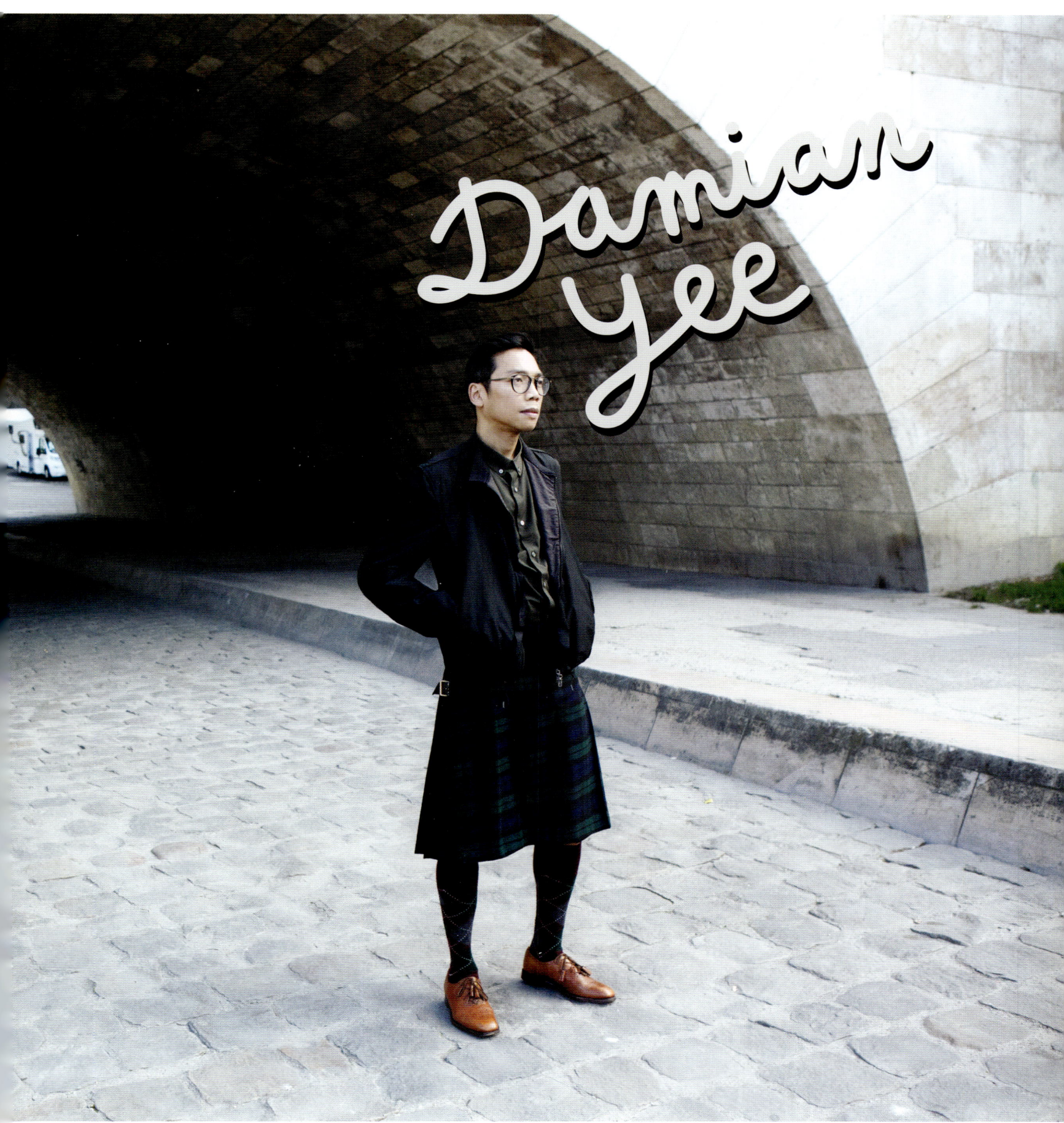

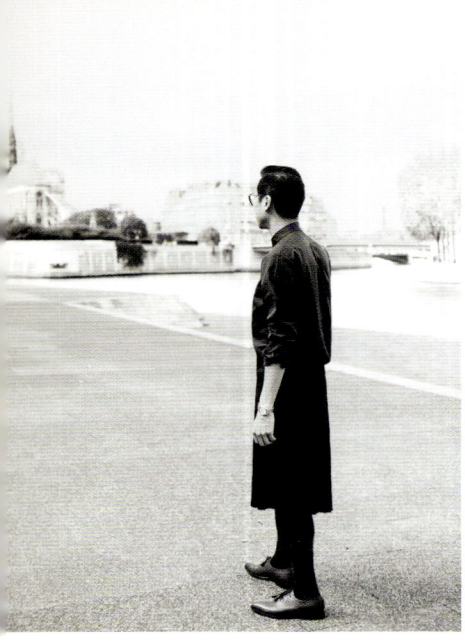
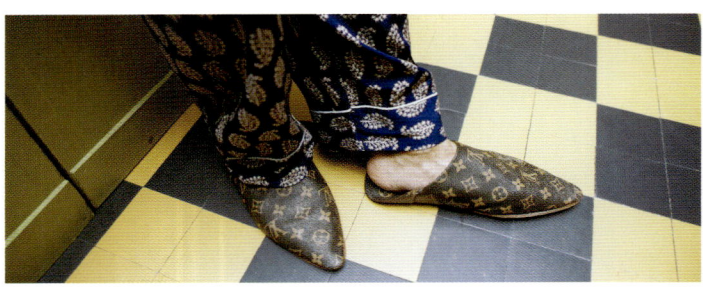
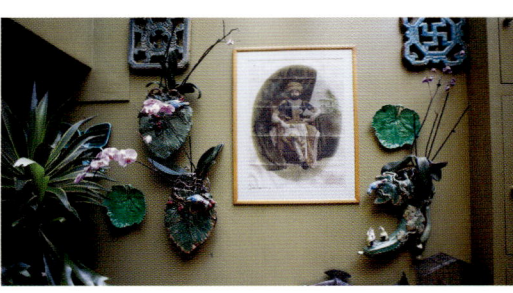
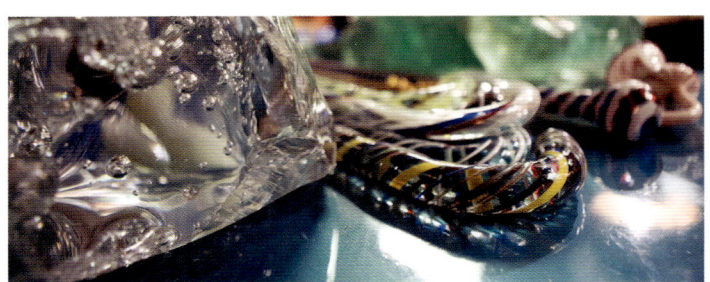
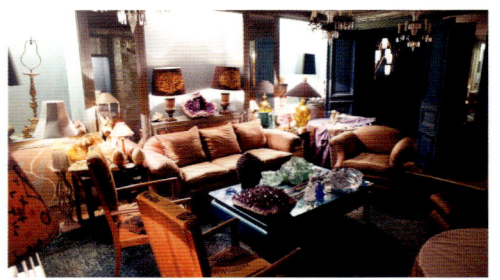
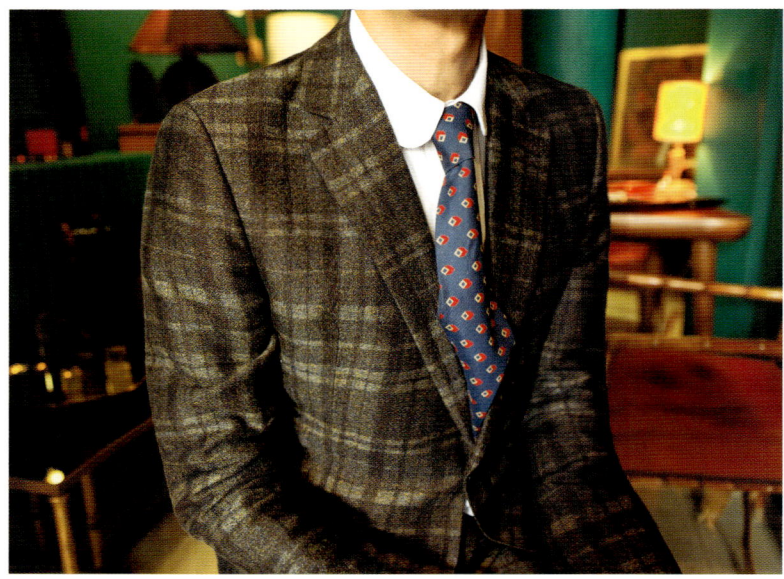
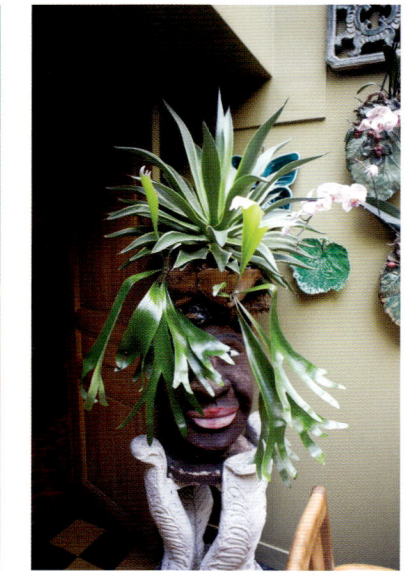
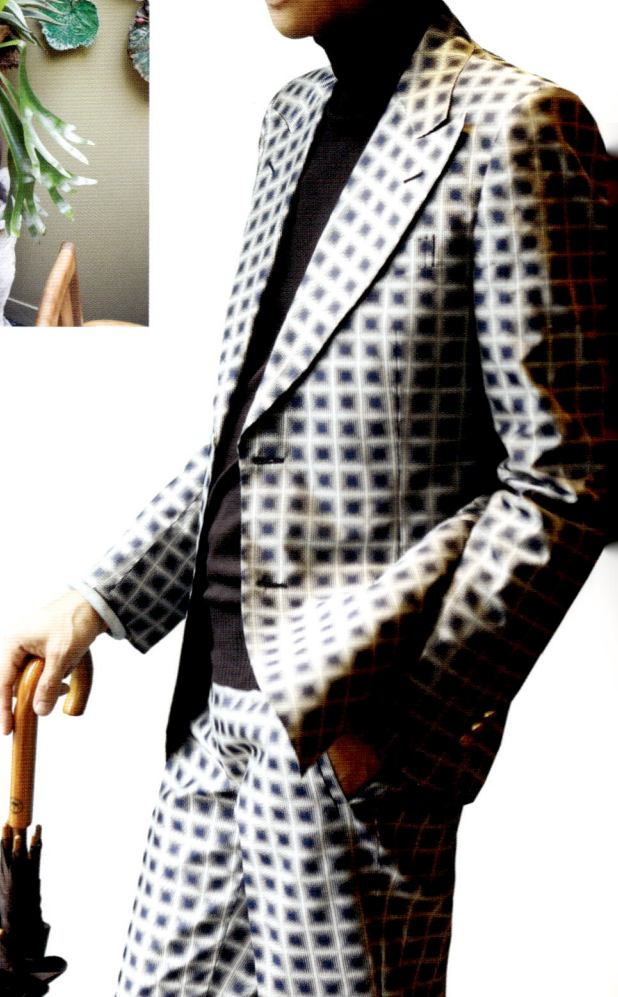
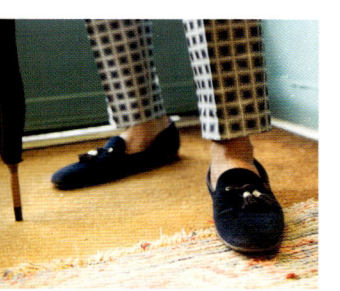
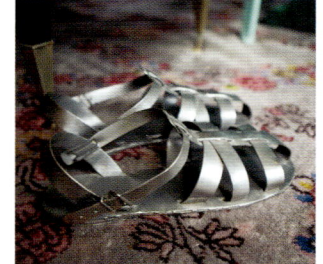
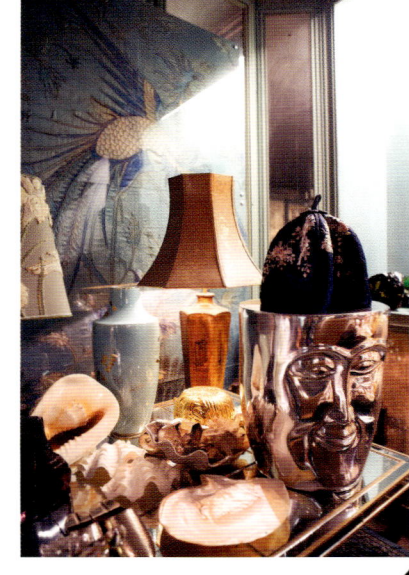
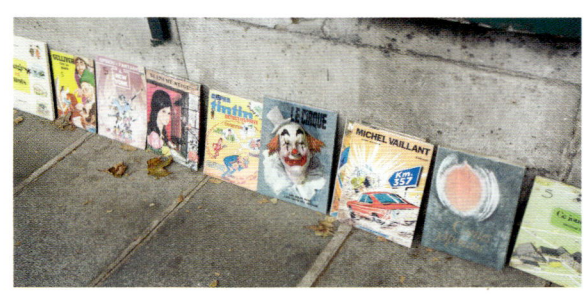

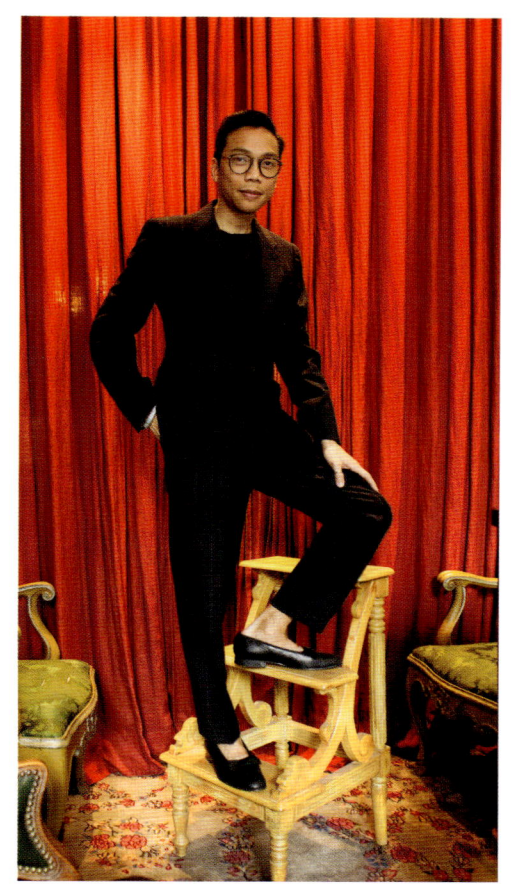
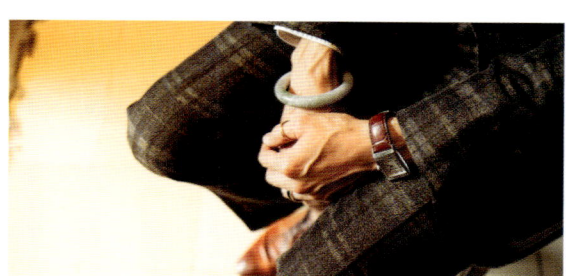
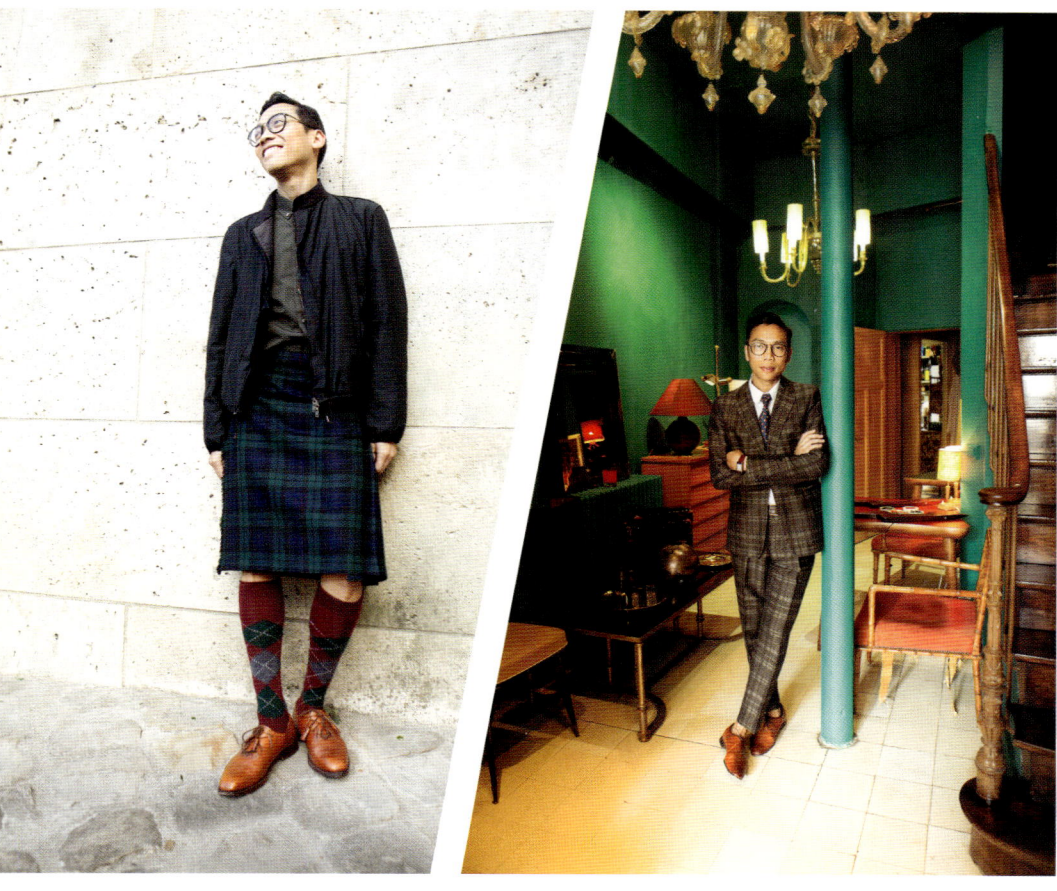
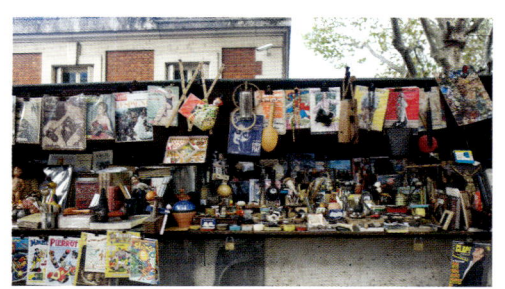
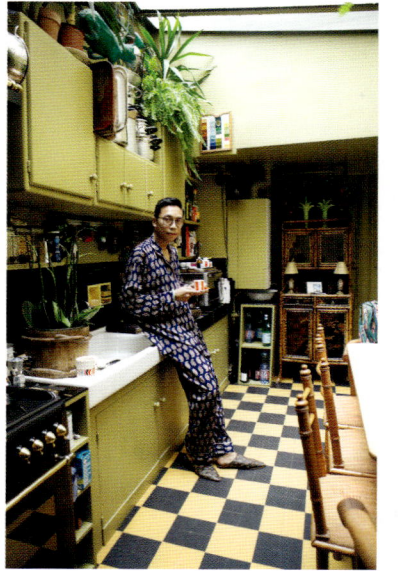
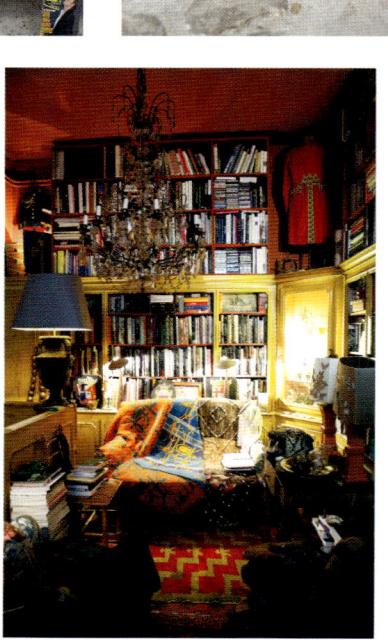
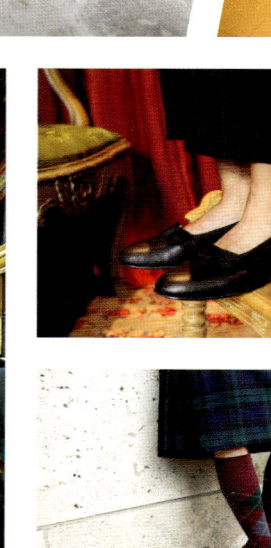
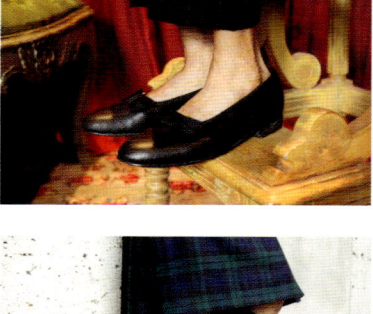
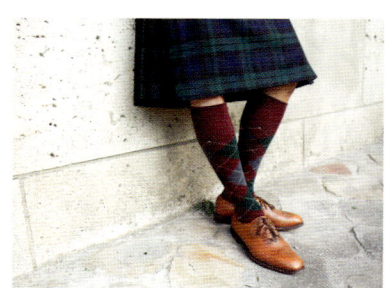
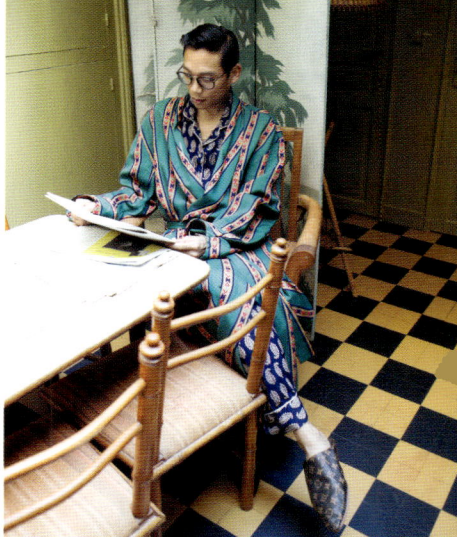

ELIZA DOOLITTLE
SERENDIPITY

I can see his giant black lens glisten across the street. A man, dressed in black, holding a professional camera, is posted behind a car and ready for action. He's anything but inconspicuous and clearly aiming at us, but somehow Eliza doesn't notice the paparazzi photographer. I nudge her as we exit the Primrose Hill bakery with our coffees. "You know he's taking pictures of you, right?" I whisper in her ear. "Oh," she shrugs, barely looking up. "They're always there. I really don't understand why. It's silly." Our meeting is definitely not front page news but let's see: she produced two Top 40 hits, her eponymous first album went Platinum in 2010, she just had a massive hit with Disclosure and is about to perform at Madison Square Garden. I'm pretty sure some people in the UK are curious to know whom she's mingling with. Sadly it's just a middle-aged woman in Birkenstocks today...

I jogged to that Disclosure song all summer. It was so clearly about my life and my future. I was head over heels in love with this boy who, in my humblest and most confident of opinions, was unaware of his love for me. In my head, it would take him a while to realize it, but eventually we would become a happy "You & Me," everything we ever dreamed, and everything we were meant to be. Alas, as autumn reared its ugly, gloomy head, I was still jogging, but the boy had still not seen the light, and I am at Eliza Doolittle's house instead—a serendipitous moment, if anything.

She'd been up late the night before, playing a gig and writing music. I don't think she's hungover, but the coffee helps. Any other artist would have canceled, but not Eliza. She's chatty, funny, and animated. Her voice is husky, her hair visibly unruly, and her accent so clearly London. She grew up in Camden Town as Eliza Sophie Caird, one of nine kids to a stage director father and a theatre actress mom. Music came naturally to her; she always wanted to be a musician, and has been playing and singing since she was 15 years old. And life is going well for her. She's recording new music and meditating, "trying to get a little peace each day," she says, "light some incense or something, close my eyes, stop thinking for a bit."

The platinum album hangs on the wall in the kitchen, but she doesn't want me to shoot it. "It's kind of cheesy, no?" she insists. Nor the family pictures, or the hand-painted piano in the living room – those are too personal, and just the thing those papps are after. She's going through a mental and material purging phase. "I used to actively search for new clothes and be quite obsessed, but now I just wear what I already have and if I come across something I love and can't stop thinking about it, I'll get it. But I'm trying to place less importance on materials." Her look is 90s pop with a bit of rock and techno and by the looks of it, the occasional, accidental side boob. "Oops, don't want to scare the kids off!" she laughs when I point out the impending malfunction of her white overalls.

Eliza and I stay in touch for a while after our shoot, because she's due in New York with Disclosure and I want her to visit my vintage store in Brooklyn. When that doesn't work out, we connect again in Los Angeles a few months later. I send her a text to come see me at my Venice Beach pop-up but she regretfully declines, because she's headed to the airport and needs to run more errands. But then something funny happens. As I sit in the store an hour later, she casually walks in the door and starts looking at the clothes. She hasn't seen me yet but I clearly startle her when I yell: "Eliza!" She looks at me with big eyes and gasps: "Oh my god, this is your store?? I just saw the sign 'vintage' outside and had to walk in. This is really, really serendipitous!" We're in shock for a little while longer and then decide that all our meetings should be kismet. Vintage kind of does that.

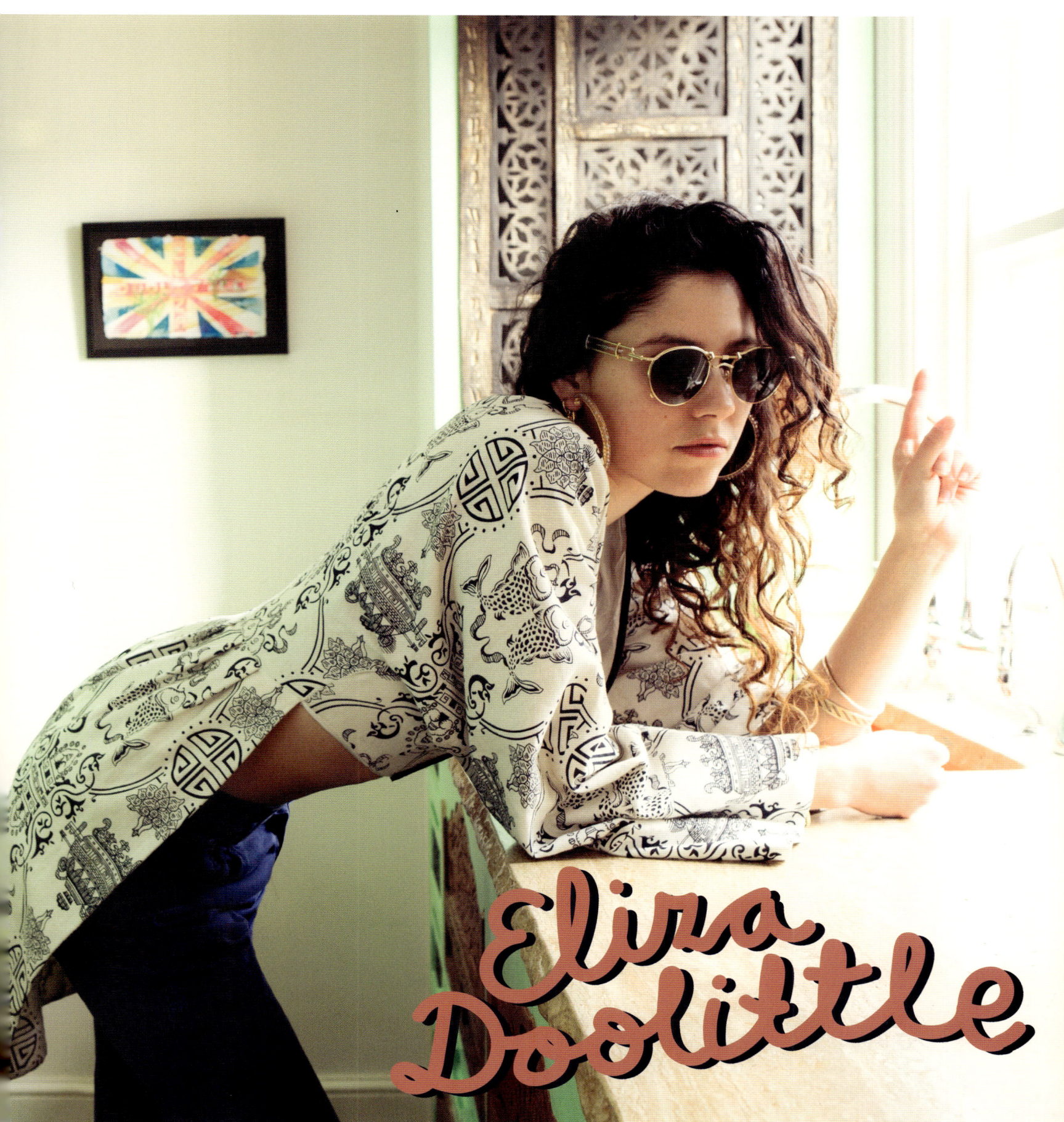

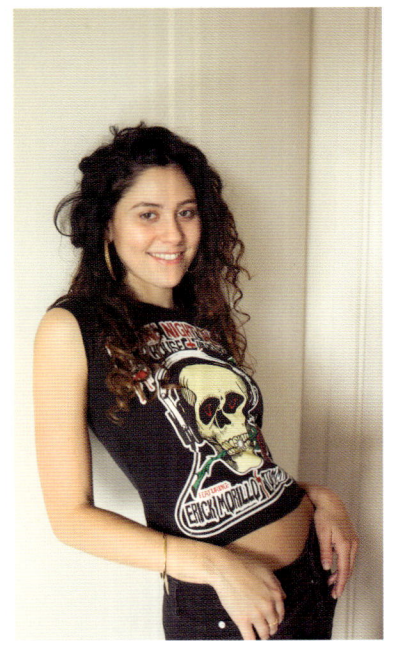
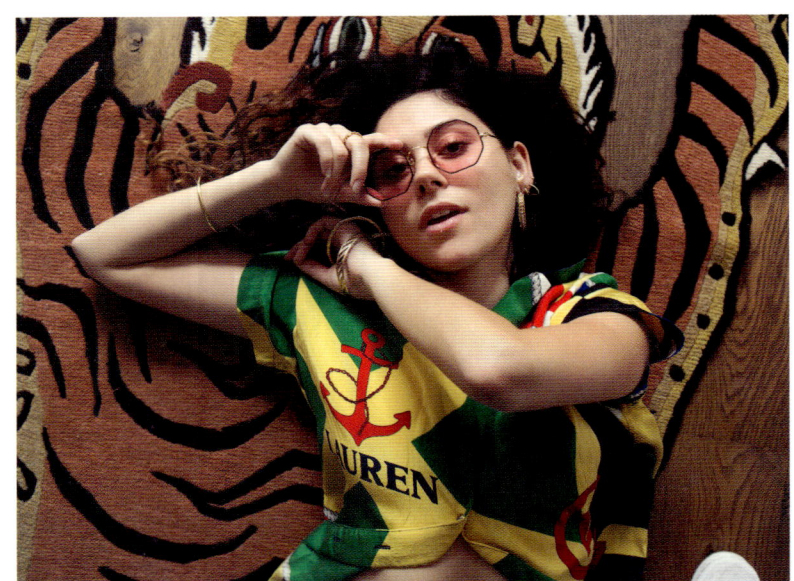
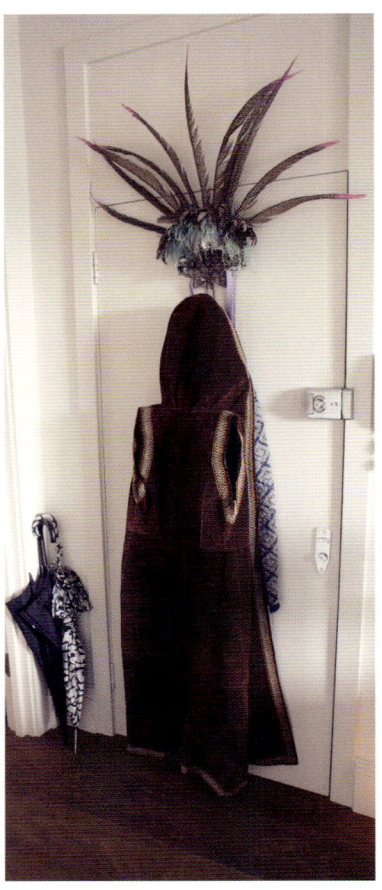
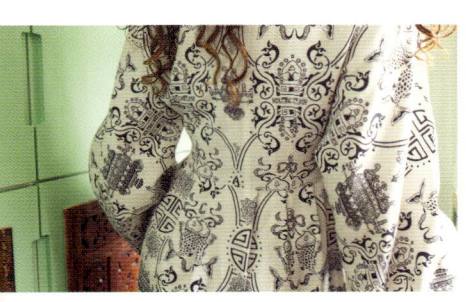
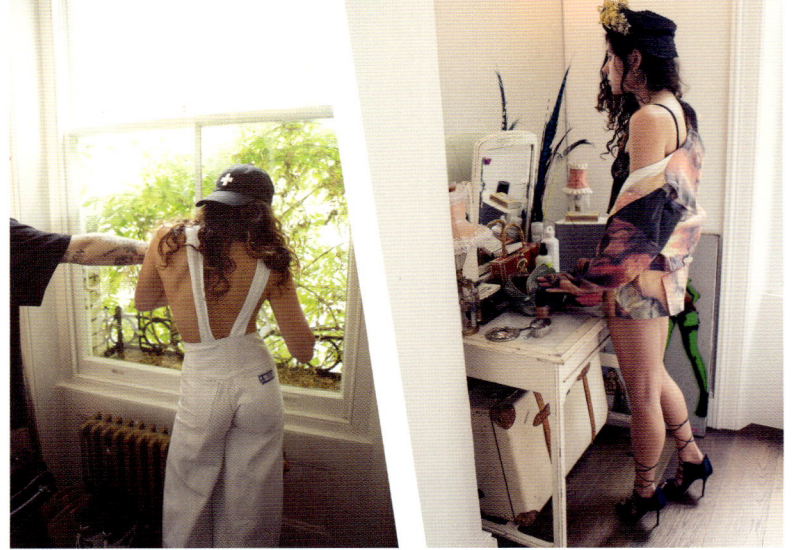
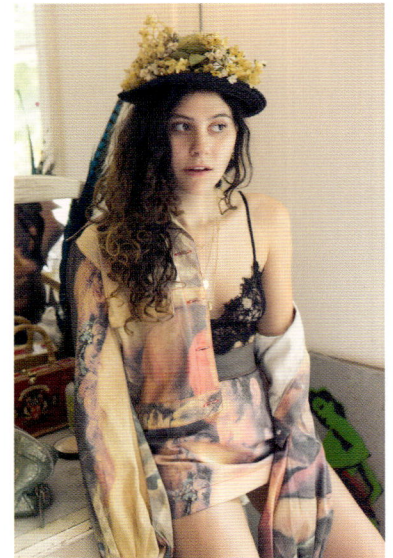
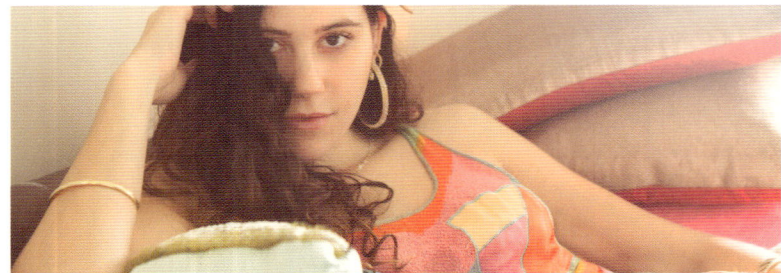
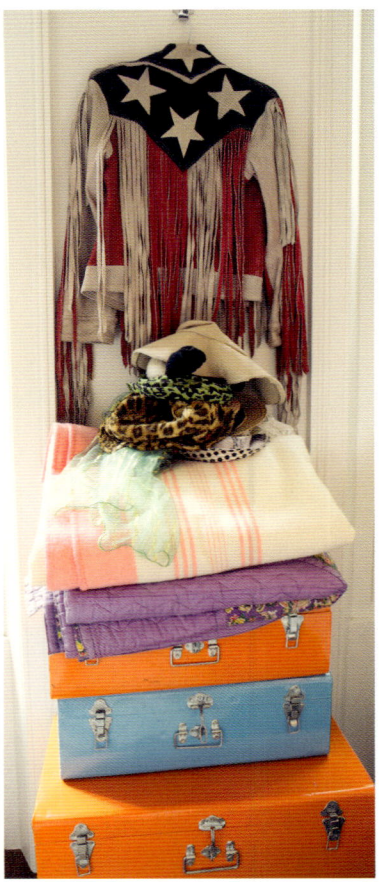
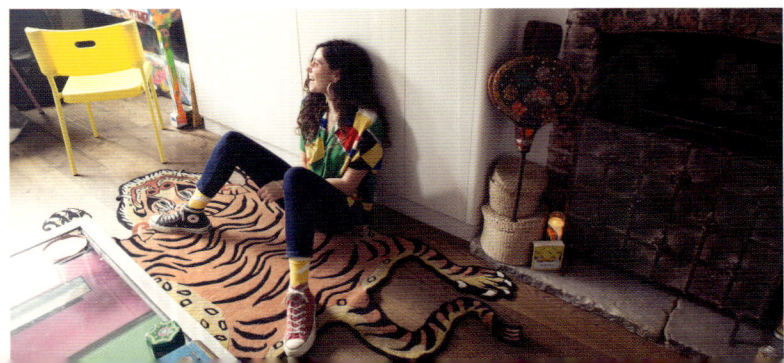
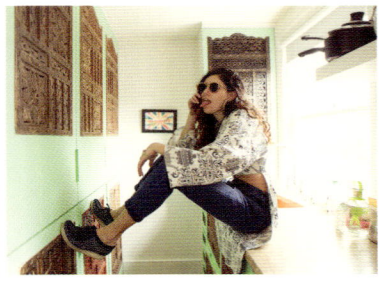

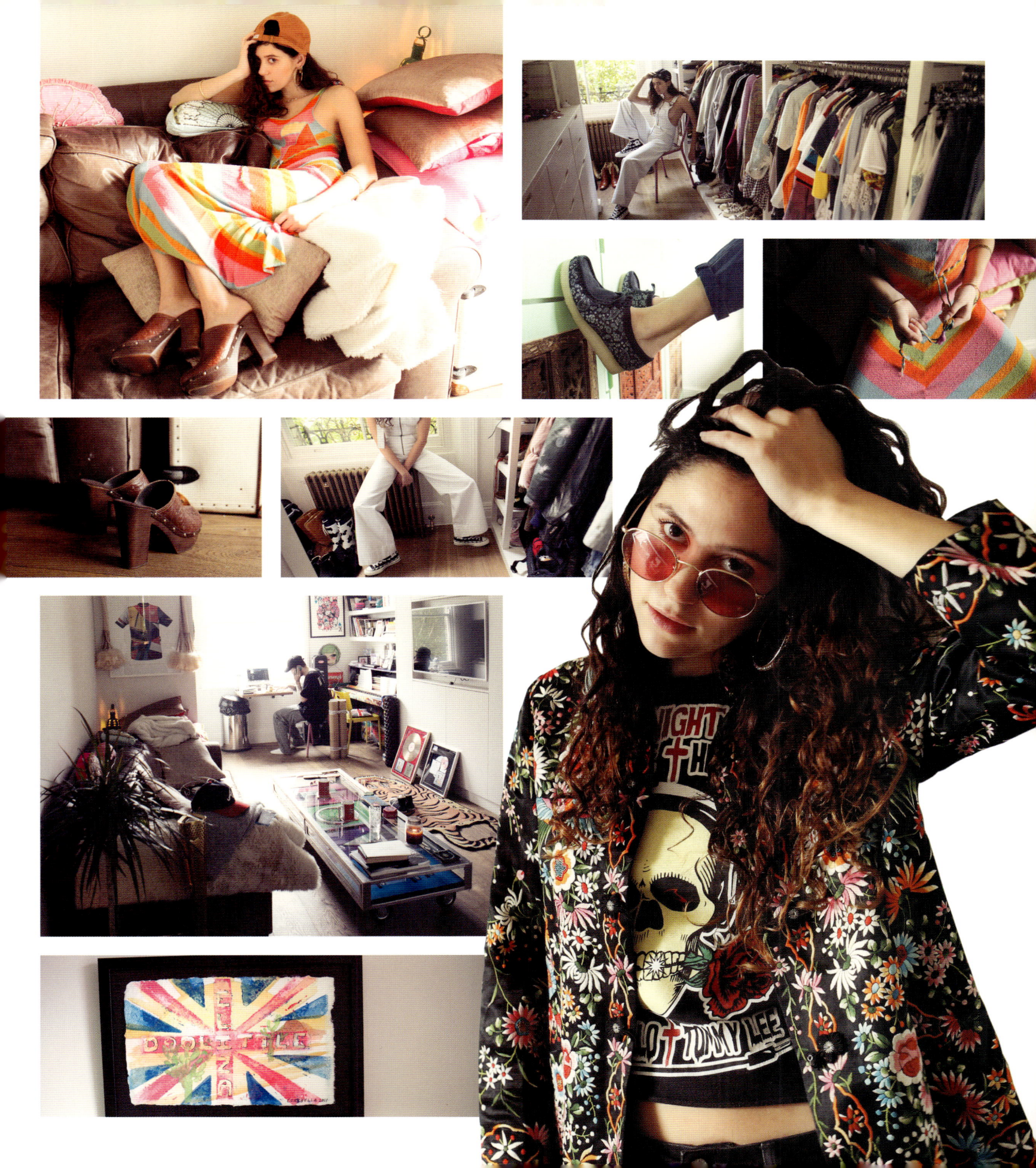

KYLEIGH KÜHN
THE FATE OF DISASTER

She had decided to sell—that rickety shell of a 1979 houseboat named *Whim*. She had bought her for $3,000 on Craigslist a few years ago, shotgun hole in one of her windows, 1980s dusty shag-carpeting, infested with bees nests, and sealed only by sun-bleached, chipped paint. She was destined for the dump, but Kyleigh loved her. She was her phoenix, a manifestation of her need to restore love in this world. "I could see she had good bones," she remembers, "with gorgeous wrap-around windows and a strong hull. In retrospect, I think she was a metaphor for my personal state: lost, broken down, and in desperate need of care. I wanted to pour myself into her, to make all the negative, neglected, and lost elements she evoked into something beautiful, cared-for, and inspiring."

Whim became a gem: a marvelous, charming little floater ensconced in Sausalito shimmer, and Kyleigh was at peace. "I see her clean white walls and her flowing curtains, and her driftwood shelves, and I feel my confidence rise. I'm reminded of my ability to turn even the most wretched of disasters into something to be cherished. We all have this ability to recast the fate of disaster." For Kyleigh Kühn and her family, this meant having born witness to a deadly terrorist attack by the Taliban in Afghanistan, at the headquarters of their non-profit organization *Roots of Peace*. "Miraculously, none of our employees or security were hurt, but the violence of the event left us shaken to the core," she recalls. "I had been working on some creative projects, making jewelry and carpets with artisans in rural villages. After the attack, everything stopped and I was forced to reconsider my efforts."

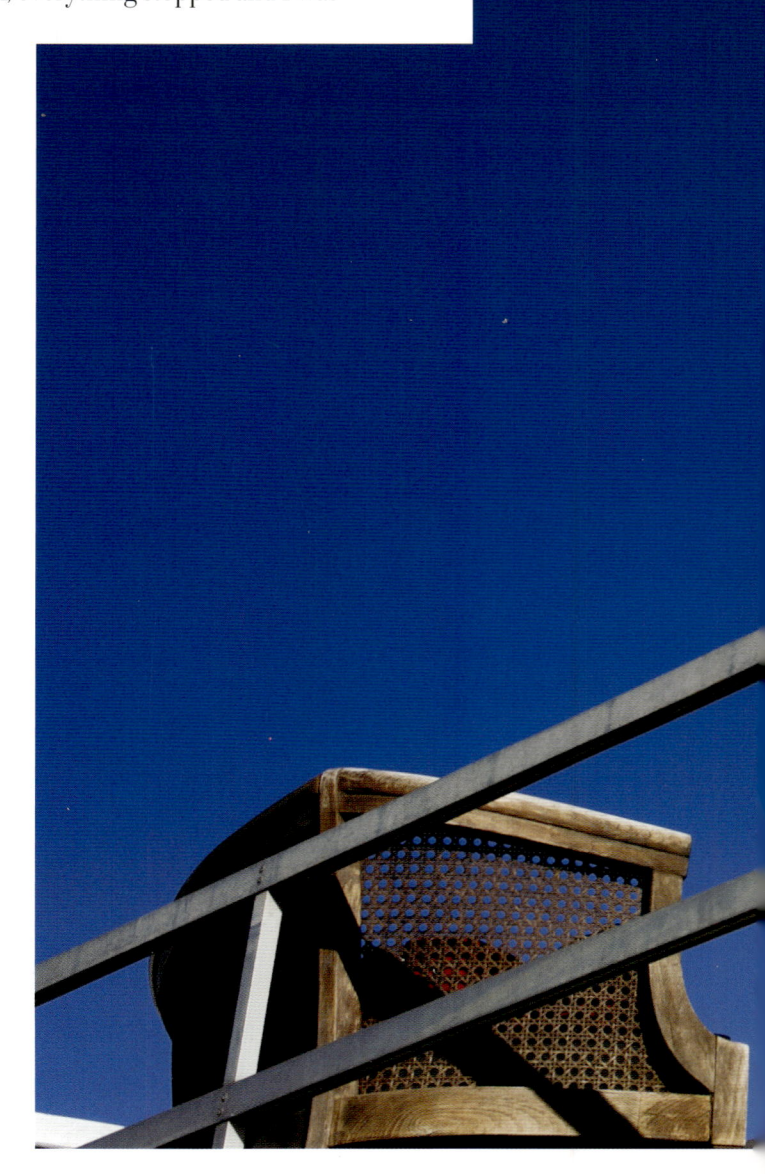

She was no longer modeling at that time, but the fashion industry had always been a kind and powerful vessel for raising awareness of her causes, so she decided to launch her #87daysofvintage campaign. "On my travels to war-torn areas, I've encountered tons of kids who are lucky to own a single jacket," she told *Elle* magazine in 2015. "It has become increasingly difficult to reconcile that reality with our culture of conspicuous consumption." She encouraged her friends to wear secondhand for a few weeks. "These days, new clothes often lack that element of love or personality," she says. "In new things, I tend to feel like I'm just imitating a style rather than embodying the magical grace of adornment." Or, like her dad once told her: "Kyleigh, look at all the girls in your class, they all part their hair in the center. Why don't you part it on the side and be different?" His support of me embracing a unique identity was so earnest, and welcoming it helped me realize that fitting-in wasn't important."

You kind of get it by now: Kyleigh Alessandra Clementine Kühn is a particularly rare and intelligent kind of activist. She's 30 years old, married to her best friend, and a self-proclaimed dreamer. She stems from a strong gene pool of do-gooders, the McNears. Her great-grandfather, John A. McNear, used his ranch as a safe haven for Chinese immigrants during the Chinese Exclusion Act in San Francisco. He later donated the land to the Park Service, and his ranch is known as China Camp. Respect for all humanity, the dignity of land, and the human spirit, runs deep in Kyleigh's blood. And it's that same sentiment that finally stopped her from selling the boat. "She's too lovely to part with...and a part of me is imbued in her bones. She floats because of my love for her, so dollars don't replace that."

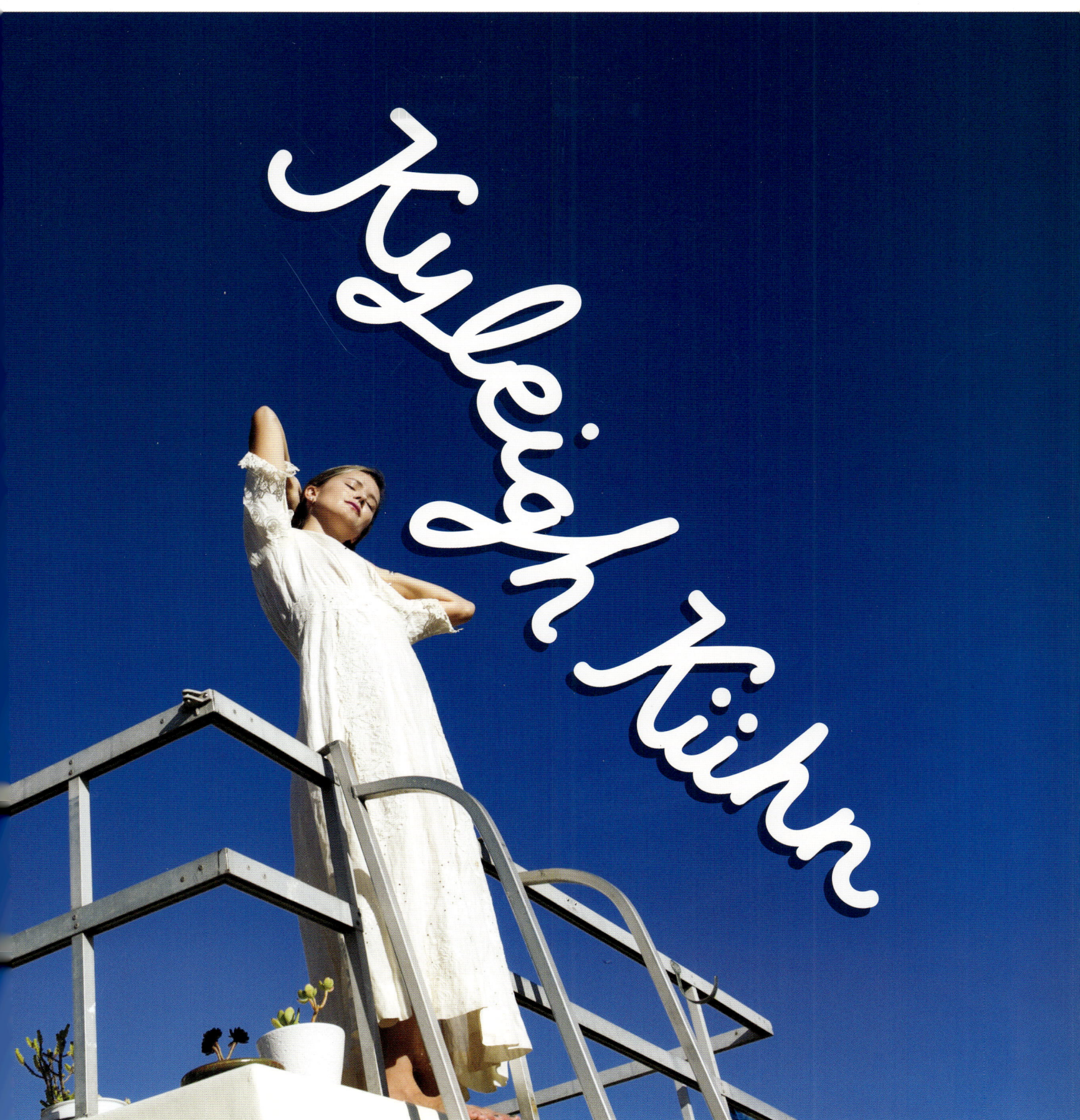

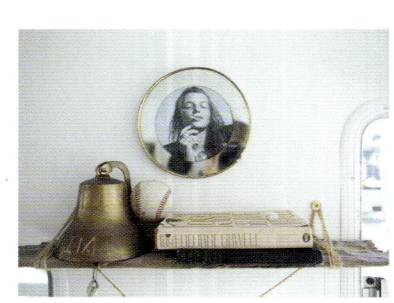
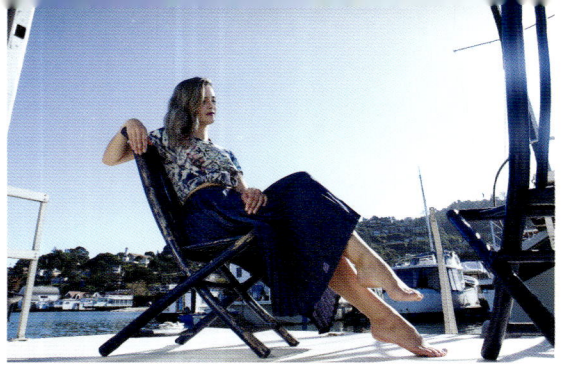
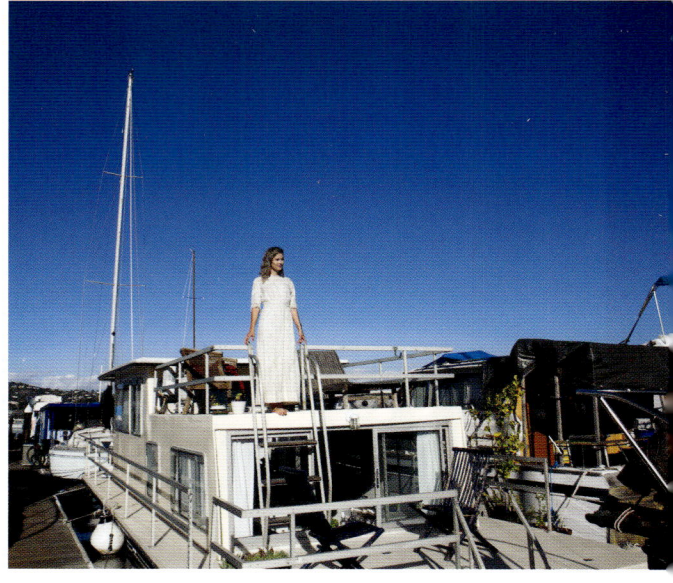
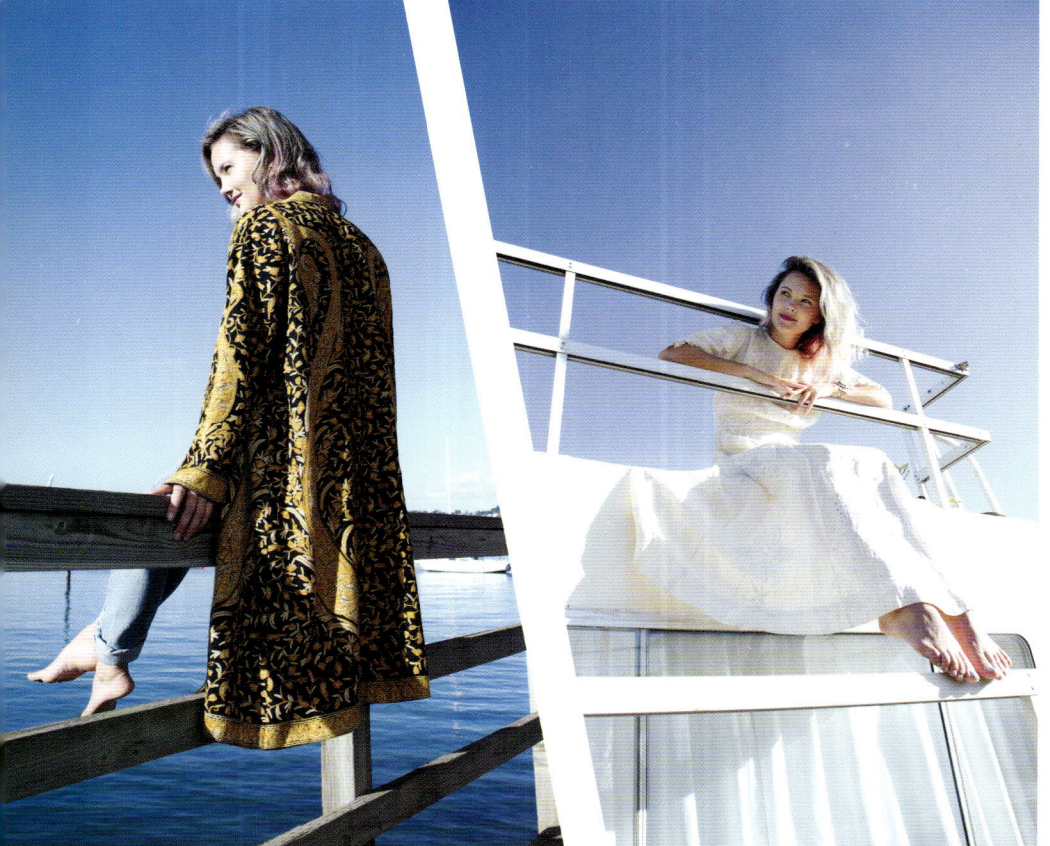
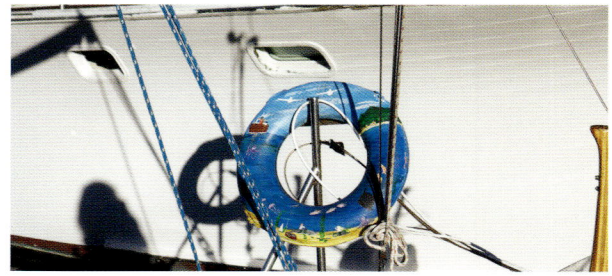
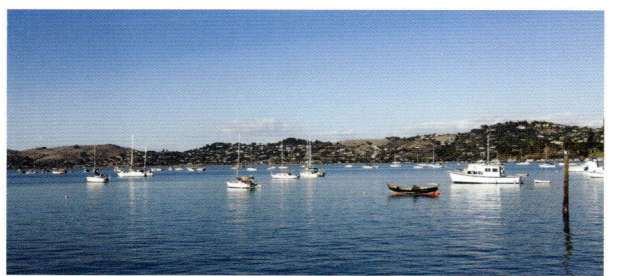
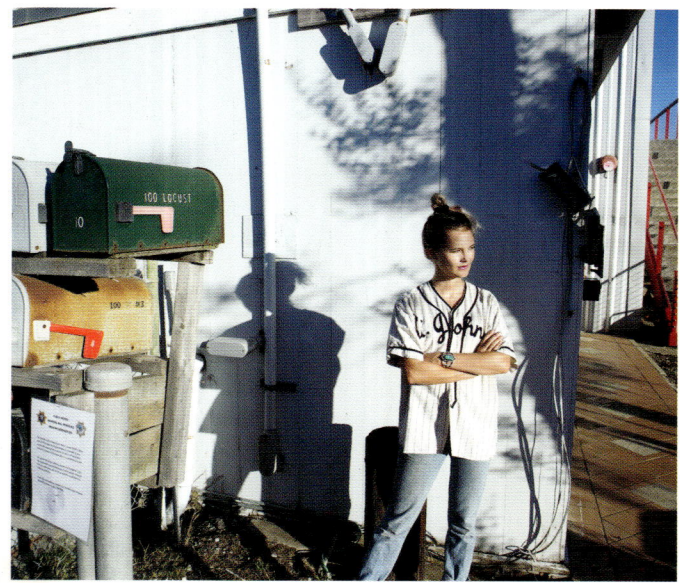
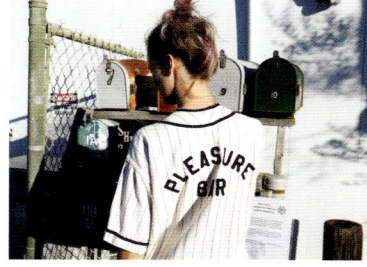
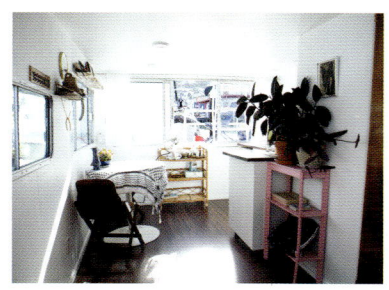
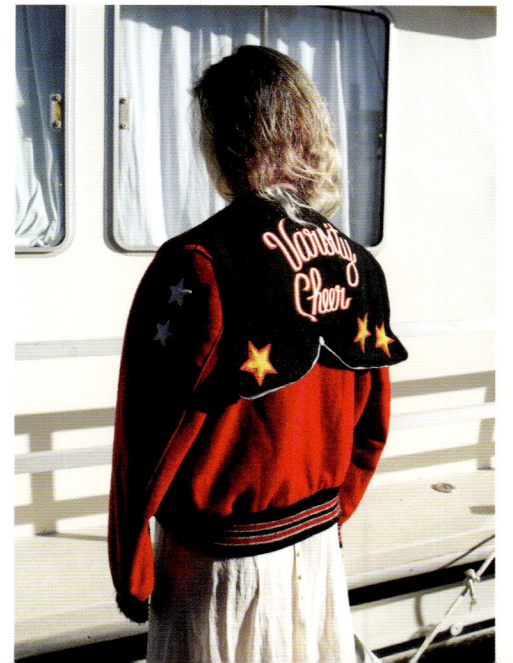

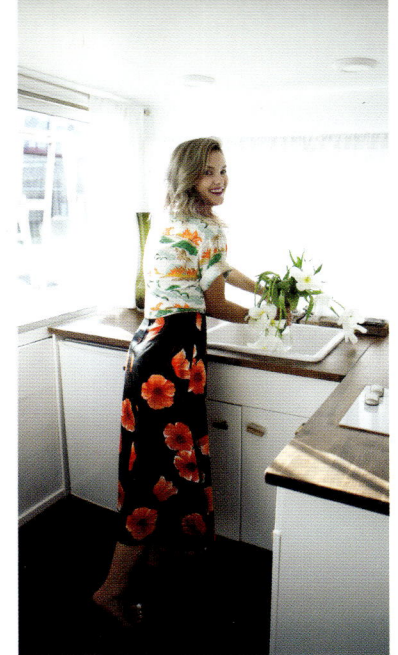
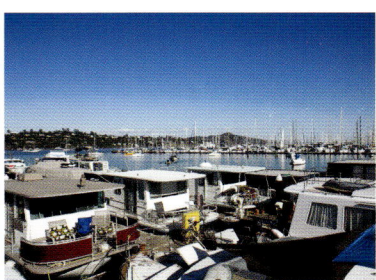
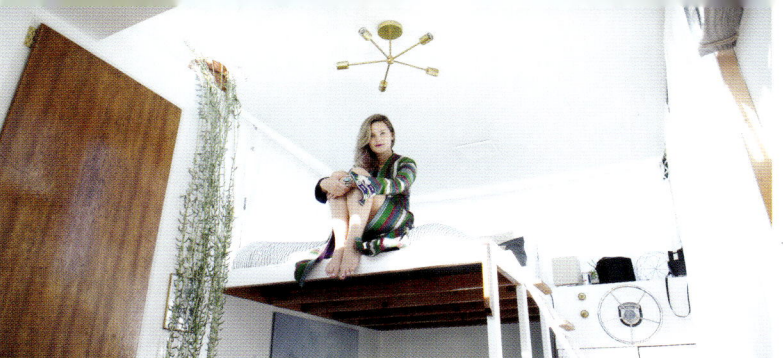
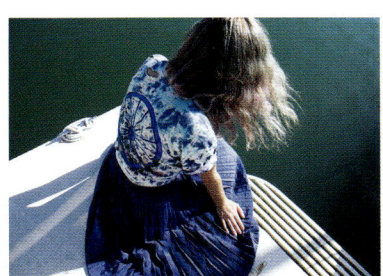
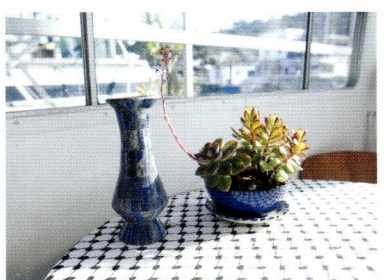
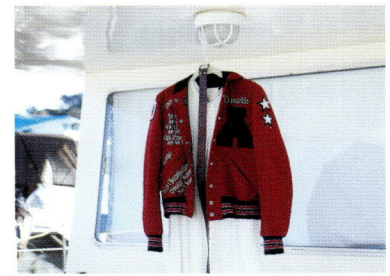
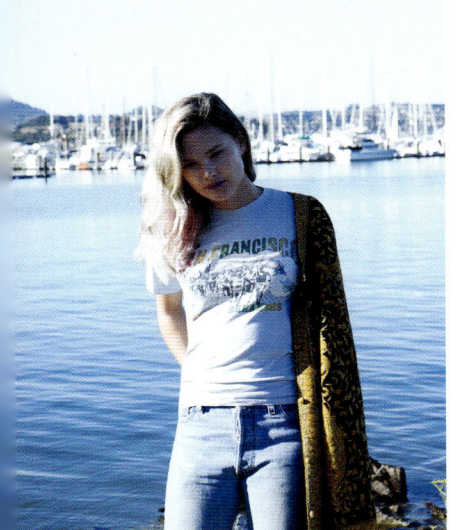
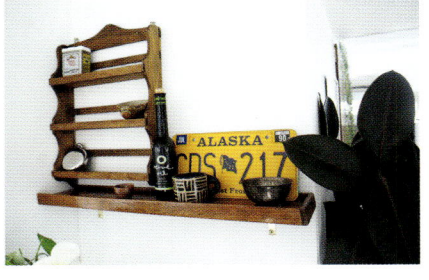
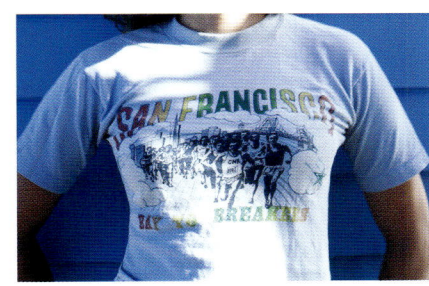
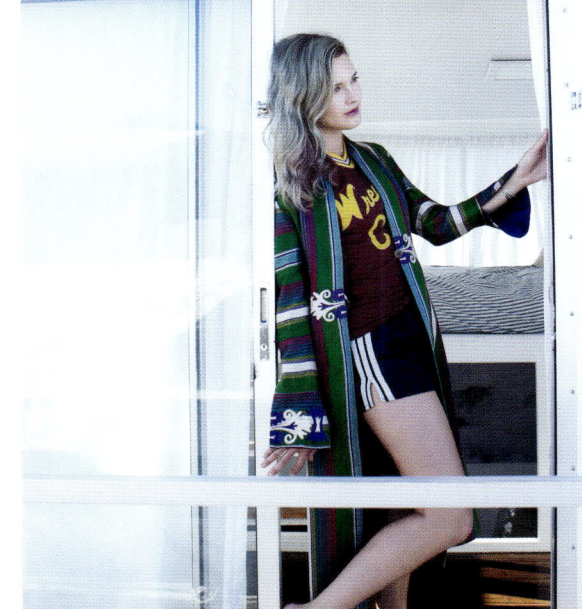
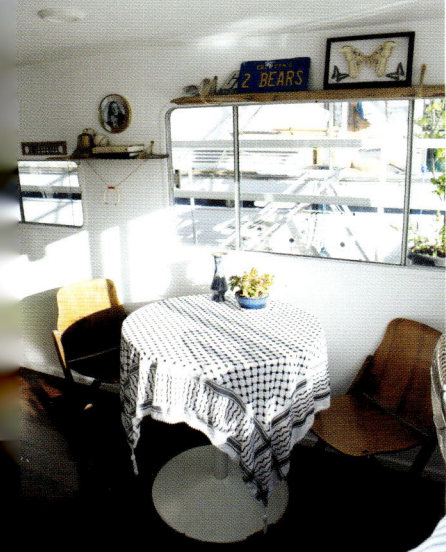
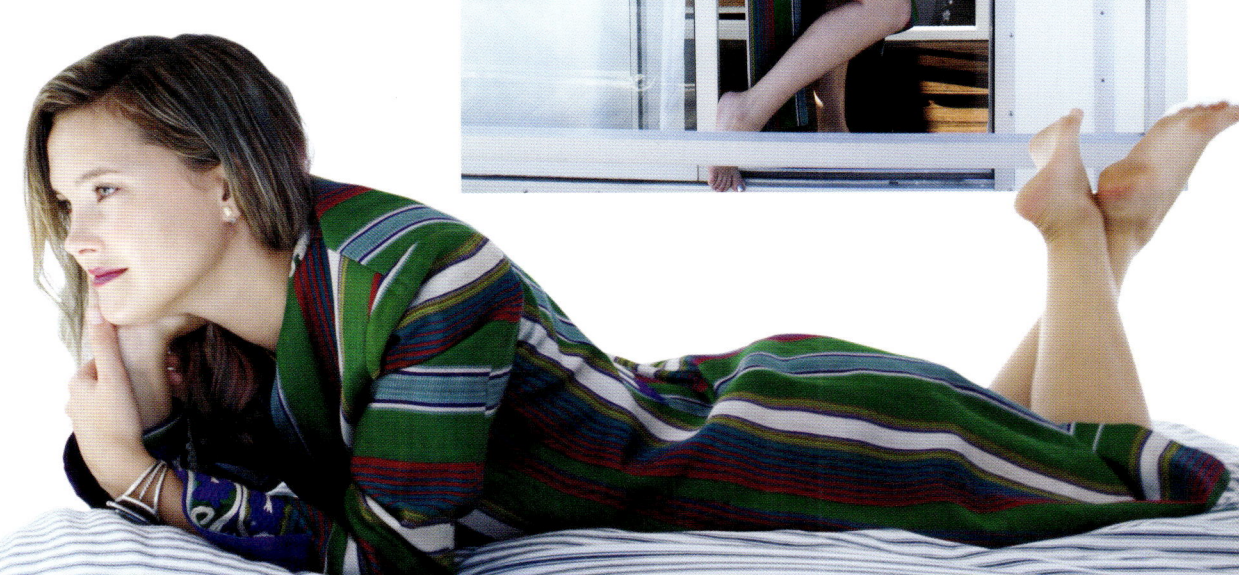

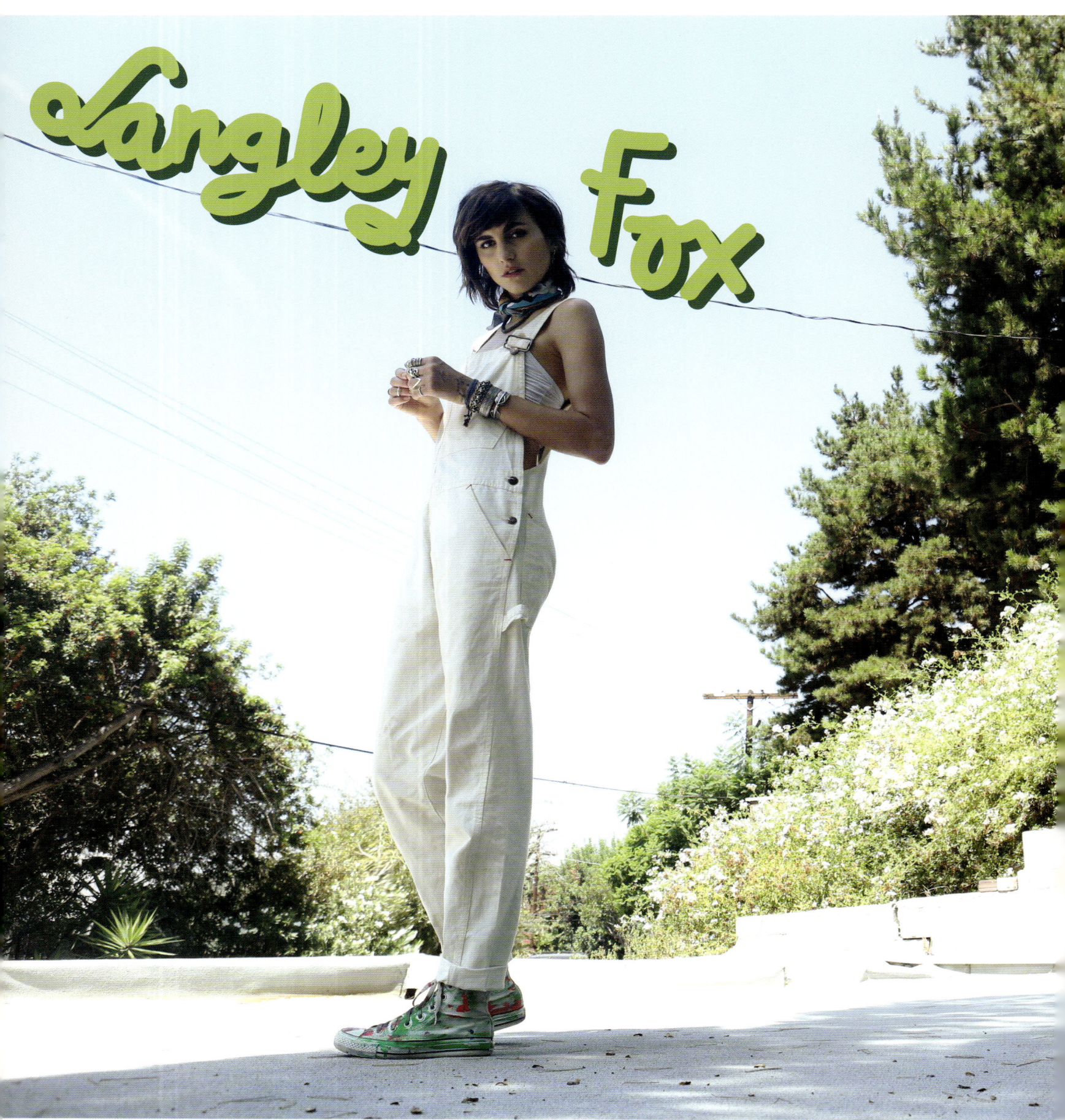

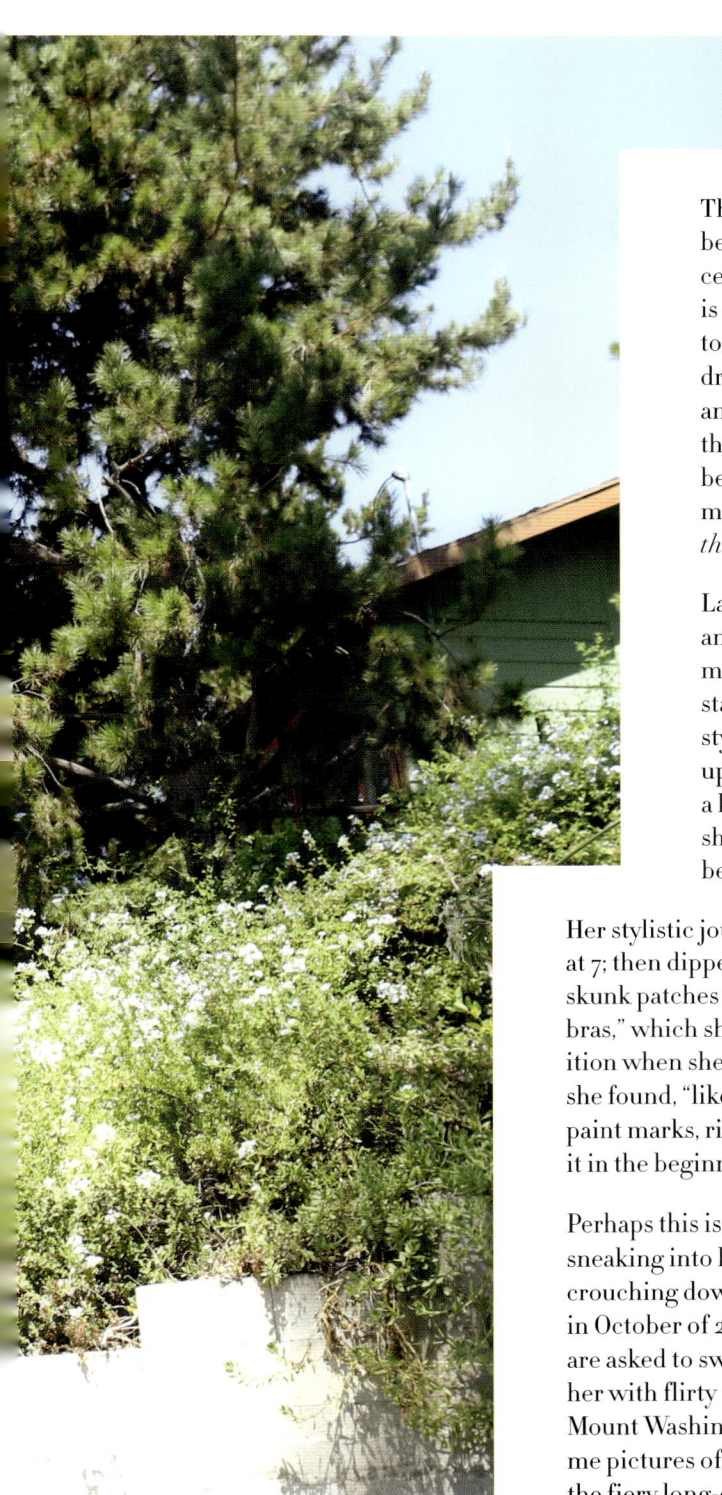

LANGLEY FOX
MEET BOB

The girl in these photos has no idea where or who she'll be in two years. On August 29, 2015 she is just a girl who celebrated her birthday in Sun Valley the week prior. She is a girl with a boyfriend and a cat named Jack Skellington that bites. She rents a pretty apartment up a hill in Los Feliz and likes to draw for a living. She models, she's goofy, she wears vintage men's overalls, and has amassed a "sick amount of neck scarves." She doesn't know that by the time this book comes out, she will not be this girl anymore. She will still be funny, make art, and be best friends with her sister Dree, but she'll have made some fundamental life choices that mark the making of a new girl. And *that* girl's name is Bob.

Langley Fox just turned 26. It's the first time we meet. She seems focused and quietly confident at first, a lanky millennial with jet-black hair, dark eye makeup, and a famous Hemingway for a great-grandfather. But she can only stay serious for so long. If she wasn't so hopelessly striking and inherently stylish, one might call her dorky. She laughs heartily at her own jokes, makes up sweeping, nonsensical stories on the spot, and juggles the vocabulary of a late-night host. She might have become a comedian one day—because she shares a birthday with Kristin Wigg?— had her love for fashion and art not become so fiercely dominant.

Her stylistic journey started with bright red hair, punk zipper pants, and ugly fleece jackets at 7; then dipped into obscure disaster when she tried "a black mullet haircut with small skunk patches around it and Invisalign that is not invisible" and wore "a lot of padded bras," which she says is a downfall for anyone as flat as her; and finally it came into full fruition when she started shopping thrift in high school. "I'm really drawn to old menswear," she found, "like jumpsuits and work wear. I like it to look like it's been heavily worked in: paint marks, rips, stains, really adds character that maybe you aren't strong enough to give it in the beginning."

Perhaps this is how and when the fundamental groundwork for Bob was laid. He was sneaking into her wardrobe, laying flat across the row of Converse on the floor, and crouching down on her mind like a baby vulture in a tux. He first reveals himself to me in October of 2016, when Langley and I take photos for *Harper's Bazaar* together and are asked to swap wardrobes. She dresses me up in suits and smelly Vans, while I adorn her with flirty dresses and heels. That's when she tells me about the house she bought in Mount Washington, and the man she hired to manage her income. That's when she shows me pictures of the Husky puppy she got and named Zeppelin, and when I find out about the fiery long-distance relationship she commenced with a photographer called Emily in London. Is that the girl in these photos? She suddenly seems like a kid. There's only one explanation, says Langley: "I think I've become Bob at this point."

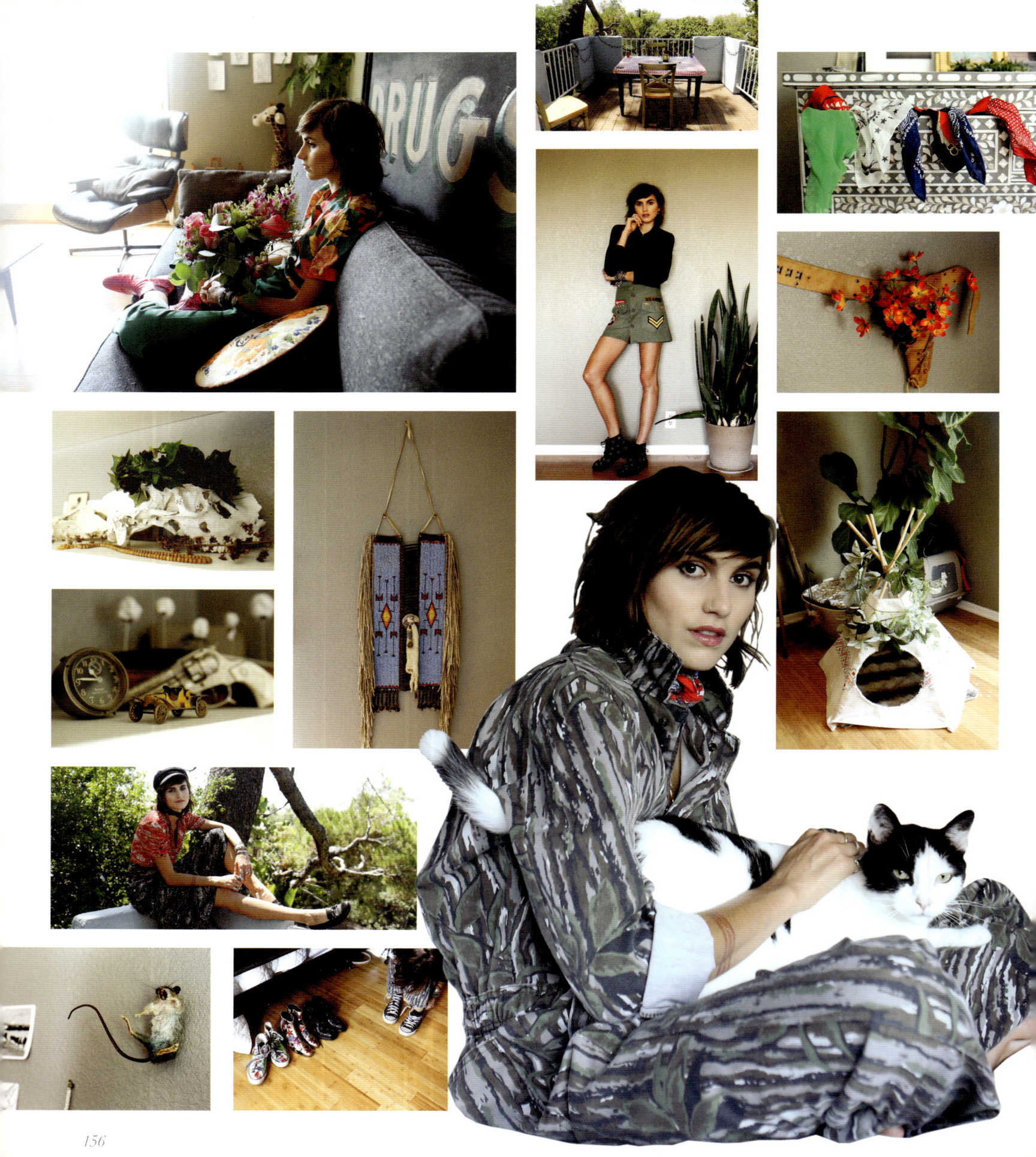

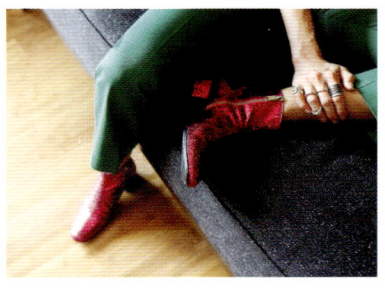
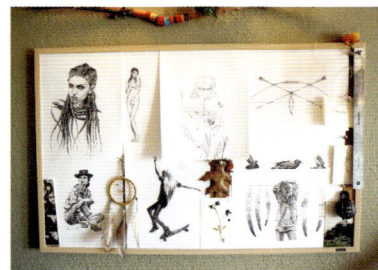
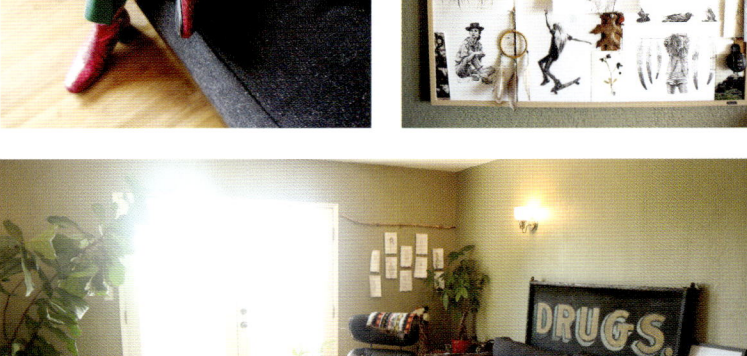
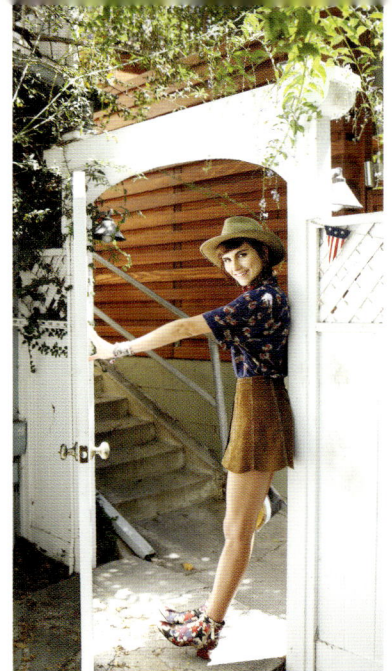
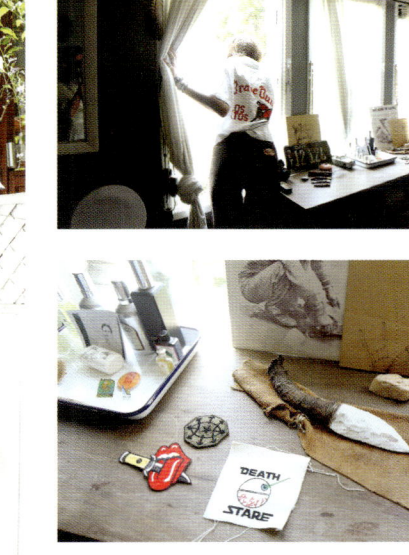
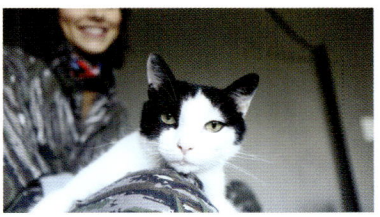
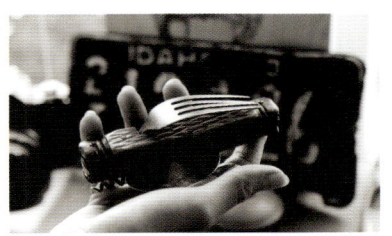
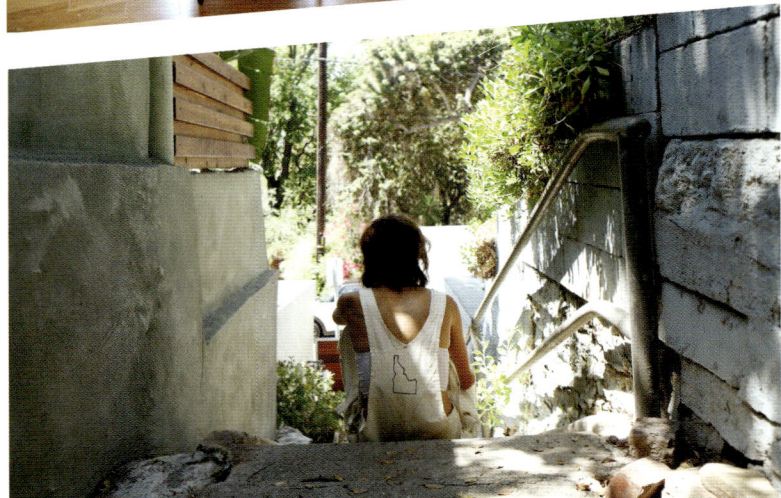
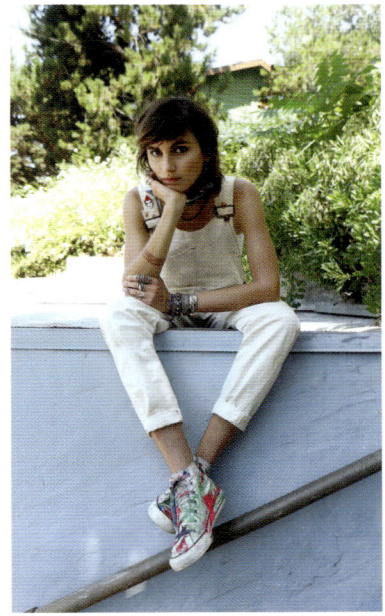
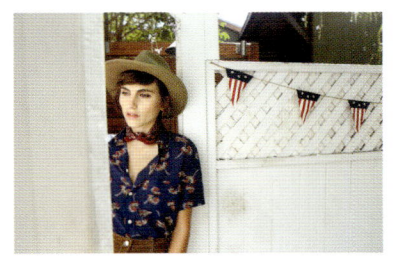
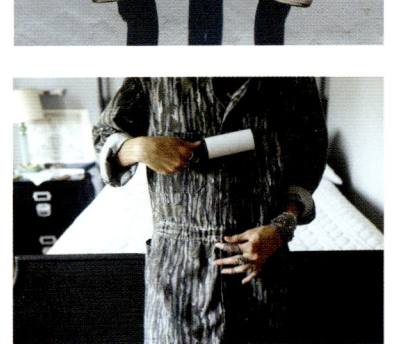
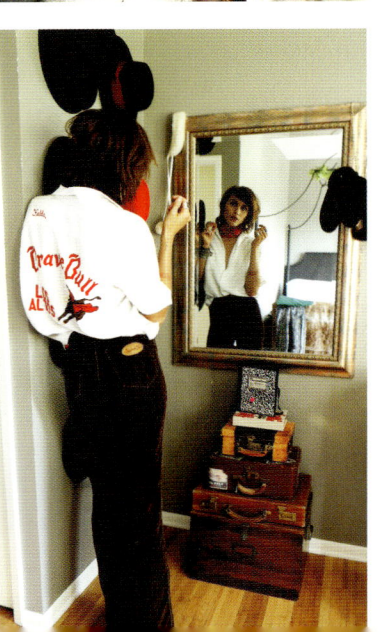
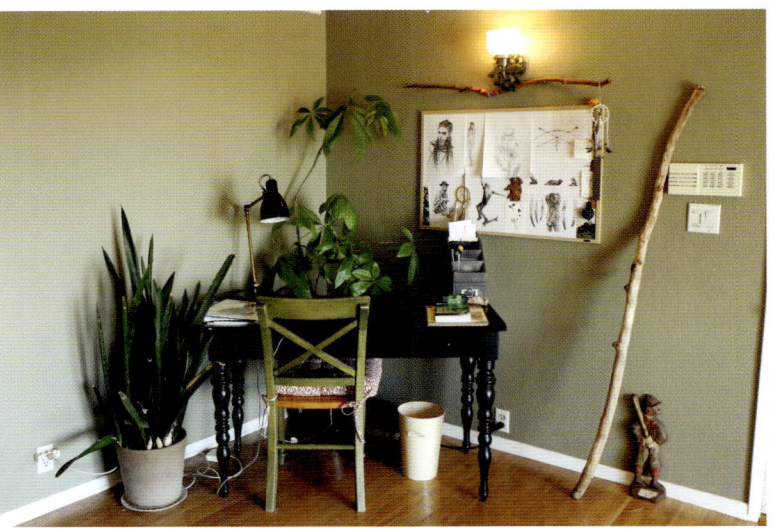

157

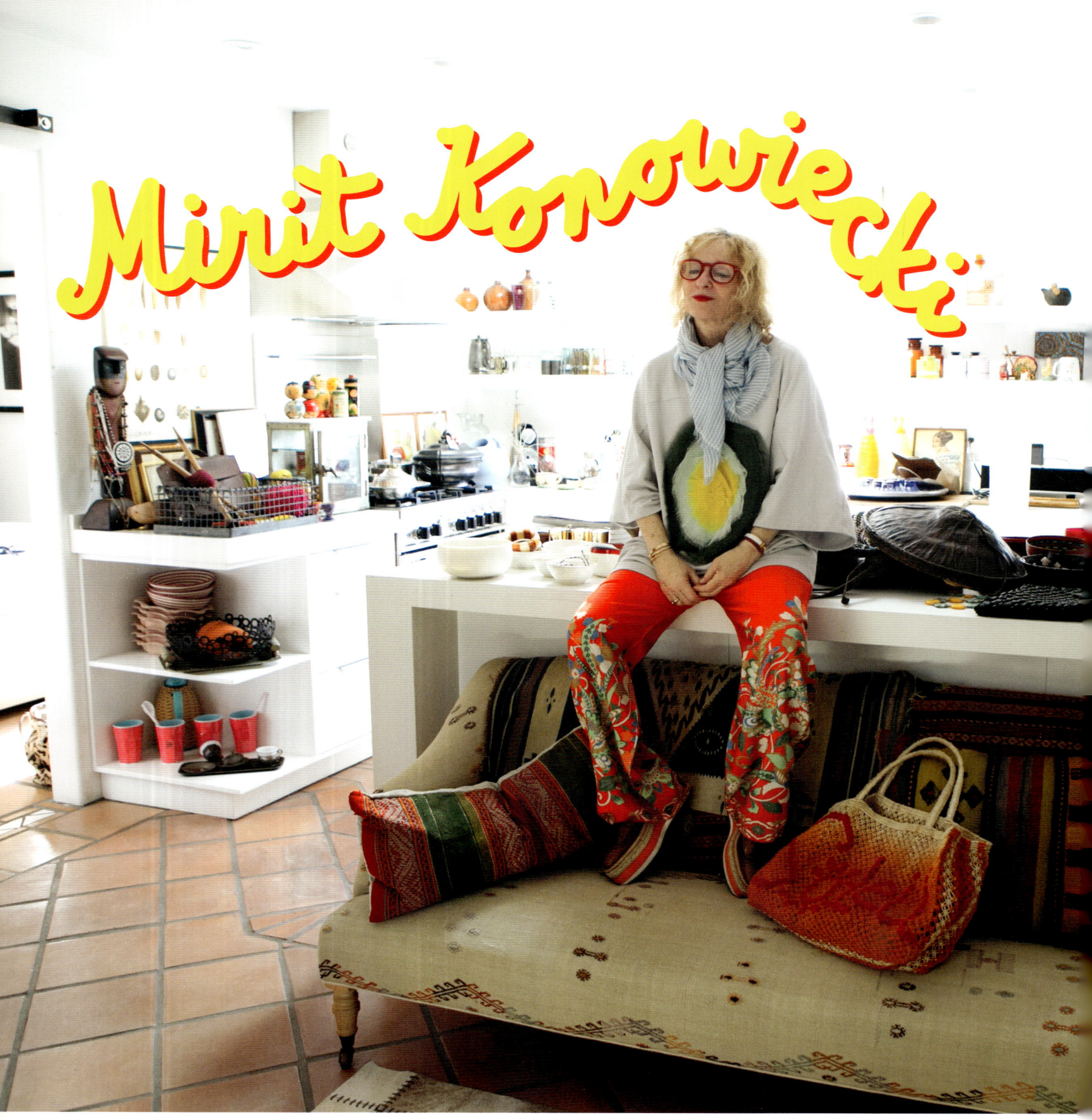

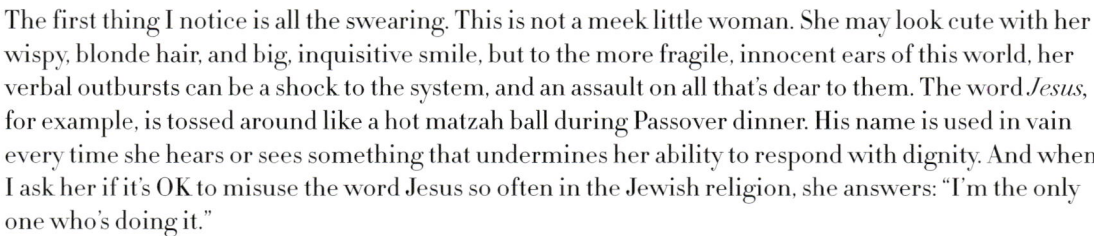

MIRIT KONOWIECKI
LITTLE GIRLS DON'T WEAR PURPLE

The first thing I notice is all the swearing. This is not a meek little woman. She may look cute with her wispy, blonde hair, and big, inquisitive smile, but to the more fragile, innocent ears of this world, her verbal outbursts can be a shock to the system, and an assault on all that's dear to them. The word *Jesus*, for example, is tossed around like a hot matzah ball during Passover dinner. His name is used in vain every time she hears or sees something that undermines her ability to respond with dignity. And when I ask her if it's OK to misuse the word Jesus so often in the Jewish religion, she answers: "I'm the only one who's doing it."

So I guess no one's really getting hurt, least of all me. I've come to know Mirit Konowiecki quite well. I call her my adoptive Long Beach mother, although she prefers the idea of us being sisters. In her own words, she was my super fan, or rather stalker, for a few years. She started following me, on Instagram and to all the vintage fairs I hosted, each time asking for a photo, which I willingly submitted myself to, but then never remembered the following meeting. It bothered her, but she persisted. "I didn't think you were funny," she says later in an attempt to make me feel guilty. "You were nice, but distant." When I moved to Los Angeles with my vintage business she became my best customer, and she was never to leave my mind and heart again. Now I dine at her table, swim with her dogs, and call on her landline. In fact, most of this book was written in her Malibu vacation home.

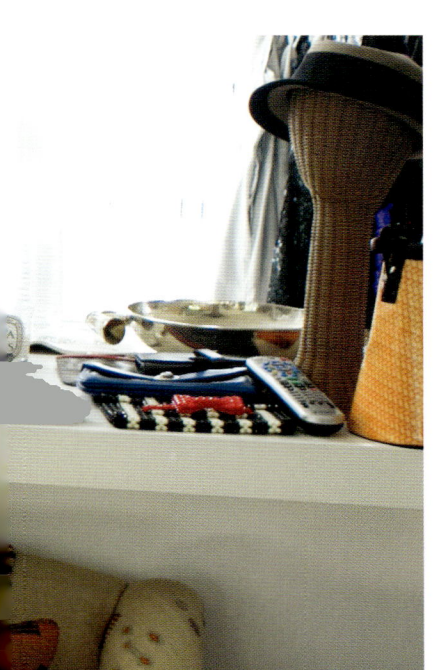

Mirit was born in Tel Aviv to a mother who survived Auschwitz and a father who was saved by Oskar Schindler. She had a very strict upbringing. The family lived modestly, but fashion was always on her mind. Being an only child meant having to spend hours and hours with her mom's Polish friends whose greatest pursuit was gossip. "They were all wearing navy blue tweed midi skirt suits," remembers Mirit, "except for my mom. She wore red! My mom had an aunt in Paris that owned a clothing store, so when she returned from her visits, she'd walk the city with her mod dresses and coats, and embarrassed the heck out of me!" Mirit also remembers her purple turtleneck sweater when she was nine years old: "I wore it when [my mom] was out of the house. I was told that little girls do not wear black or purple."

London was a huge stepping-stone to vintage. The day she bought herself a secondhand Laura Ashley maxi dress and huge, lime-green and yellow platforms at 18 years old will go down in history as one of her most satisfying days. Then she joined the army and things went south again. "Not much vintage dressing while in the army," she winks, "but the funny thing is that any time I pass by an olive-green army sweater I have to buy it! I tried to be creative in the army and got into lots of trouble for it." After the army, she started traveling, which "opened the door to the vintage Pandora's box."

Now she's married to Joseph, has three grown-up sons, and runs her own business, buying and selling vintage from the guesthouse of her home in Long Beach. And I believe this is her true calling. After spending most of her life working as a teacher and director at two Jewish schools, and caring for her mother when she got sick, this feels like a reward, or an awakening, or a much-needed dispensation of self-expression. Something had to be done to release all that shopping and styling talent. "I am ecstatic when I get compliments on a day when none of my clothes match or make sense, yet it somehow works," she admits. Her personal style is a "mishmash" of vintage, colors, ethnicities, and an absurd amount of humor.

Mirit thinks I'm funny now—maybe even hilarious, if I'm lucky. We may laugh and get stupid and make people feel very uncomfortable around us, but at the end of the day we are also human, with flaws and tragedies, mishaps and regrets, and we take as much pleasure and solace in our serious talks. Mirit is tough, but only because her softness was tested and tried to the limit. What she'll never do though, is break. "I understood life at a very young age," she acknowledges, "and I understood pain at a very young age. I feel that I was always at an advantage because of it. Pain makes you sensitive and understanding, gives you the tools to deal with whatever life throws your way. I think the best thing my parents did for me was that in spite of it all, we knew how to laugh and love life."

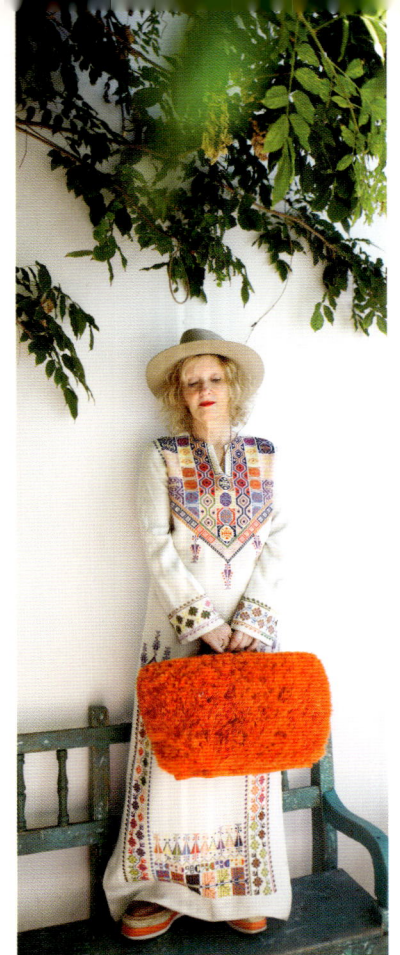
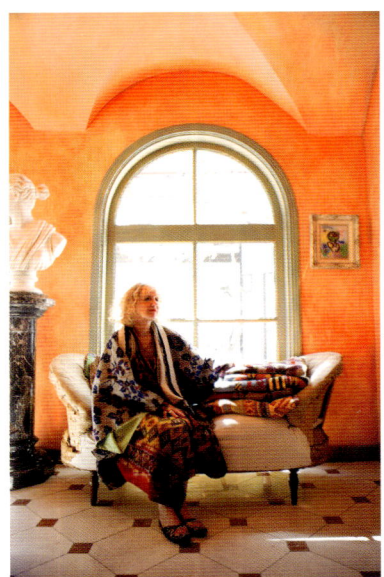
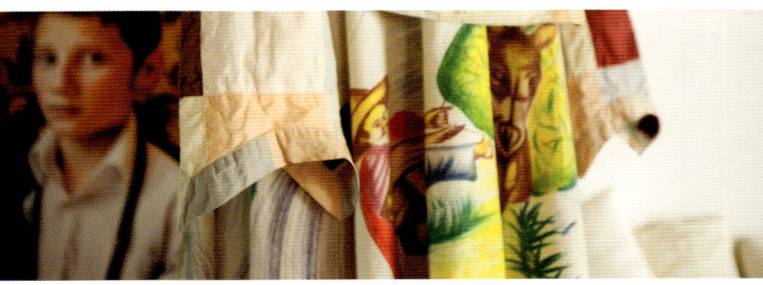
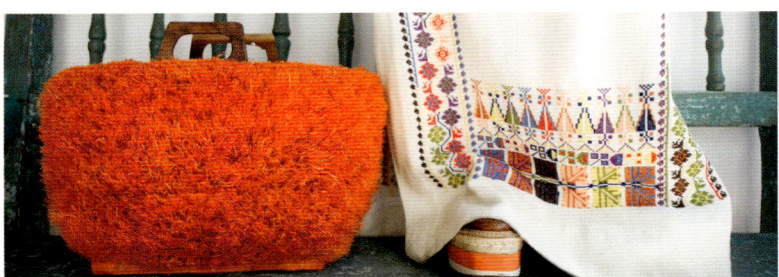
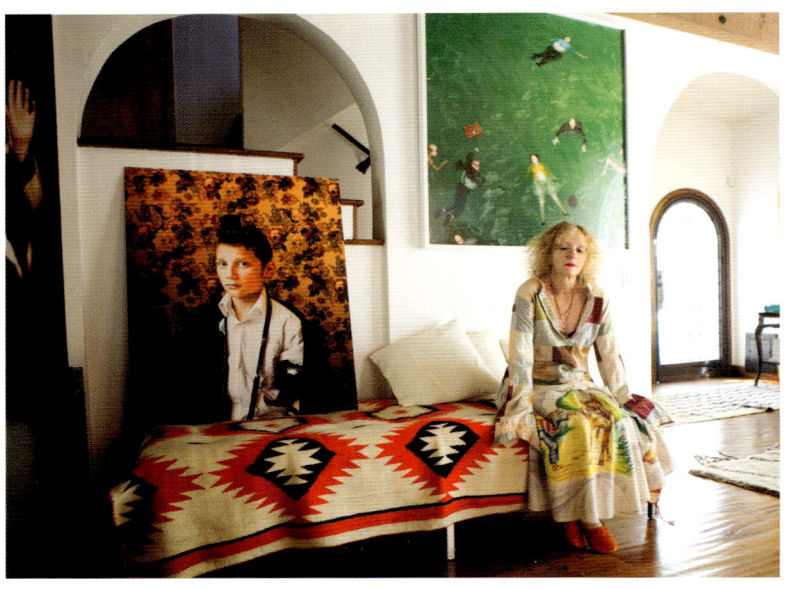
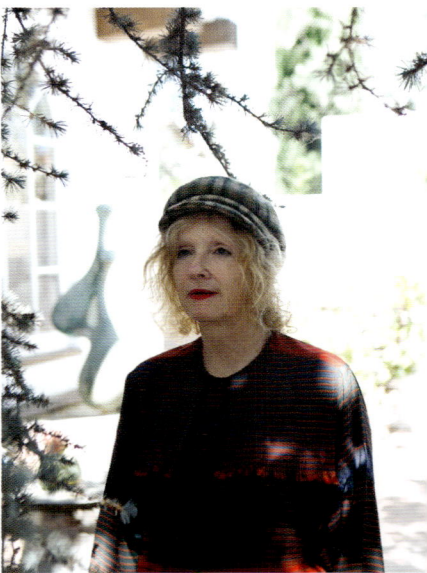
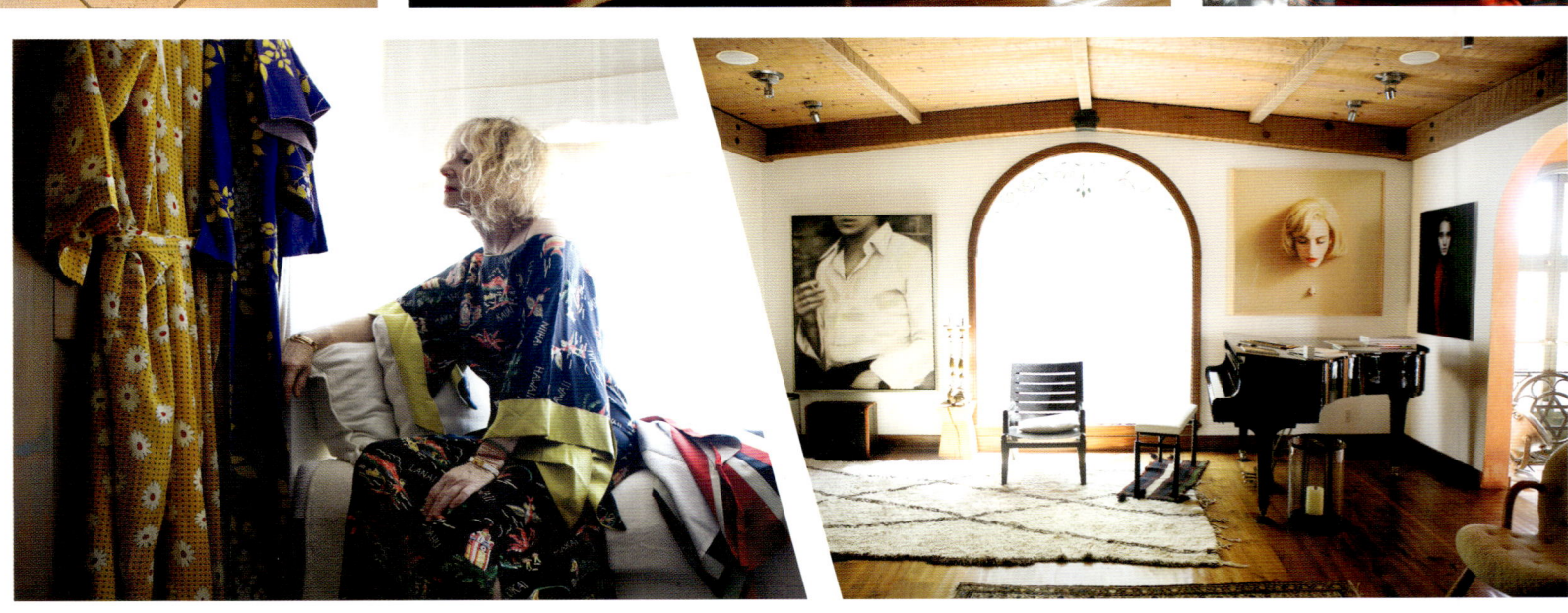

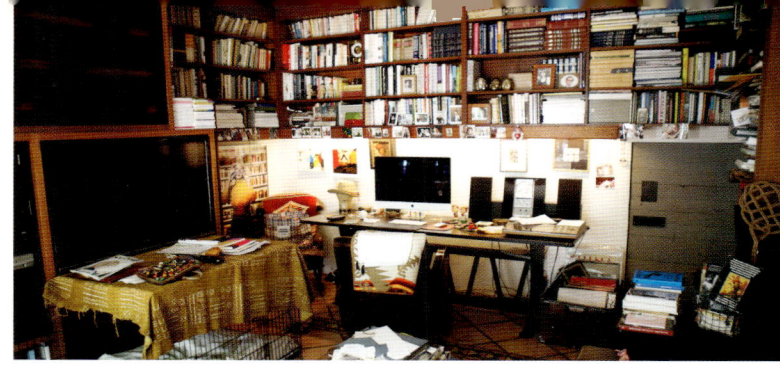
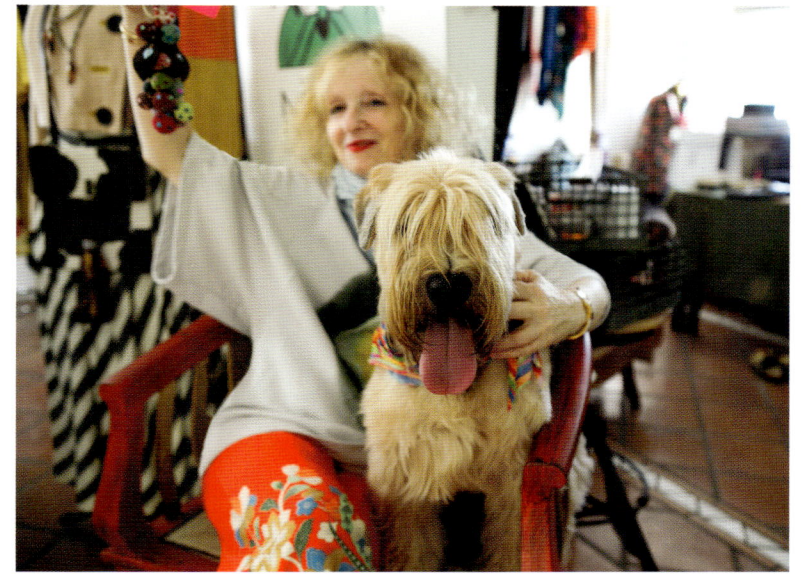

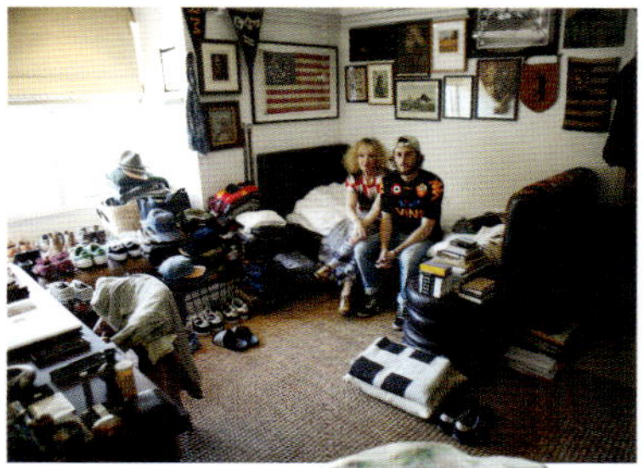

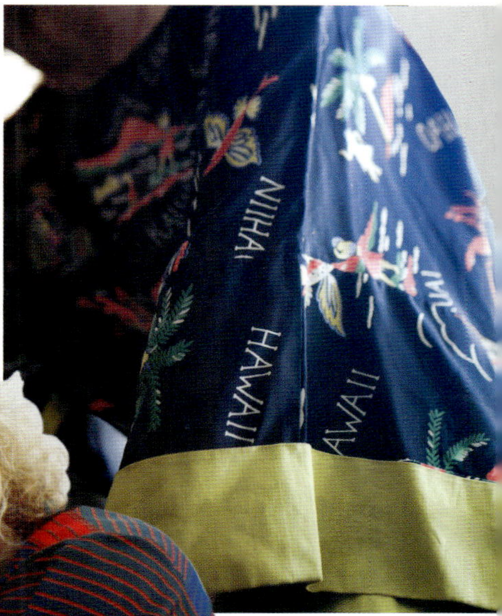

161

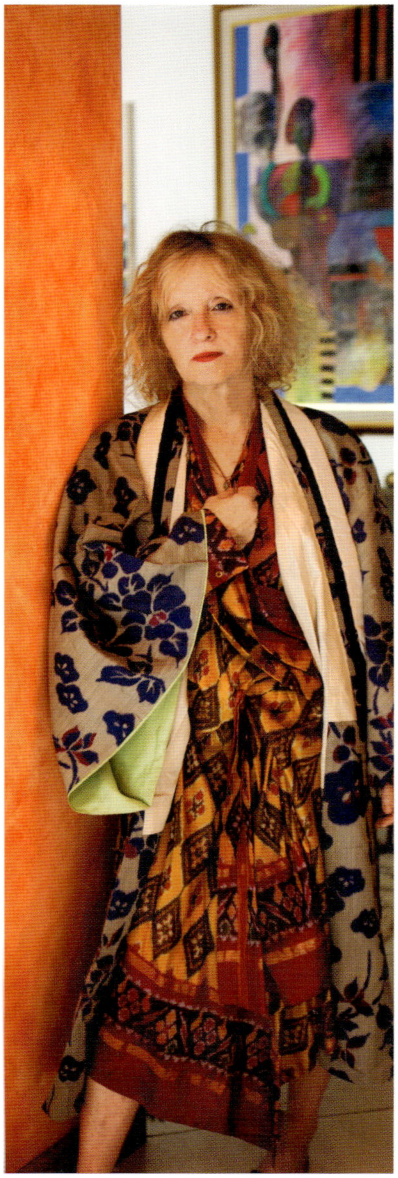

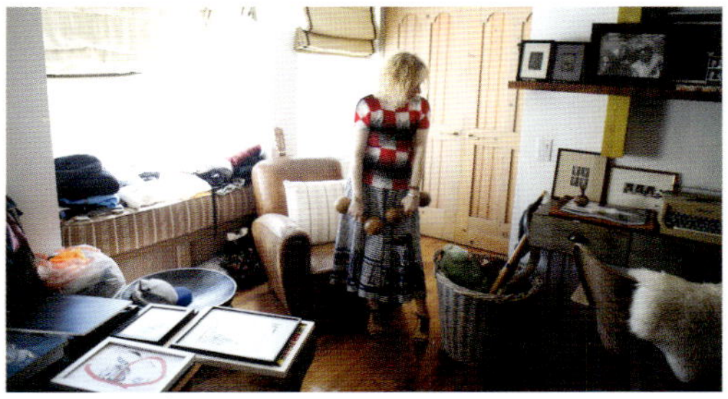

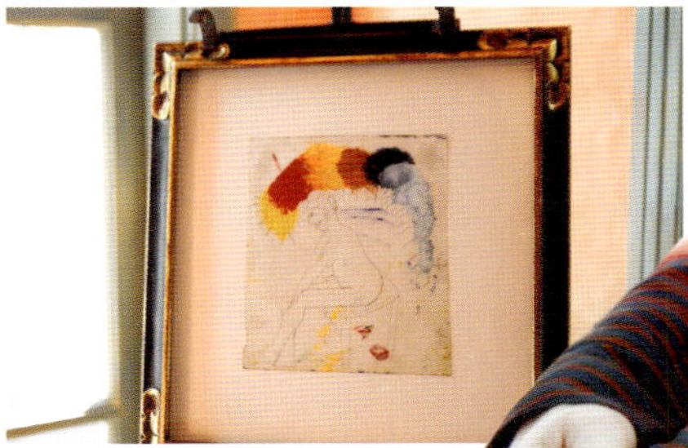

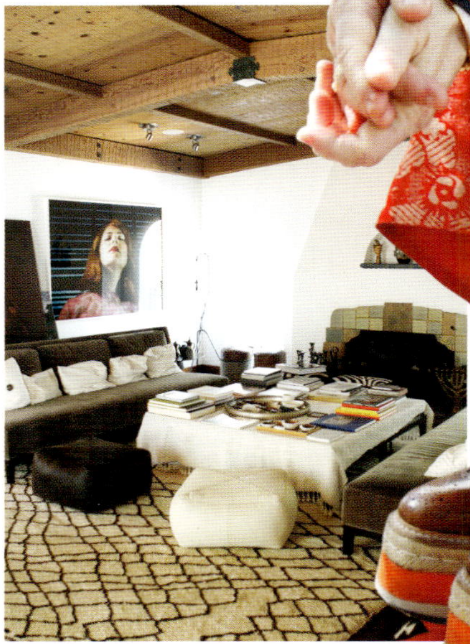

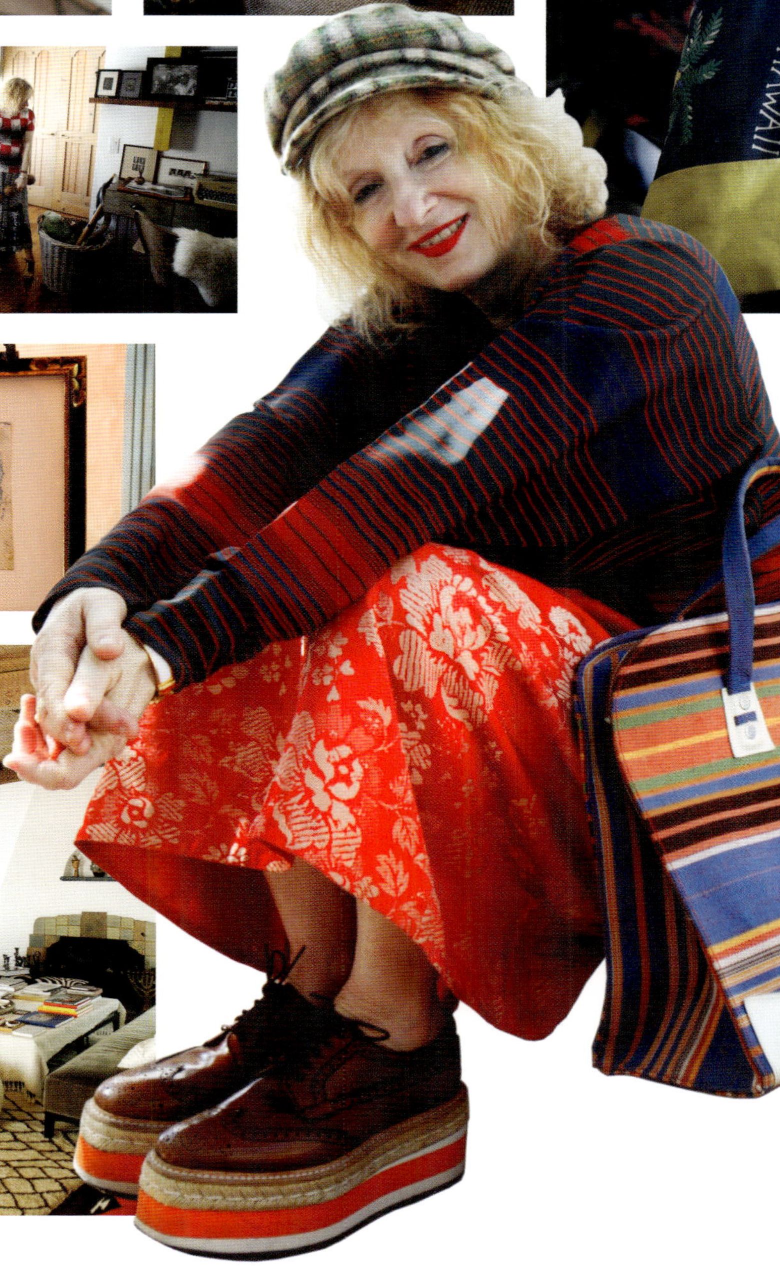

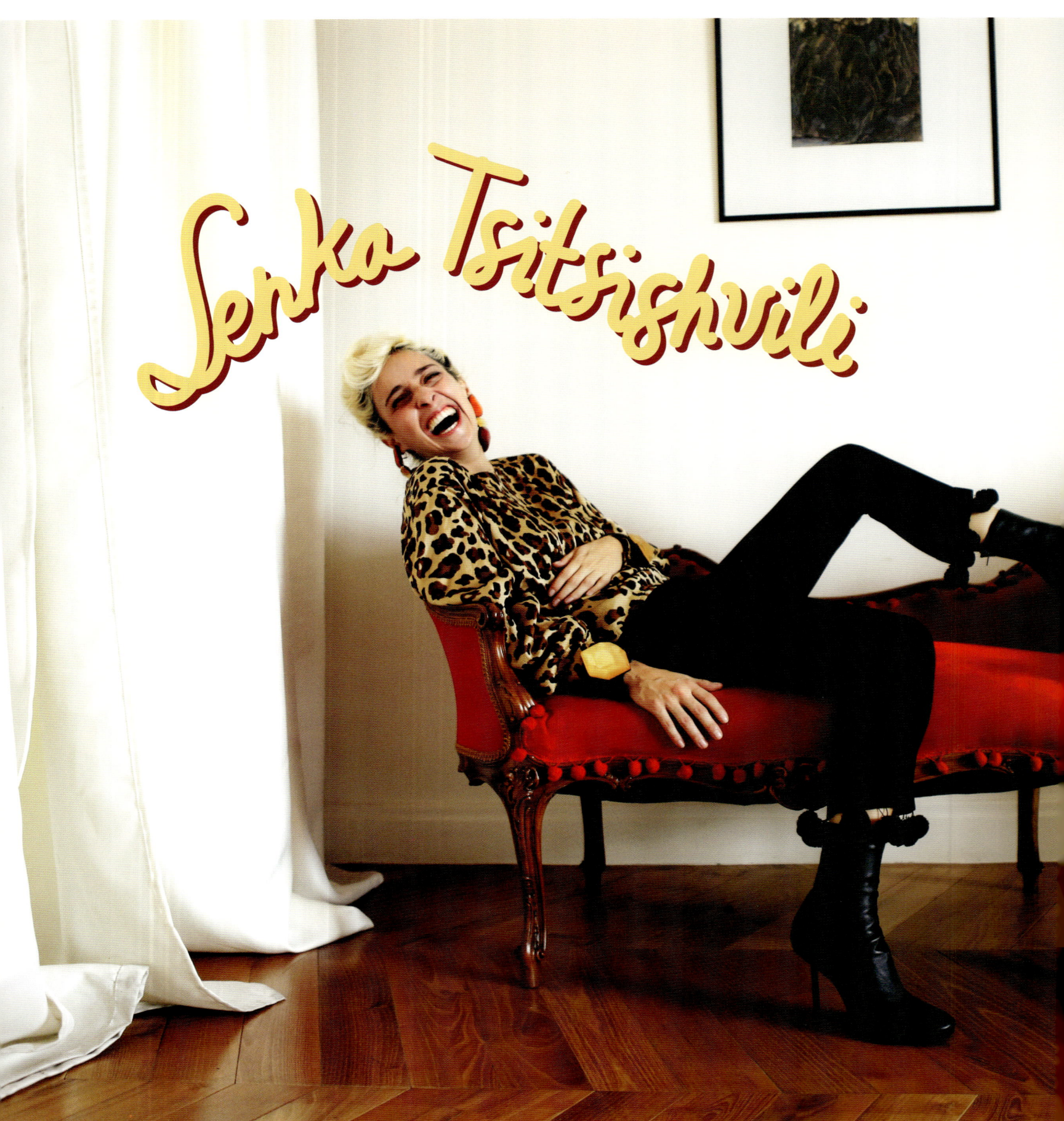

LENKA TSITSISHVILI
PIERROT LE FOU

It takes a good deal of practice and willpower to pronounce Georgian family names, but it becomes fun after a while. They are predominantly patronymics, and the most common suffixes imply you are a "son" or "child" of whomever came before you with the same name. Lenka's last name, Tsitsishvili, is royal and means *prince* or *princess*. This may sound like an incredible blessing, but it wasn't always. "There have been 11 queens with this name in Georgia," she explains in her endearing Georgian accent, "and in the beginning the communists killed and destroyed families like this. I don't remember the Soviet era much myself, but we were raised in a family where some of the grandparents of my parents were killed, and some of them were deported to gulags, so the ambience at home had always been very anti-Soviet."

Lenka doesn't live the typical life of a royal. She studied architecture, just like her father. She never even dreamed of becoming anything else; it was a clear and chosen path. Her first project was a private house in Tbilisi at the age of 19. "They were doing every crazy thing I told them," she laughs. "It seems so unbelievable to me now. After the exterior was built, we went up to interior designs, but the owners went bankrupt so it was never done exactly as we wanted."

In 2007 Lenka designed and opened her own concept store in the center of Tbilisi, Pierrot Le Fou. She carries mostly

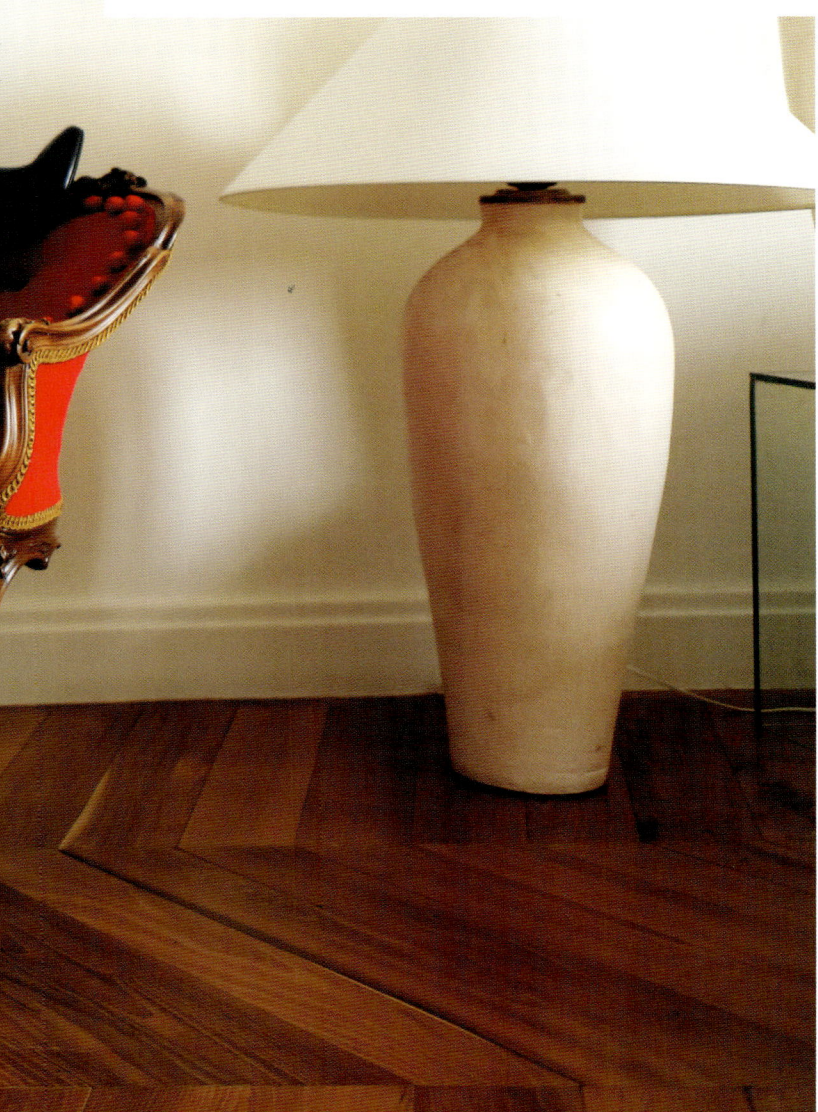

avant-garde, contemporary brands like Yohji Yamamoto, Haider Ackermann, Margiela, as well as some perfumes, accessories, and shoes. One look inside her closet at home is enough to understand the style references. She's a minimal dresser with a flair for dramatic accessories. She finishes each outfit with corset belts, or layers of jewelry, or lace gloves, or oversized hats.

When it comes to vintage though, we have a problem. There isn't any in Georgia, nor in any of the other former Soviet countries, "only if you have something from grandma or mother." As a kid, Lenka says she "loved to spend a lot of time in [her] grandmother's wardrobe, which was so interesting and different from what everybody wore in these days; it was difficult to get different clothes in those days." She only discovered real vintage when she visited Paris for the first time.

Lenka has a beautiful, spirited soul. She's endlessly positive and energetic, even with the back injury she says she's recovering from. She comes off as shy at first, but that's just because she's overtly polite and considerate. She speaks with a deep voice and giggles incessantly, but with caution. Her friends tell me she's always in a good mood, and I can only concur. She plays Bach at home, but pop music in her car because she says it makes her happy. She never sits still. "I don't like to be relaxed for too long," she confesses, "but the best way to relax is still a good dance, dance, dance!" I'm sure she's a super fun mom. At 36 she already has four children: Zaza, 15; Niko, 12; Gio, 11; and Ketevan, 9; and she may even want more. I don't know how she does it, but don't you just love those Georgian names?

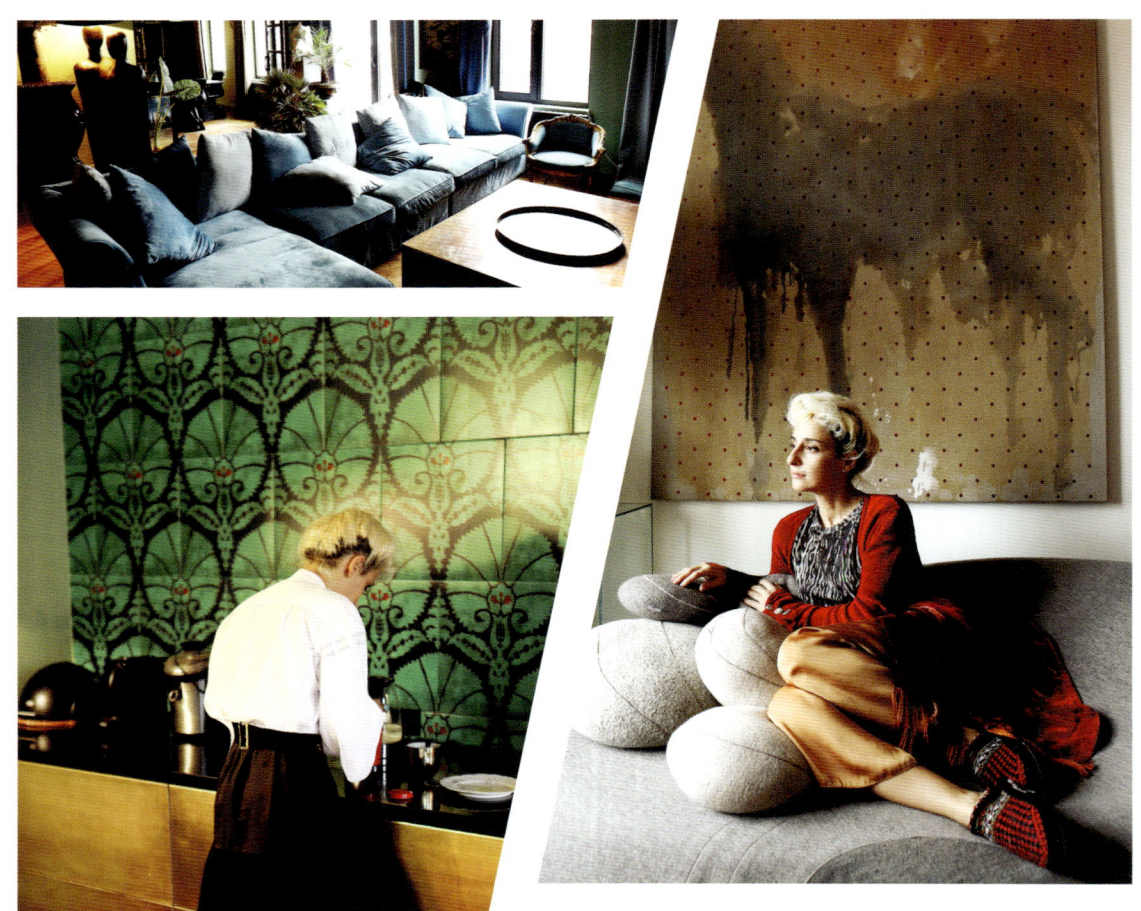
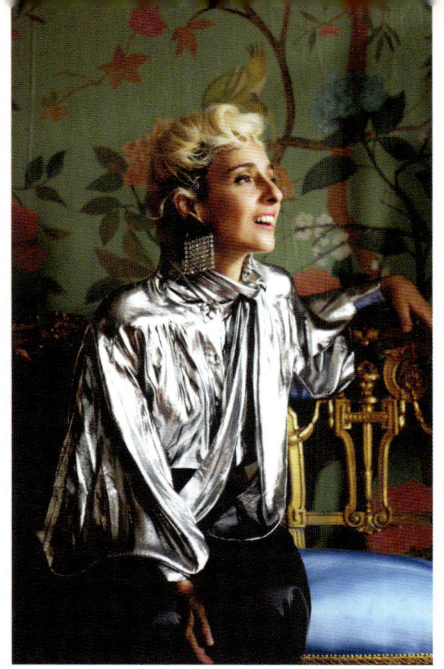
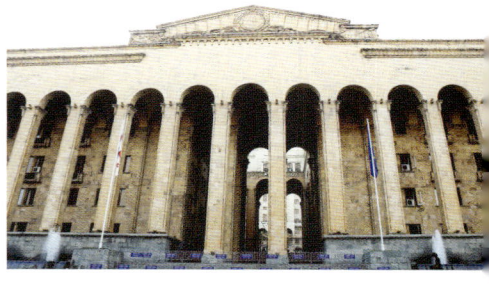
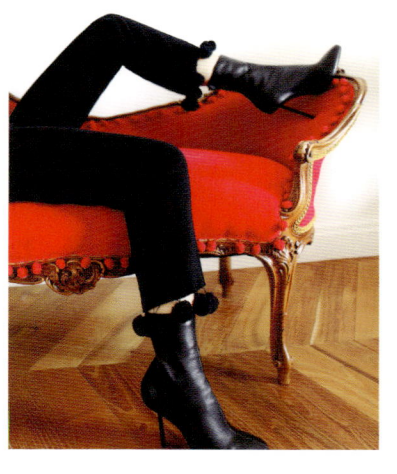
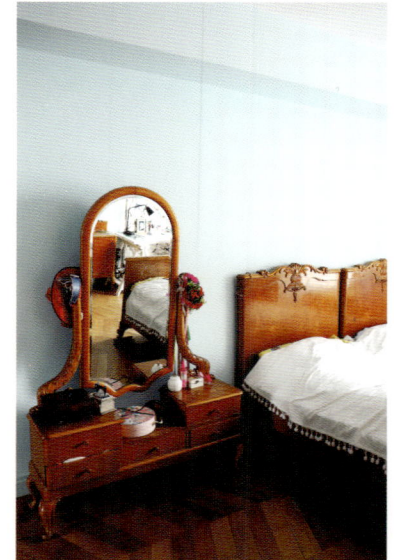
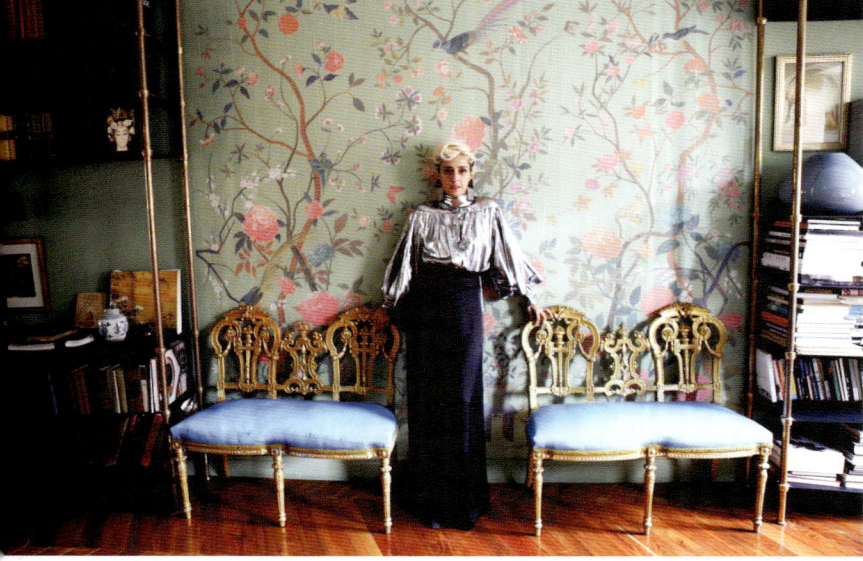
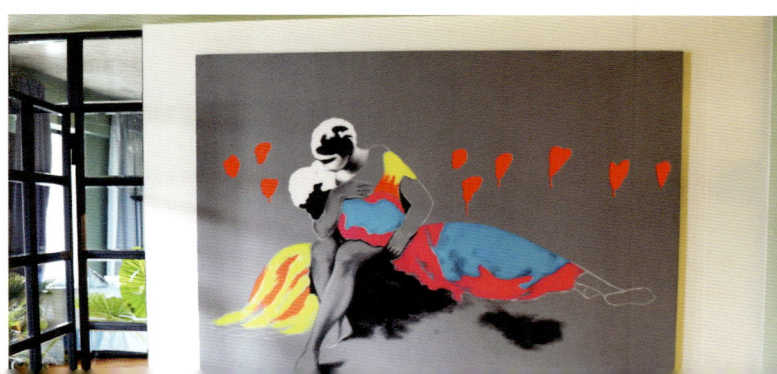

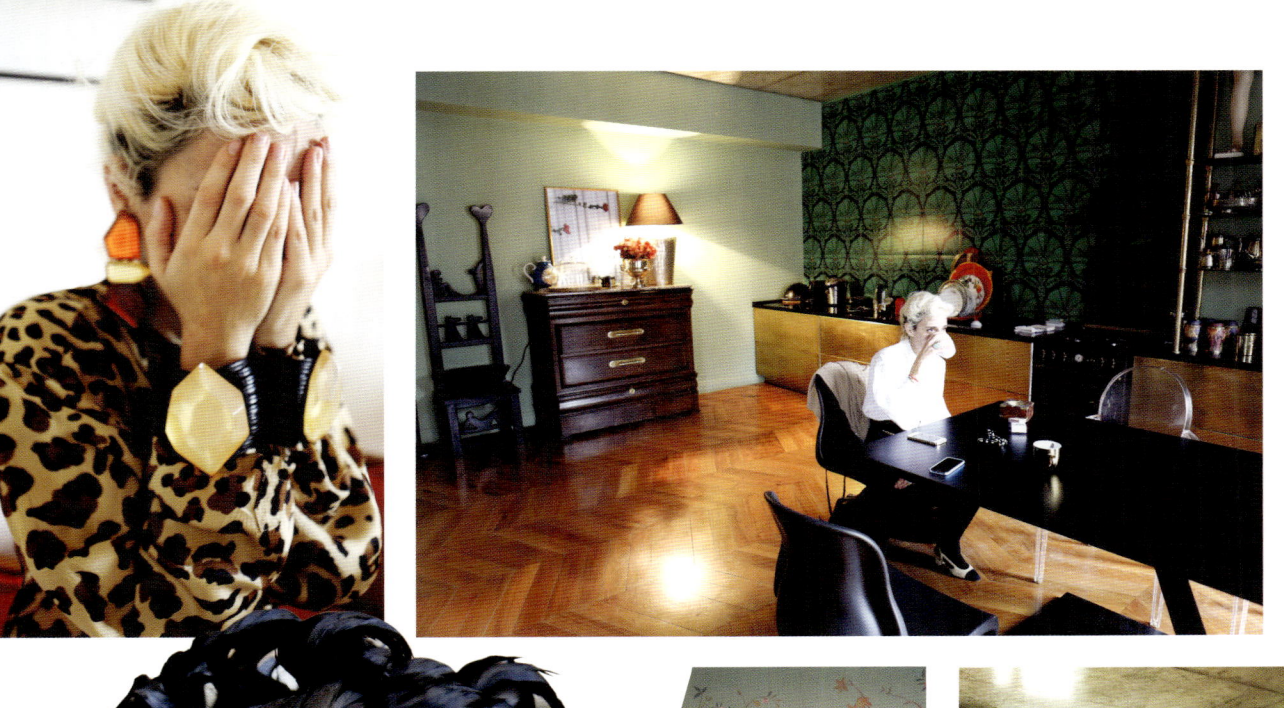
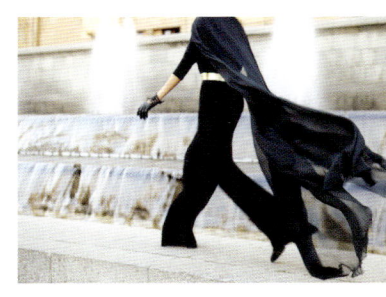
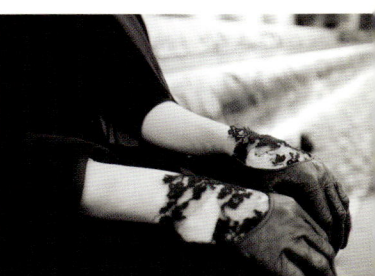
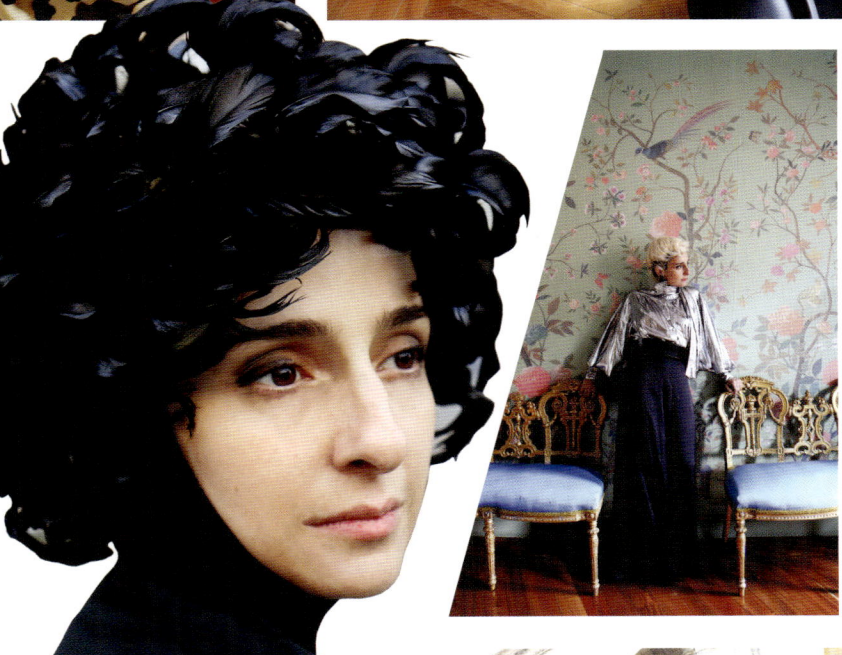
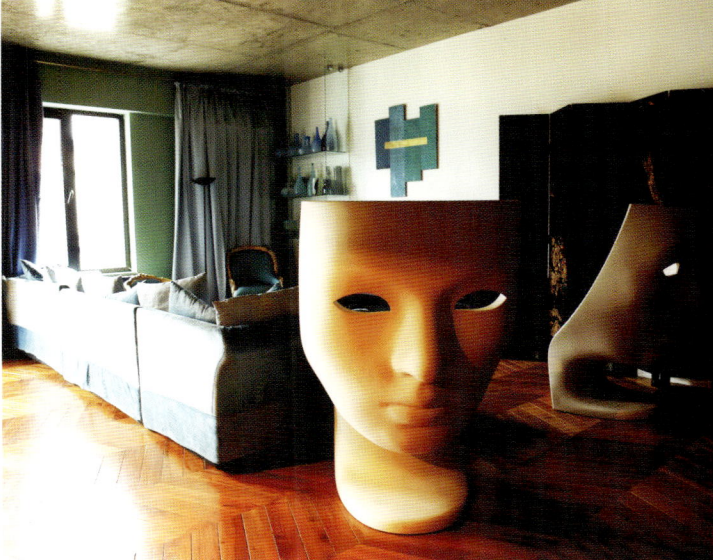
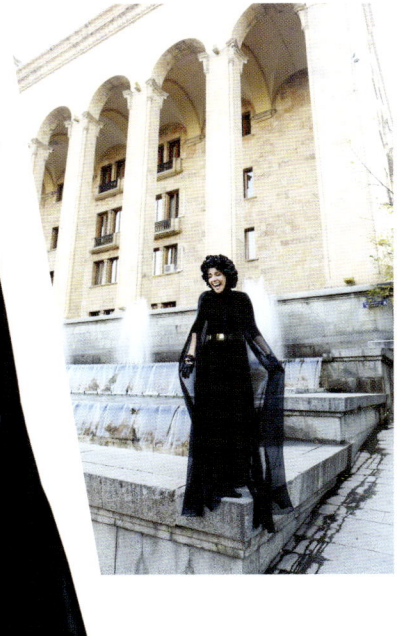
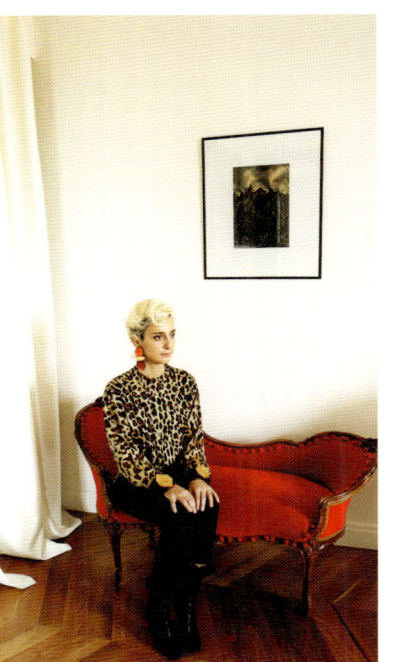
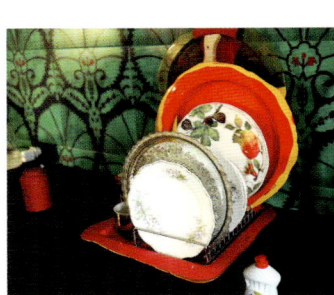
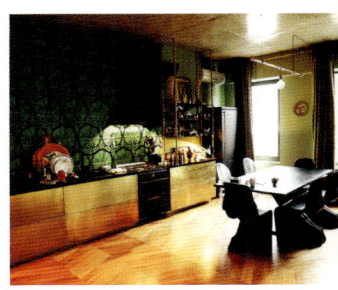

LINDA RAMONE
A PINK ODE TO LEGEND

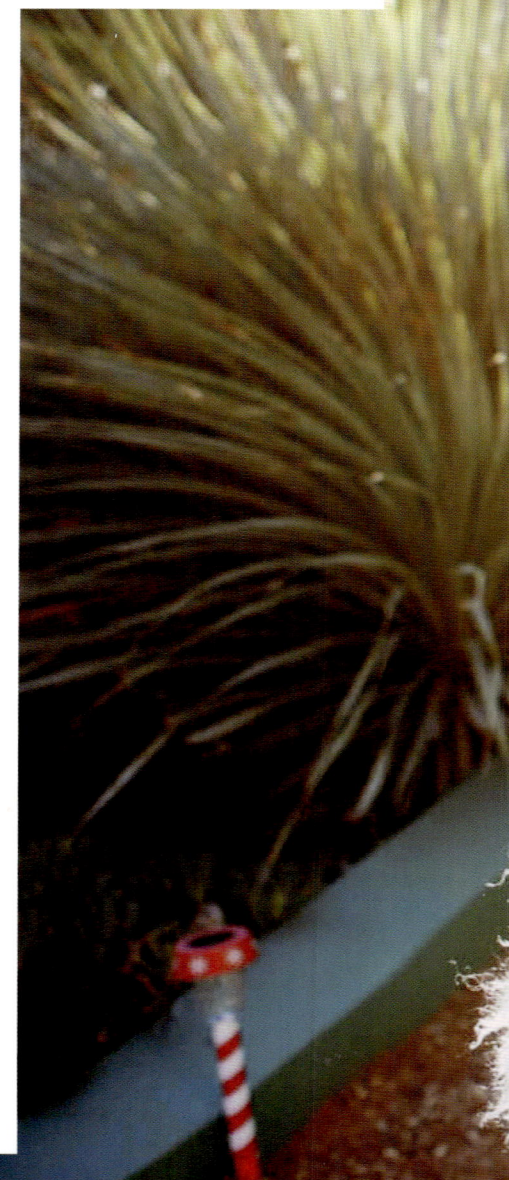

The first indication is the house I am standing in front of. It is *pink*: a bright, unapologetic, screaming, Pepto-Bismol pink with prairie-green roof and window trimmings, candy canes planted on the front lawn, and life-size figurines depicting the Nativity of Jesus in the driveway. Part of me wishes it were dark; then I would be able to see all these Christmas decorations in their intended luminous insanity. Mind you, the holidays have come and gone—it is January—but something tells me there is more at stake here than a mere tribute to Santa. This is the work of a fanatic enthusiast who dreams of December in August, and pines for snow in Sherman Oaks.

The buzzer sounds just like mine at home in Brooklyn. It's a comforting little ring, but all familiarity vanishes as soon as I step into the garden. It's so many kinds of fantastic and overwhelming. First of all, it's strange to see toy soldiers, reindeer, snowmen, and penguins propped up against palm trees, and a kidney-shaped, aqua-blue pool. They must feel like most New Yorkers do when visiting Los Angeles: lost in translation. Then there's all the hummingbirds motoring around the sugar water feeders. They're almost invisible, but their buzzing frenzy resonates throughout the entire yard. I'd be content to just sit and watch the spectacle in awe, were it not for the happy "Hello!" and bowl-cut-framed smiling face greeting me by the front door. "I'm Linda Ramone! How are you?"

It's extraordinary how tightly she's held on to her Queens accent, even after living in Los Angeles for nearly 20 years. Maybe it's another way of keeping her late-husband, Johnny Ramone's legacy alive. Never mind the hundreds of concert pictures on the walls, or the themed rooms they designed together (there is a Disney bathroom, a horror media room, a rock 'n' roll bedroom, an Elvis foyer, and a Nancy Sinatra living room), or the Johnny Ramone tribute she organizes at the Hollywood Forever Cemetery annually: "Last year I had over 3,000 people!" Linda Ramone lives and breathes his heritage, as he intended it when they packed up and moved out West: "Out there having fun in the warm California sun." She even cuts other people's hair like his, I hear.

"How about three?" she challenges me. You have to understand that Linda yells rather than speaks, as if you're in the next room and she needs to get her point across through a thick concrete wall. Her voice is high and pitchy, and she finishes every sentence with a raspy, mischievous giggle. You can't help but listen, really. "I can just hold up the clothes against my body, instead of putting them on. Seven outfits is a bit much I think." I mean, she's right. One look at her pink-and-turquoise brocade outfit today is enough to understand her Barbarella-meets-mod-meets-CBGB's aptitude. However, I think, with this much vintage under one roof, why not flaunt it? "I dress up every morning," she finally agrees. "And it takes me about an hour [to get ready]. A typical day involves metallics, velvets, tiaras, hats, boots, vintage furs, matching pocketbooks, and shades." Even when you're sick or sad, I ask incredulously?! "Then I just wear a caftan with matching scarf and slippers."

Though she works every day as the President of Ramones Productions, Linda's life is sunny and less than cumbersome. She never had kids—"Apparently they are so much work!"—but she drives a brand new Porsche, travels to Rome as often as she can, loves "fine dining and road trips," buys custom leather pieces from Romulus at South Paradiso Leather, enjoys the company of a big, one-eyed cat named Munchkin whom she and Johnny adopted after she was thrown off a roof, and dates a gorgeous, young musician who reminds me of Johnny. "Pookie!" she sings proudly when she leads me to his studio/magical man cave. "Last year he released a great record called *The Olms* with Pete Yorn. At the moment he's working on a new record, completely on tape, that he produces himself." J.D. knows he's being summoned for a picture because he follows us up to his rainbow rooftop without a word. They look so freaking good together I want to scream. And just like that, with my new Ramones T-shirt in hand and hundreds of incredible pictures on my memory card, I have my final indication that this pink bubble is bliss.

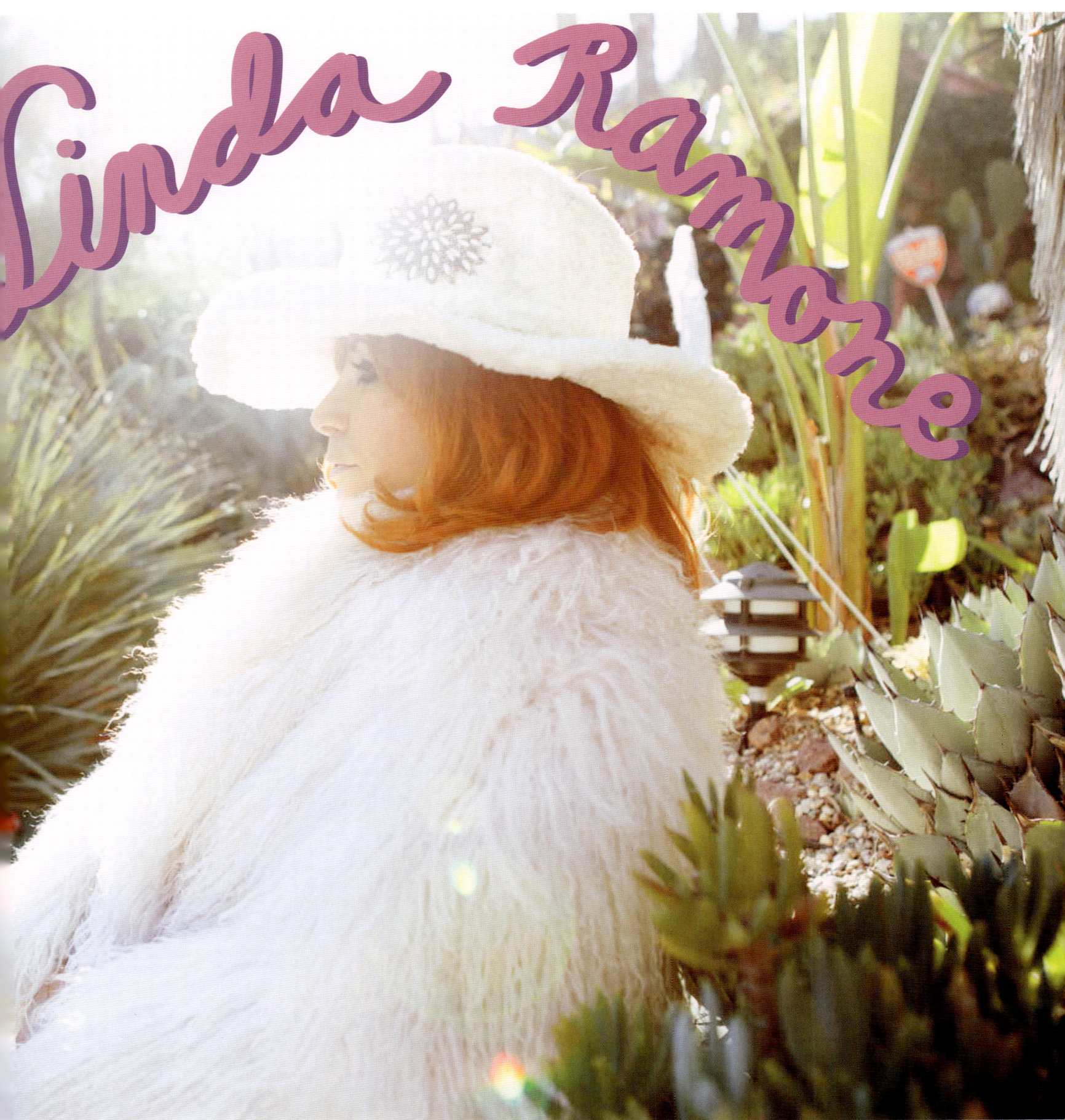

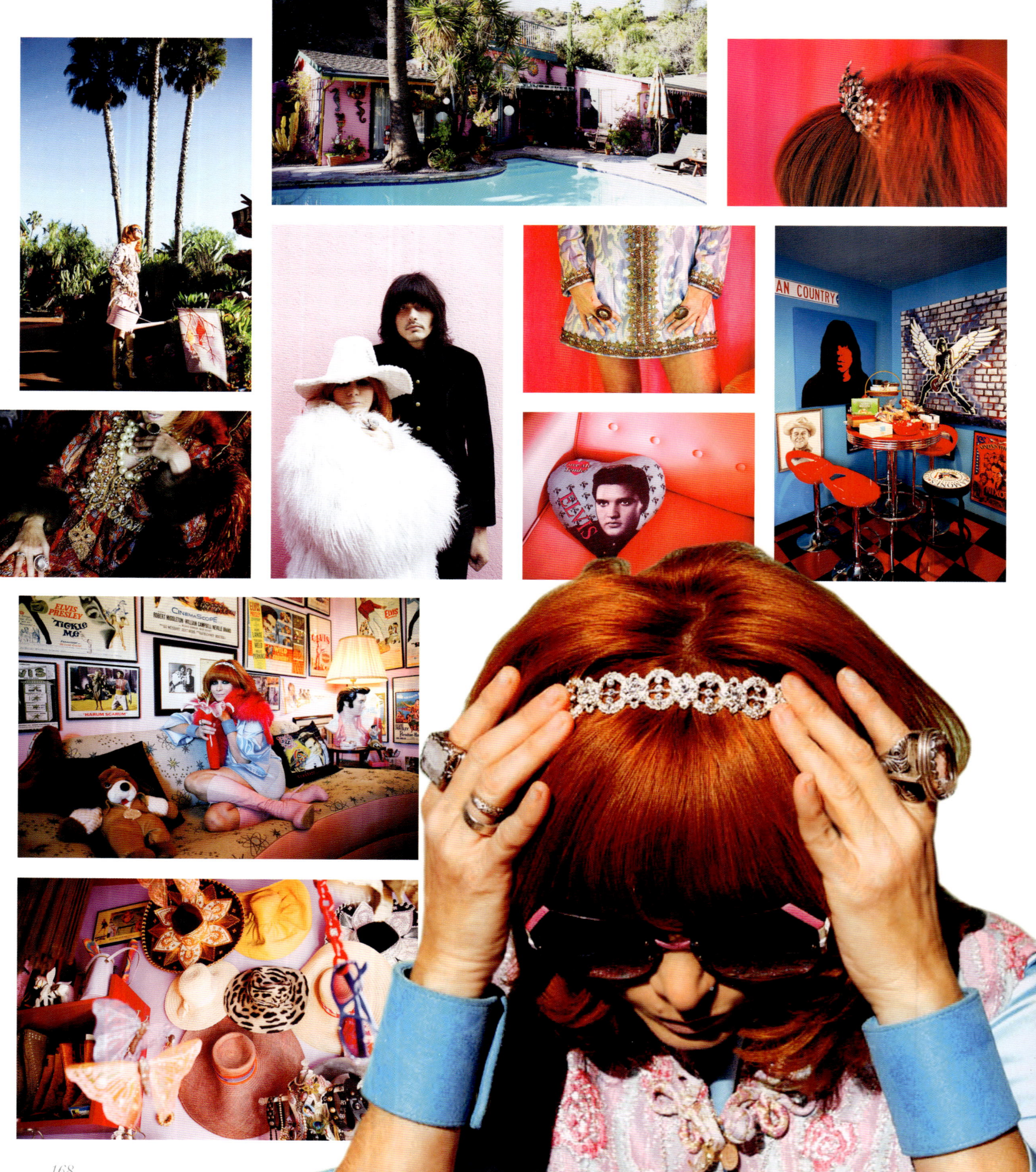

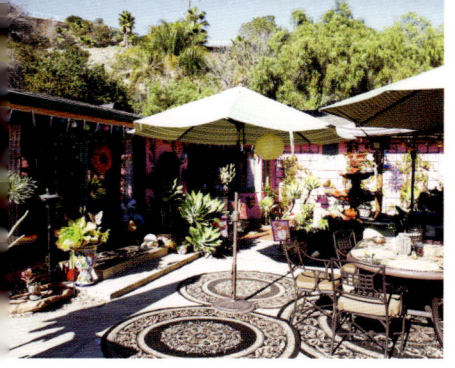
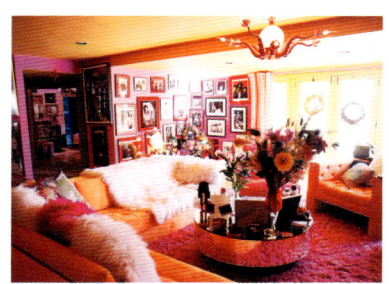
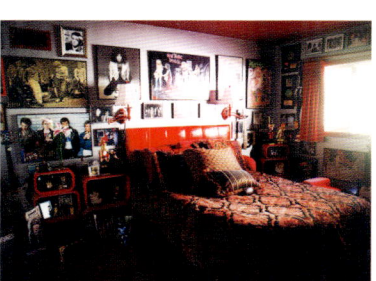
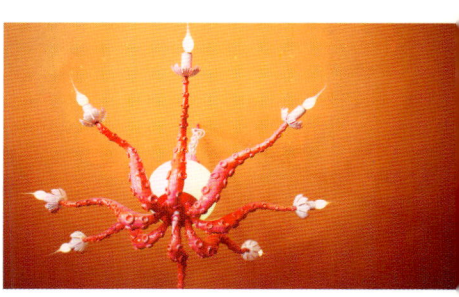
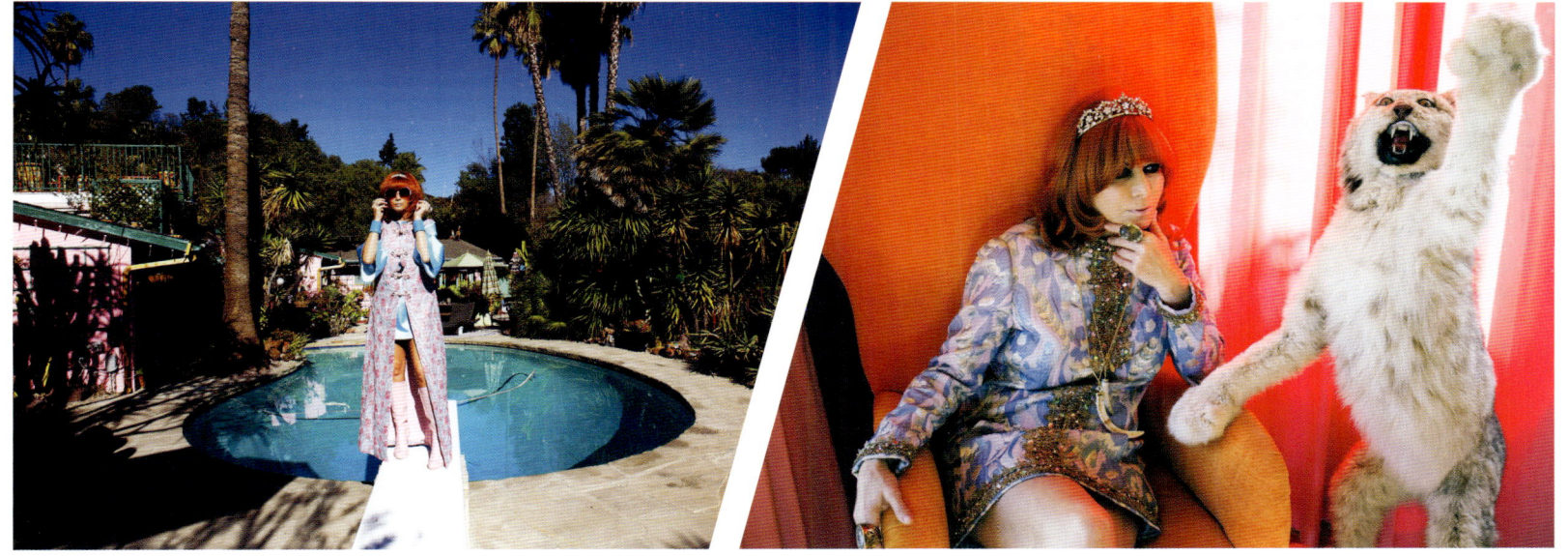
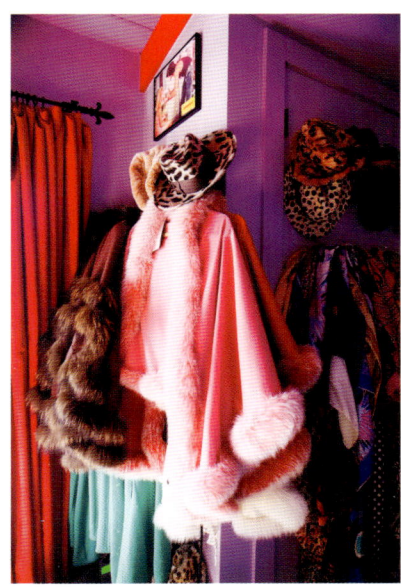
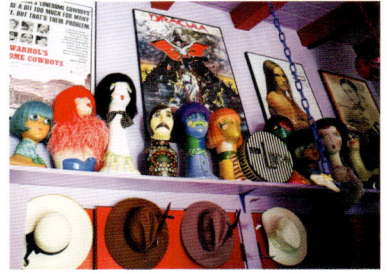
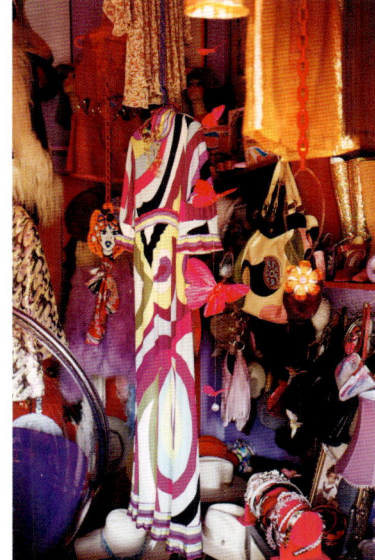
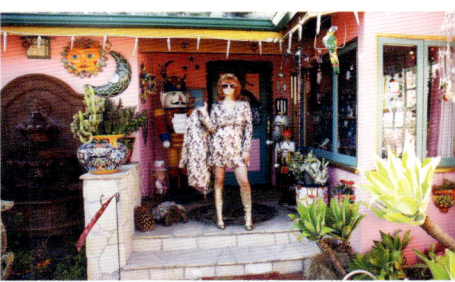
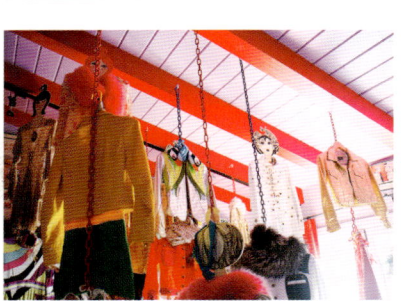
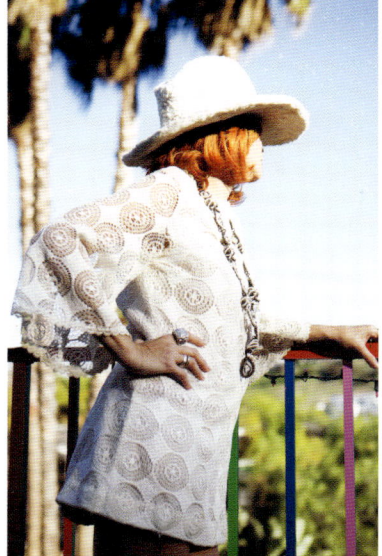
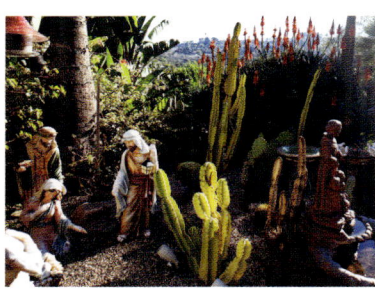
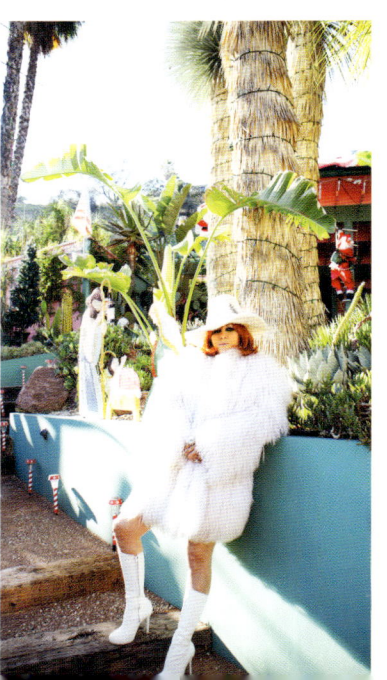

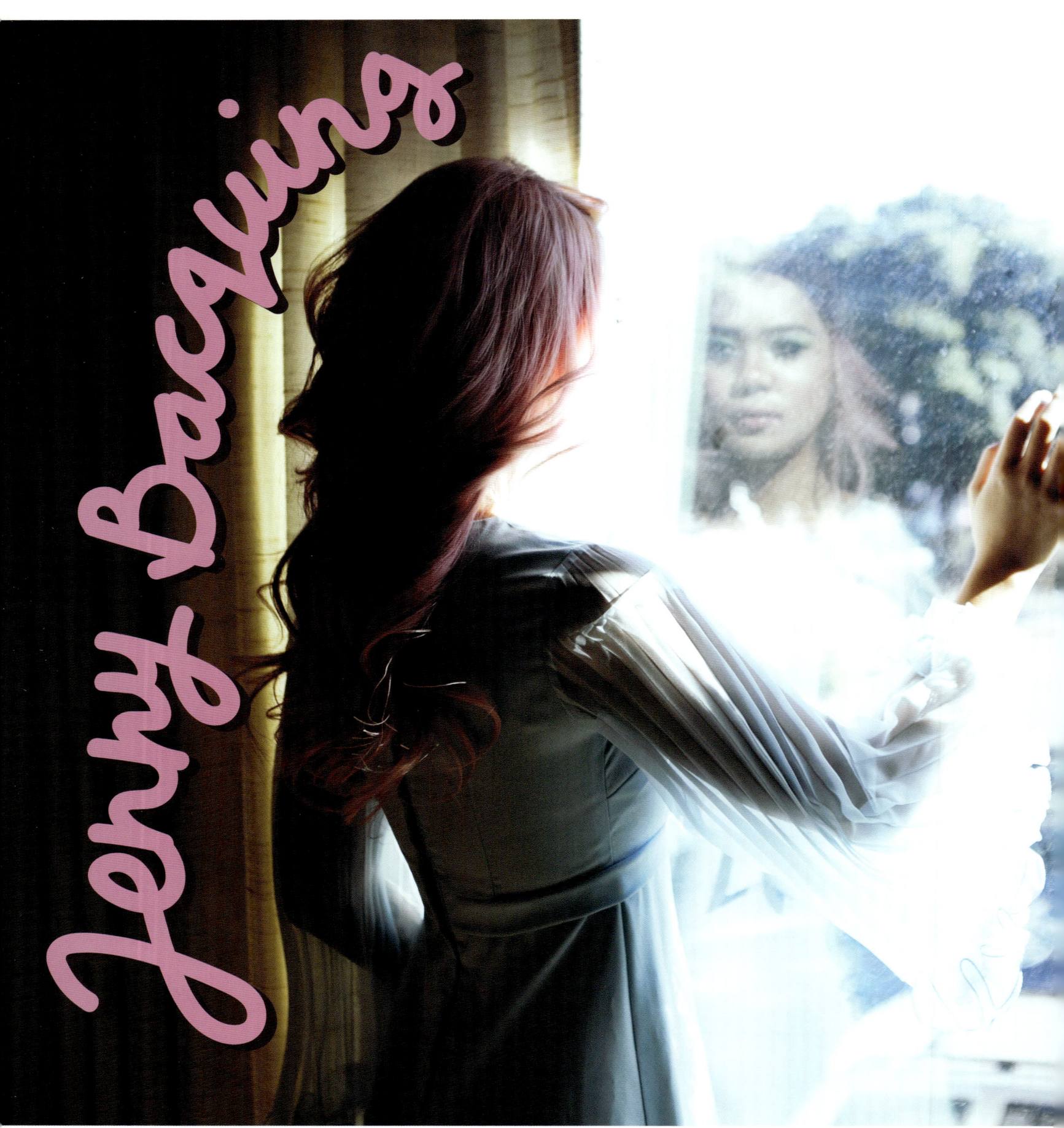

JENNY BACQUING
FIGHTING IN TULLE

I got the fateful text at 8 a.m.: Jenny had suffered a massive anxiety attack during the night and was incapable of doing the photo shoot this morning. Well, damn, I had come all the way to San Francisco to photograph her. She was such a unique and adorable little creature. I had been stalking her Instagram feed—@shelovesdresses—for months. I loved her unwavering dedication to pastel, tulle, and baby dolls. She was unapologetically different: always smiling, always perfect, always wearing these cute prom dresses and 1970s hairstyles. She seemed a little shy maybe, but definitely not like someone who is prone to chronic hyperventilation.

Fast-forward one and a half years, and I am back in the Bay Area. Jenny's divorced now and she has pink hair, and she did not have a panic attack last night. She opens the door in an oversized gray teddy onesie with a bunny tail in the back, and walks me up one floor to her aunt's old apartment. She's only here for a short while until she moves into her new place in Ohlone Land. Nothing has been touched since auntie relocated to a nursing home in the early 90s, but the furniture—the pots and the pans, the carpet, the lamps, and everything else inside this dusty space—is actually much older, probably late 70s, and makes for *the* coolest set location. The soft, muted tones of beiges and velvety browns, and low light coming through the old nylon curtains, are a photographer's dream—and I'm not mad we didn't get to do this last year.

"I have had social anxiety since I was very young," explains Jenny. "I was outgoing with my close family members, but at school, and in sports, I kept to myself. I always had a drawing pad or a book to read." In high school she wanted to be a politician, and ultimately a Congresswoman. "I now know that I do NOT have the temperament for formal government politics," she shares, "as I would probably die of a rage-stroke from all the Republican bullshit."

Twenty-nine-year-old Jennifer Marie Baquing is known to be a very vocal activist on her social media channels. When Trump was elected, she offered her services as a wedding photographer free-of-charge to any and all LGBT couples who wanted to move up their wedding date in the event the new president would revoke their right to be married. "What don't I fight for?" she laughs when I ask about her grievances. "I fight against systemic racism, white supremacy, against capitalism, against heteronormativity, against Islamaphobia, against transphobia, against Trump, against white feminism, against cultural appropriation. I fight for #BlackLivesMatter, for equity of PoC in the USA and abroad."

That strong voice and no-nonsense attitude stand in stark contrast with the charm of her delightful, naive appearance, but there's an explanation. She started thinking about fashion after she saw a picture of her maternal grandmother wearing a cream, bell-sleeve, lace I. Magnin mini dress the day she eloped in the 60s. The image stuck with her, and encouraged her to only wear what makes her happy. "I think that especially we, as women, are socialized to measure ourselves based on a lot of problematic beauty and fashion standards," Jenny posits, "when the most important thing is being happy and respectful of our clothes. That being said, I did once wear a pair of suede sandals every day for a whole semester, and they smelled really bad. I probably should have thrown them away." Ultimately Jenny would like to stop fighting. "In 20 years I hope that I'm not still fighting against the same things I'm fighting against today. I hope that I'm happy, and safe, and loved."

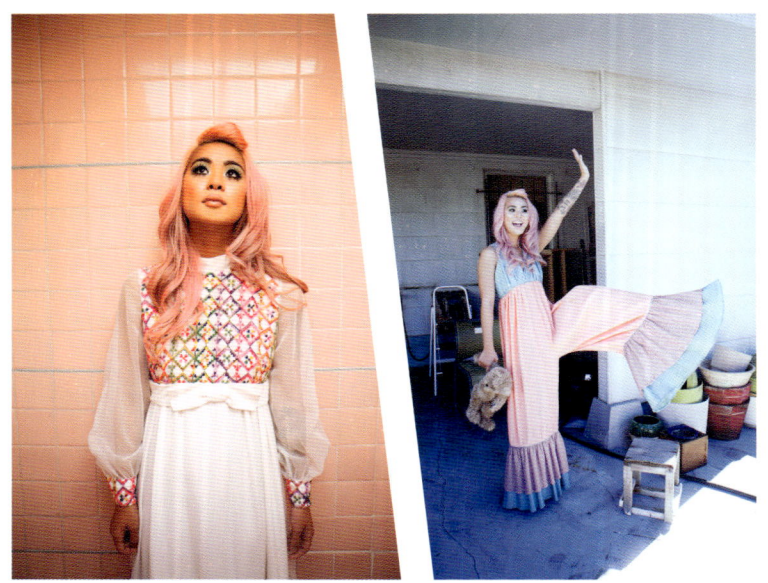
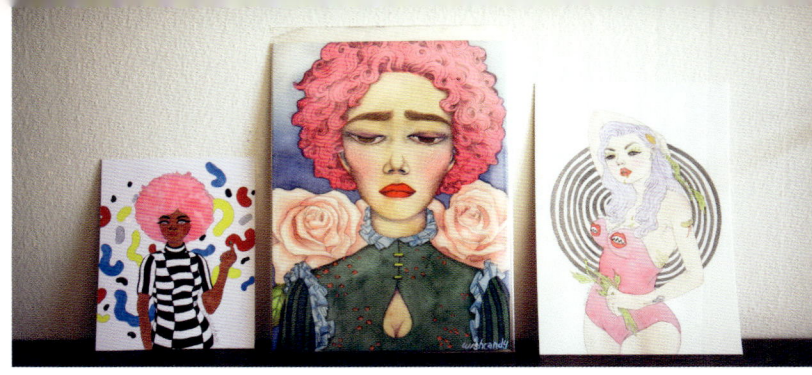
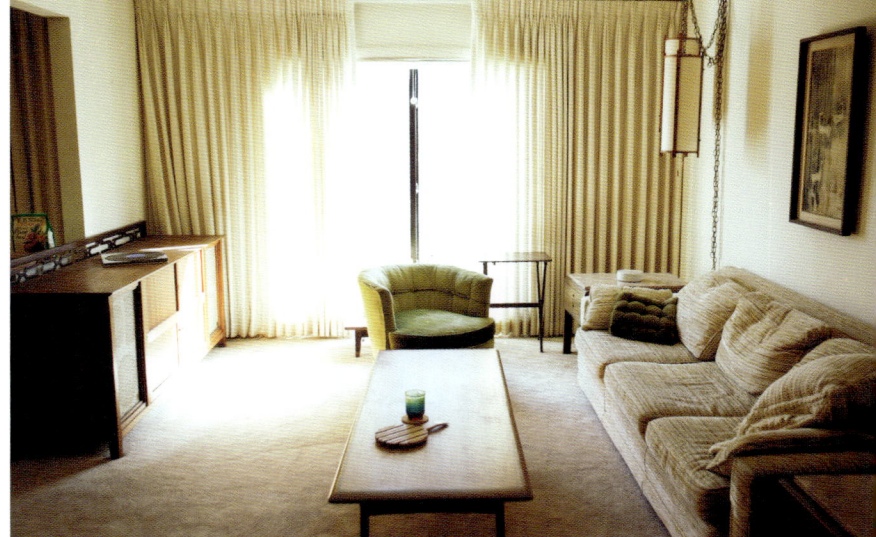
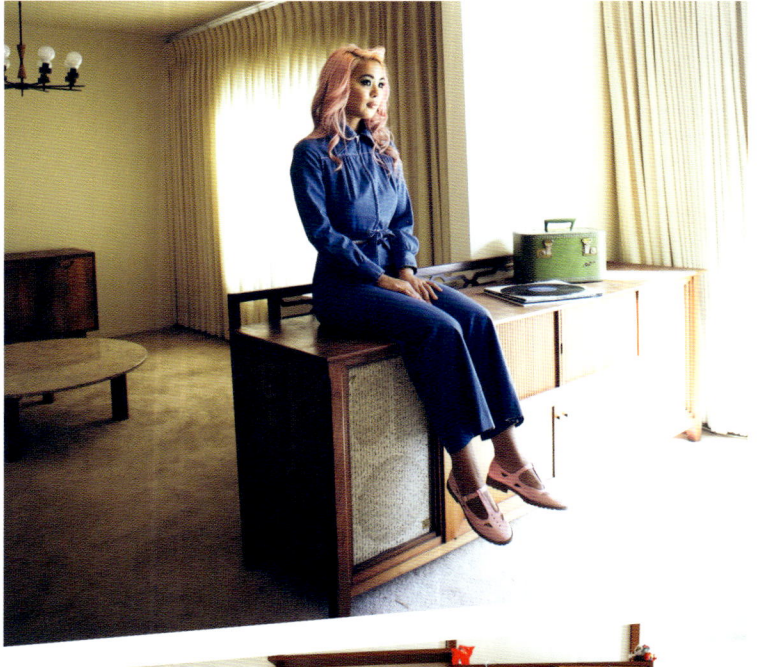
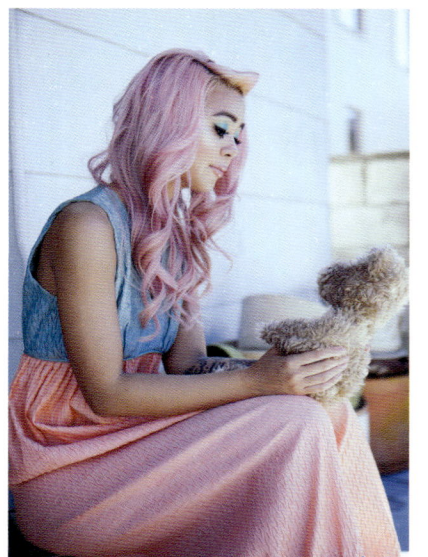
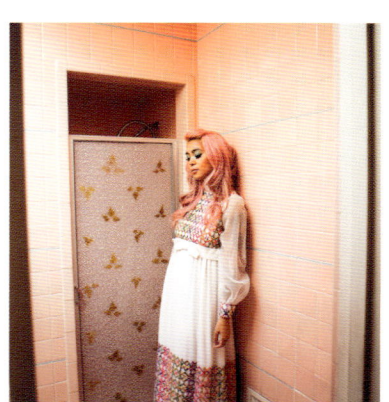
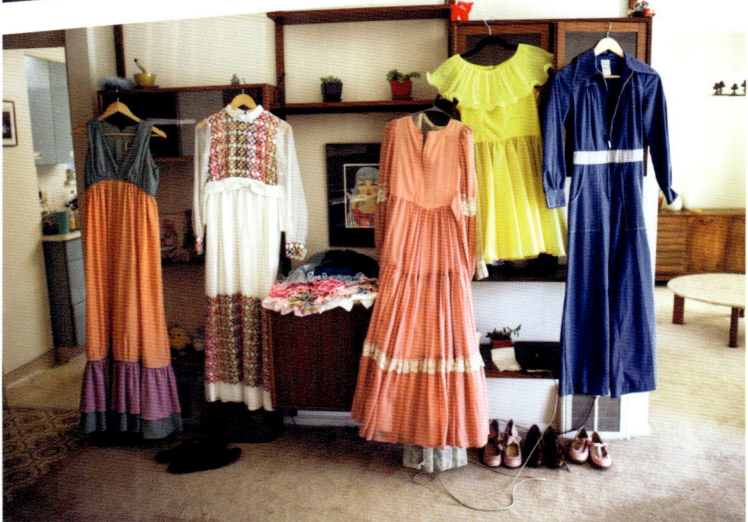
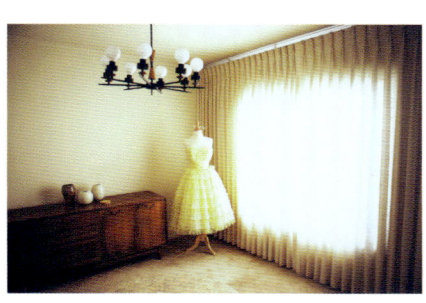
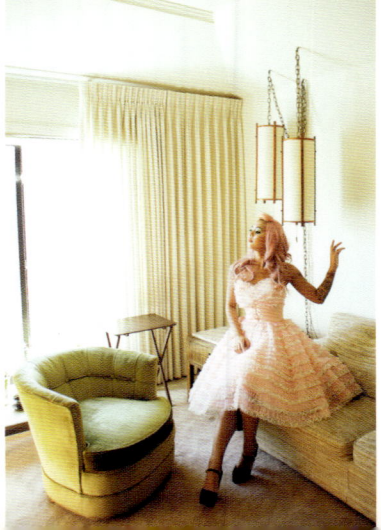

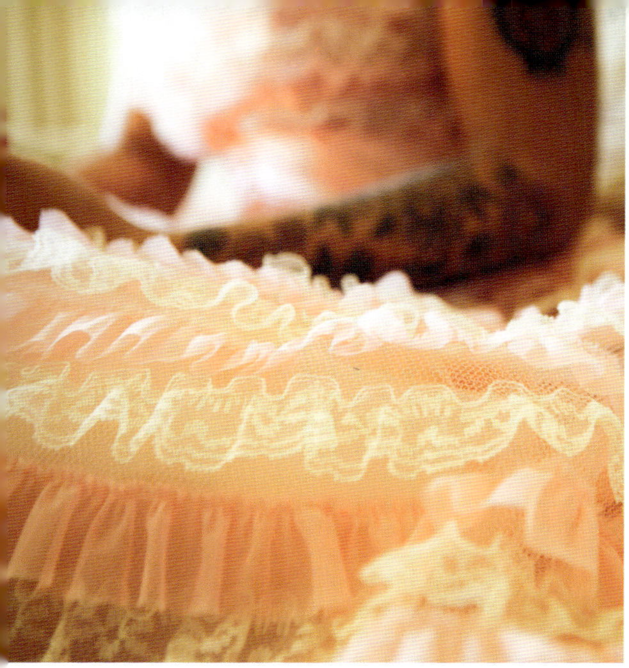

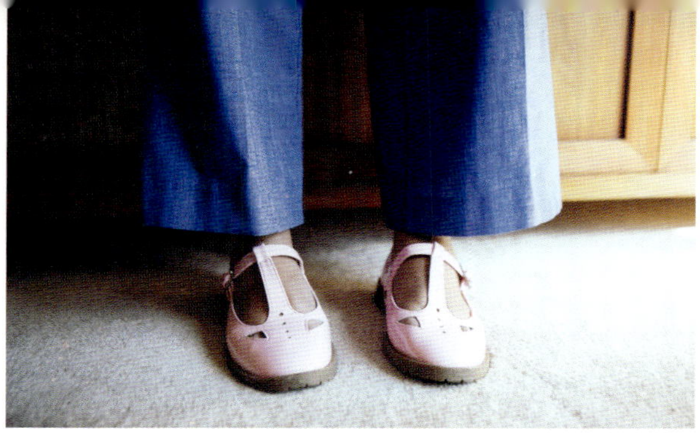

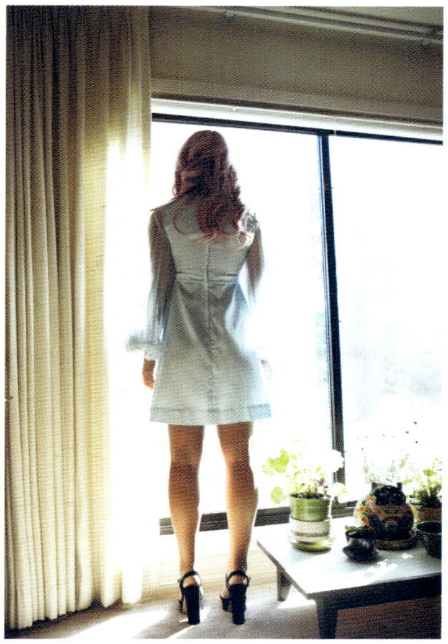

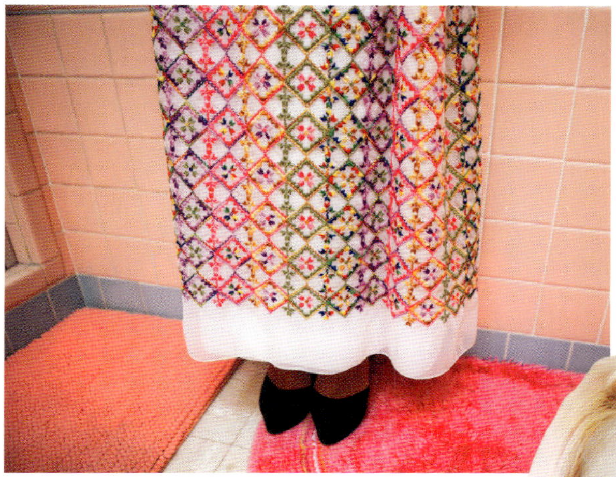

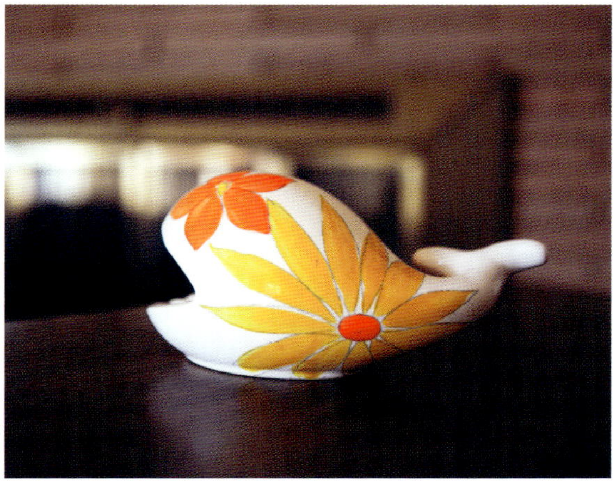

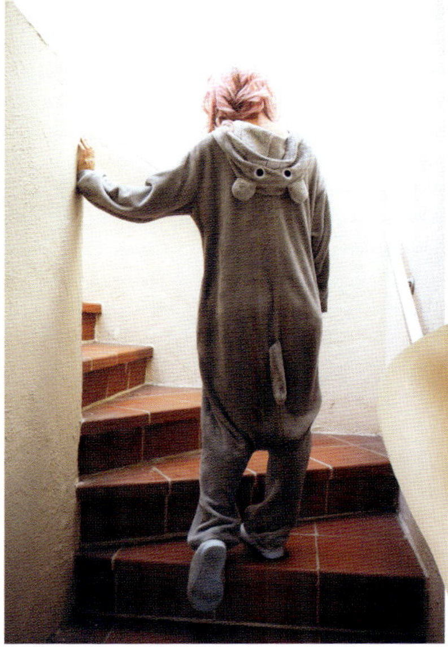

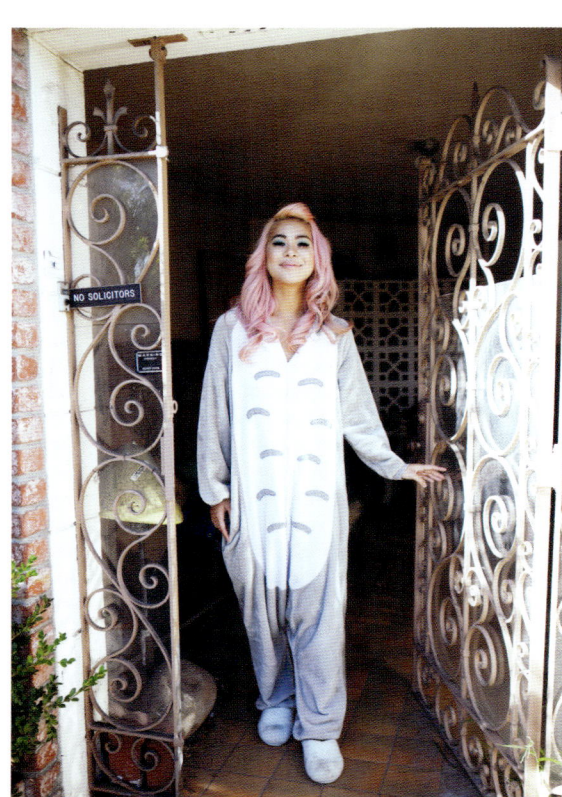

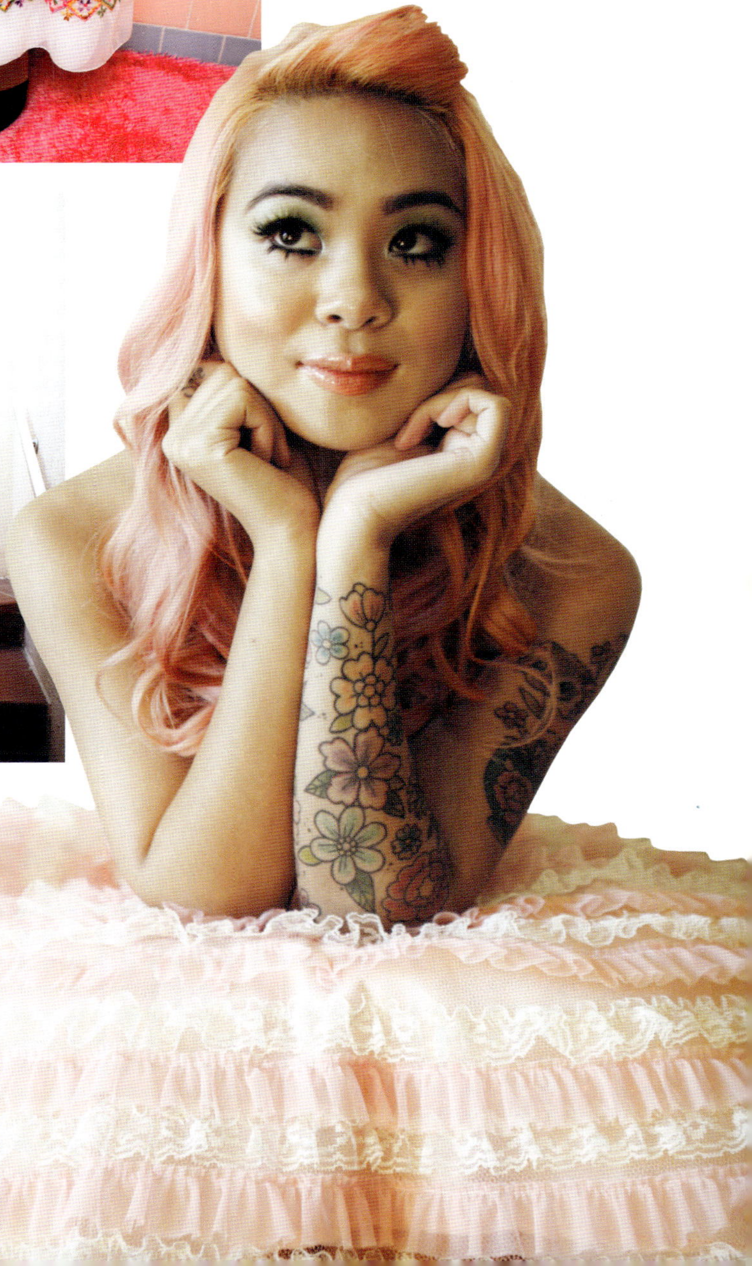

**MARGOT
HOW TO RAISE
A PRODIGY**

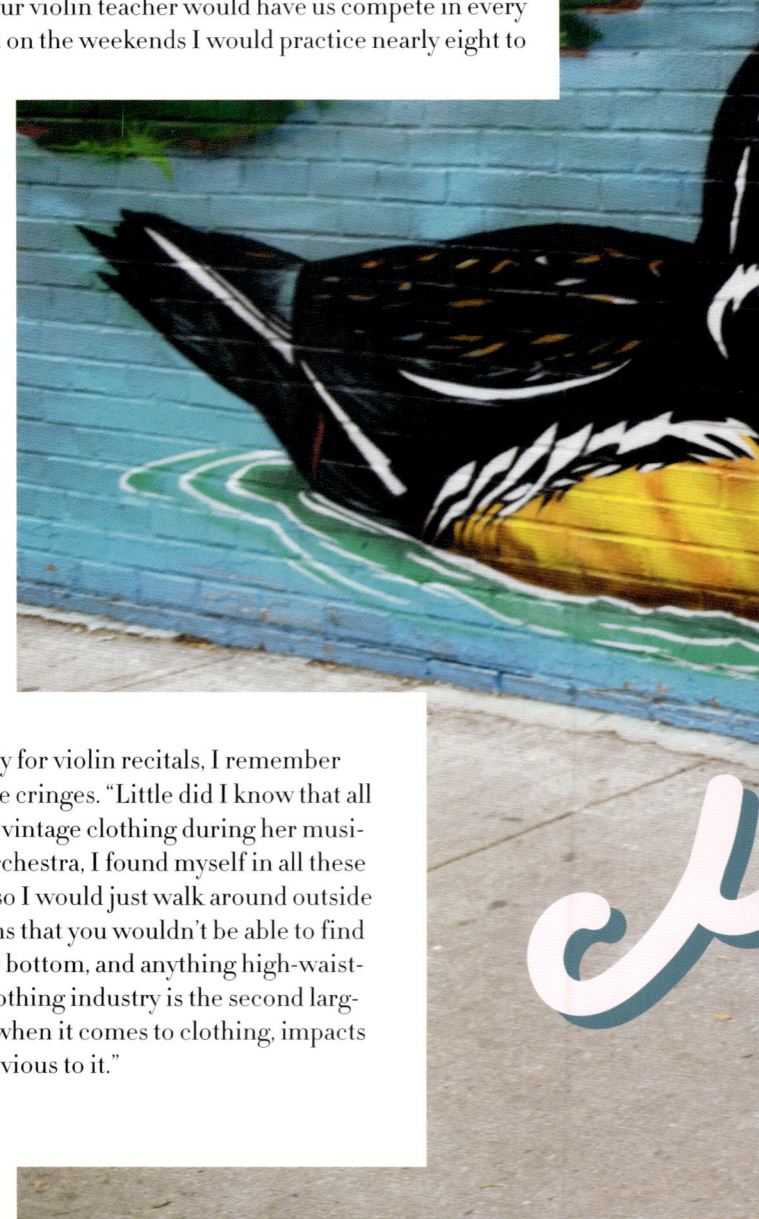

Dear future parents, do you wish for smart, conscious, talented, focused, ambitious children who make you proud and stress-free? You do? Then keep reading.

Caitlin Lowery was only four years old when she picked up the violin. She came home from preschool on the first day of summer and told her mom: "I'm bored. What are we doing?" Mom expected her daughter to just want to play outside and hang out, but she did not conceive that kind of girl. Caitlin was not destined for sand castles and pillow fights. Instead, mom remembered having seen a violin in her grandfather's closet and decided to put her daughter in violin lessons. Caitlin loved playing the wooden instrument from the moment she first held it, and for the next 24 years this would be all her household would hear.

"My whole childhood revolved around playing," recalls Caitlin. "I was wildly obsessed. I played in multiple orchestras, quartets, trios, and duets; you name it. There was a state competition that our violin teacher would have us compete in every year, and I remember preparing for so many solo and ensemble pieces that on the weekends I would practice nearly eight to twelve hours a day. I was super-disciplined and dreamed of being a solo violinist when I grew up. I didn't know anything else and never thought about anything else. I also don't remember ever going to a high school party, which is extremely ironic considering that the first few years of living in New York were spent performing violin in clubs!"

Caitlin now goes by her stage name, Margot, and her career has reached soaring heights. She signed a record deal with Warner Brothers last year. She performs and records with DJ Mia Moretti as The Dolls, who toured with Katy Perry in Asia for six weeks and played in front of massive arena crowds. She also sings and records solo work. And she writes pieces for movies. But now there's also a man in her life, "A very lovely boyfriend who is a phenomenal musician and writer and who keeps me laughing," and she desperately wants a corgi. But the violin is still her lifeline, a force so habitual she's like a puppet on its strings. I ask her if it's like driving a car a she laughs: "Not even! Driving a car seems like more work. I don't think about it when I play at all. When you start so young you don't know any better. It's second nature at this point, it's like an extension."

The violin even decides what goes in her closet. "Getting ready for violin recitals, I remember how much I used to hate putting on a slip under my dress," she cringes. "Little did I know that all I would want to wear out now is just the slip!" She discovered vintage clothing during her musical travels. "Once I started touring with the Trans-Siberian Orchestra, I found myself in all these small towns all over the United States. Malls give me anxiety, so I would just walk around outside and come across these adorable shops full of such special gems that you wouldn't be able to find anywhere else." She loves anything that has a matching top or bottom, and anything high-waisted. She wears vintage for ethical reasons: "It is said that the clothing industry is the second largest polluter in the world. Every decision we make, especially when it comes to clothing, impacts so many people around the world, and we are completely oblivious to it."

And that, dear future parents, is how it's done.

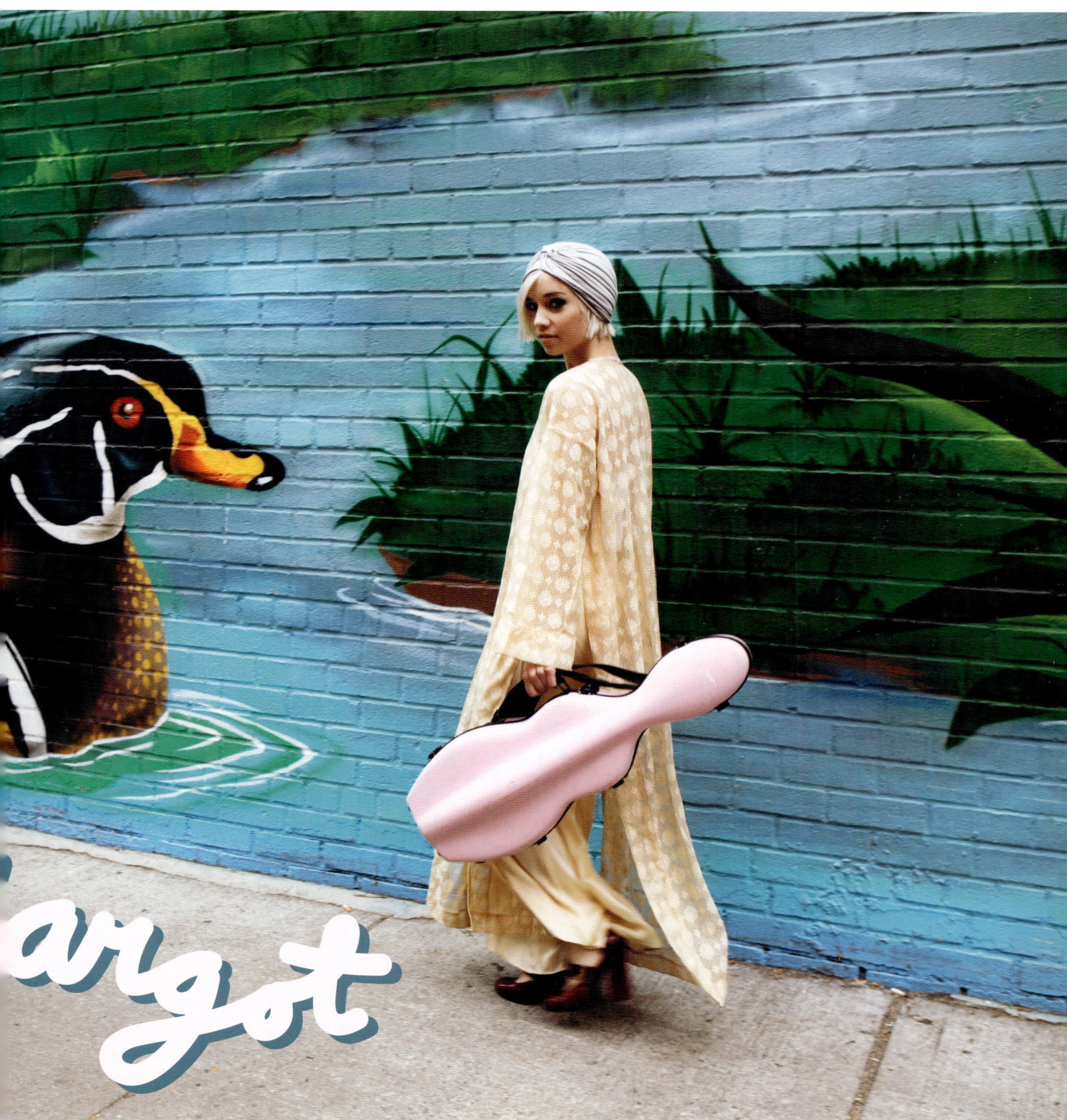

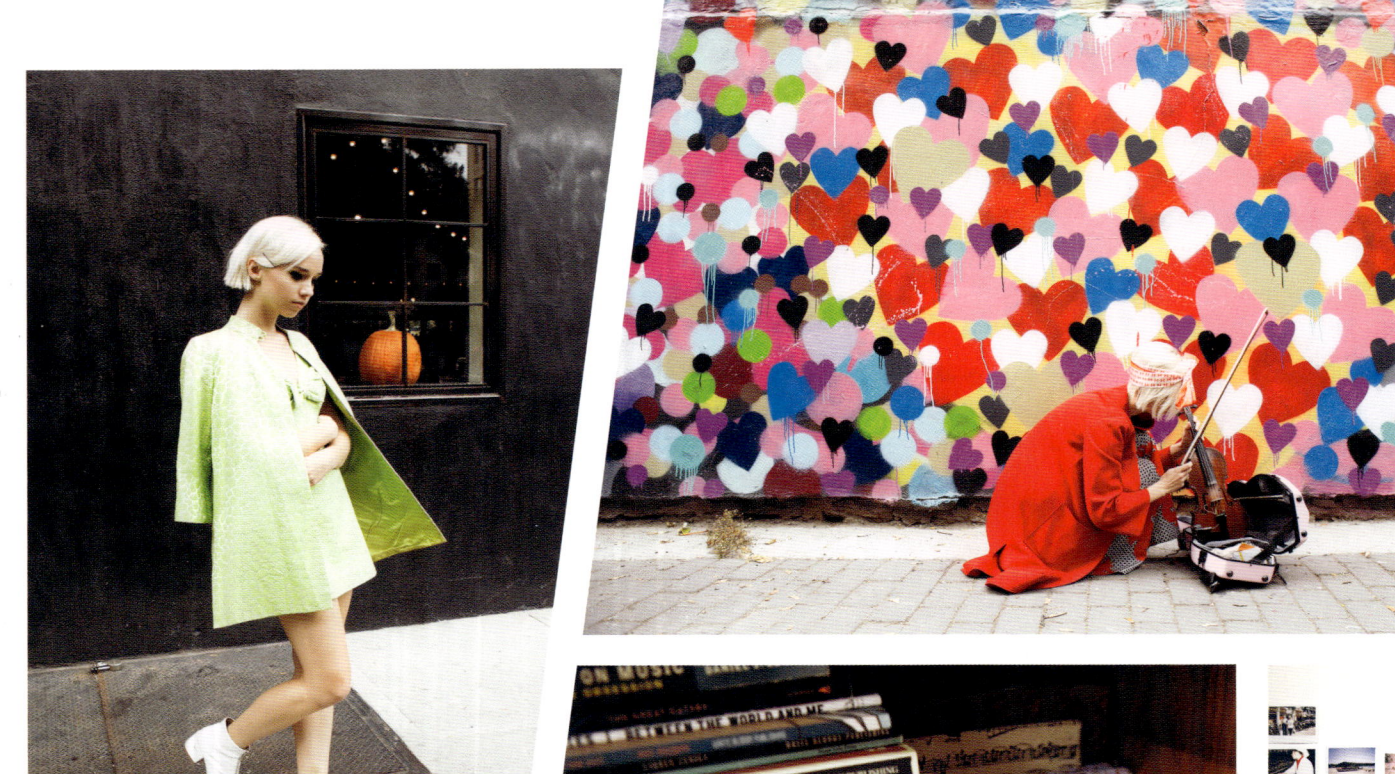
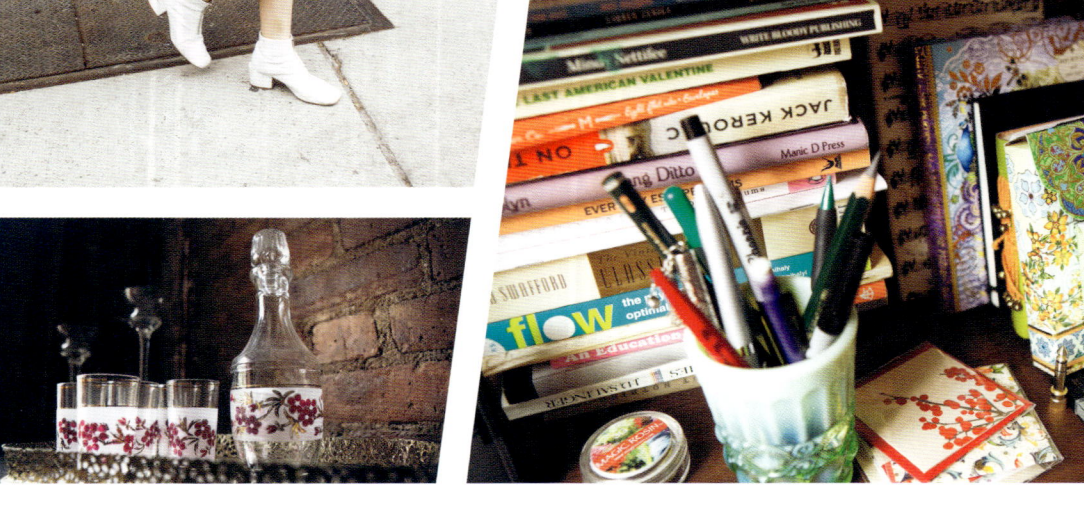
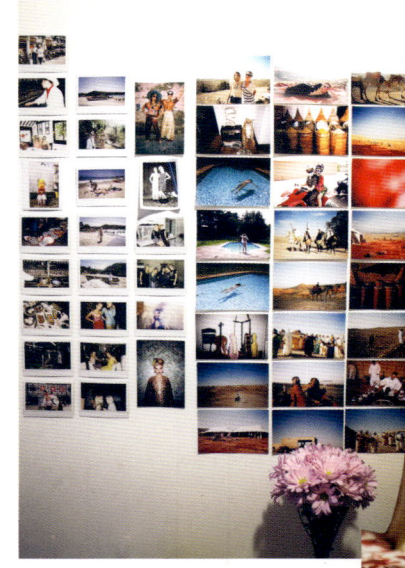
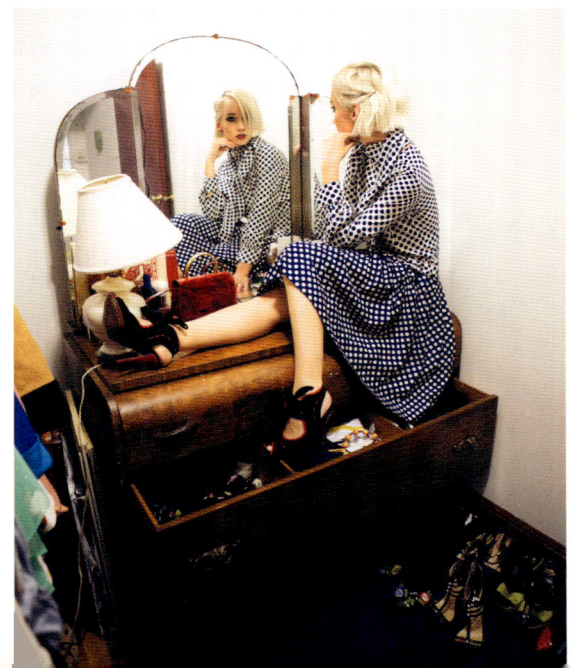
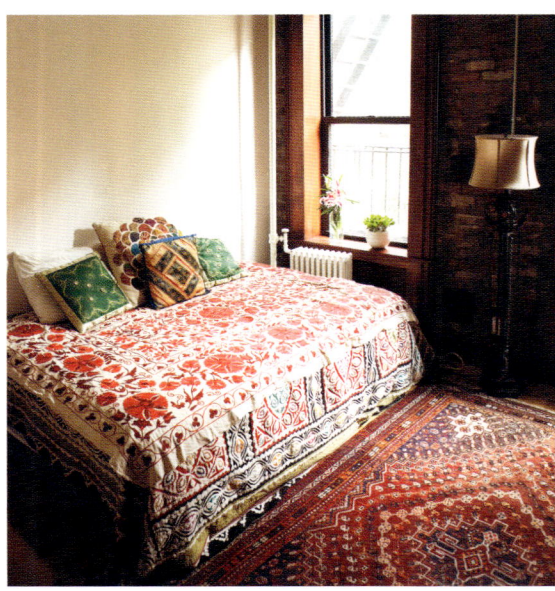
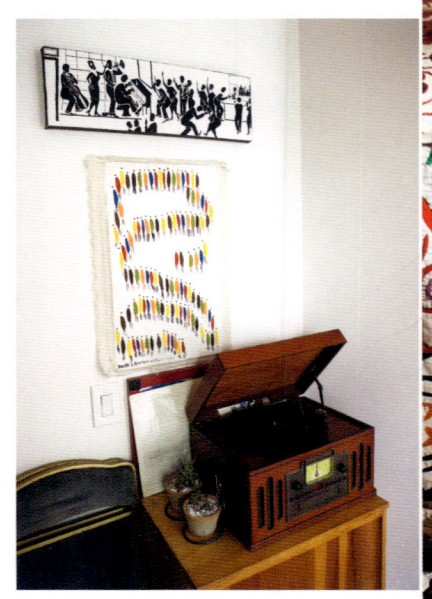

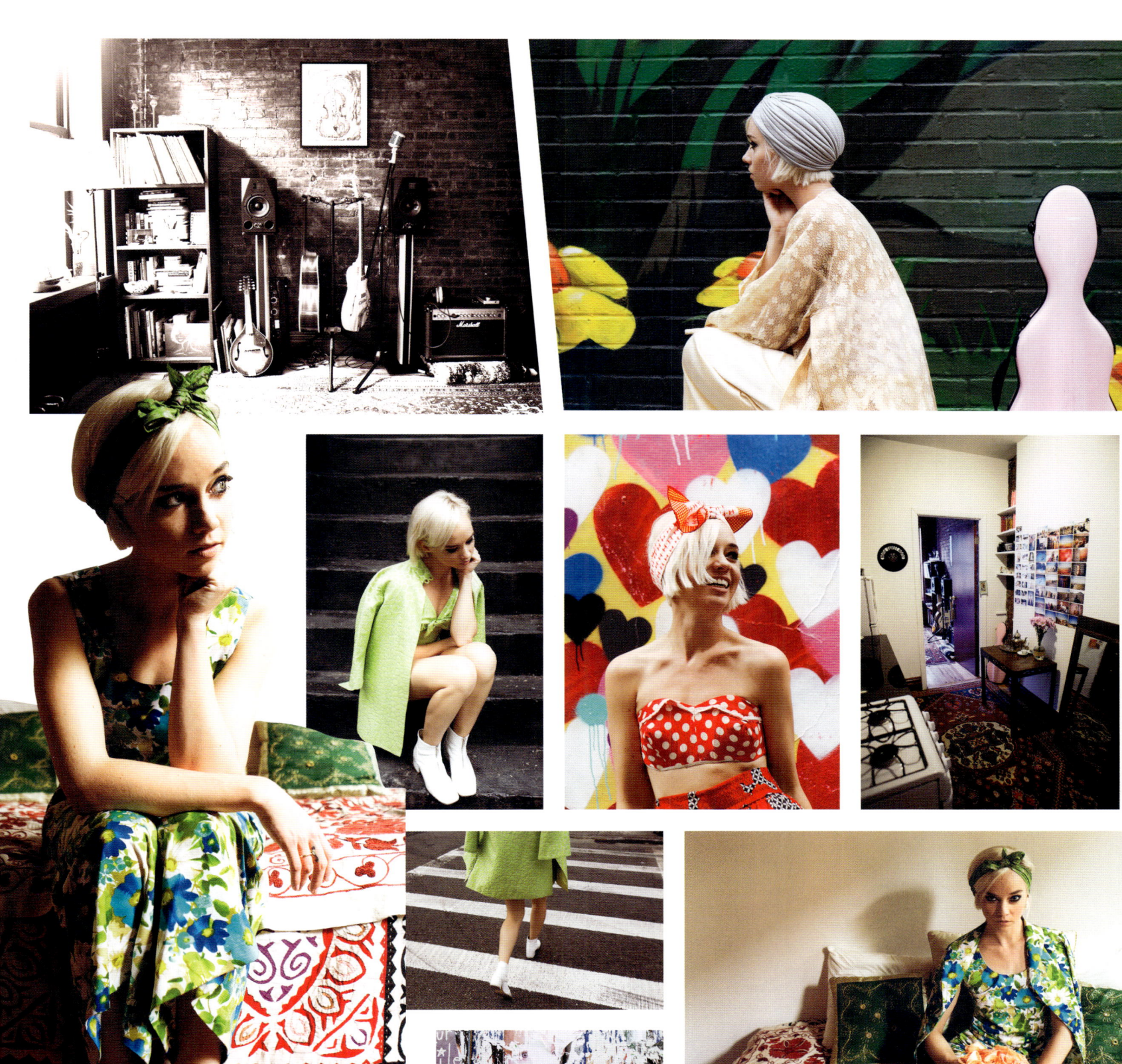

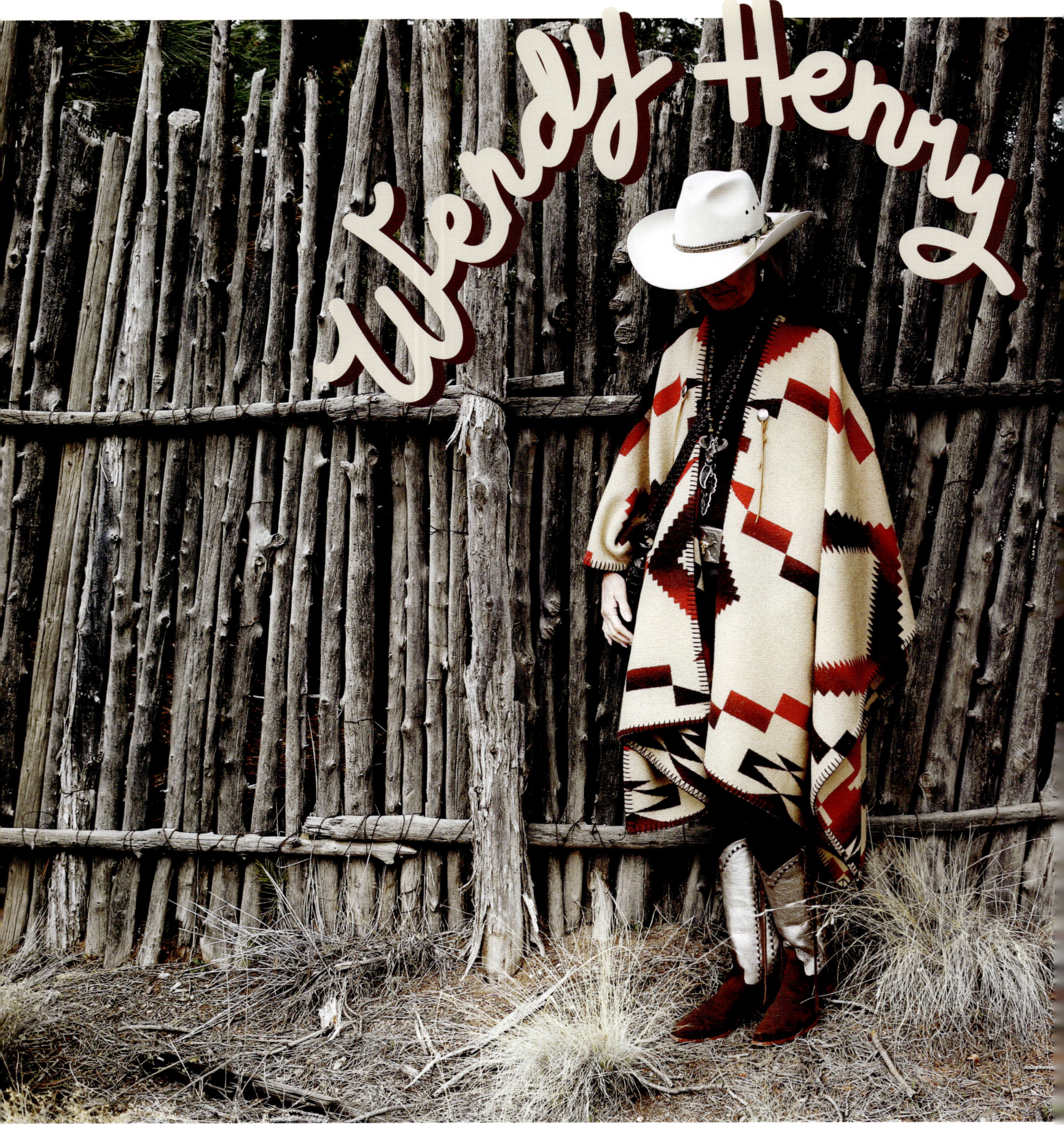

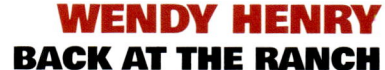
WENDY HENRY
BACK AT THE RANCH

The wondrous world of Wendy Henry starts to unfold by the backdoor parking-lot, where her white Mercedes is stationed. The Albuquerque license-plate spells the name, "Wendy." Simple. Like Cher. Or Madonna. She had been very agreeable and generous in her e-mails; she said she would lend us whatever we wanted for the shoot, and would personally give us a tour of Back at the Ranch, the vintage and custom boot store she opened in Santa Fe 25 years ago. I have not glimpsed the woman so far, until she sticks her skinny frame and blonde bob out the door of the office—faithful, smiling employees and dog Lola in tow. She's wearing belted beige khaki-and-leather Ralph Lauren jeans, a faded denim shirt, chestnut alligator booties, a long pearl-and-suede necklace, and turquoise jewelry. And the only thing I can think to say at that very awestruck moment is: "Do you have six more of those outfits?"

And so I find myself buried even deeper and cozier in Wendy's world the next day. Her (second) husband Cowden kindly picked me up at the hotel and dropped me off at the house, an old adobe overlooking the Sangre de Cristo mountain range, and Colorado on a clear day. "Oh, don't worry!" Wendy coos, when I humbly thank the man for his trouble. "He loves it!" While Cowden retreats to his office, Wendy and I get to talking and dressing, and it's immediately clear that this meeting is not just in passing; it's lasting. For starters, she hands me a shopping bag with a pair of Back at the Ranch boots she knows I'll love. Because, according to Wendy, every man and woman should own a pair. "Cowboy boots are definitely a fashion statement," she claims. "They are timeless and purely American. They never go out of style." When Tom Ford came in the store last year, he wanted one simple black pair, but by the time Wendy was done with him, he left with three, in all different colors.

Wendy will be turning 65 in June. Originally from Pennsylvania, she grew up in Hollywood, Florida, and opened her first store in Miami in 1972. It was called Avant Garde Leotard. In the early 80s she moved to New York and opened Wendy Lane, a women's wear store on 78th and Broadway. When she visited a friend in Santa Fe in 1989, she stayed. "It was time to leave the hectic lifestyle of New York," she remembers. "I needed wide open spaces, beautiful light, and clean air. I had always wanted to live out west." She met Cowden at a block party. He lived just down the street from her. It was the first outing his friends managed to drag him to after his wife died, he told me in the car. Wendy pulled him out of his rut. "Yeah, she's very special," he said to me. "I just adore her."

The thing is though: Wendy has *always* dressed like a Southwestern Ralph Lauren model, even when she lived in Florida. She defines her style as "classic, not really trendy." Her staple pieces are "blue jeans, white T-shirts, cowboy boots, tooled leather belt with my gold-and-silver trophy buckle. A cognac croc tote by Anthony Luciano, Coreen Cordova one-of-a-kind charm necklaces, and a Hermés scarf (thanks to Cowden who likes to buy them for me). The other day I was trying to calculate how many pairs of jeans and white T-shirts I have bought in my life…the amount is scary!" She says her mother is her biggest inspiration. "She had wonderful taste. She was casual and had an understated elegance." So basically, all Wendy had to do to fit in was adopt a Southern twang and learn how to say, "Howdy." When it's time to go, Wendy stuffs more of her things in my hands: a black turtleneck sweater, a coat she made from vintage blankets, a pair of her size-28 jeans, and a belt for show. "You will be freezing in Taos tomorrow," she insists. "Where do you need to go now? Whole Foods?" she asks patiently. "Cowden will take you. He loves it!" The hotel is just fine, I say. "Whatever you want," says Wendy, "you're family now." She gives me the biggest hug and sees me off to the car. And in that instance, as I take my seat, I realize that just like her employees, who have worked for her for more than ten years, and the thousands of customers who have loyally ordered Back at the Ranch boots for years, and her husband who has not left her side for the past ten years, I have fallen hard and good for Wendy's charms. She is ruthlessly funny, impossibly generous, and the kind of youthful very few people can pull off. I walked into a world where friendship is instantly imperative, and age is measured by authentic grace, not numbers. And if it were up to me, I'd never leave either.

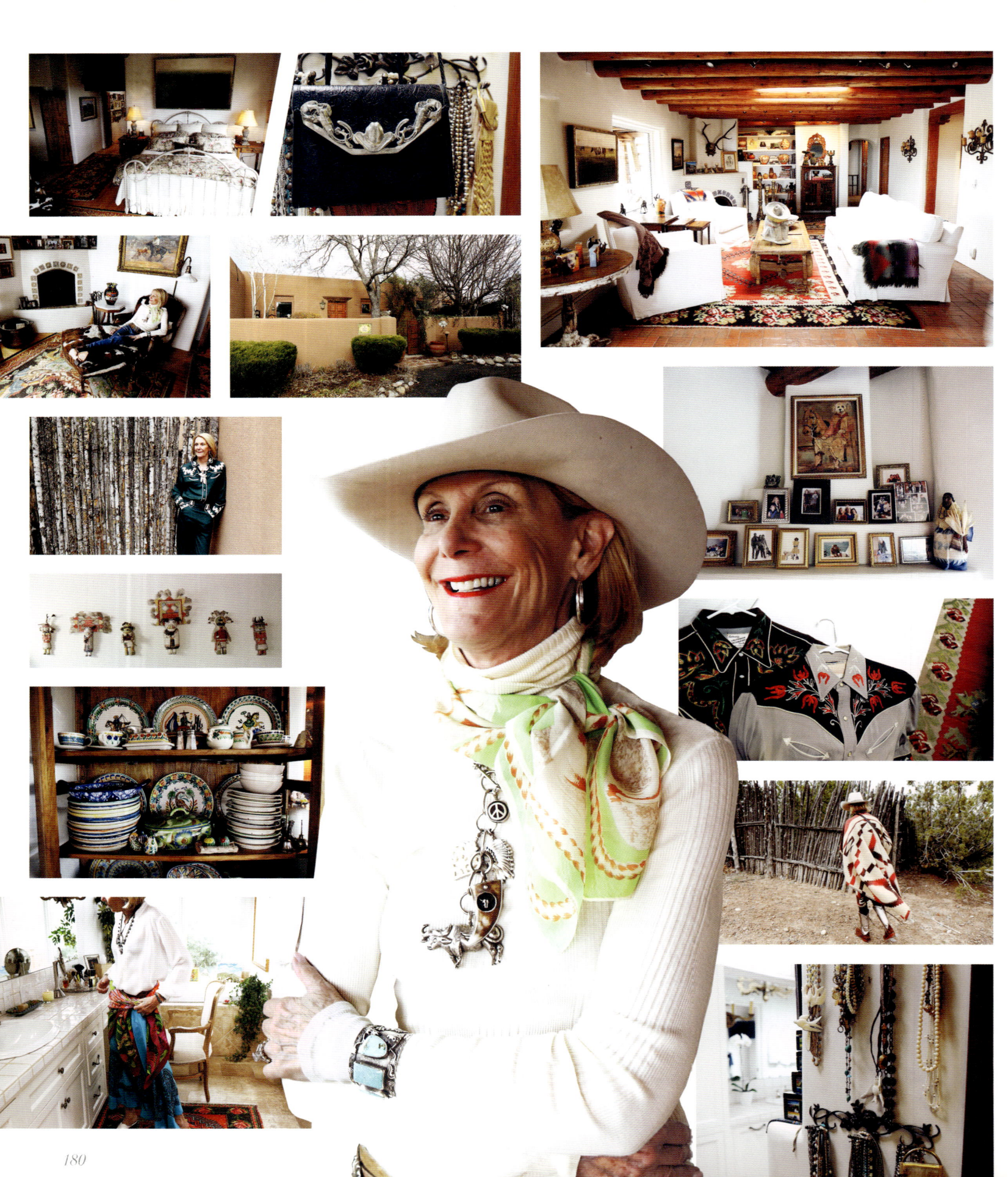

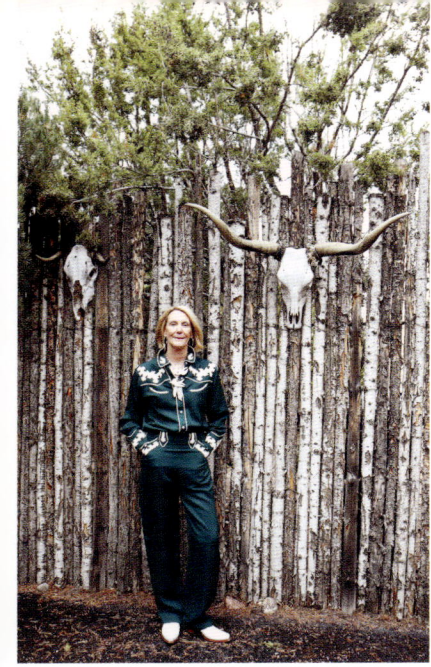
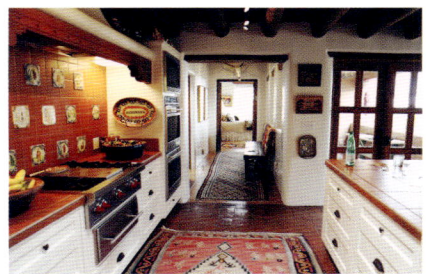
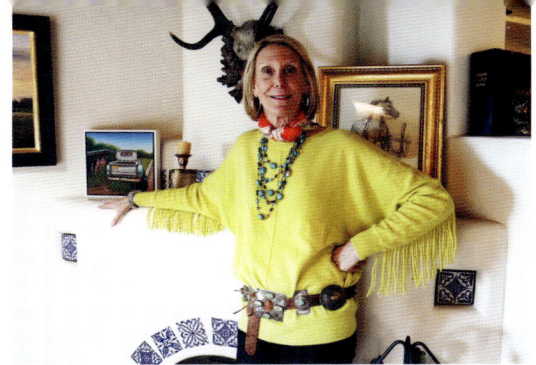
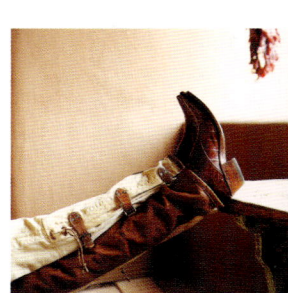
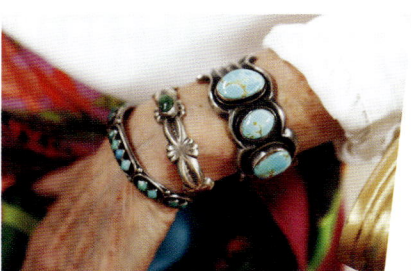
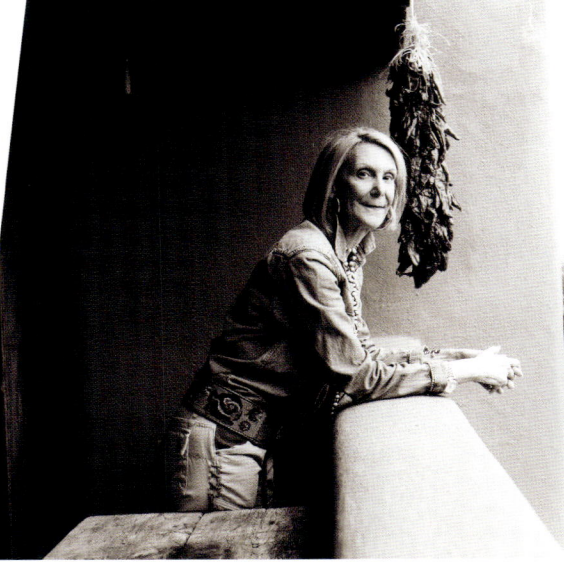
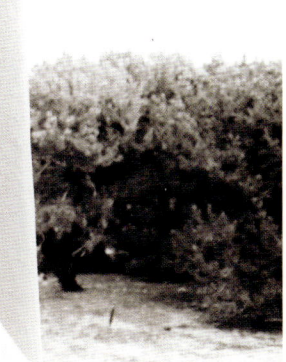
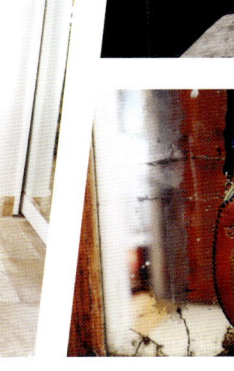
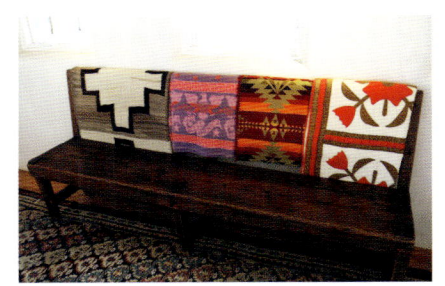
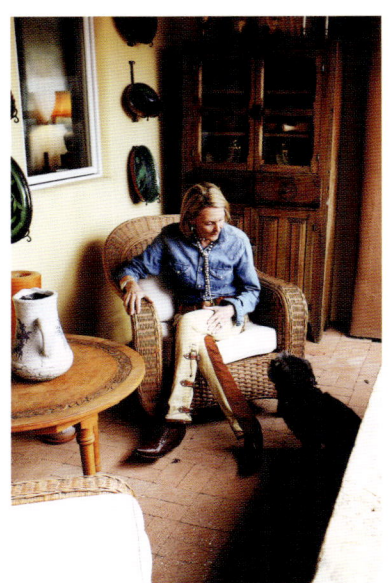
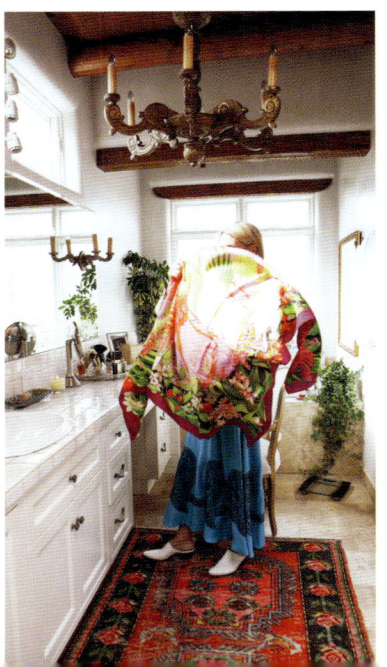
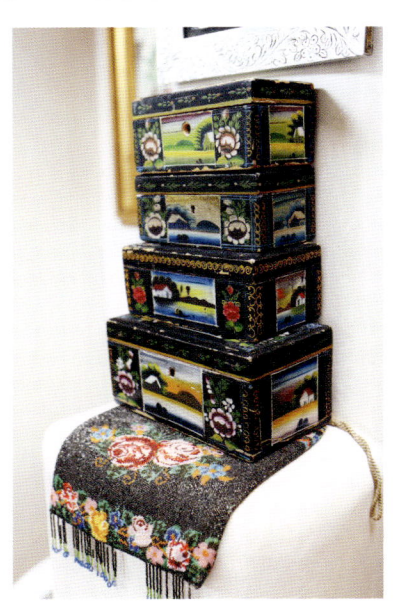
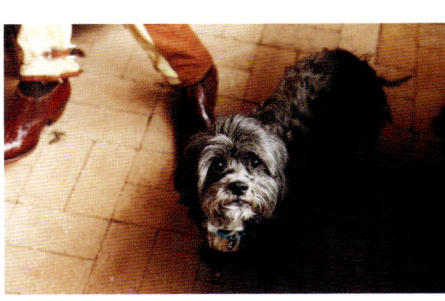
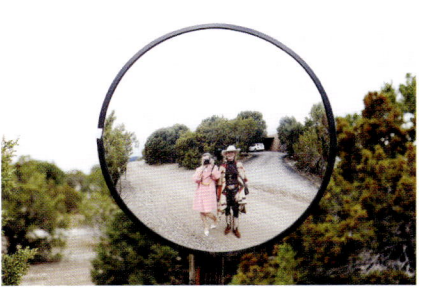

TENNESSEE THOMAS
I CRIED WHEN I WATCHED THE ROLLING STONES

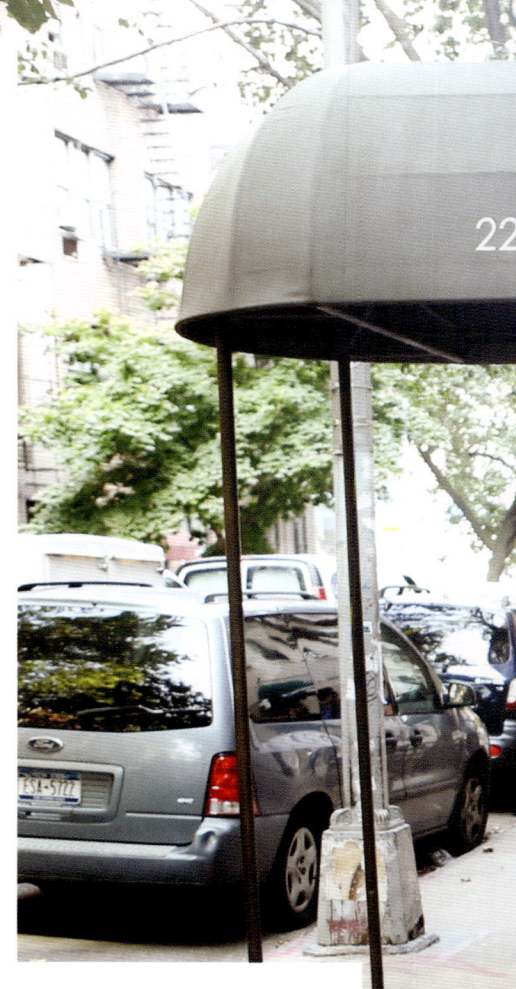

Tennessee Thomas's apartment looks just as I'd imagined: cute, retro, and little. It reminds me of the house in *Alice in Wonderland* where everything seems to be shrinking, but really it's just Alice growing bigger and bigger. Everything in this house, from the cups to the hangers to the rug, is part of the same adorable theme, and curiously enough in-sync with its owner's quirky voice, soft British accent, and batting lashes. I'd simply call it "mod," but Tennessee's imagination is much wilder. "It feels like a little boat!" she smiles. She has been living here for two years now, and has made it her very own. "I looked at 17 places in one day during a blizzard!" she recalls with a shiver. She relocated from Los Angeles. "When I saw this place it had great energy! An artist had lived here and all the walls were painted with insane murals of cats and grasshoppers in technicolor! And with the big windows it was bright, even though it's tiny. I love my loft bed. It's like a little cave! Or a tree house! I considered keeping the murals but decided that all my own stuff is already crazy enough. I didn't need any inherited wackiness!"

Thirty-year-old Tennessee is a bit of a jack-of-all-trades these days, but her first love is always music. She formed a band called The Like with a few girlfriends from high school and toured the world for ten years. "When we were 18, just after graduation, we signed a record deal and made an album," she says. "An incredible dream! We were very lucky girls!" They made follow-up albums, kept touring, and then, sadly, broke up. "We needed to go off and do our own thing; we were very codependent! I hope at some point we will reunite." When she settled in New York she got regular DJ gigs. She plays, "only 60s soul, girl groups, freakbeat, British Invasion, psych, French yé yé girls." She collaborates with friends like Leith Clark of *Lula* magazine, Gia Coppola, and Alexa Chung on fashion projects, and started The Awareness Experiment with activists Sarah Sophie Flicker and Maximilla Lukacs. "We make mini-documentaries to raise awareness about critical issues," like fracking, women's health rights, the rainforest, and so on. "Our directing team is called The Department of Peace," she says proudly.

But the biggest impromptu career move happened when she took over the lease of an empty storefront in the East Village. "I kept walking past empty shops and had a fantasy of having a space of my own..." she says dreamily, "a headquarters for think tanks and salons and community-based collaborative projects. I mentioned the idea to a few friends, and a few months later I hit the jackpot. The owners of one of my favorite antiques shops, A Repeat Performance, took the lease on the shop next door to them, basically to protect the integrity of the East Village as an artistic community and to keep out a Starbucks or whatever! I was introduced to them and we decided to split the shop. We sold some of their incredible mid-century antiques and I pulled in local artists and designers! It was so fun to have a clubhouse!"

Tennessee is a colorful, happy girl with lingering teenage crushes and a serious 60s addiction. She collects Ponytail record cases, 45-inch girl group and garage vinyl, and loves all the Motown artists. Her favorite colors are pale pink and bright red. Her middle name is Bunny. And she describes her style as "Beatle-fan! 1965 screaming teenager!" She never wears heels ("too clumsy"), and swears by Peter Pan collars and dorky saddle shoes ("I wore that long before *Moonrise Kingdom*! Haha."), and not surprisingly she adores vintage. "I love the hunt!" she tells me. "Nothing better than finding a vintage treasure! It's so exciting...The other day I found an incredible black-and-white cape, and when the label said PARAPHERNALIA I nearly died! That was Betsey Johnson's first clothing company in New York in the mid 60s! Edie Sedgwick was her fit model and she did all the costumes for *Ciao! Manhattan*. These pieces should be in a museum! My mum was a BIBA girl..." It's clear Tennessee was born in the wrong era, but she's making up for it by creating her own little 60s world. For the two hours I spend in her little apartment, I am her 60s teenage BFF and I, too, want to cry at a Rolling Stones concert.

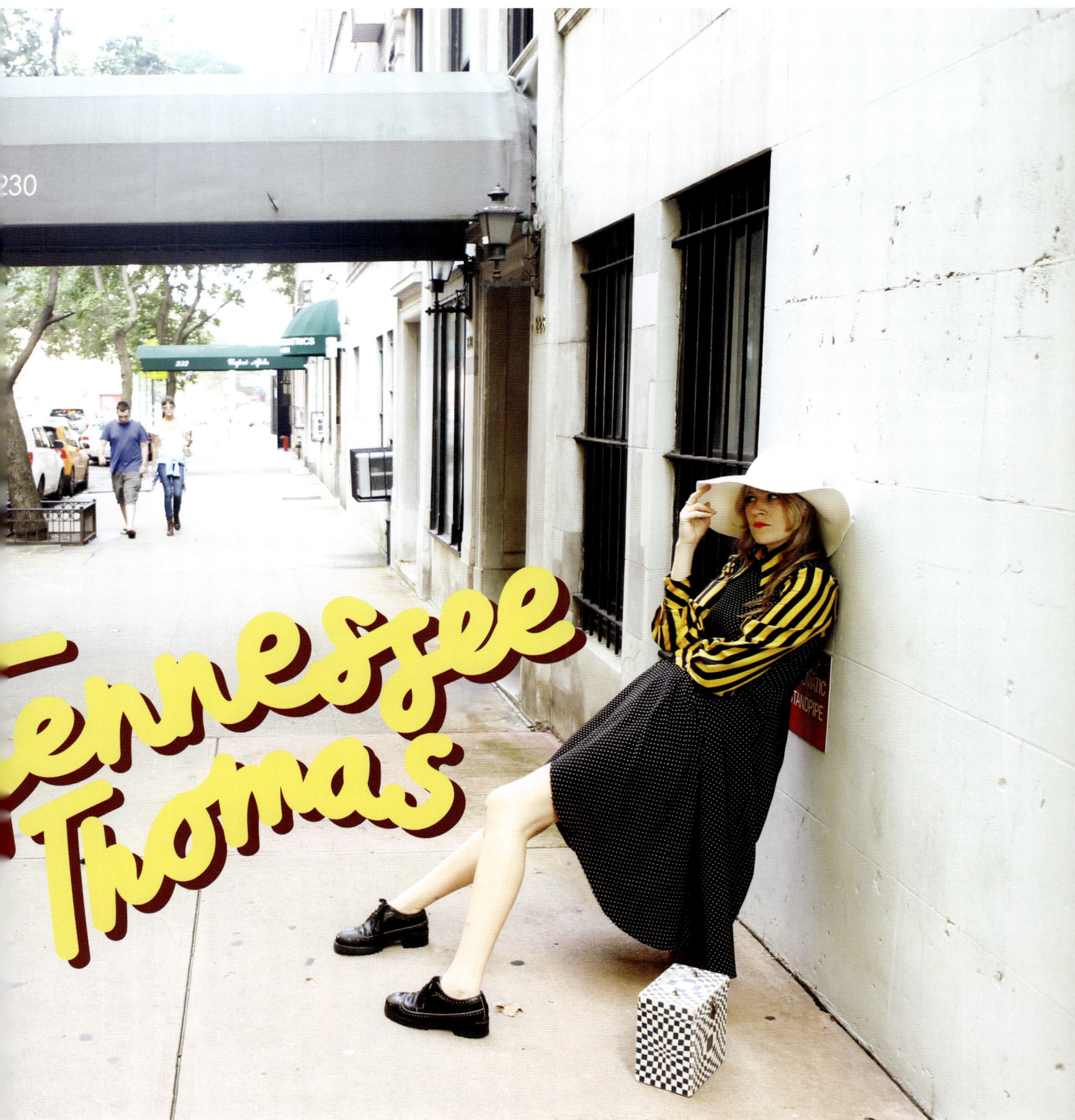

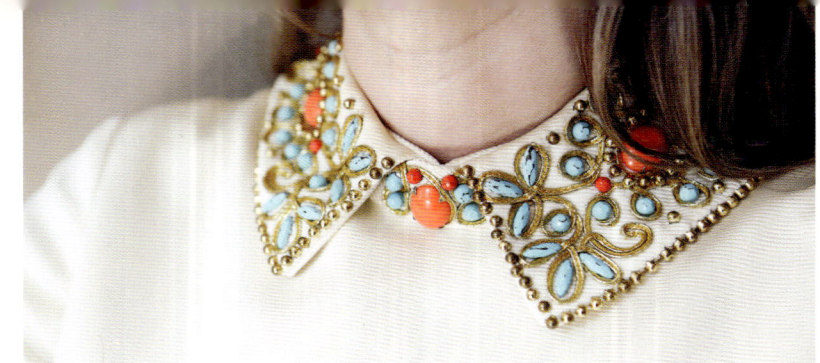
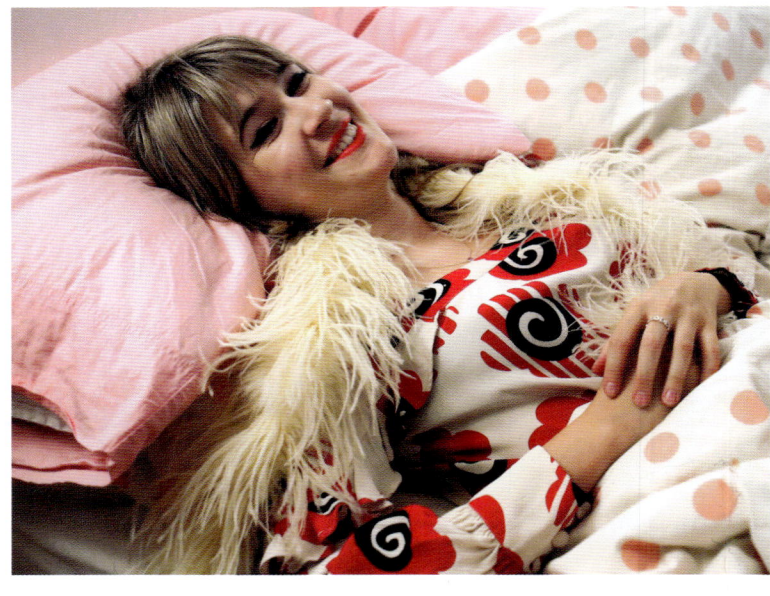
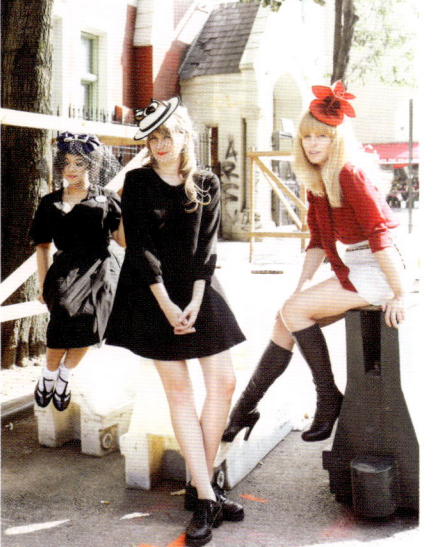
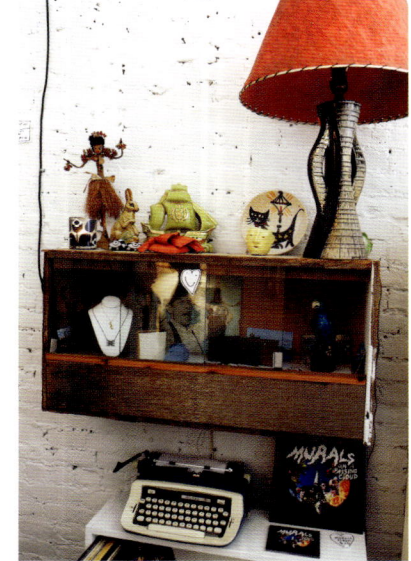
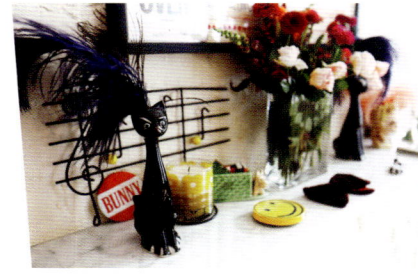
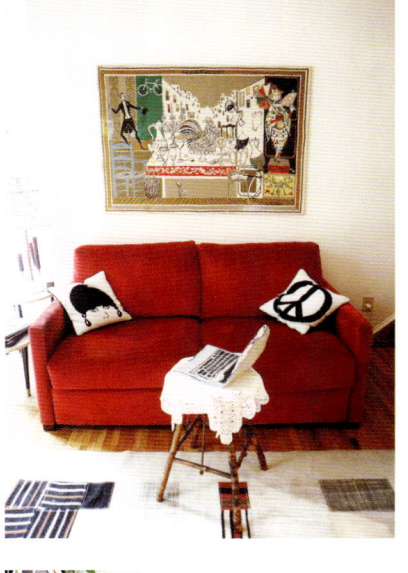
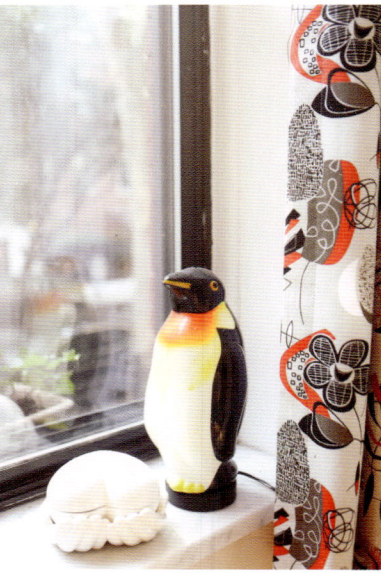
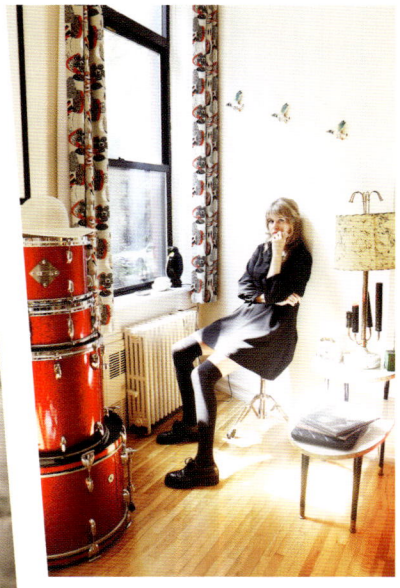
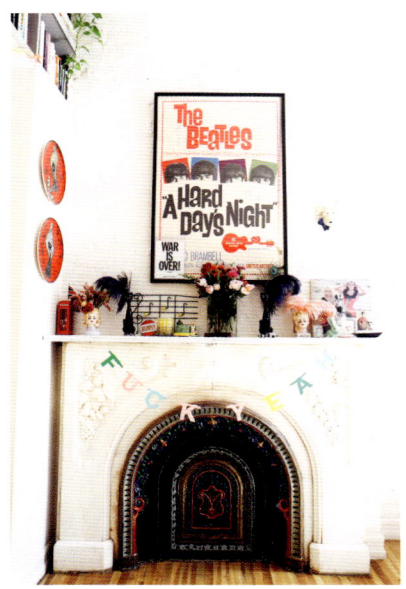
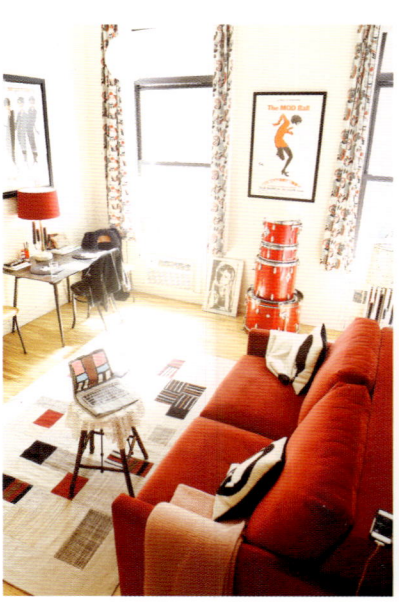
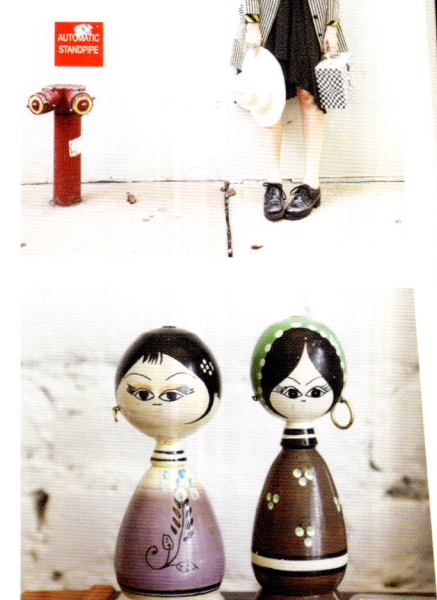

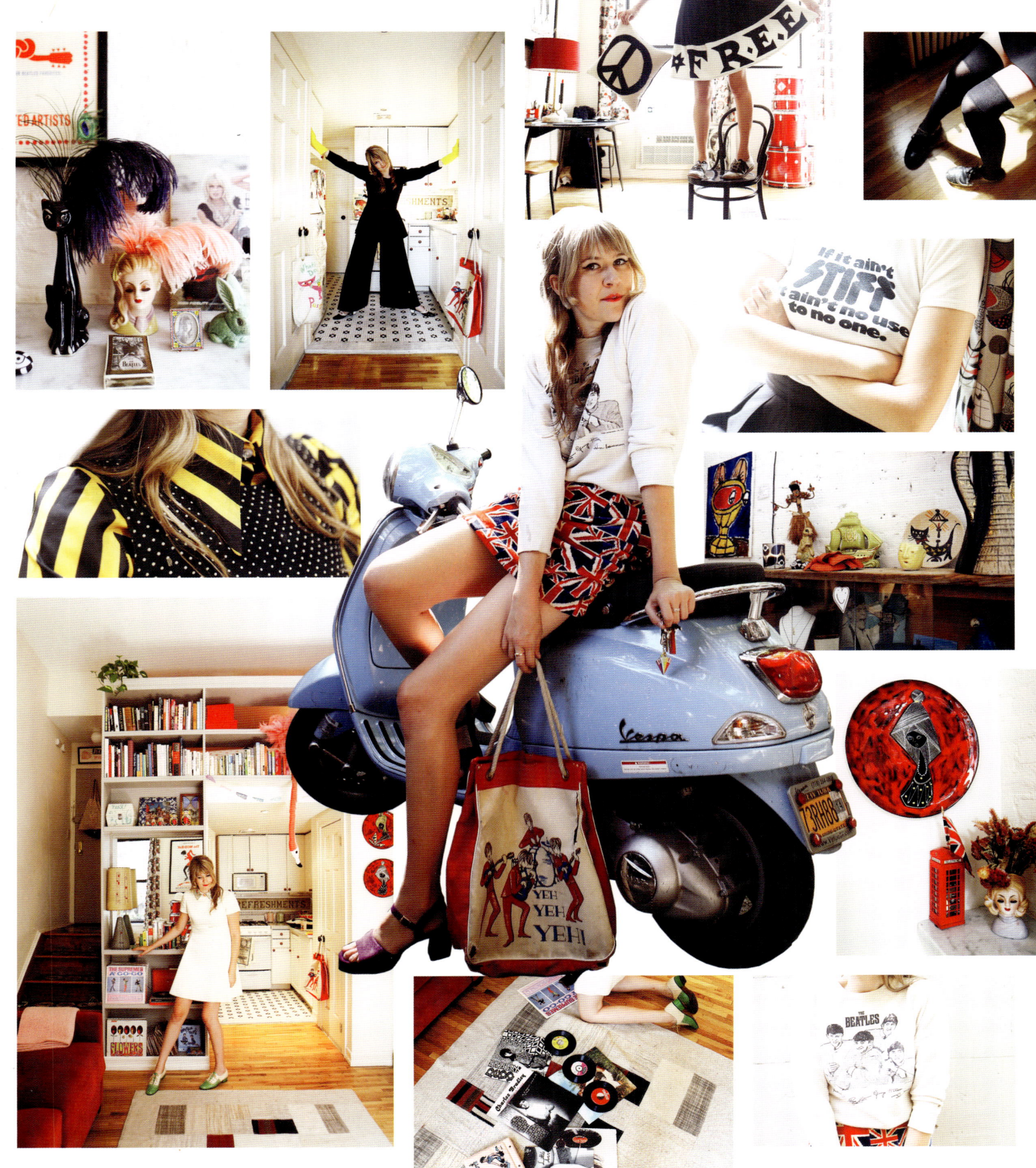

EMMANUEL DEMUYNCK
UNSUITED LIVES

It takes a strong pair of shoulders to carry the weight of such intrigue with elegance. I guess it's a Belgian thing. It's a small country and people gossip because people have both time and secrets. But they're never secrets for long. For Emmanuel Demuynck the revelations were not only shocking, they were also formative. Here's this shy, sophisticated man sitting in front of me, with his perfectly coiffed white beard and his soft, soothing voice, who lives in a beautifully decorated apartment in Gent, with a wife and no kids, and a head full of colorful inspiration, but no hint of drama. When he speaks, he's relaxed and curious, eloquent and interesting, deeply jazzed about his home accessories project, and in no shape or form demonstrates any cause for concern, nor prepares me for the stories he's about to tell.

I don't know Emmanuel. A mutual friend insisted we meet because we both love vintage, and there's very few such enthusiasts in Belgium. Most notably, Emmanuel has found a creative way to make his passion profitable. As a window dresser and interior designer he had amassed an enormous collection of old and unused fabrics and felt the need to repurpose them. "I didn't study fashion, so clothes were out of the question," he remembers. "So I decided to do these patchwork silk scarves. I knew many retailers in Belgium, so I immediately had a great clientele." He founded the Monsieur Maison label in 2010. Every season he makes a limited edition collection of scarves with deadstock couture fabrics, old Valentino, Chanel, Leonard, and others he finds at flea markets and antiques stores in Europe.

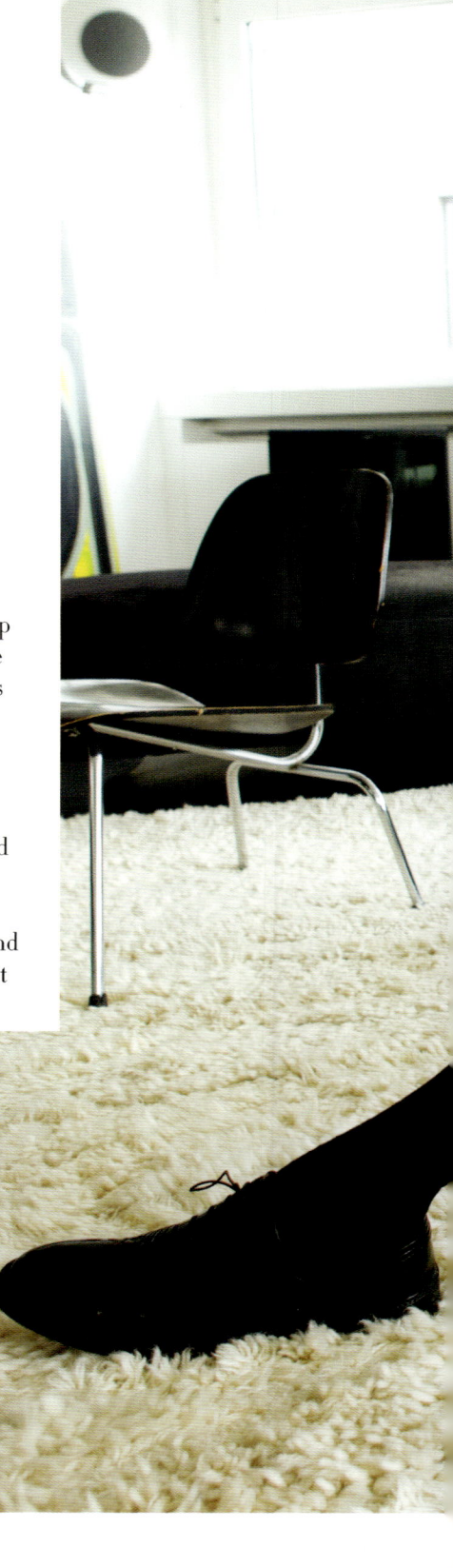

We talk for a while about his technique and love of art. At 17 he wanted to study Design in Paris but his mother thought he was too young to leave home. As a compromise she let him pick a school of his choice in Belgium. He moved to Gent and studied painting at the Royal Academy. It was also around this time he discovered his sexuality, but he repressed the feelings. "There was no 'room' for these kinds of thoughts," he regrets. "It was difficult. And it disappeared." He got married and threw himself into the professional realm. "I work like a painter," he says. "I make a composition and leave it to sit for a while. If it's good, I keep it, if not, I wipe it out, similar to a painter who chooses his colors. It's like a ripening process." Ironically, he tried to steer his collection into women's and men's, but it didn't work. "The men were choosing the florals and the women the plaids, so I gave up," he laughs.

Then he begins to unravel a string of recent events and discoveries that have me glued to my seat. Emmanuel grew up in a small village on the Belgian coast. It was dead in the winter but bursting with life and tourism in the summer. His mom and dad ran a guesthouse and worked hard. The village doctor would visit regularly, but not to make the usual kind of house calls. Emmanuel remembers his mom making supper for the doctor and he'd stay for a while. That doctor, it turns out, was his real father. "I'm a love child," he decides. "They had a relationship for 20 years. Everyone in the village knew except for my dad and I. I also discovered I'm not really Belgian; I'm Armenian, and Jewish." All of a sudden the roots he had built his entire existence on were useless. He was stunned to the core and his very identity was at stake.

Partly because his wife got sick and he was left to his own devices and partly because she had revealed she was lesbian, Emmanuel began to tug again at the feelings he had so long ignored and smothered. His world was upside-down and it left him grasping at any ends to keep afloat. He struck up a conversation with a man online and explored his impulses. Before long he had a full-fledged, but secretive relationship that ratified his deep longing. There is much more to this story, but I promised to keep things private and rated PG. The man before me had opened his heart and accepted his inspiring journey. Sometimes people don't come to life until they have lived a few different, unsuited lives. I believe that people dwell and stir until they find the niche that nurtures them fully. This new path may be unsettling and treacherous at first, but if it leads to the truth then there's no turning back.

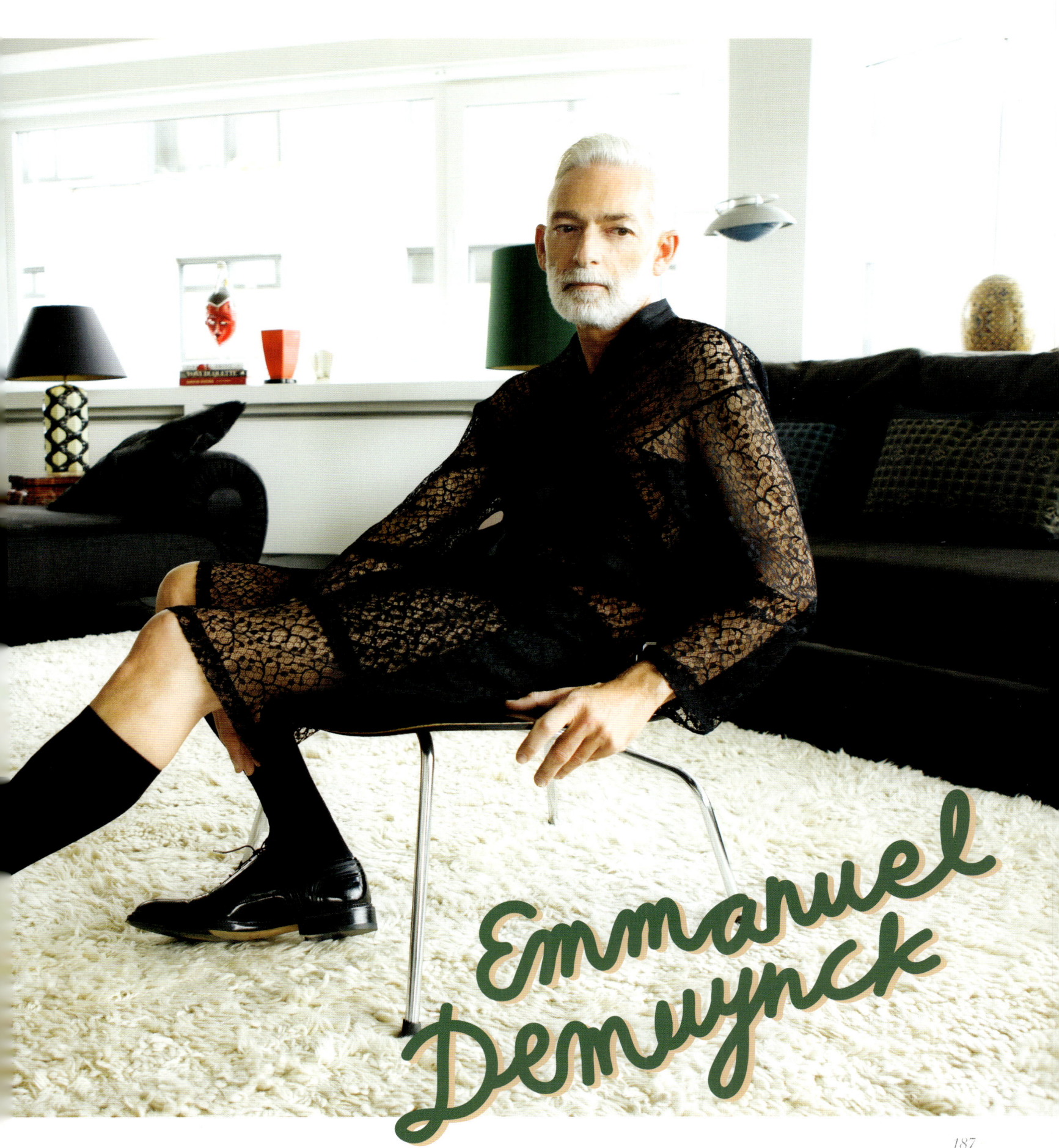

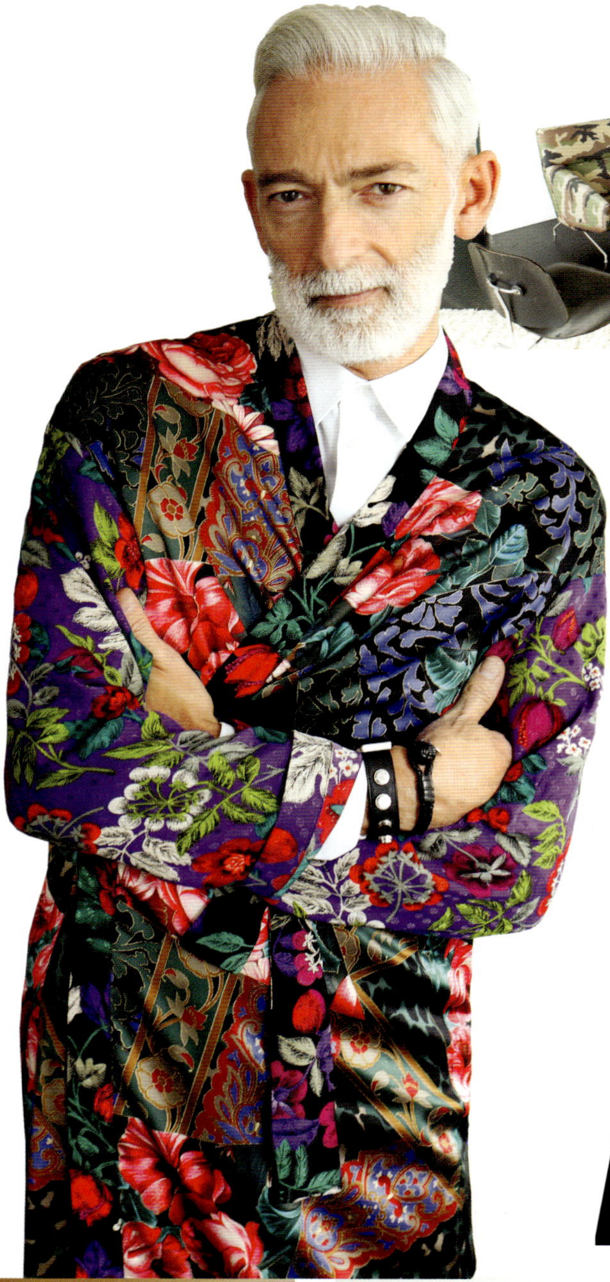

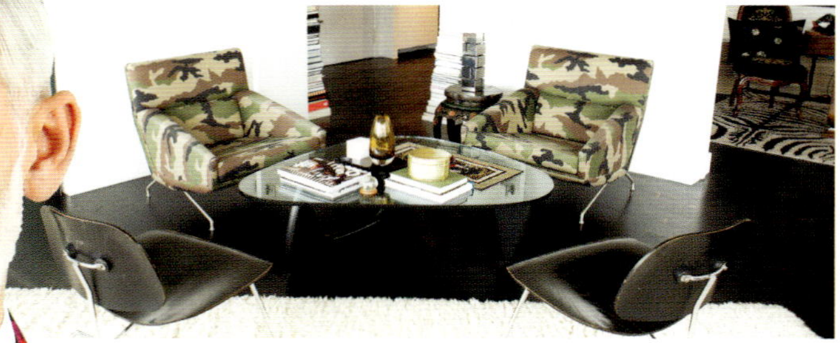

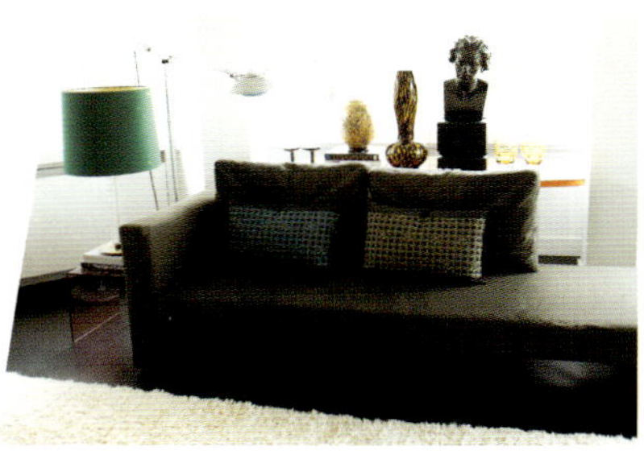

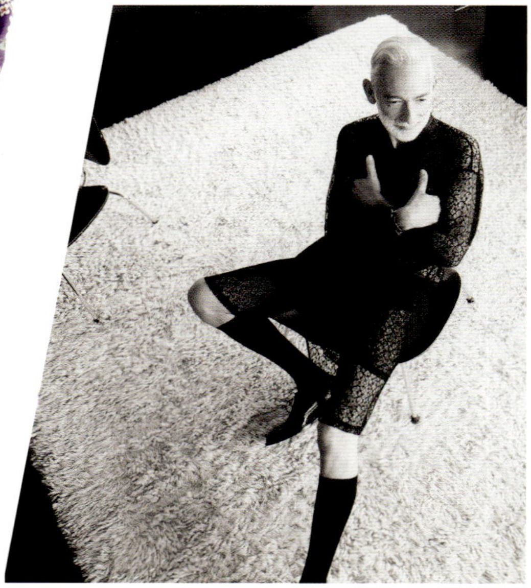

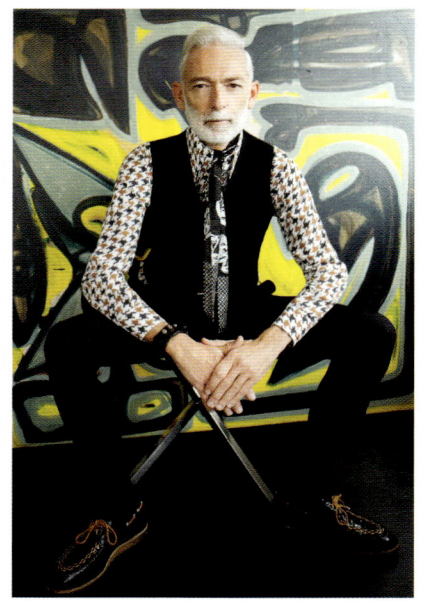
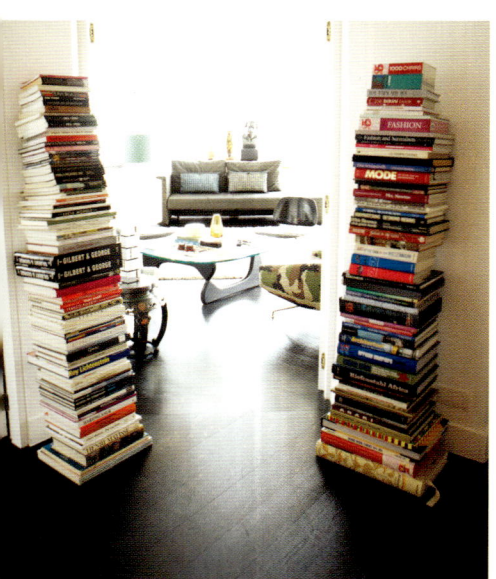
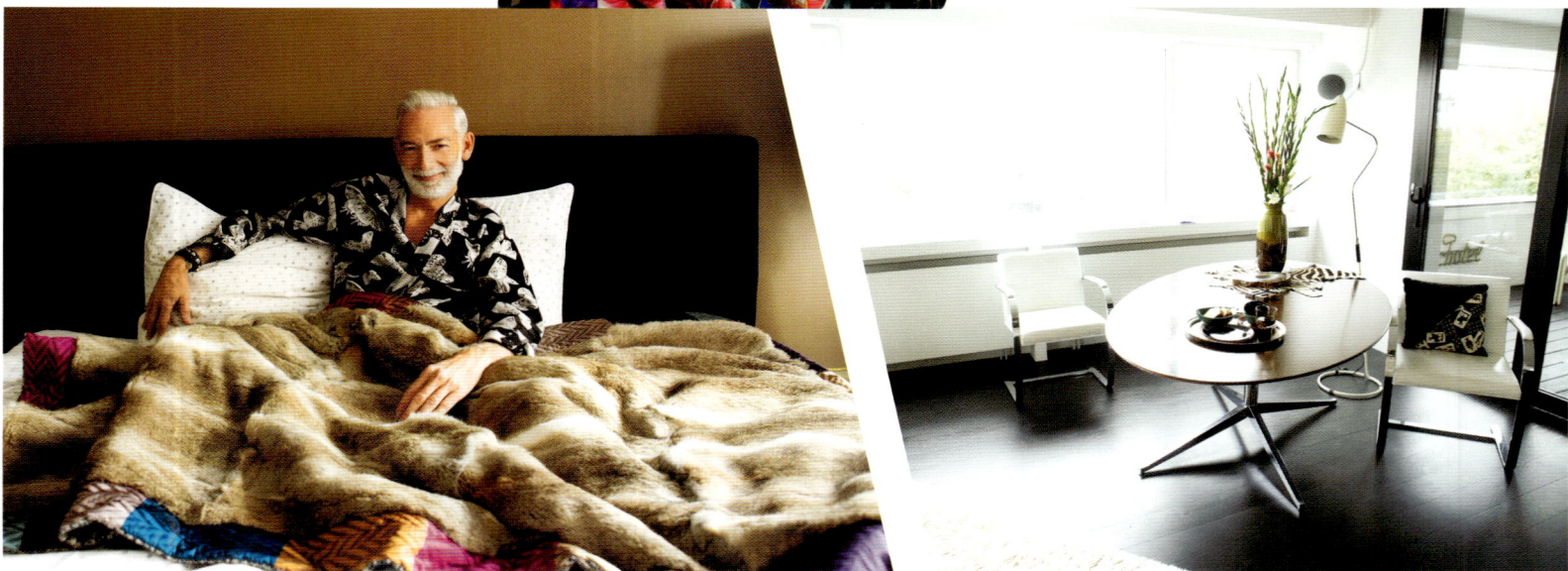

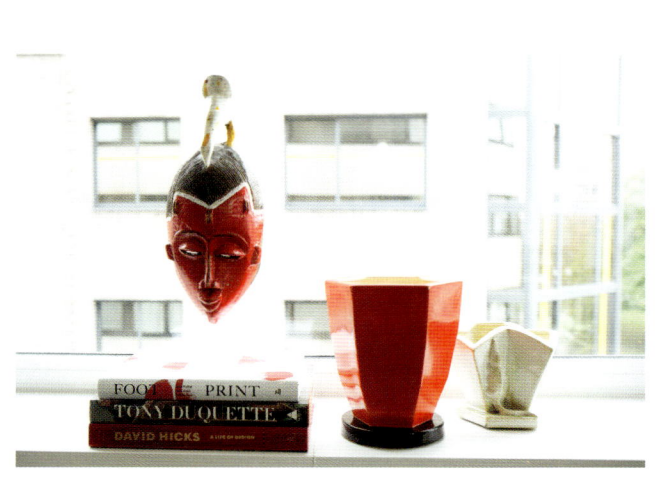
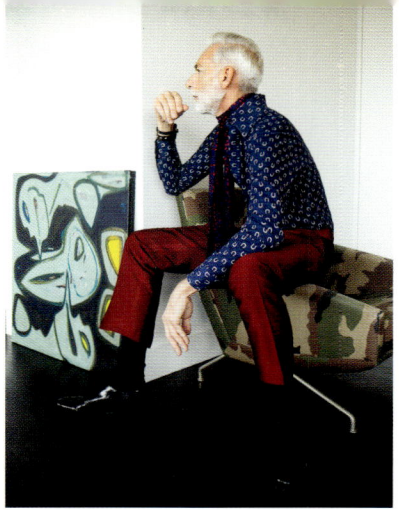
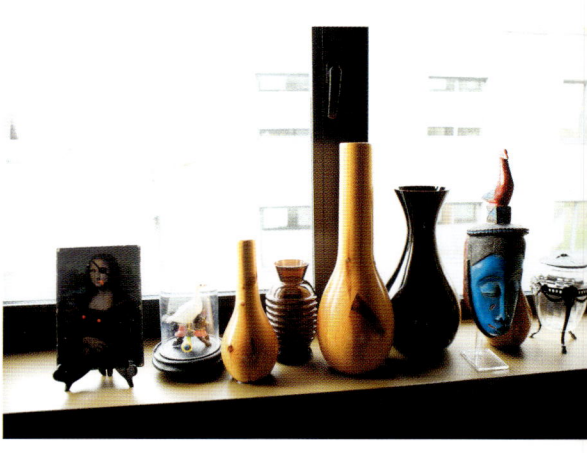
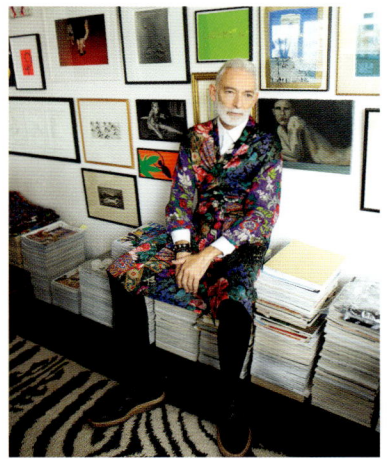
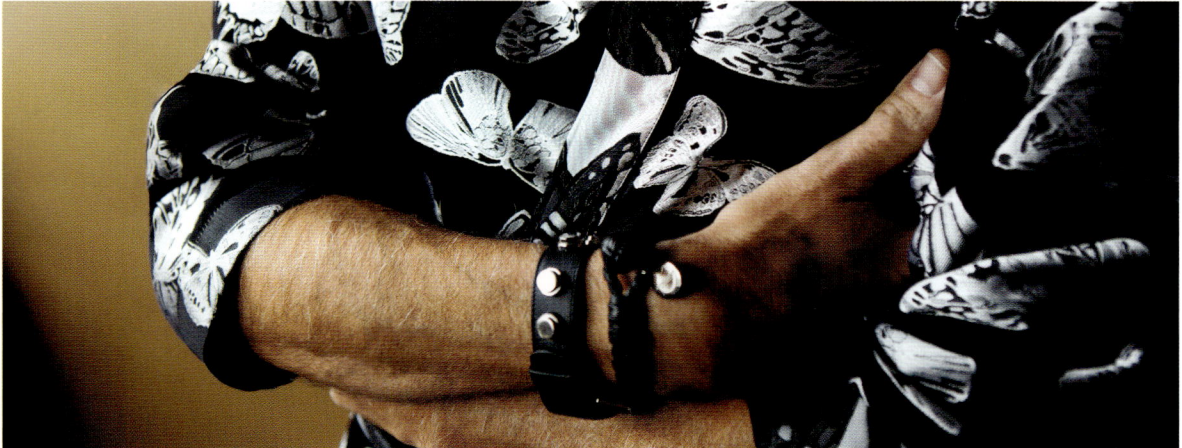
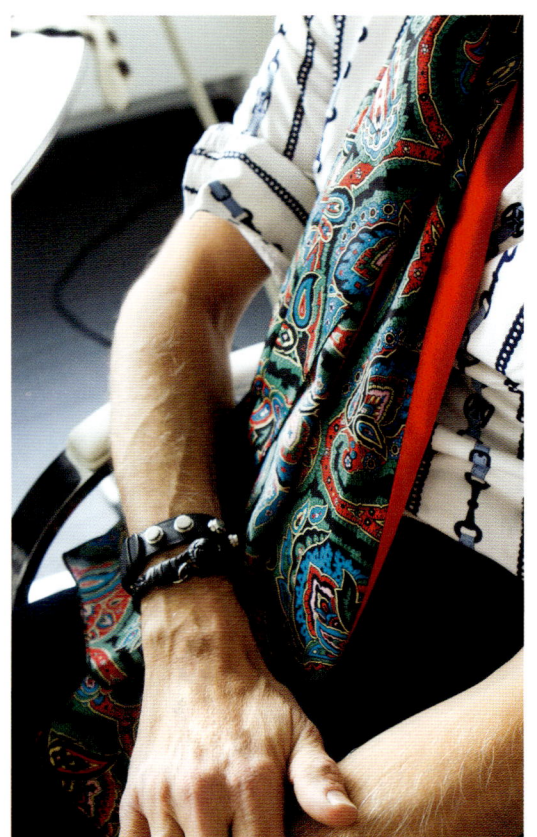
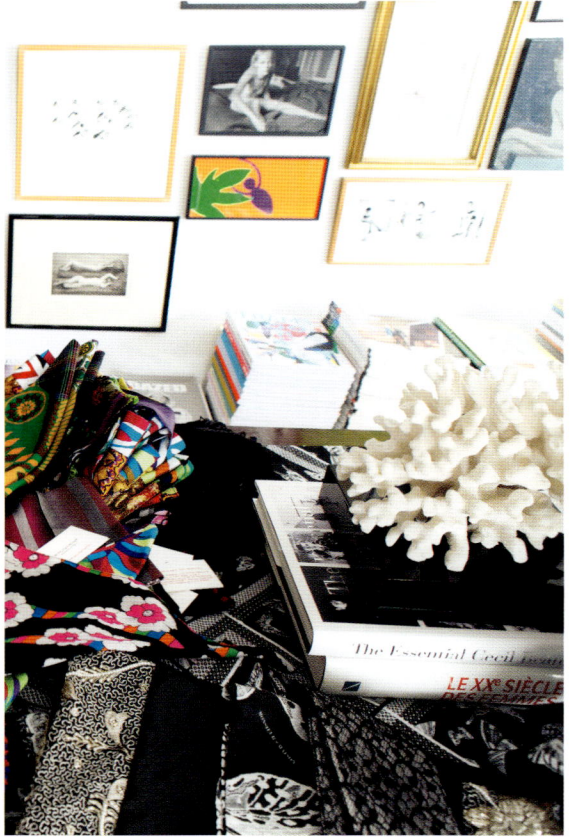
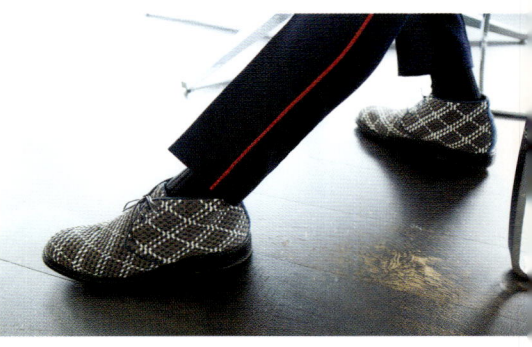
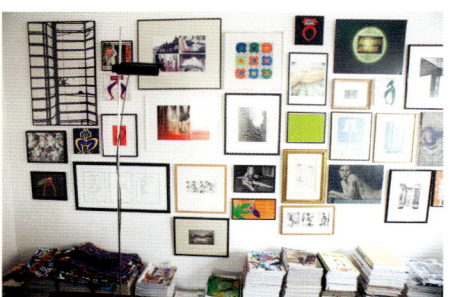
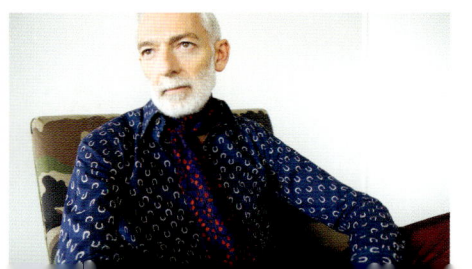

PAIGE ELKINGTON
SEVENTIES PORN CHIC PLUS TURTLENECKS

"Should I buy these?" she asks, crouching down in front of her laptop on the bed. She's looking at a pair of vintage, 90s shoes. And that was not a rhetorical question by the way. There's a science to this search, and an entourage of girls in the room who jump up in unison and scurry over to peer at the screen. Paige is a self-proclaimed "Etsy-loyalist." She doesn't randomly browse for pieces; she kind of invents them. "I always know what I want, so all I have to do is type 'metallic lace-up pants' into the search bar and see if they exist." I'm guessing today's pursuit is about purple and orange booties, and behold: they exist! The response from the floor is mild but encouraging.

Paige Elkington is no stranger to *Tales*. She's a consistent presence on my pages, and a recurring vision in thigh-highs at LA parties. Her pout has become a trademark, and a happy reminder that life in La La Land is "flirtatious and sassy." She has a husky low laugh, a knack for costumes, and a rather twisted sense of humor that's increasingly dominating her Instagram feed. Have you seen her Marc Jacobs call girl video? I've watched it 30 times. "I'm working with a company called Super Deluxe, hosting comedy videos and other entertaining content," she explains dryly. "I'm also writing a short to direct and star in, and developing a talk show concept. And yes, please go buy my handbags on paigeelkington.com! They're cute as hell." Voila. That's Paige's hyphenated SoCal professional life in a nutshell; she's funny and she designs purses.

Paige grew up in Knoxville, Tennessee, and went to college in Charleston, South Carolina. "I appreciate my Southern roots," she thinks back, "but, c'mon, I'm undeniably a big-city girl! I decided to come to LA because I wasn't quite ready for New York. It just seemed easier. Now I've been here for six years and have no real plans to leave." She has a long-term boyfriend, Mickey Madden, the drummer of Maroon 5, "and the best human," and two dogs named Toast and Jam. Needless to say, she's not going anywhere. The rest of her family is spread across different states. Mom is a child psychologist and her sister, she says, is even funnier than she is. When can I meet *her*?

Tonight's a big night. Saint Laurent is producing a huge show and after party at the Palladium in Los Angeles, and "everyone is going." Wristbands are exchanging hands, phone calls are made to friends of friends of PR people, and outfits are carefully orchestrated. Eleanor Wells is the stylist on call and procures a vintage, orange Dolce & Gabbana dress for Paige. Her knee-jerk reaction is to hike up the hem, just like she used to do when she and her mom co-designed her elementary school talent-show outfits. "I made sure to sew my skirts an inch or two shorter when her back was turned," she winks. There's just one thing missing—shoes! Paige and Eleanor think hard and long, and then it hits them, hard, like a brick over the head: *Where are the purple and orange booties when you need them?*

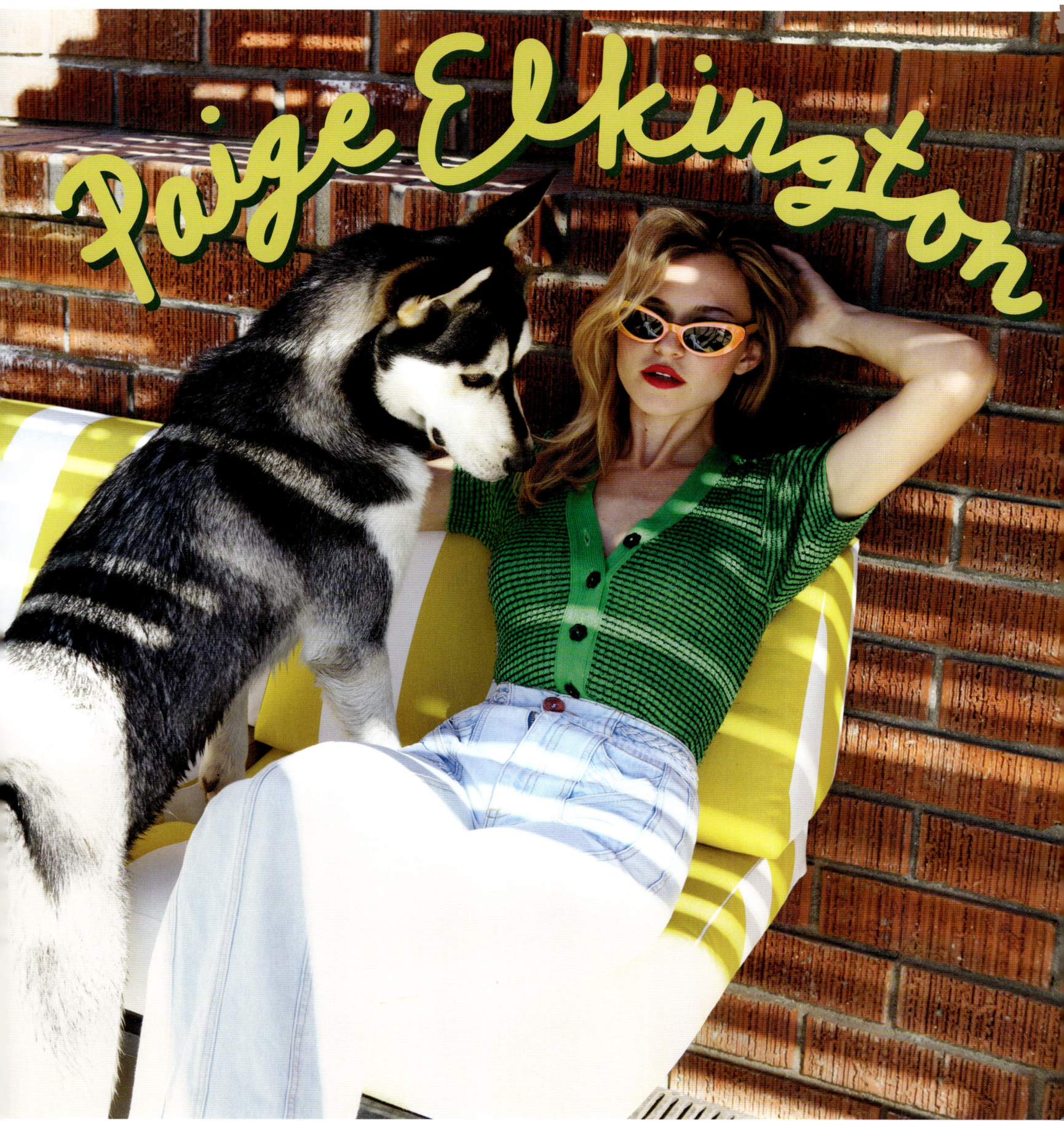

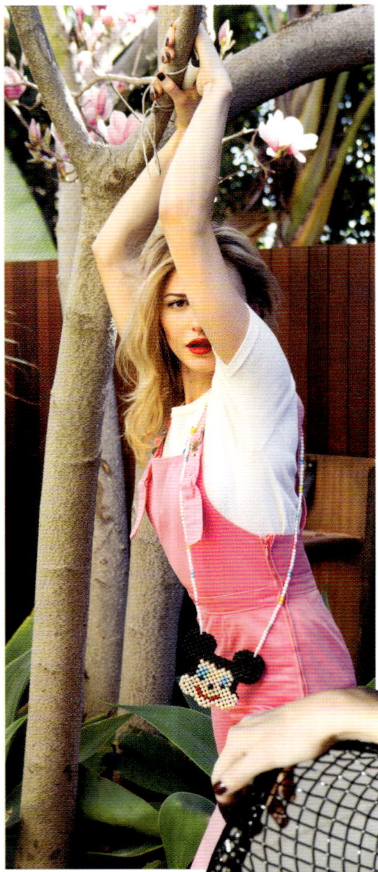

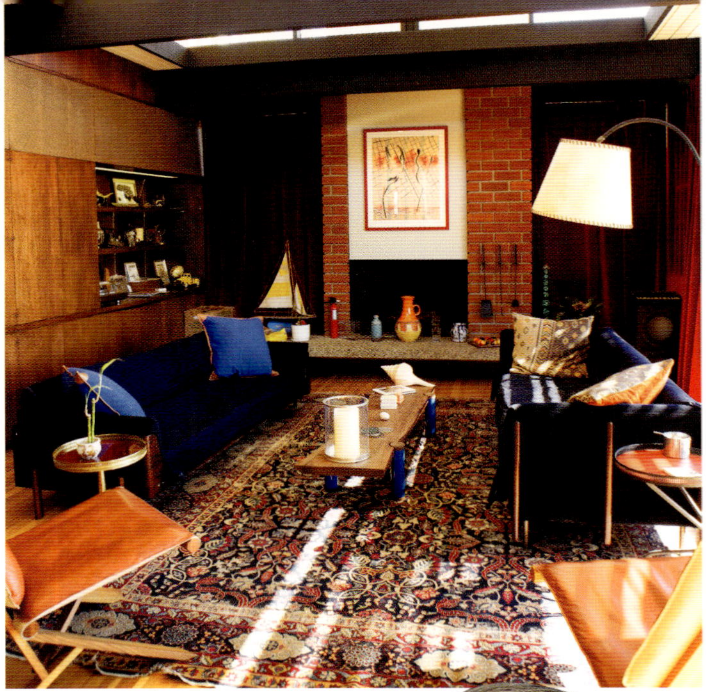

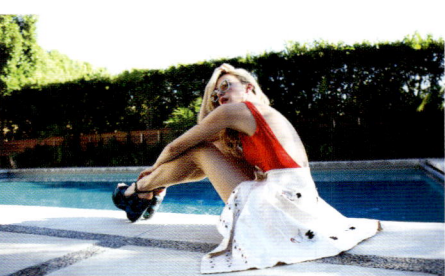
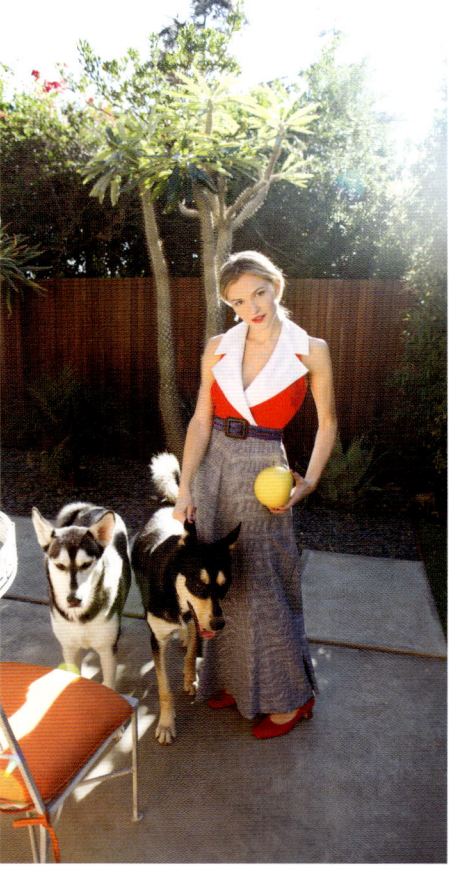
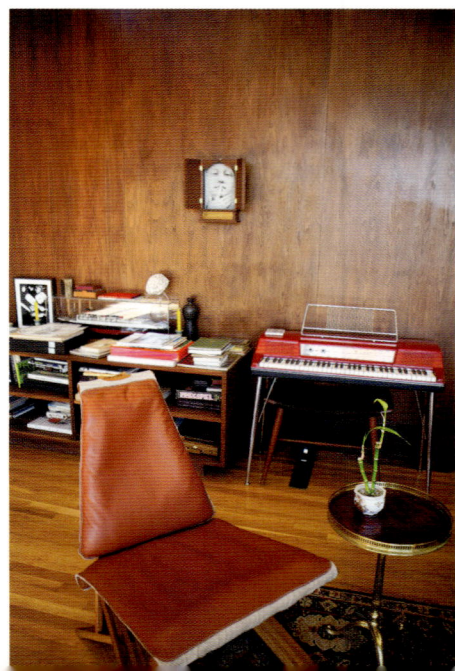

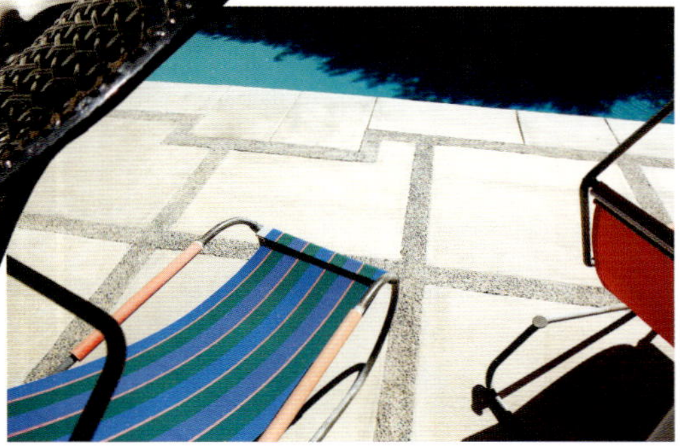

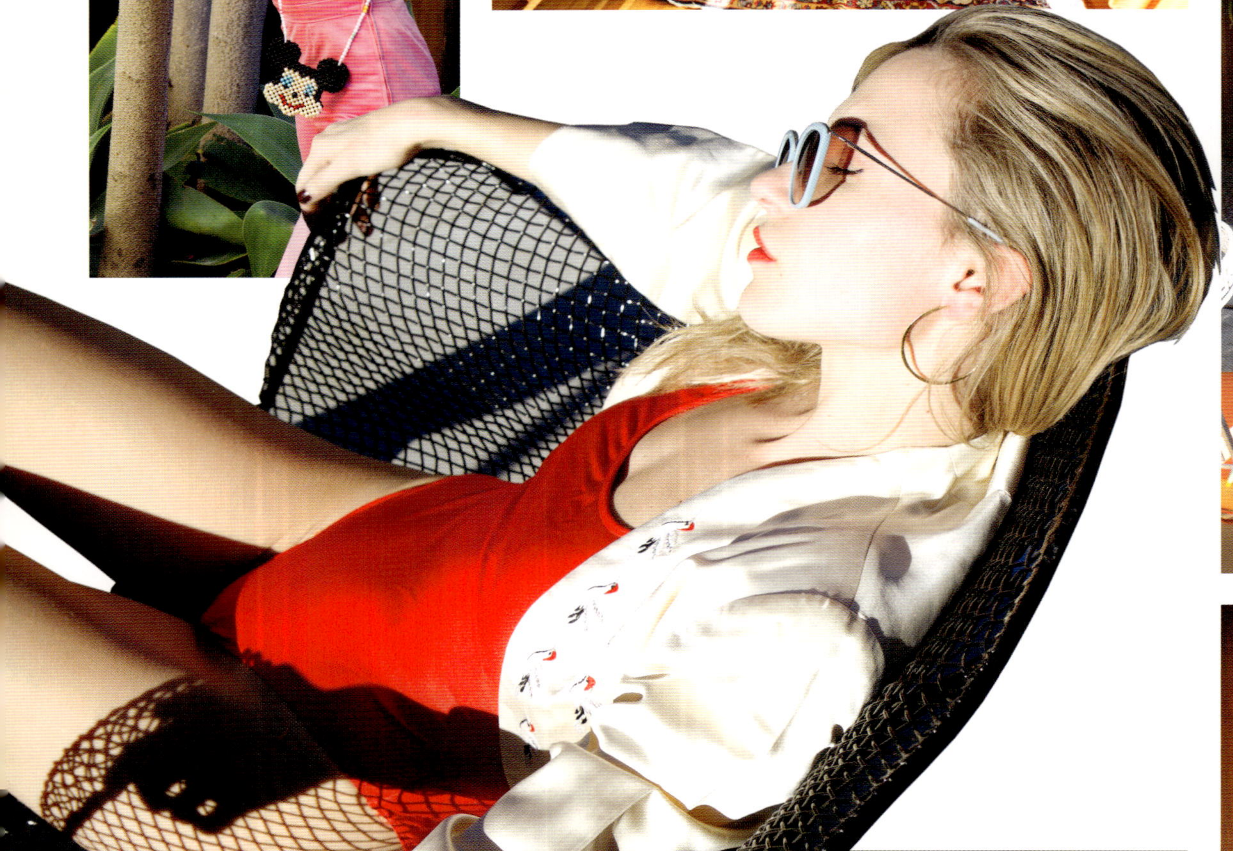

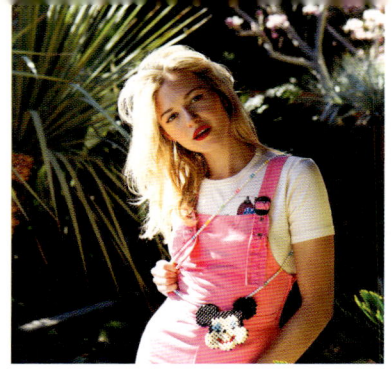
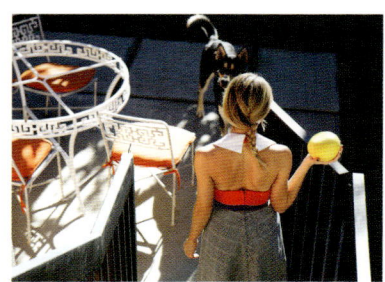
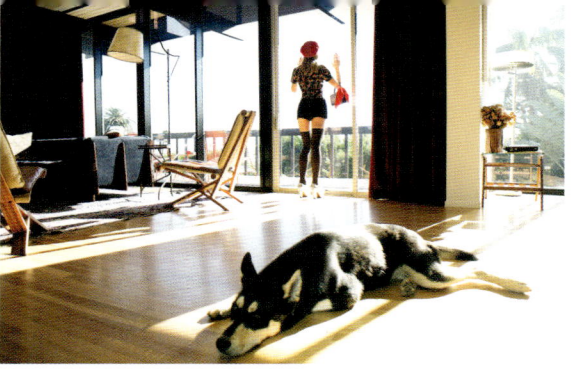
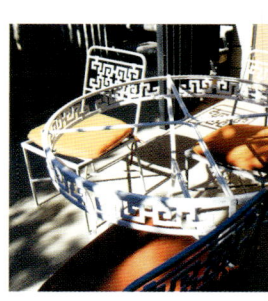
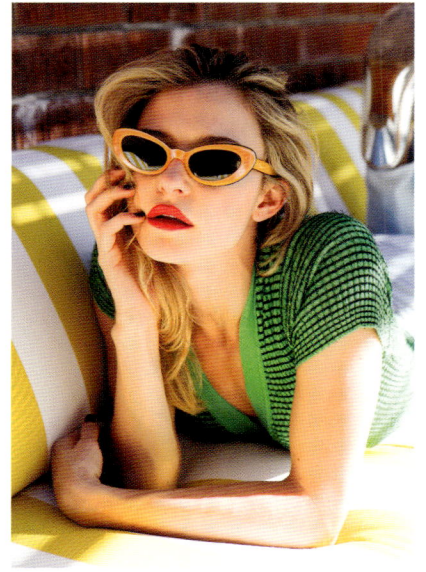
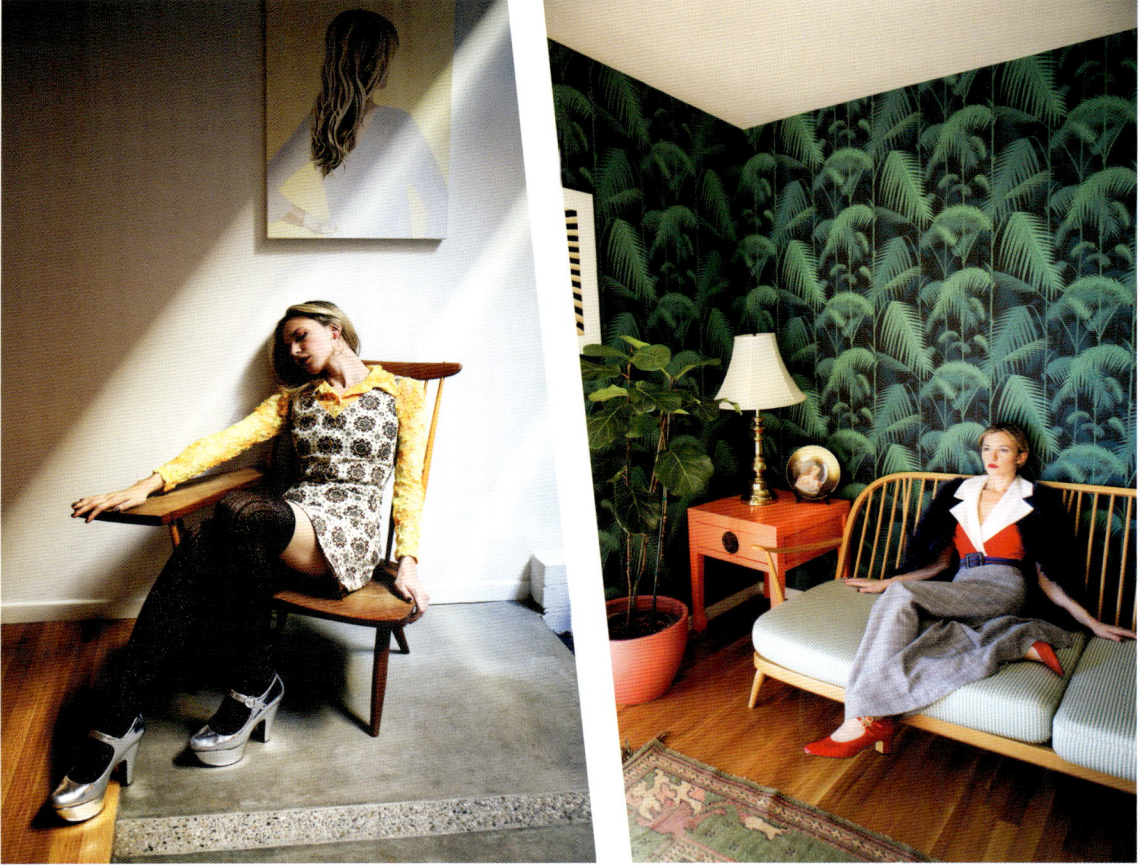
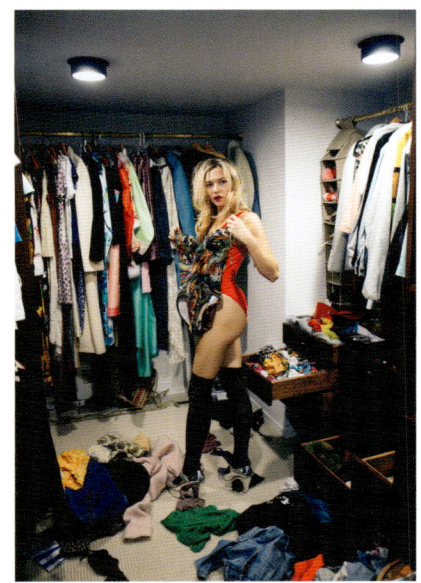
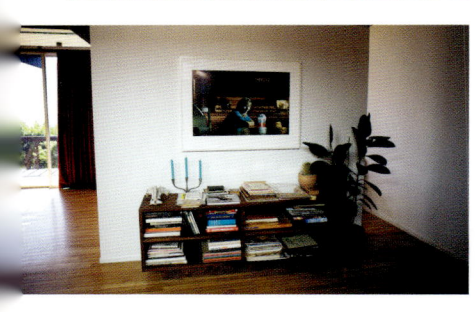
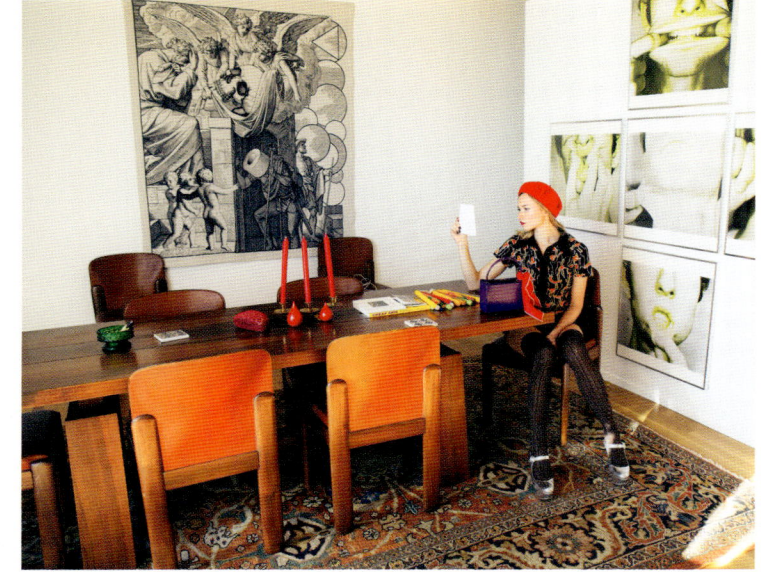
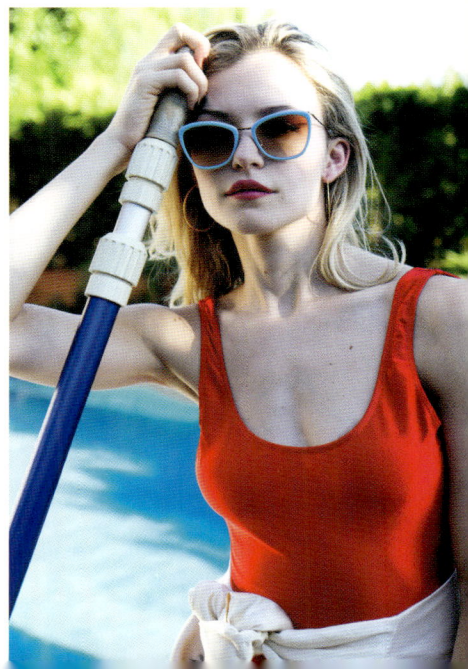

PAULA GOLDSTEIN
UNPLANNED, BUT MUCH LOVED

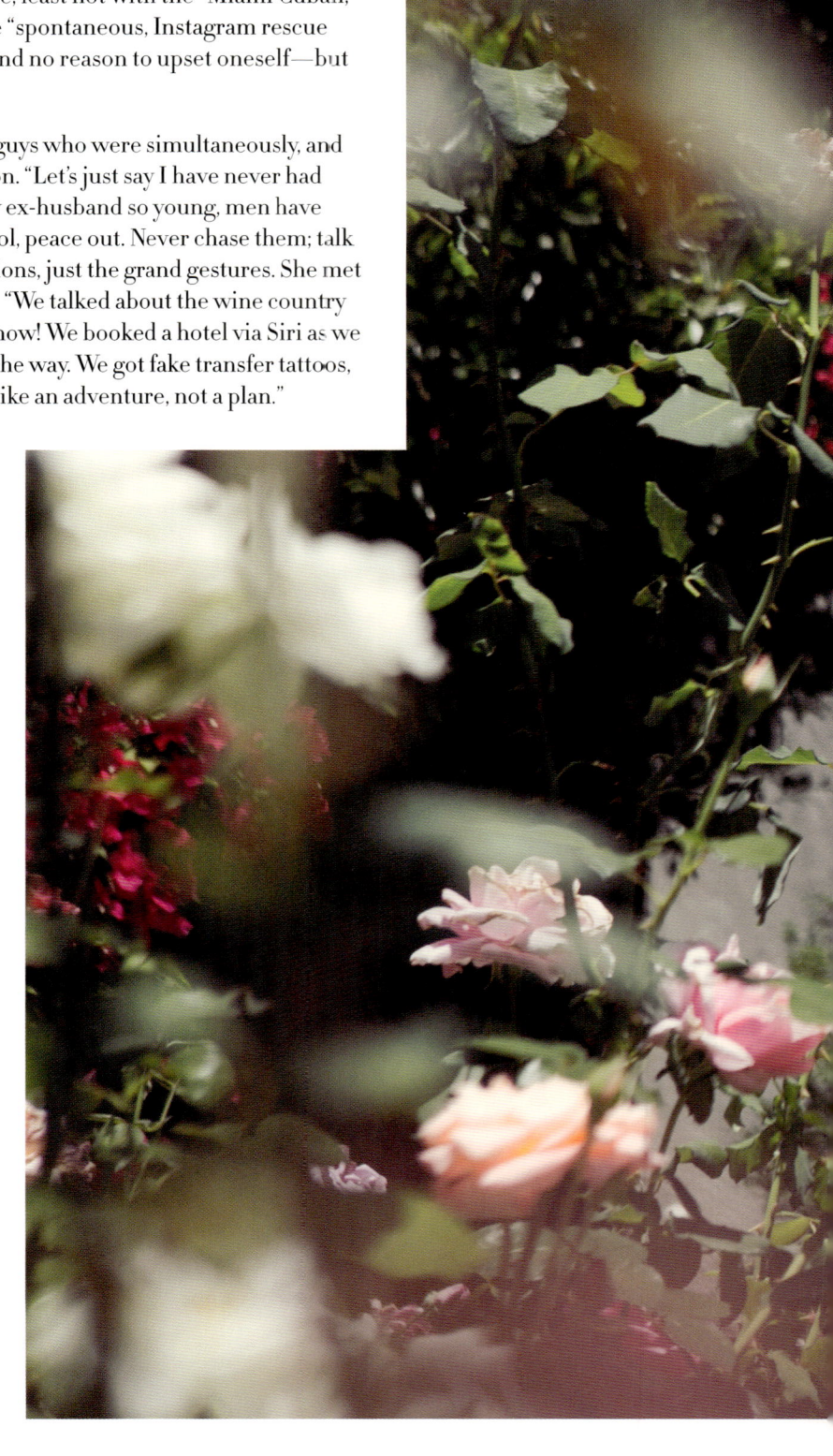

Paula Goldstein only recently moved to Los Angeles. She has barely unpacked; most of the boxes with her vintage clothes haven't even arrived from New York yet. She's a little uneasy and she seems tired today. "I gained so much weight since I got here," she sighs. "I guess it's because I am driving everywhere, and not walking?" It's a common complaint, but most certainly not detrimental to a happy, new life, least not with the "Miami Cuban, gentle genius" boyfriend she picked up in San Francisco, and the "spontaneous, Instagram rescue puppy" they named Dobby. It's just a matter of time, we decide, and no reason to upset oneself—but we would soon find out that there's more to the story...

Paula was always destined for love. There would always be a few guys who were simultaneously, and often in different continents, pining and pleading for her devotion. "Let's just say I have never had any problem meeting men," she winks. "I think because I met my ex-husband so young, men have always been friends, approachable. If they aren't that into you, cool, peace out. Never chase them; talk to boys like human beings." She never understood the complications, just the grand gestures. She met Anthony on a hike the day she was meant to fly back to New York. "We talked about the wine country and how I'd never been, and he was like: let's go to Sonoma right now! We booked a hotel via Siri as we drove, and I bought a sundress and toothbrush in a tiny town on the way. We got fake transfer tattoos, and I had my first s'more. Life and love should always be treated like an adventure, not a plan."

The same is most definitely true about her unpredictable sense of style. She dresses "emotionally,"—like that time she regrettably wore a furry, neon-pink outfit the first day of school—and only in vintage. "Very unplanned. It sort of just happens." She got fascinated with vintage when she studied at the London College of Fashion. "We learned about how clothing was made, like for real," she remembers, "about sweatshops and pollution, about the tiny children's hands that had touched that ten-dollar tee before you bought it. I was horrified, so I decided to buy vintage instead; clothing that wasn't harming people or the environment, and was still in my student budget. Now I think it's part of my identity, the uniqueness of it. Or as my ballet teacher once told me: I dance to the melody, not the beat. (It wasn't a compliment.)"

So, is anything deliberate in this Essex girl's life? Sometimes... She got kicked out of school at 16 because she never went. She locked herself inside the car because she didn't want a blood test, only to come out when her mom bribed her with a pair of velvet mules. She never answers her phone, "like *ever*." She'll debate you about politics "until the cows come home," a trait she most definitely picked up from her grandmother, who had once stabbed a member of the SS in the leg with a bread knife. And she's donating 15% of sales from her *Voyage d'Etudes: Scrapbook of America* to Planned Parenthood. Which brings me back to a text I get from Paula three months after our shoot: "I guess I found out why I felt so fat: I'm pregnant LOL. Her name will be Luna—my latest unplanned, but much loved, adventure."

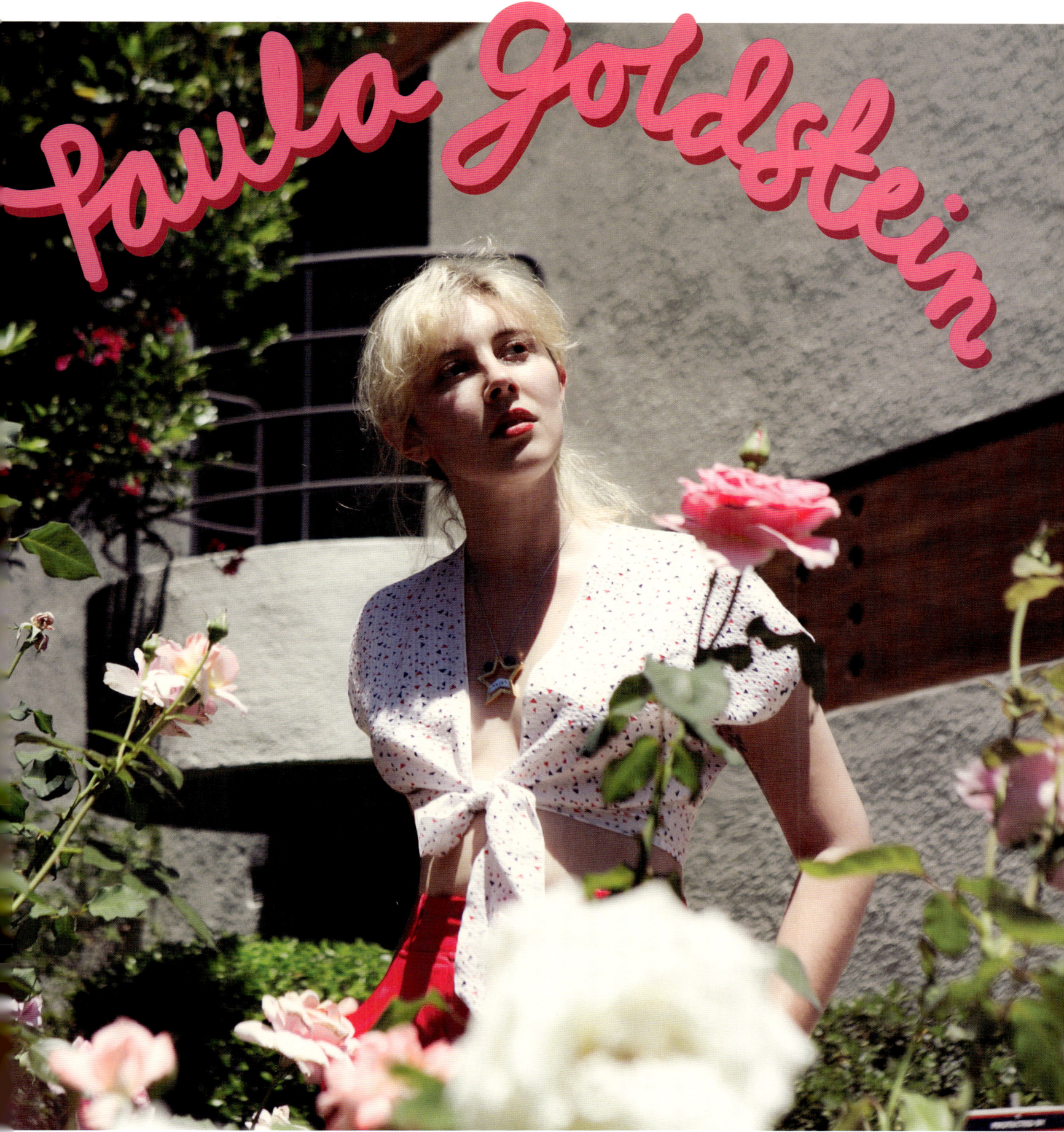

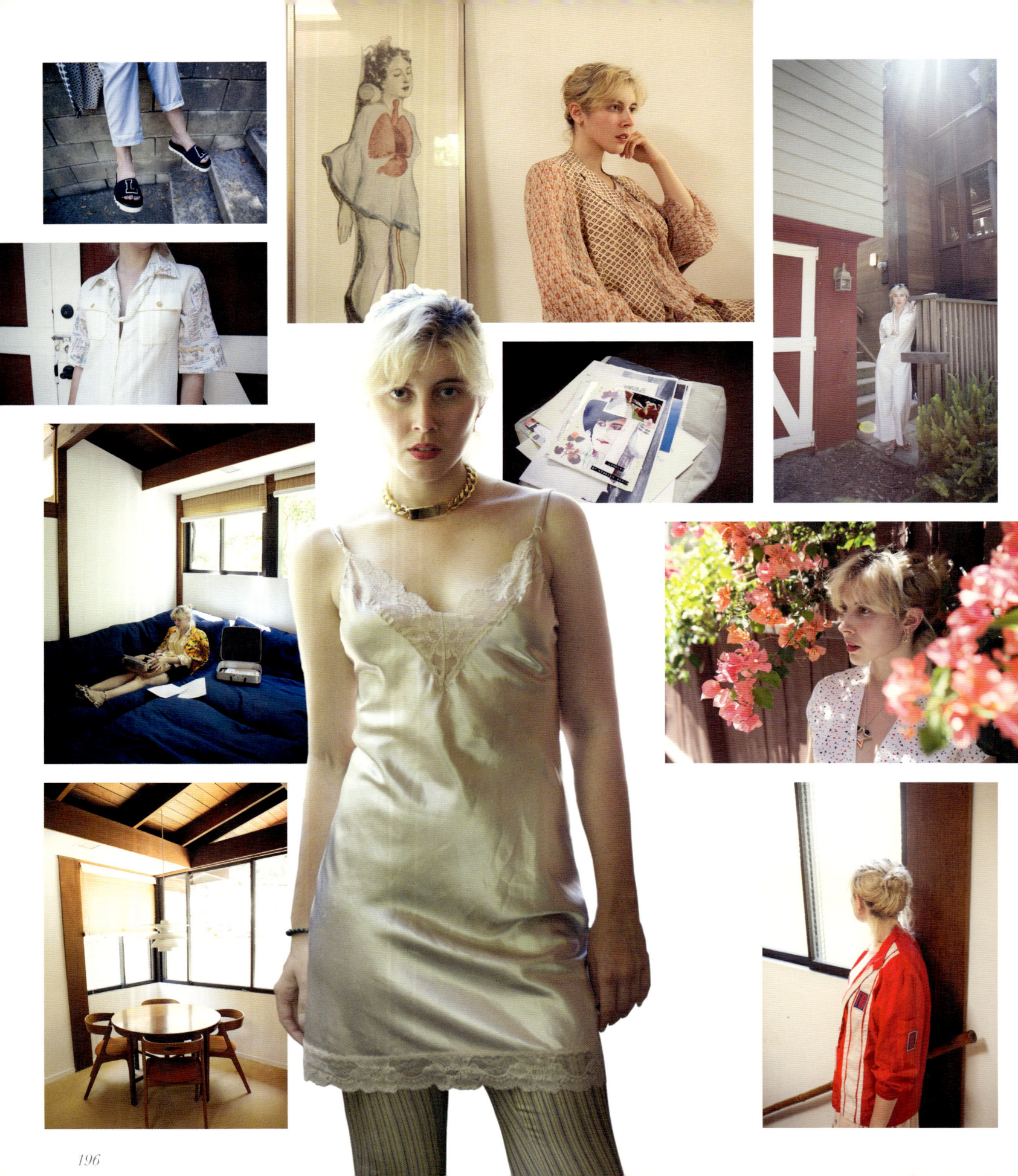

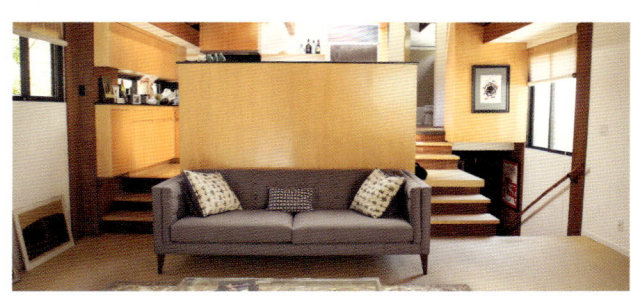
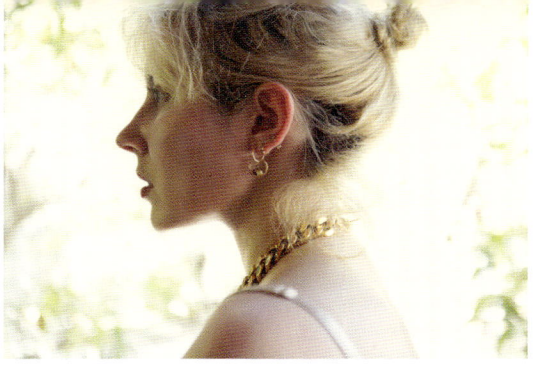
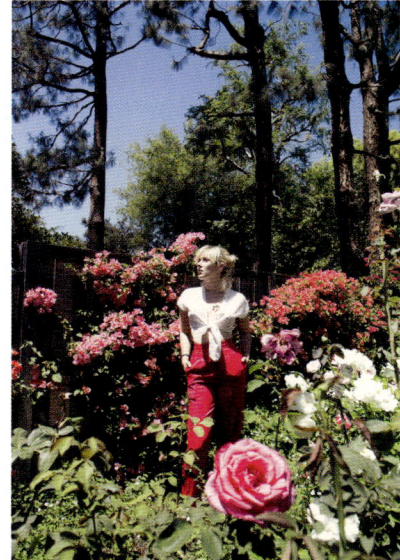
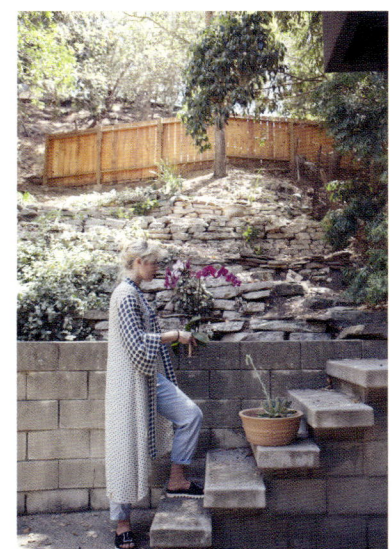
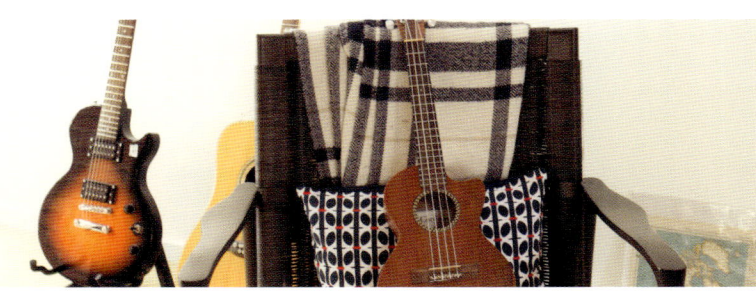
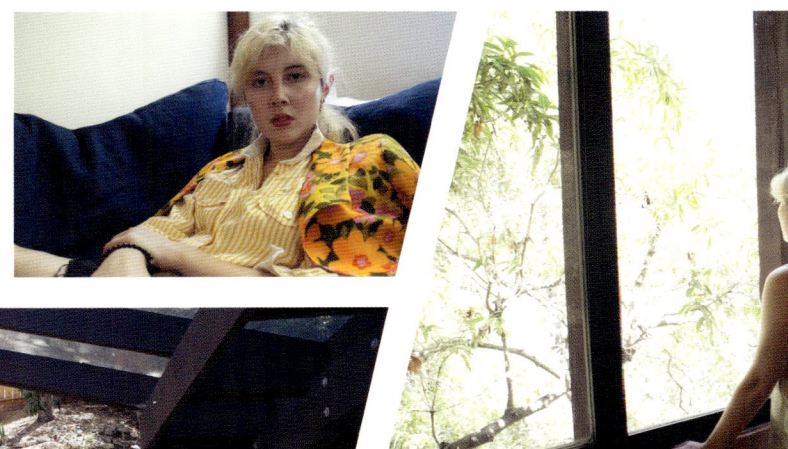
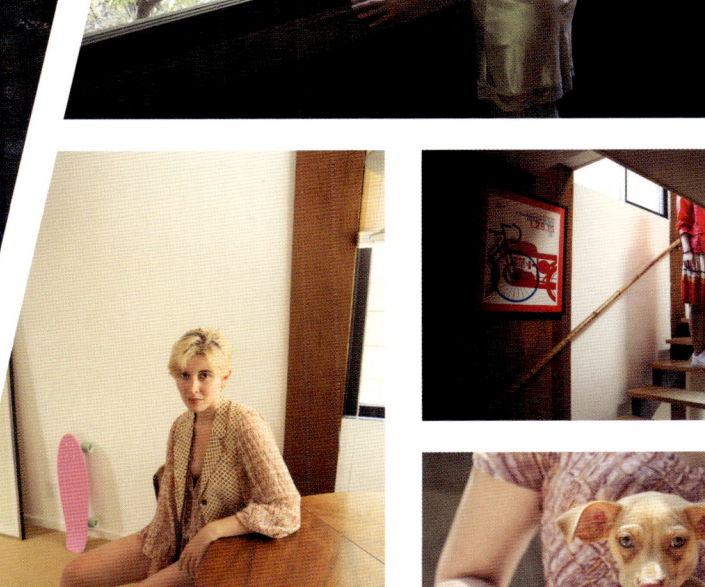
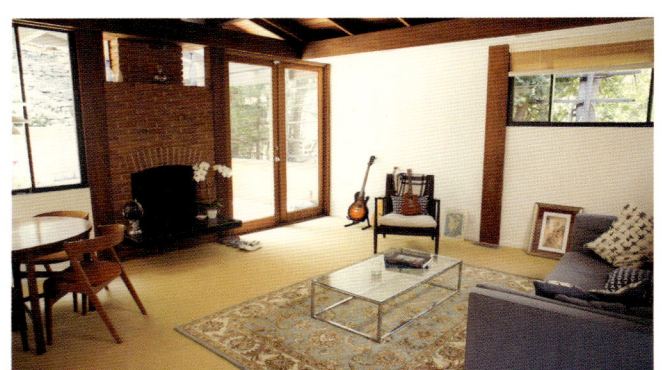

STAZ LINDES
THE AMBASSADOR'S GRANDDAUGHTER

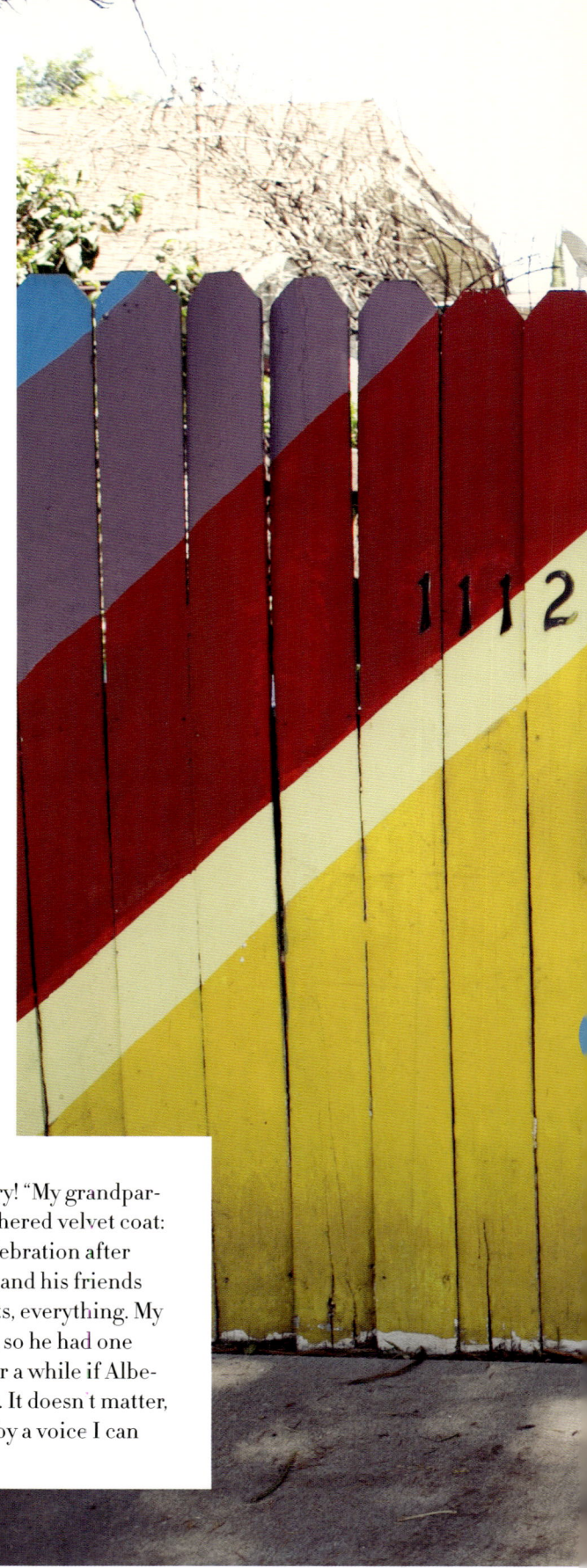

"If you found a vintage piece that was $1, but you had to go through 150 other pieces to find it, does that mean the piece is worth more than $1?" It's a pertinent question, perhaps of a more philosophical than economic nature. And it's especially relevant in this studio apartment on Sunset Junction, because both its inhabitants live and breathe vintage. It's the red thread that runs along every shelf of their cluttered, little home, through sequined sleeves and corduroy pant legs, underneath the bed and across the carpet. It's the thread that ties them together, for better or for worse. "Travis and I have to help each other to stop thrifting sometimes," says Staz, shaking her head. "He loves T-shirts and vintage. He is insanely good at thrifting. It's an amazing but dangerous talent! Thrifting or antiquing is really relaxing to me. I will literally dumpster dive. This is where the problem starts!"

You probably know Staz Lindes. Maybe you saw her shaggy blonde hair and cute pout on the February '16 cover of *CR Fashion Book*, or in the new Yves Saint Laurent beauty ads, or walking for Jeremy Scott and Moschino. At just five-foot-seven she didn't expect to have a big modeling career. Her look is unconventional, and being in Los Angeles, she never took her job seriously. She was busy playing, recording, and touring with The Paranoyds, the band she put together with high school girlfriends. She never even traveled for work until four years ago. All that changed however, when she caught the eye of LA compatriot Hedi Slimane. He made her one of his Saint Laurent muses and kick-started a full-blown frenzy. "It's a super conflicting, strange job," she says, "but it has given me so many amazing experiences and brought so many amazing people into my life. I think it's still headed in the right direction! You never friggin' know!"

"Where's the rest of the patches?" asks Travis seated on the floor, rummaging through a bag. "Mine or yours?" asks Staz. She looks up. "Oh, you can have that one, by the way. It's scary." Staz will collect anything: "Right now I'm into horror VHS, horror t-shirts, good books, and I continue to add to my longstanding vinyl and clothing collection." Her most prized possessions belonged to her Russian grandfather or her parents, and each piece tells an amazing story. She shows me a tiny cardigan Twiggy knit for her mom, and a custom piece by Ossie Clark. Mom was a model in London during the late 60s and early 70s, who went on to set-decorate Fran Drescher's shows after she moved to Los Angeles. Dad is Hal Lindes, a composer who played guitar for Dire Straits.

But the greatest story is the one that produces today's best outfit, *and* a fake country! "My grandparents barely escaped the horrendous reign of Stalin," she begins, holding up a weathered velvet coat: "They both had to flee and eventually made it to America. They treated life as a celebration after that. My grandfather, "Gaga," had a huge personality. He was such a funny man. He and his friends decided to make up a fake country. They made fake pamphlets, postcards, passports, everything. My grandfather, of course, was the ambassador of this country, and needed a costume, so he had one made. I am so lucky to be wearing the Ambassador of Alberia's coat!" We debate for a while if Alberia is or could be a real country. "Isn't that the airline you just flew on?" asks Travis. It doesn't matter, because in that exact moment, the record starts to play a French song, performed by a voice I can only identify as Miss Piggy. Who says things need to make sense to be true?

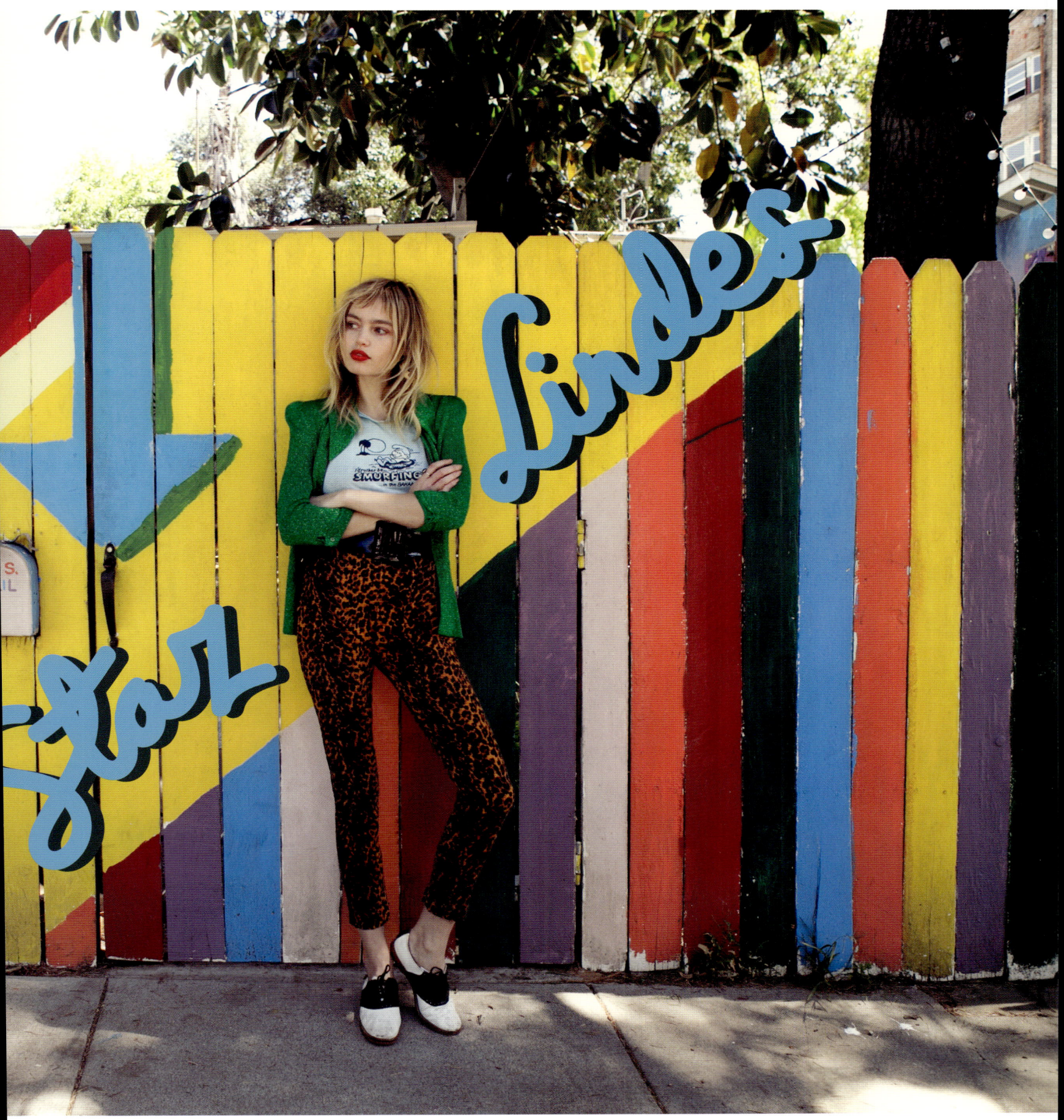

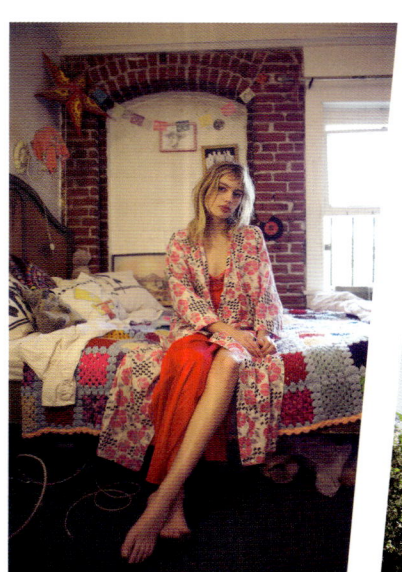
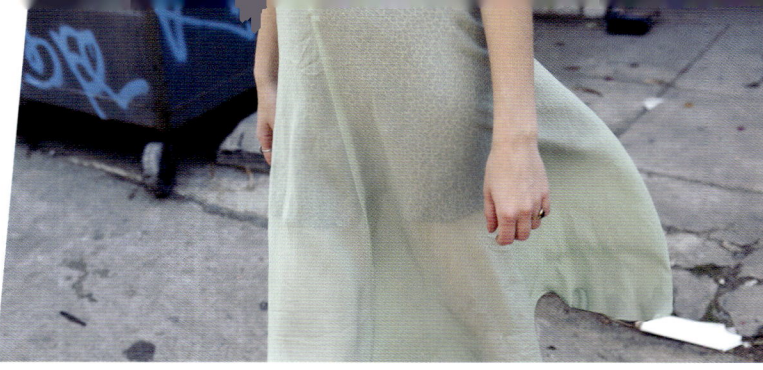
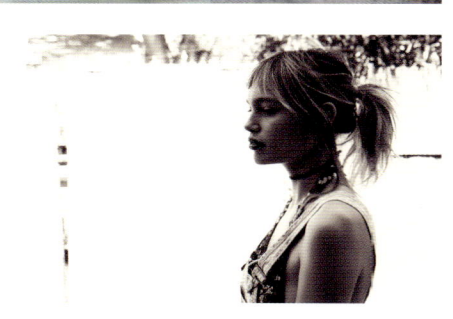
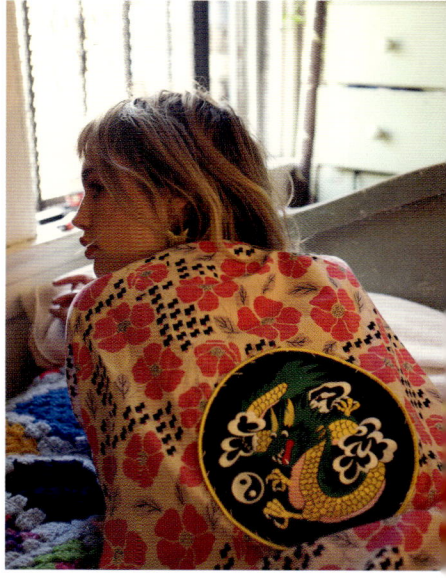
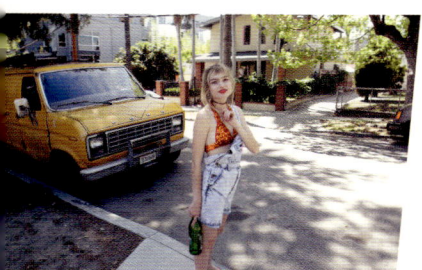
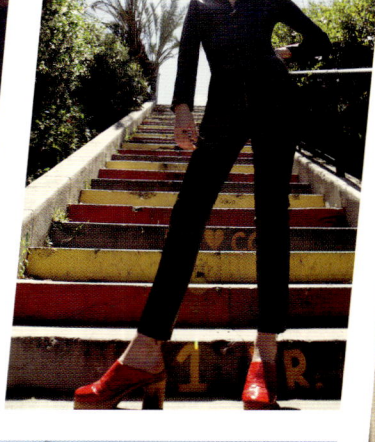
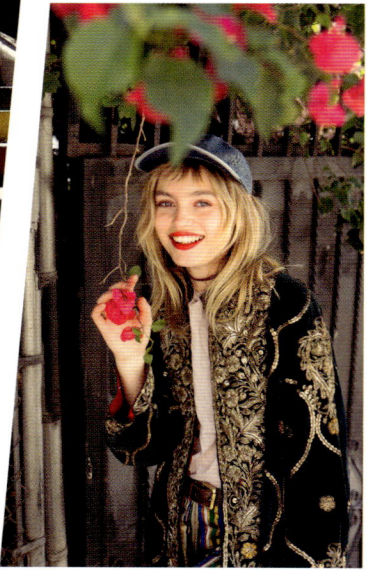
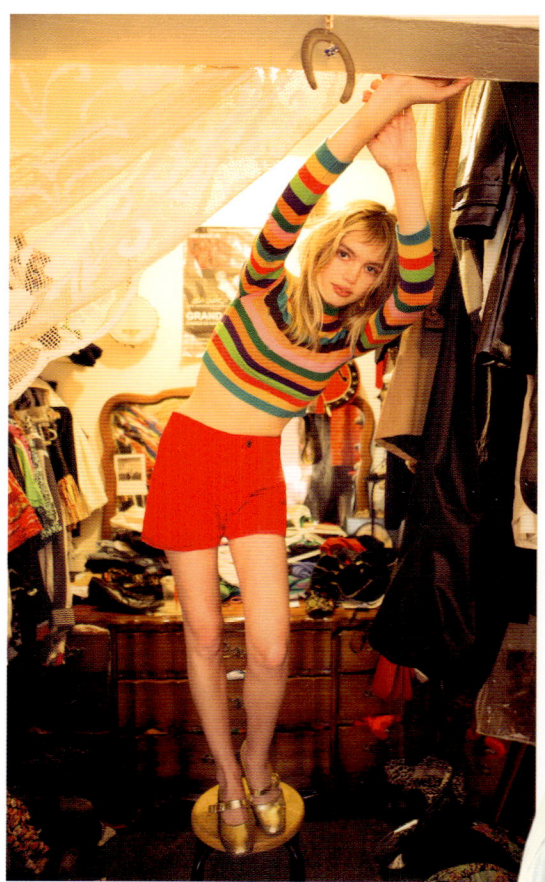
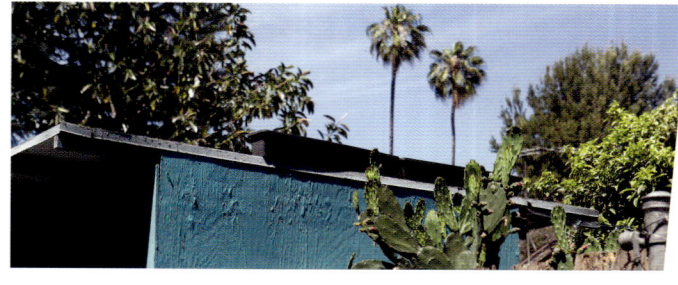
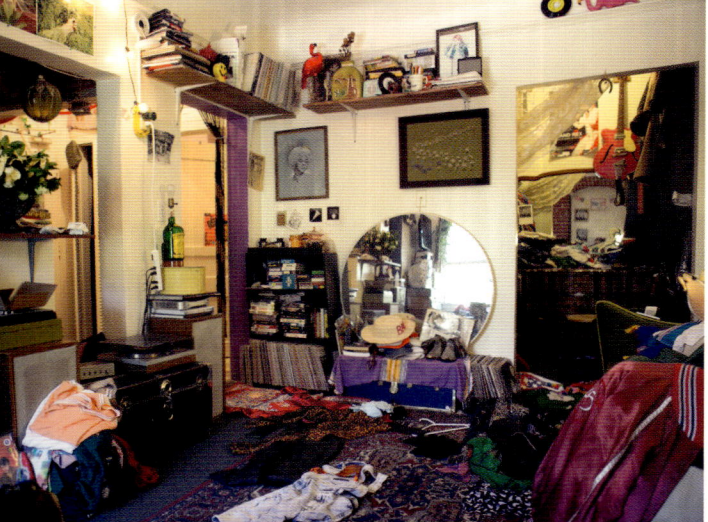
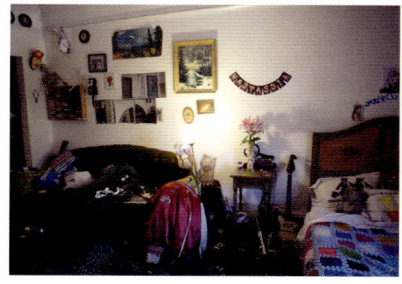
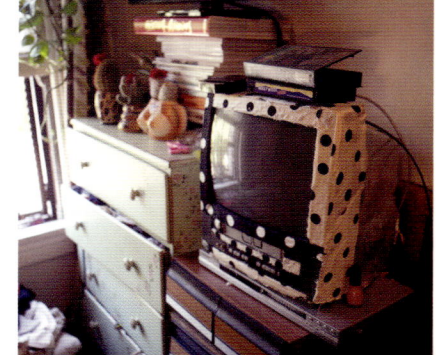
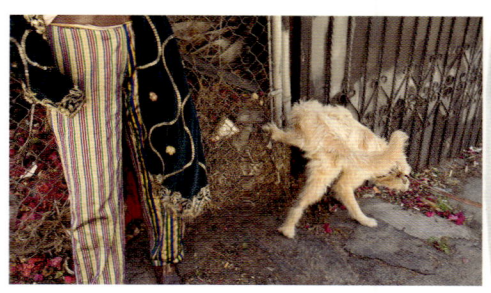

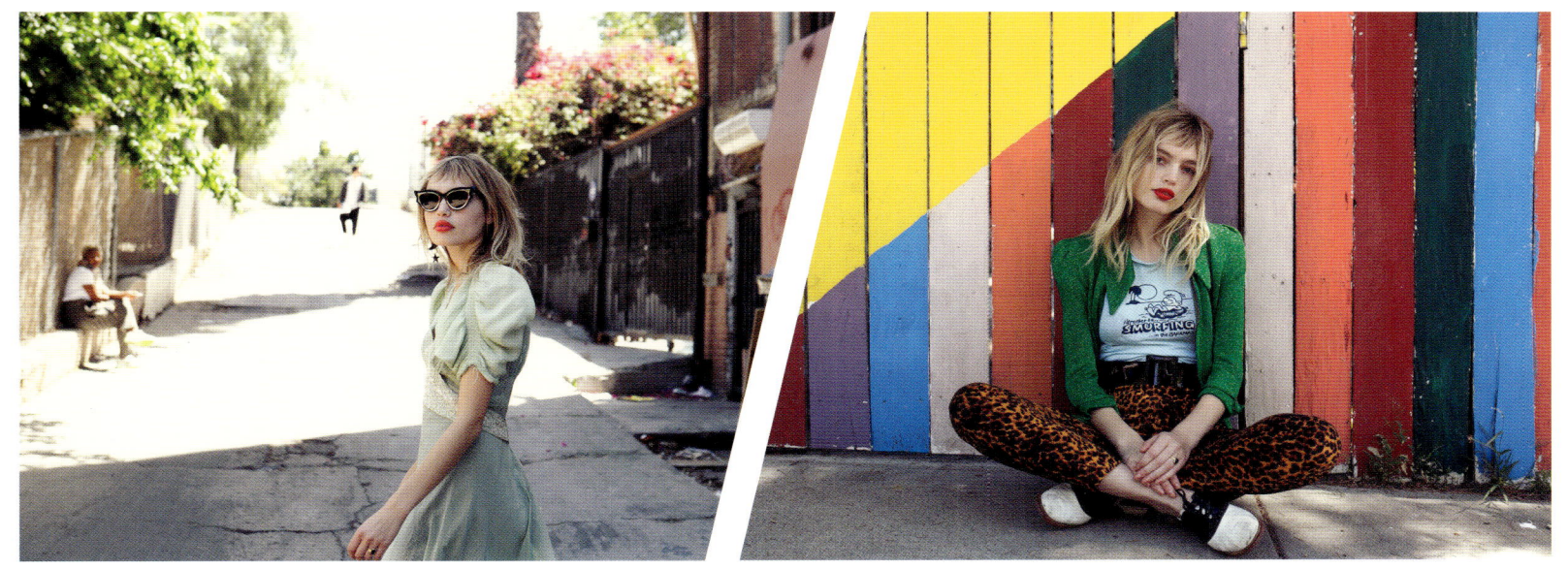
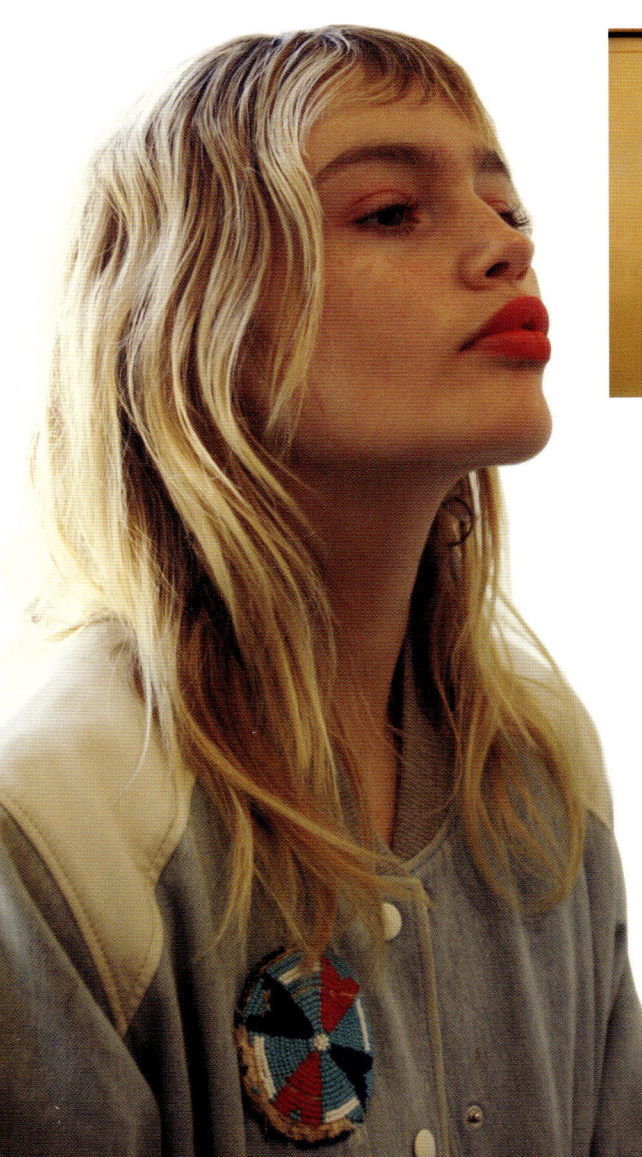
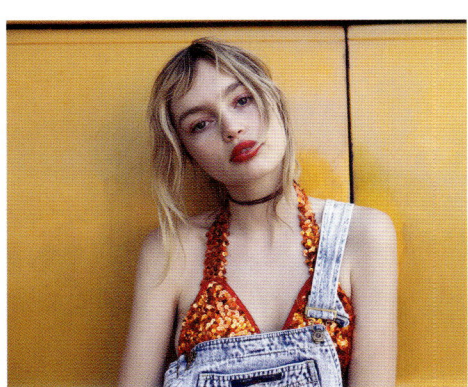
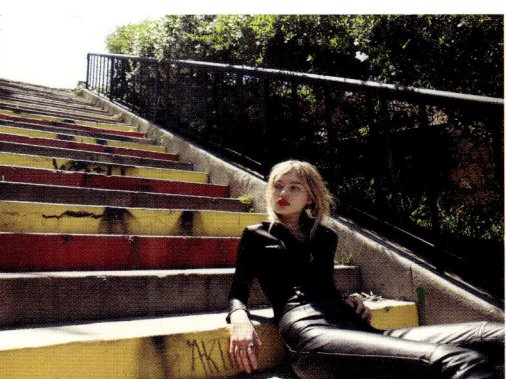
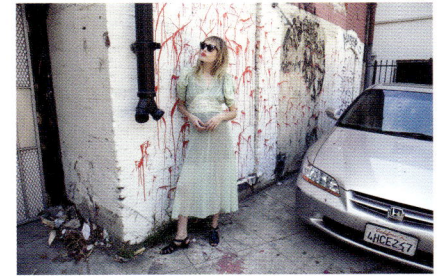
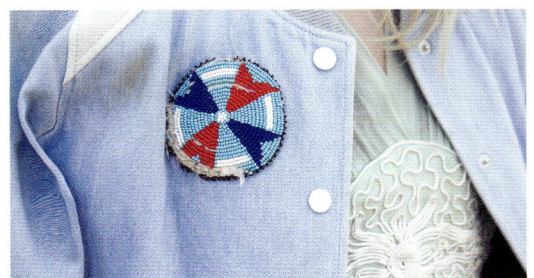
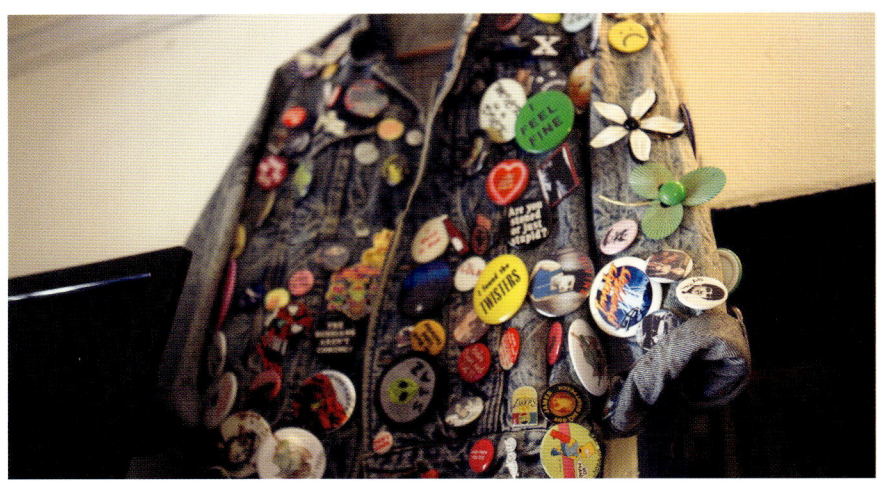

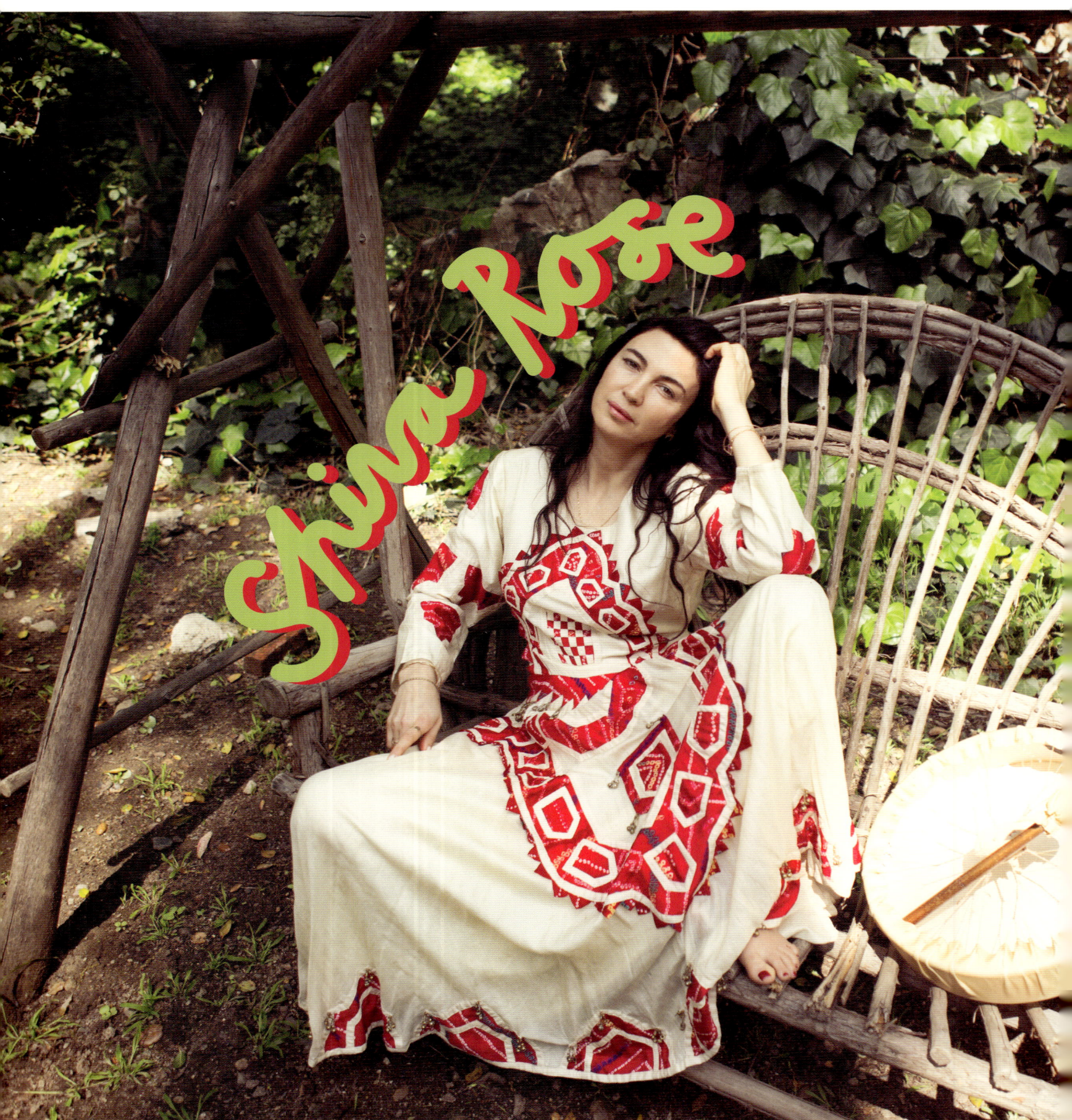

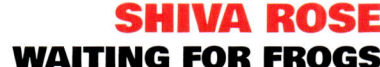

SHIVA ROSE
WAITING FOR FROGS

It's early morning in the Santa Monica Mountains. The dew lingers daintily on sprigs and weeds. The sunbeams flicker through foliage overhead. A bird sings, a gong sounds. This is not your ordinary backyard. This is a sanctuary, a tranquil oasis of earthy wellness. It is the home of a few healthy chickens, a swarm of honey bees, three gigantic oak trees, a dog named Luna, a cat named Fig, and a beautiful woman with red lipstick. Every morning she sits in the wooden pagoda at the end of the downward path and serves tea. It's a powerful, live potion, made from the twigs of thousand-year-old trees in Taiwan. And with every sip, she connects deeper and more profoundly to nature. It's a self-fulfilling ritual. But there is one thing that saddens her as she watches her perfect green garden: the creek has run dry, and every day she prays to hear the frogs again.

Shiva Rose was always a sensitive child. She grew up in the countryside of Iran, living in a dreamworld filled with dragonflies and cherry trees. But her youthful imagination was abruptly compromised when the Revolution broke out. "My family and I had to escape in the middle of the night," she remembers. "My mother is American and my father was very liberal in his thinking, so our lives were in danger. After a very traumatic escape, we landed in London for a moment, before coming to California." She found solace in dance, books, plays, and old movies. Her dream was to be a ballerina, but she soon realized that what she loved best was to lose herself in great stories. She studied drama, theater, and world arts, became an actress, married Dylan McDermott, and had two lovely daughters.

But tragedy struck again. At 26, after the birth of her first daughter, the doctors told her she had just one year to live. "I had severe auto-immune conditions," she says quietly. "I felt so depleted and exhausted. It took me many, many years to get back to a healthy place. What helped me was organic food, clean pure water, no chemicals in the home, using all-natural products, and adding more fats to my diet. Also, having a spiritual connection to the source of all things." But it is perhaps the divorce that grounded her more solidly. She found this gorgeous house and the practice of Kundalini yoga. During one of her meditations, she got the idea for a non-toxic beauty line. "It started with one product," she remembers, "a rose face oil that I had been making for myself for decades. I saw the need for an upscale, chic, yet powerful beauty line that actually nourishes the skin rather than drying it out. It's all based on Ayurvedic teachings and blessed with mantras and crystals."

And vintage? That's her one vice, the only thing she allows herself to get high on. "Once you've tasted the adventure of discovery, it stays in your blood," she smiles. For Shiva it's about the stories the pieces tell and the characters she can become. "I realized I could wear a vintage velvet cloak and be a Russian aristocrat, or I could wear a 1950s western blouse and be a cowgirl of sorts. And what would Nastassja Kinski in *Paris, Texas* be without that iconic and sexy, pink angora sweater? Or Charlotte Rampling without her erotic suspenders and black SS cap in *The Night Porter*? These films became even more powerful because of the costumes that helped the story along." Sometimes she dreams of being one of these women who wears an easy, daily uniform, but then she realizes how much she loves her kimonos. Life is good and green in this house—despite the tardy frogs.

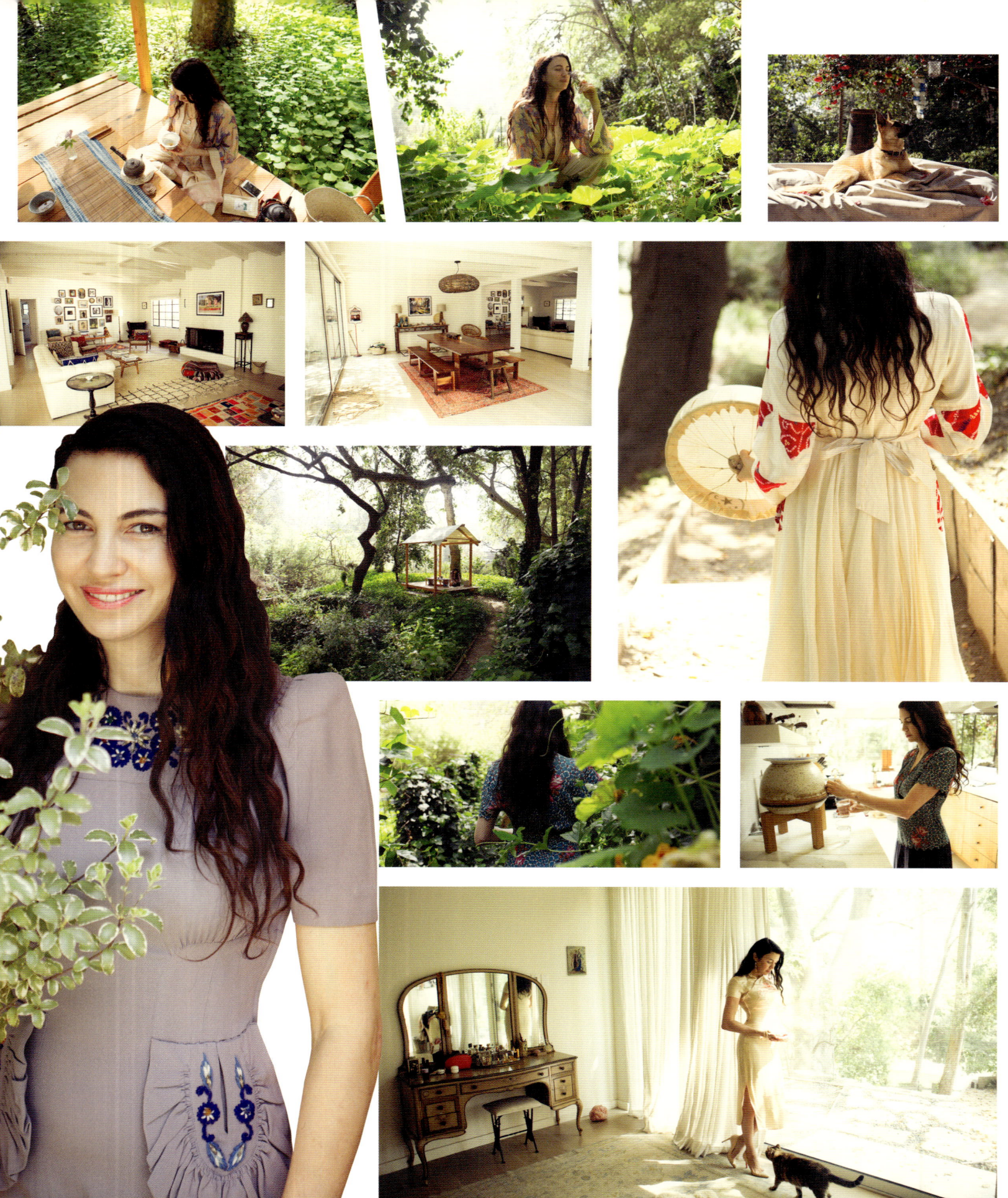

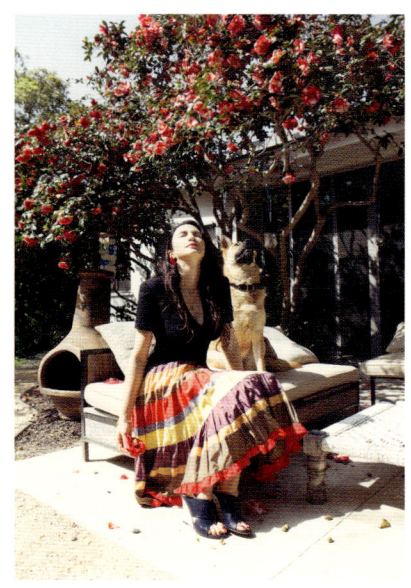
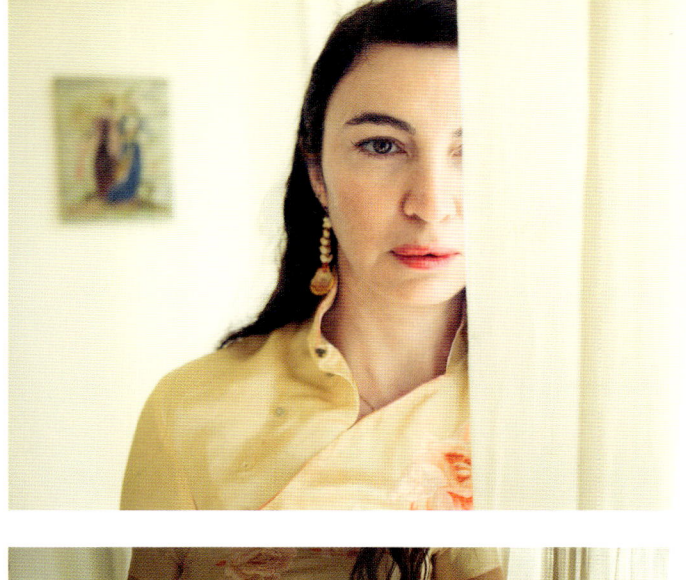
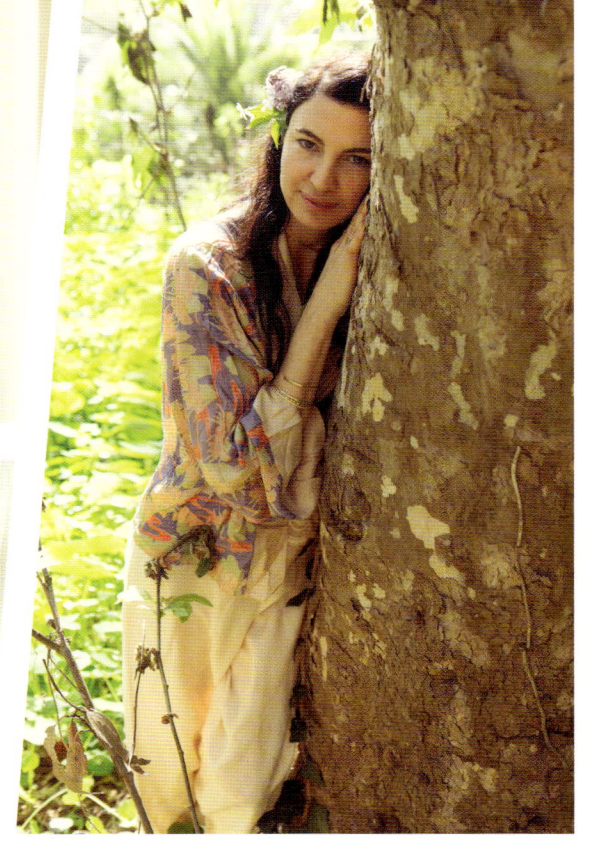
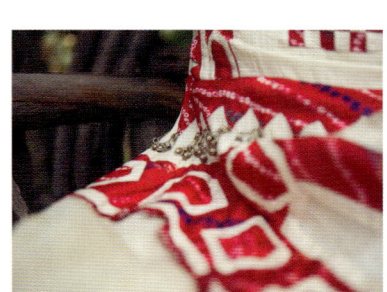
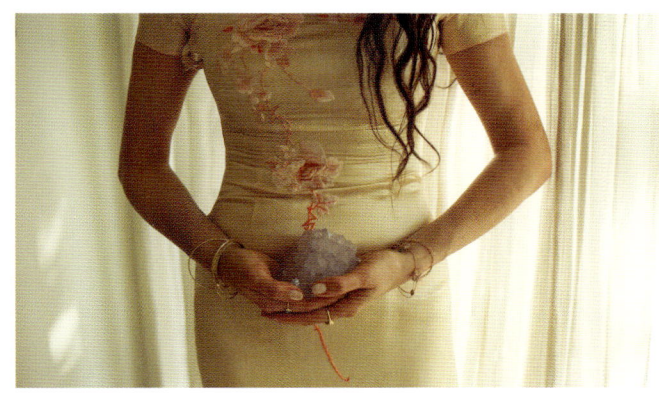
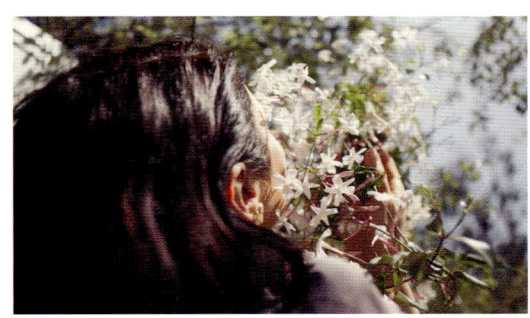
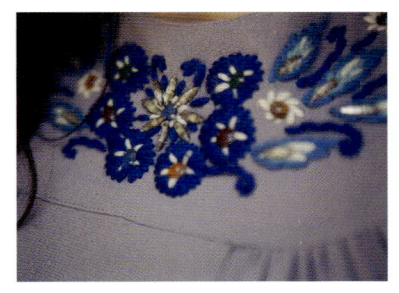
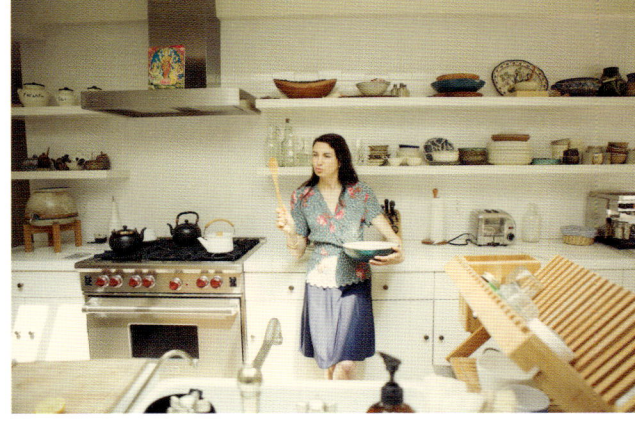
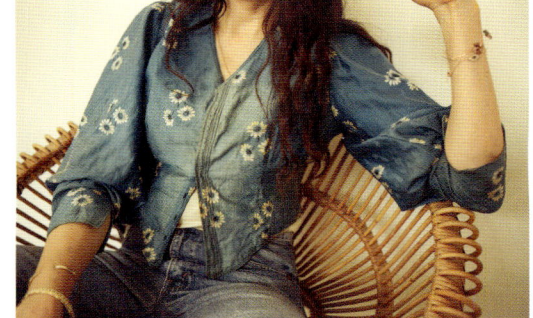
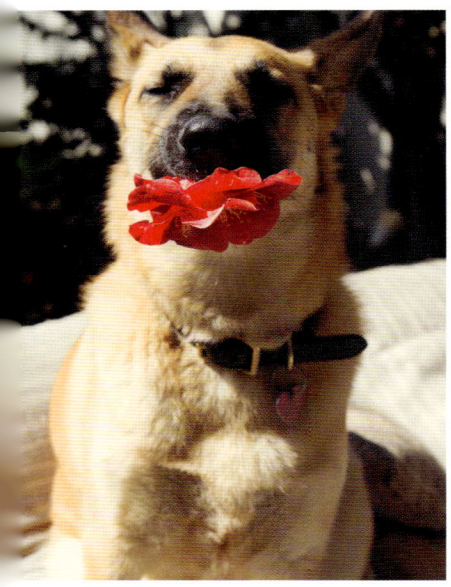
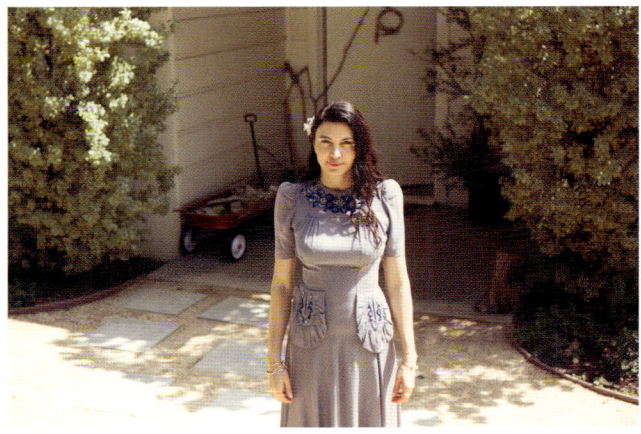
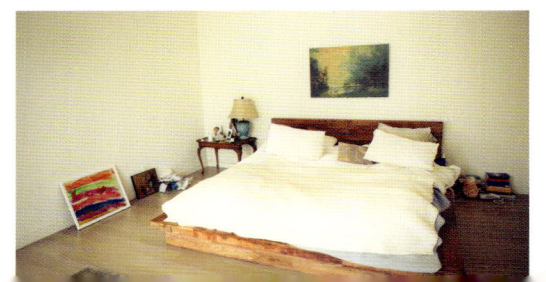

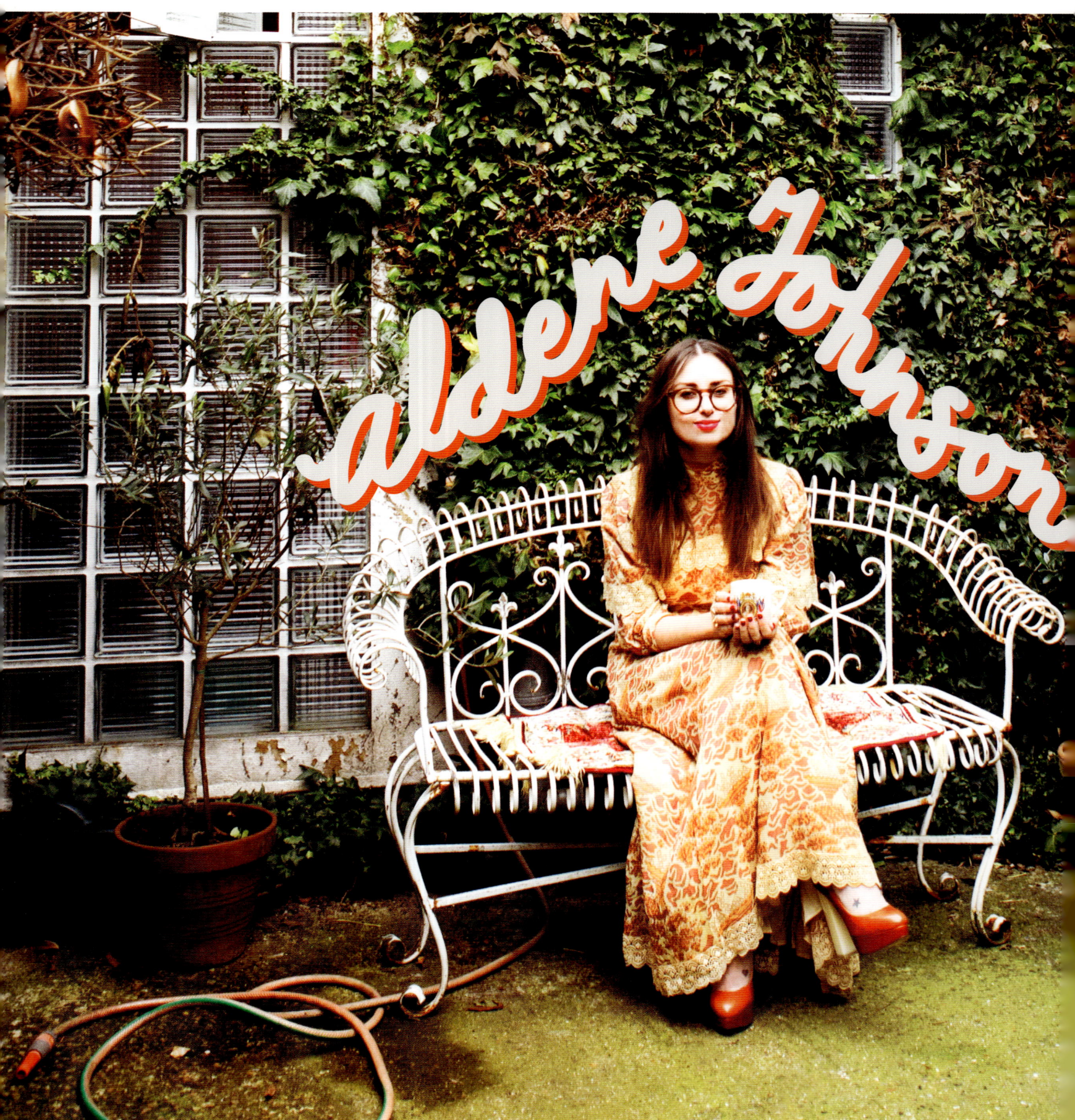

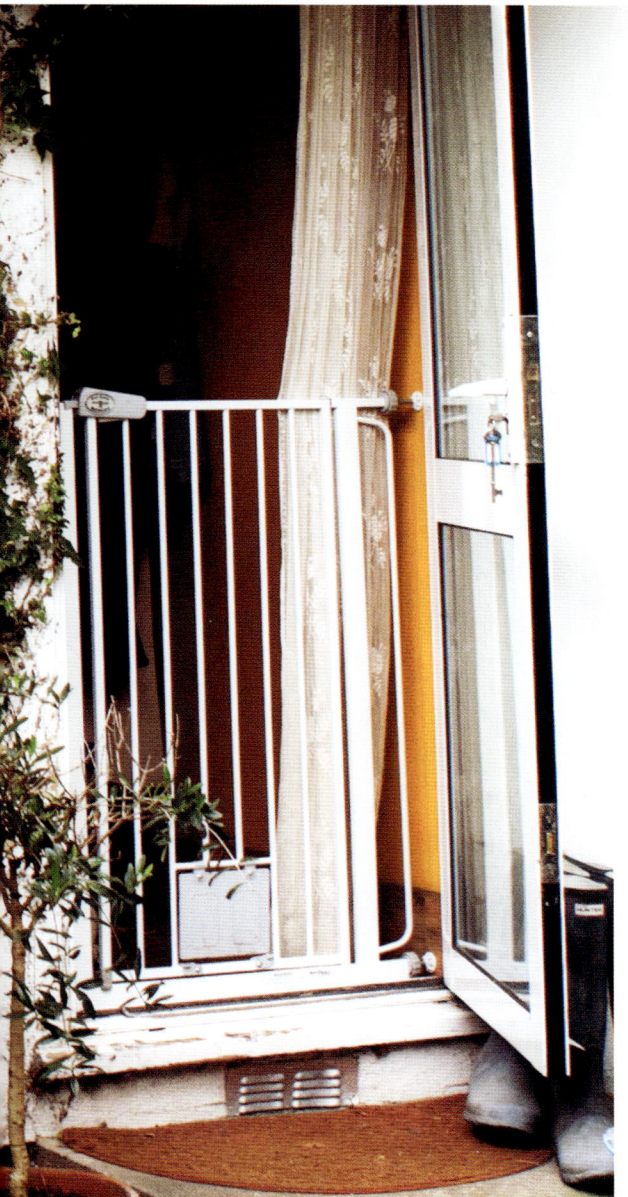

ALDENE JOHNSON
EXIT LONDON

Walthamstow is quite a mouthful. And it's pretty far too, about an 18-mile drive to the outskirts of London in the northeast. It's a cute and leafy, but uneventful, little neighborhood with a bustling Middle Eastern market on weekends. According to Wikipedia, Walthamstow is often referred to as Awesomestow, which is not only easier and more fun to pronounce, it also implies its recent gentrification and soaring real estate prices. Apparently, it's the new Shoreditch and everyone's moving there. Except Aldene Johnson and her family—they're leaving, and perhaps setting a new trend. "Last year we started visiting Margate, as a few friends have houses there," she explains. "There's a really good vibe there, with creatives all moving from London. Having such beautiful beaches on our doorstep will be so wonderful for the boys."

For now though, Aldene and her lads are still in their two-bedroom townhouse in the "Stow." When she opens the door, baby Buddy Miles is on her arm, smiling because he's just woken up from a nap. Bix, the labrador, walks up carrying an old blanket, and there's a cat somewhere too. Her name is Lola. Husband Kevin is at his music studio in the city, and the other boy is on a play date. Everything in this little house breathes nostalgia and vintage, from the curtains to the bedspreads to the salt and peppershakers in the kitchen. It seems perfectly congruous with Aldene's whimsical, almost witchy, look. The contents of her walk-in closet provide ample proof of a severe infatuation with antiquities. She loves kimonos and jewelry, and combines elements of masculinity with touches of femininity. But she's not as ritzy anymore. "Since having children I find I wear fewer dresses," she says. "My go-to outfit is a cream silk blouse, jeans, and accessories."

Aldene Johnson is probably best known for her work with Florence Welsh. She's been styling the frontwoman of Florence + the Machine for shows, appearances, and photo shoots, since "Lungs" came out eight years ago. "After assisting, I started working for *Vice* magazine," she looks back. "I became their first Fashion Editor. It was there I met Tabitha Denholm [who was] art directing Florence's first album cover. She made the introduction. We share an incredible love for vintage, for beautiful things really. One memorable [look] for me is the 1920s soft-pink chiffon-and-cream lace piece that she wore at Somerset House."

Aldene was born in Zimbabwe and grew up in South Africa. Nothing in her early years hinted at a career in fashion. She wanted to be a marine biologist and spent all her summers at the aquarium, feeding sharks and hanging out with dolphins. But then she went on to study Psychology in university, and that didn't stick either. It wasn't until she moved to London that she realized styling was an actual job. Besides Florence, she has collaborated with incredible artists like Corinne Bailey Rae, Aluna George, MØ, and Goldfrapp. "I'd like to think that there is an elegance to my work," she considers, "but also an edge. I form a real bond with the wonderful women I work with. It's really important that they trust and feel confident in me as their stylist."

It's interesting to hear so many of the people in this book credit London for their love of vintage. Camden Town, Portobello Market, the King's Road, Carnaby Street, were all such epicenters of subcultural shifts and youth identity. It was thought, and encouraged, that one could dress and act as freely as one wanted to; the crazier, the better. London always had that experimental, creative spirit that all the other big cities lacked. It was rougher and more explosive. Growing up in Belgium, which is just across the Channel, I'd hop on a boat or the Eurostar as often as I could. I moved to London after university to study at the London College of Fashion. That year was pivotal for my personal growth and my confidence as a vintage girl. The city grows on you, and long lingers after you leave—even in places as remote as Margate.

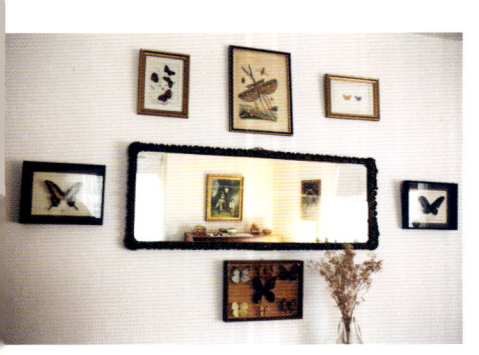
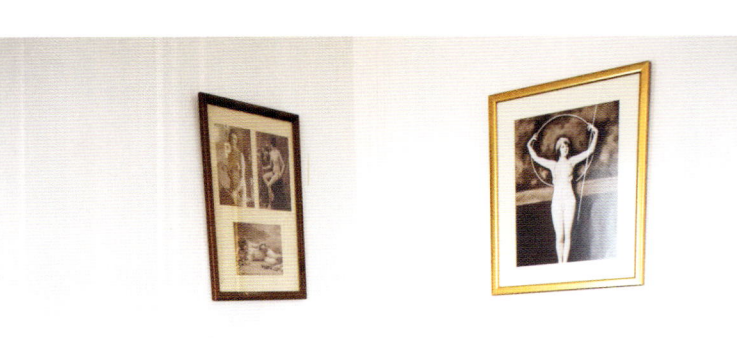
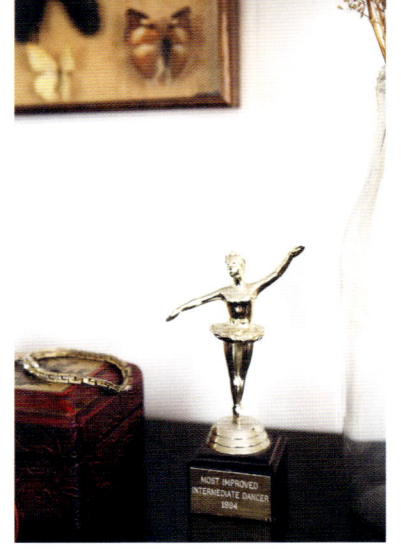
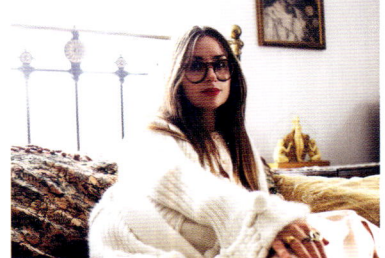
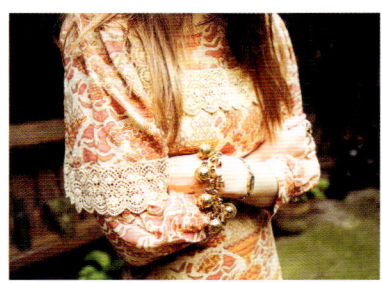
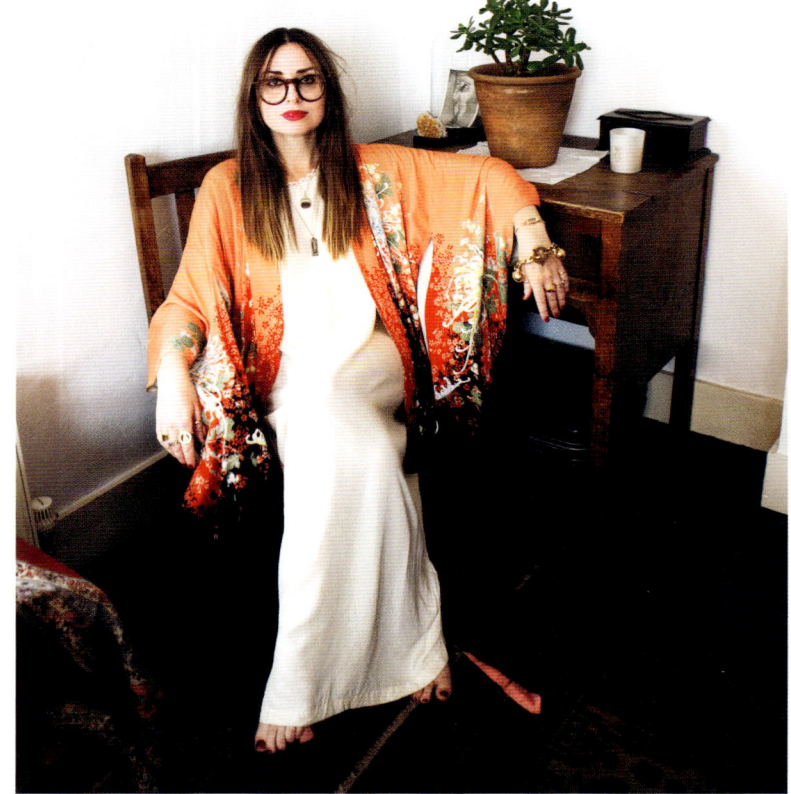
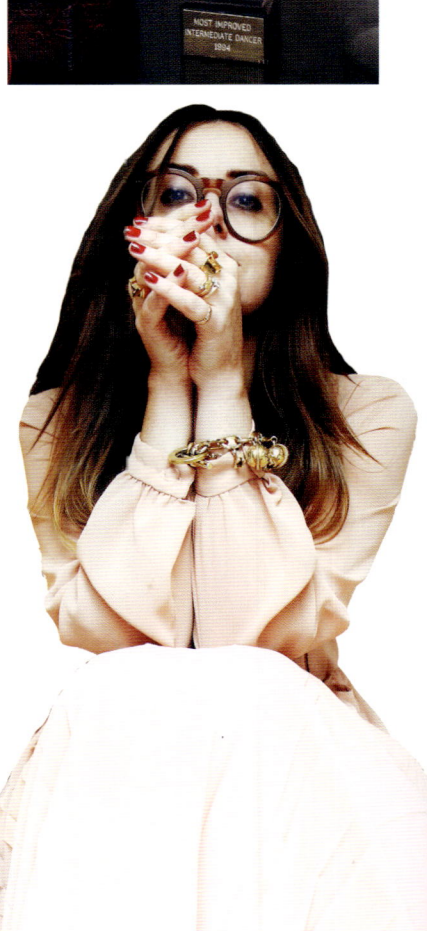
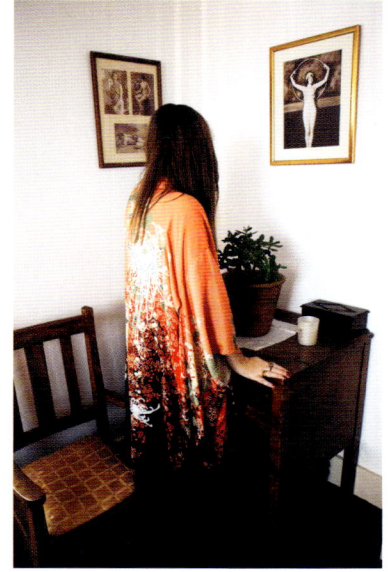
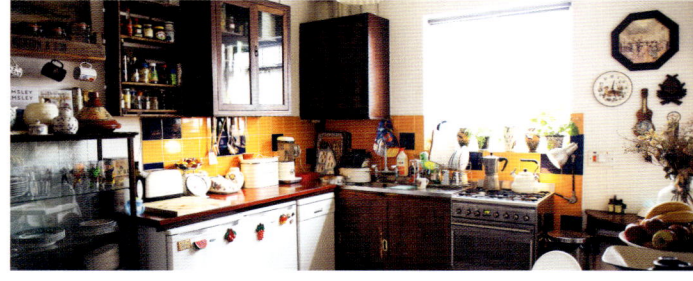
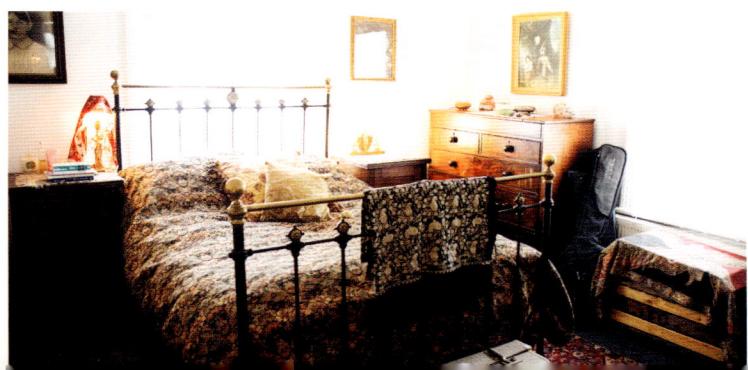
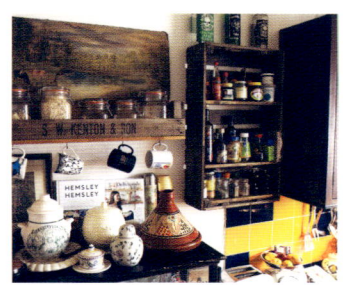

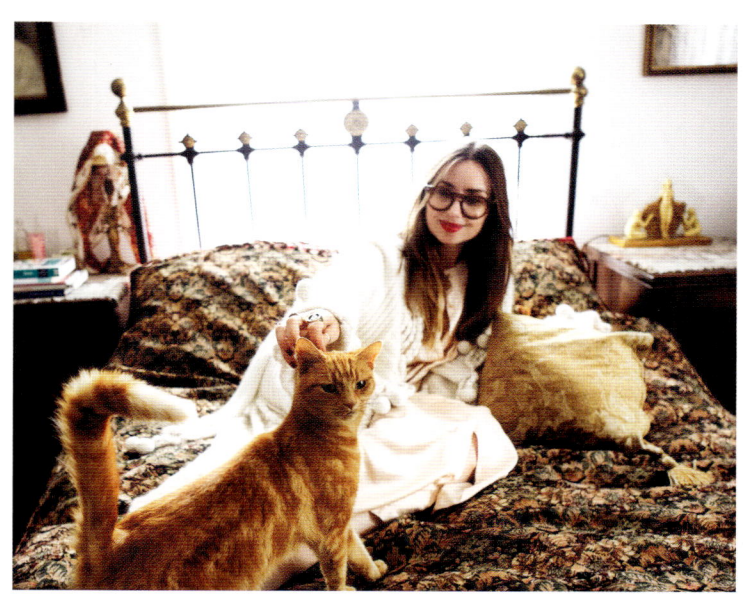
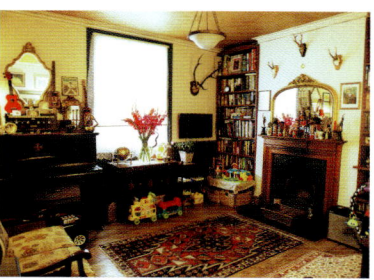
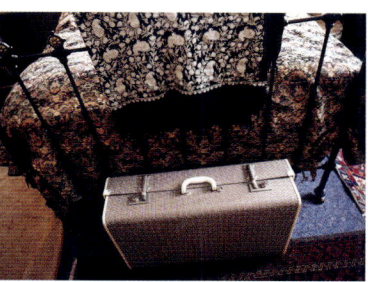
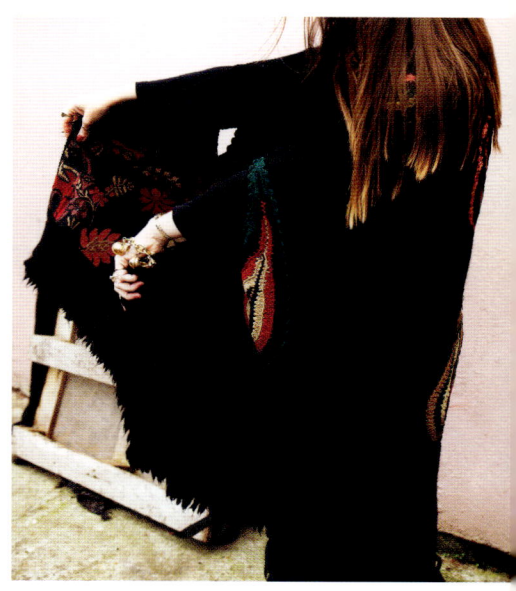
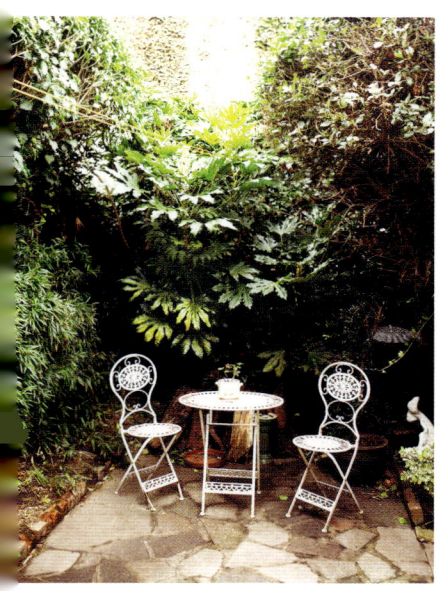
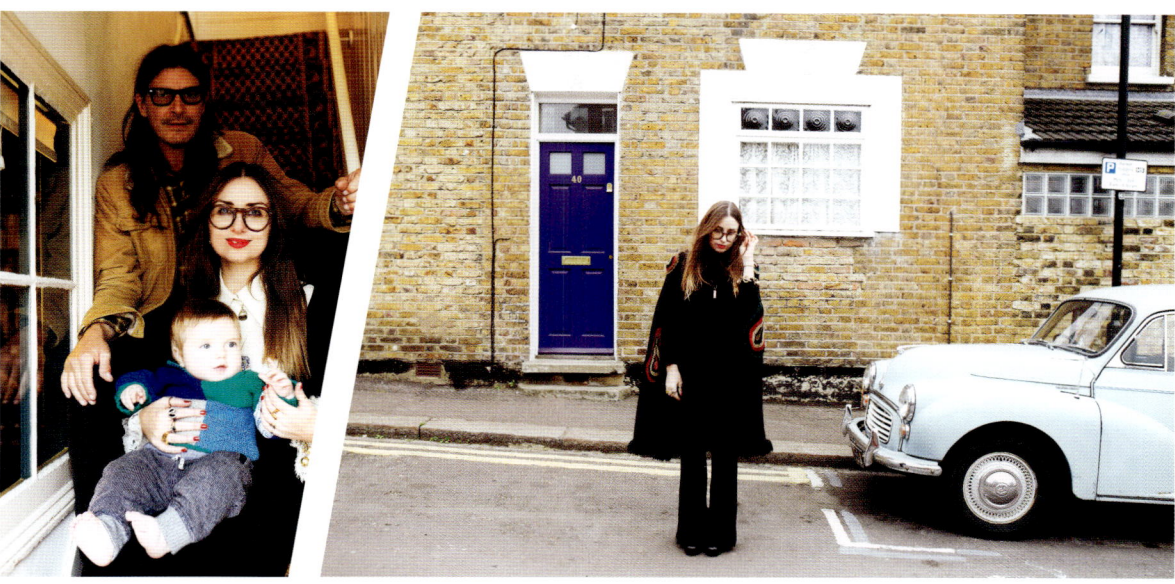
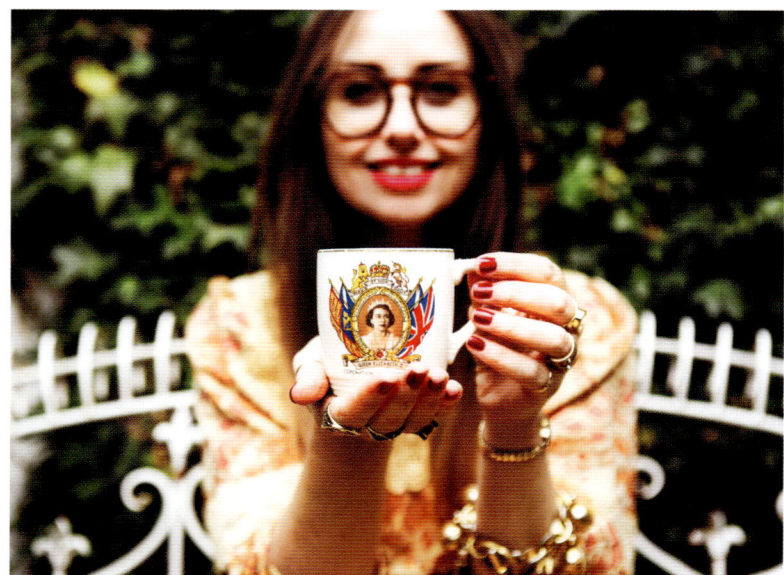
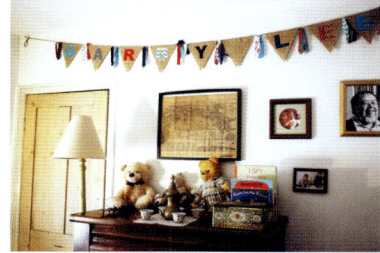
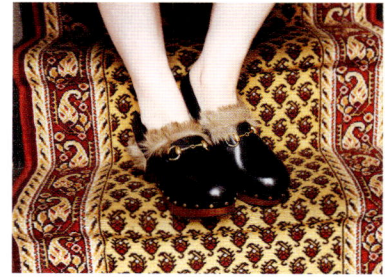
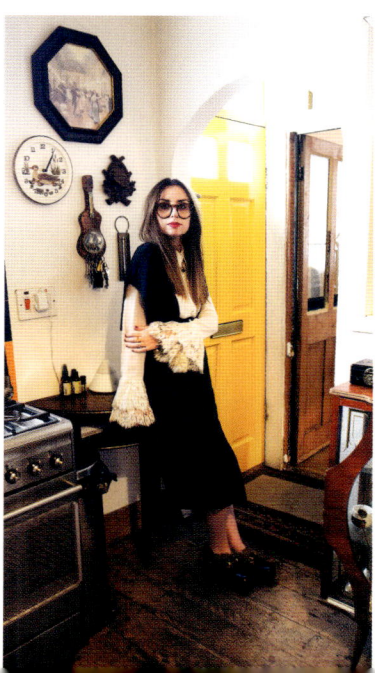

STEVEN ONOJA
ALL THESE DAMN BELLS 'N WHISTLES

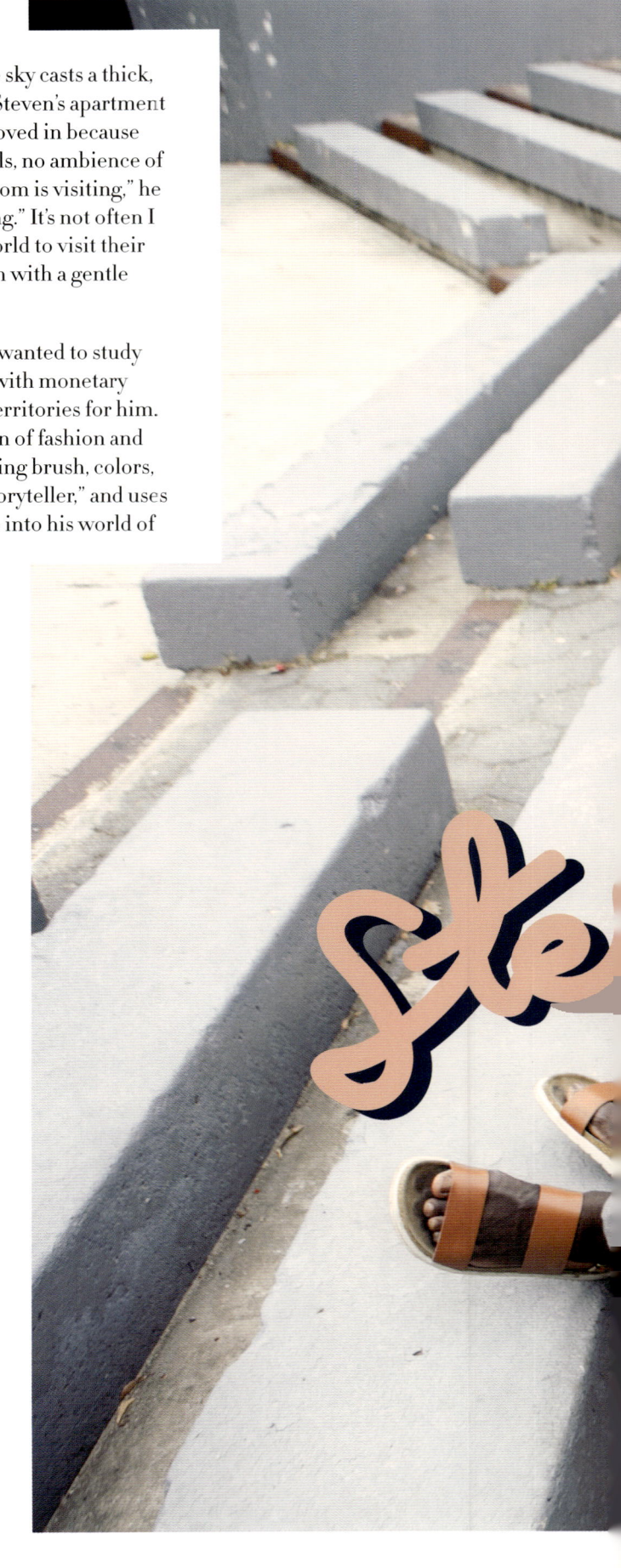

It's 10 a.m. on a Sunday morning in Brooklyn. The sky casts a thick, lackluster gray on the near-empty streets below. Steven's apartment is quiet, almost soundproof. He must have just moved in because there's barely any furniture, no frames on the walls, no ambience of any kind, just a few bottles of Scotch on a side table and shoes on the floor. "My mom is visiting," he motions when it's time to change into his first look. "She's in the bedroom, reading." It's not often I meet the parents, especially not ones that have just flown half-way around the world to visit their only child. Ms. Onoja is in town from Nigeria. She's an attractive, reserved woman with a gentle demeanor, but the sort of eyes that mean business.

Steven left home at 18 to study accounting at Berkeley College. In all fairness, he wanted to study fine and applied art but his family refused. They wanted him to have a "real job" with monetary prospects. But living in New York eventually did open up new and unchartered territories for him. "Style has been a form of art for me now," he says, about discovering the explosion of fashion and menswear. "As an artist, style is a different platform to express myself without using brush, colors, and canvas." He likes to refer to himself as an "Art Director, Consultant, Visual Storyteller," and uses his blog Ostentation and Style to showcase his sartorial pursuits and draw people into his world of vintage suits and berets.

Even more fascinating are the life lessons he generously discloses on his Instagram feed. He dispenses a book deal's worth of mantras on a daily basis. For example: "Sometimes a single step forward is enough for a day. That alone is progress, and any kind of progress is powerful." Or, "Sometimes you have to unlace your shoes and step into someone else's." And, "The concept of Western education is now obsolete to me, fancy degrees hold no weight without innovation." He says he's an old soul, and a far from perfect person, "but it's been such a whirlwind to go from point A to point B. My favorite part about all of this is my ability to connect with others."

Steven is a very private person he says, which must be causing all kinds of conflicting emotions, given that he's so clearly a public persona. He admits he never does interviews and was impressed with himself for answering my questions. And even though he seems grounded and spiritual, there's something tortured about him too. "At 18 I was fearful, almost like a mad man, that I wouldn't know how to get where I wanted to be. But now that I'm doing what I love, I realize it's much more about liking who you are. When you get to where you wanna be, don't settle for anything less. Life is far too short to just be OK—though some days it's all you can be."

He's grateful for the opportunities he's been given, but not entirely content with the way things are run. "It's not because I am rich that I'm in New York," he warns, "it's because I want to show mainstream media how much can be achieved with little. All these damn bells and whistles and for what? Function outlasts fame. Convenience has cost us our ability to connect. It has improved technologies and speed, but slowed our pace of genuine communications. I am here to try and change that. Call it prideful arrogance, bullshit, or whatever, but that's why I'm here. My goal in life is to die a decent man after having lived like one too." Just don't take off the suits while you're doing it. We love them.

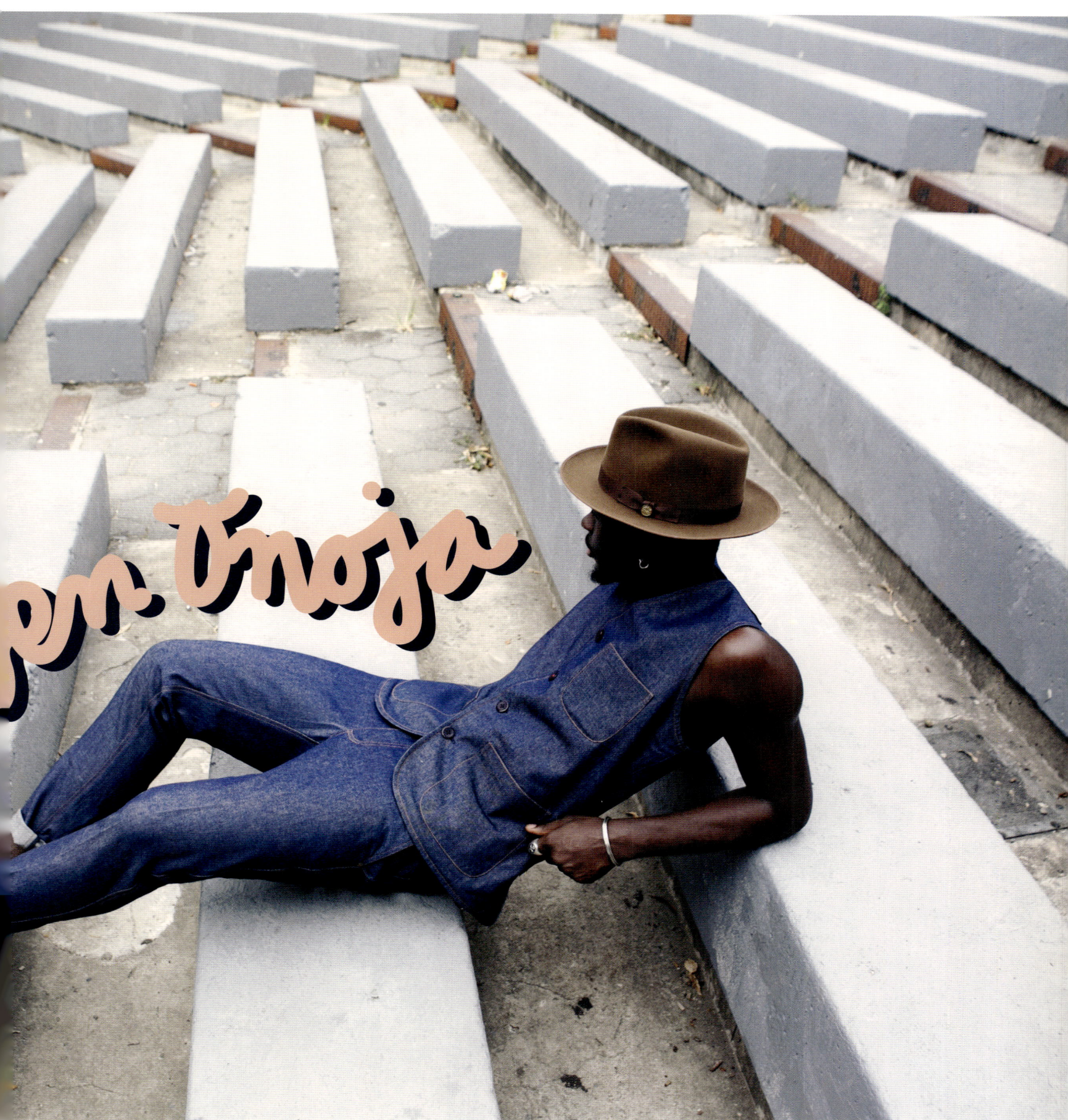

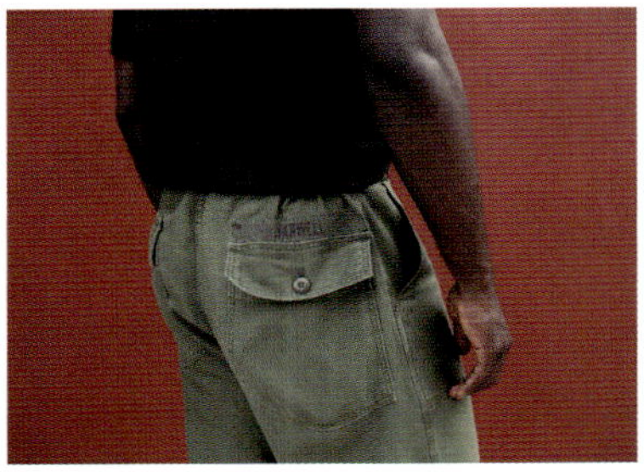

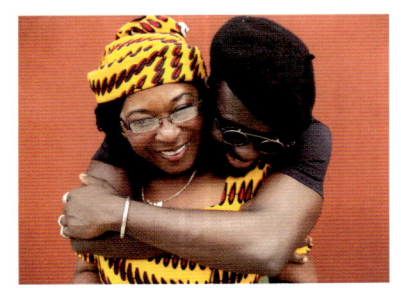
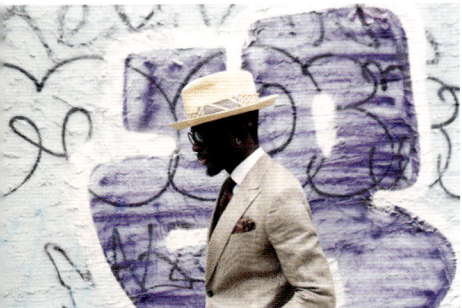
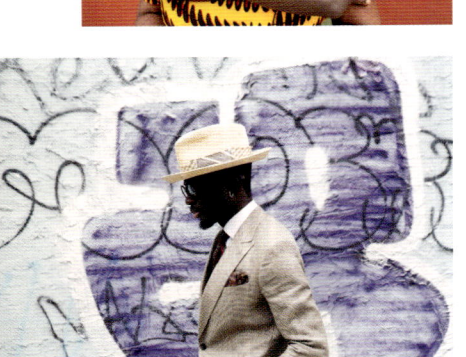
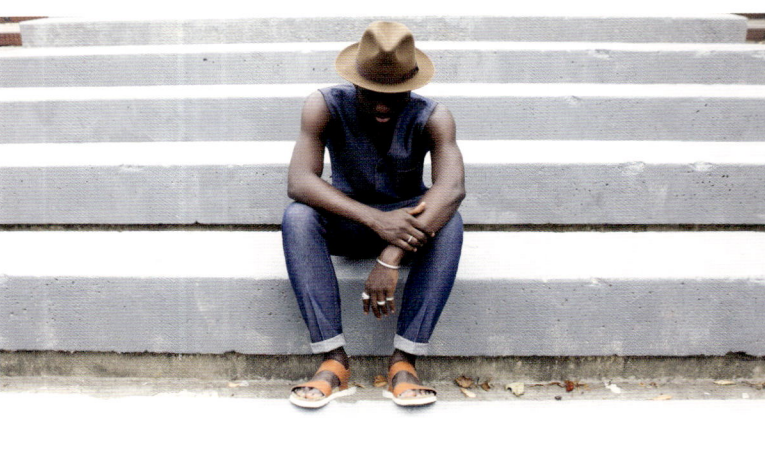
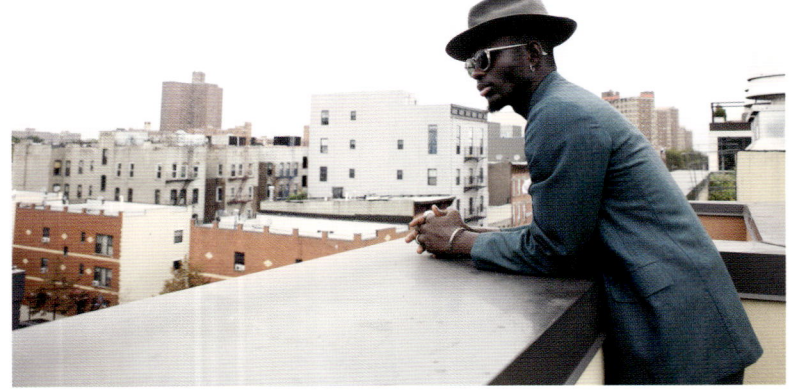
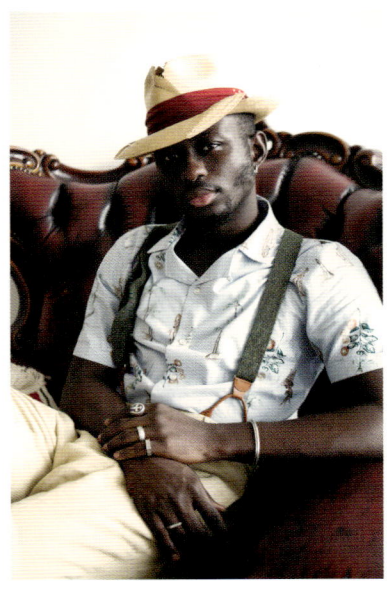
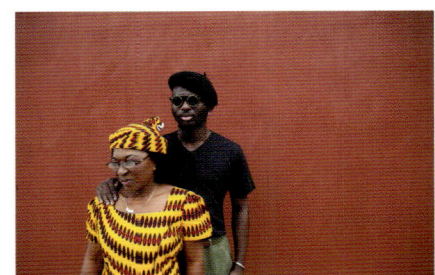

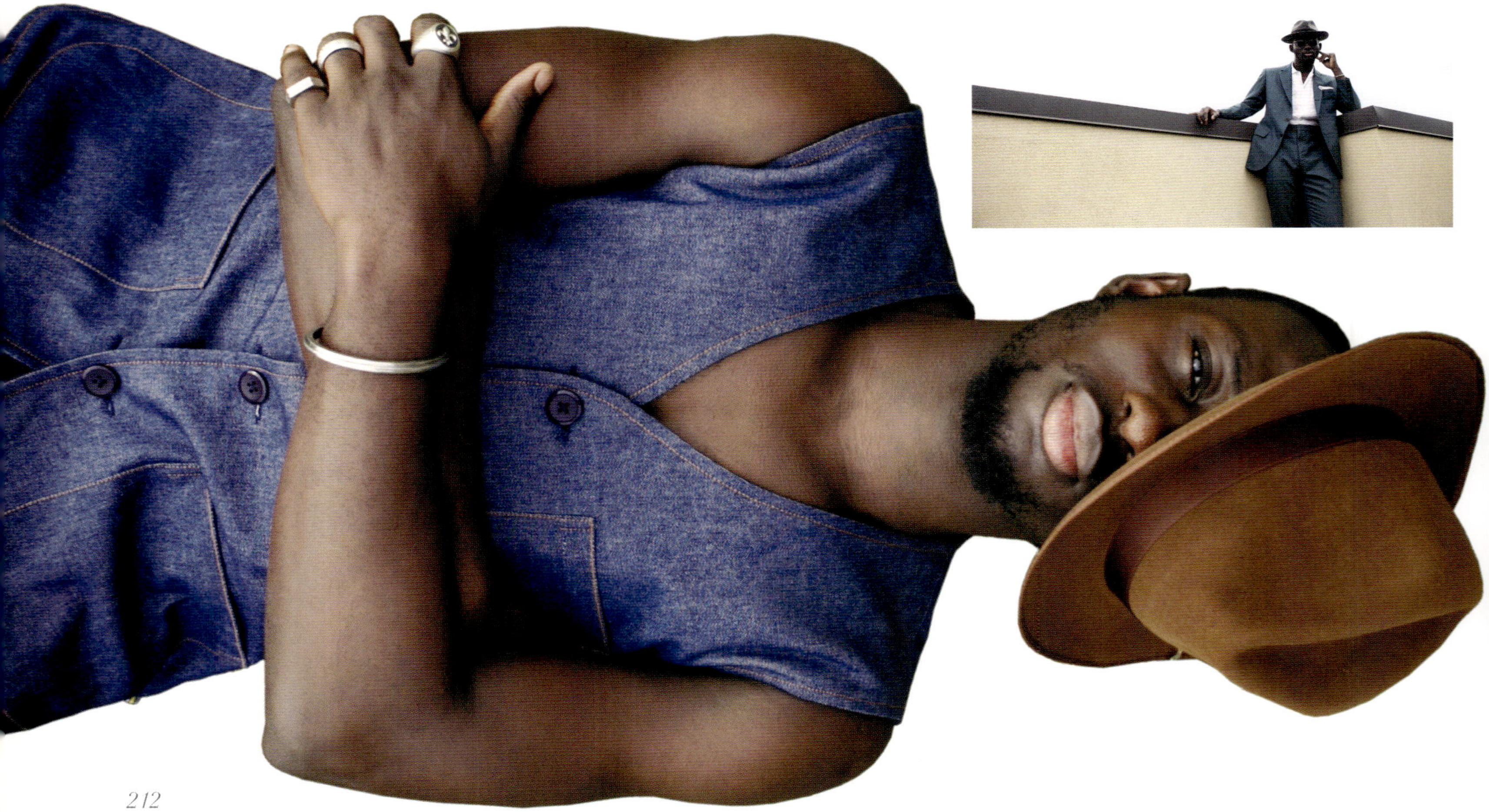

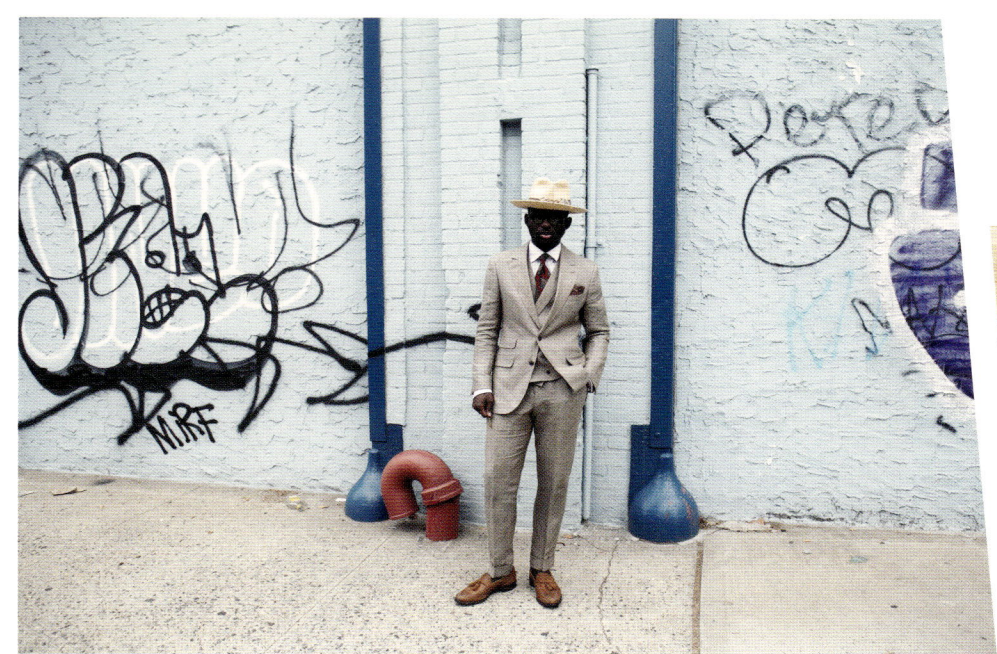
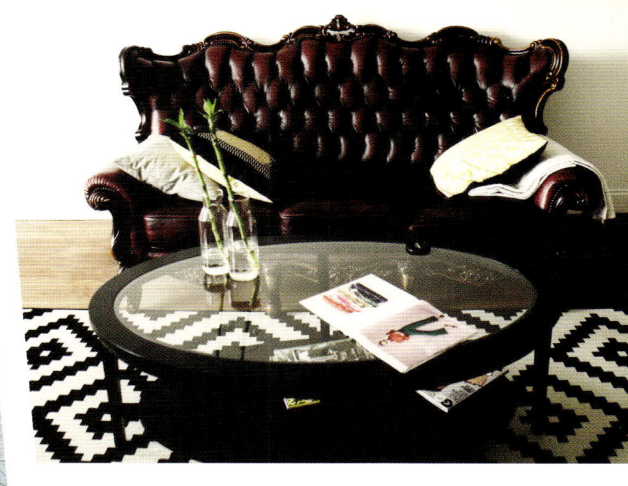
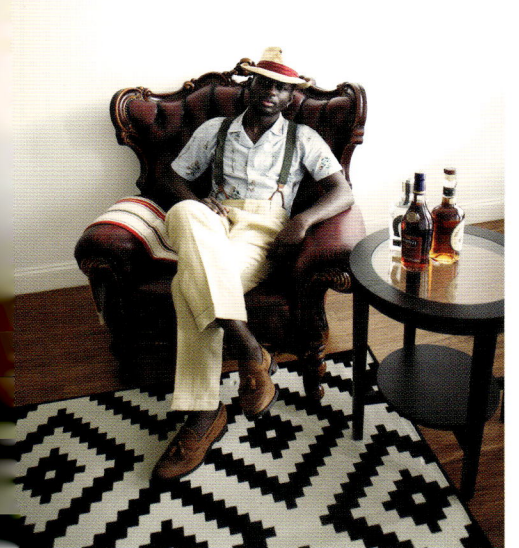
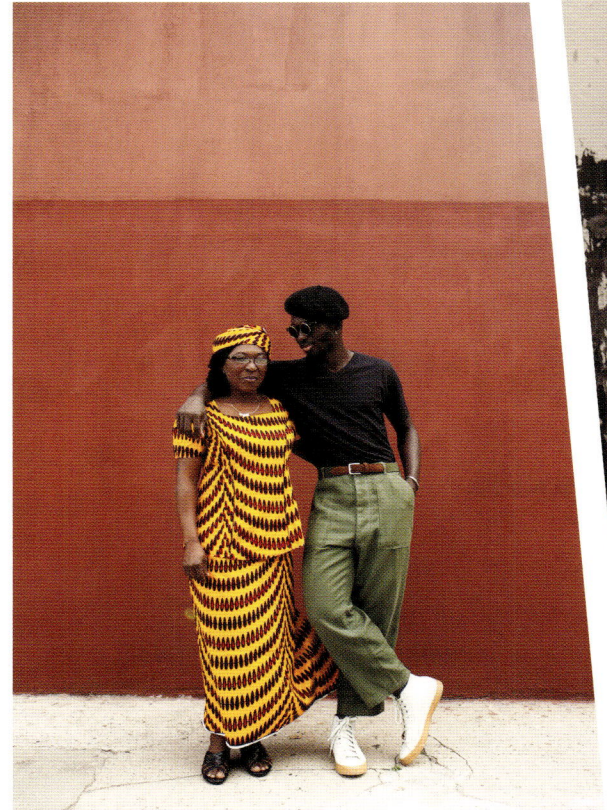
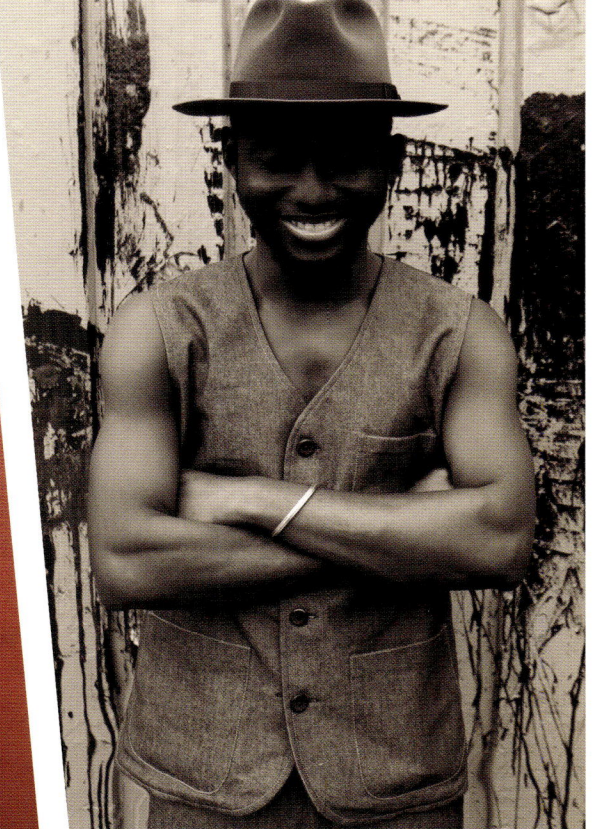
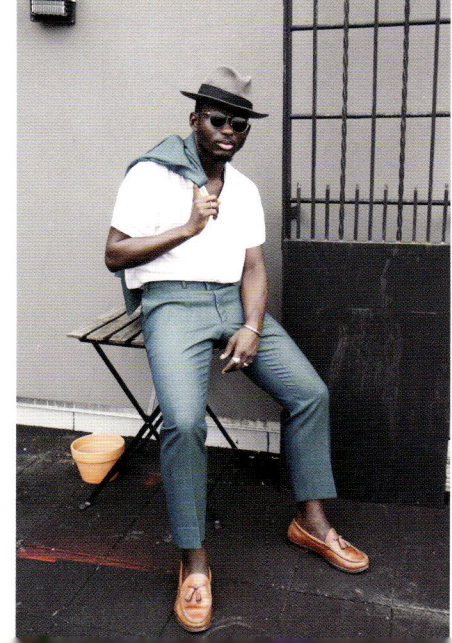
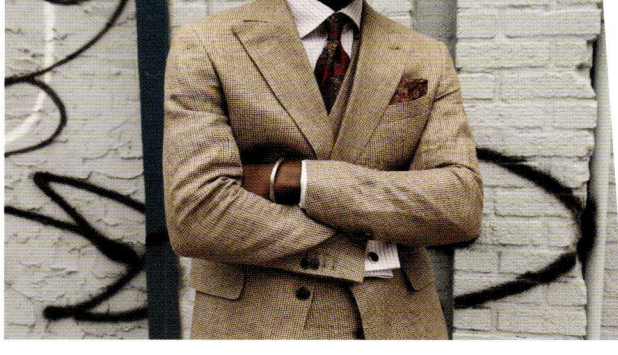
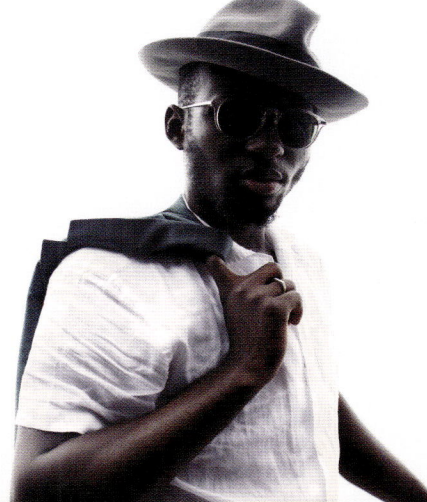

VALY BAX
IT STARTED WITH BARBIE

It's not raining yet, but it probably will. It's the sort of thing you can count on in Belgium, next to getting mayonnaise on your pommes frites without asking. Valy lives in Dilbeek, a municipal town just outside of Brussels, in a white farmhouse that's more than a hundred years old. She has a big, grassy backyard, an unobstructed view of cows in the field across the street, and a gravel driveway that runs to the back of the property, where a 1970 Mini Cooper is parked. It's a slice of real country living in the heart of Flemish Brabant.

It's funny and kind of disorienting to see Valy Bax in this rural, earthy locale. She's the exuberant woman you see backstage at Chanel shows, lining up the models; or at Giovanna Battaglia's wedding, styling the guests; or behind the desk at her vintage store in the Rue des Teinturiers, designing displays. She's always stood out in Belgium because she is different and unafraid. Her personal style was never dictated by trends or the ways of the land. "I dress differently from Belgians," she says. "I have my own style that I created, throughout the years, by mixing different influences. It's eclectic, accessible, timeless, and always with elegance. Style and elegance are something you create on your own."

And to think it all started with a Barbie. "I was six years old," she remembers. "She represented modernity, very stereotyped, and I identified with her as she was blonde like me. She was the first 'adult' doll, and the perfect woman. It was a big change for me. Barbie was a doll representing a woman. She was not like the dolls I had when I was younger." And dressing her was a creative outlet. She made garments out of every piece of leftover fabric she could find. Had her parents not refused, Valy would have studied Fashion Design at the Royal Academy of Fine Arts in Antwerp. (Just like me actually.) Alas, being a "designer" was not considered a real job in Belgium at the time. She studied tourism instead, and says sarcastically she "played tourist" her whole life.

Valy spent most of her student years at Mirano, Brussels' most illustrious nightclub, and eventually worked there as a "barmaid" and dancer. (The owner of the place was Etienne Russo, now the man behind Villa Eugenie, one of the world's biggest fashion and event production companies, who still employs Valy.) On weekends she hung out with the cream of the creative crop: models, designers, actors, musicians, and during the week she started doing street castings and booking models.

In 1997 she opened a vintage store with her best friend Ramon. "I've loved vintage since I was a kid," she says. "The first spark came from the movie *Breakfast at Tiffany's*, which I saw in the 80s. Audrey Hepburn wearing Givenchy, the symbol of elegance and beauty. She had a big influence in fashion, and she inspired me." She sources her pieces mainly in Belgium. "I look for *nobles matières* and as far as fit is concerned, it's mainly a *coup de coeur*. I like to find exceptional pieces with a soul and a story. I'm very attracted to fabrics that have had several lives and have been worn by several people for decades."

Her nine-year-old son Louen is home from school this week. He's watching cartoons upstairs, and comes down now and again to ask a question or grab one of the croissants on the kitchen table. Valy also has a teenage daughter. Valy's husband Mamadou, is at work—he's a chef. "Oh, I think I have something that will suit you," she jumps up. "You know, Natalie, I am not an XS anymore, so I think you should have it." She pulls a cream colored Courrèges skirt-suit from the dense rack of vintage in her bedroom and asks me to try it on. "Are you sure you don't want to sell it?" I ask incredulously. "Nah, I'd rather give it to someone who will look good in it." In the car on the way to her store, we remember the good old days, when life was fun and full of change, but she promises, "I will forever feel the need to learn, discover, and invest. I find balance in my family life with my wonderful children." But the party's over.

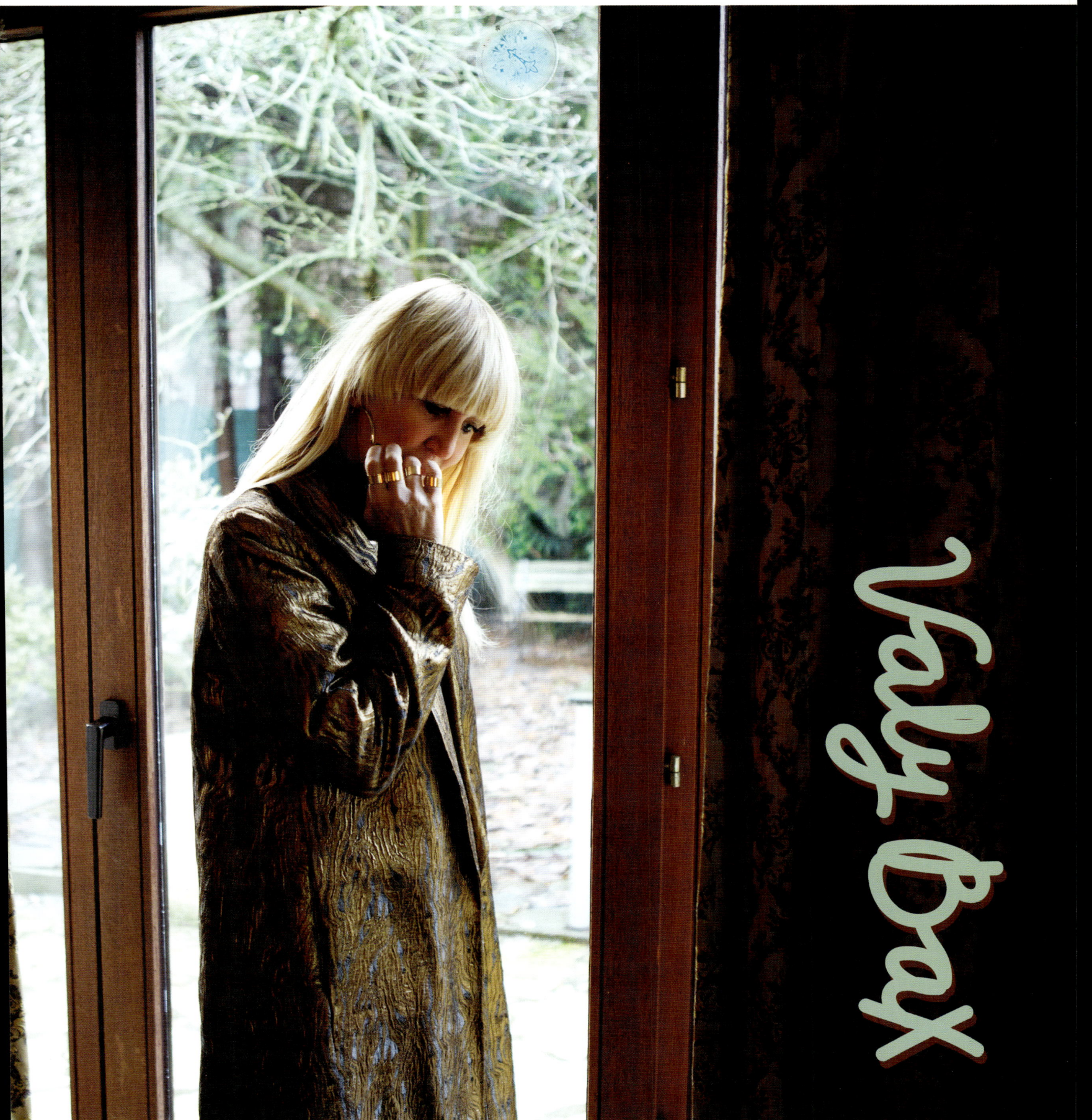

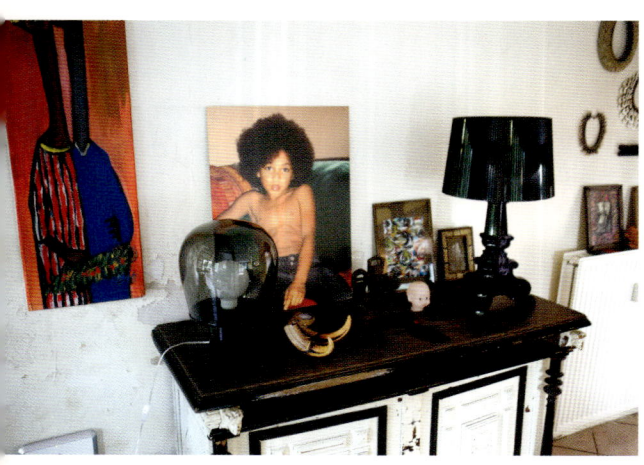
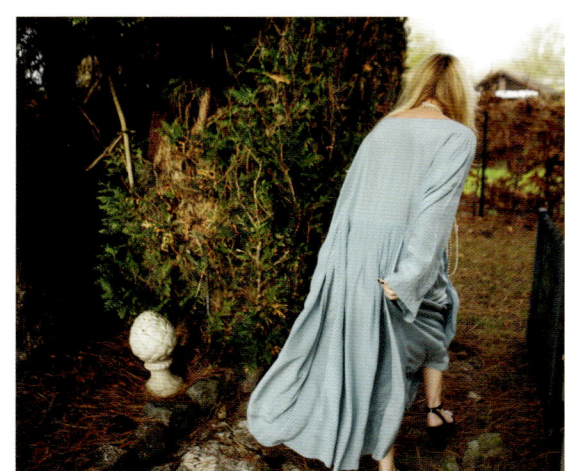
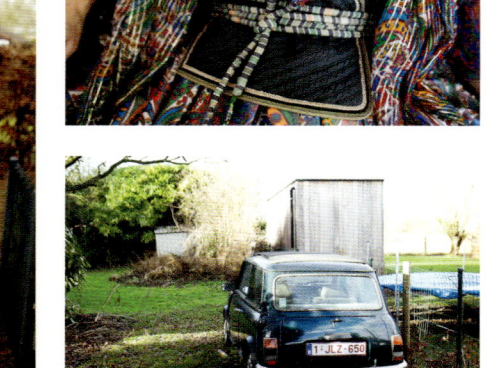
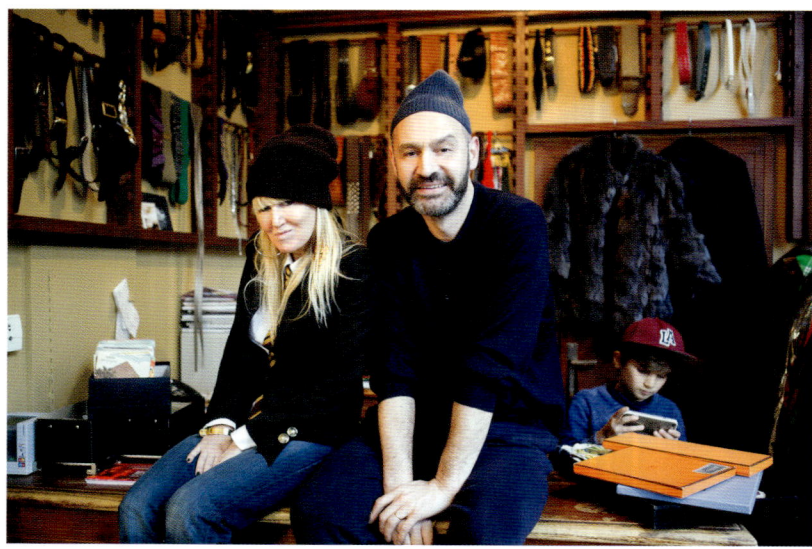
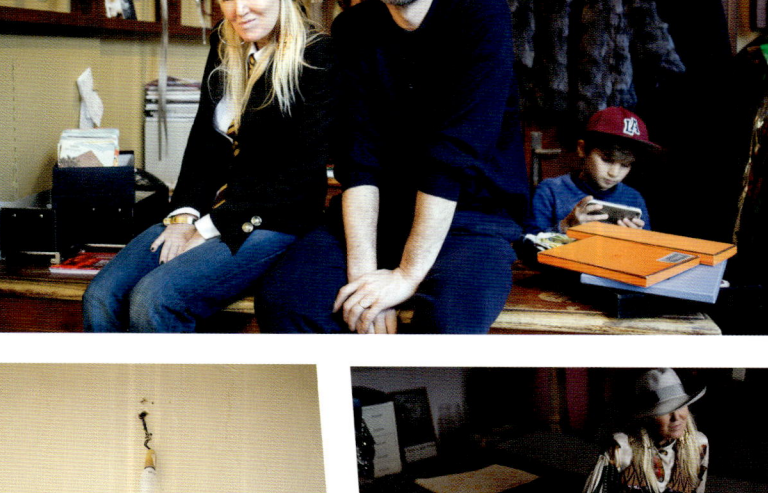
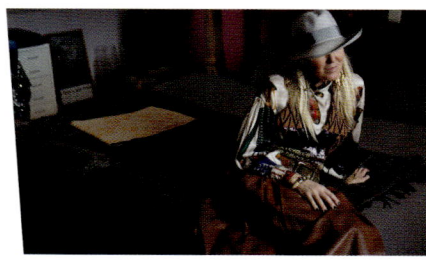
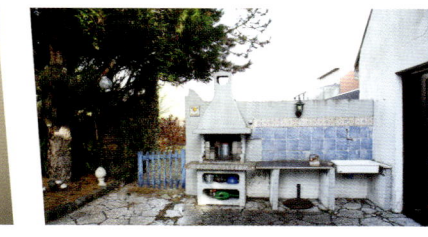
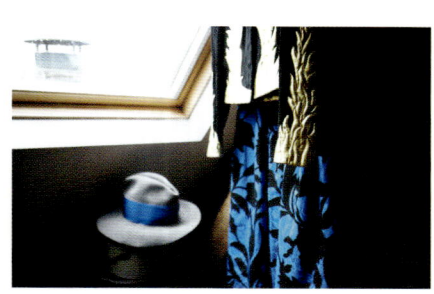
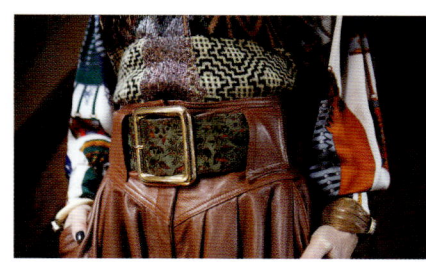
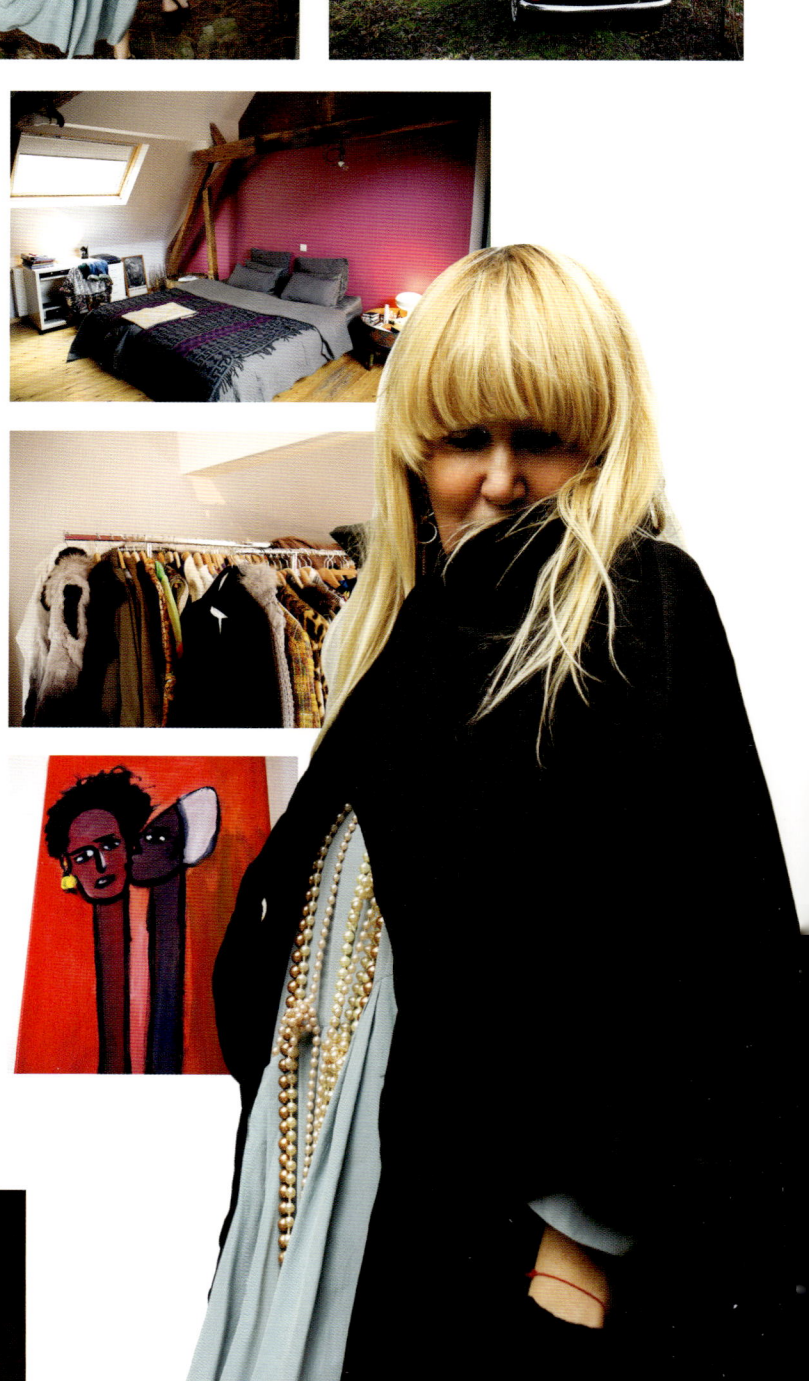

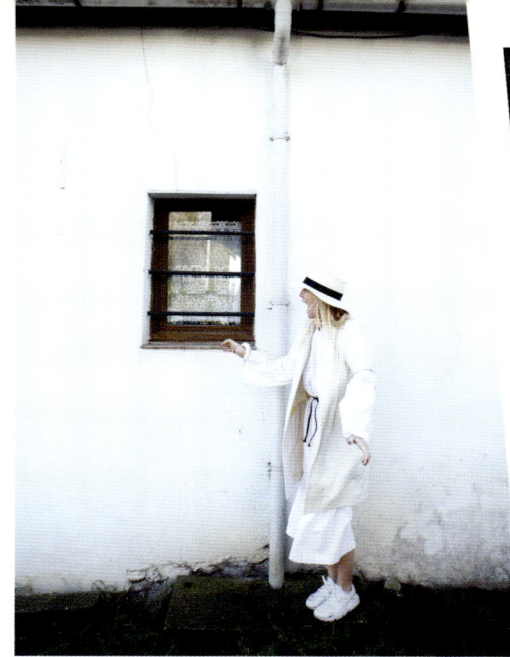
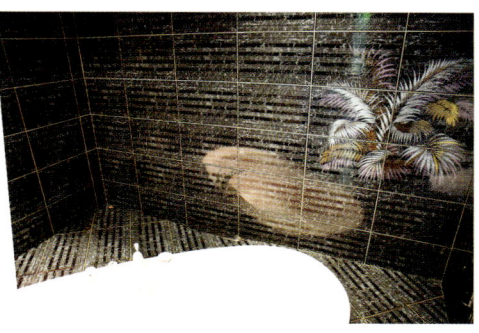
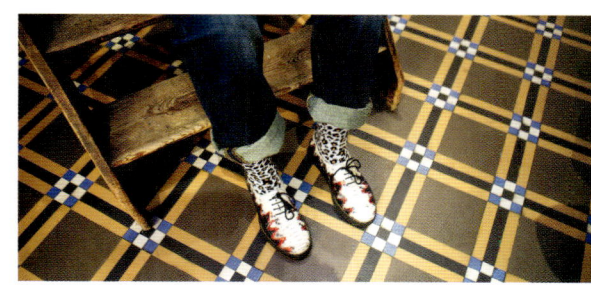
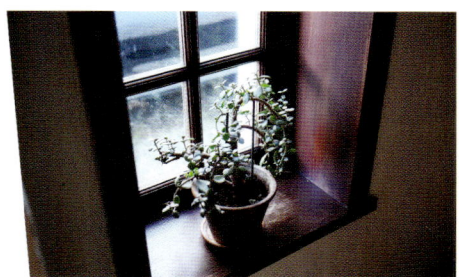
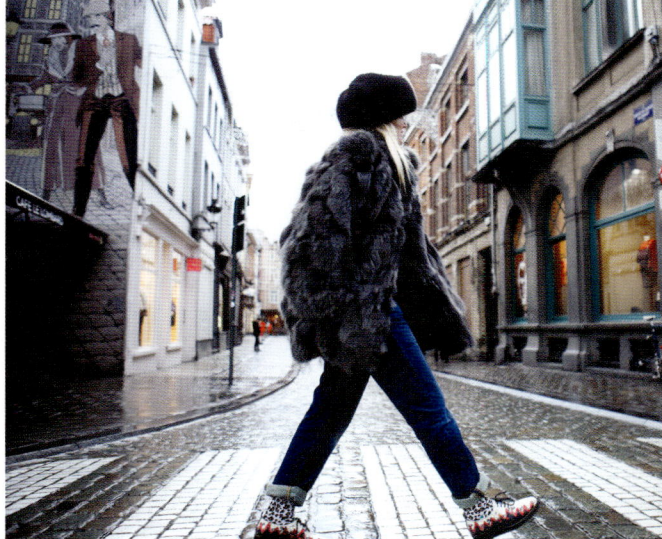
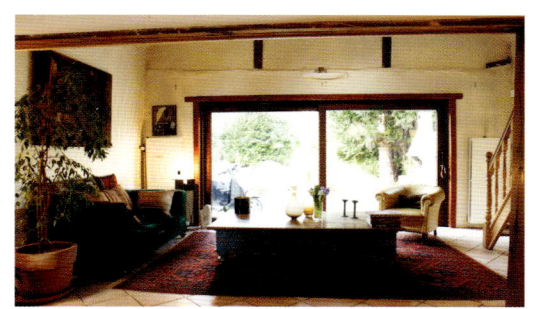
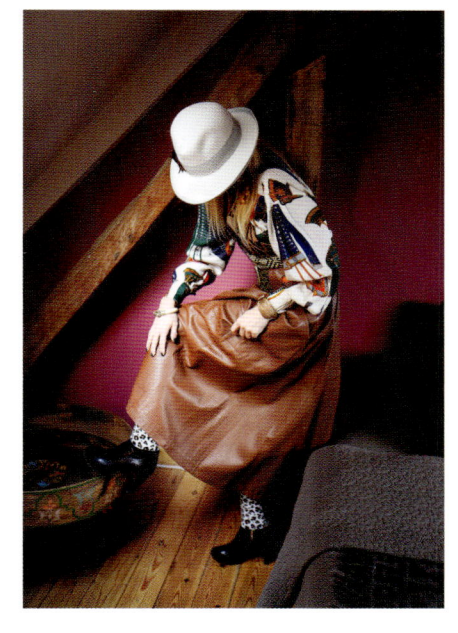
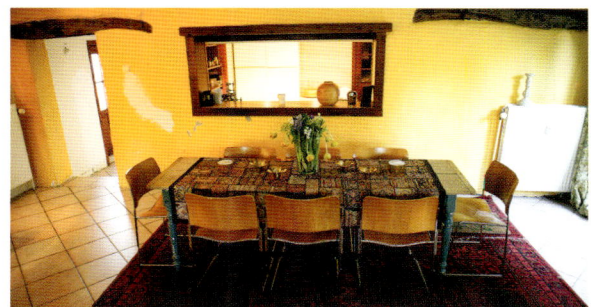
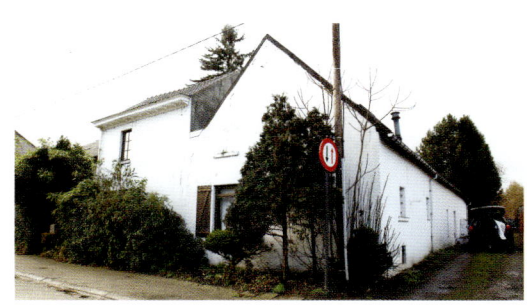
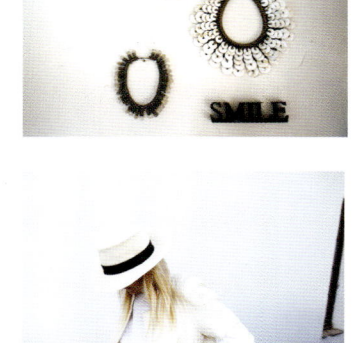
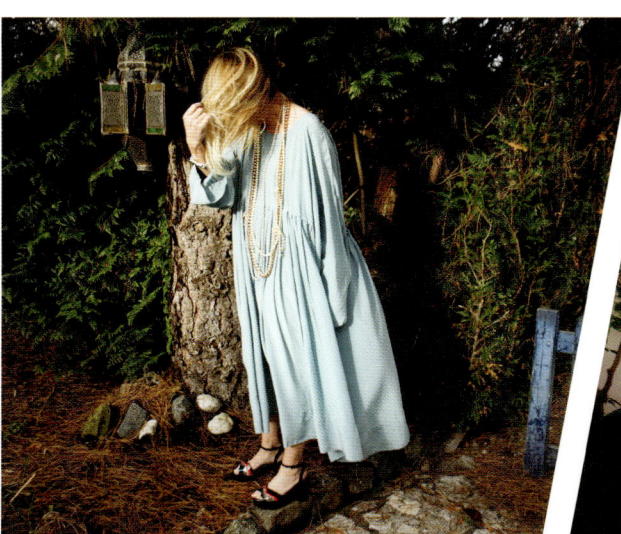
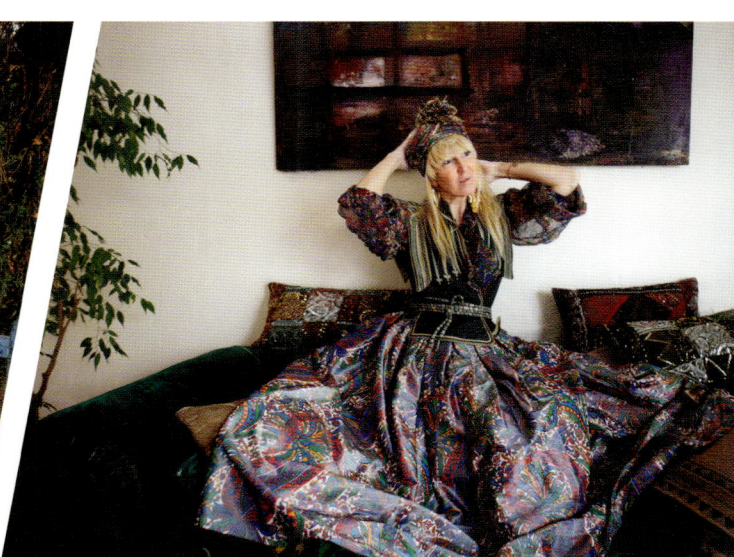

DESANKA FASISKA
I LOVED BRIDES

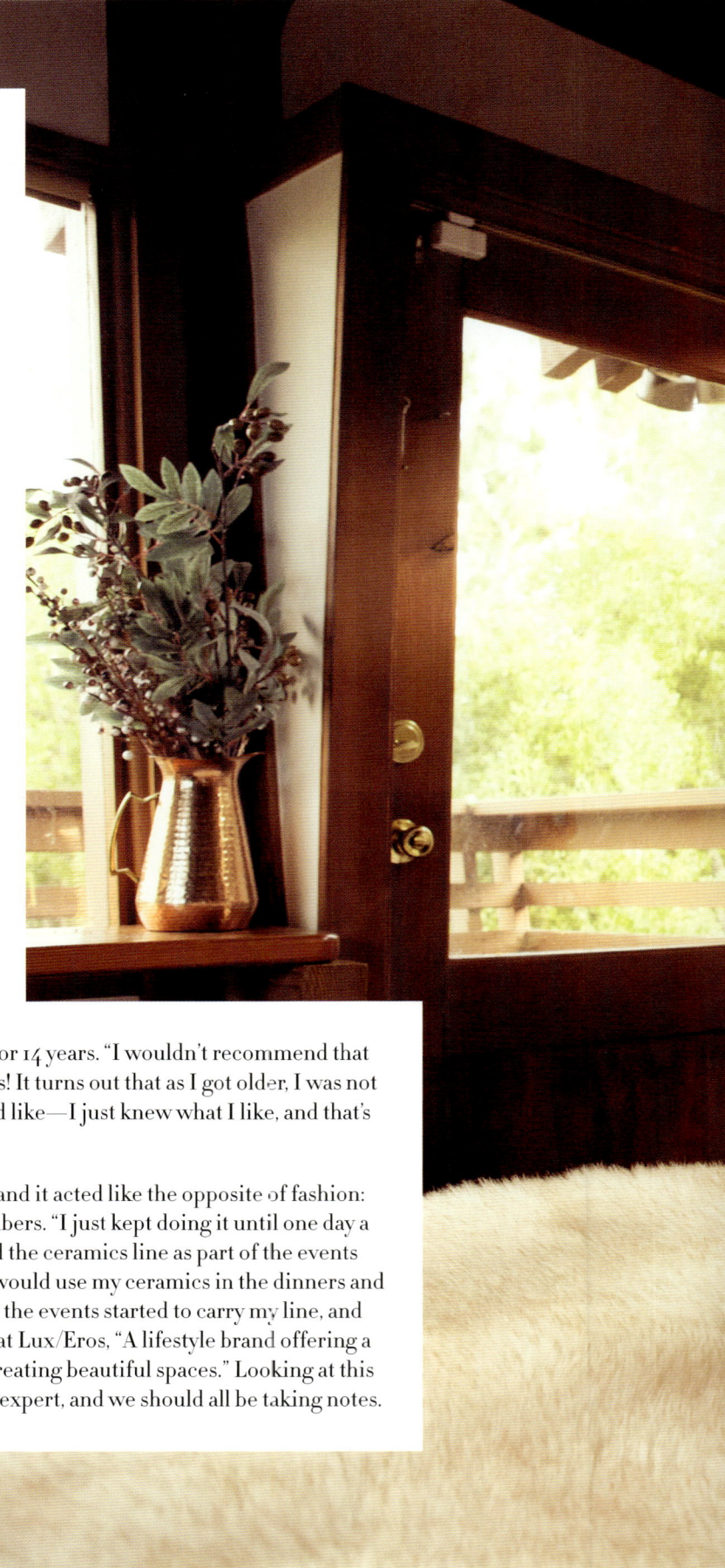

There was something about the A-frame she couldn't resist. She was drawn to it like a moth to a flame. It was a powerful attraction, and it wasn't aesthetic. It was purely nostalgic, undeniably channeling her childhood. The shape of the house transported her to the long summer days she spent with her family by the lake in West Virginia, and the cabin her father had built that looked just like it—unforgettable summers filled with bonfires and water skiing. So she bought the house in Hollywood Hills and fixed it up. She modernized it without rattling its original charm. And it became the home for new memories with her own family.

Desanka Fasiska—everyone calls her Desa—was adopted at birth in Pittsburgh, Pennsylvania. Her adoptive dad was a mad-scientist and her mom a lawyer. After their divorce, she moved to California with her mom at three years old. She was a confident child and pretty independent. She loved to try new things and got bored quickly; she blames ADHD. She always knew she wanted to become a fashion designer. She was obsessed with brides and bridal dresses. "I used to draw and design brides and wedding dresses," she laughs. "When we were on vacation and there was a wedding happening at the hotel, I used to make my mom take me over to the bride so I could meet her! Only a little girl could get away with that kind of stalking!"

Ironically Desa was not the marrying type herself. At the time of our shoot she didn't have a baby yet; she wasn't even pregnant. She was just sipping wine, freewheeling around the house, and like any other single LA gal, conjuring up her next date and party. But now she has Rocky with her live-in boyfriend and, besides politics, he is all she dedicates her time to. Not even clothes or vintage play a big role anymore, even though fashion was her life for 14 years. "I wouldn't recommend that job to my worst enemy!" she cries. "It's not as glamorous as it seems! It turns out that as I got older, I was not very fond of chasing trends and knowing what other people should like—I just knew what I like, and that's not always in fashion."

It was only by chance that she discovered her new creative outlet, and it acted like the opposite of fashion: pottery. "It was dirty, non-technical, and it felt freeing," she remembers. "I just kept doing it until one day a collection seemed to emerge from my tinkering, and so I launched the ceramics line as part of the events and creative community project I was running out of my home. I would use my ceramics in the dinners and workshops I hosted, and then people that had stores who attended the events started to carry my line, and eventually I put all the focus on my ceramics." Her work is on sale at Lux/Eros, "A lifestyle brand offering a fully immersive experience in California Living, with a focus on creating beautiful spaces." Looking at this amazing house, and that motivating A-frame, Desa's definitely the expert, and we should all be taking notes.

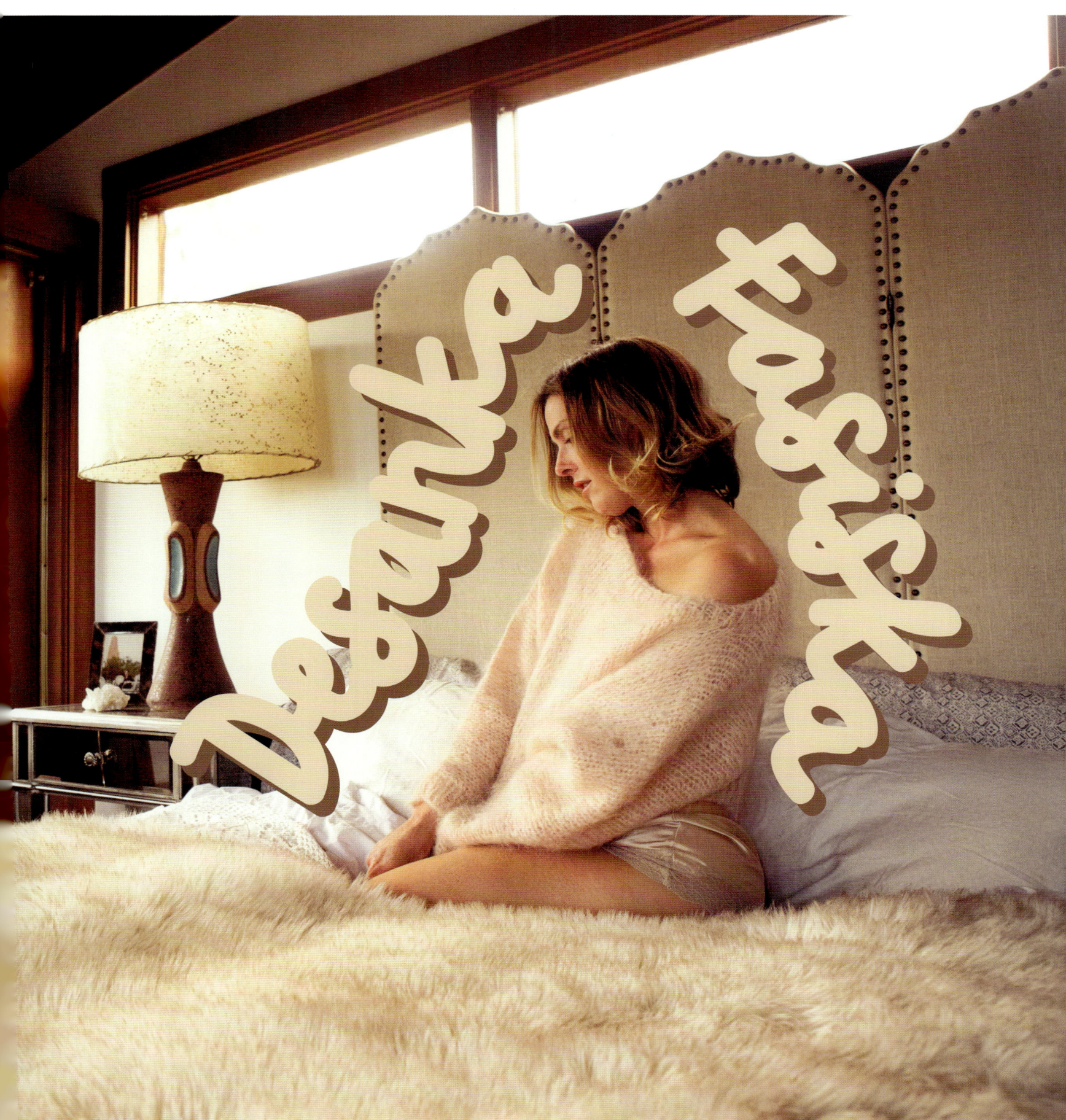

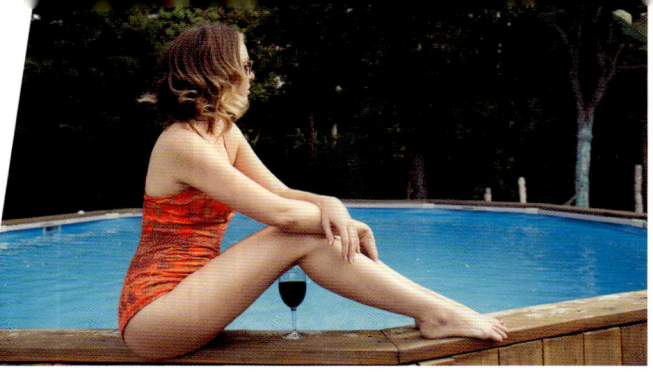
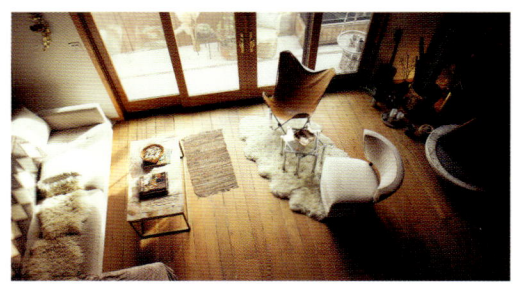
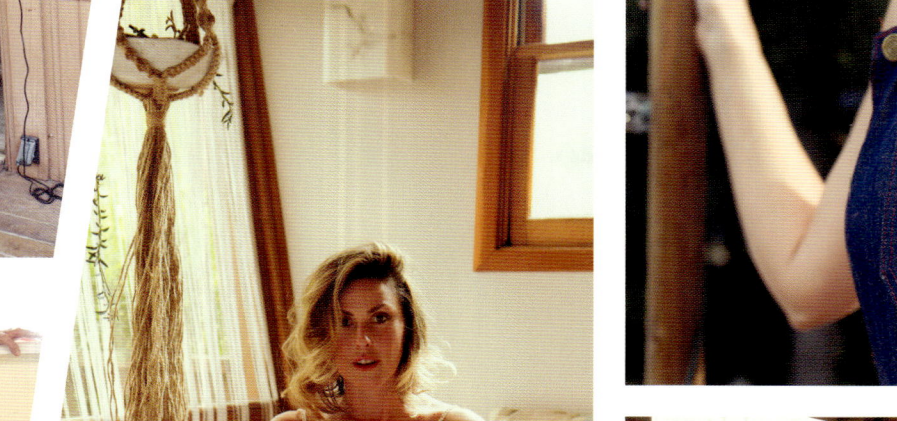
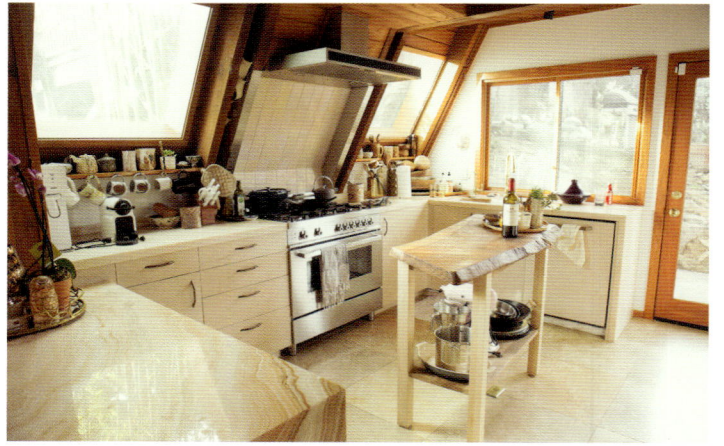
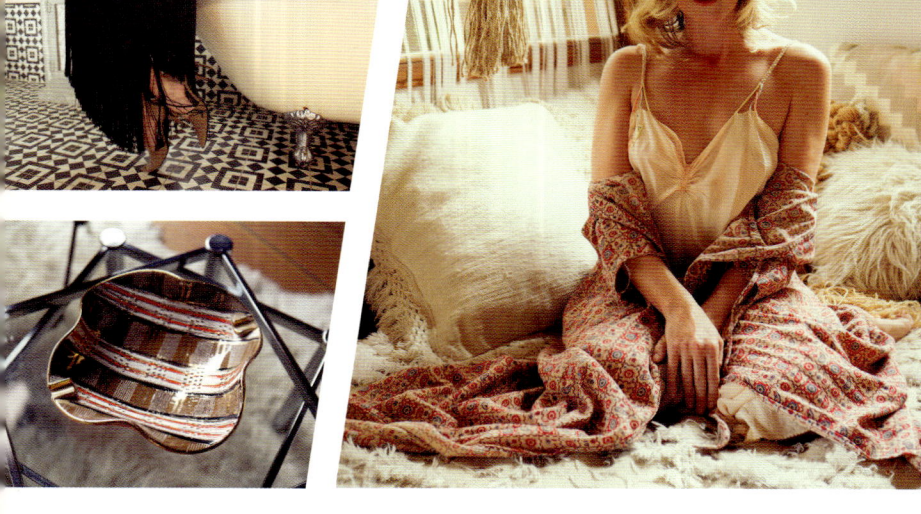
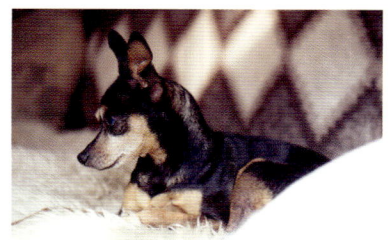
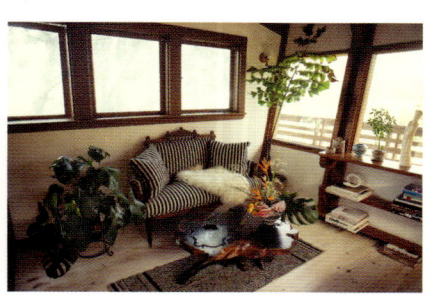
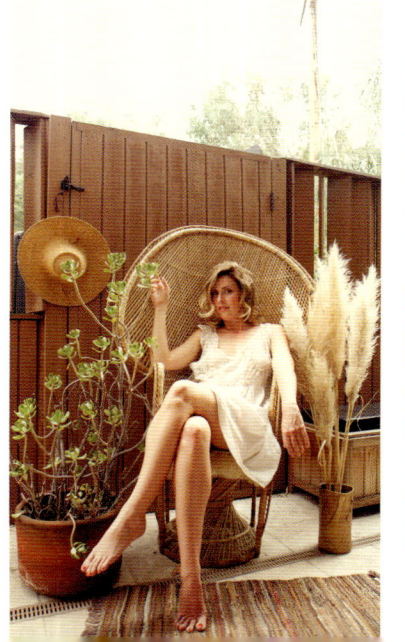
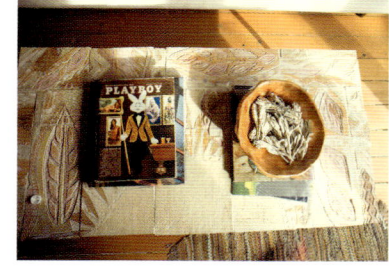
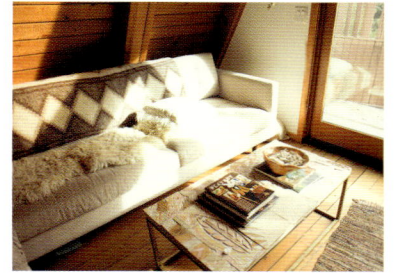
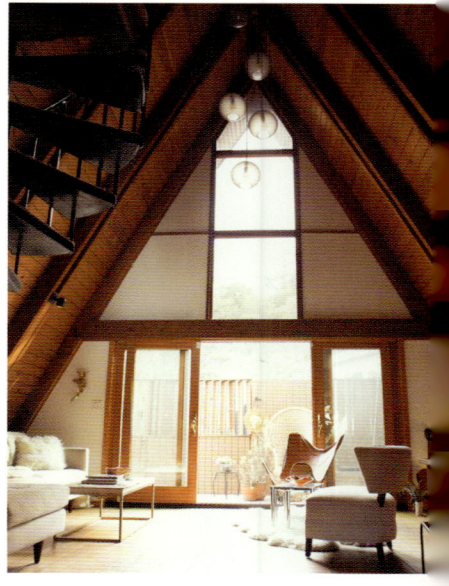

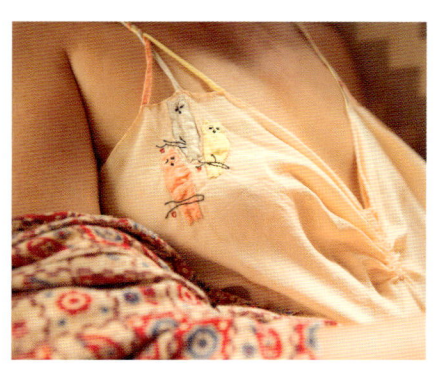
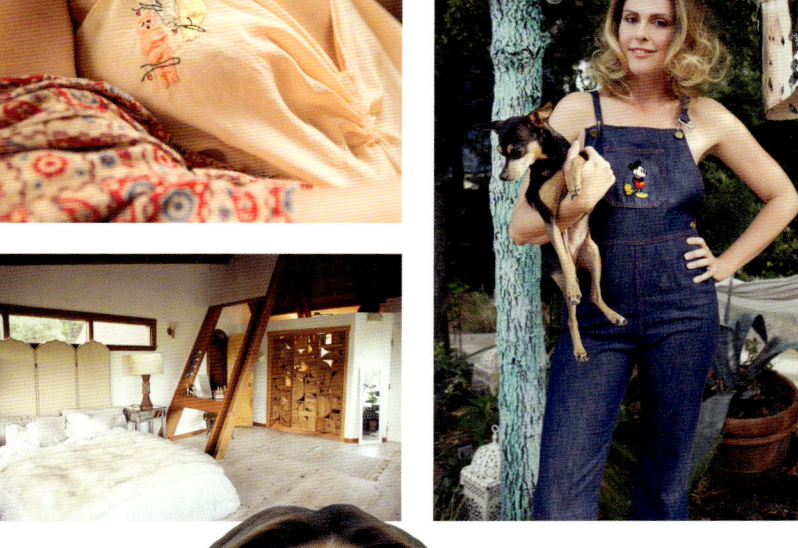
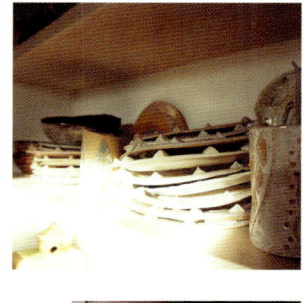
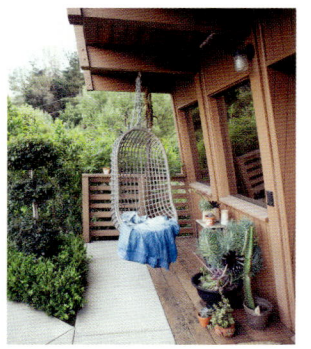
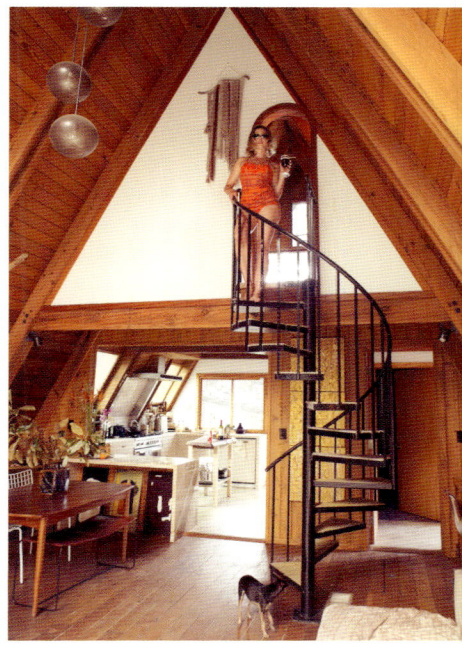
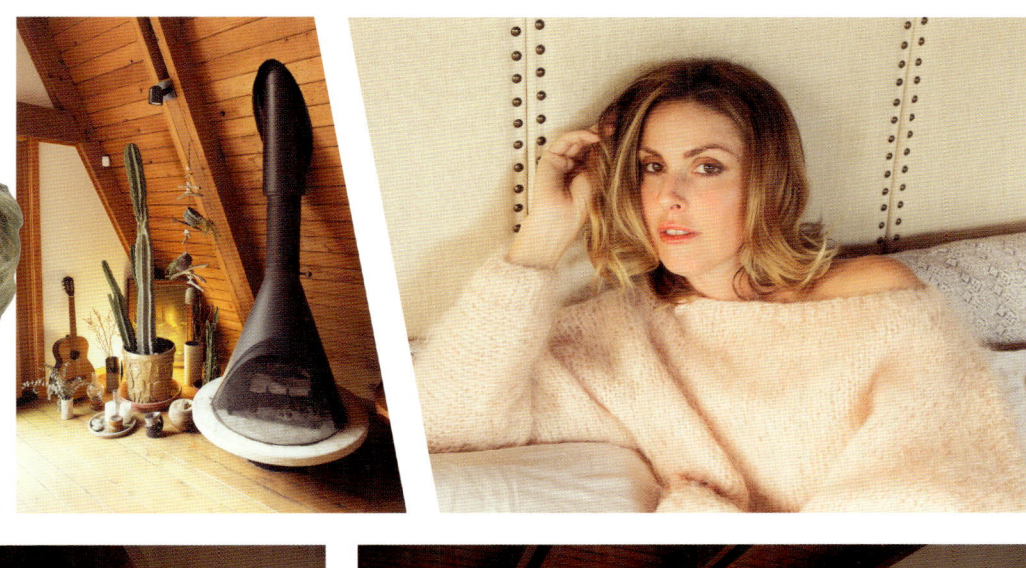
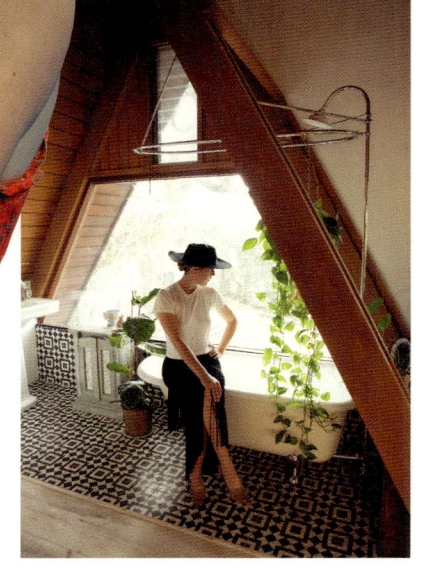
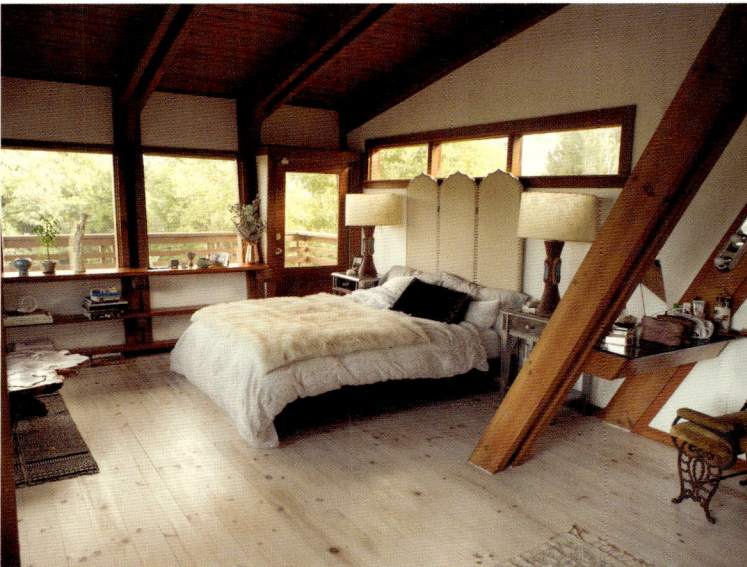

ZOË BLEU SIDEL
BECOMING A TOOTH FAIRY

There was that one year Zoë Bleu only wore Barbie bridal dresses. Her parents were going through a divorce, and she guesses it was her way of coping with the trauma. She shows me a picture frame in the living room of herself at four years old, reclining in a leather couch, barefoot, in a white poufy satin dress and veil. "Usually I had a do-rag under my crown!" she laughs. Zoë Blue was the only girl in school who was obliged to wear a uniform, because the other parents started complaining about her outlandish outfits. "I wore ruby slippers every day," she explains, "and then all the kids wanted ruby slippers and that upset the parents. I don't know why, because I think every kid should have a pair of ruby slippers, right?" They forced her in a pair of Sketchers and shorts with a T-shirt—"It was the worst thing ever." There's a video of Zoë Bleu crying in her closet, stomping the light-up sneakers, screaming: "I feel ugly! I want to be a princess today!"

It set a harrowing precedent, because Zoë Bleu Sidel would never, and will never, walk the line of conventional adornment. She's always searching, exploring, hunting, twisting, and turning, never resistant to change. She's safe to play in Los Angeles, and in London, her new home. She never gets shit from anyone; not because she's the daughter of a famous actress, but because she has the confidence and peer support to be herself. That was drastically different when she left home to attend Sarah Lawrence College in Bronxville, New York, a few years ago. It was her dream school, but she had to drop out. "I felt isolated," she says regretfully. "I know I'm a very eccentric person and I thought a school like Sarah Lawrence would embrace that. But people did not have a good reaction to me at all. They were looking at me like: "Where are you going? A carnival?" For the first time in my life I felt ashamed and uncomfortable. I felt like I couldn't have friends. So I bought a pair of jeans and tennis shoes and a T-shirt. I never owned a pair of jeans before! And then people hung out with me."

The look she's feeling today is Little-Bo-Peep-meets-Gypsy-fortune-teller. She's concocting elaborately layered, dramatically studied vintage costumes that give her the allure of a romanticized Cassiopeia. "I love to layer things that don't make much sense together," she states. "It's like throwing a dinner party for a bunch of people you like, who you really want to get along." She mixes all the eras, but still feels very connected to her first pieces. "My mother collected Victorian tea dresses and 1920s flapper dresses," she says. "She passed these down to me around the age of 12 and it was all over from there." She loves the "fragility" of vintage. She's increasingly drawn to pieces that took the most care to make. "Everything was made by hand and therefore super painstaking," she fawns. "These old garments are precious because they were precious to whomever made them! I understand and appreciate the time it takes to create something so special. It makes me feel special to find these treasures and wear them."

In the kitchen Zoë Bleu notices how tan her mom looks. It's unusual because Rosanna Arquette never goes in the sun without a hat. She just returned from an anniversary trip to Tahiti with her husband and a few friends. "I know," she retorts, "but I was covered up. It went right through my clothes!" We discuss how Zoë Bleu inspired John Galliano when she posted a picture of the long, red-haired tabby shoes she made. And how she developed a painful crush on Leonardo DiCaprio, who was vacationing on the island. And the trip the family is taking to Israel this summer. "I have beautiful photos of my mama pregnant with me floating in the Dead Sea. It will be nice to be there with her again," she says. Zoë Bleu is also trying to find funding for a clothing line, and will be starring in a period movie. She calls herself "an actress, a stylist, a collector of *stuff*, and a beginner beekeeper." She's also still working on becoming a tooth fairy, something she badly wanted to achieve as a child. If ever there was such a fairy, she *should* look like Zoë Bleu, and perhaps she'd leave the girls ruby slippers instead.

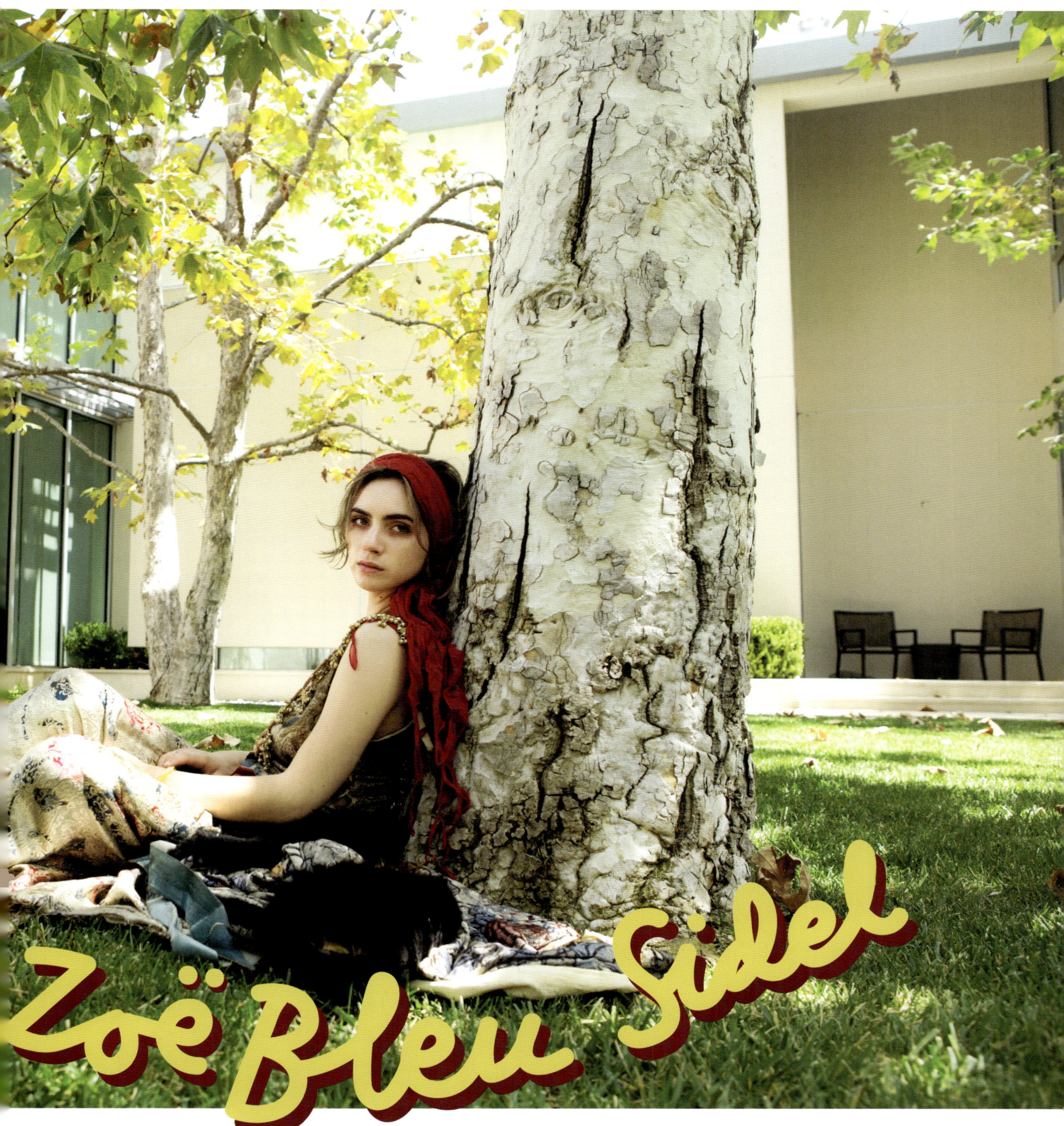

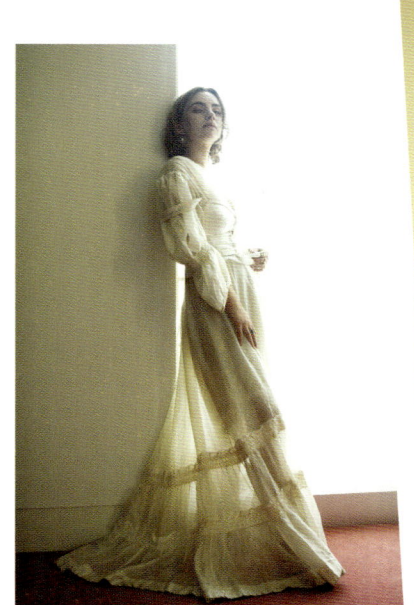
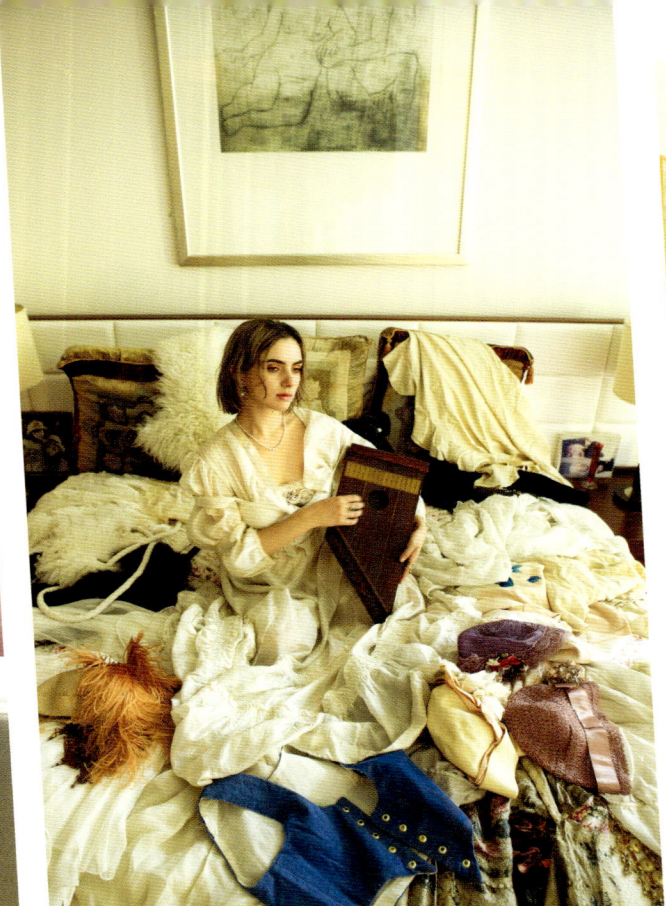
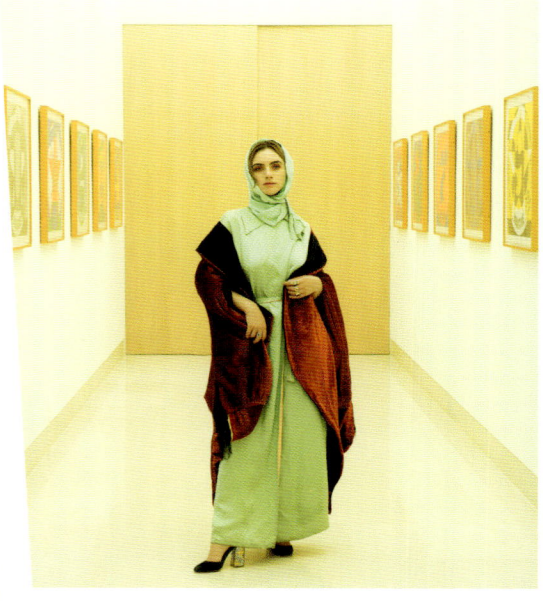
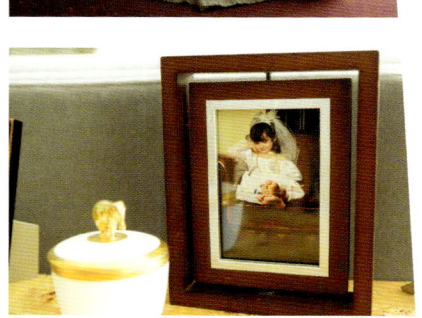
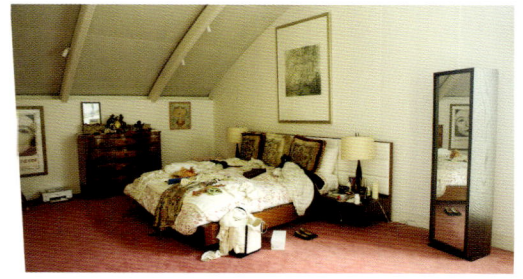
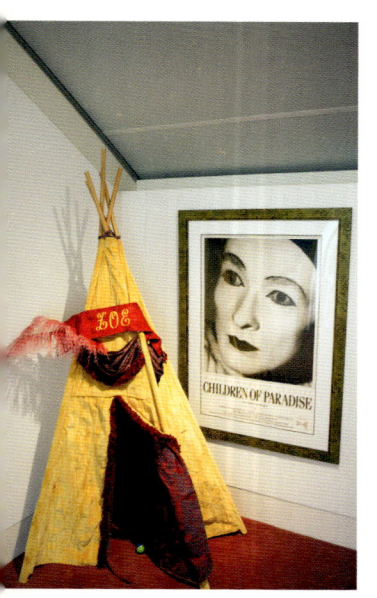
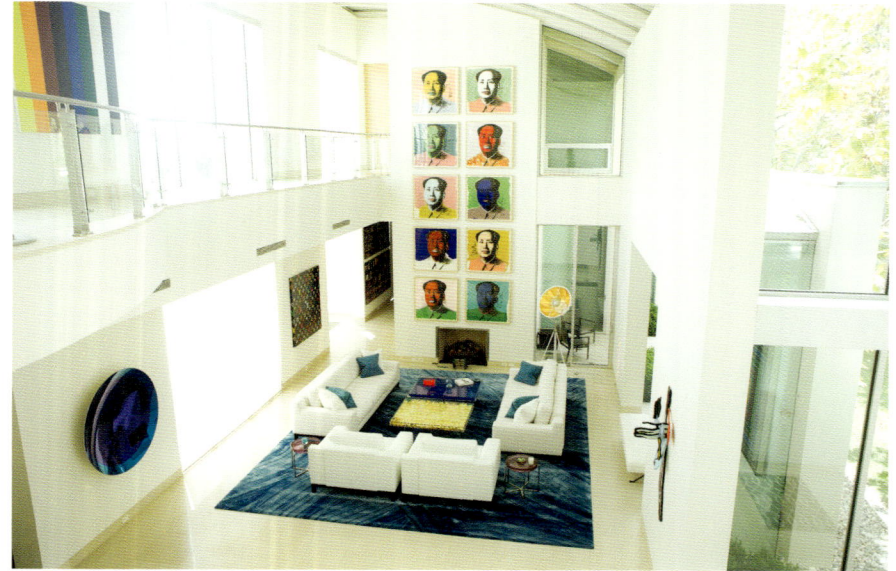
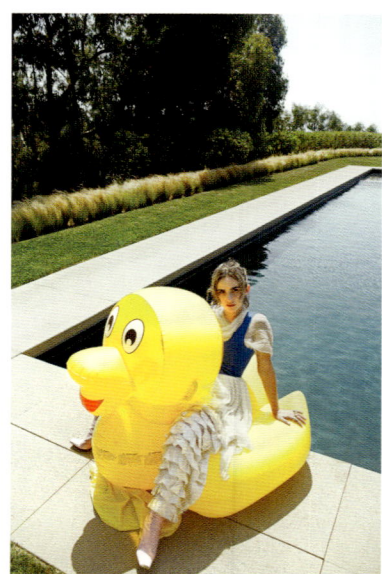
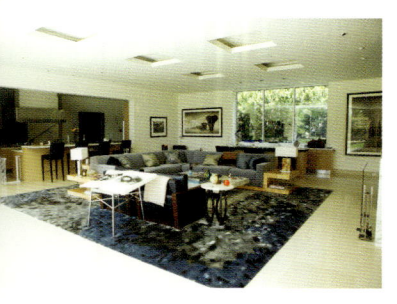
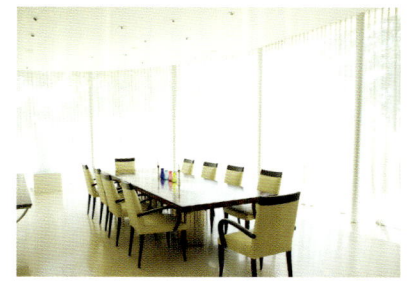
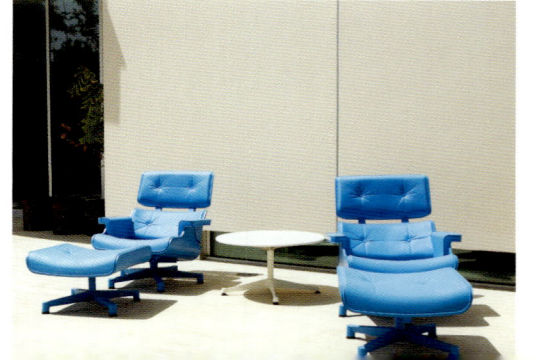
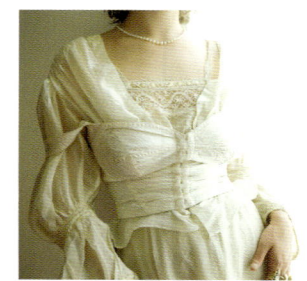

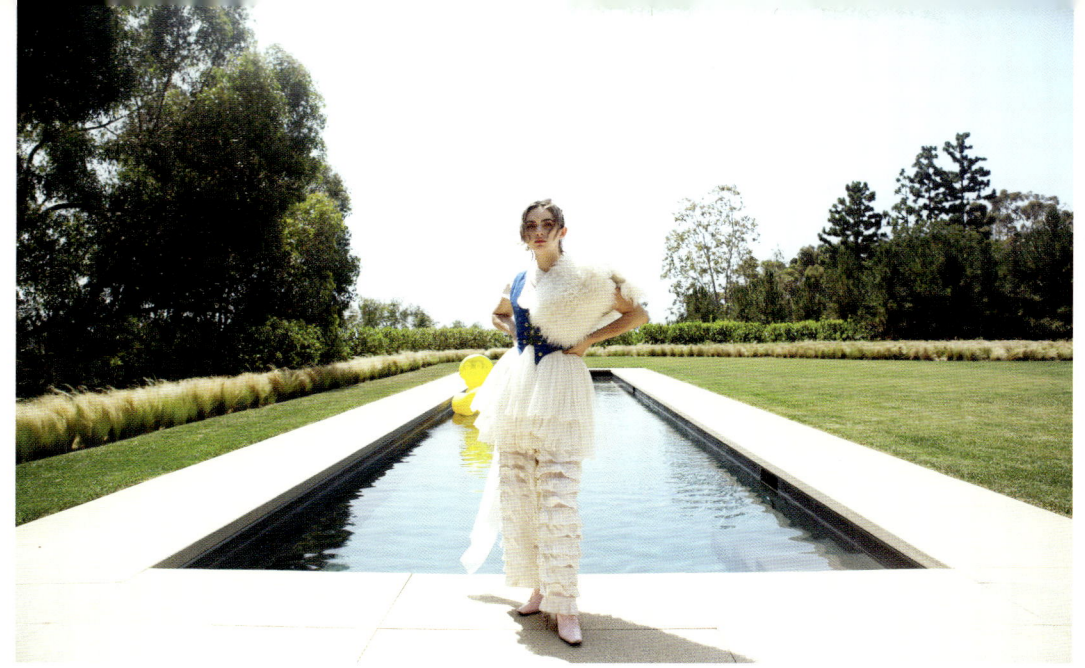
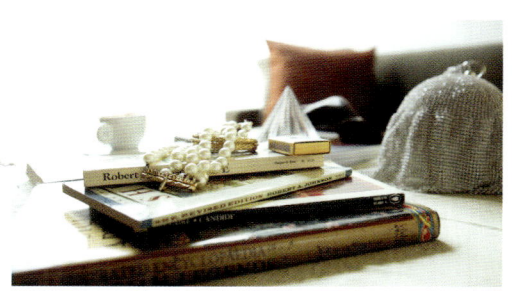
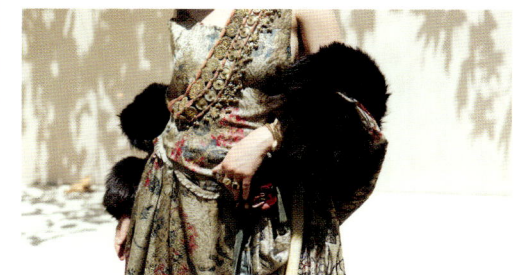
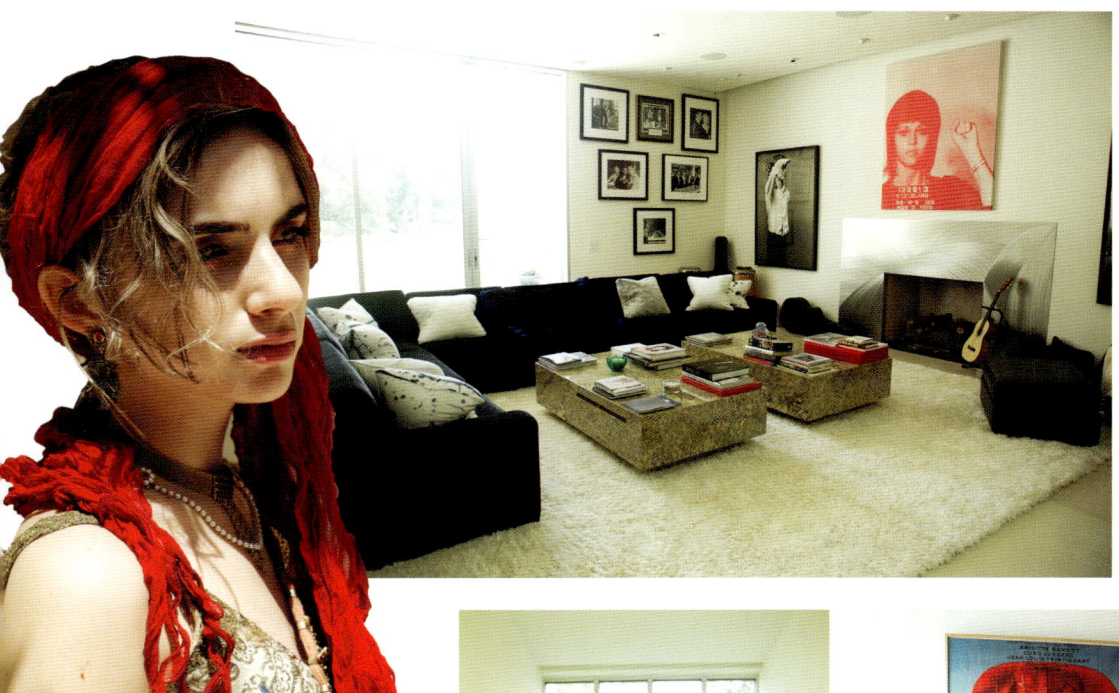
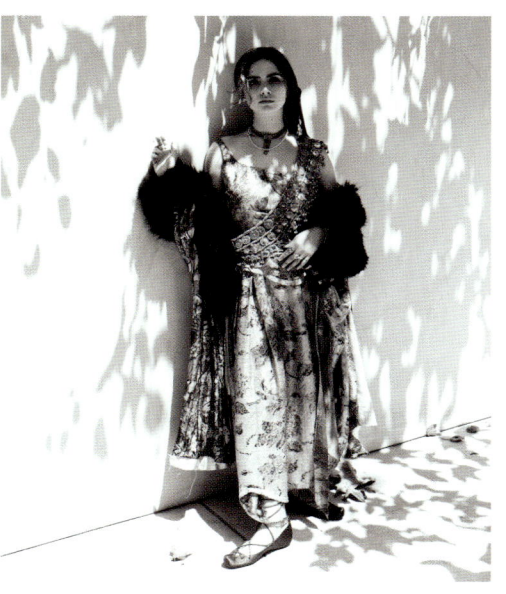
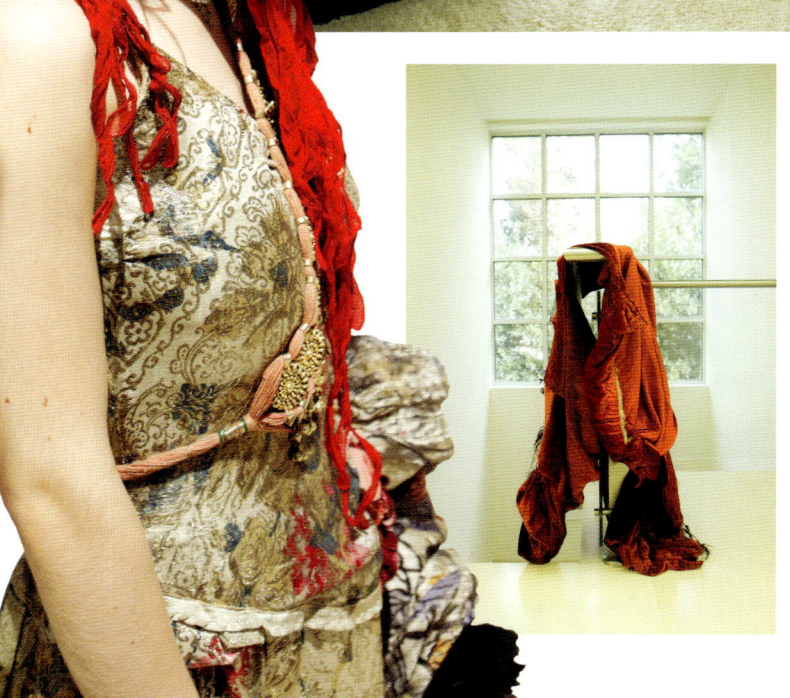
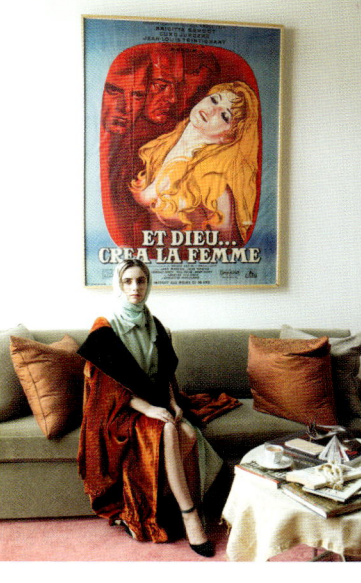
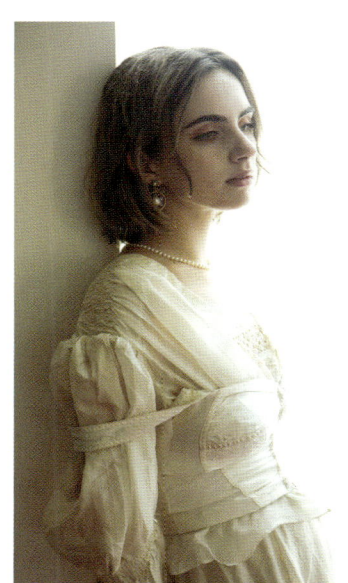

SASHA SPIELBERG
SASHA, TANYA, AND THE REST

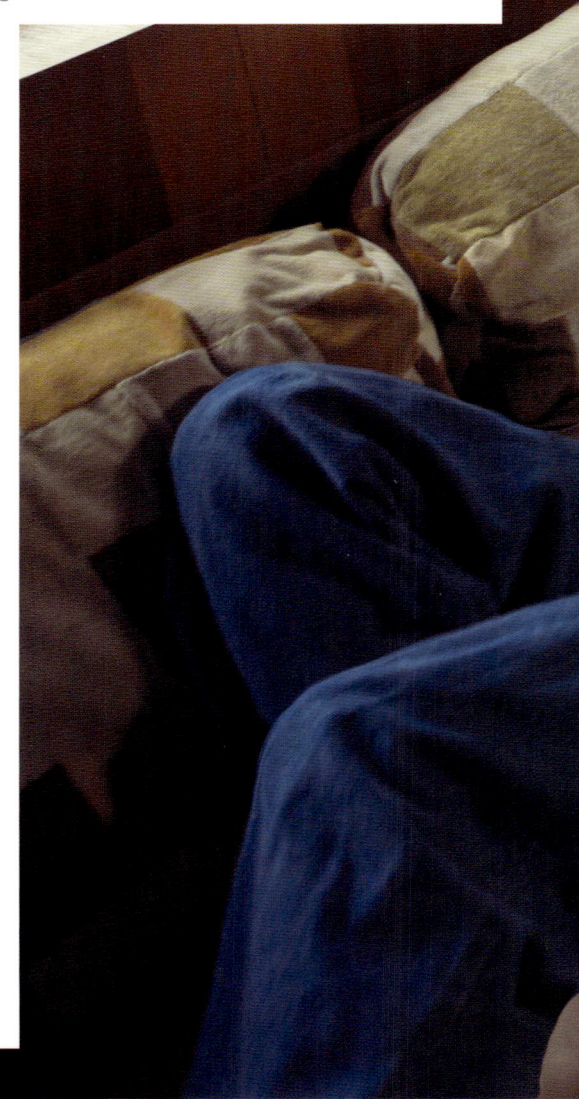

I get a glimpse of Sasha's acting skills when she shuts the door on me. We're pretending this is an episode of *MTV Cribs* and I'm taping my exit. "It's time to go!" she growls and makes a big scene of shoving me onto the driveway of her Silver Lake duplex. I know how seriously she takes her band, Wardell, and flourishing musical career, but should that ever dwindle she certainly has a splendid comedic talent to fall back on. "I love making people laugh so much," she admits. "It's one of my greatest joys. And I think I am a very naturally performative person, but I was in a sketch comedy group at Brown and I felt I wasn't as passionate about it as I thought I'd be. I gravitate more towards the spontaneity in humor. Maybe that's why I resort to my Instagram for ten-second spur-of-the-moment characters."

I also get a glimpse of Sasha's writing skills when I read the hilarious answers to my follow-up questionnaire. Her life of 27 years can be written in a few telling chapters and characters:

Ages 3 to 5 were pretty volatile. She adopted a personality her parents called, "Tanya." She was "a raging, temper tantrum-throwing, possible psychopath."

Ages 6 to 12 were more docile: she was a great kid, but not entirely out of the water. She had a lot of imaginary friends. "Most were unicorns," she writes, "and a lot were fairies, and then I had a really rad dinosaur friend who lived in the basement. Then I had a lot of imaginary boyfriends… A LOT." This was also the time she started experimenting with fashion. "I would go to my mom's closet and try on every pair of her high heel shoes and all her slips," she remembers. "I would put on her dark-red lipstick and attempt to strut around. It was borderline-inappropriate as I was about six years old, but not much has changed since then."

Ages 12 to 14 are best left forgotten. "Can I say my face was a malfunction from 12–14? No, that's being mean to my younger self."

Then the boobs started to come in. "I actually used to PRAY for boobs," she says. "My mom had them, my older sister had them, all I wanted were boobs. And I got them! I thought I was going to get a perfect set of 34Cs and move on with my life, but then they just kept growing and growing!" There's nothing inherently wrong with triple Ds—I'm sure her boyfriend doesn't mind them at all—but there are some instances when they became a nuisance. She remembers a 2014 show at SXSW in particular: "I was in a see-through black-lace bodysuit and the bralette underneath—if you can even call it that—fell down. This entire show was also being live-streamed. So everyone saw my boobs. And my boobs aren't just like perfect 32Bs that are meant to be seen by everyone. They're National Geographic."

They also limit her wardrobe choices. The conventional fashions don't cut it, but vintage does, she discovered. "It has to be tight at the waist, whatever it is," she states. "I find that vintage is the only thing that looks good on me because I have a very specific body type." When I ask her to describe a typical outfit, she has to think deeply, then decides to "phone a friend." One friend said, 'Some jumper situation or a colorful short sundress.' Another said, 'Levi's and a vintage tee.' Another said, '40s dress.' I wonder if I wear different things with different friends? Oh no! Like split personality disorder with clothing!" she cries.

Buying vintage always reminds her of playing pretend and dressing-up as different characters, much like the actress she always wanted to be. "I think as we get older we lose that side of us, and I aim to keep that inquisitive, imaginative side alive in me forever." The next chapters of her life will most likely continue to present a continuous range of personalities, but that's why we love her and we can't wait to meet them. "I also like to imagine the stories vintage clothing carry with them," she goes on. "I fantasize that I'm the outfit's second owner ever, but really deep down I know it came from a hip 20-something who lives in Silver Lake and is a hoarder like myself."

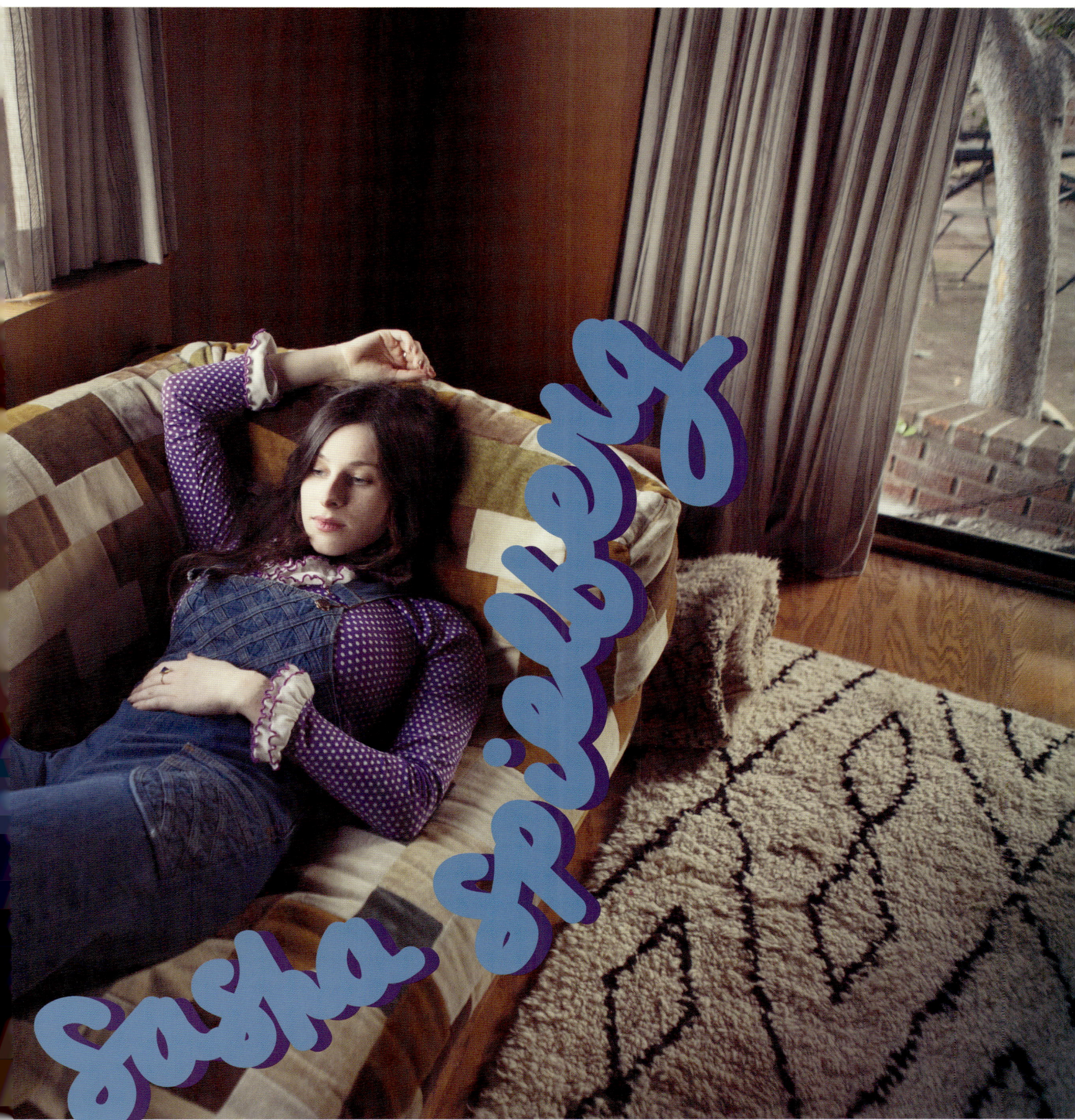

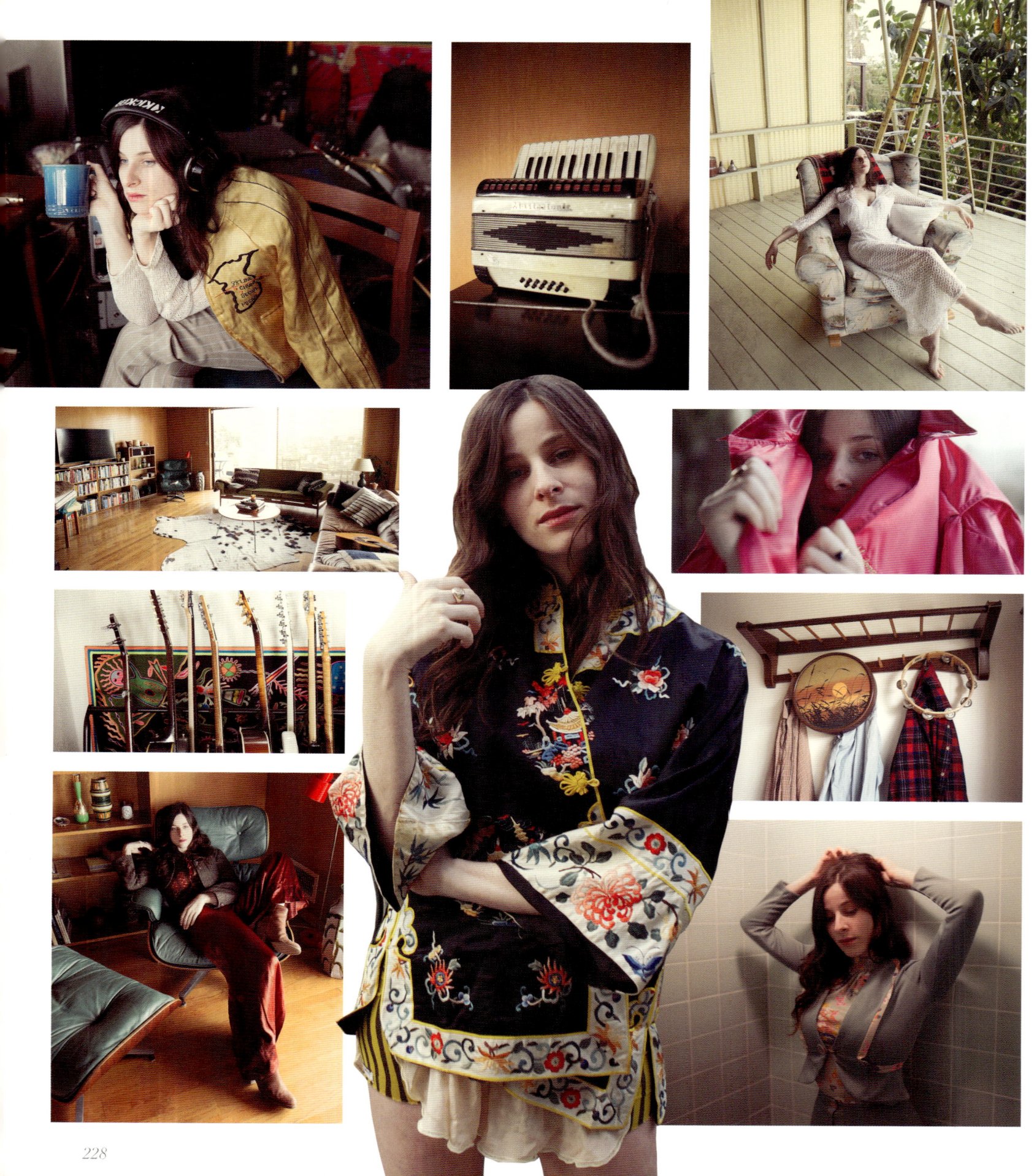

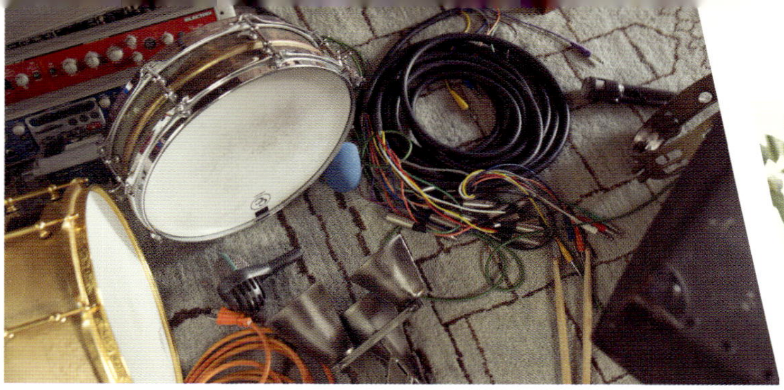

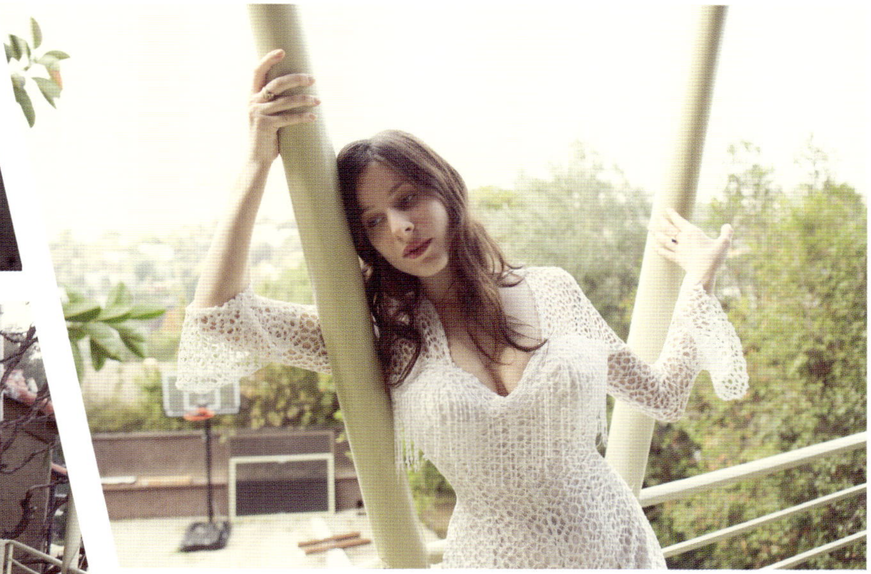

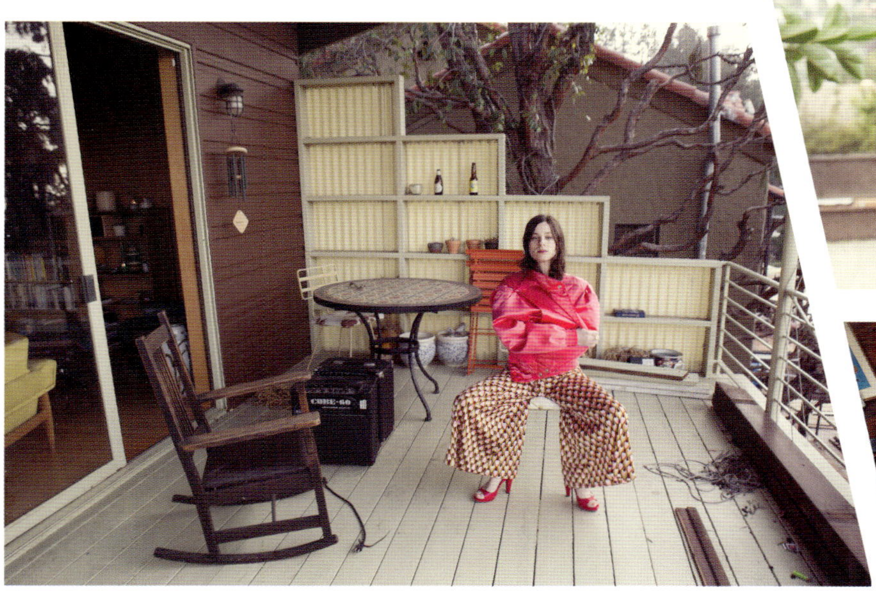

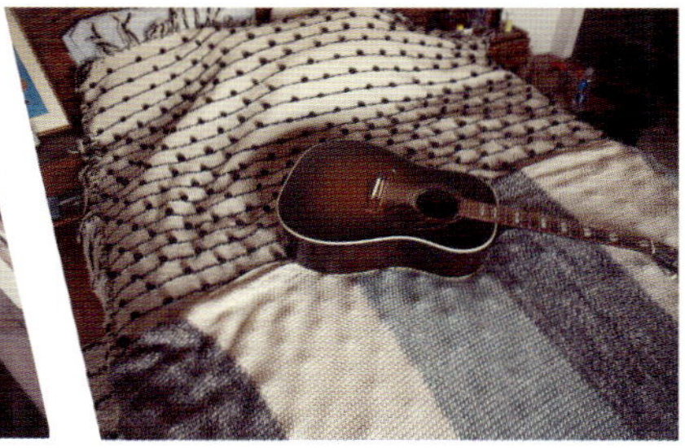

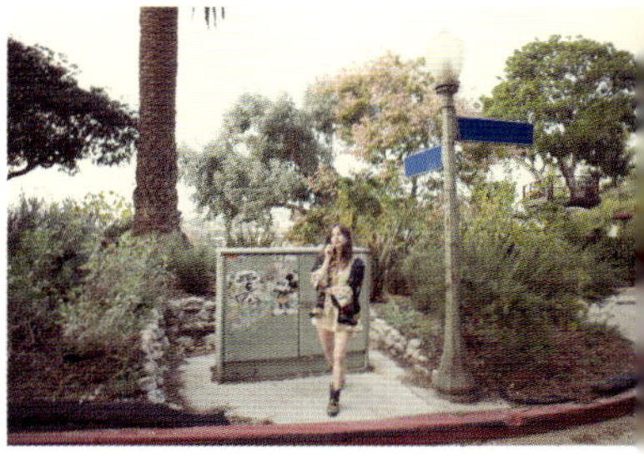

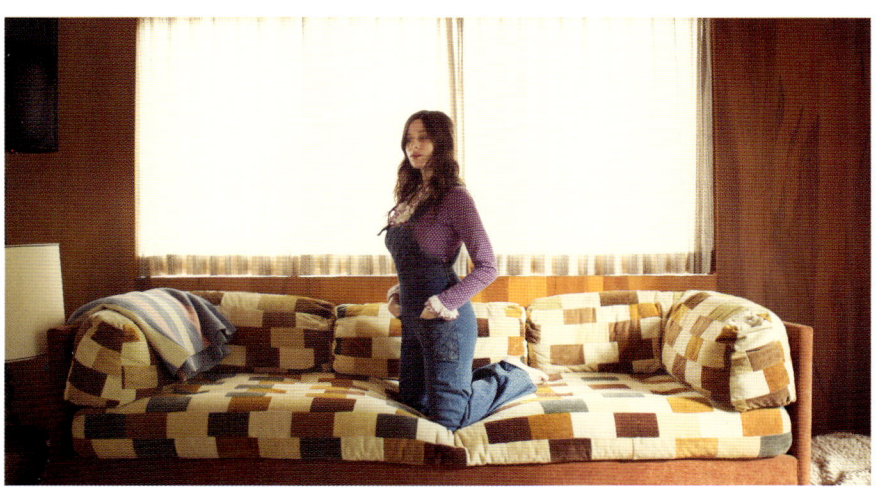
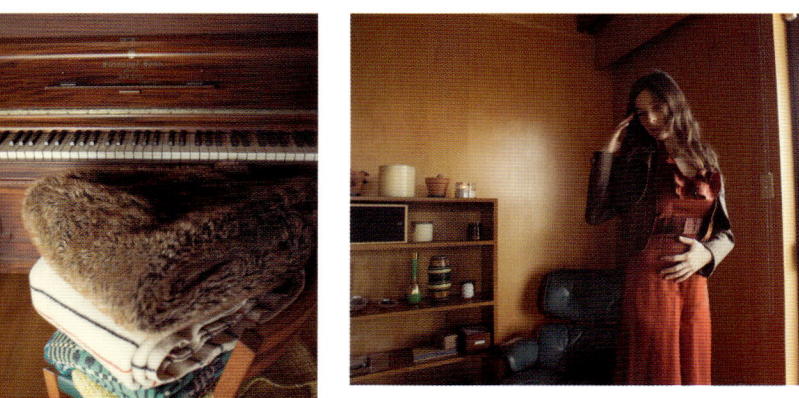
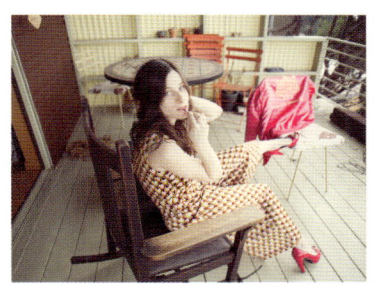
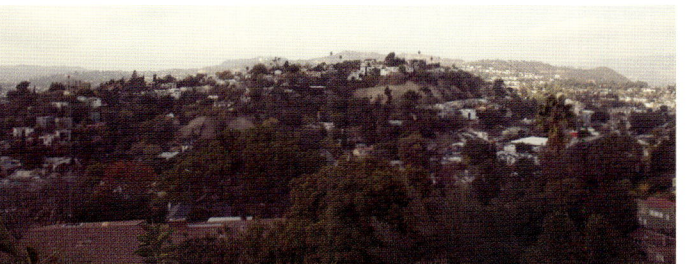
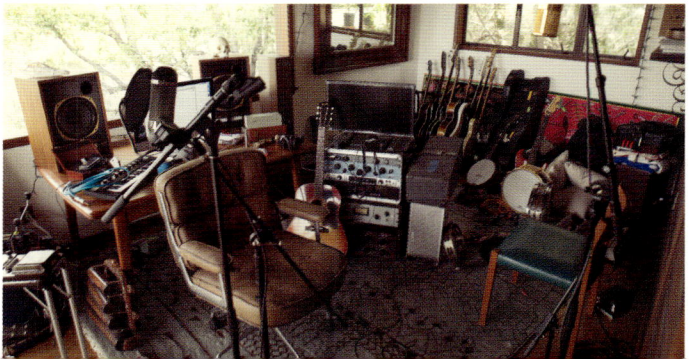
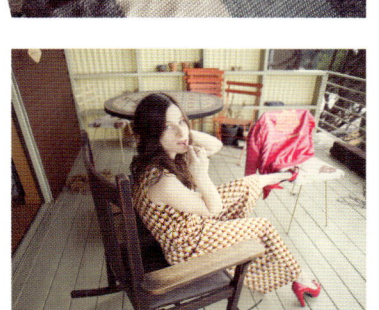
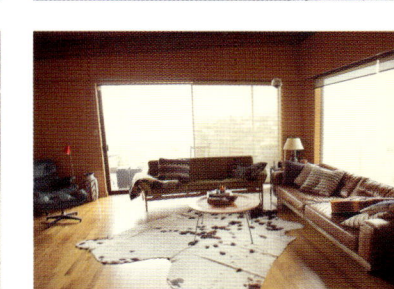

WARIS AHLUWALIA
IT'S JUST FABRIC

The gas station is packed. I figure we are halfway there, considering the traffic we are about to face heading east on Route 27. We've been on the road since 11:30 this morning and we're starving. And we have to pee. There is the prospect of fresh lobster and grilled fish once we arrive, but for now we have to settle our rumbling stomachs with salty nuts and canned tuna. Waris slides back into the passenger seat with a big grin on his face and a giant protein bar in his hands. "I'm trying to maintain a diet that contains 200% of the daily required protein intake," he says in a clear, scientific voice. That's admirable, I say, but why? "I have a fast metabolism and I'm constantly on the move. I need the protein to keep me going." But, he adds, "I only eat protein bars in hunger emergencies at gas stations off the LIE. Otherwise I tend to keep processed foods to a minimum—if it has a complex label, I'm not interested." I can learn something from this guy, I think. He's skinny, lean, *and* good looking. Write that down.

Turns out this is just one of many facts I learn about Waris Ahluwalia, the 40-year-old Sikh most people outside of New York have come to know as "the mysterious, bearded man with turban" from the Wes Anderson movies. Spending four hours in a car with someone will do that. But I don't mind, because he's funny. "How long ago did we first start talking about our shoot?" he asks me casually. "A year ago!!" I fire back. "Yeah, I was kind of waiting for your site stats to go up," he reasons, then chuckles when I shoot him an offended look. It's the sort of humor that doesn't get old because you're never prepared for it. He doesn't have an accent either, in case you're wondering. He grew up in the city. His family moved from the Himalayas—he took his first steps at the Golden Temple—to New York when he was five years old. But he still enjoys his mom's daal, keeps his beard long, and takes five minutes every morning to tie his signature, black turban—he doesn't sleep with it. When I ask him if it's limiting his swag, he objects: "Darling, a turban goes with everything. It's an important part of me—yet it doesn't restrict or limit me, or even enhance. It's a reminder of the values my family and religion taught me. It doesn't make me inherently more religious or spiritual—it's just fabric. It's how I behave day-to-day with the world around me that defines me. My interactions with the universe."

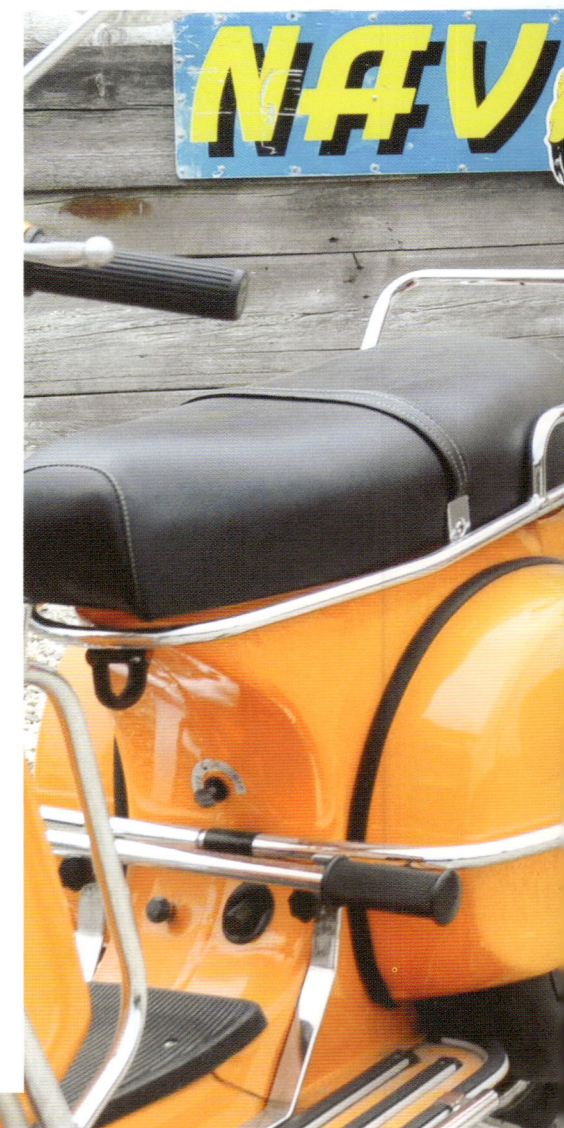

When we arrive at Melet Mercantile the sun is wrapped in a haze of hungry humidity. We learn (on Twitter) that a nasty storm is headed our way from the city, but it doesn't make it any cooler—I'm sweating. Waris takes his time. He loops the store a few times before he makes up his mind about the pieces he's going to wear. He's picky and determined. Most photographers want to put him in suits, probably because "I tend to wear suits quite a lot," he guesses. "It's simplicity blended with complexity to create a dashing uniform. The hope is that if one looks like a gentleman, one may behave like a gentleman. What a world that would be." But today is different. "No bottoms!" he yells. "I'm not going to wear any bottoms! Where do you keep your loin cloths?" The sales girls giggle and present him with a few colorful sarongs instead. "Yes!" A grey Mercedes station wagon pulls up in the driveway. It's Bob, the owner, and he's beaming. "How can one put a bromance into words?" gushes Waris. "Bob is charming, insightful, and utterly talented at what he does. It's Bob's passion that makes Melet a gem. And his wife Pam. There's no place like it."

And with the promise of rain and a great meal we commence our fashionable dress-up, dress-down party. He picks out shoes, jackets, even a white mesh tank top, which he finds hilarious. We drive to the Bay with a change of clothes and an enormous beaded necklace. The air is thickening, the storm dangerously close and looming. We probably have an hour left before the storm slaps us in the face. But Waris is a professional. He stays in character the entire time, a serious, serene version of himself. And what do you know? Underneath that svelte, protein-laced body lies a buffness even Waris is not fully aware of. That close-up of his arms stirs up all kinds of questions. "Are you single?" I ask him, genuinely. "At the moment I am indeed very single," he answers willingly, "are you running a dating service on your site? Maybe you could help me with some pick-up lines." Oh, ladies...did I mention House of Waris makes amazing jewelry? Go pick out yours.

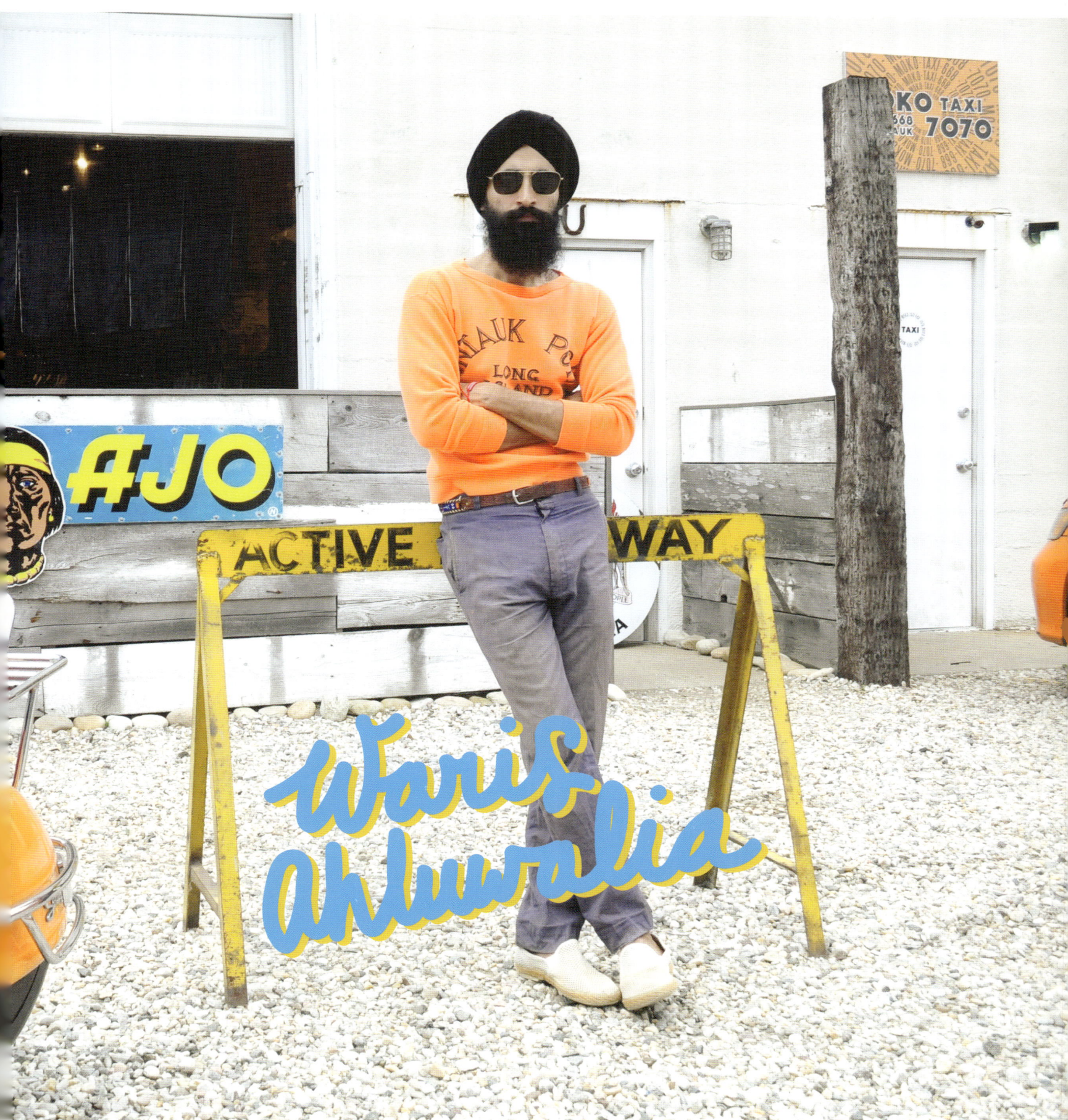

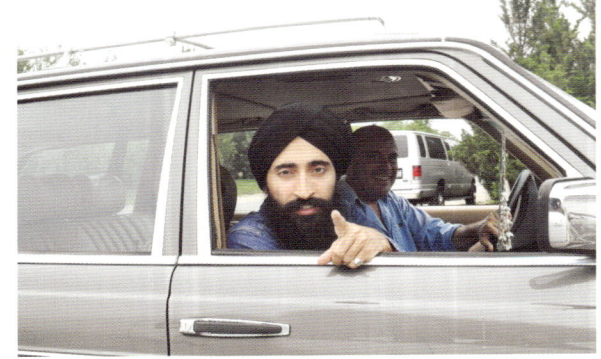
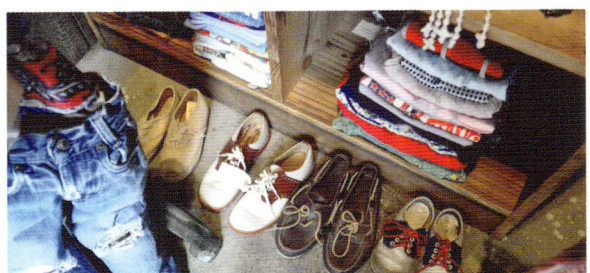
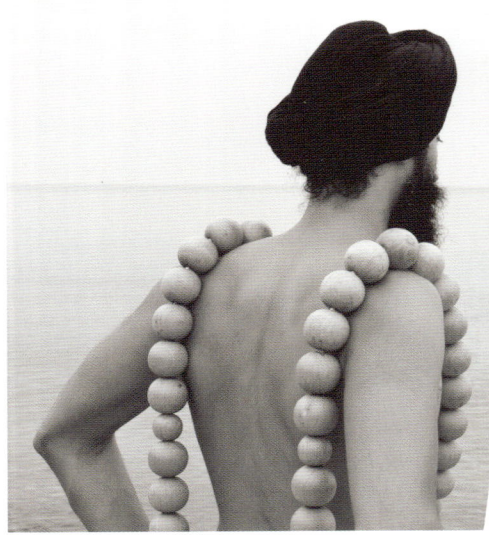
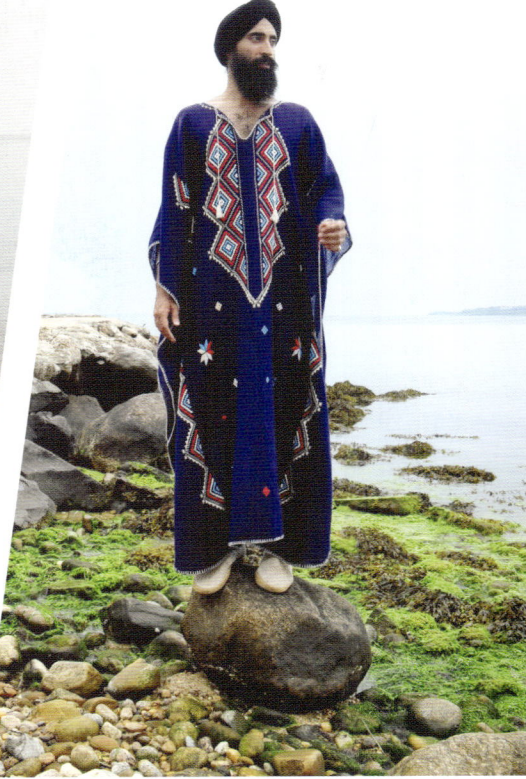
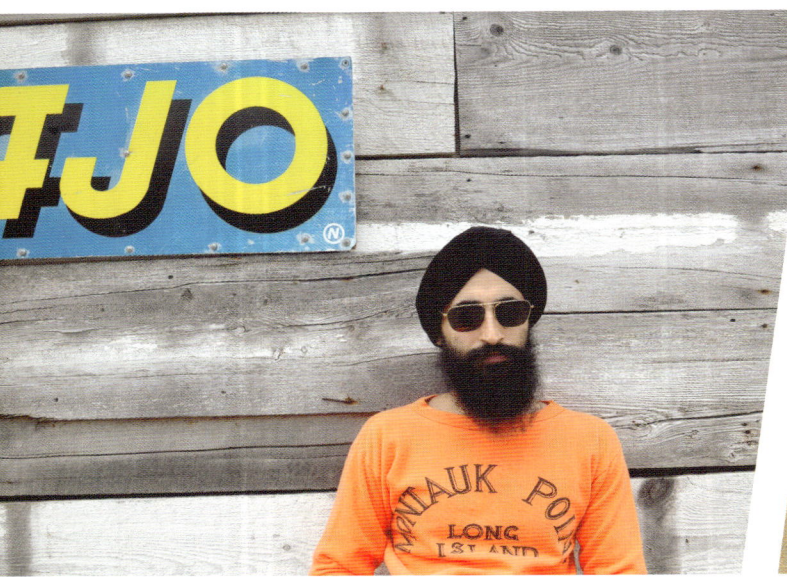
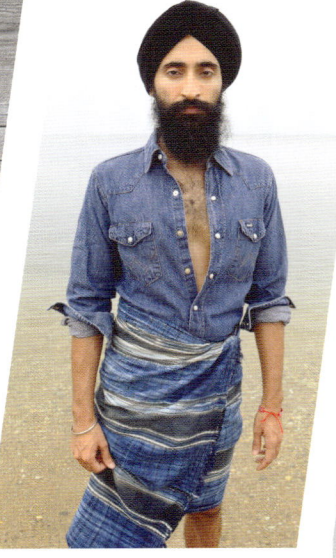
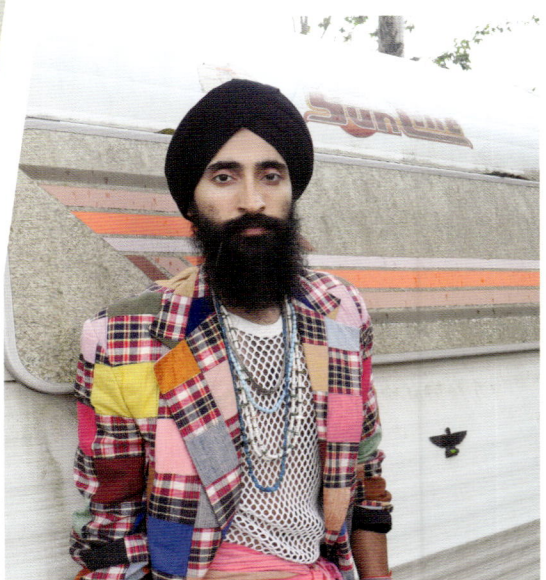
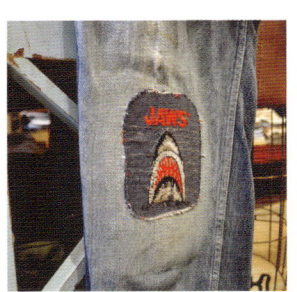
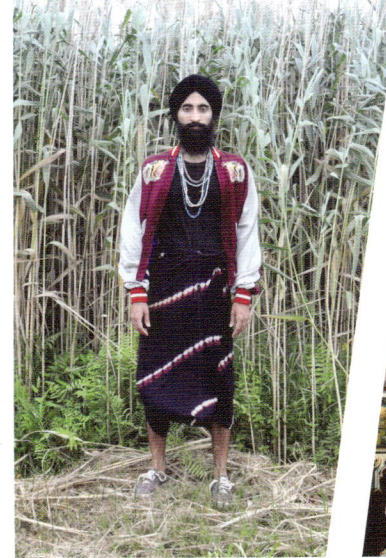
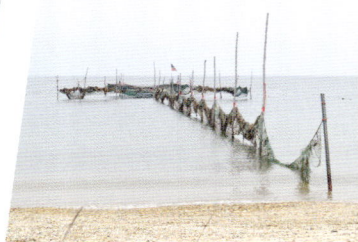
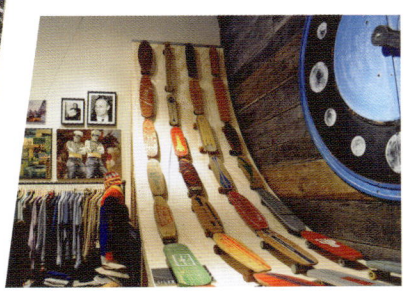
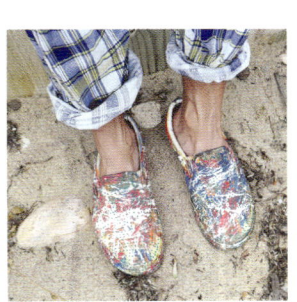
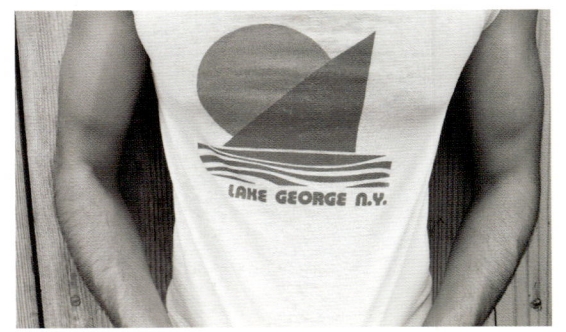

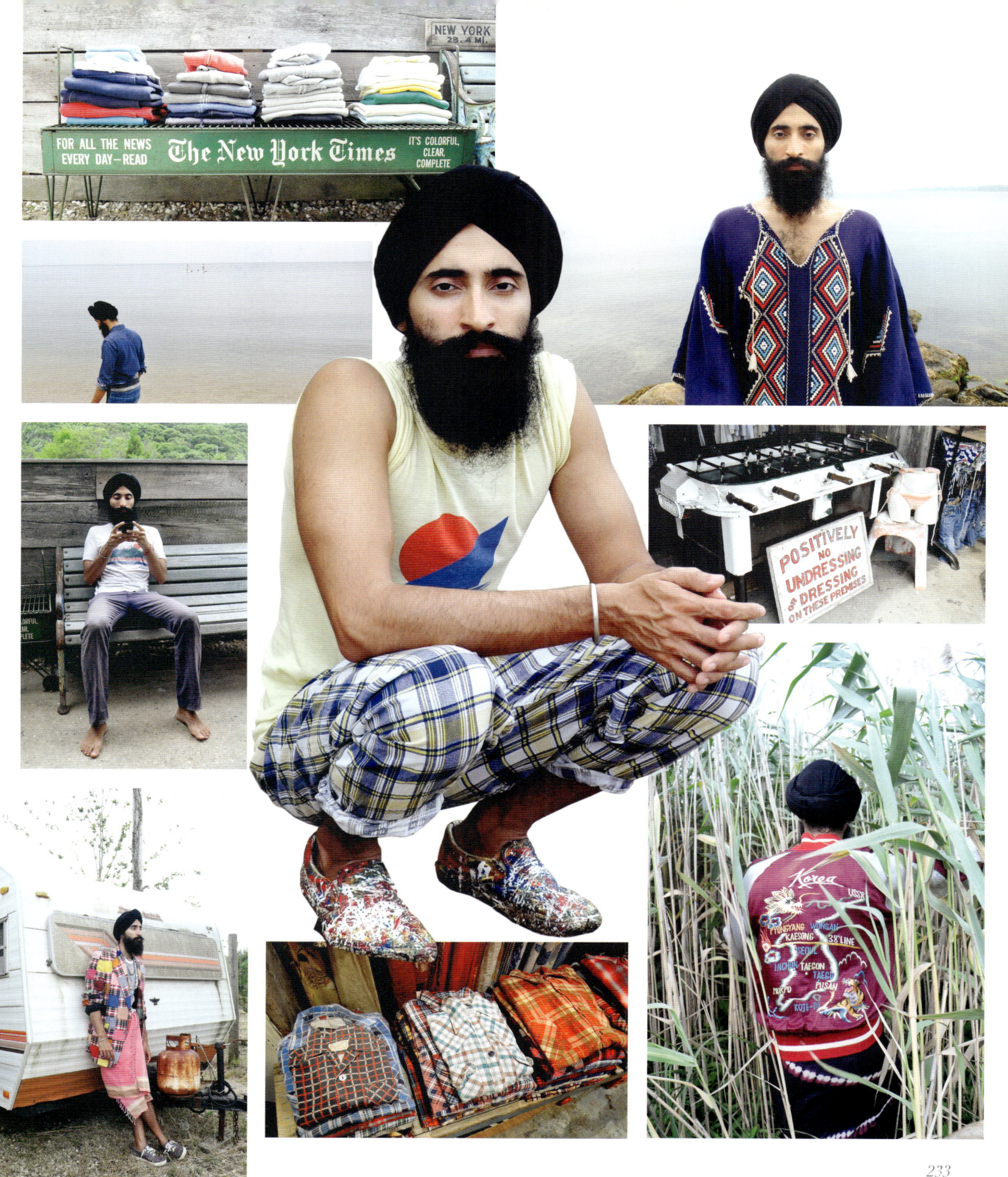

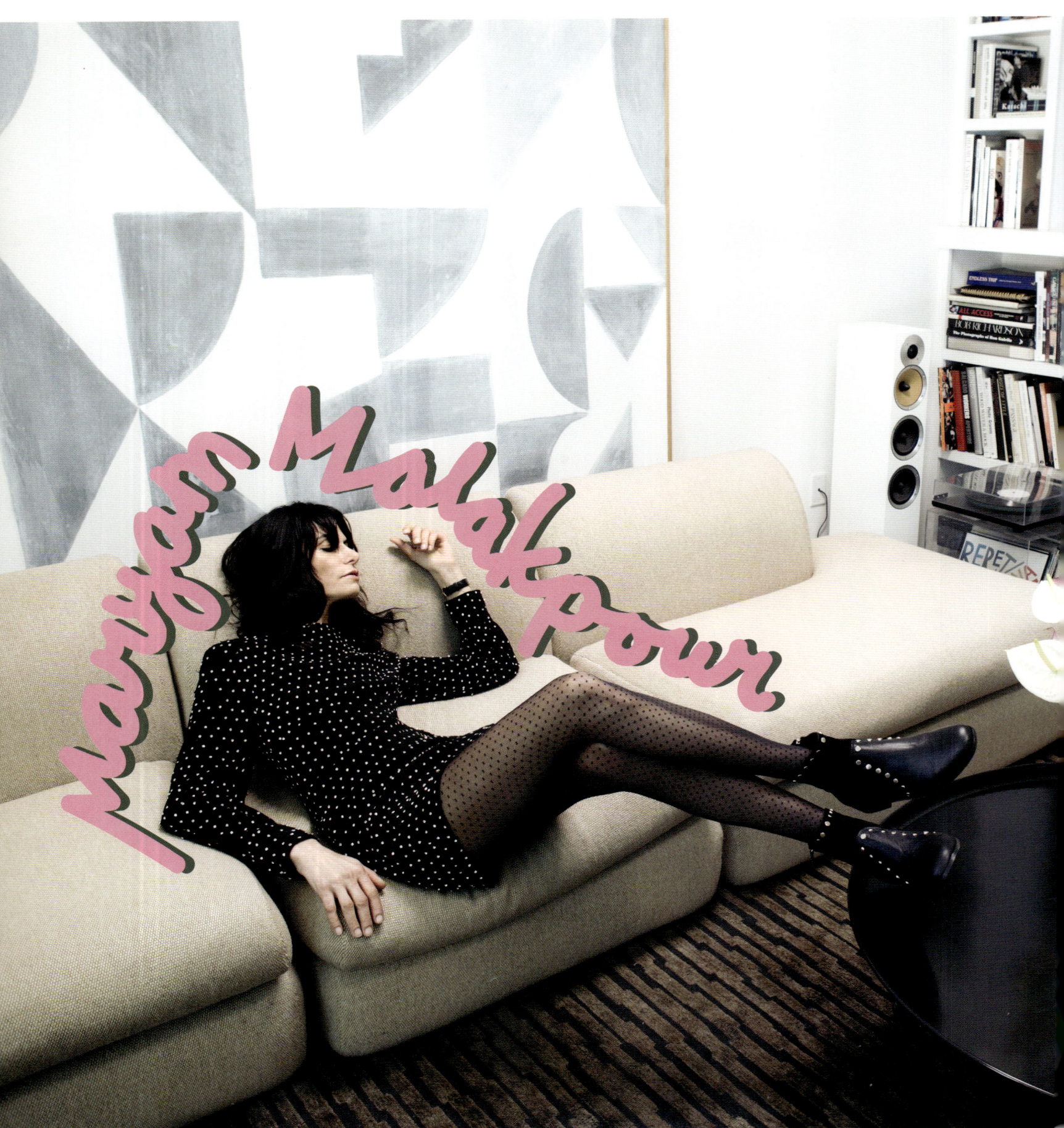

MARYAM MALAKPOUR
LAUREL CANYON

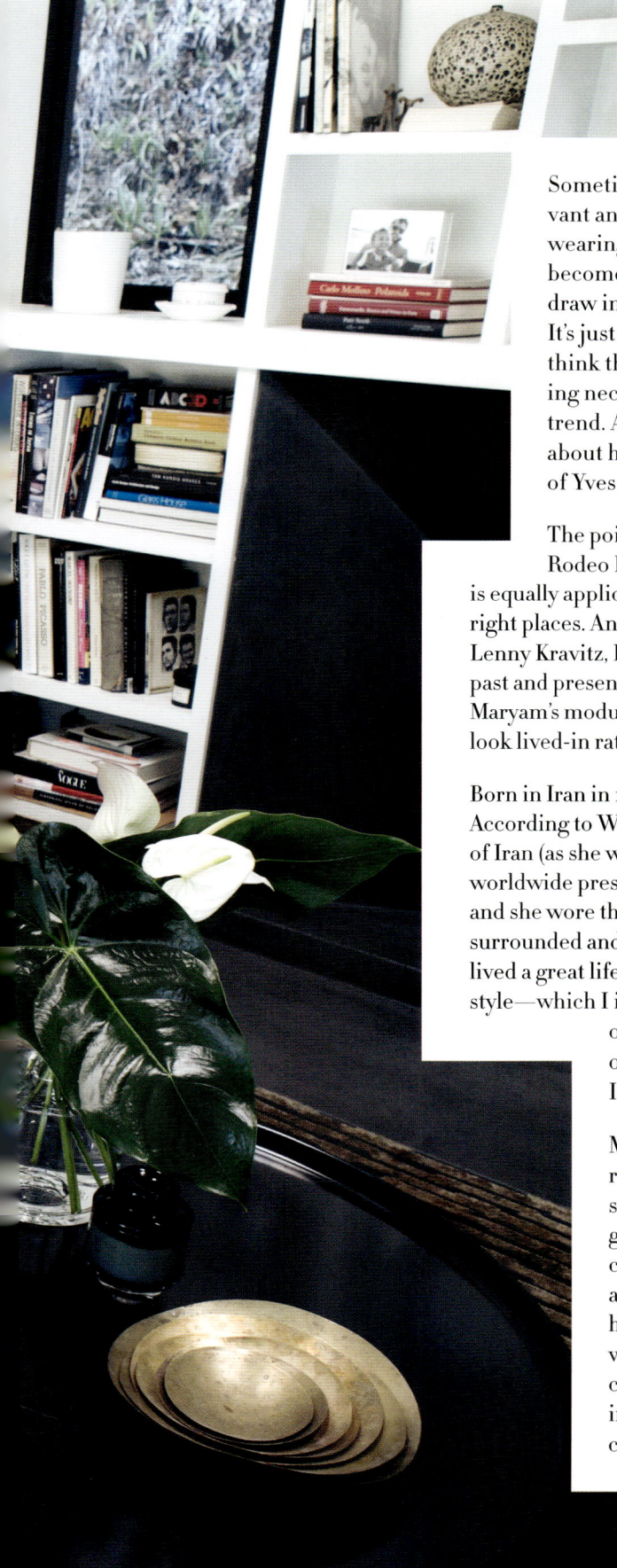

Sometimes the art of wearing vintage well is to appear so relevant and updated that everyone automatically assumes you're wearing the latest, hottest threads. Ultimately everything old becomes new again, and it's no secret that most design teams draw inspiration from the past, with some level of blatancy. It's just a matter of interpretation and how well they can paraphrase redundancy. You think the whole off-the-shoulder ruffle trend is new? Technically it's as old as the prevailing necklines of the Baroque period. And more recently, it's a direct copy of an early-70s trend. And what about Hedi Slimane's Saint Laurent? There was absolutely nothing new about his silhouette and some of his prints and patterns were nothing more than remakes of Yves' original designs.

The point I'm trying to make is that Maryam Malakpour may *look* like she's just cleared out Rodeo Drive, but in actual fact she's just really good at mixing old and new. And the reverse is equally applicable: she may *look* vintage, but in actual fact she's just finding the right pieces in the right places. And not just for herself—she's been dressing musicians and rock stars since the 90s. Lenny Kravitz, LL Cool J, Seal, U2, the Strokes, Aerosmith, and the Rolling Stones are all clients, past and present. And wouldn't you say they all have that same retro rock 'n' roll edge? It's kind of Maryam's modus operandi. She prefers to put her men in vintage Ts, jeans, and leather jackets that look lived-in rather than off-the-rack.

Born in Iran in 1968, Maryam names Queen Farah Diba Pahlavi as her preeminent style icon. According to Wikipedia, "Farah Diba married Shah Mohammed Reza at age 21. The young Queen of Iran (as she was styled at the time) was the object of much curiosity and her wedding received worldwide press attention. Her gown was by Yves Saint Laurent, then a designer at the house of Dior, and she wore the newly commissioned Noor-ol-Ain Diamond tiara." As a young girl Maryam was surrounded and heavily influenced by the sumptuous splendor and glamour of her country. "We lived a great life in a great era—where fashion, music, and lifestyle were the ultimate metaphor of style—which I idolize and am inspired by to this day," she swoons. "Tehran, like any big city, was full of life and vibrancy. The streets were filled with cars and people of all ages and walks of life." When her family migrated to the United States in the late 70s to escape the Islamic Revolution, they settled in California.

Maryam was a quiet, studious kid who graduated early from high school and enrolled right away in fashion school. When the record label budgets began to dwindle, she shifted her attention towards fashion consulting, advertising, and editorials. She's a guest editor at various magazines such as *V*, *V Man*, *CR Fashion Book*, and *Elle*, but continues to engage mostly in projects that involve music or emerging talents. She also dresses Heidi Klum. Her latest project though, is shoes—a joint venture with her sister Marjan. "At the time when we started NewbarK," Maryam explains, "there were not a lot of choices for flat shoes as an alternative to ballerinas. We wanted to create something with a lot more heritage and culture, shoes that you can wear day into night with great aesthetic and super comfort." And this is just an extension of her creative ability to make everything old become new again.

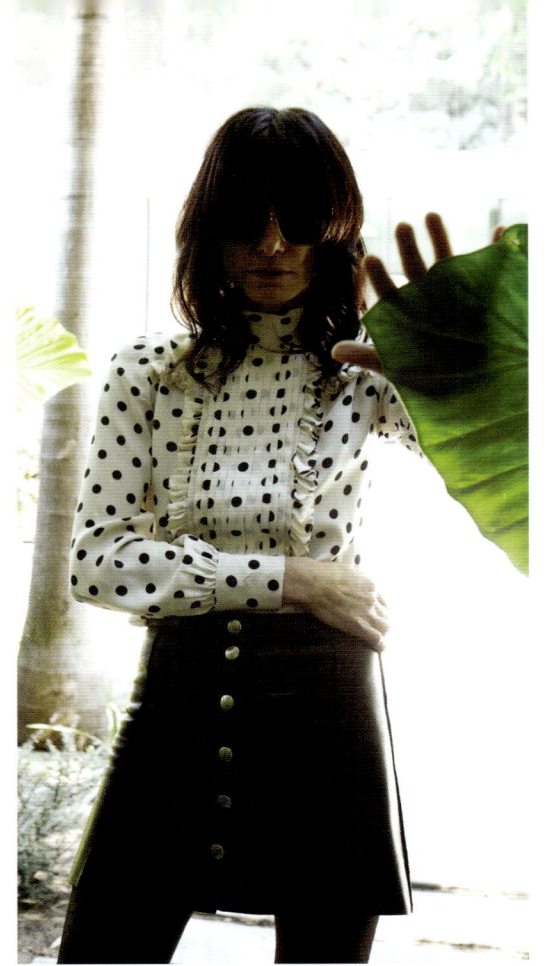
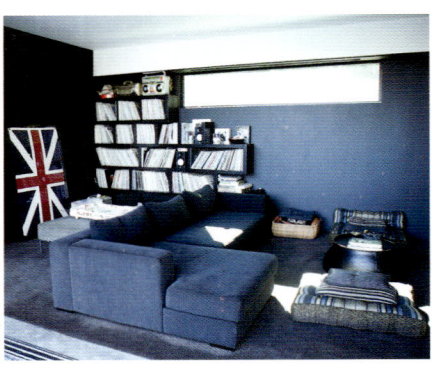
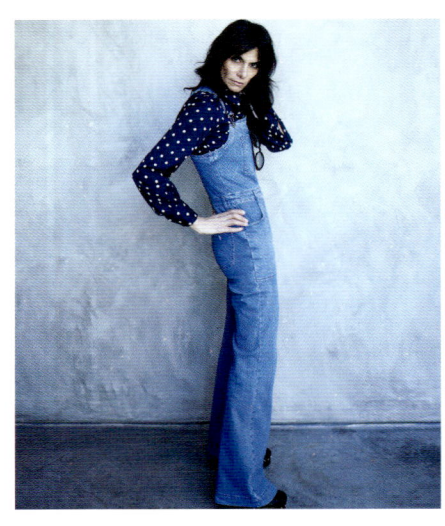
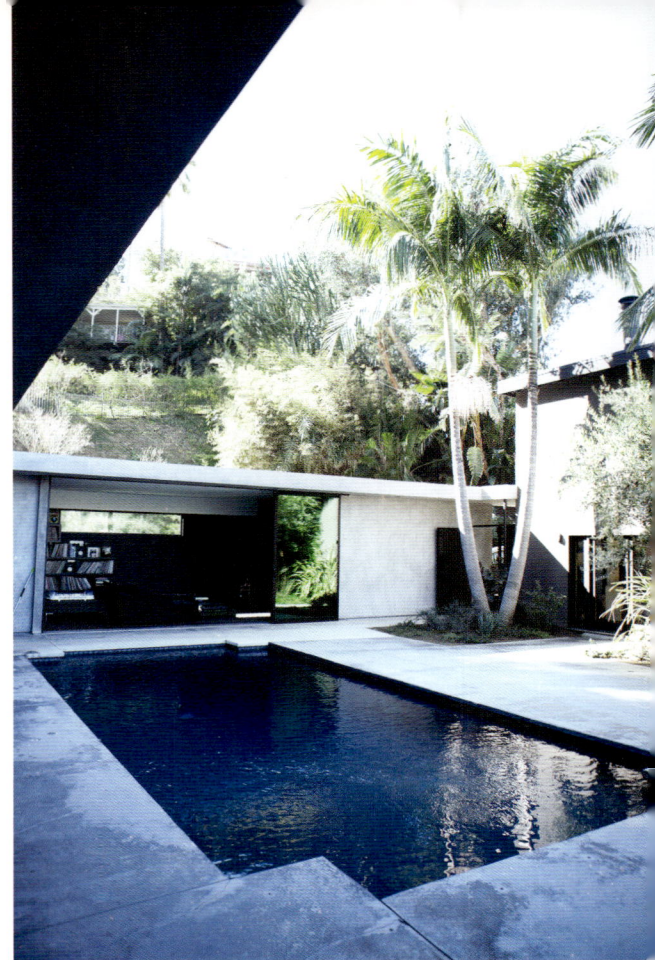
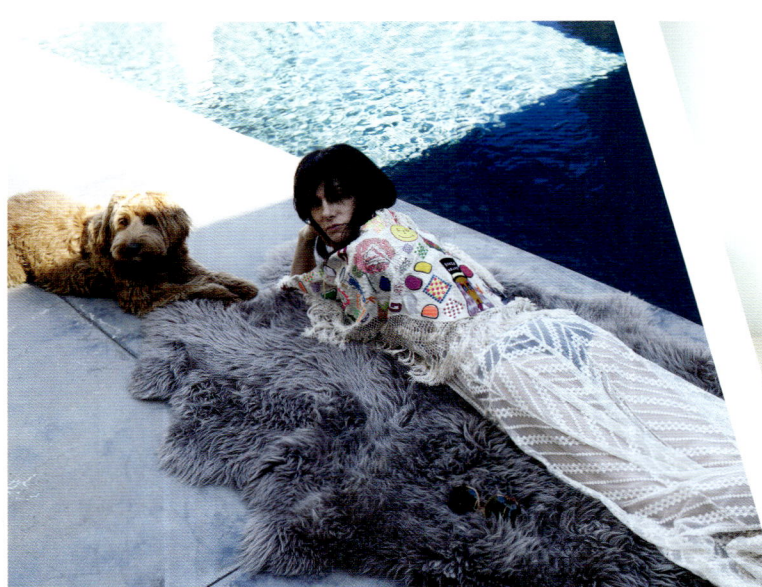
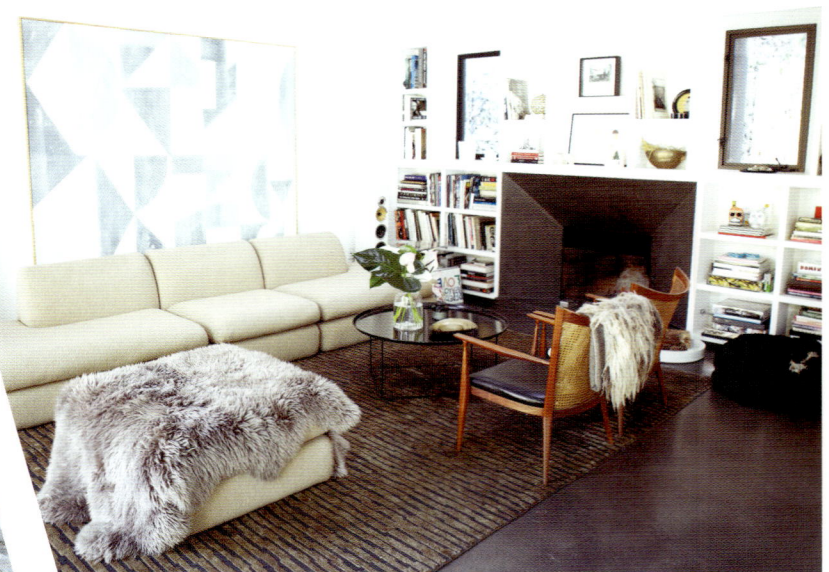
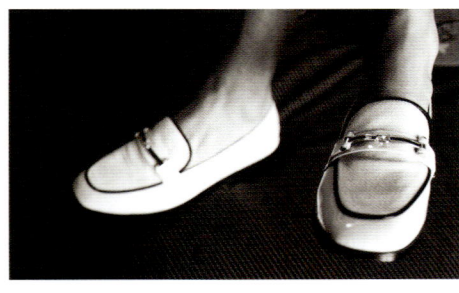
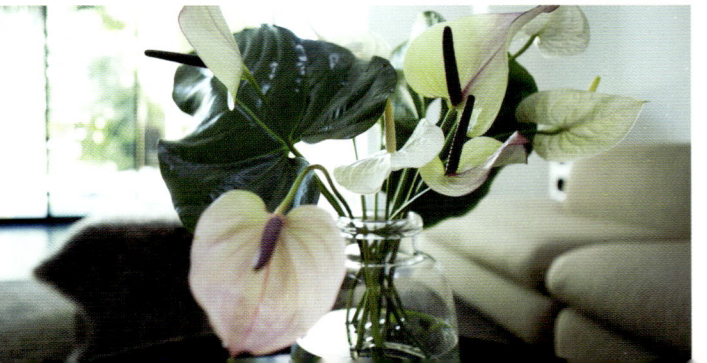
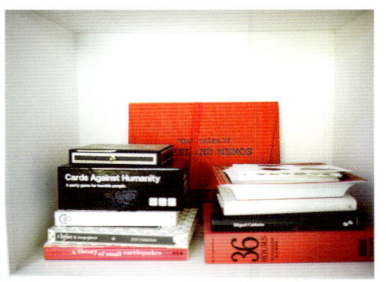

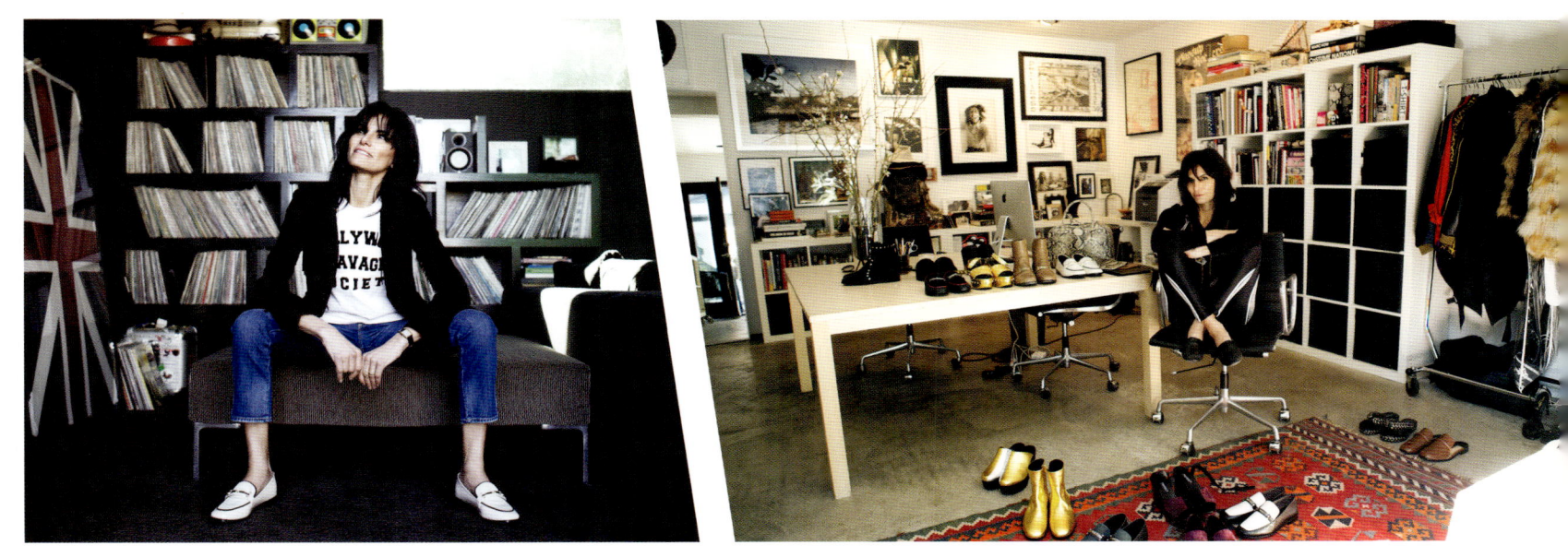

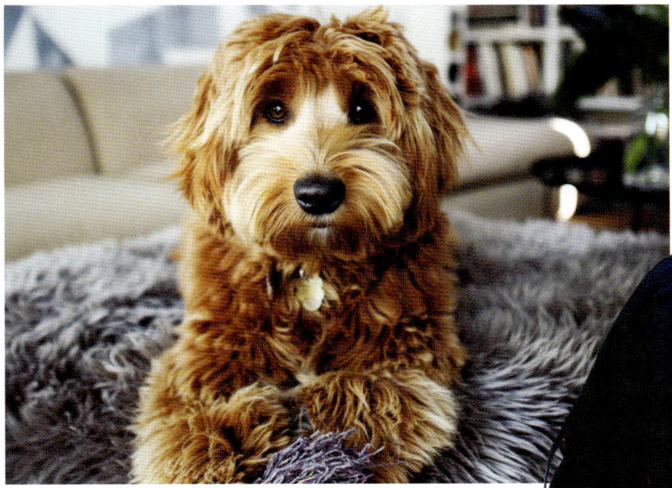

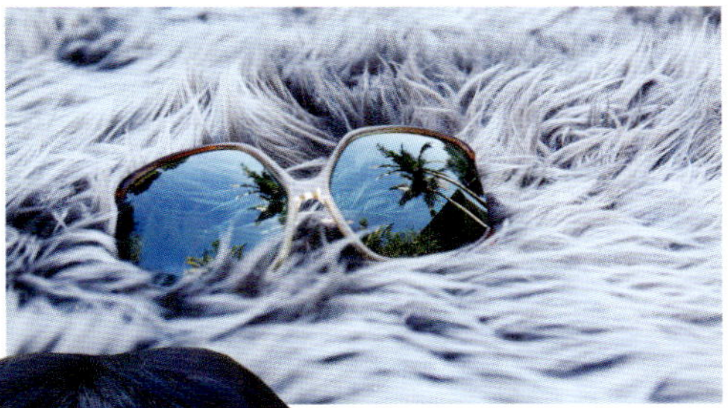

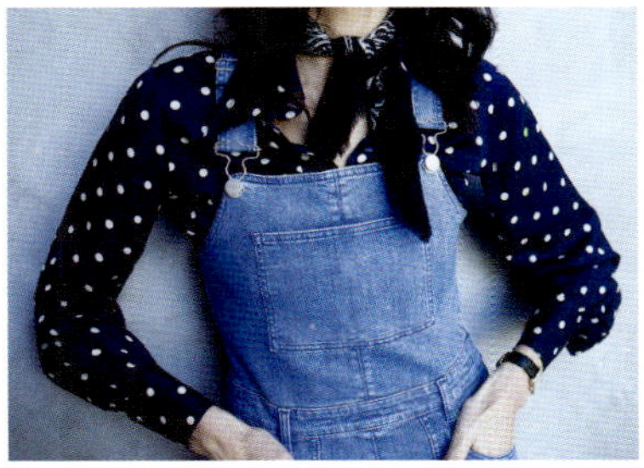

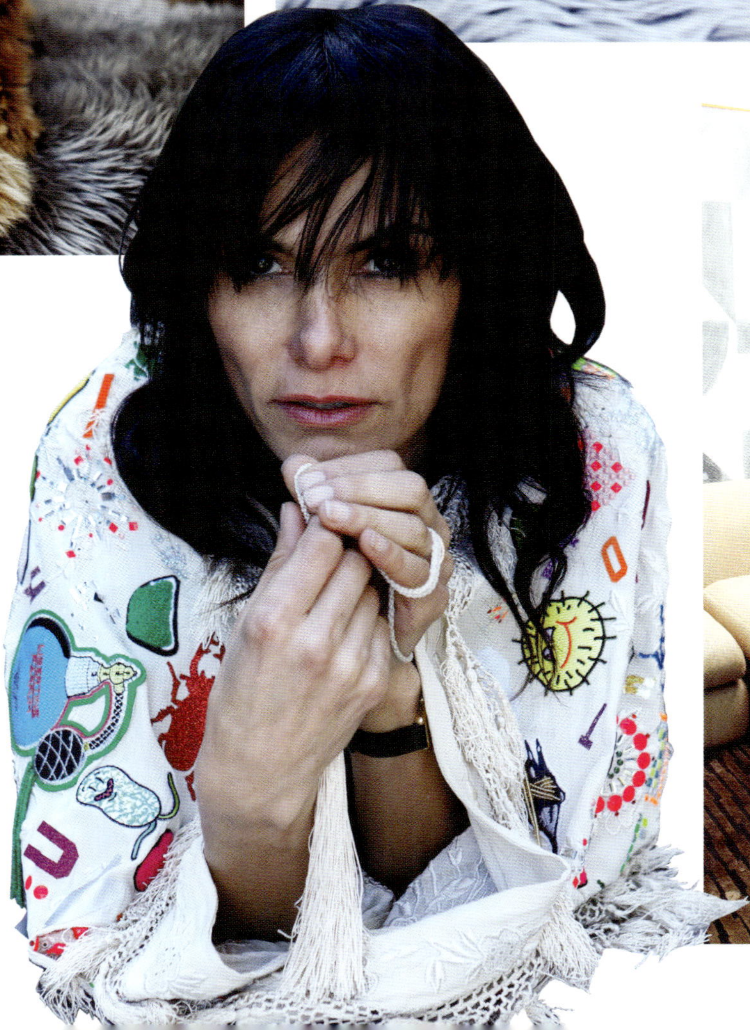

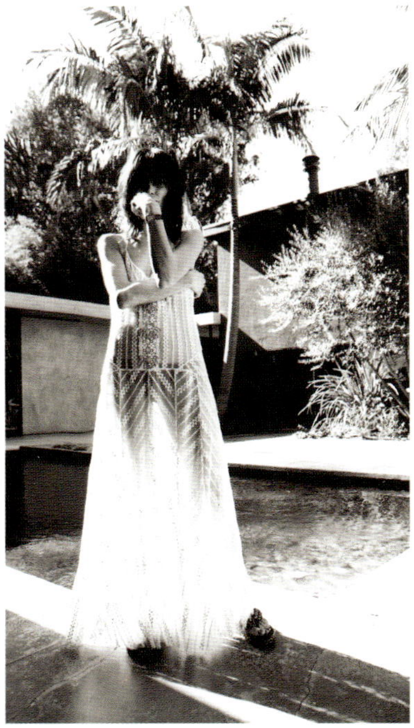

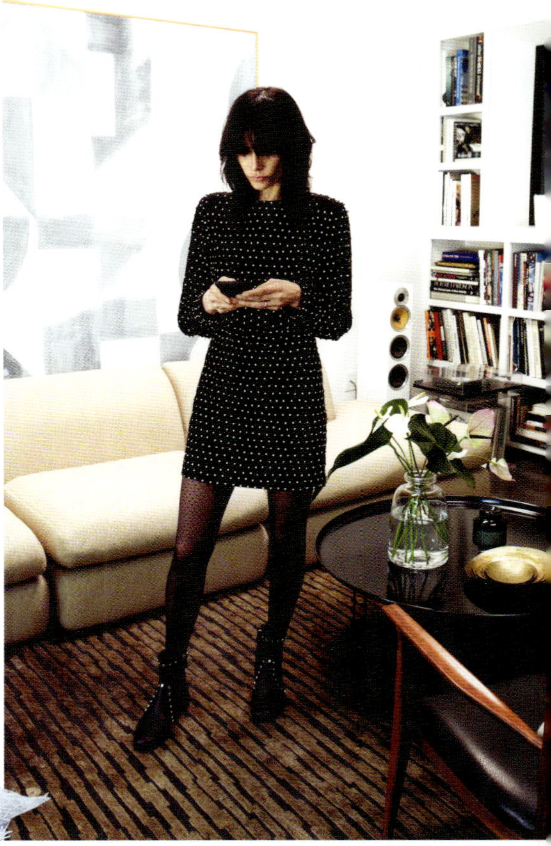

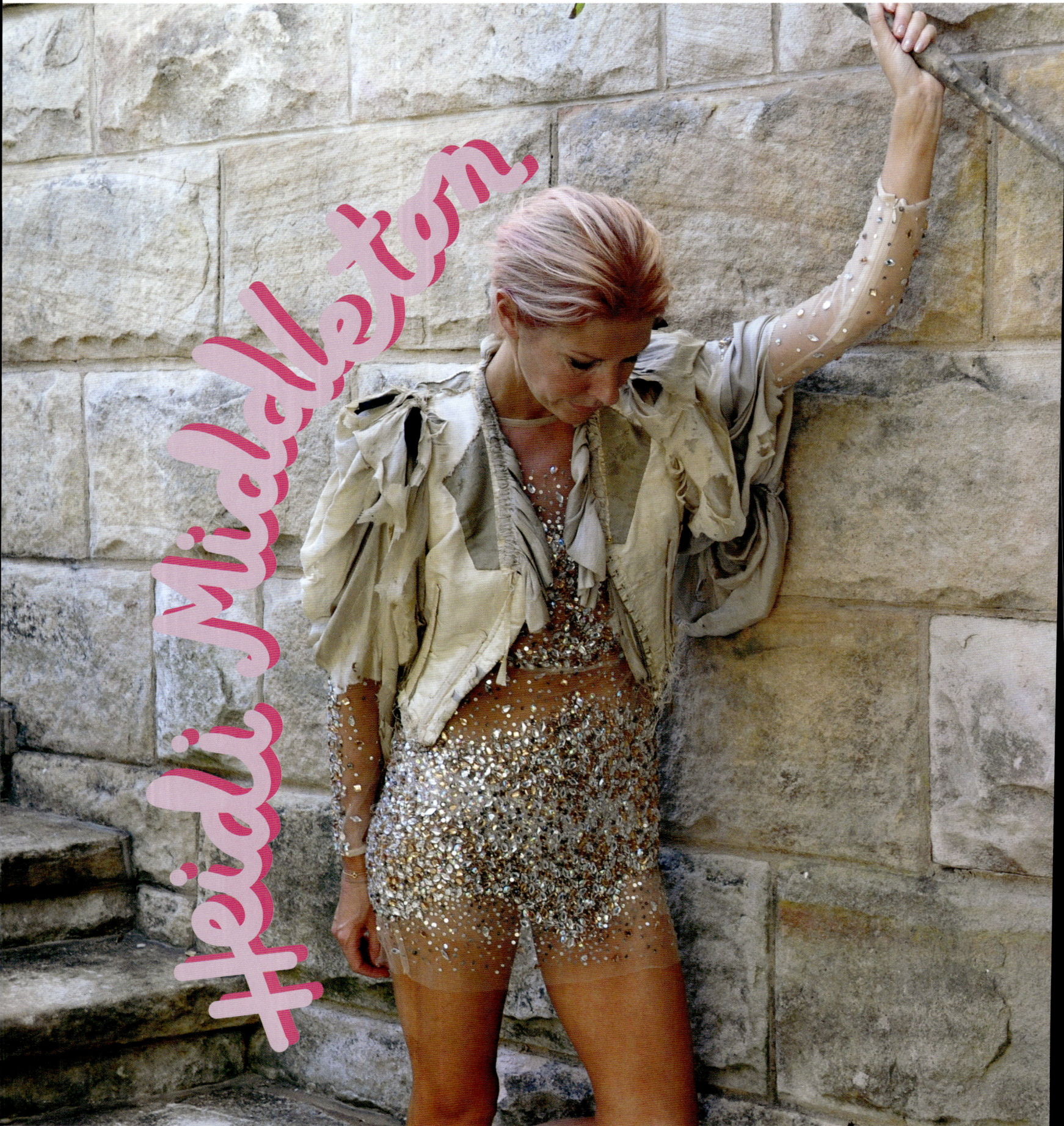

HEIDI MIDDLETON
A COLORFUL HISTORY

The road to Palm Beach, Australia, is a pretty uneventful strip of concrete. I am supposedly going to some incredible place in the Northern Beaches region, 25 miles north of Sydney, but so far the landscape is just getting a little bit greener going inland, and a little bit more winding going upward. Halfway into the trip I can make out a few lakes on either side of us, surrounded by thick bush and tall palm trees, and I ask the driver if there are any crocodiles, but he informs me that they only live in the salt waters of northern Australia. That would explain the unguarded picnics on the grassy banks... I don't see any koalas either, or kangaroos, so I wait patiently for the magic. And then out of nowhere, on my left, appears the ocean beneath us, a shimmering bay of the deepest blue you've ever seen, dotted with tiny white sails, and reflected by an even bluer sky. The air is so crisp you can almost hear the waves. The high-noon sun casts a spellbinding light on my view. I need look no further. I have found paradise.

Heidi has set the table on the patio with a light lunch: goat cheese, olives, cured trout. Classical music is playing softly over the speakers. "The kids are at the beach," she winks when I remark how peaceful it is. "Would you like a glass of wine?" she enquires. I nod, taking in my new surroundings. It's a hot day and I'm in blissful heaven: *this* is my dream house. Built in the 1940s, and at one point occupied by a flamboyant gay fashion designer and a celebrated Australian painter, the house resembles an Italian terraced villa. The entire front of the house, facing the bay, is open, basking in sunlight throughout the day and displaying breathtaking sunsets at dusk. The walls are covered in smooth, white stucco, and the windows kept in their original floor-to-ceiling frames. "The house has a colorful history," begins Heidi. "We have slowly been chipping away at the diamond with small to medium-sized renovations, and now have plans at council to make some significant changes, like adding another story to the top level. I have designed a large room/walk-in closet as part of the new floor."

When her husband comes home with the two girls (India Grace is six and Elke Bay is five), Heidi lights up. They will only be staying a minute to change—they've gotten clear instructions not to disturb mommy while she's working. At the time of this shoot, Heidi Middleton is Creative Director and Head Designer at Sass & Bide, a position she held for 13 years. That the brand is doing well is an understatement. You may have heard about the 65% stake purchase by Myer for $42 million in 2011, and the company plans to open flagships in Los Angeles, London, and New York. Heidi and her partner Sarah-Jane Clarke have appeared on every subsequent "Young Rich List" but have remained perfectly unaffected and modest—they are lovely, down-to-earth women with fulfilling, healthy lives and wonderful families. Despite a bout with cancer in 2007, Heidi is the picture of happiness and health. She's poised, soft-spoken, a little bit shy, curious, sexy, and in the best shape of her life. I may very well check off "dream body" on my list of marvels today too.

Heidi excuses herself for not having her entire wardrobe on hand. She packs and sends a new storage box of clothes to the garage every month. "Our entire garage is full of both vintage and archived Sass & Bide. My new bedroom cannot come fast enough!" Her outfits begin and end with vintage. "It is what first fueled my love of fashion. I am at my happiest when I am clashing favorite vintage pieces with 'fallen-in-love with' new purchases. It is also what inspires me daily in the design room." In a few words her style is "intuitive, nomadic, contradicted, spirited, modern, and free." She's laid out what seems like a lifetime collection of Sass & Bides and vintage accessories on the bed and pulls out whatever vintage pieces she has in her bedroom this month. I am amazed at the ease and confidence with which she dresses. She has the natural ability to make any garment look cool. It's a gift. We could have done this for a few more hours but the sun is setting and I have to snap back to reality. Maybe when Heidi itches to move abroad again—she lived in Europe for a few years—we can swap homes. Now wouldn't that be a dream...?

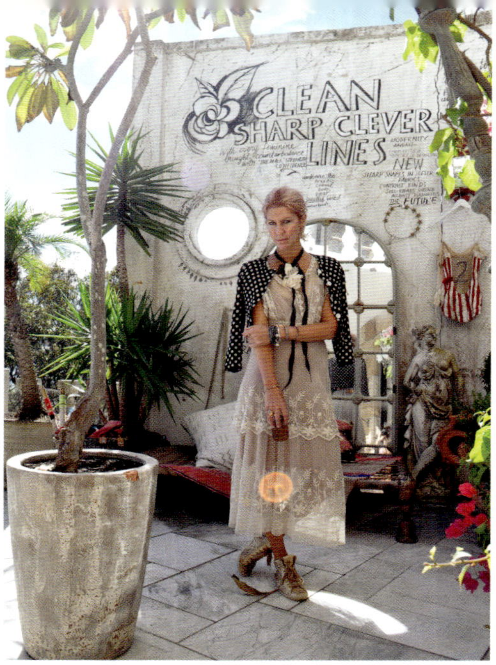

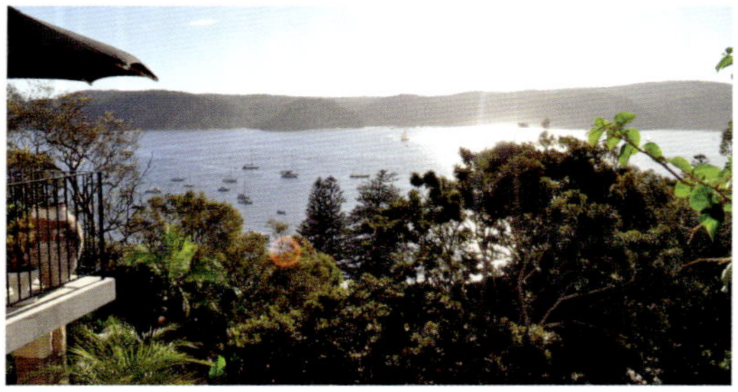

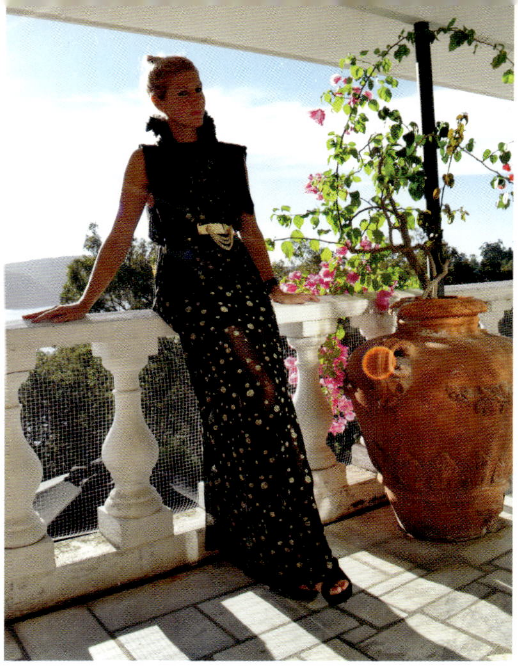

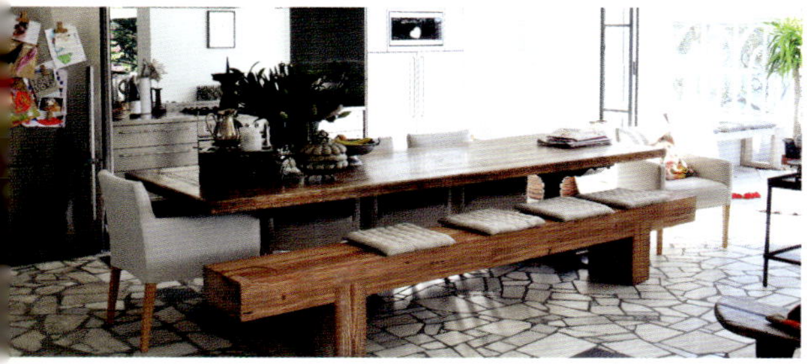

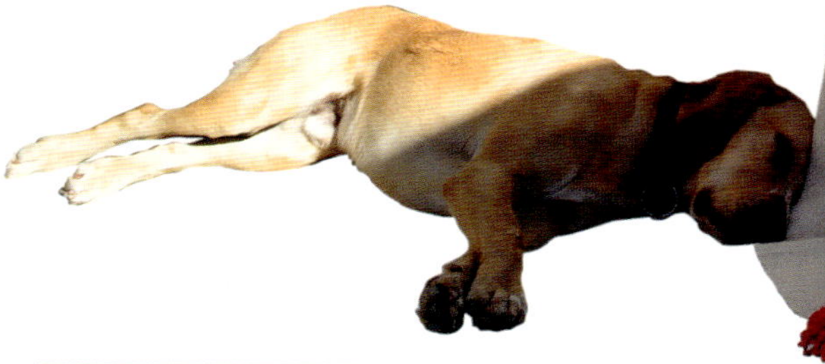

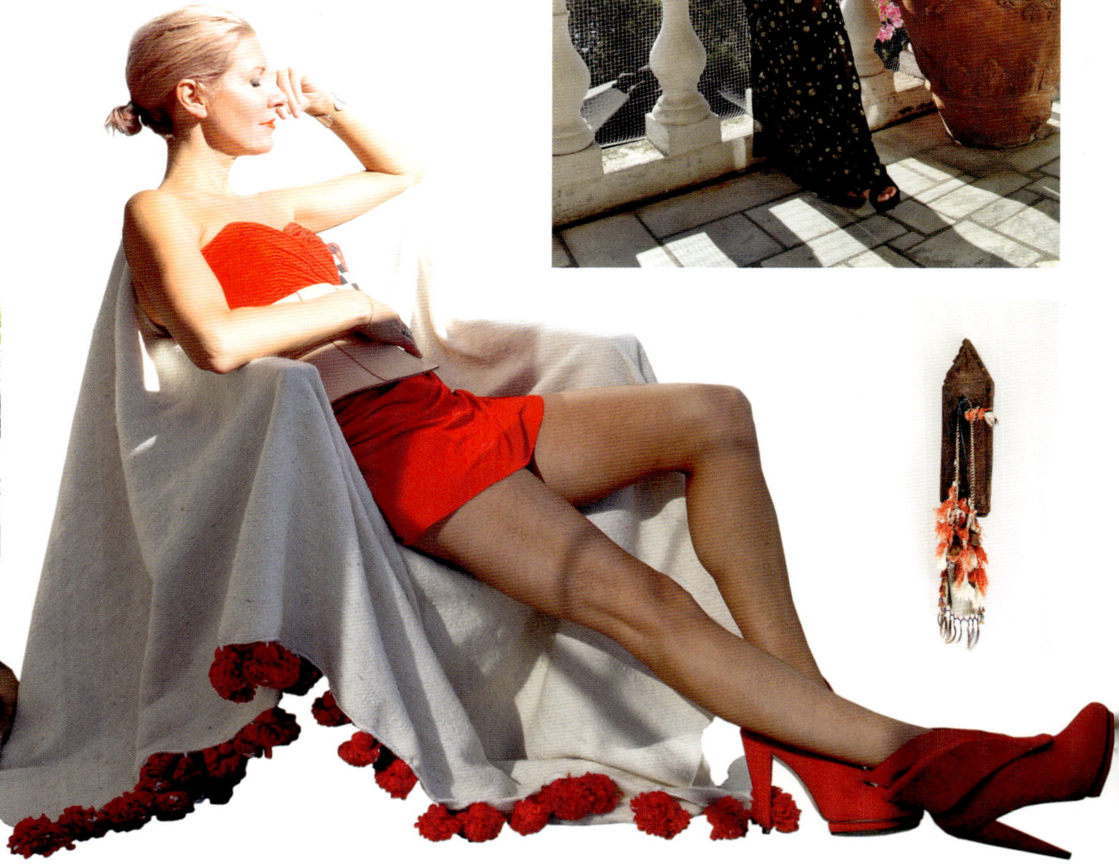

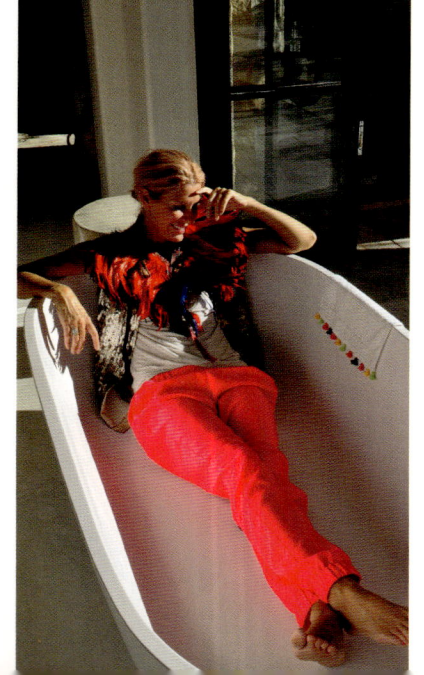
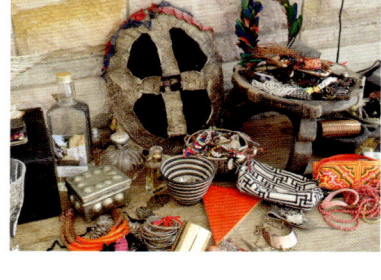
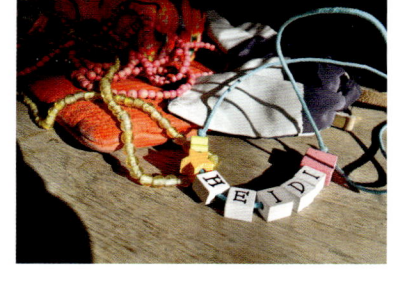
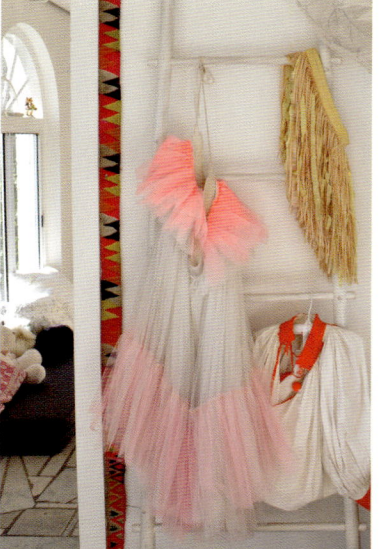
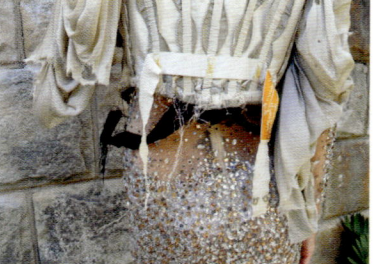
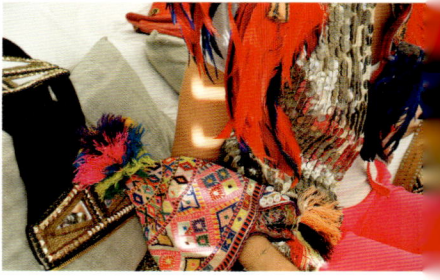

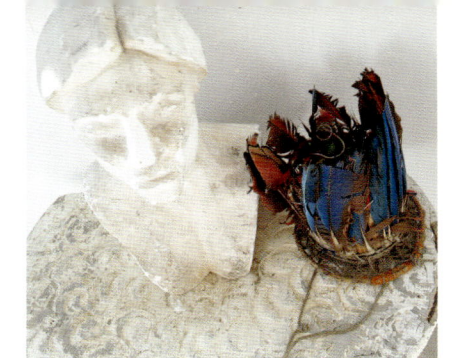
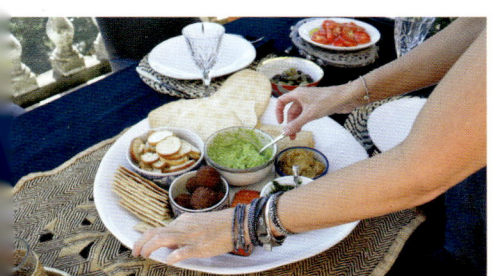
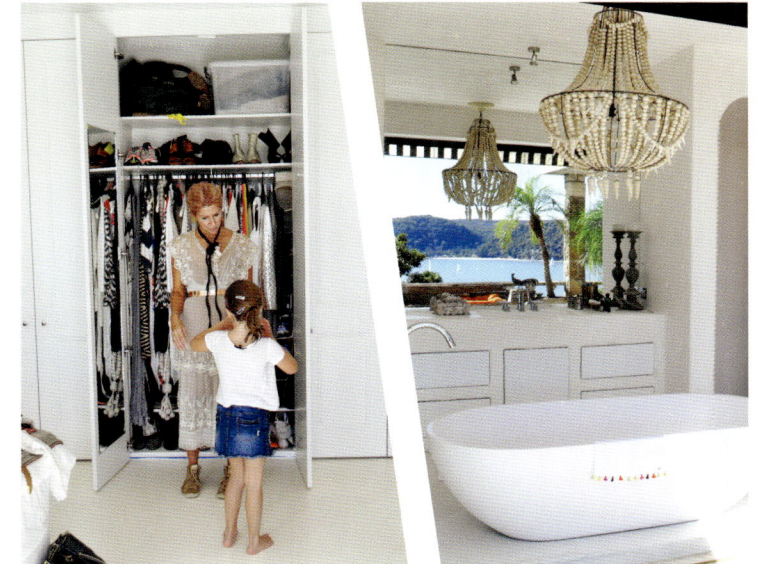
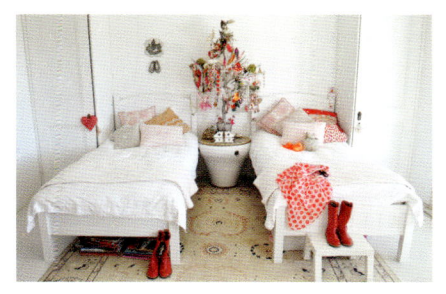
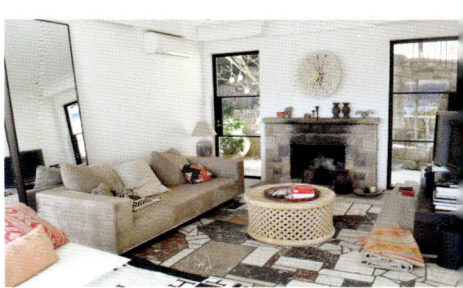
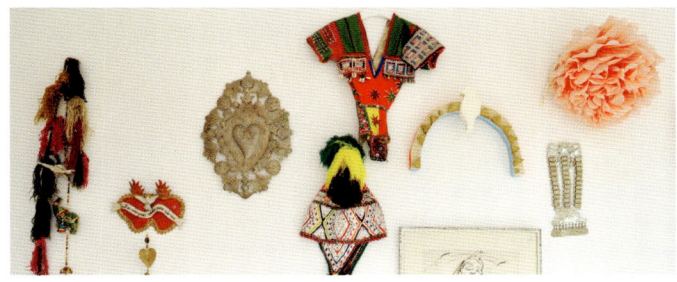
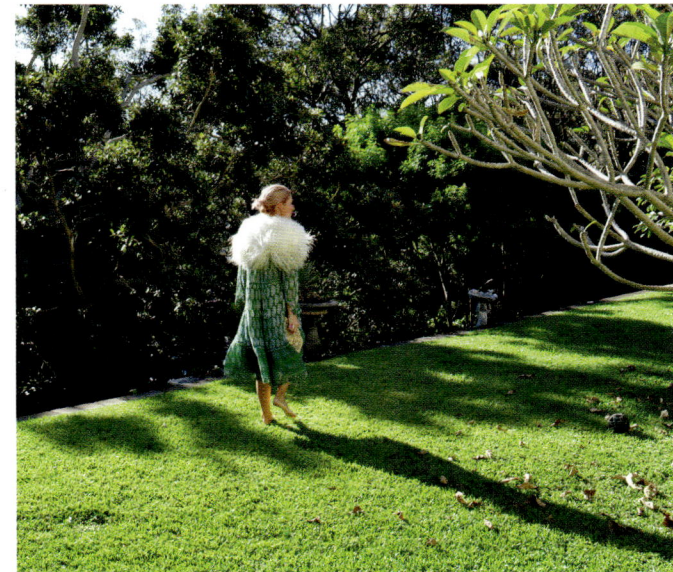
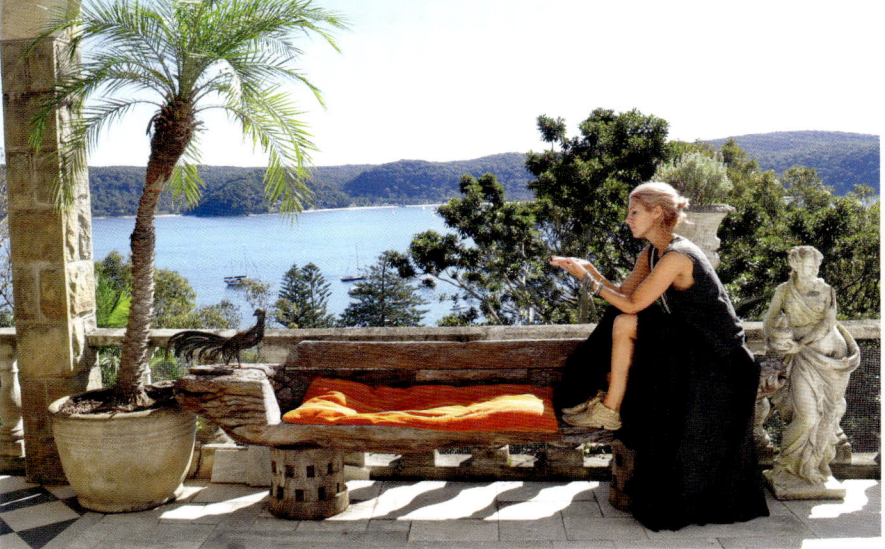
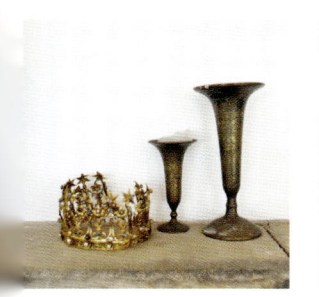
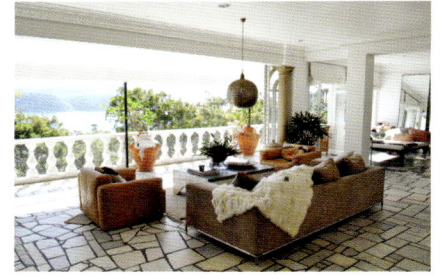
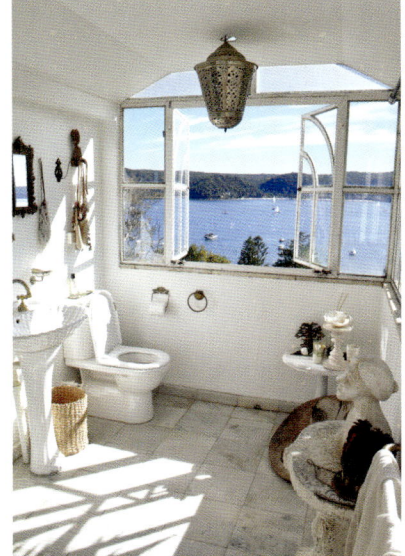
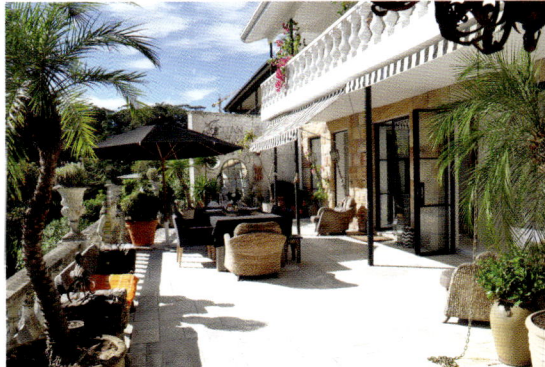
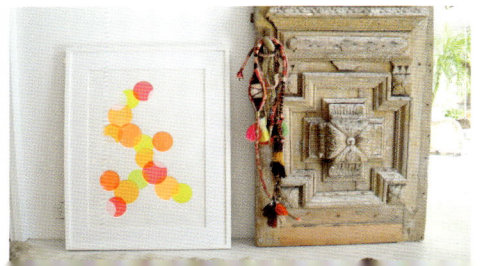

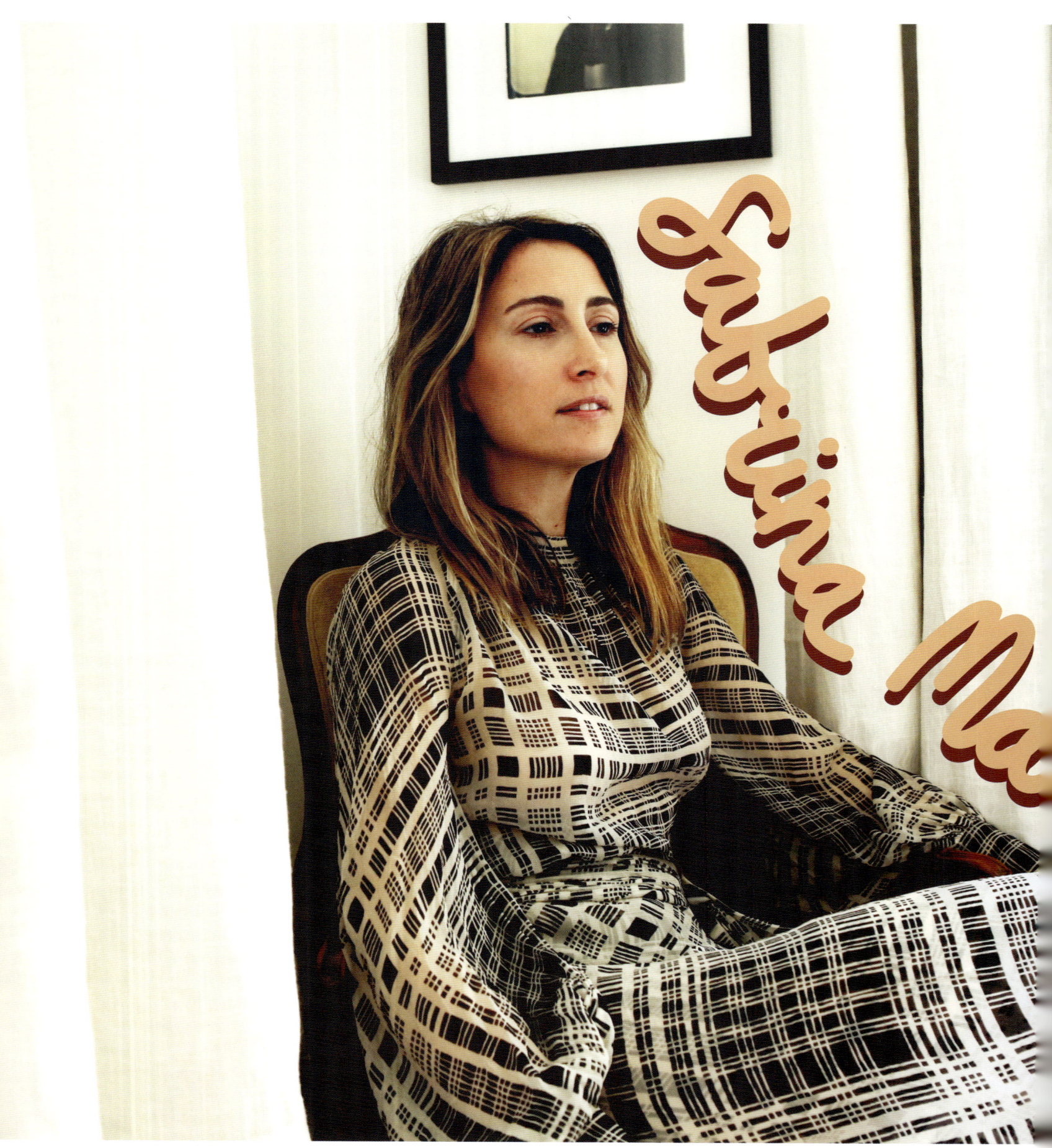

SABRINA MARSHALL
IT DOESN'T ALWAYS LOOK THE SAME

We're standing in front of Sabrina Marshall's closet in Paris. She's about to demonstrate the essence of her wardrobe, and reveal the foundations of her inner-workings. Sabrina's closet is like a map to her mind. It's minimal, curated, sensible, and elegant, with just a few unexpected bursts of bohemian deviation. Despite the fact that she's a vintage collector and vendor, you won't find any ruffles, tassels, pompoms, or crazy colors here—in part because she says such things don't suit her anymore, but more likely because Sabrina's palette is muted and swings along a pendulum of 70s to 90s inclinations. A typical look usually consists of "high-waisted denim, a silk blouse, a double-breasted blazer, and a 1960s Boucheron watch." It's simple, chic, and more importantly, manageable. Sabrina Marshall is not the kind of girl who has time to stand in front of said closet for too long.

"You're gonna see only Yves Saint Laurent because that's all I wear," she apologizes. She pulls out a vintage Yves Saint Laurent blouse, then a blazer, then a belt, then a dress, then a jumpsuit, then another blazer. "I have a lot of Yves Saint Laurent blazers," she admits. "They're the best! Everyone copies them!" I agree, of course, and admire the consistency of her aesthetic. As the daughter of a French mother who works in the art world, and an American father who still lives in Los Angeles, both influences are apparent, and not just sartorially. "Being around art throughout my life most likely shaped my eye and sensitivity to artistic expression," she suggests. Her interior is just as classic, practical, and warm as the human fabric she's made of. She collects 1950s mid-century modern furniture ("My favorite piece is a Raffia Sideboard by Florence Knoll"), as well as contemporary design ("My favorite being anything by the Bouroullec Brothers"). Nothing in this scenario is an accident.

Sabrina's affiliation with vintage started in Los Angeles in the mid-90s. "When I was about 13 years old, I used to go to Melrose Avenue to hunt for vintage slip dresses, mostly in tie dye, to pair with clogs!" And since 2013 she has made it her business. She quit her position as Fashion Editor at *Self Service* magazine and started Re-SEE after a conversation with a friend about "great pieces from past seasons that we missed out on, and how amazing it would be if there was a curated, trustworthy, global site where one could find them, without having to sift through hours of product." They wanted to create a platform that educates people on the best pieces from past collections: collections that changed fashion, like Yves Saint Laurent's first prêt-a-porter collection in 1964, or Helmut Lang's final collection at his eponymous brand, or Phoebe's first collection at Céline.

When the store launched I wrote: "It's a completely different, undeniably French way of looking at vintage, and a far cry from my own personal mix and clash of prints and patterns. Re-SEE has a minimal, monochrome view on vintage. None of the pieces look dated or retro, not just because some of them are as fresh as last season's, but also because, like me, Sabrina and Sofia try to reinvent the old and pre-owned for the modern world." We're all in this together, for the same reasons, and with the same intentions, but it doesn't always look the same. And thank the mighty gods for that.

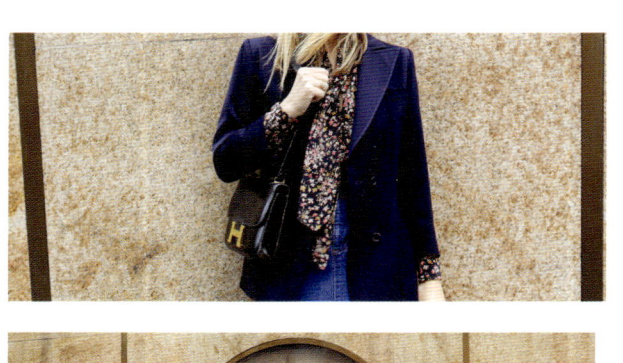
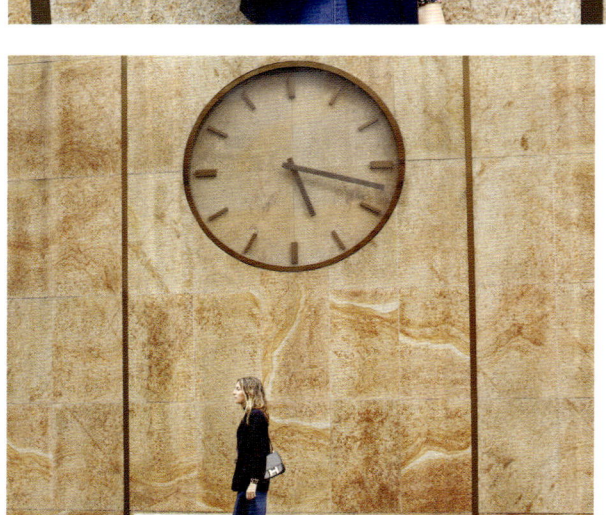
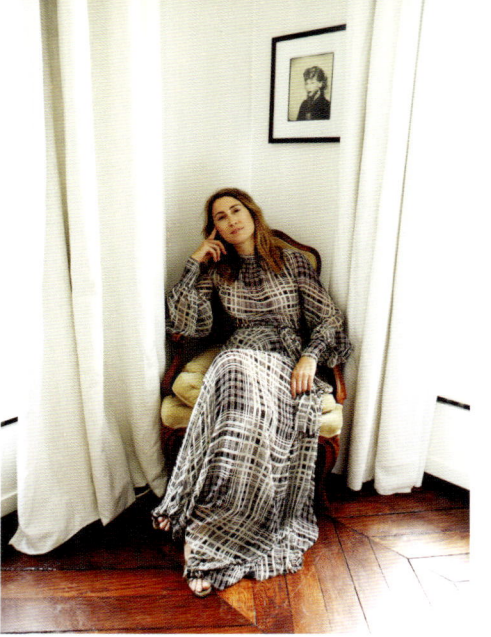
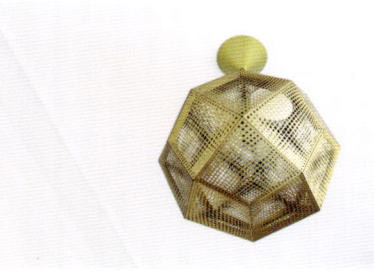
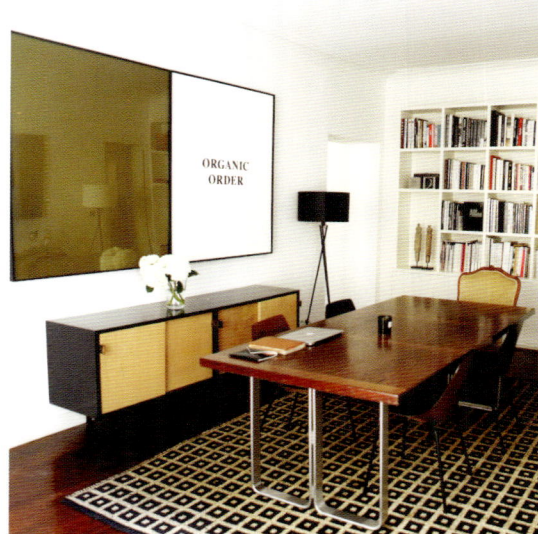
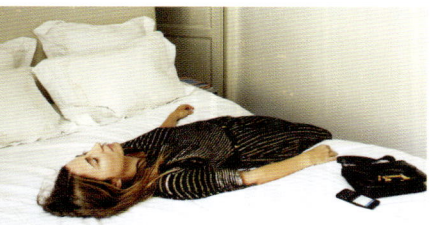
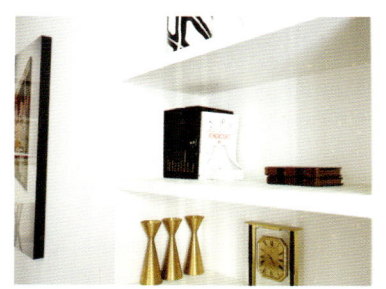
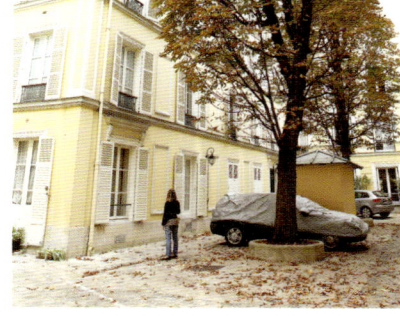
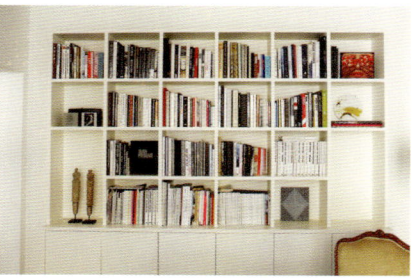
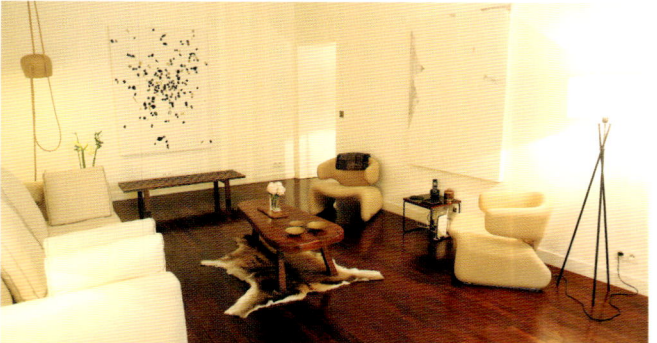
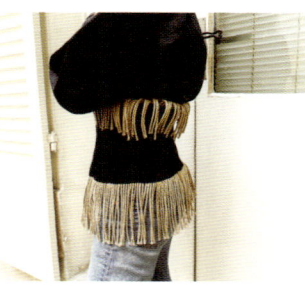
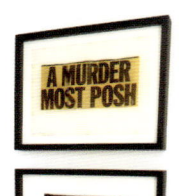
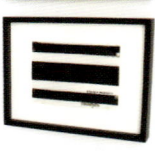
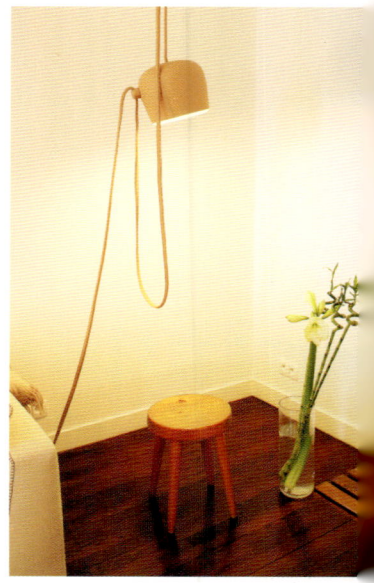

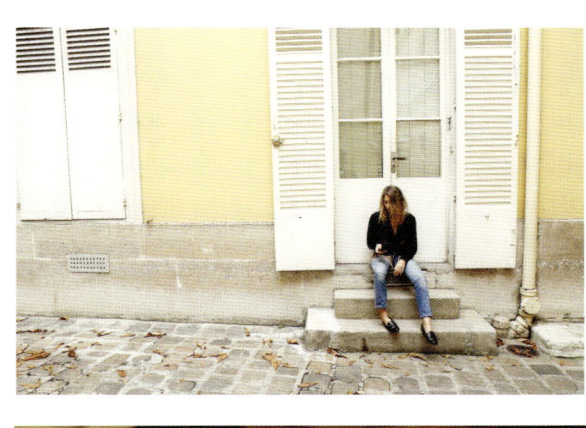
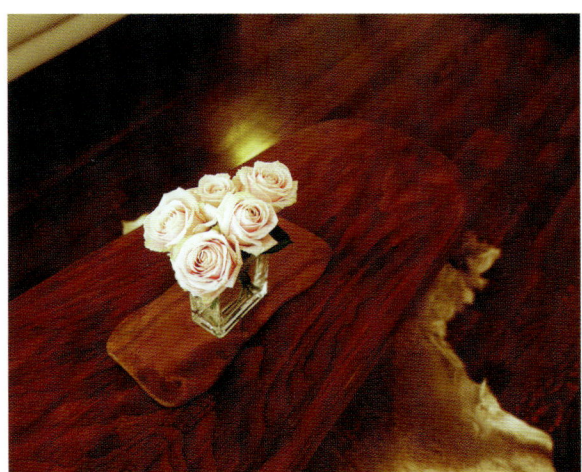
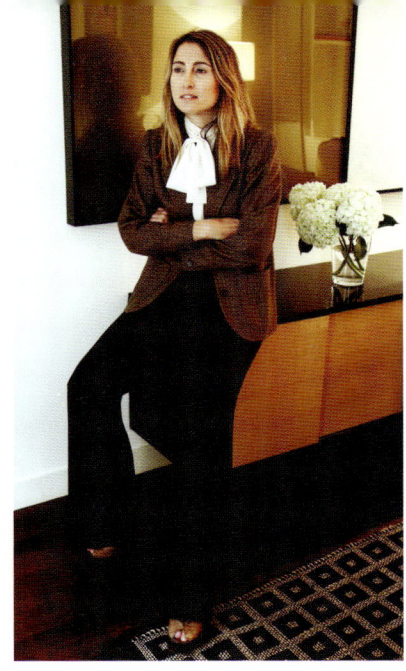
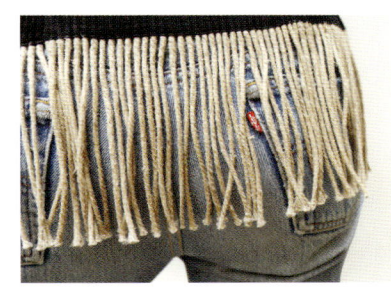
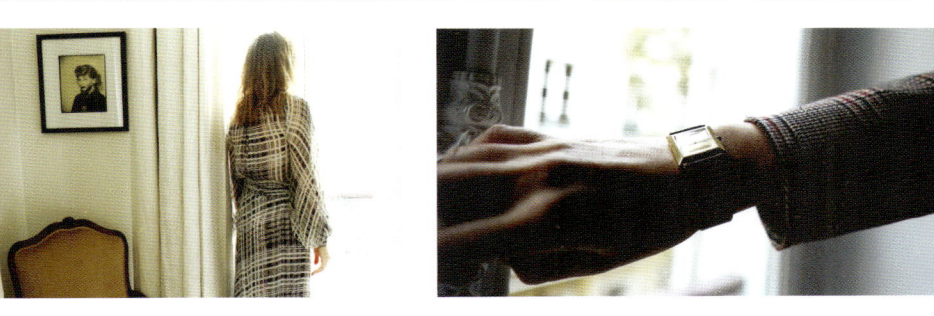
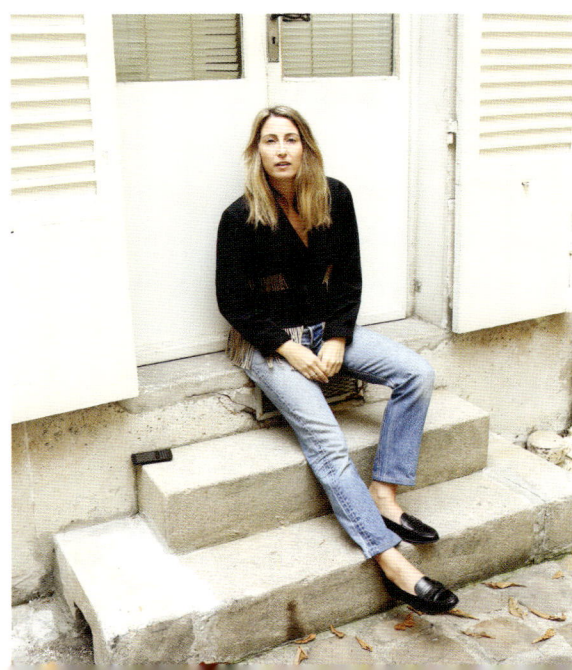
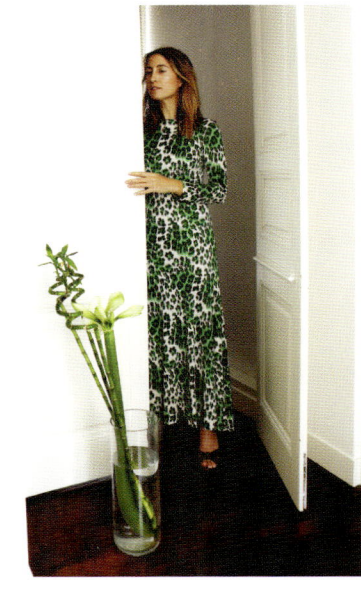

245

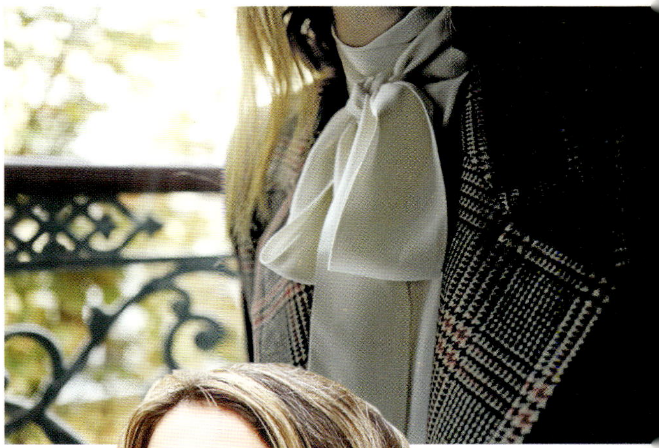

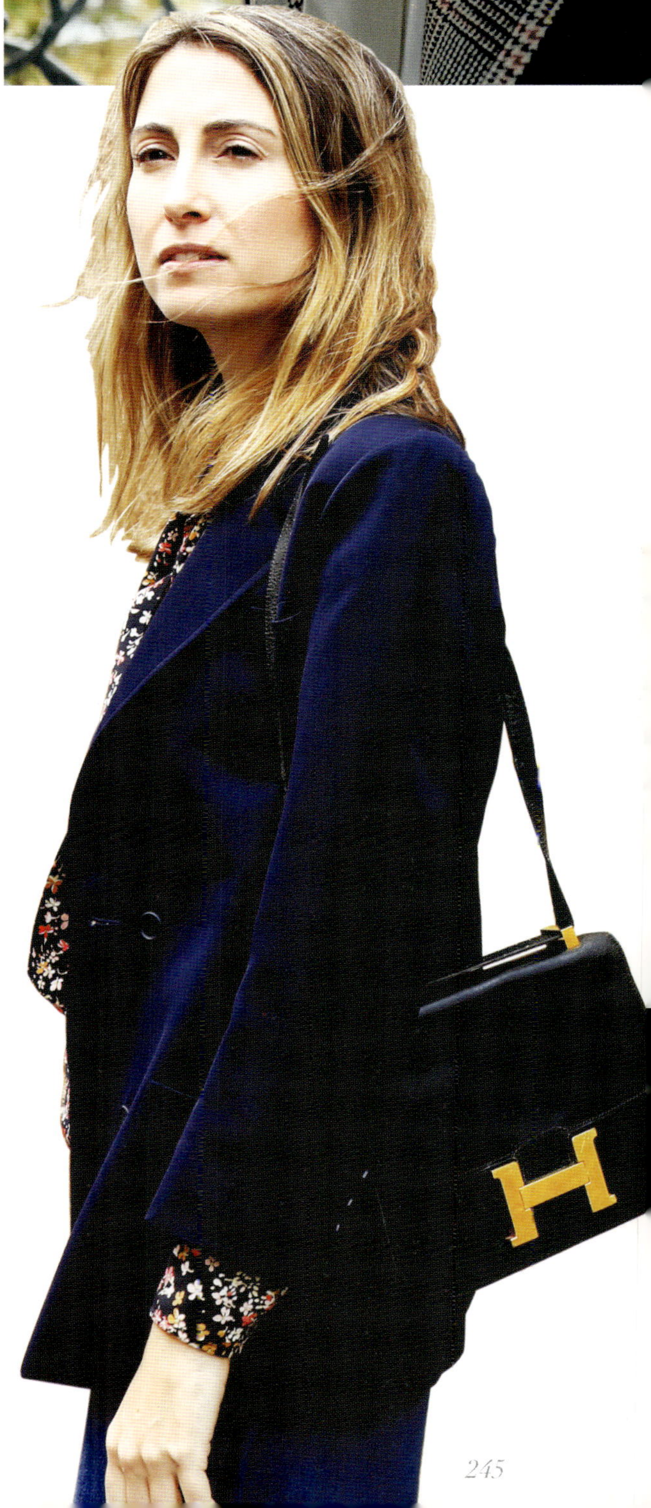

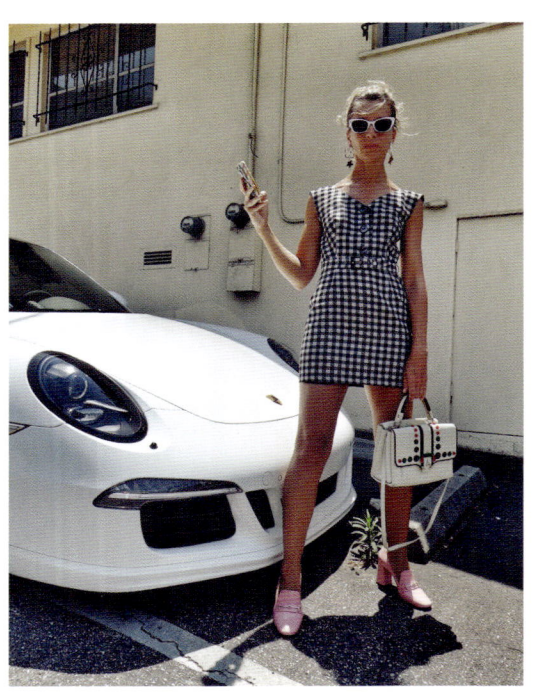

Born and raised in Belgium, *Natalie Joos* began her career in fashion when she moved to New York in 1997. Armed with a university degree in Journalism, she first started working as Personal Assistant to writer Glenn O'Brien, followed by six years as Studio Manager for acclaimed photographer Craig McDean. Natalie eventually created her own casting company in 2003. Over the next 10 years she built up an impressive roster of fashion clients and eventually also contributed to magazines as a writer and a stylist. In 2010 Natalie launched Tales of Endearment, a blog with stories about "friends, vintage, love, style and life." Besides personal travel, dating, and style posts, she takes her readers inside the homes of vintage-loving women and men. Natalie is also a favorite of the street style photographers and has become a sought-after influencer. Vintage is her unwavering niche and passion. Natalie now lives in Los Angeles and *Tales of Endearment* is her first book.

TALES OF ENDEARMENT
Modern Vintage Lovers and Their Extraordinary Wardrobes

Photographs © 2017 Natalie Joos
Introduction © 2017 Natalie Joos

All rights reserved. No part of this book may be reproduced in any manner in any media, or transmitted by any means whatsoever, electronic or mechanical (including photocopy, film or video recording, Internet posting, or any other information storage and retrieval system), without the prior written permission of the publisher.

Published in the United States by powerHouse Books,
a division of powerHouse Cultural Entertainment, Inc.
32 Adams Street, Brooklyn, NY 11201-1021
telephone 212.604.9074, fax 212.366.5247
e-mail: info@powerHouseBooks.com
website: www.powerHouseBooks.com

First edition, 2017

Library of Congress Control Number: 2017950418

Hardcover ISBN 978-1-57687-840-8

Book design by Krzysztof Poluchowicz

Printing and binding by Asia Pacific Offset

10 9 8 7 6 5 4 3 2 1

Printed and bound in China